To Mike S.

From - Grandma Snyder

Fraternally Yours
Theodore F. Lang.

LOYAL WEST VIRGINIA

FROM 1861 TO 1865

WITH AN INTRODUCTORY CHAPTER ON THE STATUS OF VIRGINIA

FOR THIRTY YEARS PRIOR TO THE WAR

BY

THEODORE F. LANG

MAJOR 6TH W. VA. CAVALRY AND BREVET COLONEL

———

"Child of the storm"
"Born amid the throes of war"

———

BALTIMORE, MD.

THE DEUTSCH PUBLISHING CO.

1895

New Edition
Published in 1998 by
BLUE ACORN PRESS
P.O. Box 2684
Huntington, W.Va. 25726

ISBN 1-885033-19-2

PREFACE.

The best testimony to an act is the testimony of one who saw the act done. Modern criticism, not content with mere tradition, demands a record of facts.

The last chapters of the great Civil War are now being recorded. Those who participated in the struggle, those who saw it, are fast passing away, and what is now obtainable from eye-witnesses must soon become tradition.

From this point of view any facts relating to the war are valuable, and he who helps to preserve them has, in a measure, done a duty to his fellow man.

This work has been written in deference to the Author's convictions that a great neglect exists at this time, and has existed for many years, in relation to the history of the part taken in the late war by the loyal West Virginians, both civil and military, who stood so firmly for the preservation of the Union.

It was largely with this incentive to guide him that the following pages were written, though indeed, without a full appreciation of the great labor necessary to gather from authentic sources the facts which have been here collected. By no means the least difficult task has been to digest the large amount of material at hand. Indeed, the work has assumed greater proportions than at first intended, largely due to the incorporation of extracts from official reports for the verification of statements which would otherwise stand entirely upon individual assertion.

The Author's personal reminiscences are largely taken from notes kept during his term of over three years' service in the field and, having been made at the time the acts occurred, their accuracy has not been impaired by time.

The Author is under profound obligations for valuable data furnished by Generals Thomas M. Harris, William H. Powell, Isaac H. Duval and Henry Capehart, Captain Thos. H. McKee, Lieut. L. W. V. Kennon, U. S. A., Judge J. Marshall Hagans, Hon. Isidor Rayner, M. C., and especially to Capt. Jos. W. Kirkley, War Records Department, ex-U. S. Senator Waitman T. Willey, Colonel John G. Kelley, Frank S. Reader, Esq., author of "History of 5th W. Va. Cavalry" and editor of the *Beaver Valley Daily News*, at New Brighton, Pa., Major Alexander Shaw, Captain John K. Shaw, and Captain C. M. Hoult.

To no one more than to the writer are apparent the imperfections of the work. His aim has been to impartially record the facts, believing that sufficient time has passed since the events occurred for just criticism to take the place of partisan abuse.

THEODORE F. LANG.

BALTIMORE, MD., *August*, 1895.

CONTENTS.

CHAPTER IV.

GENERAL GEORGE B. McCLELLAN'S OPERATIONS IN WESTERN VIRGINIA IN THE SPRING OF 1861.

CHAPTER V.

GENERAL McCLELLAN'S OPERATIONS—(CONTINUED).

CHAPTER VI.

McCLELLAN'S OPERATIONS—(CONTINUED).

CHAPTER VII.

PERSONAL REMINISCENCES OF THE AUTHOR.

CHAPTER VIII.

PERSONAL REMINISCENCES—(CONTINUED).

CHAPTER IX.

PERSONAL REMINISCENCES—(CONTINUED).

CHAPTER X.

PERSONAL REMINISCENCES—(CONTINUED).

CHAPTER XVI.

PERSONAL REMINISCENCES—(CONTINUED).

CHAPTER XVII.

PERSONAL REMINISCENCES—(CONTINUED).

CHAPTER XVIII.

PERSONAL REMINISCENCES—(CONTINUED).

CHAPTER XIX.

ORGANIZATION OF THE PEIRPOINT GOVERNMENT.

CHAPTER XXII.

LOYALTY OF PRESIDENT JOHN W. GARRETT TO THE UNION, AND HIS CLOSE RELATIONS TO PRESIDENT LINCOLN.

CHAPTER XXIII.

FIRST REGIMENT W. VA. CAVALRY VOLUNTEERS.

CHAPTER XXIV.

SECOND REGIMENT W. VA. CAVALRY VOLUNTEERS.

CHAPTER XXXV.

SIXTH REGIMENT WEST VIRGINIA INFANTRY.

CHAPTER XXXVI.

SEVENTH REGIMENT W. VA. INFANTRY VOLUNTEERS.

CHAPTER XXXVII.

NINTH REGIMENT W. VA. INFANTRY VOLUNTEERS.

CHAPTER XXXVIII.

TENTH REGIMENT W. VA. INFANTRY VOLUNTEERS.

CHAPTER XXXIX.

ELEVENTH REGIMENT W. VA. INFANTRY VOLUNTEERS.

CHAPTER LVIII.

BREVET MAJ.-GEN'L W. W. AVERELL—(CONTINUED).

CHAPTER I.

INTRODUCTORY:—WESTERN VIRGINIA AND ITS RELATIONS TO THE MOTHER STATE FOR MANY YEARS PRIOR TO THE WAR.

Virginia, One of the Thirteen Original United States :—Its Boundary, Principal Cities and Towns, Rivers, Mountains, Minerals, Natural Curiosities, Climate, Products, Canals, Railways, Public Buildings, Newspapers, etc.—Early Settlement.—Mother of Presidents.—First to Prepare the Federal Constitution.—Hostility Between the People of the Eastern and Western Part of the State.—The Causes Therefor.—Constitution of 1850.—Talk of Separation of the State.—Hons. W. T. Willey and John S. Carlisle Stand for Separation.—A Proclamation by Governor Letcher.—Western Virginians Incredulous.

SSUMING that this book may be read by those who were but little children—or, perhaps, unborn at the time of the Rebellion of 1861 to 1865, this chapter is intended more for their edification than for the reader who participated in the terrible struggle for supremacy in that contest. Virginia, one of the thirteen original United States of America, was bounded on the north by Pennsylvania and Maryland, east by Maryland and the Atlantic, south by North Carolina and Tennessee, and west by Kentucky and Ohio. It was divided into 148 counties. The chief towns were Richmond (the capital), Petersburg, Norfolk, Wheeling, Staunton, Waynesborough, Alexandria, Portsmouth, Lynchburg, Clarksburg, Fredericksburg and Parkersburg. The Chesapeake Bay, which divides the southeastern portion of the State, affords deep and spacious harbors. The chief rivers are the Potomac, forming the northeastern boundary; the Ohio on the northwest; the James, York, Chickahominy, Rappahannock, Rapidan, Appomattox, Shenandoah, and Kanawha.

Eastern Virginia is level or rolling land, rising gradually from the ocean and Chesapeake Bay. The western portion also rises rolling and hilly from the Ohio, while through the center, from northeast to southwest, run four ranges of mountains: (1) a low range on the east, commencing with the Bull Run Mountains near the Potomac; (2) the Blue Ridge, more elevated, through which the Potomac passes at Harper's Ferry, and which forms the eastern boundary of the Shenandoah Valley; (3) the Alleghany or Front Ridge; (4) the Laurel Ridge and Cumberland Mountains in the southwest. The highest peak—White Top, in Grayson County—is 6000 feet; other peaks rise from 4000 to 4500. The valley of Virginia or of the Shenandoah is from 1200 to 1500 feet above the sea.   In the eastern part of the State are found gold, copper, iron, etc.; there are also two belts parallel to the Blue Ridge, crossing the James River above Richmond, with rich coal deposits. On the western borders of the State are coal fields, mineral springs (hot and cold), sulphur, salt, gypsum, lead, marble, porcelain clay, fire-brick clay, granite, and soap-stone slate.

Among the natural curiosities are the Natural Bridge in Rockbridge County, Luray Caves in Page County, Weir's Cave in Augusta County, Blowing Cave (which sends out a blast of cold air in summer, and draws in air in the winter), flowing and ebbing springs, the Hawk's Nest, a pillow of rock 1000 feet high, and a wealth of mountain scenery which has justly named Virginia the Switzerland of America.

In eastern and southeastern Virginia extremes of temperature are found. In summer it is intensely hot, and in the swampy river bottoms malaria prevails.   In winter the higher regions are extremely cold, but the climate of a large part of the State is delightfully pleasant and proverbially healthy. The soil of the eastern portion is light and good.   In the valleys rich, producing wheat, Indian corn, tobacco and the hardier fruits.   The chief exports are tobacco, flour, cotton, wool, coal, lumber and oysters (15,000,000 bushels per annum).

The people of the western part of the State enjoyed a climate as genial as that of the Italians who dwell on the slopes of the Appenines; they had forests of hard wood more valuable than those that skirt the upper Rhine; rich fields of coal and petroleum that are not excelled in the world; a soil which yields abundant crops of grain and fruit; its rivers and creeks are bountifully supplied with fish.   Game of all kinds are found in the mountains, and the air is rendered musical by the songs of birds of many kinds.

The internal commerce was carried on by means of the navigable rivers, the James River Canal, Potomac Canal, and 1771 miles of railway.

In 1860 there were 3105 churches, of which 1403 were Methodist, 787 Baptist, 437 Catholic, 290 Presbyterian, 188 Episcopalian.   There were a university, 23 colleges, 398 academies, 3778 public schools, and a large fund for the education of the poor.   In 1860 there were 15 daily newspapers, 16 tri-weekly, and 103 weekly; also 21 public libraries.   There were State institutions for the blind and for the deaf and dumb.   The insane asylum at Staunton is the oldest in the United States.

Virginia was the earliest settled, largest, and most populous of the thirteen original States; called "the Old Dominion" and also the "Mother of Presidents," four out of the five Presidents before 1825 having been Virginians; she was the first to propose the Federal Constitution.   In 1769 Thomas

Jefferson, a member of the House of Burgesses, which had been established in 1619, asserted for the Colony the right of self-taxation, denying the right of the English Parliament to tax the Colonies. In 1773 Patrick Henry, Thomas Jefferson and Richard Henry Lee were appointed a committee to confer with the other Colonies, and urged upon their delegates the Declaration of Independence. In fact, Virginia with her grand array of brilliant men, stands upon the very pinnacle of the nation's greatness. George Washington, Thomas Jefferson, James Madison, James Monroe, and John Tyler in turn became the nation's choice for President; beside these names, the honor roll of the State numbers its heroes, statesmen, divines and artists by the hundreds. But had the State furnished but *the* Washington, she would still excel in her contribution of exalted manhood to the country.

With a commonwealth so rich in natural resources and so pre-eminent in great achievements, it would seem that every impulse would move her sons to preserve intact their common heritage. But such was not the case, and it will be shown that power of conflicting opinions and antagonistic aims prevailed against the more sentimental influence of State pride. For thirty years before the Rebellion the people of the eastern and western part of the State had been in a condition of absolute hostility, and from the writer's earliest recollection the candidate for the State Legislature from the western part of the State, in order to secure the suffrage of the people of his district, was compelled to pledge his influence, if elected, to the principle of a division of the State, and this pledge had to be given, no matter of what political faith he was. Indeed, from the very origin of the settlement of western Virginia, when the Federal Constitution was adopted, its citizens were in a large degree alienated from the eastern and older section of the State. The men of the west were hardy frontiersmen, a majority of them soldiers of the Revolution and their immediate descendants, without estates, with little but the honorable record of patriotic service and their own strong arms for their fortunes. They had few slaves. They had, however, land patents, which were certificates of patriotic service in the Revolutionary War, and they depended upon their own labor for a new home in the wilderness. A population thus originating, a community thus founded, was naturally uncongenial to the aristocratic element of the Old Dominion. As the terms were formerly used, the Blue Ridge was the boundary between eastern and western Virginia.

In 1850 the former contained 401,540 whites, 45,783 free colored persons and 409,793 slaves ; the latter 492,609 whites, 8,123 free colored and 62,233 slaves.

The long-standing dispute between these sections, growing mainly out of the questions of taxation and representation, were temporarily compromised by amendments to the Constitution made in 1850, by which a mixed basis for representation was adopted, giving to the west a majority in the House, and to the east a majority in the Senate. By this compromise, slaves under twelve years of age were not subjects of taxation, while upon those above that age $1.20 was levied. The west complained that a large proportion of the property of the eastern planters, which consisted of slaves, was either wholly or in effect free from taxation, while all of theirs was taxed ; and, moreover, affirmed that they derived little benefit from the sums expended for internal improvements, which substantially comprised a few thousand dollars each year for turnpike and road improvements and an appropriation to erect an insane asylum at Weston, in Lewis County, while the tide-water districts were liberally provided for. From this time many leading men in the western part of the State began to devise means for a separation between the two sections. As early as 1851 Hon. Waitman T. Willey, of Monongalia County, member of the State Convention of Virginia, in a speech before that convention, made an impassioned and eloquent argument on the question of "A Just Basis of Representation," taking the ground that the western part of the State had been unfairly dealt with by the east. He said : "More than one-half of the people of Virginia, by at least one hundred and fifty thousand—more than one-half of the voters of Virginia, by at least fifteen thousand—are standing this day knocking at the doors of this hall; after long years of delay, after mature deliberation and a quarter of a century's discussion and patient endurance of their grievances, they are now, to-day, at this moment knocking at the doors of this hall, demanding their proper political power, and an apportionment of representation upon the principles of the Declaration of Rights."

Hon. John S. Carlisle, in a speech at a convention in Wheeling, in May, 1861, said : "There is no difference in opinion between the advocates of a separation of this State. If I may be allowed, I can claim some credit for my sincerity when I say that it has been an object for which I have labored at least since the year 1850. The convention which met at Richmond in that year, and adopted our present State Constitution, clearly disclosed to my mind the utter incompatibility consistent with the interests of the people of northwestern Virginia of remaining in connection with the eastern portion of the State."

Governor Letcher,* in his proclamation to the people of northwestern

---

* On the 14th of June, 1861, Governor Letcher having posted troops at Huttonsville, in Randolph County, issued that proclamation. It further insisted that the majority of the State should rule the State, and called upon western Virginians, in the name of past friendship and historic memories, to co-operate with Secession and join the Southern army. The vote referred to was the vote upon the question of Virginia seceding from the Union, held on the 4th Thursday in May, referred to in following chapters.—T. F. L.

Virginia, June 14, 1861, admits that these complaints were well founded. He says : " There has been a complaint among you that the eastern portion of the State has enjoyed an exemption from taxation to your prejudice. By a display of magnanimity in the vote just given, the east has, by a large majority, consented to relinquish this exemption, and is ready to share with you all the burdens of government."

The unprejudiced reader will recognize the " magnanimity " of the vote referred to by Governor Letcher in his proclamation, and, assuming that the overture was sincere, coming as it did at the very threshold of a revolt by a long-suffering, waiting and patient people, it failed to impress with any degree of faith the masses to whom it was addressed. Had that spirit prevailed, and justice been meted out in the years that had passed, there was a remote possibility that western Virginians might have become educated to conform to the laws and customs governing the people of the east. But, for reasons already expressed, the convictions of the westerners were as indissoluble as were the imperishable mountains that divided the commonwealth.

CHAPTER II.

LOYALTY OF WESTERN VIRGINIANS WHEN THE CONFLICT CALLED THEM TO ARMS.

Habits, Customs, Manners and Character of the People of the State.—The City and Towns-people.—The Farmer and the Country People.—The Improvident Mountaineer.—Bush-whackers and their Methods.—Western Virginians Allied to Northern Sentiments and Institutions.—Gov. Letcher Assembles Legislature in Extra Session.—Proceedings of Same.—Virginia Convention Passes Ordinance of Secession.

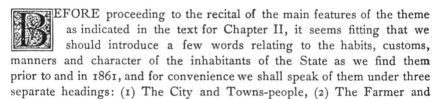EFORE proceeding to the recital of the main features of the theme as indicated in the text for Chapter II, it seems fitting that we should introduce a few words relating to the habits, customs, manners and character of the inhabitants of the State as we find them prior to and in 1861, and for convenience we shall speak of them under three separate headings: (1) The City and Towns-people, (2) The Farmer and the Country People, and (3) The Improvident Mountaineer.

In the Cities and Towns

of West Virginia we find that characteristic energy and push, in a business way, that pertains to other enterprising cities; lawyers, doctors, artists, bankers, merchants, mechanics and all professional and trades-people trying to excel in their specialty, turning night into day in their eagerness to grow wealthy. And in this endeavor they maintained a courtesy and suavity of character that was Chesterfieldian in its way. The older men were really solid in their habits, and the young men generally followed their example. There was no time or place then where a later day excrescence, in society called a "dude," could endure for a single day.

The legal fraternity and the ministry of West Virginia in those days numbered some of the most brilliant and noted intellects in this country, and the writer recalls the prompt reply of a prominent eastern wholesale dry goods dealer to the question, "where do you find your most reliable and trusted retail purchasers?" and he replied without reserve, "from Western Virginia." And the women of these cities and towns were cultured and refined in all the domestic relations of the home. They had no true conception of the advanced or "strong-minded" woman, and they knew little of Paris dressmakers; their highest ambition was to make good wives and a happy home.

The Farmer and the Country People.

It was this element of West Virginia's population that stood pre-eminent as an illustration of a happy, contented and satisfied class. There were farmers of large and of small estates, but *all* were in sympathy and stood by each and for each other. The larger and more fortunate operators, in addition to producing wheat, corn, buckwheat, fruits, etc., for their family use, generally had an extra amount of each to sell; beside, they raised large numbers of fine horses, cattle, sheep and hogs, which were shipped to eastern markets; but, no matter whether the farmers were of extensive or small estate, they always stood together, they endorsed notes, borrowed and loaned, and extended a helping hand each to the other. If a house or barn was to be built, a field of corn to be husked, a log-rolling to be done, the neighbors for miles around would assemble on the day set apart, and would accomplish in a day what would require months to perform single-handed. And these occasions usually furnished a day and evening of refined enjoyment, for the women would not be left out. To illustrate, a farmer would have, say a field of corn to husk, and his wife and daughter would have a quilt to make ; so the farmer would strip his corn, say 200 or 300 barrels, from the stock, haul and pile near by the corn-crib, and his wife would place her quilt in the frame, when a day would be designated for the joint husking and quilting, when all the neighbors would be invited, the farmers and their sons to the husking, and the farmers' wives and their daughters to the quilting. Reader, did you ever attend one of those country affairs? If not, your life has passed in blissful ignorance of that acme of joyous entertainment, as compared with which the present day "tea," or " german," is indeed dull and unimportant. But the entertainment, let us explain. When the men assemble at the corn pile, an equal division is made of both, the pile of corn and of the huskers; each set of men are posted at either side of the corn pile, when, at the command, the men make the husks fly, until the work is completed, when the side husking the greater number of bushels is declared the winner of a prize that had been proffered. And similar proceedings have taken place with the ladies relating to the quilting. Finally, when the work has been finished, supper is in order, and just here our power of description cannot do justice to one of those country suppers. Delmonico receives you in his magnificent "dining parlors " and hands you a "menu " to select from, but these fancy French dishes rarely agree with your plain American stomach, and the thought of the inevitable headache robs the feast of half its pleasure. Not so with our country supper of light rolls, stewed chicken, a boiled country-cured ham, with broiled venison and appropriate vegetables, and pumpkin pie that would make a New England housewife knit her brows in envy. Yet, that is not all, for the young folks' hour has arrived, and they are in full dress; not in the conventional full dress of the city belle, for the bright, cheerful, laughing country girl needs no decolleté gown, rouge or powder to make her attractive, nor does an orchestra rendering scientific selections from Mozart, Strauss or Schubert furnish music for the dance; instead, the best violinist of the neighborhood plays familiar airs (if dancing were in order). But without the music and without the dance, the young country folks have endless ways to while away the happy hours. Although a most interesting topic, space will not permit a more extended reference to the social customs which prevailed among the better element of the rural population at that time.

THE IMPROVIDENT MOUNTAINEERS

are not referred to here as having furnished any considerable part of the population whose methods and aims in life contributed to the advancement and elevation of the State. On the contrary, their life work was little above the savage who inhabited these same hills when the country was yet a "howling wilderness." Their abode was in the mountains of the middle and southwestern counties of the State. They were generally squatters, paying nothing for the land of which they had taken possession; they would clear a few acres, build a rude cabin, and thus isolated they would raise a small patch of corn and potatoes, sufficient to meet their necessities from year to year, and for other food they depended upon wild game and fish, a generous supply of which was found in that part of the State. They were without education, or the means of getting it even had they desired to do so. They would make periodical visits to the county towns with a supply of furs, ginseng and other roots, which they would exchange for clothing, coffee, sugar and, of course, whiskey. Perhaps it would have been just as well not to have referred to this improvident element of the country, nor would we have done so but for the fact that our description of the people of the State would not be complete without such a reference. Moreover, when the war did come, a few of them had the courage of their convictions and enrolled themselves as soldiers either in the Union or the Confederate armies. The majority of them, however, became the terror of the Union soldiers by their irregular and cruel methods of warfare, known in military parlance as "bushwhackers," "guerillas," etc. Having allied themselves with the Confederate cause, they felt secure in their murderous attacks on Union troops while on the march or at out-posts, nor did they spare the defenseless women and children of the sparsely settled country. They usually did their fiendish work under cover of darkness, but it was a common practice to conceal themselves in the dense wood of the mountain side and fire into the ranks of the marching soldiery without warning, and with no possible chance of returning an effective shot. The Union troops dreaded this one-sided method of warfare more than the pitched battle, where each combatted with equal chances to win. This species of warfare, now forbidden by the law of nations, has existed from the earliest times. Rome, both imperial and republican, was harassed by similar bands. The mountain fastnesses of Greece and of Spain have long been the rendezvous of just such desperadoes, and our own Mexico has become noted for her bushwhackers. Let us, however, turn our thoughts from these stragglers engaged in their despicable work to that larger body of patriotic people who, imbued with an unselfish devotion to principle, were entering that "irrepressible conflict," not as the champions of Virginia or of South Carolina, not as the champions of Ohio or Pennsylvania, but as defenders of what was greater than any State, the Union.

By every natural association West Virginia was allied to Ohio and Pennsylvania, and therefore to Northern sentiments and institutions. Bordering on the Ohio River for two hundred and fifty miles, she was adjacent to Pennsylvania for a distance of one hundred and twenty miles, half on the southern line, half on the western line of that State. Her extreme point—the Pan-handle—stretched to the northward of Pittsburg, and was within twenty-five miles of the parallel of latitude that marks the southern boundary of the New England States. When, therefore, the loyal people of western Virginia declined to yield to the demand of the Secessionists of the State it very naturally created a great deal of enthusiasm in the States of Ohio and Pennsylvania, and did much to attract the sympathy and help of those States to the support of the brave loyalists of this section. At this time the people of Virginia found themselves confronted with the most important question that had as yet come up in the history of the State since the days of the Revolution.

Governor Letcher had called an extra session of the State Legislature to meet on the 7th of January, 1861, among other things " to take into consideration the condition of public affairs and determine calmly and wisely what action is necessary." People in western Virginia did not comprehend that a terrible war was about to be inaugurated, and many were incredulous at the idea of secession. The Legislature convened in extra session on the 7th day of January, and on the 14th passed a bill calling a convention of the people of Virginia, whose members were to be elected on the 4th of February, and were to meet in Richmond on the 13th of that month. A substitute for this bill, offered in the House of Delegates, providing that a vote of the people should be taken upon the calling of the convention, was defeated by a large majority. Thus, for the first time in the history of the State, a convention would assemble without the sanction of the people. A clause of the bill, however, provided that the sense of the voters should be taken at the election for members of the convention, "as to whether any action of said convention dissolving our connection with the Federal Union or changing the organic law of the State shall be submitted to the people for ratification or rejection."

The convention assembled at Richmond on the 13th, and organized by electing the Hon. John Janney, of Loudoun County, president; Hon. W. T. Willey, of Monongalia County, was appointed a member of the Committee on Federal Relations.

Fulton Anderson, a commissioner from Mississippi, Henry L. Benning, a commissioner from Georgia, and John S. Preston, a commissioner from South Carolina, addressed the convention, all urging Virginia to join the Southern Confederacy. Mr. Willey answered the address of Preston in an able and eloquent speech.

While the convention was still pouring in resolutions relating to the great subject of Union upon the Committee of Federal Relations, and before it had made any report, an event took place at the Federal capital which was designed either to bring matters more rapidly to a crisis, or restore order and harmony to the country. Mr. Lincoln was inaugurated President of the United States on the 4th of March for four years. The inaugural address, whilst of a tone and character that did not threaten or wound, still announced the doctrine that nothing had yet taken place, according to the Constitution, which was sufficient to tie the hands of the Executive or deter him from retaking the forts and arsenals and repossessing the property belonging to the Government in the States where secession had been instituted.

This address was received and interpreted by the people of Virginia and the convention according to the prevailing opinions of parties on the questions then being agitated. The extremists argued and asserted that it was equivalent to a declaration of hostilities, and by the superior vehemence which characterizes revolutionists, together with a resort to the sophistry of public commotions, they drew to them many who were filled with alarm at the aspect of affairs and found a temporary relief in the shadow of violent spirits.

The pressure of events brought from the Committee on Federal Relations a partial majority report on the 9th of March, the tenor of which exalted any and everything relating to secession and States' rights, whilst pretty much everything relating to the Federal Union was lightly referred to.

By permission of Judge J. Marshall Hagans, of Morgantown, we are pleased to quote from his admirable

SKETCH OF THE ERECTION AND FORMATION OF THE STATE OF WEST VIRGINIA FROM THE TERRITORY OF VIRGINIA,

pertaining to that convention. "The report of the committee was a signal for a general onset between the parties. One of the most animated and spirited debates which modern times has witnessed immediately began. It was characterized by a warmth and ability which the great interests of the occasion demanded and the high order of intellect engaged brought forth. The vehemence and rancor of the Secession cabal was met by the sturdy determination and lofty eloquence of the Unionists, in defense of all that was honorable and revered in the history of their country. Every influence that could be exerted by the factionists was brought to bear in the arguments. State pride, that fatal deity of the Virginian, was urged with all the eloquence of the most accomplished orators. On the part of the Unionists, the traditions and the glory of the past, and the magnitude of a mighty future, were portrayed with a zeal and faithfulness which the proudest intellects of any age never excelled. The most gifted minds of the times poured the rich treasures of their maturity into the agitated flood of patriotic duty. After elaborate discussion a vote was had on the 4th of April. Both parties desired it, for the purpose of ascertaining the progress of accretion and defection. The resolutions were voted on separately, and were amended or stricken out, on a basis generally favorable to the Union cause. But the great test vote was on the sixth, for which a substitute was offered providing that an ordinance of secession from the Federal Union should be submitted to the people of Virginia at the annual election in May following. This proposition met with a most signal rebuke, by a vote of forty-five for and eighty-nine against it. The spirits of the Union members rose triumphant with the results, which evinced such a decided majority against direct secession, however much diversity of sentiment might exist on questions of adjustment involving neutrality or non-coercion. Prior to this time a few days, a scheme had been concocted by the Secessionists designed to accomplish, in the most revolutionary manner, what they feared could not be done through the convention in its present temper. A circular was issued, signed by six members of the convention, two members of the House of Delegates and the clerk, and extensively distributed throughout the State. It called upon the parties to whom it was addressed to present themselves in Richmond on the 16th day of April, to consult with the friends of Southern rights as to the course Virginia should pursue in the present emergency; and to send from each county a full delegation of true, reliable men. The object of this, viewed in the light of subsequent events, as to the time of meeting and other circumstances, cannot be misunderstood. It was one link in the chain of combination which had brought about such a disordered state of public affairs, and was designed to effect secession with or without even the semblance of the forms of law, which many would have attached to such action by the regular convention.

"After the vote on the report of the committee a new system of tactics was inaugurated. No longer was it a discussion in which giant minds wrestled for the supremacy. The voice of reason and the impassioned appeals to the conscience were soon interrupted by the low mutterings of those discordant passions ever heard when physical force, having been overcome by the sublime powers of moral causes, raises its ghastly tones to animate the fury of its might. Terms of obloquy and reproach were applied to those who still resisted the secession mania; they were scornfully denominated 'submissionists.' The galleries and lobbies of the hall were filled with a wild, excited throng, hounded on by negro traders of Virginia and bands of negro hunters from South Carolina. They frowned and hissed when patriots below were pouring out upon the altar of their country the most magnificent tributes from their noble hearts and enlightened consciences. When they left the hall it was to be insultingly met at the door and on the streets by epithets of ignominy and reproach. Another part of the infernal devices was the employment of bands of music, which traversed the streets, collecting a motley crowd of lewd fellows and desperate characters who tore down from the market places and public squares the flag of the Republic and hoisted in its stead the palmetto and Confederate emblems.

"These same characters roamed the streets at night from place to place, and called out the public men from the South sojourning in the city, and applauded the most extreme sentiments with the wildest echoes. It was a part of their duty also to intimidate the Union members of the convention, especially those from the northwestern part of the State; and these, on arising from their beds in the morning, would discover, in close proximity to their windows, ropes with suggestive nooses at their ends pending from an adjoining tree or lamp-post. But they remained firm, proudly conscious of the integrity of their position, rejoicing in the knowledge that they were in the best of earthly causes—supporting a good government; they stood like the eternal hills, secure in their foundations. The policy adopted by the conspirators produced its effect on the people. That portion of society which takes but little interest in public affairs in ordinary times is the element from which the factionists draw the largest agency in furthering their purposes. They are ready to distinguish between ordinary and extraordinary periods in the passing events; and when they discover violent measures controlling the hour, either from timidity or ignorance, they hasten to join themselves with those who are usurping the reins of power or who occupy the largest share of public attention. This class also became attached to the party of the conspirators, and thus swelled to the proportions of respectability, they deemed the hour for action had arrived. A prominent actor in the scenes in Virginia was dispatched to Charleston, South Carolina, to announce that everything was in readiness in Virginia for the inauguration of the final act of the drama. He told the Carolinians that they must strike the blow, and 'in an hour, by Shrewsbury clock, his State would be with them.'

"This was a welcome announcement to the Southern leaders. For months the public mind had been frenzied by anticipations; society had experienced some of those upheavals which precede revolutions and go far towards resolving it to its original elements. War had been the theme of conversation in all circles, and those who had dared lift a voice against the universal rage had been silenced without mercy. Armies had been equipped and disciplined, and in the gush of their enthusiasm the young soldiers were crying to be led to the field. Public expectation was at the highest point and was clamoring for gratification. The chiefs, however, were awaiting the auspicious moment when the greatest moral force could be set in motion to aid their schemes. This promise, then, from the 'mother of States,' which to the people would give sanction to the enterprise and success if it were in the range of possibility, was the signal for the boasts and efforts of thirty years to culminate in the first direct assault of active warfare and the opening of hostilities. The fruits of this advice was the firing on the walls of Fort Sumter, in Charleston harbor, the echoes from which were returned by the mountains of a continent, and only ceased when the national honor was baptized in the blood of a million of citizens.

"During the progress of the bombardment of Fort Sumter the excitement in Richmond and in the convention was intense. Bonfires and illuminations blazed high in the streets and public squares; the national flag was torn from its place over the dome of the capitol and trampled under the feet of an infuriated mob; stores and public places were closed and the populace sought the streets to give vent to their feelings. Strangers rushed to the city from all parts of the State and helped to swell the throngs; many who had come in advance of the call before mentioned, to meet on the 16th of

April, assembled together in a large hall and sat with closed doors. No ingress could be obtained to the sessions of this mysterious body. To add to the alarm of the times, the convention went in secret session and all further knowledge as to its operations, to the Union people at least, was at an end. But the scenes witnessed within the walls of that room, as detailed by members, have no parallel in the annals of ancient or modern times. The Union men began to appreciate their position only when they saw those who had been their active co-laborers bowing before the storm and yielding before the pressure of events. In vain did they appeal, exhort, entreat them to remain firm in the adhesion to the national bond. On the morning of the 17th, Mr. Wise, the member from Princess Anne, rose in his seat and drawing a large Virginia horse pistol from his bosom, laid it before him, and proceeded to harangue the body in the most violent and denunciatory manner; he concluded by taking his watch from his pocket and with glaring eyes and bated breath declared that events were now transpiring which caused a hush to come over his soul; at such an hour, he said, Harper's Ferry and its armory were in the possession of Virginia soldiers, at another period the Federal navy yard and property at Norfolk were seized by troops of the State. It was then that the Union members saw the object of the other assemblage which had sat with closed doors from its beginning, and whose concealed hand seizing the reins of government, had left them the form without the power to resist. It was true as he had spoken; the volunteer companies which had been organized after the raid by John Brown in the Shenandoah Valley had, under orders from some mysterious power, assembled to the number of two thousand or more, and moved on Harper's Ferry with the design of seizing the armory and arsenals at that point belonging to the Federal Government ; the small garrison of marines, after destroying the most valuable property, fired the buildings and fled in precipitate haste.

"On the 17th of April, after much confusion and excited discussion, the convention came to a vote on an ordinance of secession from the Federal Union. The vote stood eighty-one for and fifty-one against it.

* * * * * * *

"Immediately after the passage of the fatal ordinance the convention began to diminish in numbers. The delegates from the northwestern part of the State, from the counties which now compose the State of West Virginia, finding themselves in a hopeless minority, quietly, and in some instances secretly, took their departure for their native mountains, where their humble yet more faithful constituents received them with open arms and anxious minds."

CHAPTER III.

LOYALTY OF WESTERN VIRGINIANS WHEN THE CONFLICT CALLED THEM TO ARMS—(CONTINUED).

Virginia Annexed to the Southern Confederacy.—Treason and Secession an Incentive to Western Virginia Loyalty.—Moral Courage Required to be for the Union.—Speakers Mobbed and Meetings Broken up.—Escape of Union Members of the Convention.—Public Meeting of Unionists at Clarksburg.—The Beginning of the War of the Rebellion.—Secession of Southern States.—Convention at Montgomery, Alabama.—Constitution Adopted and Jefferson Davis made President.—Firing on Fort Sumter.—Correspondence Between Governor Letcher and Mayor Sweeny.—Prompt Action in Western Virginia.—Loyalty of the M. E. Church.—Summary of War-Time Events.—Enlistment in the Union Army.

N the 25th of April the State, by Secession Commissioners acting under authority of the convention in session at Richmond, was annexed to the Southern Confederacy at Montgomery, Alabama. Of the preliminary action the people knew nothing; they were afterwards called upon to go through the farce of an election, on the 4th Thursday in May following, to vote on the adoption or rejection of the Ordinance of Secession.

The treason at Richmond furnished abundant incentive to the west to assert its dignity and independence. The triumph of Secession upon the James naturally led to the triumph of loyalty among the mountains. And while Governor Letcher was training the State militia for service against the general Government, Union meetings were held all over the western counties for the support of that Government. The moral courage required to espouse the Union cause at this time was, perhaps, never surpassed. The majority of the people of the State being naturally for the principle of State's rights, the Unionists bore much at their hands, both socially and financially, so that it was no easy matter, after all, to be for the Union. Speakers were mobbed, meetings were broken up, rough and tumble fights were frequent, and neighbors and kinsmen were arrayed against each other; yet, there was no yielding of the loyalty of the Union people of western Virginia.

The news of the passage of the Ordinance of Secession spread like wildfire. The Union members of the convention escaped from Richmond, some at the hazard of their lives. Hon. John S. Carlisle was among the first to escape. As soon as he arrived at Clarksburg, his home, he called a public meeting for April 22d, and, notwithstanding but twenty-four hours' notice had been given, the courthouse, where the meeting was held, was filled to overflowing, and this meeting was one of the many exciting incidents of that period that vividly impressed the writer's memory. Mr. Carlisle was the principal speaker. He was an educated and talented man and an effective orator. For two hours he addressed his eager hearers upon the issues of Union or Secession, and only those who heard his inspiring words can estimate the effect they had upon the action of his auditors. There is no room for doubt that Mr. Carlisle's appeal saved many waivering ones to the cause which he had espoused, and many of those who before were discouraged, now took up the fight with renewed force and a determination to win. This was the first important public meeting held in the State after the passage of the Ordinance of Secession; and that meeting called for an assembly of delegates, to be composed of ten men from each county, to a convention to be held in Wheeling on the 13th of May following. In pursuance of this call, public meetings were held in every county, the shortest notice calling out the largest concourses. These assemblies were addressed by Union men and by Secessionists. It must be remembered that at this early period there was still a bond of local attachment or State kinship that had not as yet been rudely severed, and not only at these public meetings were Secessionists permitted to speak and state their cause, but in the stores and offices, and upon the street corners, and at county cross roads could be seen groups of men entertaining antagonistic views, discussing—oftentimes impassionately—the great and ruling question of the hour. In succeeding chapters these matters will be fully presented.

February 8th, 1861, the date of the formal inauguration of the Southern Confederacy, marks the beginning of the War of the Rebellion. All of the previous acts of the Secessionists were within the limits of a peaceful solution, this act called for heroic treatment—it was no longer a question of ideas, but of physical force—the people were entering upon a civil war.

South Carolina, on the 20th of December, 1860, was the first to secede. In the month of January following it was in turn joined by these States, viz.: Mississippi, Alabama, Florida, Georgia and Louisiana. These States met in convention at Montgomery, Alabama, on the 4th of February, 1861, and in four days all preliminary arrangements were completed ; a provisional Constitution, almost identical with that of the United States, framed, and Jefferson Davis elected President, and Alexander H. Stevens, Vice-President of the new Nation. Then followed five other States, but in a majority of them a strong Union sentiment prevailed, and their dissolution from the

Union was obtained by a very slight majority. Texas was the first to follow, and then came at intervals Arkansas, Virginia, North Carolina and Tennessee.

We do not propose to discuss here the issues which led to this unhappy condition of affairs, only to say that it was the culmination of an insane revel of partisan license, which, for thirty years, had in the United States worn the mask of Government.

The fullest realization that the war was on was the firing upon Fort Sumter, on the 12th of April, 1861. The first shot fired—at 20 minutes past 4 o'clock, A. M.—when, in the dark and quiet of the night, the flash and the dull roar of a monitor came from the Confederate battery on Sullivan's Island. The conscious shell went up shrieking and wailing along its fiery curve, and lingering reluctantly before its downward plunge, burst as it fell over the doomed fortress. No meteor of more direful portent ever lit the sky; for this told surely of the beginning of a civil war, compared to which all civil wars before it were as squabbles of children in a corner. A war in which millions of men were to be engaged, and which was to scatter ruin and want through the country in which it raged; which was to convert half a continent into one great battlefield, and strew it from east to west with the graves of its citizens, slaughtered to gratify the base ambition and the disappointed pride of a small faction who justified to themselves their attempt to destroy a government upon the monstrous assumption of the right of one man to own and use another as his property.

No sooner had Virginia, on the 17th of April, passed the Ordinance of Secession, than Governor Letcher addressed a letter to Hon. Andrew Sweeney, mayor of Wheeling, informing him of the fact, and ordering him to "seize at once upon the custom house of that city, the postoffice, and all public buildings and documents in the name of the sovereign State of Virginia." The mayor promptly replied: "I *have* seized upon the custom house, the postoffice and all public buildings and documents in the name of Abraham Lincoln, President of the United States, whose property they are." And this reply of Mayor Sweeney reflected the opinion of the masses of the people in western Virginia, and they were not slow nor uncertain in their expression of opinion. They realized, however, that with the secession of Virginia completed and proclaimed they must do one of two things : either proceed at once to organize a State government which would be faithful to the National Constitution, or drift hopelessly into anarchy, and thus contribute to the success of the Rebellion.

Their prompt and intelligent action is a remarkable illustration of the trained and disciplined ability of Americans for the duties of self-government.

And it must be remembered that the people who were so intensely interested did not hold to any wild theories or communistic tendencies.   All along the border of the State there were a number of avowed abolitionists, and a few scattered through the interior, but at this early period they remained on the defensive side of the issues.   The preachers of the M. E. Church North had a large membership in the State, and they were intensely loyal to the Union cause.

Hon. F. H. Peirpoint, one of the leading men of the State, though not a member of that church, wrote one of his most effective letters and published it in a local paper, extolling the preachers of the M. E. Church, maintaining that they were simply living under the rule promulgated by Wesley. This letter had wide circulation and tended to strengthen the Union sentiment, not only with the membership of that church, but other religious denominations as well.

The following summary will call to mind of the war-time reader how rapidly and exciting did one event follow another, until every fibre of our nervous system was stretched to its fullest tension:

April 17, 1861.—Ordinance of Secession adopted by Virginia Convention.

April 18.—United States Armory at Harper's Ferry abandoned and burned by its garrison.

April 19.—Conflict between United States troops and mob in Baltimore, Md.

April 20.—General Butler's command arrives at Annapolis, Md.

April 23.—Maj.-Gen'l Robert E. Lee assigned to the command of the military and naval forces of Virginia.

April 27.—Col. Thos. J. Jackson, Virginia Volunteers, assigned to command of State troops at and about Harper's Ferry.

May 1.—Volunteer forces called out in Virginia.

May 3.—Governor of Virginia issues call for additional forces. *

May 4.—Col. A. G. Porterfield assigned to command of State forces in northwestern Virginia.

May 5.—Alexandria, Va., abandoned by State troops.

May 9.—Exchange of shots between the United States steamer Yankee and the batteries at Gloucester Point, Va.

May 13.—Baltimore, Md., occupied by United States troops.

May 13.—Maj.-Gen'l George B. McClellan, U. S. Army, assumes command of the Department of Ohio, embracing West Virginia.

---

* This call was sent into western Virginia to all the commanding officers of the State militia, and was practically disregarded by all.—T. F. L.

May 14.—Seizure of a train of cars at Harper's Ferry.

May 15.—Brig.-Gen'l Joseph E. Johnson, C. S. Army, assigned to command of troops near Harper's Ferry.

May 18 and 19.—Engagement at Sewell's Point.

May 24.—Advance of Union Army into Virginia and its occupation of Arlington Heights and Alexandria.

May 26 to 30.—Advance upon and occupation of Grafton, Va., by Colonel Kelley's Union forces.

June 2.—Brig.-Gen'l G. T. Beauregard, C. S. Army, given command of the Department of Alexandria.

June 3.—Action at Philippi.

June 6.—Brig.-Gen'l Henry A. Wise, C. S. Army, ordered to command of troops in the Kanawha Valley.

June 8.—Brig.-Gen'l R. S. Garnett, C. S. Army, assigned to command of troops in northwestern Virginia.

June 10.—Engagement at Big Bethel.

June 13.—Descent of Union troops upon Romney.

July 10.—Skirmish at Laurel Hill.

July 11.—Battle of Rich Mountain.

July 13.—Battle of Carrick's Ford.

July 13.—Surrender of Pegram's Confederate forces to General McClellan at Beverly.

July 15.—Harper's Ferry evacuated by the Confederate forces.

July 16.—Union advance toward Manassas, Va.

July 17.—Confederate Army retired to the lines of Bull Run, Va.

July 17.—Skirmish at Fairfax Courthouse.

July 18 to 21.—Confederate forces from the Shenandoah Valley, under Gen'l Joseph E. Johnson, re-enforced the army of General Beauregard at Manassas.

July 21.—First Battle of Bull Run.

The foregoing summary contains only a few of the many fagots that served to kindle the flame of patriotic devotion in western Virginia : nearly her entire territory had, within three months, seen and felt the effect of terrible war, and she illustrated her devotion to the Union by the most practical method, namely, the voluntary enlistment in the army of many of her brave sons.

CHAPTER IV.

GENERAL GEORGE B. McCLELLAN'S OPERATIONS IN WESTERN VIRGINIA IN THE SPRING OF 1861.

GEORGE BRINTON McCLELLAN was born in Philadelphia, Penna., December 3, 1826. His school education was in that city, in the preparatory school attached to the University of Pennsylvania. He entered the Military Academy at West Point in 1842, graduating in 1846, when he was assigned to the Corps of Engineers as Second Lieutenant. In September of the same year he went with the army to Mexico, where he served with distinction during the war. He was breveted First Lieutenant for gallantry at Contreras and Churubusco, Captain for Chapultepec.

On the 22d of May, 1860, he married Ellen Mary Marcy, daughter of Captain (afterward General) Randolph B. Marcy, and established his residence at Cincinnati, O., as President of the Eastern Division of the Ohio and Mississippi Railroad Co., where he was occupied as such when the Civil War began and he offered his services to his country.

He was commissioned Maj.-General of Volunteers in Ohio on the 23d of April, 1861. On the 14th day of May he was made Major-General in the United States Army and placed in command of the Department of Ohio, which included Ohio, Indiana and the western portions of Pennsylvania and Virginia.

McClellan's services as military engineer in Mexico had brought him great distinction; but the office he then assumed was novel and promised

GEORGE B. McCLELLAN
Major General U.S.A.

many trials and difficulties. The training of a single company of recruits required great patience and executive ability, but an army to be created out of undisciplined volunteer forces required genius and great tact. Happily for General McClellan, the men who first enlisted to defend the Union were patriots—business men, who readily grasped the situation—and in a fortnight, from communities of business and professional callings, sprung an army of intelligent, disciplined soldiers. It was not, however, the formation of a military department which included West Virginia that furnished the incentive that impelled her sons to espouse the Union cause, for they had shown since the day of the passage of the Ordinance of Secession that they regarded that act with the same significance as if it had been a shot fired into their midst from the cannon's mouth, the influence of which awoke a peaceful people into a frenzy of war that went out into every city and town and mountain road. Then every loyal man and woman in western Virginia became a worker in the cause which moved the nation's soul. Men went to enlisting, officers to organizing companies and regiments, following which came the mighty gathering of our heroes. The doors of the workshops were closed, the fields were deserted, armed men poured down from the hilltops and surged up from the valleys; the middle wall of partition was broken down between classes until it seemed like the good days of old "when none were for party but all for the State." The whole of our boundary became one vast military camp. But during this time the Confederates were not indifferent, but, to the contrary, were equally active in the matter of preparation for war. And there was foreshadowed at the time what history afterwards verified—that both sides were very much in earnest.

"Though," said some, "will brothers fight brothers?" "Aye," said our people, "even brothers will fight when their mothers have been struck."

History has been slow to give that full meed of praise to the sturdy loyalty of West Virginians that their early stand in the conflict merited.

It cannot be truthfully denied that the purposes and aims of the Confederate authorities in sending troops so early into the western part of the State was:

(1) To capture and impress into their ranks all subject to military service.

(2) To establish their lines along the borders of Ohio and Pennsylvania, thus making those two States the battle-ground. And had West Virginia concurred in this opinion the war in all probability would have been greatly prolonged.

Believing that the early proceedings of the Confederate authorities pertaining to western Virginia would be interesting reading, we quote (from Rebellion records) a few official acts promulgated at that time, to wit:

EXECUTIVE DEPARTMENT, RICHMOND, VA., *April* 23, 1861.

Major-General Lee having reported to the Governor, he will at once assume the command-in-chief of all the military and naval forces of the State and take in charge the military defenses of the State.   JOHN LETCHER.

GENERAL ORDERS, }
    NO. I.   }   HEADQUARTERS, RICHMOND, VA., *April* 23, 1861.

In obedience to orders from his Excellency, John Letcher, Governor of Virginia, Maj.-Gen'l Robert E. Lee assumes command of the military and naval forces of Virginia.

R. E. LEE, *Major-General.*

HEADQUARTERS, VIRGINIA FORCES,
RICHMOND, VA., *April* 29, 1861.

MAJ. A. LORING, *Commanding Volunteers, Wheeling, Va.*:

Major : You will muster into the service of the State such volunteer companies as may offer themselves, in compliance with the call of the Governor, take command of them, and direct the military operations for the protection of the terminus of the Baltimore and Ohio Railroad on the Ohio River, and also that of the road. It is desirable that the business operations of the company and peaceful travel shall not be interrupted, but be afforded protection. Major F. M. Boykin, Jr., has been directed to give protection to the road in the vicinity of Grafton. You will place yourself in communication with him with the view to co-operate, if necessary. You are requested to report the number of companies you may muster into the service, the state of the arms, condition, and all the circumstances connected therewith.   Respectfully, etc.,

R. E. LEE, *Maj.-Gen'l Commanding.*

HEADQUARTERS, VIRGINIA FORCES,
RICHMOND, VA., *April* 29, 1861.

LIEUT.-COL. JOHN MCCAUSLAND :

You will proceed to the Valley of the Kanawha and muster into the service of the State such volunteer companies (not exceeding ten) as may offer their services, in compliance with the call of the Governor; take the command of them, and direct the military operations for the protection of that section of the country. Your policy will be strictly defensive, and you will endeavor to give quiet and assurance to the inhabitants. It has been reported that two companies are already formed in Kanawha County, Captain Patten's and Captain Sevann's, and that there are two in Putnam County, Captain Beckett's and Captain Fife's. It is supposed that others will offer their services. The number of enlisted men to the company, fixed by the convention, is eighty-two. You will report the condition of the arms, etc. of each company, and, to enable you to supply deficiencies, five hundred muskets, of the old pattern, will be sent ; I regret to state that they are the only kind at present for issue. Four field pieces will also be sent you as soon as possible, for the service of which you are desired to organize a company of artillery. The position of the companies at present is left to your judgment, and you are desired to report what points below Charleston will most effectually accomplish the objects in view.   I am, Sir, etc.,

R. E. LEE, *Maj.-Gen'l Commanding.*

HEADQUARTERS, VIRGINIA FORCES,
RICHMOND, VA., *April* 30, 1861.

MAJOR F. M. BOYKIN, JR., *Virginia Volunteers, Weston, Va.*:

You are desired to take measures to muster into the service of the State such volunteer companies as may offer their services for the protection of the northwestern portion of the State. Assume the command, take post at or near Grafton, unless some other point should offer greater facilities for the command of the Baltimore and Ohio Railroad and the branch to Parkersburg. It is not the object to interrupt peaceful travel on the road or to offer annoyance to citizens pursuing their usual avocations; but to hold the road for the benefit of Maryland and Virginia, and to prevent its being used against them. You will therefore endeavor to obtain the co-operation of the officers of the road and afford them, on your part, every assistance in your power. You will also endeavor to give quiet and security to the inhabitants of the county. Major A. Loring, at Wheeling, has been directed, with the volunteer companies under his command, to give protection to the road near its terminus at the Ohio River, and you will place yourself in communication with him and co-operate with him, if necessary.

Please state whether a force at Parkersburg will be necessary, and what number of companies can be furnished in that vicinity. You are requested to report the number of companies you may muster into the service of the State; their arms, condition, etc., and your views as to the best means for the accomplishment of the object in view.

To enable you to supply any deficiencies in arms in the companies, two hundred muskets, of the old pattern, flint-locks, will be forwarded by Colonel Jackson,* the commanding officer at Harper's Ferry, to your order, from whence you must take measures to receive them and convey them in safety to their destination under guard, if necessary. I regret that no other arms are at present for issue.   Very respectfully, etc.,

R. E. LEE, *Maj.-Gen'l Commanding.*

EXECUTIVE DEPARTMENT, RICHMOND, VA., *May* 1, 1861.

HON. L. P. WALKER:

Arrangements have been made to call out, if necessary, 50,000 volunteers from Virginia, to be rendezvoused at Norfolk, Richmond, Fredericksburg, Alexandria, Harper's Ferry, Grafton, Kanawha, Parkersburg, and Mounsdville. Convention has authorized a provisional army of 10,000. Our troops are poorly armed. Tolerable supply of powder; deficient in caps.   JOHN LETCHER.

[BY THE GOVERNOR OF VIRGINIA.]

A PROCLAMATION.

RICHMOND, *May* 3, 1861.

The sovereignty of the Commonwealth of Virginia having been denied, her territorial rights assailed, her soil threatened with invasion by the authorities at Washington, and every artifice employed which could inflame the people of the Northern States and misrepresent our purposes and wishes, it becomes the solemn duty of every citizen of this State to prepare for the impending conflict. These misrepresentations have been carried to such extent that foreigners and naturalized citizens who but a few years ago were denounced by the North and deprived of essential rights have now been induced to enlist into regiments for the pur-

---

* Thomas J. Jackson.

pose of invading this State, which then vindicated those rights and effectually resisted encroachments which threatened their destruction. Against such a policy and against the force which the government at Washington, relying upon its numerical strength, is now rapidly concentrating, it becomes the State of Virginia to prepare proper safeguards. To this end and for these purposes, and with a determination to repel invasion, I, John Letcher, Governor of the Commonwealth of Virginia, by authority of the convention, do hereby authorize the commanding general of the military forces of this State to call out and cause to be mustered into the service of Virginia, from time to time, as the public exigencies may require, such additional number of volunteers as he may deem necessary.

Given under my hand, as Governor, and under the seal of the Commonwealth, at Richmond, this 3d day of May, 1861, and in the eighty-fifth year of the Commonwealth.

JOHN LETCHER.

By the Governor:
GEORGE W. MUNFORD,
Secretary of the Commonwealth.

HEADQUARTERS, VIRGINIA FORCES,
RICHMOND, VA., *May 4*, 1861.

COL. GEORGE A. PORTERFIELD, *Harper's Ferry, Va.*

Colonel: You are directed to repair to Grafton, Taylor County, Va. and select a position for the troops called into the service of the State for the protection and defense of that part of the country. It is desired to hold both branches of the railroad to the Ohio River, to prevent its being used to the injury of the State. You must, therefore, choose your position with this view, that you may readily re-enforce troops on either branch. Major A. Loring, at Wheeling, has been directed, with the volunteer force under his command, to give protection to the terminus of the main road at the Ohio River, with whom you will communicate and co-operate. You will also place a force on the Parkersburg Branch, at such point as you may select, under a suitable officer with necessary orders for his guidance. Major F. M. Boykin, Jr., of the Virginia Volunteers, who will act under your orders, has been previously authorized to call out volunteers from that section of country, and you are authorized, under the proclamation of the Governor, of the 3d inst., to extend the call to the Counties of Wood, Wirt, Roane, Calhoun, Gilmer, Ritchie, Pleasant, and Doddridge to rendezvous at Parkersburg, and to the Counties of Braxton, Lewis, Harrison, Monongalia, Taylor, Barbour, Upshur, Tucker, Marion, Randolph, and Preston to rendezvous at Grafton.

It is not known what number of companies will offer their services, but it is supposed that a regiment composed of infantry, riflemen, and artillery, may be obtained for the Parkersburg Branch; a similar force for the main road, near Moundsville, and three regiments for the reserve, near Grafton; and you are authorized to receive into the service of the State that amount of force. You will report the number of companies mustered into service, their condition, arms, etc. Two hundred muskets have been sent to Colonel Jackson, commanding at Harper's Ferry, to the order of Major Boykin, which will be distributed under your orders, and you will cause proper receipts to be taken from the captains of the companies for the security of the State. More arms, etc., will be forwarded to you on your requisition. It is not intended to interfere with the peaceful use of the road, and you are desired to obtain the co-operation of its officers and agents in the accomplishment of the purpose of the State, and, on your part, to aid them in its management as much as possible.

Second Lieuts. J. G. Gittings and W. E. Kemble, of the Provisional Army of Virginia, have been ordered to report to you for duty.

Very respectfully, etc., R. E. LEE, *Maj.-Gen'l Commanding.*

HEADQUARTERS, VIRGINIA FORCES,
RICHMOND, VA., *May* 11, 1861.

MAJ. F. M. BOYKIN, JR., *Grafton, Va.*

Major: Your letter of the 7th has just been received, and I regret to learn that the prospect of assembling the Virginia forces at Grafton is so unfavorable. You must persevere, however, and call out companies from the well affected counties, and march them to Grafton or such other point in that vicinity as you may select. Four hundred rifles and some ammunition have been ordered from Staunton to Major Goff, Virginia Volunteers, at Beverly, Randolph County, who has been directed to communicate their arrival to Colonel Porterfield and take his directions as to their disposition. You can by this means arm certain companies and prepare them for service preparatory to receiving those from Harper's Ferry. I do not think it prudent to order companies from other parts of the State to Grafton, as it might irritate instead of conciliating the population of that region. On Colonel Porterfield's arrival at Grafton communicate this letter to him.

Very respectfully, etc.,

R. E. LEE, *Major-Gen'l Commanding.*

GRAFTON, VA., *May* 16, 1861.

COL. R. S. GARNETT, *Adjutant-General Virginia Army, Richmond, Va.*

Colonel: In my last report I stated that I would first get possession of the arms consigned to Major Goff, and then try to collect a force and occupy this place. I accordingly sent a messenger to Major Goff, at Beverly, about fifty miles distant, and proceeded to ascertain what force I could get, its condition, and the sentiment of the people in the counties of Taylor, Barbour, and Harrison.

I also sent orders to the captains of companies, supposed to be armed, in the surrounding counties to bring their companies immediately to a designated point near Grafton and there await my orders. The messenger from Beverly returned with the reply that nothing had been heard of the rifles, nor had Major Goff been informed that they were to be sent to him. This is a serious disappointment. Several companies in this vicinity are organizing and expecting to be furnished at once with arms and ammunition. I found a company organizing at Pruntytown, in this county, which will be ready to receive arms in a day or so. There is another at Philippi, Barbour County, awaiting arms, and another in Clarksburg which will soon be ready. I have seen the officers of these companies. There are other companies forming in the surrounding counties, but all without arms and ununiformed. This force, when received, will not for some months be more effective than undisciplined militia.

There are but two companies in this vicinity known to be armed. One of these, Captain Boggess, at Weston, about forty-five miles distant, has the old flint-lock musket, in bad order, and no ammunition. The other, Capt. Thompson's, at Fairmount, twenty miles from this place, has a better gun and some ammunition. These companies are now marching towards this point; are ordered to do so at least. This is the only force on which I have to depend, and it is very weak compared with the strength of those in this section who, I am assured, are ready to oppose me.

I have found great diversity of opinion and much bitterness of feeling among the people of this region. They are apparently upon the verge of a civil war. A few bad men have done much mischief by stirring up rebellion among the people, and representing to them the weakness of the State and its inability or indisposition to protect them, the power of the Government at Washington, and their willingness to give any aid required to resist the

State authorities. I am too credibly informed to entertain doubt that they have been and will be supplied with the means of resistance. They and their accomplices have also threatened the property and persons of law-abiding citizens with fire and the sword. Their efforts to intimidate have had their effect both to dishearten one party and encourage the other. Many good citizens have been dispirited, while traitors seized the guns and ammunition of the State to be used against its authority. Arms in the hands of disbanded volunteer companies have been retained for the same avowed purpose. The force in this section will need the best rifles. Those at Harper's Ferry, which were injured by the fire, if fitted up, will do very well, as there will not be the same use for the bayonet in these hills as elsewhere, and the movements should be of light infantry and rifle, although the bayonet, of course, would be desirable. I have the honor to be,   Yours, etc.,

GEORGE A. PORTERFIELD, *Colonel.*

HEADQUARTERS, VIRGINIA FORCES,
RICHMOND, VA., *May* 27, 1861.
COL. GEORGE A. PORTERFIELD, *Commanding, etc., Grafton, Va.*

Sir : I have to inform you that I have ordered one thousand muskets, with a sufficient supply of powder and lead to Beverly, escorted by Colonel Heck and Major Cowan. Any instructions you may have for Colonel Heck address to him at Beverly. Colonel Heck has been instructed to call out all the volunteers that he can along his route.

I am, sir, with great respect, your obedient servant,

R. E. LEE, *General Commanding.*

By the foregoing proclamation, letters and orders of the Confederates in authority, it will be observed that the eagerness to possess the western part of the State, in advance of any definite action upon the part of the people thereof, proved to be premature and certainly ill advised; and the discomfiture of the local managers, who hoped to maintain absolute control of the whole State, must have been not only disappointing but humiliating indeed; and perhaps none shared in this humiliation to a greater extent than did Colonel Porterfield and Major Boykin at Grafton, and Major Loring at Wheeling, especially when they realized that their appeal for arms and munitions of war were not complied with. When, therefore, Colonel Porterfield learned that Union soldiers would probably reach Grafton in advance of the arrival of his long expected arms, he decided to retire from that town; but before doing so, he was impelled to do something in a war-like way, and therefore burned two bridges on the Baltimore and Ohio Railroad, west of Grafton, near Mannington; and this, too, in utter disregard of General Lee's proclaiming and directing that the Baltimore and Ohio Railroad was to be protected. So, for the present, we leave Colonel Porterfield and his command in possession of Philippi.

"The Department of the Ohio," already referred to in this chapter, was originally instituted to guard the line of the Ohio River, but as time advanced and the Confederates became more bold, the general Government became more aggressive, and the line of the Ohio River was lost sight of in view of a greater purpose.

When, therefore, General McClellan received orders to send troops across the Ohio into West Virginia, the occasion was hailed by the West Virginians with demonstrations of enthusiasm; for the entire loyal portion of the State had been in a condition of terror for several weeks by reason of the presence of armed soldiers of the Confederacy having full possession of the State. The advent of McClellan's troops, therefore, was not regarded as an invasion, but with rejoicing and thankfulness to friends coming to the rescue; and this feature distinguished it from the operations that were going on for the occupation of the eastern part of the State. Before the advent of his troops into West Virginia, McClellan issued two proclamations—one to his soldiers and the other to the people whom they were sent to protect. In explanation of the objects of these two official papers, McClellan says: "I addressed them to the inhabitants of West Virginia and to my troops entirely of my own volition; I had received no intimation of the policy intended to be pursued by the general Government, and had no time to seek for instructions. When, on the afternoon of May 26th, I received, at Camp Dennison, confirmation of the movements of the Secessionists to destroy the Baltimore and Ohio Railroad, I at once ordered by telegraph Col. B. F. Kelley, 1st W. Va. Infantry, and other regiments to move from Wheeling and Parkersburg along the two branches of that railway to Grafton. I wrote the proclamation and the address of May 26th to the inhabitants of West Virginia and my troops in my dining-room at Cincinnati in the utmost haste, with the ladies of my family conversing in the room, and without consulting any one. They were at once dispatched by telegraph to Wheeling and Parkersburg, there to be printed." Following is the Proclamation and the address.

PROCLAMATION.

HEADQUARTERS, DEPARTMENT OF THE OHIO, *May* 26, 1861.

To the Union Men of Western Virginia.

VIRGINIANS: The general Government has long enough endured the machinations of a few factious rebels in your midst. Armed traitors have in vain endeavored to deter you from expressing your loyalty at the polls. Having failed in this infamous attempt to deprive you of the exercise of your dearest rights, they now seek to inaugurate a reign of terror and thus force you to yield to their schemes and submit to the yoke of the traitorous conspiracy dignified by the name of Southern Confederacy. They are destroying the property of citizens of your State and ruining your magnificent railways. The general Government has heretofore carefully abstained from sending troops across the Ohio, or even from posting them along its banks, although frequently urged by many of your prominent citizens to do so.

I determined to await the result of the late election, desirous that no one might be able to say that the slightest effort had been made from this side to influence the free expression of your opinion, although the many agencies brought to bear upon you by the rebels were well known.

You have now shown, under the most adverse circumstances, that the great mass of the people of Western Virginia are true and loyal to that beneficent Government under which we and our fathers have lived so long.

As soon as the result of the election was known the traitors commenced their work of destruction. The general Government cannot close its ears to the demand you have made for assistance. I have ordered troops to cross the river. They come as your friends and brothers—as enemies only to the armed rebels who are preying upon you. Your homes, your families, and your property are safe under our protection. All your rights shall be religiously respected.

Notwithstanding all that has been said by the traitors to induce you to believe that our advent among you will be signalized by interference with your slaves, understand one thing clearly, not only will we abstain from all such interference, but we will, on the contrary, with an iron hand , crush any attempt at insurrection on their part.

Now that we are in your midst, I call upon you to fly to arms and support the general Government. Sever the connection that binds you to traitors. Proclaim to the world that the faith and loyalty so long boasted by the Old Dominion are still preserved in western Virginia, and that you remain true to the Stars and Stripes.

GEO. B. McCLELLAN, *Maj.-Gen'l Commanding.*

ADDRESS TO THE SOLDIERS OF THE EXPEDITION.

HEADQUARTERS, DEPARTMENT OF THE OHIO,

CINCINNATI, *May* 26, 1861.

Soldiers: You are ordered to cross the frontier and enter upon the soil of Virginia. Your mission is to restore peace and confidence, to protect the majesty of the law, and to rescue our brethren from the grasp of armed traitors. You are to act in concert with the Virginia troops, and to support their advance. I place under the safeguard of your honor the persons and property of the Virginians. I know that you will respect their feelings and all their rights. Preserve the strictest discipline ; remember that each one of you holds in his keeping the honor of Ohio and of the Union.

If you are called upon to overcome armed opposition I know that your courage is equal to the task ; but remember that your only foes are the armed traitors, and show mercy even to them when they are in your power, for many of them are misguided. When under your protection the loyal men of western Virginia have been enabled to organize and arm they can protect themselves, and then you can return to your homes with the proud satisfaction of having preserved a gallant people from destruction.

GEO. B. McCLELLAN,

Maj.-Gen'l U. S. Army, Comdg. Dept.

On that memorable 26th of May another event transpired that was specially gratifying to all loyal West Virginians. It was McClellan's order to Colonel Kelley, at Wheeling, to proceed to Grafton and take possession of that place, and to protect the Baltimore and Ohio Railroad at that point, where the Confederates had burned several bridges.

When Colonel Kelley's call for troops was made, his own 1st W. Va. Infantry and several companies of the 2d W. Va. Infantry appeared upon the field as promptly as the friends of Roderick Dhu burst into view upon their Alpine hills.   The 1st Regiment, Colonel Kelley's, the first recruited in the State, was mustered into the service of the United States on the 25th day of May, 1861.   Colonel Kelley at once reported to General McClellan, then at Cincinnati, O., for orders, when the General directed Colonel Kelley to fortify the hills surrounding the city of Wheeling.   Colonel Kelley's familiarity with the topography of the State reasoned that that would be a useless expenditure of time and means, and at once made his conviction known in a letter to General McClellan, and suggested instead that the true policy was to prevent the enemy from occupying the rich valleys of the Ohio and Kanawha, by driving him out of that part of the country.   McClellan telegraphed in reply that he concurred in Colonel Kelley's plan, and ordered him to get ready to move as soon as possible on Grafton, then occupied by Major Boykin's Confederate force.   This order, already referred to, was received in the afternoon of the 26th, and on the morning of the 27th, before day-break, the 1st W. Va. Infantry was on the cars bound for Grafton.   All went well until the arrival of the regiment at Mannington, when it was found that the Confederates had burned two bridges on the Baltimore and Ohio Railroad four miles from that place.   Colonel Kelley moved forward to the burned bridges, went into camp, and with a strong force proceeded to rebuild the bridges.   During the day Colonel Kelley received a telegram from General McClellan advising him that troops from Ohio and Indiana were on the way to support him.   Upon their arrival they proved to be the 16th Ohio Inft., Colonel Irvine, and the 9th Indiana Inf., Col. R. H. Milroy.   When Colonel Kelley arrived at Grafton he found the Confederates had, like the Arabs, "folded their tents and as silently stole away."   So the occupation of Grafton had been effected without the firing of a single gun.   In addition to the regiments named, a brigade of Indiana volunteers, under Brig.-Gen'l Thomas A. Morris, was sent forward by rail from Indianapolis.   Morris reached Grafton on the 1st of June, and was intrusted with the command of all the troops in West Virginia.

In conference with Colonel Kelley he found that Kelley had already planned an attack on Porterfield at Philippi.   So well pleased was General Morris with the plan that he approved it in its entirety, but having more troops at command, he enlarged it by sending another column, under Col. Ebenezer Dumont, of the 7th Indiana, to co-operate with Colonel Kelley.   The plan was a night march, to be made in two columns, starting from points on the railroad about twelve miles apart and concentrating on Philippi, and making the attack at day-break of June 3d. Each column contained about 1500 infantry, and two field pieces of artillery, smooth-bore, 6-pounders, with Colonel Dumont's column.

Grafton and vicinity had many spies, who readily obtained every information in regard to Morris' movements. It was necessary, therefore, to arrange the expedition so as to give a false impression, and thereby secure the advantage of a surprise of the enemy. With this view the following order was given to Colonel Kelley.

HEADQUARTERS, U. S. VOLUNTEERS,
GRAFTON, W. VA., *June* 2, 1861.

COL. B. F. KELLEY, *Commanding First Regiment Virginia Volunteers.*

Colonel: With six companies of your regiment, nine companies of Colonel Milroy's Ninth Indiana, and six companies of Colonel Irvine's Sixteenth Ohio, you will proceed this morning to a point about six miles eastward from this place on the Baltimore and Ohio Railroad, and march by the shortest and most practicable route towards Philippi. You must regulate your march according to your own discretion, and your bivouac or rest at night in such manner that you are sure of coming before the town of Philippi as near 4 o'clock to-morrow morning as possible. Should you this evening receive certain information that the rebels have retreated eastward from Philippi, you will make the resting time of your troops as short as possible in order to follow them up with all the speed the strength of your troops will allow. In such case you will, as early as possible, inform Golonel Dumont on the other bank of the river, and direct his co-operation with you in the pursuit, which, if in your discretion you are in sufficient force, you will continue until they are beyond Beverly, and you will also apprise these headquarters in order that supplies may be forwarded to you

By command of

JOHN A. STEIN, *A. A. A. Gen'l.*   BRIG.-GEN'L T. A. MORRIS.

This column (the left of the attack) moved by railroad train on the 2d, at 9 o'clock A. M., to the eastward, and was generally understood to be an advance on Harper's Ferry. After leaving the cars the distance to Philippi was about twenty-five miles, on a road but little traveled. The instructions required a rapid march during the day and early part of the night to a point from which, after a sufficient rest, Philippi could be certainly reached at 4 o'clock next morning.

The night column, under Colonel Dumont, was organized in conformity with the following order.

HEADQUARTERS, U. S. VOLUNTEERS,
GRAFTON, W. VA., *June* 2, 1861.

COLONEL DUMONT, *Comdg. Seventh Regt. Ind. Vols., Grafton, W. Va.*

Colonel: You will proceed by railroad this evening, at 8.30 oclock, to Webster, with eight companies of your regiment. At Webster you will be joined by Colonel Steedman with five companies of his regiment and two field pieces, also by Colonel Crittenden with six companies of his regiment. From Webster you will, with this command, march on Philippi, using your own discretion in the conduct of the march, keeping in view that you should arrive in front of the town at 4 o'clock precisely to-morrow morning. Information is received that the rebels are in some force at Philippi.

The object of your column will be to divert attention until the attack is made by Colonel Kelley, and should resistance be offered you are to aid him to the extent of your ability. In the conduct of your column you must use your discretion, being governed by such circumstances as may occur.

When joined by Colonel Kelley, the whole force will be under his command.

The companies of your regiment will take two full days' rations. Should you receive instructions from Colonel Kelley that the rebels have retreated, you will join him at once and act under his command.   By command of

BRIG.-GEN'L T. A. MORRIS.

JOHN A. STEIN, *A. A. A. Gen'l.*

This force, in leaving Grafton after dark, had reasonable assurance of reaching the enemy in advance of any information from their friends, and, as events proved, did so. The enemy was entirely off his guard, and the surprise was complete. But for the terrific storm of wind and rain that night the capture of the entire Confederate force must have taken place.

The elements seemed to have conspired on that march, to test the physical endurance of this young army, and they received their baptism like veterans. In a march of fifteen miles in pitchy darkness, drenching rain, over a mountainous country, both officers and men displayed a wonderful courage, and the march was followed by an irresistible attack and stampede of the enemy. The last five miles of Colonel Dumont's column was made in an hour and a quarter, many of his men fell by the roadside from shear exhaustion, others threw away their haversacks and provisions to keep up, rushing forward in order to be in at the fray. It is remarkable that under such circumstances the two columns were but fifteen minutes apart at the time assigned for their meeting.

As soon as Dumont's column began the attack in front, the enemy's pickets commenced firing and our artillery opened upon the surprised camp and threw it into utter confusion. But Kelley arrived only in time to aid in the pursuit, notwithstanding the enemy were in disorder rout. Porterfield succeeded, by personal coolness and courage, in getting them off with but few casualties and the loss of quite a large number of arms; the camp and all their supplies were of course captured.

It was a remarkable coincidence in the history of battles that no injury should occur on the Union side, save the severe wounding in the breast of brave Colonel Kelley, by a pistol shot in the hands of a Confederate quartermaster. No prisoners were taken, nor did any dead or wounded fall into our hands.   Porterfield retreated to Beverly, 30 miles to the south of Philippi. The telegraphic reports had put the Confederate force at 2000, and their loss at 15 killed.

The campaign thus opened with laurels for General McClellan, and the "Philippi races," as they were locally termed, greatly encouraged the Union men of West Virginia, and of course greatly depressed the Secessionists; and thus ended the first battle of the war in West Virginia.

CHAPTER V.

GENERAL McCLELLAN'S OPERATIONS—(CONTINUED).

Crosses the Ohio River and Establishes his Headquarters at Grafton.—Issues Two More Proclamations.—Gen'l R. E. Lee's Plans.—General Garnett at Beverly.—General Wise in the Kanawha.—Stupidity of Confederate Authorities.—Garnett's Force on the 1st of July. —Re-enforced and Entrenched at Rich Mountain and Laurel Hill.—Isolated from Base of Supplies.—General McClellan Posted Troops from Wheeling and Parkersburg to Grafton. —20,000 Troops in his Campaign Against Beverly, Rich Mountain and Laurel Hill.— July 2d, McClellan's Headquarters at Buckhannon.—July 10th, at Middle Fork.—Advancing on Confederate Forces.—Rosecrans' Assault on Laurel Hill.—Confederates Beaten at Every Point.—In Retreat.—Skirmish at Carrick's Ford.—General Garnett Killed. —Surrender of Colonel Pegram's Forces.—McClellan Transferred to the Army of the Potomac.—General Comments.—McClellan's Congratulatory Address Upon Taking Leave of His Army.—Rejoicing Throughout the Country.

FOR three weeks following the "Philippi races" matters military, with both the Union and the Confederate sides, were on the *qui vive*. McClellan had maintained his headquarters in Ohio; but having received reports that the enemy were concentrating at Beverly, on the 22d of June he crossed the Ohio River at Parkersburg with his official staff, and on the following day established his headquarters at Grafton and issued the two following Proclamations:

HEADQUARTERS, DEPARTMENT OF THE OHIO,

GRAFTON, VA., *June* 23, 1861.

To the Inhabitants of Western Virginia :

The army of this department, headed by Virginia troops, is rapidly occupying all western Virginia. This is done in co-operation with, and in support of, such civil authorities of the State as are faithful to the Constitution and laws of the United States. The proclamation issued by me under date of May 26, 1861, will be strictly maintained. Your houses, families, property, and all your rights will be religiously respected ; we are enemies to none but armed rebels and those voluntarily giving them aid. All officers of this army will be held responsible for the most prompt and vigorous action in repressing disorder and punishing aggression by those under their command.

To my great regret, I find that enemies to the United States continue to carry on a system of hostilities prohibited by the laws of war among belligerent nations, and of course far more wicked and intolerable when directed against loyal citizens engaged in the defense of the common Government of all. Individuals and marauding parties are pursuing a guerrilla warfare, firing upon sentinels and pickets, burning bridges, insulting, injuring, and even killing citizens because of their Union sentiments, and committing many kindred acts.

I do now, therefore, make proclamation and warn all persons that individuals or parties engaged in this species of warfare—irregular in every view which can be taken of it— thus attacking sentries, pickets or other soldiers, destroying public or private property, or committing injuries against any of the inhabitants because of Union sentiments or conduct, will be dealt with in their persons and property according to the severest rules of military law.

All persons giving information or aid to the public enemies will be arrested and kept in close custody, and all persons found bearing arms, unless of known loyalty, will be arrested and held for examination.   GEO. B. McCLELLAN,
Maj.-General U. S. Army, Comd'g Depart.

HEADQUARTERS, DEPARTMENT OF THE OHIO,
GRAFTON, VA., *June* 25, 1861.

To the Soldiers of the Army of the West:

You are here to support the Government of your country, and to protect the lives and liberties of your brethren, threatened by a rebellious and traitorous foe. No higher and nobler duty could devolve upon you, and I expect you to bring to its performance the highest and noblest qualities of soldiers—discipline, courage and mercy. I call upon the officers of every grade to enforce the strictest discipline, and I know that those of all grades, privates and officers, will display in battle cool, heroic courage, and will know how to show mercy to a disarmed enemy. Bear in mind that you are in the country of friends, not of enemies; that you are here to protect, not to destroy. Take nothing, destroy nothing, unless you are ordered to do so by your general officers. Remember that I have pledged my word to the people of western Virginia that their rights in person and property shall be respected. I ask every one of you to make good this promise in its broadest sense.

We come here to save, not to upturn. I do not appeal to the fear of punishment, but to your appreciation of the sacredness of the cause in which we are engaged. Carry with you into battle the conviction that you are right, and that God is on your side.

Your enemies have violated every moral law; neither God nor man can sustain them. They have, without cause, rebelled against a mild and paternal Government; they have seized upon public and private property; they have outraged the persons of Northern men merely because they were from the North, and of Southern Union men merely because they loved the Union; they have placed themselves beneath contempt, unless they can retrieve some honor on the field of battle. You will pursue a different course. You will be honest, brave, and merciful; you will respect the right of private opinion; you will punish no man for opinion's sake. Show to the world that you differ from our enemies in the points of honor, honesty, and respect for private opinion, and that we inaugurate no reign of terror where we go.

Soldiers! I have heard that there was danger here, I have come to place myself at your head and to share it with you. I fear now but one thing—that you will not find foemen worthy of your steel. I know that I can rely upon you.

GEO. B. McCLELLAN, *Maj.-Gen'l Commanding.*

If the reader will consult a map of West Virginia it will be seen that as the Potomac route was at that time in the hands of the Union forces, the Confederates, in order to occupy West Virginia, would have to do so either by the Staunton and Beverly turnpike or by the Kanawha route, the key of which, west of the mountains, was Gauley Bridge. General Lee's plan was to send columns upon both of these lines. Gen'l Robert S. Garnett was placed in command at Beverly, and Gen'l Henry A. Wise upon the Kanawha. General Garnett had been an officer in the United States Army, and it was supposed that this fact would stimulate recruiting and organizations of regiments from the Secession element of the population; and to still further this idea, some Virginia regiments, recruited in the eastern part of the State, were sent with him. General Wise was a distinguished Virginia politician, who had been Governor of the State, and had held many places of honor and trust in his State.

As we review the situation at this time, we marvel at the seeming stupidity of the Confederate authorities. General Lee did not illustrate that military genius that later in the war characterized the actions of that great general. To have held the position selected for General Garnett after the battle of Philippi, except with a force so large as to make defeat impossible, was simply a military blunder. On the 1st of July Garnett reported his force as 4500 men; and his efforts to recruit, he declared, had proven an absolute failure; in a whole month only 23 men had been induced to join his command. Garnett was, however, receiving re-enforcements daily from southeast Virginia, Georgia and other States, until his command numbered about 8000 men. The several points held by these Confederates were ranged from twenty to thirty miles southward from Philippi. Camp "Rich Mountain" is a gap in the Laurel Hill range, where the Staunton and Weston turnpike crosses it, about five miles west from Beverly. Garnett regarded this pass as naturally very strong and easily held; he therefore intrenched about 2000 of his men and 4 pieces of artillery under command of Colonel Pegram of Virginia forces, while he himself, with about 6000 men and 4 pieces of cannon, occupied Laurel Hill, fifteen miles further to the westward. This place was very strongly fortified; in fact, both at Rich Mountain and Laurel Hill the Confederate commander had selected the very strongest natural position for defense to be found in that part of the country. The fortifications consisted of heavy breastworks of timber and earth; but the stupid part of the whole business just referred to was that they had completely isolated themselves from all accessible base of supplies, with but one rough road as a line of advance or retreat, and this in face of the fact that the first principle in military operations is to be sure of your base of supplies and lines of retreat.

General McClellan had gradually posted his forces along the Baltimore and Ohio Railroad from Parkersburg and Wheeling to Grafton, and upon taking the field in his campaign against Beverly, Rich Mountain and Laurel Hill, he had about 20,000 men, consisting of 16 Ohio regiments, 9 from

Indiana, and 2 from West Virginia, with 4 batteries of artillery of 6 guns each, and 2 troops of cavalry. Of these forces, about 500 were guarding the railroad under the command of Brig.-Gen'l C. W. Hill, of Ohio. Brigadier-General Morris, of Indiana, was at Philippi with a strong brigade, and the rest of the forces were designated into three brigades, forming the immediate command of General McClellan. The brigade commanders were Brig.-Gen'l W. S. Rosecrans, U. S. A., Gen'l Newton Schleich, of Ohio, and Col. Robert L. McCook, of Ohio.

On July 2, McClellan's headquarters were in Buckhannon, an important strategical position; from there he could cover his base of operations and supplies and move readily, by good roads, in any desired direction; from there he could communicate by telegraph with his troops wherever located; from this point he had directed the commanding officers at Grafton, Webster, Clarksburg and Parkersburg to intrench their positions.

On the 10th of July, we find McClellan at Middle Fork Bridge, having ordered an advance all along his lines. His personal command is in sight of the enemy at Rich Mountain, with General Morris in sight of the Confederate works at Laurel Hill. The advance of both columns to these points had been made with only a skirmishing resistance. A reconnoissance made on the 10th showed that the position at Rich Mountain would be difficult to take by a direct assault from the front, so preparations were made to attack the following day. Morris was directed to hold firmly his position before Garnett, and lead him (Garnett) to believe that the main assault would be made upon his works. On the evening of the 10th General Rosecrans took to McClellan a young man named Hart, whose father lived two miles in rear of Pegram's position, who said he could direct a column of infantry to his father's farm by a circuit around Pegram's left flank, south of the turnpike. This information decided McClellan in his method of attack; so, with the main body of his army, he passed around by Buckhannon to the western slope of Rich Mountain. McClellan here divided his force into two columns, giving one to General Rosecrans, with young Hart for his guide; he (Rosecrans) did go to the rear of Pegram, while McClellan remained in front ready to attack simultaneously. When Rosecrans secured his place in the rear, he sent a courier back to McClellan to give the signal; the messenger missed his way and fell into the hands of the enemy, thus giving them full information of the movement; so when Rosecrans reached his point of attack he found that Pegram had detached about 350 infantry, with one piece of artillery, to meet the advance. The Confederates had thrown up hasty breastworks of logs and rails, and the Union troops were received with both musketry and cannon.

The combat lasted two or three hours, with varied results as to vantage gained by either side, when a charge was ordered by Rosecrans and, with a few heavy volleys from another position of vantage his forces had secured, broke the enemy's lines; and this proved to be opportunely, for Pegram had just sent re-enforcements with another cannon, but the rout was complete, and Rosecrans was in possession of the field. As was so often the case during the war, the march and the battle had been made in a rainstorm.

Rosecrans did not follow the retreating enemy, but directed his men, who were greatly exhausted by their long march, to rest upon their arms until next morning. On the morning of the 12th it was found that Pegram and his army had disappeared from their position. McClellan with his immediate command did not share in the attack; but why he did not has not as yet been explained.

By this event there fell into Rosecrans' hands, as trophies of the fight, all of Pegram's artillery, tents and camp equipage, with many stand of arms, etc.

Rosecrans' loss had been 12 killed and 49 wounded. The enemy left in their deserted camp 20 wounded, and 63 surrendered.

Pegram reports 2 officers and between 40 and 45 men killed; wounded, 5 officers and about 20 men. On the night of the 11th, after the fight of Rich Mountain, Pegram's forces made their way towards Laurel Hill. Garnett, who held that position, having been warned of Pegram's fate and his own danger, hastily left his intrenchments and proceeded southward, hoping to reach Beverly before McClellan, but on his way thither he met the fugitives of Pegram's army and learned of them that Beverly was already in possession of the Union forces, and that his retreat to the southward was cut off. The only way, then, for escape left to Garnett was to follow the course of the Cheat River towards the northeast, hoping thereby to gain an outlet into the valley of Virginia. Morris' troops followed in swift pursuit, overtaking the retreating Confederates about noonday on the 13th, Captain Benham leading the advance of Morris' troops. Then followed continuous skirmishing, and pursuing and being pursued for over two hours, Garnett himself in command of his rear guard. When Carrick's Ford was reached a pitched battle ensued. When Garnett realized that he could no longer stay the impetuous attack of the Union forces he ordered the retreat; and while withdrawing (in person) his skirmishers from behind a pile of drift-wood, the brave Garnett was killed. One of the enemy's cannon and about 40 wagons fell into Morris' hands, as did also the body of the dead general. The pusuit was then discontinued. In the meantime, Colonel Pegram and his command were floundering around in the mountains, endeavoring to make their escape.

Believing his own account of the affair would be more edifying reading than either the words of McClellan or of the author's version of it, we shall submit an extract from his report, War Records, Vol. II, to the Adjutant-General at Richmond, as follows:

BEVERLY, VA., *July* 14, 1861.

EXTRACT.

*   *   *   *   *   *   *   *   *   *   *

I then went back up the mountain,* where I found the whole force, composed of five companies of the 20th Va. Infantry and one company of Colonel Heck's regiment, drawn up in line in ambuscade near the road, under the command of Major Nat. Tyler of the 20th regiment. I called their attention and said a few encouraging words to the men, asking them if they would follow their officers to the attack, to which they responded by a cheer. I was here interrupted by Captain Anderson, who said to me : "Colonel Pegram, these men are completely demoralized and will need you to lead them." I took my place at the head of the column which I marched in single file through laurel thickets and other almost impassable brushwood up a ridge to the top of the mountain. This placed me about one-fourth of a mile on the right flank of the enemy, and which was exactly the point I had been making for. I had just gotten all the men up together, and was about making my disposition for the attack, when Major Tyler came up and reported that during the march up the ridge one of the men in his fright had turned around and shot the first sergeant of one of the rear companies, which had caused nearly the whole of the company to run to the rear. He then said the men were so intensely demoralized that he considered it madness to attempt to do anything with them by leading them on to the attack. A mere glance at the frightened countenances around me convinced me that this distressing news was but too true, and it was confirmed by the opinion of the three or four company commanders around me. They all agreed with me that there was nothing left to do but to send the command under Major Tyler to effect a junction with either General Garnett, at Laurel Hill, or Col. Wm. C. Scott, who was supposed to be with his regiment near Beverly. It was now 6½ o'clock P. M., when I retraced my steps with much difficulty back to camp, losing myself frequently on the way, and arriving there at 11¼ o'clock. Soon after I called a council of war, and it was determined to leave camp and attempt to join General Garnett. We started at 1 o'clock A. M., without a guide, over the mountains. As I remained in camp to see the last company in column, by the time I reached the head of the column, which was nearly one mile long, Captain Lilley's company of Colonel Heck's regiment had disappeared, and has not been since heard from.

The difficulties attending my march with the remaining eight companies it would be impossible for me to exaggerate. We arrived at Tygart's Valley River at 7 o'clock P. M., having made the distance of about 12 miles in 18 hours. Here we were met by several country people who appeared to be our friends, and who informed us that General Garnett had retreated that afternoon up the Leading Creek road, in Tucker County, and that he was being pursued by 3000 of the enemy.

This, of course, rendered all chance of joining General Garnett, or escape in that direction, utterly impossible. I found, on examining some citizens, that there was, if any, only one possible means of escape, and that was by a road which, passing within three miles of the enemy's camp at Beverly, led over precipitous mountains into Pendleton County. Along this road there were represented to me to be but a few miserable habitations, where it

*Referring to the engagement at Rich Mountain.

would be utterly impossible for even one company of my men to get food ; and as it was 11 o'clock P. M. it would be necessary to leave at once, without allowing them to get a mouthful to eat where they were. I now called a council of war, composed like the one of the preceding night, when it was agreed almost unanimously (only two members voting in the negative) there was left to us nothing but the sad determination of surrendering ourselves prisoners of war to the enemy at Beverly. I was perfectly convinced that an attempt on our part to escape would sacrifice by starvation a large number of the lives of the command. I now dispatched a messenger to Beverly, which was distant some six miles, with a note, of which the following is the substance :

HEADQUARTERS, AT MR. KETTLE'S FARM HOUSE,
July 12, 1861.

To the Commanding Officer of the Northern Forces, Beverly, Va.

Sir : Owing to the reduced and almost famished condition of the force now here under my command, I am compelled to offer to surrender them to you as prisoners of war.

I have only to ask that they receive at your hands such treatment as Northern prisoners have invariably received from the South.

I am, Sir, your obedient servant,
JOHN PEGRAM, *Lieut.-Col. P. A. C. S. Commanding.*

Between 7 and 8 o'clock next morning two officers of General McClellan's staff arrived with his reply, of which the following is an exact copy :

HEADQUARTERS, DEPARTMENT OF THE OHIO,
BEVERLY, VA., *July* 13, 1861.

JOHN PEGRAM, ESQ., *Styling himself Lieut.-Col. P. A. C. S.*

Sir : Your communication, dated yesterday, proposing to surrender as prisoners of war the force assembled under your command has been delivered to me. As commander of this department I will receive you, your officers and men as prisoners of war, but it is not in my power to relieve you or them from any disabilities incurred by taking arms against the United States. I am, very respectfully, your obedient servant,

GEO. B. MCCLELLAN,
Maj.-Gen'l U. S. Army, Comdg. Department.

I then formed the companies and found that 1 officer and about 40 men had left during the night. I now found my force to be 22 officers and 359 men of Colonel Heck's regiment, and 8 officers and 166 men of my own (the 20th Va.) regiment ; with these I marched towards Beverly.

On the way we were met by wagons containing hard bread for my men. On arriving at Beverly we stacked arms, our men were at once put into comfortable quarters, under charge of a guard, and rations issued to them. The officers are on their parole, with the liberty of the town. I deem it my duty to return my thanks, and the thanks of the officers here with me, to General McClellan for the kind treatment our men have received from his troops.

I find on examination that I have failed to mention my whole force at Rich Mountain on the 11th inst.; it was about 1300 men, of whom certainly not more than 350 at the utmost were engaged in the battle at Hart's farm house.

*   *   *   *   *   *   *   *   *   *   *   *   *

I am, Sir, very respectfully, your obedient servant,
JOHN PEGRAM, *Lieut.-Col. P. A. C. S.*

This event was practically the ending of active operations in that early campaign. McClellan did, however, move southward upon the Staunton turnpike, and on the 14th occupied Huttonsville.

In the meantime two regiments of Confederate troops had been hurriedly sent from Staunton to the relief of Garnett, but they were halted at Monterey, and upon them the retreating forces rallied. Gen'l H. R. Jackson was assigned to the command in Garnett's place, and both Governor Letchei and General Lee endeavored to increase this army, and resume the attempt to capture that part of the State.

General McClellan remained inactive until the 22d, when he was called to Washington and placed in command of the army that had so recently been defeated at the first battle of Bull Run.

Viewed in the light of subsequent military events, and especially when we compare the battles of Philippi, Rich Mountain and Carrick's Ford with Antietam, Fredericksburg, Chancellorsville, Bull Run, Gettysburg, Chickamauga and a hundred others that could be named, the " powder burning " of these early episodes would scarcely attain to the dignity of a lively skirmish.

But the importance of these days of *small things* stands high in the history of the nation, and it is worth while to consider how the progress of the war might have been affected or changed had West Virginia, the first theatre of the war, been other than what we found her to be in 1861. And when we take a retrospect of those exciting days, when the country hung breathless on the dispatches of General McClellan from Clarksburg, Grafton, Beverly, Buckhannon, Huttonsville and other points during the months of May, June and July, we can truthfully say that at no time during the progress of the war did the nation have greater cause to rejoice at the results of its victories than it did over these, now insignificant affairs.

President Lincoln and his Cabinet, General Scott and the officers of the Army and Navy rejoiced as the news of victory followed victory. The loyal people of the North, and the East, and the West drank in the good news and predicted the end of the war in sixty days. But the loyal hearts of the people of the border States of Delaware, Maryland, West Virginia, East Tennessee, Kentucky and Missouri had the greater cause to rejoice. The colonists of the Revolutionary struggle were not more excited over the early conflicts of Lexington and Bunker Hill, than were the loyal people of the Union at the result of Philippi, Rich Mountain and Carrick's Ford.

It is no part of the author to discuss here the war record of General McClellan, that question has furnished a theme for writers of both song and story, and volumes have been given to the world in friendly and unfriendly criticism. But in relation to the part he bore that tended to redeem and disenthral West Virginia from the curse of secession and rebellion cannot be fully appreciated, and the *finale* of his operations then, furnishes an irrefutable illustration that "*the pen is mightier than the sword.*"

The results of his campaign, as given to the country in the way of written orders to his subordinates, his proclamations to the people and to his troops, his telegrams and letters to the heads of the army at Washington, beginning with his first occupation of West Virginia and ending with the following congratulations to his troops, were marvels of word painting.

CONGRATULATORY ADDRESS FROM GENERAL McCLELLAN.

ARMY OF OCCUPATION, WESTERN VIRGINIA,
BEVERLY, VA., *July* 16, 1861.

Soldiers of the Army of the West: I am more than satisfied with you. You have annihilated two armies, commanded by educated and experienced soldiers, intrenched in mountain fastnesses fortified at their leisure. You have taken five guns, twelve colors, fifteen hundred stand of arms, one thousand prisoners, including more than forty officers. One of the two commanders of the rebels is a prisoner, the other lost his life on the field of battle. You have killed more than two hundred and fifty of the enemy, who has lost all his baggage and camp equipage. All this has been accomplished with the loss of twenty brave men killed and sixty wounded on your part. You have proved that Union men, fighting for the preservation of our Government, are more than a match for our misguided and erring brethren ; more than this, you have shown mercy to the vanquished. You have made long and arduous marches, often with insufficient food, frequently exposed to the inclemency of the weather. I have not hesitated to demand this of you, feeling that I could rely on your endurance, patriotism and courage. In future I may have still greater demands to make upon you, still greater sacrifices for you to offer. It shall be my care to provide for you to the extent of my ability ; but I know now that by your valor and endurance you will accomplish all that is asked. Soldiers ! I have confidence in you, and I trust you have learned to confide in me. Remember that discipline and subordination are qualities of equal value with courage.

I am proud to say that you have gained the highest reward that American troops can receive—the thanks of Congress and the applause of your fellow-citizens.

GEO. B. McCLELLAN,
Maj.-Gen'l U S. Army Comdg.

Furthermore, this campaign will be recognized as the first great military school for the preparation and education of men who finally became distinguished soldiers. And the first military telegraph erected in this country was the line constructed that followed McClellan from Grafton to Huttonsville, upon which he was enabled to transmit, while on the march, messages at any hour. Finally, as the country was at all times eager for good news, everything emanating from McClellan was regarded as literally true. The people were pleased with him, and he was lionized as the young Napoleon that was to lead the armies of the Union to final victory.

CHAPTER VI.

McCLELLAN'S OPERATIONS—(CONTINUED.)

Gen'ls Henry A. Wise and John B. Floyd in Command of Confederate Forces in the Kana-
wha.—Gen'l J. D. Cox in Command of Union Forces.—General Rosecrans Succeeds
General McClellan in Command of the Department of Ohio.—Reorganization of his
Forces.—Confederates Re-enforced.—Col. E. B. Tyler at Cross Lanes.—Rosecrans Issues
a Proclamation.—General Floyd Captures Cross Lanes.—Wise and Chapman Defeated
by Cox.—Rosecrans in the Kanawha.—Floyd Defeated at Carnifex Ferry by Rosecrans.—
Wise and Floyd at Loggerheads.—Rosecrans at Big Sewell Mountain.—In Winter
Quarters at Gauley Bridge and Vicinity.—The Cheat Mountain District.—Gen'l Joseph
J. Reynolds in Command.—His Fores at Elkwater.—Substantial Breastworks.—Con-
fusion in Uniforms.—General Loring at Huntersville with 8500 Men.—Gen'l Robt. E.
Lee in Command.—His Campaign Against General Reynolds.—Lee's Defeat and Retreat.
—Col. John A. Washington Killed.—Flag of Truce.—General Reynolds Called to Other
Fields.—Gen'l R. H. Milroy in Command—At Cheat Mountain and Elkwater.

DURING the period that General McClellan was driving the Confederates southward along the Alleghany Ridge, Gen'l Henry A.
Wise had, on June 6th, been appointed by the Confederate
authorities to be a brigadier-general and assigned to command in the valley
of the Kanawha. Wise's orders were to proceed with the force placed at
his command, and he was further instructed to rally the people of that valley to
resist the invading army. He was also informed that he must rely upon the
arms among the people to supply the requisite armament, and upon their
valor and knowledge of the country as a substitute for organization and discipline. Not a very encouraging situation for an advance ; but Wise was
ambitious and energetic, so, with the meagre nucleus of an army he
advanced to Lewisburg, thence down the Kanawha Valley, his force gradually increasing until, by the accession of Colonel Tompkins' detachment,
already in the valley, it numbered full 4000 men, including considerable
cavalry and four batteries of artillery. In addition to this force, Gen'l John
B. Floyd, of Virginia, who had been secretary of war under President
Buchanan, and who had also been made a brigadier-general, had been
assigned to the protection of the line of the Tennesse and Virginia Railroad;
the two commands, however, were in close proximity and could be readily
consolidated when necessary. At the time, word had gone out from Wise
and Floyd, that their armies were to proceed northward to Parkersburg and

Clarksburg, and even to Wheeling. This laudable enterprise was however reconsidered, when on the 2d of July General McClellan appointed Brig.-Gen'l J. D. Cox, then at Camp Denison, Ohio, to the command of a brigade of Ohio and Kentucky regiments, and to move at once to Gallipolis, then cross the river and occupy Point Pleasant, Va. The selection of General Cox for this service proved to be a most excellent one. He was a man of military attainments, with plenty of vim and push to carry out his plans.

Upon the appointment of General Rosecrans, on the 23rd of July, to succeed General McClellan in command of the Department of the Ohio, Rosecrans, at Grafton, July 25th, issued Special Order No. 1, in which he designated "the fourth brigade of his command, to consist of the first and second Kentucky, the eleventh and twelfth Ohio regiments, U. S. Volunteer Infantry, the nineteenth, twenty-first, and portions of the eighteenth and twenty-second Ohio Volunteer Militia, the Ironton Cavalry, and such other as may hereafter be attached will be called the 'Brigade of the Kanawha,' and will be commanded by Brigadier-General Cox, U. S. Volunteer Infantry," thus continuing General Cox in command of that region. Cox occupied the Kanawha Valley and fought several engagements in that territory with Floyd and Wise during the months of July and August, and the early part of September.

The Confederates in the meantime had been re-enforced by the militia of Raleigh, Mercer, and Fayette counties to the number of 2000 men, under General Chapman. The Confederates at this date, August 14th, numbered 8000 men, and it was expected that Gen'l Robert E. Lee would lead the force in person against General Cox, who occupied Gauley Bridge.

On the 13th of August, Col. E. B. Tyler with his seventh Ohio Infantry, was ordered by General Rosecrans to Cross Lanes, covering Carnifex Ferry, on the Gauley River, twenty miles above Cox's position.

On the 20th of August, General Rosecrans, following the example of Governor Letcher and General McClellan, issued a Proclamation to the citizens of West Virginia, as follows :

HEADQUARTERS, ARMY OF OCCUPATION,
CLARKSBURG, W. VA., *August* 20, 1861.

To the Loyal Citizens of West Virginia :
You are the vast majority of the people. If the principle of self-government is to be respected, you have a right to stand in the position you have assumed, faithful to the Constitution and laws of Virginia as they were before the Ordinance of Secession.

The Confederates have determined at all hazards to destroy the Government which for eighty years has defended our rights and given us a name among the nations. Contrary to your interests and your wishes they have brought war on your soil.

Their tools and dupes told you you must vote for secession as the only means to insure peace; that unless you did so, hordes of abolitionists would overrun you, plunder your property, steal your slaves, abuse your wives and daughters, seize upon your lands, and hang all those who opposed them.

By these and other atrocious falsehoods they alarmed you and led many honest and unsuspecting citizens to vote for secession. Neither threats, nor fabrications, nor intimidations sufficed to carry western Virginia against the interests and wishes of its people into the arms of Secession.

Enraged that you dared to disobey their behests, eastern Virginians who had been accustomed to rule you and to court your votes and ambitious recreants from among yourselves, disappointed that you would not make good their promises, have conspired to tie you to the desperate fortunes of the Confederacy or drive you from your homes.

Between submission to them and subjugation or expulsion, they leave you no alternative. You say you do not wish to destroy the old Government under which you have lived so long and peacefully; they say you shall break it up. You say you wish to remain citizens of the United States; they reply you shall join the Southern Confederacy to which the Richmond junta has transferred you, and to carry their will there. Jenkins, Wise, Jackson, and other conspirators proclaim upon your soil a relentless and neighborhood war. Their misguided or unprincipled followers re-echo their cry, threatening fire and sword, hanging and exile, to all who oppose their arbitrary designs. They have set neighbor against neighbor and friend against friend; they have introduced a warfare only known among savages. In violation of the laws of nations and humanity, they have proclaimed that private citizens may and ought to make war.

Under this bloody code peaceful citizens, unarmed travelers, and single soldiers have been shot down, and even the wounded and defenseless have been killed; scalping their victims is all that is wanting to make their warfare like that which seventy or eighty years ago was waged by the Indians against the white race on this very ground. You have no other alternative left you but to unite as one man in the defense of your homes, for the restoration of law and order, or be subjugated or driven from the State. I therefore earnestly exhort you to make the most prompt and vigorous measures to put a stop to neighborhood and private wars. You must remember that the laws are suspended in eastern Virginia, which has transferred itself to the Southern Confederacy. The old Constitution and laws of Virginia are only in force in western Virginia. These laws you must maintain.

Let every citizen, without reference to past political opinions, unite with his neighbors to keep these laws in operation, and thus prevent the country from being desolated by plunder and violence, whether committed in the name of Secessionism or Unionism. I conjure all those who have hitherto advocated the doctrine of Secessionism as a political opinion to consider that now its advocacy means war against the peace and interests of western Virginia. It is an invitation to the Southern Confederates to come in and subdue you, and proclaims that there can be no law or right until this is done.

My mission among you is that of a fellow-citizen, charged by the Government to expel the arbitrary force which domineered over you; to restore that law and order of which you have been robbed, and to maintain your right to govern yourselves under the Constitution and laws of the United States.

To put an end to the savage war waged by individuals, who without warrant of military authority lurk in the bushes and waylay messengers or shoot sentries, I shall be obliged to hold the neighborhood in which these outrages are committed responsible; and unless they raise the hue and cry and pursue the offenders, deal with them as accessories to the crime.

Unarmed and peaceful citizens shall be protected, the rights of private property

WILLIAM S. ROSECRANS
Major General U.S.A.

respected, and only those who are found enemies of the Government of the United States and peace of western Virginia will be disturbed. Of those I shall require absolute certainty that they will do no mischief. Put a stop to needless arrests and the spread of malicious reports. Let each town and district choose five of its most reliable and energetic citizens as a committee of public safety, to act in concert with the civic and military authorities and be responsible for the preservation of peace and good order.

     Citizens of western Virginia, your fate is mainly in your own hands. If you allow yourselves to be trampled underfoot by hordes of disturbers, plunderers, and murderers, your land will become a desolation. If you stand firm for law and order and maintain your rights, you may dwell together peacefully and happily as in former days.

W. S. ROSECRANS,
Brig.-Gen'l U. S. Army Commanding.

On the 26th of August, General Floyd crossed the Gauley at Carnifex Ferry, with 2500 men, and surprised Colonel Tyler at Cross Lanes, routing the regiment, with a loss to Tyler of fifteen killed and one hundred captured, of which fifty were wounded. Major Casement rallied a greater part of the regiment and led them over the mountains to Elk River, and thence to Charleston.

Floyd intrenched the position just gained and felt secure, but this occupancy interfered with the line of communication between Cox and Rosecrans.

On the 3d of September, Wise and Chapman planned a concerted attack upon Cox's position at Gauley Bridge; they met with a decisive repulse, the retreating Confederates were pursued, and for two or three days were severely punished by Cox's troops.

ROSECRANS IN THE KANAWHA.

On the above date, Sept. 3d, Rosecrans began his march to the Kanawha from Clarksburg, with three brigades commanded as follows: General Benham, Col. R. L. McCook and Col. E. P. Scammon, consisting of cavalry, infantry and artillery, and an extensive supply train. His route of march was *via* Weston, Bull Town, Sutton and Summerville to Gauley Bridge.

On September 10th, after having marched 17½ miles, Rosecrans reached the enemy's intrenched position in front of Carnifex Ferry, driving his advanced out-post and pickets before him. The enemy was strongly intrenched, covered by a forest too dense to admit its being seen at a distance of three hundred yards. Floyd's force was six regiments, with probably sixteen pieces of artillery. At 3 o'clock P. M. Rosecrans began a strong reconnoissance; led by the first brigade, under General Benham, the column soon reached a camp which had been abandoned, leaving some camp equipage and private baggage, which gave rise to the impression in the mind of General Benham that the enemy were in full retreat. General Rosecrans directed a continuation of the forward movement which soon revealed the fact that the enemy were in order of battle at their stronghold, and the battle raged. until darkness terminated the fight for the night, when the Union forces were withdrawn behind a hill and slept upon their arms.

On the following morning, while General Rosecrans was preparing to renew the attack, a runaway negro came into the camp with the information that the enemy had abandoned their position during the night, crossed the Gauley and destroyed their boats and bridges. The Gauley here runs through a deep gorge, a continuous fall for 12 or 15 miles; Rosecrans finding no means whatever of crossing the ferry, which is here 370 feet wide, pursuit was impossible. Orders were therefore given to go into camp that his troops might rest.

Union loss 17 killed, 141 wounded. Colonel Lowe, of the 12th Ohio, was among the killed.

The casualties in Floyd's command reported to be twenty. The abandoned camp contained a few prisoners, two stands of colors, a considerable quantity of arms and quartermaster's stores. His hospital containing the wounded prisoners taken from Tyler fell into Rosecrans' hands.

The reader will observe that in all the foregoing engagements of the Confederate forces in the Kanawha operations, at no time had the forces of Floyd and Wise participated in the same engagements, but it will be observed that Cox at one time had engaged Floyd, and at another time Wise, whilst Rosecrans encountered only the forces of Floyd. There was evidently no co-operation between these commanders, and the country and history would perhaps have been uninformed as to this family disaffection, had it not have been partly solved by the publication of the Confederate records. The two generals were old and wily Virginia politicians, holding deep prejudices toward each other.

Floyd was the ranking officer, and should have commanded the respect and obedience of Wise, but he refused the assistance Floyd demanded, nor could the authority of General Lee compel the ex-Governor of Virginia to real subordination, and the Confederate cause no doubt suffered by this inharmony, whilst the Union side reaped an advantage by the lack of unity.

There was little activity here during the balance of the month of September on either side. Before the 1st of October, Rosecrans had concentrated his entire command, including Cox' brigade, at Big Sewell Mountain. But his force became reduced by sickness and by detachments, until he had but 5200 effective men. The autumn rains set in early in September, and con-

L.M. Strayer

JACOB D. COX
Major General U.S. Volunteers

tinued daily until the 1st of October. Rosecrans' base of supplies were 60 miles away. The roads became so difficult that the horses and mules were being destroyed in their effort to transport supplies. The Confederates were in a similar position; hence it was not likely that any aggressive operations would take place soon by either side.

Rosecrans, therefore, very considerately, on October 5th, withdrew his forces gradually towards Gauley Bridge, and encamped as follows: Schenck's brigade, 10 miles from Gauley Bridge; McCook's, eight miles; Benham's, six miles; Cox', at Gauley Bridge, with Rosecrans' headquarters at Camp Gauley Mountain. The object in taking these several positions was to be near enough to water transportation to enable our transportation to bring forward, not only forage and subsistence, but the clothing of the troops. Orders were also immediately dispatched to have the paymasters come to pay the troops, none having received any pay since they entered the service.

So, with the troops comfortably quartered, with an abundance of forage, new clothing, plenty to eat, and with the paymaster in camp, we now turn from the Kanawha to

The Cheat Mountain District

and the operations of Brig.-Gen'l Joseph J. Reynolds.

After the brilliant achievements of our troops that terminated at Carrick's Ford, General Reynolds occupied Beverly, Huttonsville, Elkwater, etc.; and as the Confederate forces had been driven from that section of the State, the troops for the time being were principally engaged in driving from the country the bushwhackers, and in protecting the peaceable citizens in their pursuits of farming, merchandising, etc. With the exception of the 2d West Virginia and Daum's battery, General Reynold's command was composed of Ohio and Indiana regiments, and they were mainly recruited under the three months' call. All of the regiments had shown conspicuous gallantry in the several battles in which they had participated. Notably among those three months' regiments were the 7th and 9th Indiana, commanded respectively by Colonels Dumont and Milroy, both of whom were early promoted to brigadier-generals.

The military operations of General Reynolds at Elkwater and vicinity have much in them of interest. His command at this date (about August 15th) consisted of a battalion of 2d West Virginia, Colonel Moss; 14th Indiana, Col. N. Kimball; 24th Ohio, Colonel Ammen; 15th Indiana, Col. G. D. Wagner; 3d Ohio, Colonel Beatty; 13th Indiana, Col. J. S. Sullivan; 17th Indiana, Col. M. S. Hascall; 6th Ohio, Colonel Anderson; 4th U. S.

Artillery, Battery G, Captain Howe; Loomis' Michigan Battery, two guns; West Virginia Battery, Captain Daum; one company Indiana Cavalry, Captain Bracken, numbering in all about 9000 men. The base of supplies for this army was Clarksburg and Grafton. Captain Bracken's cavalry company were used as couriers between these points and headquarters.

General Reynolds was not idle, but prepared his position for defense, and was not long in placing himself behind such substantial breast-works as would defy an assault from double his numbers. The troops under his command had not yet learned the necessity of all uniforming alike, each State or community using their own fancy as to uniform. Several of these regiments appeared in the gray uniform the Confederate army had adopted. This condition of affairs proved to be very perplexing on several occasions, and serious mistakes were made. Of course that matter was soon corrected, and our whole army wore the Union blue.

But why all this array of troops? Why all this preparation for defense? Well, let us see. Only a few miles away, immediately in our front, at Huntersville, was the Confederate General Loring, with 8500 men, as follows: three Tennessee regiments of infantry, commanded by Colonels Maney, Hatton and Savage; Mumford's battalion of Virginia State Regulars; 48th Virginia, Colonel Campbell; W. H. F. Lee's cavalry; Gilliam's Virginia infantry regiment; Lee's 6th North Carolina; Burk's Virginia infantry; a regiment of Georgia infantry; two batteries of artillery, commanded by Marye and Stanley. Also Gen'l H. R. Jackson, at Greenbrier River, with 6000 men, as follows: 12th Georgia, Col. R. Johnston; 1st Georgia, Colonel Ramsey; three Virginia regiments, Colonels Scott, Fulkerson and Baldwin; one Arkansas infantry regiment, Colonel Rust; Anderson's and Shoemaker's batteries and Major Jackson's cavalry. The figures, with the commanders given above, are official.

The most interesting part of the situation presenting itself at this time is that Gen'l Robert E. Lee had been sent by the Richmond Government to take charge in person of the above-named Confederate forces. It was his first command in the field, and notwithstanding General Loring was his ranking officer in the United States Army before either rebelled against the Government that had educated and protected them, those in authority gave to Lee the command, when he at once concentrated the forces of Loring and Jackson at Big Springs, on the Valley Mountain, and proposed to march at once from there to Clarksburg and Grafton, without even consulting General Reynolds as to whether he was willing or not. But General Reynolds objected to such an uncordial arrangement. Accordingly, he placed his command at Cheat Mountain and Elkwater, and awaited the coming of the hosts; but in this instance our gray uniforms served a good purpose, for our Indianians frequently penetrated the camp of General Lee and returned freighted with the very latest news.

General Lee's plans of attack were very complete. Sending a portion of his force, under General Loring, to Cheat Mountain, while he (Lee) was to attack Elkwater direct, the plan was for Loring to capture our forces at Cheat Mountain, then to make a forced march to join Lee; the latter to await Loring's coming before he (Lee) should assault Elkwater. But the great general miscalculated, as Loring came to grief, for his forces got the worst of it, and retreated in the direction from whence they came. It was Lee's plan also that Loring should join him at early morn, and it was not until after 11 o'clock that he learned of Loring's defeat and retreat.

At this juncture an incident occurred that brought mourning to General Lee and his army. The episode is soon told. Lee sent out a reconnoitering party to investigate our position at Elkwater. The party was led by his Chief of Staff, Col. John A. Washington and Maj. W. H. F. Lee. They were on the Elkwater road, on our west flank, and about one mile from our position. At the same time they were investigating, General Reynolds had also sent a reconnoitering party of the 17th Indiana in the direction of Lee's lines, when Colonel Washington's party ran into our advance, and Sergeant Weiler and two others fired their pieces and Colonel Washington fell from his horse, pierced by three bullets. Major Lee and the balance of his party fled to their lines. Colonel Washington was lifted into an ambulance that was sent for and taken to the headquarters of Colonel Wagner. He lived but a few minutes. The death of Colonel Washington put an end to the skirmishing that had been going on all the morning, and General Lee, without attacking our position in force, withdrew his army from our front.

The following day a flag of truce brought to our out-post a small squad of the enemy, with the following communication addressed to General Reynolds:

HEADQUARTERS, CAMP ON VALLEY RIVER, *Sept.* 14, 1861.

To the General Commanding United States Troops, Huttonsville, Va.

General: Lieut.-Col. John A. Washington, my Aid-de-Camp, whilst riding yesterday with a small escort was fired upon by your pickets, and, I fear killed. Should such be the case, I request that you will deliver to me his body; or should he be a prisoner in your hands, that I be informed of his condition.

I have the honor to be   Your obedient servant,

R. E. LEE, *General Commanding.*

Of course General Reynolds sent the body under flag of truce as requested. The body which had been tenderly and neatly laid out and placed in an ambulance, was sent in charge of Colonel Hascall of the 17th Indiana, who was met at the out-post by Maj. W. H. F. Lee and others. The transfer of the body was attended with a great deal of courteous military ceremony. Upon Colonel Hascall's arrival he advanced and meeting Major Lee, saluted and handed him the following letter:

HEADQUARTERS, CAMP ELKWATER, VA., *Sept.* 14, 1861.
To the Commanding Officer Confederate Forces, Tygart's Valley:

Sir: By direction of the general commanding this post, I forward under flag of truce the remains of Col. John A. Washington, that his friends may with more certainty obtain them. There was not time last night after his recognition to communicate.

Very respectfully, etc.,   GEO. S. ROSE, *A. A.-General.*

After the transfer of the body from our ambulance to their own, officers shook hands and parted, each going to the northward and southward as duty called, and all being deeply impressed with the solemnity of the occasion. And thus ended that campaign of the Cheat Mountain district.

The vistors to Camp Elkwater, after the foregoing episode, could see carved in good, legible letters upon a large, smooth-bark beech tree, just where Colonel Washington fell, this inscription:

"Under this tree, on the 13th of Sept., 1861, fell Col. John A. Washington, the degenerate descendant of the Father of his Country."

From the date of the aforementioned occurrence, Sept. 13 till Dec. 13, there had been no general engagement in the vicinity of Elkwater, only the usual skirmishing between scouting parties, but many changes had been made in the status of the command. General Reynolds had been called to other fields, likewise several regiments had been transferred, some of them to the western and some to the eastern armies, and in turn new regiments had been added to the Cheat Mountain district, and Gen. R. H. Milroy had been assigned to the command of the district.

CHAPTER VII.

PERSONAL REMINISCENCES OF THE AUTHOR.

Early Devotion to the Union.—Formation at Clarksburg, Va., of Union and Confederate "Home Guards."—Intolerant Attitude of Secessionists.—Unionists place themselves on the Defensive.—Union and Confederate Companies Organized.—Vituperation must give place to Sober Criticism.—Early Occupation of West Virginia by Confederates.—Prominent Men for the Union.—Unique Armament of Union Home Guards.—Clarksburg the Home of Some of the Most Noted Leaders of the Southern Cause.—Collision between the two Companies of Home Guards.—The Humanity of both Sides.—Captain A. J. Smith's Sketch.—The 31st (Confederate) Virginia Infantry.

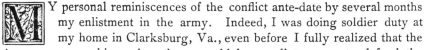

" Dissolve the Union ! Roll away
The spangled flag of glory's day ;
Blot out the history of the brave,
And desecrate each patriot's grave,
And there above the wreck of years,
Quaff an eternity of tears !

" Dissolve the Union ! can it be
That they who speak such words are free ?
Great God ! did any die to save
Such sordid creatures from the grave,
When breast to breast and hand to hand
Our patriot fathers freed the land ? "

MY personal reminiscences of the conflict ante-date by several months my enlistment in the army. Indeed, I was doing soldier duty at my home in Clarksburg, Va., even before I fully realized that the time was approaching when there would be a call to arms, to defend the constitutional integrity of the Nation. The duty to which I allude was as a member of a "Home Guard," formed for the protection of the city of Clarksburg and the adjacent country. The necessity for such an organization was suggested by the action of those of our fellow citizens who believed in the principles of secession, and who championed the Southern cause. For, as early as January, 1861, Southern sympathizers in the city of Clarksburg formed a company for military purposes, which met two or three nights in the week, in the courthouse, for drill and instructions. But here again the reader may inquire, why should this circumstance call for a Union Home Guard ?

It was not because an estimable body of the citizens were pleased to form a military organization among themselves, but it was because of the open, boastful and intolerant attitude of these people towards all who ventured to differ from them upon the questions of the day—notably the right of secession.

And this intolerance was intensified by threats of extermination to all "Yankees" and "Yankee" institutions generally. In view of the fact that among those who made these threats were some of the most influential citizens of the State, their words were received by the Unionists as authoritative, and being thus forewarned, the Unionists very naturally decided to place themselves on the defensive, and they too, as early as February, formed a Union Home Guard and occupied the courthouse, for "drill and instructions," on alternate evenings with the Southerners. For three months or more, these two military companies (soon to become Federal and Confederate soldiers), formed a theme for local excitement that vied with the larger and more important events in which the country was involved at that time.

I extract no pleasure in referring to the days of contentions between former friends, but it is part of the record of events of the period immediately preceding the war, and therefore not without interest. The hot blood of those days has now been cooled by the lapse of years. The war demonstrated the fact that the soldiers North and South were American soldiers, and the courage and prowess of both were tested on many a battlefield, and I am always glad to witness the generous tone and spirit, which now so generally prevails between these former opponents. Vituperation must give place to sober criticism. Lee and Jackson must be gauged by the same standards as are applied to Grant and Sherman. That they were good men and great military leaders none can deny, and all that was best and greatest in them belongs to our common country. Our foreign enemies must not ignore this fact, for in any attack from without they must consider that they will have to fight the Grants and the Lees, and the Shermans and the Jacksons, who would in such an event stand side by side. President Lincoln was altogether right and wise—as he always was—when he addressed the body of men who came to serenade and congratulate him on the final victory, a few days before his lamented death. He listened to their bands play and said: "Why, I wish the band would play Dixie; that is our tune now; we captured it." Truthful words fitly spoken; cavillers may wail, but the logic of events is plain—for to-day the children of Federal and Confederate march shoulder to shoulder, common citizens of a common country, inheritors of a common destiny, to be perpetuated, may it be, for ages to come.

The two opposing companies heretofore referred to continued to drill, and to keep the city in a state of political effervescence. Early in May, 1861, a Confederate force occupied Grafton, and during the month, Philippi, Beverly, Rich Mountain and the Kanawha Valley fell into their hands.

Our company of Union Home Guards were acting under no special

THEODORE F. LANG
Major 6th West Virginia Cavalry

authority, save that natural law of self-preservation. About May 1st, we began to perform police and picket duty in the city and on the roads leading into the place. The Guard consisted mainly of young men; there were, however, some notable exceptions, whose names were either on the roll or gave encouragement by a strong and outspoken approval. We recall such prominent men as Colonel Richard Fowkes, Waldo Goff, Nathan Goff, Lloyd Lowndes, Walter Ebert, Alstorphius Werninger, Luther Haymond, William A. Harrison, Thomas W. Harrison, Lloyd Moore, Jasper Y. Moore, Peter H. Goodwin, Samuel R. Steel, John and W. P. Irwin, Lloyd L. Lang, Col. Thos. S. Spates, Ira Hart, James G. Bartlett, John and Edwin Stealey, Edwin Maxwell, Burton Despard, Wm. R. Alexander, Elisha Owens, Benj. F. Shuttleworth, Noah Dunnington and others.

This guard was not generally uniformed, and the variety, quality, and quantity of their armament ranged from a dirkknife to a double-barreled shot-gun. My own equipment for service will illustrate. I did, however, wear a suit of soldier clothes, having been, prior to the beginning of hostilities, orderly-sergeant of "the Harrison Rifles," a uniformed and armed company of the State militia. So, with my uniform, when on duty, I carried my orderly-sergeant's sword, a six-shooter pepper-box revolver, and a monster cutlass, made to order by the city blacksmith from a worn-out file. The thing was two-edged, sharp as a razor, about 18 inches long, and of course made of the best steel and tempered to perfection.

No two of us were armed alike, but the home-made cutlass was a recognized necessity for both defensive and offensive warfare. Homely and impractical as these instruments of war now seem, they were then, nevertheless, in the hands of courageous men, who would have used them to the death.

Perhaps no other portion of West Virginia was so severely tried in the balance of loyalty as was Clarksburg.

It was the home of some of the most noted leaders of the Rebellion in the western part of the State. It was here the first full company west of the Alleghany mountains was recruited for the Confederate army, and notwithstanding the fact that since May 1st our Union Home Guard had been doing good service day and night in the way of picketing the approaches to the city, and keeping scouting parties out in all directions to the southward, frequently meeting with questions requiring careful but stubborn treatment, the climax of our indignation came when, on the afternoon of May 23, our home company of Confederates (before referred to) of about 60 men, appeared upon the streets, armed and equipped for active service. This occurrence came very near producing a local collision that bid fair to be a very serious one. It was a question of loyalty *vs.* disloyalty of neighbors and former friends. The Union Home

Guards were not slow to resent this insult to the United States Government. The courthouse bell, which we had previously designated to ring the danger signal, sounded the assembly, and with the alertness of the tiger springing from his lair, the courthouse was soon filled with the Union Home Guards and the excited inhabitants of the city. A hasty conference of the members of the Guard, and a committee was appointed to wait upon the Confederate company and demand their objects and intentions. Our committee was treated with that characteristic bombast of the original F. F. V.'s, who believed that one Southern gentlemen could annihilate half a dozen "Lincoln hirelings"; but our Union Guards didn't believe any such nonsense as that, and after a second council of war, demanded the unconditional surrender of their arms. Realizing that we were desperately in earnest and meant business, a conference with us was agreed upon to meet at the courthouse at once. The reader must not disguise the fact that this was an occasion of desperation between men goaded to the extreme tension of maddened endurance.

The conference developed the humanity of both sides, and speeches by both parties were made to a crowded audience. Our side, however, were firm in their demands for the surrender of their arms and a disbandment of the company. The terms finally agreed upon were the surrender of the arms until the following day, when they were to be returned, provided the company would leave the city in a body. This was concurred in, and the following day witnessed the departure of the company, with their arms and accoutrements, for Grafton to join the Confederate forces stationed there, and the shedding of blood was averted.

The leading spirits of both sides of that exciting episode afterwards became conspicious in the War of the Rebellion. From those leading actors sprung the 3d W. Va. (Union) and the 31st Va. (Confederate), and the fortunes or misfortunes of war gave the opportunity to these noted regiments to meet face to face upon several occasions on the field of battle, and I speak the sentiments of the survivors of my regiment, I know, when I say that we have no occasion to exult over the fallen 31st Va., and they should feel no humiliation at having been conquered by veterans worthy of their steel. Each did their best, each fought a good fight.

* Captain A. J. Smith's Sketch.

In anticipation of hostilities between the States, a company of volunteers was organized in Clarksburg, Va., in January, 1861, to be held subject to the orders of the Governor of Virginia. It was composed of some of the best

---

* The following sketch is contributed by Capt. Augustine J. Smith, a member of the company of Confederates just referred to.   T. F. L.

citizens of the town and vicinity, and included in its membership eight attorneys-at-law, two editors, one civil engineer, several merchants, clerks, mechanics and farmers, and numbered about 60 men.

Uriel M. Turner was elected captain and Wm. P. Cooper and Norval Lewis, lieutenants. The company drilled two or three nights in the week until the 23d day of May, 1861, when they were ordered to rendezvous at Grafton, Taylor Co., and on that day took up their line of march for that place. On the second day they arrived at Fetterman; on the night of their arrival, Bailey Brown, a member of a Union Company at Grafton, fired on our pickets, and he was shot dead, being the first blood shed in West Virginia. We took possession of Grafton next day. As large bodies of Union troops were advancing on Grafton, we retreated to Philippi where the command was surprised on the 2d day of June, 1861, by a large force of Union troops, under Col. Kelley. From there we retreated to Huttonsville, when we were reinforced by several regiments and marched back to Laurel Hill, 12 miles from Philippi, which was occupied by Union forces under General Morris, who attacked our force about the 8th of July. Finding our position untenable, by the defeat of General Pegram at Rich Mountain, the forces under General Garnett retreated toward Beverly; finding that our retreat had been cut off by our cavalry having blockaded the road, we turned off the Beverly pike, six miles from that town, and took the road across the tributaries of the Cheat River. On the second day of the retreat, we were compelled by the rains and mud to abandon our wagons, trains and one piece of artillery.

The Federal forces not being encumbered, caught up with our rear guard, and in a skirmish General Garnett was killed; thereupon a stampede ensued, which continued until next morning, when we arrived at the "Red House," on the N. W. Va. turnpike. After resting a few hours, we retreated towards Petersburg, Hardy Co. As we were pursued by Federal forces from behind and threatened in front by forces at Oakland, Md., we continued to Petersburg and Franklin, to Monterey, where we were met by large reinforcements under General Robert E. Lee, having been on the retreat one week and without food for several days. In consequence of the hardships on the march, large numbers of our men died. The company having been formed into a regiment composed of ten companies of West Virginians, was designated company "C," 31st Va. Vols., a regiment known as a *crack regiment* in the army of northern Virginia.

From Monterey, after a few days' rest, we went west about 25 miles to the west side of the Alleghany Mountains, on the east fork of the Greenbrier River, where we camped until the latter part of November. While here we were attacked by General Reynolds of the Union forces, and after five hours' fight, repulsed him. At this camp, the first death occurred in company "C;" Daniel S. Sumner, O.-S., died with the measles. After leaving Camp Barton, we took up winter quarters on the top of the Alleghanies, where we staid until April 1, 1862. On the 13th December, we were surrounded and attacked by a large force of Federals under General Milroy, and after eight hours' fighting, repulsed him, the losses on both sides being heavy. Company "C" lost five men killed, viz., Ethelbert Smith, James Smith, Alvin Nutter, A. J. Cropp and John W. Whitman, and had ten wounded.

About the 1st of May the command returned east to within 5 miles of Staunton, where we joined General "Stonewall" Jackson and returned west, and fought General Milroy at McDowell; defeated and followed him to Franklin; we continued with General Jackson and were under his command until his death at Chancellorsville in May, 1863; afterward with Early until the close of the war. The "Co." lost about 20 men killed, and 10 men died from disease; among the killed, in addition to those above mentioned, were Samuel Dawson, Lt. Wm. West, Jno. W. Wallingham, H. H. Holden, Joseph Snyder, Jonas Greathouse, Luther Dawson. Among those who died were Lt. Norval Lewis, Silas Greathouse and Aaron Young.

Scarcely a member of the company escaped being wounded, some as many as five times. Louis Carmack, John W. Pridmore, Wm. Taylor, were disabled from wounds. The company participated in the following battles: Surprise at Philippi, Laurel Hill, Greenbrier River, Alleghany Mountains, McDowell, Front Royal, Winchester, Cross Keys, Port Republic, 1862; seven days' fight at Richmond, Cedar Mountain, 2d Manassas, Antietam, Fredericksburg, Chancellorsville, Monocacy, Winchester, Fisher's Hill, Wilderness, Spottsylvania Court House, Cold Harbor, Welden Road, Hatchers Run, 1864; and were in the trenches at Petersburg and on the retreat to Appomattox. The company was reorganized in May, 1862, viz., Wm. P. Cooper, captain, Norval Lewis, 1st lieutenant, Wm. J. West, 2d lieutenant, O. T. Bond, 3d lieutenant.

It was recruited to about 100 men while at Philippi and had very few accessions afterward. From death, promotions, and transfer the company surrendered about six men at Appomattox.

The following members were promoted from the ranks to be commissioned officers: Robt. Johnston, Confederate Congress; John S. Hoffman, colonel 31st Va. Infantry; Wm. P. Cooper, major 31st Va. Infantry; Augustine J. Smith, captain Army of Tennessee; Benjamin M. Smith, captain Jackson Cavalry; Robert J. Smith, captain Jackson Cavalry; J. M. Blair, captain Company "C," 31st Va. Infantry; G. D. Camden, major 25th Va. Infantry; Thomas D. Armsy, major Jenkins Cavalry; Hugh H. Lee, captain Jackson's

Staff; S. M. Sommers, captain and asst.-quartermaster; Asbury Lewis, captain Jackson Cavalry; Joshua Rodabaugh, lieutenant Company "C," 31st Va. Infantry; W. F. Gorden, captain Jenkins Cavalry; O. T. Bond, lieutenant Company "C," 31st Va. Infantry; Wm. J. West, lieutenant Company "C," 31st Va. Infantry; James M. McCann, captain Jackson Cavalry.

The following members are known to be surviving, Captain Augustine J. Smith, Captain B. M. Smith, Captain J. M. McCann, Private A. W. Lang, Lieutenant Joshua Rodabaugh, A. J. Queen, David Slocum, Wm. T. Smith, J. H. Preston, Captain J. M. Blair, Captain Asbury Lewis, T. M. Golden, Jno. W. Rector, Marcellus Armstrong. But two deserters, viz., Jacob Runnion and Wm. McCoy.

Native and adopted citizens of Clarksburg, Va., who held commissions in the Confederate army: Lieut-General Thomas J. Jackson (Stonewall), Brigadier-General Wm. L. Jackson, Colonel Geo. Jackson, Colonel Jno. S. Hoffman, Lt.-Colonel Alfred H. Jackson, Colonel Chapin Bartlett. Majors, Wm. P. Cooper, P. B. Adams, G. D. Camden, Jr., Andrew T. Owens, Rezin C. Davis, Jno. L. Sehon. Captains, John G. Gittings, Charles McCally, Uriel M. Turner, Augustine J. Smith, Benj. M. Smith, Robert J. Smith, Silas Owens, Wm. F. Gorden, Hugh H. Lee, Warren Lurty, Alvin N. Bastable, Samuel M. Sommers. Lieutenants, Norval Lewis, Fred. W. Bartlett, Edward Lynch.

CHAPTER VIII.

PERSONAL REMINISCENCES—(CONTINUED).

Recruiting and Organization of the Third Virginia Union Infantry Regiment.—Trials and and Disappointments of the Confederates in Filling their Ranks in West Virginia.— Third Regiment in Company Detachments Fighting Guerrillas.—Author's Experience as Post-Adjutant in Issuing Passes.—Consolidation of the Third Regiment.—Ludicrous First Experience in Soldiering in the Field.

THE incidents relating to the recruiting and final muster-in of my regiment—the Third Virginia Union Infantry Volunteers—will recall, no doubt, the experience of all other regiments recruited in western Virginia. Governor Peirpoint entrusted the formation of this regiment to Col. David T. Hewes, of Clarksburg. The camp or rendezvous, named "Camp Hewes," was located near the city, and was well supplied with tents and other necessaries for the comfort of the men. I was designated recruiting officer for the regiment, and in that capacity assisted in recruiting companies B, F and G.

My success as recruiting officer depended upon circumstances. Within the limits of Clarksburg but little argument was required to find men willing to sacrifice themselves upon the altar of patriotism, but in the smaller towns some argument and explanation was necessary. I will relate my experience at the town of Weston, in Lewis County, 29 miles south of Clarksburg. Being well acquainted there, I naturally anticipated a hearty welcome and easy time in securing a full company for my regiment; but the Secession element was flourishing there, and as usual they were the men of influence—the officeholders—devoted to Governor Letcher and General Lee. So my uniform didn't impress that element with the importance of my mission, but as I realized that I had the full sanction of "Uncle Sam" at my back, I cared little for their objections and growling. I assumed my right to do as I pleased. Accordingly, I distributed printed circulars through the town, calling a general meeting at the court house for the following day. This was the first official visit that quiet town had received from the "Lincoln hirelings," and this innovation upon my part so incensed the great men (officers) of the town that they waited upon me with "official" importance, and informed me that I could not hold my advertised meeting in the court house, and that if I attempted to enter it for such an unholy purpose my arrest would soon follow, and in place of the court house I would find myself in the county jail.

I challenged their authority to interfere with even so small a part of the United States as a recruiting officer, and I don't know whether it was my determination or their timidity, but the advertised call was held at the court house and no interference was offered. I made my speech to the interested audience which filled every part of the large room, and then called for volunteers, when twenty good, loyal men signed the roll. Soon after, I procured the services of a fifer and drummer, and treated the town to a parade. I then secured transportation, and with colors flying left for Clarksburg with my recruits, much to the indignation of the Secession element and the gratification of the loyal men, and that event proved to be only the introduction that finally secured 750 men to the credit of Weston and Lewis counties to the Union cause.

The Confederates, however, were not so successful at recruiting their regiments, as the following correspondence would indicate. I quote from Brig.-Gen'l R. S. Garnett, C. S. A., to Gen'l R. E. Lee:

HEADQUARTERS, DEPARTMENT OF NORTHWESTERN VIRGINIA,
CAMP AT LAUREL HILL, VA., *June* 25, 1861.

*   *   *   *   *   *   *   *   *

* I have been, so far, wholly unable to get anything like accurate or reliable information as to numbers, movements or intentions of the enemy, and begin to believe it an almost impossible thing. The Union men are greatly in the ascendency here, and are much more zealous and active in their cause than the Secessionists. The enemy are kept fully advised of our movements, even to the strength of our scouts and pickets, by the country people, while we are compelled to grope in the dark as much as if we were invading a foreign and hostile country. My hope of increasing my force in this region has, so far, been sadly disappointed. Only eight men have joined me here and fifteen at Colonel Heck's camp—not sufficient to make up my losses by discharges, etc. These people are thoroughly imbued with an ignorant and bigoted Union sentiment.

*   *   *   *   *   *   *   *   *

(Signed),   R. S. GARNETT,
                    Brig.-Gen'l Provisional Army Commanding.

Also, extract from Gen'l Henry A. Wise's report to General Lee:

BUNGERS MILL, VA., FOUR MILES WEST OF LEWISBURG, *Aug. 1st*, 1861.

Gen'l R. E. Lee, Commanding, etc.

*   *   *   *   *   *   *   *   *

The Kanawha Valley is wholly disaffected and traitorous. It was gone from Charleston down to Point Pleasant before I got there. Boone and Cabell are nearly as bad, and the state of things in Braxton, Nicholas, and part of Greenbrier is awful. The militia are nothing for warlike uses here. They are worthless who are true, and there is no telling who is true, you cannot persuade these people that Virginia can or will ever reconquer the northwest, and they are submitting, subdued and debased. I have fallen back not a minute too soon, and here let me say, we have worked and scouted far and wide and fought well, and marched all the shoes and clothes off our bodies, and find our old arms do not stand service. I implore for some (one thousand) stand of good arms, percussion muskets, sabers, pistols, tents, blankets, shoes, rifles and powder.   Respectfully,

HENRY A. WISE.

The full quota of companies for the third regiment was secured about the 1st of July, and when the regiment by general consent selected its field and staff officers (see Regimental History), I was made adjutant.

In the meantime Clarksburg had become the most important military post in West Virginia. It was the base of supplies for quartermaster and commissary stores during that series of battles at Philippi, Rich Mountain, Laurel Hill, Carrick's Ford, etc., and continued to be an important military headquarters till the close of the war.

In addition to my duties at the date of muster-in as regimental adjutant, I was also designated as post-adjutant, and as such had special charge of issuing passes and administering the required oath of allegiance to the United States to all persons, not soldiers, coming into or leaving the city. My office was usually the headquarters of the commanding general, who would perchance remain at the post for a day or more. I recall with interest the season when General Rosecrans, with Captain Hartsuff as Adjutant-General, occupied my office. I was complimented by the confidence of General Rosecrans, and rendered him material aid in his plans to march to the Kanawha.

I missed the genial society of General Rosecrans and Captain Hartsuff who went to other fields, but I continued to keep open house at the same place, and for some time had extra duty in my specialty of administering the oath of allegiance to many West Virginians who had, in an unguarded hour, joined the Confederate forces, and being among the number captured at Rich Mountain, came with their parole to take the oath and become law-abiding citizens again. Among that number was one of my near relatives, and in reply to my inquiry as to how he liked soldiering, said that his camp experience was delightful, the life of a soldier was charmingly exciting, and that he would not have given it up but for the fact that " when you ———— Yankees called you were mean enough to bring your guns along." He took the oath and remained faithful to his obligation.

The position of "pass-giver" at this period afforded abundant opportunity to study and to become familiar with the true inwardness of the applicants. I will refer briefly to some of their characteristics, and for convenience will do so under three distinct headings: *The truly loyal, the undecided, and the truly rebel.* The first referred to gave little annoyance. They would walk boldly to the desk, and with free, open willingness subscribe to the required oath, seeming to regard the ceremony as a blessed privilege vouchsafed to them. The second, or "undecided" class gave the most trouble, and, like the rockets, their actions and course was "erring and unknown"; there was no positive assurance whether they held the obligation binding or not. The spy or blockade runner would take the oath with a sad and sullen assent. The doubtful ones—those who were Union when it was policy to be such, or Confederate when with Confederates—offered the greatest study; their devices and idiosyncrasies were often amusing. Some would assure me they were intensely loyal, but had conscientious scruples about swearing to that fact. Others would assure me that I had known them all my life—what was the use of swearing them? Again others would address an envelope to the Governor of the State or other official, and would assume indignation that a man with a letter to the Governor should be obliged to take an oath to be loyal to the Government. A prominent merchant of this class from a neighboring town wished a pass to go to Wheeling to replenish his stock of goods, and conceived this potent evidence of his loyalty. He had an old copy of the New York *Tribune*, and having improvised a fan so that the folding of the paper displayed the heading when he asked for the pass, I suggested the required oath, when he innocently gave a knowing wink directed towards the *Tribune*. I feigned to not understand, when he winked again and again; but as I had never kept a soda fountain he failed to make me understand. The reader will understand the potency of this device better perhaps when I state that just prior to the war only two copies of the New York *Tribune* had been sent to the postoffice at Clarksburg, and for that offense Horace Greeley, the publisher, had been cited to appear before the Judge of our Circuit Court, and he was found guilty of "publishing and distributing an incendiary document." With that indictment standing against Horace Greeley, the aforesaid merchant thought his paper fan should be an unquestioned passport. He took the oath.

I could go on *ad infinitum* relating incidents under this heading—some of them amusing, some of them touching and painful.

The third class, or "truly rebel," seldom required passes. They remained at home, and were themselves keepers of their self-made prisons. They were few in numbers, however, and gave the Government little concern. They worshiped in their isolation the institution of negro slavery and the Act of Secession, but were too cowardly to fight for their cause.

About the 10th of September came the gladsome order for me to relinquish my duties as post-adjutant and report for duty at the front. For several weeks prior to this date the officers of our regiment had been urging the authorities to relieve our scattered regiment from the irksome duties of fighting guerrillas, and permit us to take the field as a consolidated regiment. Until this date my duties had been wholly executive and clerical, and I knew nothing of the practical and exciting duties of war, but I was eager for the change, and welcomed the order that bade me report at Beverly, the place designated for the assembling of my regiment. Believing that my first experience in real soldiering would reawaken the early recollections of some of my comrades who enjoy the ludicrous side of early army life, I will draw the picture as it now vividly stands before me. The adjutants of infantry regiments being entitled to a horse, I had procured a noble animal with the finest rig—gold braid, bright ornaments, and all of the most approved army regulations—my uniform and saber to correspond. So, when mounted, I looked every inch a soldier (aside, in a bandbox). Poor, foolish, misguided young man. How little I knew of the realities of terrible war. Well, the day came when I was to take my leave. My command consisted of the regimental band and about seventy-five recruits for different companies of the regiment. Of course I had to have transportation for my personal effects, but I was a good deal perplexed when I discovered that the full complement of the regiment's transportation had been furnished, and was already far to the southward; but I was not to be repulsed so early in the engagement. I had already in my official capacity secured the friend-ship of Capt. Charles Leib, the widely-notorious depot quartermaster, and by strategic movement secured from him an ambulance and a pair of fine horses. The veteran soldier will naturally ask, "For what purpose did one common, every-day adjutant want with so much transportation?" The inquiry is easily answered. It was for my Saratoga trunk, filled with several suits of soldier clothes, with an abundance of fine linen, including night-shirts, etc. Then my camp-chest, which was filled with cooking utensils, with an abundance of hams, tongues, sausage, jellies, preserves, spices, etc., with a full line of chinaware, knives, forks, spoons, etc. Then I had a cot, with blankets, white spread and sheets, and my desk was filled with paper, envelopes, and necessary blanks for regimental purposes, not forgetting a wall tent.

The hour for departure came, the assembly sounded, and mounted at the head of my band, recruits and ambulance, it was necessary to march through the city, and that hour revealed to me that even amid the pomp and glitter and tinsel, just behind the scene lurked the heart-burning of possibly the last good-bye to family and friends. My residence in the city was on

for the night at Camp Alleghany (lately vacated by the Confederates), and whilst we were all comfortable and warm within, the night without was terrible, by reason of the bitter cold, and at the same time the rain did not cease to fall the whole night through. Consequently, day dawned with the ground and trees covered with clear, glassy ice. This, however, did not offer a barrier to the march of the soldier to duty, and we were early on the tramp. The turnpike, after leaving the camp, passed through a dense mountain forest, and as the rain fell upon the trees, freezing as it fell, the tall pines had become freighted with their load of crystal ice, the weight of which inclined them together, forming an arch of fantastic design, under which for miles and miles we marched. The clouds having dispersed, the bright sun of the morning bursting out from behind the clouds shone through, producing sparkling effects, compared with which the Kohinoor is a pebble of marble; and this is not all, for as the wind blew through the million of meshes in the archway it gave off flute-like sounds that contained every note in the scale. At the same time the swaying of the trees by the wind kept up a continuous creaking, and at intervals breaking with a report not unlike the discharge of a pistol, altogether forming a march of weird, awe-inspiring music. Realizing that no human power could in a century of time produce such effects, and that the Creator of the universe had done so in a single night, suggests the beautiful words of the poet Derzhavin on "God," from which I quote:

> " Thy splendor fills all space with rays divine."
> * * * * * *
> "As sparks mount upward from the fiery blaze,
> So suns are born, so worlds spring forth from Thee,
> And as the spangles in the sunny rays
> Shine round the silver snow the pageantry
> Of Heaven's bright army glitters in Thy praise."

Arriving at Monterey that evening, we remained a fortnight. During our stay at this place, the enemy, on the 12th of April, 1000 strong, attacked our forces. A short engagement ensued, when the Confederates withdrew with considerable loss.

On the 30th of April, Milroy occupied McDowell, 12 miles east of Monterey and 36 miles west of Staunton. On the 8th of May the battle of McDowell was fought. Generals Milroy and Schenck's forces had met the forces of Generals "Stonewall" Jackson and Edward S. Johnson, consisting of five brigades. The battle was fought with great stubbornness on both sides, lasting about five hours, when darkness put an end to it. Finding the position untenable, General Schenck (who ranked Milroy) withdrew during the night to Franklin. On the following day (May 9th) General Jackson sent the following characteristic telegram to Adjutant-General Cooper at Richmond: "God blessed our arms with victory at McDowell yesterday." In the light of the facts we fail to see the "victory," or wherein "God blessed their arms." ` " The Records of the Rebellion " contains the official reports of both Generals Schenck and "Stonewall" Jackson, and they show that the Confederates outnumbered the Unionists more than three to one. The Union loss was 26 killed, 227 wounded, 3 missing. Total, 256. No officers among the killed, eleven wounded.

The Confederate loss was 75 killed, 423 wounded. Total, 498. 16 officers killed and 38 wounded.

This was the first battle in which my entire regiment had been engaged, though they had, by company, seen hard service, and had had many skirmishes with bands of bushwhackers.

Further particulars of the McDowell engagement will be found in another chapter—title, " 6th W. Va. Cavalry."

On the 11th of May we find Generals Schenck and Milroy (after their retreat from McDowell) at Franklin. Gen'l John C. Fremont who had been placed in command of the " Mountain Department," had issued orders to his forces to concentrate at this place, when the brigades of Schenck and Milroy became a part of his personal command in the field.

It was here I first met General Fremont. I found him a man of splendid physique, with a pleasant face, affable in manner, wearing a full beard and thick suit of hair, and every inch a soldier.

Upon taking command of the Mountain Department in the field, General Fremont, at Franklin, W. Va., rearranged his brigades. In this he practically made the brigade of West Virginia troops, to wit: 2d W. Va., 3d W. Va., 5th W. Va. Infantry, 1st W. Va. Cavalry detachment, 1st W. Va. Battery G, L. A.; the 25th Ohio, and a battery of the 1st and 12th Ohio, L. A., were also of this brigade, which was commanded by Gen'l R. H. Milroy. It was fitting at this time that General Milroy should have been placed in command of this brigade, for, having spent several months in active campaign with the West Virginia soldiers, he was familiar with their methods as fighting soldiers and of their necessities.

An incident occurred at this period that served to excite mingled feelings of disgust and amusement among the West Virginia soldiers at Franklin. It was this: When General Blenker arrived with his division, which was composed mainly of Germans from Pennsylvania and New York, they were much surprised to find themselves associated with "Virginia soldiers."

At this time they were ignorant of the fact that there could be any loyalty with "Virginia" in it, and so incredulous were they that they demurred to being cast with the "Virginians" in time of battle, alleging that these soldiers could not be *true* to the country's cause, and expressed fear that they would betray them in the heat of battle.

But this stupid ignorance was short-lived, and our German comrades soon realized that there was no loyalty so intense as the loyalty of these men of West Virginia, whose love for the flag was intensified by the fact that they were fighting for home as well as for country.

Besides the regiments named in Milroy's Brigade from West Virginia, the 8th W. Va. was also in Fremont's command, and was brigaded with the 60th Ohio, the two commanded by Col. G. P. Cluseret, of General Fremont's staff; Battery C, W. Va. L. A., in General Staehl's Brigade, and the 3d W. Va. Cavalry detachment unassigned.

By reason of past service in the field and the willingness with which the West Virginia soldiers responded to every duty, Milroy's brigade during this entire arduous campaign was placed in the lead when on the advance and covered the rear when on the retreat; it opened and closed in each skirmish and battle, and was assigned to every important duty. It would be unpardonable injustice did I not specially mention the gallantry and faithfulness of the 25th Ohio, which had served with the West Virginia soldiers prior to coming to the Shenandoah Valley. The 25th was a good regiment; both officers and men were not only brave soldiers but were genial, companionable comrades as well.

To read the history of the campaign is to verify the truthfulness of this statement relating to Milroy's brigade. The West Virginians, by reason of education and circumstances, readily made efficient soldiers. They were good horsemen, and excelled in the use of the rifle; indeed, these two conditions were regarded by them as accomplishments. From childhood both men and women learned how to ride, and when in the saddle became a part of the horse's poetry of motion; and few things give more amusement to West Virginians when in the large cities than to witness a city dude or dudess on horseback in the act of fashionable horseback riding. To look upon a dude aping "English, you know," with his feet pushed through the stirrups, and then bobbing up and down in the saddle as if trying to escape the tortures of a tack with its sharp end protruding from the seat, very naturally provokes derisive laughter.

The personnel of the West Virginia regiments named in the foregoing— both rank and file—mainly distinguished themselves by their steadfast devotion to duty, and, aside from the killed in battle and died from disease, few changes were made during their full term of service. A few dismissals for cause, a few resignations and a few promotions among the officers seemed to satisfy all.

Whilst the officers were, as a rule, faithful and courageous in battle, but few of them became conspicuous for great brilliancy or dash. I do not mention this fact to the discredit of any, for they were good citizens before the war, they were good soldiers during the conflict, and when peace came, conscious of having faithfully served their country, became again good citizens.

CHAPTER X.

PERSONAL REMINISCENCES—Continued.

"Stonewall" Jackson's Raid in the Shenandoah Valley.—Fremont Ordered to the Front.—Wretched Condition of his Command.—Battle of Front Royal.—Jackson Pained.—Censures his Troops for Deserting their Colors to Pillage.—Rout of Banks' Command Down the Valley to Williamsport.

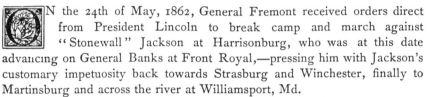N the 24th of May, 1862, General Fremont received orders direct from President Lincoln to break camp and march against "Stonewall" Jackson at Harrisonburg, who was at this date advancing on General Banks at Front Royal,—pressing him with Jackson's customary impetuosity back towards Strasburg and Winchester, finally to Martinsburg and across the river at Williamsport, Md.

Perhaps no period or campaign during the Rebellion furnished so much of disaster and direful results to the Union cause as did that period, beginning on May 24, 1862, and terminating August 30th with the second battle of Bull Run, embracing the operations of Generals Fremont, Banks, Shields, Sigel, McDowell and Pope. In the earlier operations of the campaign, the armies under consideration were designated under three divisions, viz.: The Mountain Department, General Fremont commanding; the Department of the Shenandoah, General Banks commanding, and the Department of the Rappahannock, General McDowell commanding.

The later period of the campaign contemplates the consolidation of the afore-named armies and the command of Brigadier-General Sturges at Washington, to form one army—designated the "Army of Virginia." The command of the Army of Virginia was especially assigned to Gen'l John Pope as commanding general; the order making this change came direct from the President, dated June 26, 1862. But I must return to speak of the advance of General Fremont's column from Franklin to intercept Jackson in the Shenandoah. A more inopportune time could not have fallen to the lot of an army than was this order to General Fremont to advance.

It is a conceded fact, that the Union army in the late war was the best fed, best clothed, and best paid army the world has ever known, and notwithstanding this admitted fact, as early as April, when General Fremont took command of the Mountain Department, his plans and promises to the country were hampered—indeed virtually clogged—for want of quarter-master and commissary supplies, and at the time of his taking command in the field, with headquarters at New Creek—subsequently Petersburg and Franklin, with the exception of the brigades of Milroy and Schenck—both of which, having recently passed through a severe campaign—were greatly in need of such supplies; but General Blenker's division was practically helpless; in fact, the division might be designated as in a pitiable condition, with but few horses and mules, and they broken down and starved—unfitted for cavalry, artillery, or wagons and ambulances. Forage was so scarce that the horses of the entire command were suffering, and the men were quite as destitute and were suffering not only for want of sufficient rations but also in the matter of clothing and blankets, and there was at least a month that many of the troops were without tents or other shelter to protect them from the chilling blasts of a late and stormy spring.

I was a frequent visitor to headquarters, and I know that this condition of the army was not caused by the neglect of General Fremont, for he showed me copies of requisitions made by mail and telegraph, and the demand was repeated day after day; so when the time did come for his command to advance he was in poor condition for such an emergency, and I can truthfully say that at the time Jackson made his raid into the Shenandoah Valley one-third of Fremont's command were unfit for duty by reason of sickness from exposure and the want of forage and rations.

In substantiation of my recollections as noted, I quote from General Fremont's official report of his advance movements:

"The streams were swollen by the incessant rains, and the roads had become almost impassable. With a complement of wagons much exceeding that upon the route, the supply would have been but meager even in fair weather. With the limited number available, together with the hindrances encountered, the supply was far below the need. Not so much as one-quarter forage was got forward, and except an incomplete ration of bread, no rations had been got up for the men. For days together fresh beef, with a little salt, was the only provision on hand for issue. Coffee, so essential and desirable in the field, was becoming a luxury almost unknown. Subsistence arriving under invoice to a particular brigade, was taken by order and, so far as it would go, distributed to all. Sick-lists were largely on the increase, and such was the demoralization induced by privations endured that demonstrations among the men, amounting almost to open mutiny, had in instances to be put down with the strong hand."

In justice to the troops from West Virginia and Ohio, the brigades of Milroy, Schenck, and Cluseret should not be included as among those "to be put down with the strong hand." No such forceful argument had been proposed to them, nor could it possibly apply to those troops, for at this date no dissatisfaction looking to revolt had possessed them.

With the order directing Fremont's march, authority was given him to order the purchase of horses, or otherwise, in the language of the despatch, "to take them wherever or however he could get them." But it came too late to aid Fremont. Of forage in the country near by, scarcely a single pound could be gleaned; it had already been too well stripped by the Confederate forces. Naturally, in the absence of forage, the horses and mules died or were rendered unserviceable, and as to waiting for the arrival of horses or forage from Wheeling, that was impossible; under the terms of the order Fremont was to move at once.

Of the different roads leading from Franklin to Harrisonburg, all but one had been obstructed by Jackson; bridges and culverts had been destroyed, rocks rolled down, trees felled across the way for a distance of a mile or more. It was, therefore, regarded as impractical to attempt to march on any of these roads to Harrisonburg. Fremont determined to take a route not specifically set down in his order of advance. Instead, then, of attempts through a barren district, by any of the above-named routes, Fremont moved rearward as far as Petersburg—thence, striking easterly by way of Moorfield and Wardensville, to Strasburg. At Petersburg were found rations to last the command for five days. At this place, tents, with the exception of a very few for indispensable staff and hospital purposes, were required to be abandoned and placed in store. In like manner all surplus personal baggage was directed to be cast off, it being the object to put the column in the lightest possible marching order.

The column had reached Petersburg on the afternoon of May 26th. On the 27th, at daybreak, the march was resumed. The troops fording the Shenandoah and camping at night near Moorfield, arrived on the 28th at Fabius, about ten miles easterly from Moorfield, upon Branch Mountain. At this latter point, upon the written protest of the Medical Director, George Suckley, against further marching of the command without one day's rest, a halt was called for the 29th. Hundreds of stragglers and broken-down men from the Blenker division had been left along the road in the ascent of the mountain, and it was plain their condition demanded consideration. They were weak and reduced, not only from recent fatigue and want of food, but from previous hardship and privation on the route from the Potomac. While halting here at Fabius, a despatch was sent forward to General Fremont from President Lincoln, stating that the rebels were in the valley of Winchester and Martinsburg, and Fremont was directed to move upon the enemy "by the best route he could." On the 30th the command moved from Fabius. A renewed storm had made the roads heavy, and the march was most fatiguing. On the 31st the column passed the summit of the mountain between Lost River and Cedar Creek, marching most of the night, and closing up in a drenching rain, amid intense darkness at Cedar Creek, when we went into camp.

I will at this point and date (May 31st) leave General Fremont, and speak of Jackson's operations on this celebrated raid down the Shenandoah Valley and his return. The Confederate forces was the combined commands of Gen'ls "Stonewall" Jackson and Richard S. Ewell, numbering about 20,000 men. General Banks' main force was stationed at Strasburg, Col. John R. Kenly (later General Kenly) and his command (a part of Banks' forces) were stationed at Front Royal. Kenly's command consisted of his own, 1st Maryland Infantry Regiment; 2 pieces of Knap's Pa. Battery, Lieutenant Atwell commanding; 2 companies 26th Pa. Infantry, Captain Lane commanding; a detachment of the 5th New York Cavalry, Major Vought commanding, came up an hour after the engagement begun—numbering all told 1000 men. Front Royal was an indefensible position—distant about 8 miles southeast from Strasburg.

On the 22d of May the whole Confederate force moved down the road leading from Luray to Front Royal. The advance (under General Ewell) bivouacking about 10 miles from the last named place. On the 23d, about 2 P. M., Jackson's advance force, under command of Gen'l Bradley T. Johnson, attacked Colonel Kenly's position. Kenly was without cavalry. The enemy were upon him on all sides before timely notice of the strength of their forces was known; Colonel Kenly, however, was too old and careful a soldier to be caught napping, and notwithstanding Kenly had but 1000 men, he engaged and held in check 6000 of the enemy for nearly four hours. This fight was desperate in its stubborness, and many on both sides were killed and wounded. The gallantry and skilful handling of this small force by Colonel Kenly was for months the theme for admiring comment throughout the country. Colonel Kenly, badly wounded, and a large number of his command fell into the hands of the enemy.

The Confederate forces at this time in the Shenandoah embraced Ashby's Cavalry; the First Brigade under General Winder, the Second Brigade, Colonel Campbell commanding; the Third Brigade, Colonel Fulkerson commanding. The troops recently under command of Brig.-Gen'l Edward Johnson, and the division of General Ewell, comprising the brigades of Generals Elzey, Taylor, Trimble, and the Maryland line, consisting of the First Maryland regiment and Brockenbrough's battery under Brig.-Gen'l Geo. H. Stewart, and the 2d and 6th Va. Cavalry, Colonel Flournoy.

After the engagement at Front Royal, the Confederates seemed to have had complete possession of the situation. Banks retired with the main body of his command from Strasburg. He made an unsuccessful stand at Middle-town, Newtown, Bartonsville and at Winchester; but his gallant opposition was borne down by the impetuous Confederates, while many of Banks' artillery and wagon trains filled the road, and the victors took possession of them.

In General Jackson's official report, he says: "But in the midst of these hopes I was pained to see, as I am now to record the fact, that so many of Ashby's command, both cavalry and infantry, forgetful of their high trust as the advance of a pursuing army, deserted their colors, and abandoned themselves to pillage to such an extent as to make it necessary for that gallant officer to discontinue further pursuit." The artillery, which had pushed on with energy to the vicinity of Newtown, found itself, from this discreditable conduct, without a proper support from either infantry or cavalry. This relaxation in the pursuit was unfortunate, as the enemy was encouraged by it to bring up, about two hours later, four pieces of artillery, which were planted on the northern skirt of Newtown, and opened upon our batteries. This disregard of discipline on the part of the Confederate soldiers enabled Banks to continue his retreat to his great advantage; and after the event at Winchester, Banks' rout was complete, and he made no general stand thereafter, but pushed on to Martinsburg. Here he halted a couple of hours, and then on to Williamsport by sunset of the 25th, crossing the Potomac into Maryland. The river at this point was crossed by a ferry-boat, which was barely sufficient to transport the ammunition train. The cavalry could wade and swim the stream, but there was no way to get the infantry across. Fortunately, however, a pontoon train had been brought along all the way from Strasburg; it was soon brought into service, and by noon the next day the infantry had all been got across. "Never," says General Banks, "were more grateful hearts in the same number of men than when they stood on the opposite shore." In this retreat of fifty-three miles Banks lost about 900 men, of whom 38 were known to be killed and 155 wounded, the others were captured. Of his train of 500 wagons he lost 55, besides considerable stores, captured and destroyed at Strasburg and Winchester.

General Jackson, in his report, severely censured his cavalry for lack of enterprise. He says: "There is good reason for believing that, had the cavalry played its part in this pursuit as well as the four companies had done under Colonel Flournoy two days before in the pursuit from Front Royal, but a small portion of Banks' army would have made its escape to the Potomac."

Jackson reached Williamsport just in time to see Banks safe on the Maryland side. He rested there for a single day (26th) when he assembled his command, and divine service was held for the purpose of rendering thanks to God for the success with which He had blessed their arms, and to implore His continued favor.

CHAPTER XI.

PERSONAL REMINISCENCES—(CONTINUED).

Jackson's Retreat up the Shenandoah.—Banks and Sigel Follow to Winchester.—General McDowell's Indifference.—General Fremont in Pursuit.—Harrassing the Retreating Confederates.—Colonel Cluseret's Thrilling Experience in the Dark.—Gen'l Geo. D. Bayard Joins in the Pursuit.—Constructing a Pontoon Bridge.—Swept by Flood.—Colonel Wyndham Captured.—Battle Between Confederates and Pennsylvania Bucktails.—Colonel Kane Wounded and Taken Prisoner.—General Turner Ashby Killed.

ACKSON at this time realized that he could not hold his newly gained possessions, and must of necessity return southward over the route which he had just come. So, after manœuvring for a couple of days in the vicinity of Martinsburg, Halltown, Loudoun Heights, Harper's Ferry, etc., he issued orders for his troops to return to Winchester on the 30th, when he started on his retreat of desperation, for he had at this time learned of the advance of Fremont from the West, and McDowell from the East for the purpose of intercepting him in his retreat up the Shenandoah Valley.

Immediately, upon Jackson having abandoned his pursuit, Banks gathered his scattered command, and the pursuer became the pursued. But Banks' army was in no condition for a successful advance, and, therefore, made little progress, and soon halted at Winchester and vicinity. In the meantime, and immediately upon the information that Jackson was driving Banks from the valley, the authorities at Washington hurried forward all available troops to Harper's Ferry, and sent General Saxton to organize and prepare the same for immediate service against Jackson. About 10,000 men responded to this demand, and Gen'l Franz Sigel was sent forward to take command of this force and push Jackson. Sigel did start, and tardily reached Winchester, when he, too, gave up the pursuit.

I will now return to General Fremont, where I left him at Cedar Creek, on May 31st.

At this time and at this point General Fremont confidently expected to hear from General McDowell.

The following telegrams received by General Fremont would justify this conclusion. I quote:

WASHINGTON, *May* 29, 1862 (12 M.).

Major-General Fremont:

General McDowell's advance, if not checked by the enemy, should or (and) probably will be at Front Royal by 12 noon to-morrow. His force, when up, will be about 20,000. Please have your force at Strasburg ; or, if the route you are moving on does not lead to that point, as near Strasburg as the enemy may be at that time.

A. LINCOLN.

WASHINGTON, *May* 30, 1862 (4 P. M.).

Major-General Fremont:

Yours saying you will reach Strasburg or vicinity at 5 P. M., Saturday, has been received and sent to General McDowell, and he directed to act in view of it. You must be up to time of your promise, if possible.

A. LINCOLN.

Fremont did keep his promise, but where, oh where was McDowell? The part he bore in this important campaign would indicate that he, with a war map of the Valley of Virginia and a copy of the " Articles of War," had hied himself to some lone spot to study said map to ascertain how far his " separate independent military geographical department " extended, and whether the 62d Article of War would permit him to march his army of 20,000 men over an imaginary line to fight a battle, which, if won, would be credited to General Fremont.

Whilst General McDowell's command was designated as the Department of the Rappahannock, it was in reality a part of the Army of the Potomac. To this army (Potomac) McDowell was much attached, and his ambition was to take part in any and all movements made against Richmond. So, when the order from Washington reached him directing him to hurry to the Shenandoah Valley to co-operate with Banks and Fremont against Jackson, he was much perplexed, and even telegraphed his protest to so doing to Mr. Lincoln. But the President's orders were imperative and had to be obeyed, and though complying, the results of the part taken by McDowell showed a tardiness of movement of his command that at least indicated indifference. I will refer to his command later in my sketch.

At Cedar Creek the road forks, one branch leading to Strasburg and the other to Winchester. Early on the morning of the 1st of June, General Fremont moved toward Strasburg, Colonel Cluseret, with his brigade of the 8th West Virginia and 60th Ohio, in the advance. At 7 o'clock in the morning we touched Jackson's main body, driving in the pickets of Ewell's command, and, pressing forward, he soon became engaged with cavalry and artillery. In this skirmish a detachment of the 8th West Virginia and 60th Ohio, under command of Maj. John H. Oley, of the 8th West Virginia, did gallant service. Colonel Pilson, with a section of artillery, afterward came to the support of Major Oley. At about noon the enemy's batteries ceased firing, and our cavalry being pushed forward found the enemy in retreat. A reconnoissance by Colonel Cluseret with the 8th West Virginia and 60th Ohio pushed rapidly toward Strasburg, when within a short distance of the town he learned that the enemy had vacated the place. So, with the addition of a battalion of cavalry and a section of artillery, he was ordered to take possession of the town. Night brought with it another one of those terrible storms that had become so frequent of late, and this one excelled in its down pour of rain, and the lightning and thunder were indescribable. It was simply terrifically grand.

A thrilling incident, in which Colonel Cluseret and his command were the actors, is worthy of mention. The night just referred to was simply black in its darkness, and but for the vivid flash of the lightning for the moment one could not see his outstretched hand. Colonel Cluseret, being without guides and unfamiliar with the country, passed through the town, which was in darkness, and marching on saw lights in the distance, which he supposed was the town, but upon approaching the same, about 11 o'clock, the lights proved to be the enemy's campfires, and he found himself in the midst of Ashby's cavalry, which was the rear-guard of Jackson's army. Colonel Cluseret at once gave the order to charge, but at the sharp fire of Ashby's men the cavalry broke in a shameful panic, carrying back with it the artillery. To the honor and praise of the 8th West Virginia and 60th Ohio, not a man of them followed the disgraceful example, but stood their ground like veterans, and delivered such a steady and well-directed fire that the movement of Ashby was checked.

Colonel Cluseret, having accomplished the objects of his reconnoissance, withdrew his men and returned to the main column. I will mention just here that the 8th West Virginia and 60th Ohio were new regiments, that had just been recruited and sent to General Fremont a few days before he started on his march from Franklin, and this battle in the dark was their first introduction to powder and bullet at the hands of the enemy; they were, therefore, the more to be praised for their gallantry.

At early dawn on June 2d, General Fremont's army was in motion, and we soon found that Jackson was in full retreat, and that we were then in pursuit. Passing Strasburg we were joined by Gen'l George D. Bayard, of General McDowell's command, with a cavalry force of about 800 men and four pieces of artillery, and a battalion of the Pennsylvania "Bucktails," under Colonel Kane. After passing Strasburg we came upon the scene of Colonel Cluseret's engagement of the night before. It was marked by the smoldering campfire of Ashby's men, also by one of our caissons, which had been disabled and left on the ground, and by several of the enemy's killed and wounded.

The route we were upon was a good turnpike road running from Strasburg to the southward toward Staunton, and its even surface was a welcome exchange for the mire and mountain sloughs through which we had recently passed.

The enemy being closely pressed by our advance, about 10 A. M. made a stand and showed fight; but Colonel Pilson, Chief of Artillery on Fremont's staff, had in hand Buell's and Schirmer's batteries, supported by Bayard's cavalry and 600 men from our own column under Colonel Zagonyi, Chief of Cavalry. After a sharp engagement, lasting an hour, the enemy were driven from their position, and again pursued. At intervals during the day the enemy faced about, and were as often compelled to relinquish the fight. In the pursuit it often happened that the enemy were only a few hundred yards from our advance.

By sunset the enemy had secured the high points beyond Woodstock, where they were permitted to rest in peace, as our own force was also glad to get needed rest.

The retreat of this day was a reckless one; over 500 prisoners fell into our hands, and a number of our soldiers, captured from General Banks, were recovered, besides several hundred stand of small-arms, some cast away, and others standing in stacks upon the roadside. Broken wagons, ambulances, clothing and blankets lined the route, all giving unmistakable evidence of hurried retreat. In all the fighting that day our loss was comparatively small, but two killed and less than a dozen wounded. Colonel Pilsen lost his horse, killed. We found seven of the enemy killed, with several horses. His loss during the day must have been considerable; of course they would take with them all killed and wounded, except when too closely pressed to do so.

June 3d was a repetition of the 2d, the enemy fighting and retreating, we fighting and advancing. The enemy, however, had the advantage in this— they devoted much of their time in destroying bridges and culverts, and in otherwise placing obstructions upon the road. Sometimes we would reach a burning bridge in time to put out the fire. The bridge over Cedar Creek at Mount Jackson was saved by a splendid dash of Captain Conger, with a company of his 3d West Virginia Cavalry. The Confederate General Ashby, who had covered the retreating column, barely escaped capture by Captain Conger's men. The captain pushed on with vigor, and witnessed the firing of the more important bridge beyond Mount Jackson, crossing the north fork of the Shenandoah. He made a gallant charge, but the volleys of grape and musketry drove back his small command; and, notwithstanding General

Bayard arrived with his cavalry in good time, the artillery necessary to drive the enemy from their protected position could not get up until the fine bridge was in flames.   Our loss during the day was not over one killed and a few wounded.

The burning of the bridge over the Shenandoah gave us a decided set-back, and but for the fact that General Fremont had with him pontoons our advance would have been delayed several days; but the pontoons were hurried to the front, and, notwithstanding the stream at this point was wide and rapid, having been swollen by recent rains, Major Haskell performed a most dangerous and daring feat by plunging with his horse into the current; and, by swimming to the opposite bank, secured the preparatory ropes.

Then a corps of employees, acting as pontoniers, under Lieutenant Robinson, of Ohio, with details from infantry regiments, went actively to work.   It was now nearly dark and a heavy rain was falling, but that faithful band worked on, uncomplainingly, throughout the night, and by 6 o'clock in the morning the bridge was made available for crossing and a portion of our infantry and cavalry gotten over.   Suddenly, however, the river, fed by the storm and mountain tributaries, began to rise, and in the space of a few hours it had gained fully twelve feet in height, with a current turbulent and swift, and with the drift forcing itself upon the boats, several of them were swamped, and to save the bridge from utter destruction the ropes were cut, and the pon-toons that had cost so much labor swung around to the northern shore, and our army was cut in two; but that portion that had crossed over the river was well protected by the skilful placing of batteries upon available bluffs and hills.   For 24 hours our army was compelled to give up the cherished pursuit. Toward night, however, the stream, as suddenly as it had risen, began to subside, when the working parties renewed their efforts.   The work was laborious, indeed, and tested the full capacity of endurance of the men engaged.

By 10 A. M. the next day that bridge was again in condition for crossing; so on the 5th of June we were again on the tramp, following the enemy, and though we had lost at least 30 hours, giving the enemy an advantage he proved not slow to use, and notwithstanding the suffering of our men by standing in the storm all these weary hours, they stepped out with a willing-ness that told plainly they were eager for the fray.

On this day we marched about 20 miles, passing on the way the still burning campfires of the enemy, and when we bivouacked just beyond New Market the enemy's camp was only a few miles ahead.   On the 6th, by an early start and rapid march, we gained on the retreating forces, and by 2 P. M. we drove his rear-guard through Harrisonburg.   As there are several diverg-ing roads from this city, General Fremont was uncertain as to the direction taken by the enemy; so he ordered his command into camp around about the city, when he at once sent out reconnoitering parties on the different roads.

At this time I want to do justice to that splendid soldier, Gen'l George D. Bayard, and his command, by recording it that General Fremont did, at the time he (Bayard) reported on the 2d inst., place him in command of the advance, and he practically maintained that honorable place whilst he remained with General Fremont.

Of the reconnoitering parties just referred to as having been sent out, one was in command of Colonel Wyndham, and consisted of his regiment, the 1st N. J. Cavalry, with a battalion of the 4th N. Y. Cavalry. Several miles to the southeast of Harrisonburg Colonel Wyndham came upon the enemy in a dense wood. The ambuscade was an effective one on the part of the enemy. Colonel Wyndham and his men fought desperately, but they were surrounded on all sides, and were consequently badly cut up. Colonel Wyndham was taken prisoner, the regimental colors lost, and 30 men, including Captains Shelmire, Clark, and Harris, were killed.

But this victory of the enemy was short-lived, for a little later on, just before sundown, General Bayard, with four companies of Kane's Rifles (Pennsylvania Bucktails), and the 1st Pa. Cavalry, entered the woods. Immediately after entering the Bucktails encountered a regiment of the enemy's cavalry, with artillery and a regiment of infantry, from which the Bucktails received a terrific and damaging fire. The engagement lasted only half an hour, during which the Bucktails lost upward of 40 in killed, wounded and missing. Colonel Kane was wounded and taken prisoner; Captain Taylor a prisoner, Captain Blanchard shot through both legs, Lieutenant Swayne wounded. This battalion was, and is still, entitled to the highest consideration of the Goverument for their splendid conduct. At the critical moment in this episode, Colonel Cluseret, with his brigade, came to the relief General Bayard, when the enemy retreated in disorder, leaving our forces in possession of their camp, with their dead and wounded left in our hands.

With the growing darkness the enemy continued their retreat, being continually harassed by our advancing forces.

This short but intensely-inflictive engagement was among the noted events of the war, and notwithstanding the severe loss of which I have written as having befallen our arms, our loss was small as compared with that of the enemy, and by this event the whole Confederacy was thrown into mourning scarcely less intense than that experienced by the death of "Stonewall" Jackson. It was in this engagement that the pride of the Valley of the Shenandoah, the beloved of all the army, the companion of Jackson, the brave, lion-hearted Gen'l Turner Ashby fell.

It will, perhaps, be interesting reading, especially to the Maryland soldiers, to know that the infantry regiment alluded to as being in the woods and sustaining a heroic part in this engagement was the 1st Md., Colonel (afterward General) Bradley T. Johnson commanding. The 58th Va. was the first regiment engaged, but Colonel Johnson charged through the woods to the left in support of the 58th. Colonel Johnson's regiment suffered severely, and the Colonel had his horse shot from under him at almost the same moment that General Ashby's horse was killed, and a moment later Ashby himself fell.

CHAPTER XII.

PERSONAL REMINISCENCES—(CONTINUED).

The Calm Before the Storm.—Reconnoissance in Force.—Fremont's Order of March.—Battle of Cross Keys.—Union and Confederate Forces Engaged.—Letter from Gen'l James Shields.—Retreat of Confederates from Cross Keys.—Battle of Port Republic.—Disobedience of Orders.—Escape of Jackson and his Army.

THE 7th of June dawned with an indescribable calmness that the veteran soldier learned to interpret and regard with some degree of correctness as the "calm before the storm," or the still before the battle. General Fremont knew that Jackson could not longer afford to permit his rear-guard to be annoyed with his (Fremont's) anxious advance. The loss to a retreating army is often heavier than in the actual battle, and this had been the experience of Jackson for the past two or three days. When, therefore, on the morning of the 7th, the hurry and flurry of the cavalry especially had given place to the more substantial movement of brigades in close marching order, the story was given to the soldier, without command, that a battle was near at hand. No less than three brigades were sent out on as many roads to locate Jackson. General Milroy took his entire brigade in the direction of Port Republic; others were ordered toward Keezletown and on the Staunton turnpike to Middle River. These reconnoissances developed the fact that Jackson had left the main road and had taken a narrow and difficult one in the direction of Port Republic, and that he had selected a favorable location and was preparing to make a stand and give General Fremont battle. The several brigades having returned to camp, a movement in the new direction was determined upon for the morrow, the 8th.

The entire command had orders to prepare an unusually early breakfast, and before the rising of the sun, Fremont had directed his column to take an unfrequented road leading through the woods from Harrisonburg, about six miles to the southeast, to Cross Keys, where Jackson had made his stand. It may interest those who participated in that day's march and battle to read General Fremont's order of march as published on that morning, June 8th, 1862.

THE ADVANCE.

Colonel Cluseret's brigade, consisting of the 60th Ohio and 8th W. Va., reinforced by the 39th N. Y. (Garibaldi Guards).

THE MAIN COLUMN.

1. Dickel's 4th N. Y. cavalry.

2. General Stahel's brigade, consisting of the 8th, 41st and 45th N. Y., and 27th Pa., and Dilger's, Buell's and Schirmer's batteries.

3. General Bohlen's brigade, consisting of the 54th and 58th N. Y., and the 74th and 75 Pa., and Weidrich's battery.

4. General Milroy's brigade, consisting of the 2d, 3d and 5th W. Va., 25th Ohio, and Hyman's, Johnson's, and Ewing's batteries.

5. General Schenck's brigade, consisting of the 32d, 73d, 75th and 82d Ohio, DeBeck's and Rigby's batteries, and a small detachment of cavalry.

6. Rear-guard, following ambulances and ammunition train, General Steinwehr's brigade, under command of Colonel Koltes, consisting of the 29th and 68th N. Y., 73d Pa., and Dieckmann's battery.

General Bayard's brigade did not compose a part of this column, as the severe duty performed by them the past few days made it imperative that it be left temporarily at Harrisonburg for the main purpose of shoeing the horses that were rendered unserviceable by reason of being unshod; later in the day, however, General Bayard came forward to take part in the battle. The most of his command, however, was detailed as escort to the wagon train, and to cover the line of communication against parties that would likely attack from the many by-roads and cross-roads.

About 8 A. M. heavy musketry firing was heard in our front, indicating that Colonel Cluseret was engaging the enemy. The effect of this firing accelerated the step of the whole command, and we soon learned that the enemy had placed a regiment—the 15th Alabama, Colonel Cantey—as outpost at Union Church, and it was this force that Cluseret was engaging.

The enemy stubbornly fell back through the timber a distance of a mile or more, Cluseret vigorously advancing. At this point Jackson's main force was found in line of battle, which was a naturally strong one, and selected at leisure on the preceding day, which gave to Jackson a great advantage over General Fremont; but this is one of the inevitable conditions in war, and General Fremont had no choice but to go in and make the best of it.

The placing of his command in line of battle was regarded by all as especially skillful, and was about in the following order: Colonel Cluseret's brigade, which had pushed the forces opposed to it back upon the enemy's main line, held their position, which was well to the front and near the center. General Stahel's brigade took position on the left of Cluseret and some distance from his (Cluseret's) position. General Milroy's brigade, leaving the main road, took position on Cluseret's right. Those three brigades formed the first line of battle, with Milroy on the right and Stahel on the left. General Bohlen's brigade coming up, was conducted to a position to the rear of Stahel and Cluseret, covering the gap between these two brigades.

General Schenck's brigade took to the right in the direction of Milroy, and occupied a position that secured our forces against a flank movement in that direction. This line was formed as promptly as if it had been going to position for review or dress-parade in an open field; and in addition to this prompt action of the infantry, it did not require over thirty minutes to place in the most favorable position eight batteries of artillery.

Colonel Dickel's 4th N. Y. cavalry occupied a position on the extreme left. On our right and rear was the detachments of cavalry of Schenck's Brigade. Captain Conger's company was on duty at General Fremont's headquarters.

It must not be understood that the forming of this line of battle was done in a quiet way, for the fighting was going on all the time. From the formation in line of Cluseret's brigade, each brigade in turn as it came into line became engaged, and by the time all were posted the battle was raging from right to left. Steinwehr's brigade arriving from the rear at this time was deployed in rear of the batteries as a reserve. General Blenker having arrived at this moment took charge of his division.

The severest fighting of the day was on our left, done by the brigades of Stahel and Bohlen, and especially by the 8th and 45th N. Y. of Stahel's brigade. These two regiments were mostly in open ground, and were engaged at one time with four regiments of the enemy.

Their loss was heavy, but when both brigades fought so gallantly it would be unjust to single out special deeds. The entire command was and is entitled to the warmest commendation.

I may be pardoned, however, at all times, referring especially to Milroy's brigade and to my own regiment (3d W. Va.), for it is with these brave men that my reminiscence is most closely associated.

The battle raged during the day with little change of position on either side, and when we consider the unequal numbers engaged—Fremont's entire force not exceeding 10,000 men, and were on the offensive, while Jackson's force was known to number 18,000 men, and strongly placed—it is a marvel that our army was not forced to the defensive and utterly annihilated.

The following extract from General Fremont's report of the battle, made after a careful inspection of the situation, will show how strongly the enemy were located:

"The enemy occupied a position of uncommon strength, commanding the junction of the roads to Port Republic. He had chosen his ground with great skill and with a previous full knowledge of the location. His main line was advantageously posted upon a ridge, protected in front by a steep declivity, and almost entirely masked by thick woods and covered by fences. Near his center, and on the summit of an abrupt ascent, bordered at the base by the high, perpendicular bank of a marshy creek, he had massed, in addition to his guns elsewhere, three of his best batteries. From superiority of numbers his flank, both at the right and left, considerably overlapped my own.''

Milroy's brigade was opposed to the brigades of Generals Steuart and Elzey, of Ewell's division, and the casualties on both sides will attest the severity of the battle on that part of the field.

The forces directly opposing General Milroy were the Second Brigade, commanded by Brig.-Gen'l George H. Steuart, composed of the 1st Md., the 44th, 52d and 58th Va., with Brockenbrough's and Lusk's batteries. The casualties were, Brigadier-General Steuart severely wounded; in the 1st Md., Lieut. Hezekiah H. Bean and 27 others wounded. Col. (later Gen'l) Bradley T. Johnson was in command of this regiment. The casualies in the 44th Va. were, Capt. John T. Martin wounded, with one enlisted man killed and two wounded. The casualties in the 52d Va. were, Lieut. C. M. King killed, and Maj. John D. H. Rose, Lieuts. S. Paul and T. D. Ranson and Ass't-Surg. John Lewis wounded, with one enlisted man killed and 20 wounded. The 58th Va. had five enlisted men wounded; Brockenbrough's battery, two enlisted men killed; Lusk's battery, two enlisted men killed and three wounded.

The Fourth Brigade was in command of Brig.-Gen'l Arnold Elzey, and was composed of the following regiments: the 12th Ga., 12th Va. and Raine's battery. The casualties were, General Elzey wounded; the 12th Ga., two enlisted men killed and 11 wounded; the 13th Va., Lieut. R. C. Mason wounded, with two enlisted men killed, 13 wounded, and one missing; Raines' battery, two enlisted men killed, seven wounded and eight missing.

The forces of the enemy occupying their right and opposed to the brigades of Generals Stahel and Bohlen were, the Seventh Brigade, commanded by Brig.-Gen'l Isaac R. Trimble, composed of the 15th Ala., 21st Ga., 16th Miss., 21st N. C. and Courtney's battery. The casualties among the officers of this brigade were, 15th Ala., Capt. R. H. Hill and Lieut. W. B. Mills killed; Lieuts. H. C. Brainard and A. A. McIntosh wounded, and Lieut. W. T. Berry missing; the 21st Ga., Lieut. J. M. Mack killed; the 16th Miss., Col. Carnot Posey and Lieuts. J. B. Coleman and W. R. Brown wounded; the 21st N. C., Lieut. L. T. Whitelock wounded. The total loss in this brigade was 138 killed and wounded.

The Eighth Brigade, commanded by Brigadier-General Taylor, and Patton's brigade, commanded by Col. J. M. Patton, were also of the forces opposed to Stahel and Bohlen.

Returning to the consideration of the part taken by Milroy's Brigade, that general maintained his reputation as "Fighting Milroy." Upon taking position he at once advanced his brigade well to the front, driving in a strong line of the enemy's skirmishers, attacking their main body at close quarters. His men suffered severely in an attempt to plant a battery in a desirable position. The brigade lost 23 enlisted men killed, 120 enlisted men wounded. I regret that I have not the names of all the killed and wounded in the brigade. I recall of my own regiment, however, the following killed: Wm. Cole and John J. Fredericks, of Company A; Daniel Spangler, of Company B, and James S. Phillips, of Company E. I knew these men well, and the pain their death caused me then lingers with me as I write.

When we consider the severity of this battle, so far as the burning of powder would indicate it to be severe, we marvel that so few men were killed and wounded. Another coincidence is worthy of mention: while the Union forces had few casualties among the officers, the Confederate casualties among the officers were exceptionally heavy. Our only loss in officers was Lieuts. Nicolai Dunka, Aid-de-Camp to General Fremont, Jas. M. Vance, 60th Ohio, and Frederick Leuders, 27th Pa., killed; Lieuts. Henry Grassan and Bruce B. Rice, died of wounds; Colonel Gilsa, of the 41st N. Y., Captain Miser and Lieut. Brundensteen, of General Blenker's staff, wounded.

In concluding my recollections of this battle, I do not wish to make the impression that the troops named as having been most hotly engaged were superior in prowess to others on the field, but by reason of their position in the line they had the brunt of the fighting to do. That splendid brigade of Ohio troops commanded by General Schenck had no superior in the whole army; and Steinwehr's Brigade, commanded by Colonel Koltes, were also brave soldiers. All the artillery along our line behaved with conspicuous gallantry, and every attempt of the enemy to emerge from the cover of the woods was repulsed by the assistance of our batteries. When the battle ended both armies occupied practically the positions taken by them in the morning.

Fremont had bivouacked his command a short distance from the scene of battle, but our pickets retained securely the ground temporarily relinquished by the main body. As neither army seemed to have gained any advantage by this engagement, General Fremont very naturally felt no little annoyance as to his line of operations for the morrow, when a scout brought in some welcome intelligence.   It was a note from Gen'l James Shields, commanding a division of McDowell's army.

The following is General Shields's letter :

LURAY, *June* 8 (9.30 A. M.).

Maj.-Gen'l Fremont, Commanding Pursuing Forces :

I write by your scout.   I think by this time there will be 12 pieces of artillery opposite Jackson's train at Port Republic, if he has taken that route.   Some cavalry and artillery have pushed on to Waynesburg to burn the bridge.   I hope to have two brigades at Port Republic to-day.   I follow myself with two other brigades to-day from this place.   If the enemy changes direction, you will please keep me advised.   If he attempts to force passage, as my force is not large there yet, I hope you will thunder down on his rear.   Please send back information from time to time.   I think Jackson is caught this time.   Yours sincerely,

JAMES SHIELDS,
Maj.-Gen'l Commanding Division.

General Fremont knew that General Shields was somewhere in the vicinity of Luray, but had received no knowledge of his whereabouts or intentions, and this letter gave General Fremont a pretty clear idea of what would be the program on the following day.   It was evident that Jackson would have to abandon Cross Keys, and throw his whole force against General Shields at Port Republic.   General Fremont therefore was prepared to see his front clear of the enemy in the morning.   Accordingly he made preparations for an early advance.

At dawn, as surmised, the enemy was found to have retired from our immediate front.   General Fremont made no delay in pushing his troops forward.   As we passed over the scenes of the preceding day's fighting we found the enemy's dead in great numbers upon the field, and some 20 horses lying together upon the height occupied by his center batteries, showing the wholesale effect of our artillery.

Our column had not proceeded far when a black column of smoke about five miles away showed that the Port Republic bridge was on fire, and soon after the sound of heavy cannonading met our ears.   It was now evident that Shields was engaging Jackson.   General Fremont at once put his command in quick marching order, hoping to be on hand at the interesting ceremony of bagging Jackson.   So when General Fremont reached the crest of the ridge overlooking the Shenandoah, and beyond it the town of Port Republic, his eyes met a painful surprise.   He was not to be gratified by the capture of Jackson.   To the contrary, he was just in time to witness Jackson's retreating army, which was now passing " over the hills and far away," with the bridge burned ; another illustration of the fact that " the best laid plans of mice and men gang aft aglee."

General Shields's plan, if carried out, would have accomplished his purpose. The battle that did take place was one of the stupendous mistakes that armies sometimes meet with. This bridge, which crosses the Shenandoah, was to have been burned by General Shields's order, and he sent Colonel Carroll, in command of a brigade, to burn the bridge. Had he done so, Jackson would have had no way open for retreat, but would have fallen between Fremont's aud Shields' forces. Colonel Carroll disobeyed his orders, and took it upon himself, with one small brigade, to whip Jackson's 18,000 men. The result was that Jackson fell upon Carroll with all his force, and pushing over the bridge set it on fire, thereby preventing Fremont's pursuit. Had the bridge been burned as per order of General Shields, his entire division would have had time to come to the front. As it was, only one brigade, that of Gen'l E. B. Tyler, succeeded in getting to the relief of Colonel Carroll. And thus terminated the memorable raid of Stonewall Jackson in the Shenandoah.

For Colonel Carroll's disobedience the severest punishment should have been meted out to him. I cannot, however, close this sketch without giving that meed of praise to Gen'l E. B. Tyler and his command, likewise Colonel Carroll and his men, for the heroic defense they made in the face of overwhelming numbers.

CHAPTER XIII.

PERSONAL REMINISCENCES—(CONTINUED).

A Just Criticism.—General McDowell Censured.—Mismanagement and Jealousy.—General Shields' Letters.—Fremont at Mount Jackson and Middletown.—Sickness and Discharges.—Army of Virginia Created by Order of the President.—General John Pope Assigned to the Command.—Retirement of General Fremont.

THE student of war history, who may read the account (in the preceding chapters) of the campaign terminating at Port Republic, will no doubt—if he reads from a Union standpoint—experience a sense of just condemnation of some one, or of some military authorities. If, however, it is read from a Confederate standpoint, a thrill of superior management or prowess will no doubt prevail. I feel, therefore, that a just criticism of the situation, as I saw and understood it, will interest all, no matter from which standpoint they may read.

In order, then, that my criticism may be made plain, I shall note a few introductory leading facts.

1. On Thursday, May 22, Generals Jackson and Ewell entered the Shenandoah Valley on their raid, with a force, in round numbers, of 20,000 troops.

2. At this date General Banks was at Strasburg and vicinity with 9000 troops.

3. General Saxton—later, Sigel—was at Harper's Ferry with 7000 troops.

4. General Fremont was at Franklin with 12,000 troops.

5. General McDowell was at Fredericksburg with 20,000 troops.

On May 24, General Fremont at Franklin, and General McDowell at Fredericksburg, each received from President Lincoln the same order to march with all haste to the Shenandoah Valley to the relief of General Banks. Both of these generals were distant the same number, about 75 miles from the Shenandoah.

With this statement I submit my criticism. And I do this with all the sincerity of an unprejudiced mind or motive. Both Generals Fremont and McDowell, the principal actors, have long since been called to their eternal rest.

That Jackson's raid was a Confederate success cannot be denied. Why successful? We find him with 20,000 soldiers, whilst there were opposed to him in front, and not far away, on right and left flanks 48,000 soldiers; with this superior force, how was it made possible for Jackson to march to Harper's Ferry and Martinsburg, and then march back again without capture? For convenience I will present my criticism under the following special headings:

    1. The rain and the floods.
    2. Mismanagement.
    3. Jealousy.

    1. *The Rains and the Floods.*—It is true that for a period of ten days in the midst of this raid the rain fell in torrents, swelling the rivulets into creeks, the creeks into rivers, and the rivers into seas, washing away bridges, and rendering marching almost impossible; but the elements do not respect or show partiality to individuals nor to armies. So the rain fell upon the Union and the Confederate alike, hence in this there can be no criticism or censure.

    2. *Mismanagement.*—It was cruel, wicked, idiotic "mismanagement" that placed the troops of Fremont, Banks, and Sigel in the field, and they be expected to perform active and efficient service without the means of transportation, with but little food for man or beast. But such were the facts. There was one man and one department, however, that was and is deserving of special commendation for heroic service performed under the aforementioned conditions. I refer to General Fremont and his command. He obeyed orders and his men followed him. But as I have already alluded to the distress of his army, it is not necessary to repeat, further than to say that I have not, nor could I, draw the picture sufficiently strong to depict the distress of these brave men; and yet they pushed forward and met Jackson at Cross Keys, and though numbering 12,000 when they left Franklin, 1500 fell by the wayside—either to go to the hospitals or to their graves; so when they overtook and met the enemy at Cross Keys, so severe had been the march through rain and storm, with chill and hunger, that the men were more fit subjects for the hospital than for the battle.

Fremont knew before the battle that the enemy nearly doubled his own command, and he sought aid from Banks, Sigel and McDowell. In reply to his letter to General Banks, at Winchester, that he was on the eve of a battle, and for him (Banks) to push forward with all his force, Banks replied: "I am here without supplies or transportation, and am unable to move. I have sent to-day a strong detachment of cavalry, with instructions to reach you if possible." From General Sigel, at Winchester, in response to a similar request, Sigel writes: "I am exceedingly sorry that I could not proceed at once to the scene of action to assist you, but the troops under my command brought from Harper's Ferry could scarcely reach Winchester, and were in such a condition that it is necessary to prepare them for field service before they leave this place, otherwise they would be an incumbrance and not a help to you."

And Fremont fought the desperate battle of Cross Keys alone with his own command. But have I not written enough to justify me in handing my case to an impartial jury, and asking a verdict of guilty of "count 2, mismanagement," as charged?

3. *Jealousy.*—Whilst "jealousy" applies to all in authority who could have rendered aid to Fremont, but did not, it is especially intended to apply to General McDowell and his command. As has already been stated, McDowell was ordered by the President from Fredericksburg at the same date that Fremont was ordered from Franklin, and both ordered to operate toward the same object, "in capturing or driving Jackson from the valley." Both had about the same distance to march, both were ordered to operate in the Shenandoah Valley, which was the geographical territory of General Banks; but as both these generals had been ordered there for a special duty, it was the most natural thing to expect, and would seem to be the plain duty of both generals to lose sight of departmental lines and technicalities and co-operate to capture Jackson.

When the President's orders were received by McDowell his forces were in splendid condition, well clothed, and had an abundance of forage and rations. He made a tardy march, and on June 5 his headquarters were at Front Royal. Fremont had pushed forward with his hapless command, and was at this date at Mount Jackson. He was then on the heels of Jackson, and knew he would soon overtake and engage him; whereupon he dispatched Captain Howard, of his staff, to McDowell, detailing, in writing, his position and expectations. Fremont's Acting-Assistant Adujant-General, who wrote the communication urging McDowell to join him without delay, had inadvertently made the communication read as an order instead of a request.

Notwithstanding the fact that McDowell had marched his men 75 miles for the purpose of capturing Jackson, this is the reply he sends in the face of the enemy to Fremont:

"I beg to call the attention of your staff officer to the terms he has employed in his communication to me, making it in the nature of a positive, peremptory order, as if to me under your command. Being, like yourself, the commander of a separate, independent military geographical department, with certain troops assigned to me by the Secretary of War, and being here in a neighboring department for a special temporary purpose, under the direct orders and instructions of the President, I cannot receive orders from an officer save in the accidental temporary case provided for in the 62d Article of War."

I infer that this ponderous literary production was not entrusted to his acting assistant adjutant-general, for it was signed in full—"Irvin McDowell, Major-General, commanding Department of the Rappahannock." Now, am I not justified in the use of the word "jealousy"? And I trust the reader will not be so verdant as not to understand. Let us reason. Both Fremont and McDowell were major-generals. Fremont had beaten McDowell into the Shenandoah. Fremont had already skirmished with the enemy, and had sought the aid of Banks, Sigel, and McDowell to assist him in the final attack. Banks and Sigel could not reach him, as has been stated. McDowell had no such excuse, but had he joined in the attack, and had success been the result, Fremont would have been the victor, and would have received the plaudits and congratulations of the country, as he would have deserved. McDowell realized this.

Now, impartial reader, I have fairly stated my case; draw your own conclusions. Of this I am quite sure, Banks did not object that either Fremont or McDowell had crossed over imaginary lines and were within his jurisdiction. Mr. Lincoln did not object; the Nation did not object; there could be no objections except in the jealousy of a few men.

The following extracts from letters from General Shields to General Fremont, dated Luray, June 12 and 13, will explain:

Maj.-Gen'l JOHN C. FREMONT:

My advance guard was driven back on the 9th after a sanguinary engagement of four hours. I reinforced it and determined, in connection with you, to renew the attack next morning. After handing the dispatch to your messenger a peremptory order reached me from Washington directing me to get my command together and return at once to this point, preparatory to marching to Fredericksburg. I never obeyed an order with such reluctance, but no option was left me.

    *   *   *   *   *   *   *   *   *   *   *

I have sent a communication to the War Department, in which I bear testimony to the energy, activity, and ability with which you conducted the pursuit. The general who led my advance (2500) committed two grave errors; one, in not burning the bridge at Port Republic; the other, in taking up an indefensible position and waiting until he was attacked in force by Jackson. He was compelled to fall back, which he did in good order. I joined them with the main body, and then Jackson fell back in haste. I hurried to attack him the next day. This was my proposition to your messenger, which he started to take to you, when peremptory orders arrived to set out for Fredericksburg. This was one of the mistakes of the war. We ought to have ended Jackson first. He should not have been left behind in the valley. Had we fallen upon him next morning he never would have come back to this valley, and we could have destroyed the railroad at Waynesboro and Gordonsville. General McDowell knew nothing of our situation. He acted upon some preconcerted plan, without reference to things in the valley.   (Signed)   JAMES SHIELDS, *Major-General.*

The escape of Jackson and the withdrawal of Shields ended those provokingly mismanaged operations which I have dignified by calling a campaign in the Shenandoah, which gave opportunity and justification to a large body of good soldiers to suggest a revolt, and also justified me in criticism which might truthfully have been written in much stronger terms.

On the 11th and 12th of June, Fremont withdrew his command to Mount Jackson, where a much needed rest was given to both men and animals. The excitement of the march and the battle having relaxed, the dreadful effects of the starving and the exposure of the men to the intense cold soon showed itself. For more than two hundred men after a careful examination by a board of surgeons, were discharged for physical disabilities incurred, incident to their hard service, while the sick and wounded brought along mainly in army wagons (owing to a want of ambulances), numbering more than 1000, were now in the hospital at Mount Jackson.

On the 24th of June, Fremont withdrew farther down the valley to Middletown, where he formed a junction with the forces of Generals Banks and Sigel.

The tents and baggage left at Petersburg on the 27th of May having been brought forward to Middletown, camps and hospitals were established at healthful points, the men were made comparatively comfortable, and the sick began to improve. For the first time since leaving Franklin, on the 24th of May, the men here received full rations.

Fremont at this time was preparing his command for active service, when the following Presidential order fell like a bursting shell upon General Fremont and the troops of the Mountain Department:

EXECUTIVE DEPARTMENT,
WASHINGTON, D. C., *June* 26, 1862.

Ordered :

I. The forces under Major-Generals Fremont, Banks and McDowell, including the troops now under Brigadier-General Sturgis at Washington, shall be consolidated and form one army, to be called the Army of Virginia.

II. The command of the Army of Virginia is specially assigned to Maj.-Gen'l John Pope as Commanding General. The troops of the Mountain Department heretofore under the command of Major-General Fremont, shall constitute the First Army Corps, under command of Major-General Fremont; the troops of the Shenandoah Department, now under General Banks, shall constitute the Second Army Corps, and be commanded by him; the troops under command of General McDowell, except those within the City of Washington, shall form the Third Army Corps, and be under his command.

A. LINCOLN.

LORENZO THOMAS, *Adjutant-General.*

General Fremont was greatly incensed at this taking off of his official head, and declined to pass under the command of General Pope, and asked to be relieved from the duty to which he had been assigned under General Pope, which, of course was done, and General Fremont was placed on waiting orders.

CHAPTER XIV.

PERSONAL REMINISCENCES—(CONTINUED.)

Reorganization of the Corps, under General Pope.—General Sigel in Command of the First Corps.—General Milroy Commands an Independent Brigade.—Pope's Literary Period.— Strength of his Army.—Advance to Culpeper Court House.—Battle of Cedar Mountain.— Terrible Slaughter of both Armies.—Armistice to Bury the Dead.—Interesting Episode.

N the reorganization of these corps, under General Pope, General Franz Sigel, on the 29th of June, was assigned to the command of the First Army Corps, declined by General Fremont. General Milroy was complimented by the command of an independent brigade consisting of four regiments of infantry, viz.: 2d, 3d and 5th West Virginia infantry ; 82d Ohio infantry; 1st West Virginia cavalry, companies C, E and L; Ohio light artillery, 12th battery, and was further complimented by being designated as the advance brigade of Sigel's first corps.

From the date of issuance (June 26th) of President Lincoln's order placing General Pope in command of the Army of Virginia, with headquarters at Washington, D. C., until July 31st, the date that General Pope took command in the field, headquarters at Warrenton, Va., the reorganizing, equipping and placing his army for active service can fitly be termed a military literary period. For the orders, letters and telegrams which passed between Pope and his subordinates numbered two hundred and fifty. At this date (July 21st) Pope's immediate command consisted of the first (Sigel's) corps, 19,820 men, headquarters Sperryville, Va.; second (Banks') corps, 20,442 men, headquarters near little Washington, Va.; third (McDowell's) corps, 32,239 men, headquarters Warrenton Va. At this time evidences of active operations filled the air; reconnoissances and scouting parties were being sent out on all roads leading to the southward, and the presence of "Stonewall" Jackson in force at Gordonsville and Charlottesville indicated a battle at an early day.

On August the 8th General Sigel, at Sperryville, received this telegram from General Pope: "The enemy has attacked our left, and is marching on this place (Culpeper)." Sigel was ordered to move his command at once on the road from Sperryville to Culpeper, and to continue the march the following morning at as early an hour as possible. The same order received by General Sigel was also given Generals Banks and McDowell. Gen'l

Geo. D. Bayard, on the 9th, commanding the cavalry of the army, and who was operating the most advanced position of Pope's army, sent this dispatch to General McDowell: "The enemy are advancing in force, artillery, cavalry and infantry; wagons in sight." This advance was on the James City road, and towards Culpeper Courthouse. Banks' and a part of McDowell's corps were at Culpeper Courthouse and posted along a few miles south of the town, near Cedar Mountain. Banks' corps met the Confederates under "Stonewall" Jackson about 2 P. M. of the 9th at Cedar Mountain, also called Cedar Run and Slaughter's Mountain, situated 8 miles south of Culpeper Courthouse. After some preliminary maneuvers of the two armies, the clash came at 5 P. M. The battle on the Union side was mainly fought by Banks' second corps, and it stands recorded as one of the most desperately fought battles of the war, lasting until far into the night.

It is stated in General Pope's report of the engagement that General Banks precipitated the battle, and the engagement took place at least 24 hours earlier than Pope's plans had provided, Sigel's corps not arriving till the following day. Milroy did, however, push forward with his independent brigade of West Virginians, and arrived at Culpeper at 5 o'clock A. M. on the 9th. At 5 P. M. of the same day he received orders to move immediately in the direction of Cedar Mountain, from which direction heavy firing had been heard all the afternoon. Having marched about 3 miles from Culpeper, the road was found blocked by ambulances and stragglers from the battlefield. Milroy here placed two of his regiments across the road to stop the terrified mass in their headlong retreat. Milroy was partially successful in this; the two regiments pushed the mass forward, and after much labor succeeded in camping his brigade well to the front at about 2 o'clock the following morning. Having posted his pickets at a suitable distance to our front, the men were ordered to rest on their arms.

On Sunday, the 10th, Milroy still holding his position in advance of his corps, but boiling over for a fight, which was his normal condition, he threw forward a line of skirmishers with a strong support along his entire front. We soon came upon the enemy's skirmishers, supported by their whole force, strongly posted in the woods about 2000 yards in front of us. Here skirmishing continued until about noon, the enemy occasionally firing upon us by companies. Whenever this occurred, Milroy would send a few shells among them causing their sudden withdrawal. During the afternoon our skirmishers drove the enemy from the woods, following them some three-fourths of a mile.

On the morning of the 11th, it being determined to remove the dead and wounded from the field, Milroy was ordered to advance his brigade to cover the ambulances and working parties. When he arrived at the outskirts of the woods, he found there a strong force of Union cavalry under the command of General Bayard, whilst our ambulances were busily engaged in removing our wounded from the field, General Milroy received a request from General Bayard to attend a conference with the Confederate Gen'l J. E. B. Stewart, relative to a cessation of hostilities for the purpose of attending to the dead and wounded of both armies. An armistice until 2 o'clock, P. M., was finally agreed upon, but finding the number to be burried greater than at first believed, by mutual consent the armistice was extended to the evening. The slaughter proved to be severe on both sides, most of the fighting being hand to hand. The Confederate loss was 229 killed, 1014 wounded. Union loss 314 killed, 1445 wounded. The dead bodies of both armies were found mingled together in masses over the entire field of the conflict. The burying was not completed on this day (Monday), the heat being so terrible that active work was impossible.

Believing that a reference to this armistice would be of interest, I will give to the reader what I saw and heard upon this occasion. An armistice, it must be known, is a suspension of hostilities by mutual agreement between two armies. It sometimes takes place when both are exhausted, and other times when an endeavor to form a treaty of peace is being made, or when an exchange of prisoners is desired, or, as upon this occasion, for the purpose of burying the dead.

There seems to be some question as to which side asked for a cessation of hostilities, " Stonewall " Jackson, in his official report, says: " On the 11th a flag of truce was received from the enemy, who requested permission until 2 o'clock to remove and bury his dead." Milroy says in his report "that he was called to a conference by General Bayard with General Stewart of the Confederates." But no matter which requested the truce, the act was a Christian one, and deserving of commendation. The method of determining an armistice is for one side to send one or more messengers, usually officers, with a flag of truce (white flag) to the opposing army. The flag is always recognized by hostile forces, and a cessation of fighting at once follows, and the courtesy of civilized nations at once succeeds to the horrors of war. This event was certainly an interesting one, and brought out fully the better humanity of the soldiers of both armies. As I have already stated, the battlefield was covered with the dead bodies of both armies, mingled together. Following immediately after the formal declaration of agreement between Generals Bayard, Milroy and Stewart, a detail of several hundred from each army was made for the purposes of burial.

The reader unacquainted with the facts will be incredulous, no doubt, when I state that while in the midst of the battle, when each side were trying to kill the entire opposition, that they could come together in the most friendly relations, believing at the time that in a few hours the fight was to be renewed. But such was the case, and the commingling of the Blue and the Gray, of both the living and the dead was a marvelous illustration of the fact that the soldiers of both armies were fighting for a principle that each believed to be right without any personality in it. In this humane duty the soldiers of both sides vied with each other in the gentleness with which they would handle the now swollen and discolored dead, and but for the uniform of the dead it would have been difficult to distinguish to which side the body belonged. It was therefore the common procedure for the Union and the Confederate to join hands in conveying to the ambulances the first body approached, no matter to which side it belonged. And the soldiers further showed their friendship by transactions like this: "Say, Johnny Reb," or "Say, Yank," let us exchange clothes awhile, I want to see how it feels to be a "Yank" or to be a "Reb," and off would come the coat and hat, and in less than an hour it was difficult to distinguish which was Union or which was Confederate, and thus several hours were spent, and it was a common scene during that time for a squad of both sides to be enjoying together a cup of good Union coffee with sugar in it, or to be smoking a Confederate pipe of Old Virginia tobacco. So, when the hour arrived for the close of the armistice, all believing that the battle was to be renewed, there were genuine expressions of regret, and the hearty hand-shake and " God bless you and keep you," went out from many a sincere heart.

My personal experience at the time with a prominent Confederate officer will further illustrate. I had at the time a very fine field-glass, the lenses the best I had seen in the army; the Confederate was testing the glass, and found that he could plainly distinguish objects 15 miles away, he wanted to purchase the glass, and proffered me a fabulous price in Confederate money for it, which had no value to me. But the officer had a handsome blooded horse that I had admired. So I proffered to exchange my glass for his horse and give him the difference in value in either gold or greenbacks, both of which were above par in the Confederacy. But the horse had been presented to him by some lady admirers in the Shenandoah Valley, and he could not part with it on any such terms. He therefore made this proposition, that, as the battle was to be renewed in a very short time, and in the event that I was killed or wounded, or fell into their hands, the glass was to be his property; or, in the event that my side should be victorious and he be killed or wounded, and himself and horse should fall to my side, the horse was to be my property.

A number of officers of both armies being present, they were called to witness the transaction, when the officers of both sides, with a great deal of courtesy, bade each good-bye, and thus ended the armistice, but at an hour too late to renew the battle, so Pope's army bivouacked for the night.

On the evening of the 11th, the soldiers' delight (the mail) came to camp; beside letters from home, I received promotion from Governor Peirpoint, my commission as major of my regiment.

CHAPTER XV.

PERSONAL REMINISCENCES—(CONTINUED).

Retreat of Confederates from Cedar Mountain.—Pope's Busy Operations.—Capture of General Pope's Headquarters by General Stewart's Cavalry.—Battle of Manassas, or Second Bull Run.—Death of Colonel Cantwell.—Captain Gibson's Premonition of Death Verified.—Repulse of Pope's Army.—West Virginia Troops Engaged.—Losses Sustained by Union and Confederate.—Army of Virginia Merged into the Army of the Potomac.—General Pope Relieved of his Command at his own Request.—Milroy in Camp at Fort Ethan Allen.—Orders to Return to Western Virginia.

N the morning of the 12th, when Pope was engaged in arranging his forces for an early attack, he learned that the enemy had retreated during the night. Jackson had learned of the arrival of Sigel's Corps, which decided his course. Following the battle of Cedar Mountain, Pope's army was engaged in that series of marches and battles at Crooked Creek, Sulphur Springs, Rappahannock Station, Freeman's Ford, Hedgeman's River, Waterloo Bridge, Warrenton Springs, Warrenton, Broad Run, Gainsville, Manassas, or Second Bull Run.

During the series of battles just named, General Pope—on the night of the 22d of August—was visited by a calamity that will be interesting reading, especially to the survivors of the Army of Virginia; the interest will be intensified no doubt when it is known that the incident was suppressed by General Pope in all of his reports of that campaign. The incident, or calamity would seem to be the better word, was the capture by Gen'l J. E. B. Stewart's cavalry of General Pope's headquarter tents and wagon train.

In his report to Gen'l R. E. Lee—from which I quote—General Stewart says: "Gen'l Fitzhugh Lee's Brigade was in advance, the head of the column pushed on by the village of Auburn, reaching the immediate vicinity of Catlett's Station after dark. Rosser being in front, by his good address and consummate skill captured the picket, and we soon found ourselves in the midst of the enemy's encampments, but the darkest night I ever knew.

"Fortunately we captured at this moment, so critical, a negro who had known me in Berkeley, and who, recognizing me, informed me of the location of General Pope's staff, baggage, horses, etc., and offered to guide to the spot. After a brief consultation it was determined to accept the negro's proposition, as whatever was to be done had to be done quickly, and Brig.-

Gen'l Fitz. Lee selected Col. W. H. F. Lee's regiment for the work. The latter led his command boldly to within a few feet of the tents occupied by the convivial staff of General Pope and charged the camp, capturing a large number of prisoners, particularly officers, and securing public property to a fabulous amount. While this was going on the First and Fifth Virginia Cavalry were sent to attack another camp beyond the railroad and obstruct the latter. This was gallantly done under the dashing lead of Colonels Rosser and L. T. Brien, over ground exceedingly difficult, crossing a heavy filling of the railroad, with ditches each side, amid darkness and a perfect torrent of rain.

"As day dawned I found among the great number of prisoners Pope's field quartermaster, Major Goulding. The men of the command had secured Pope's uniform, his horses and equipments, money-chests, and a great variety of uniforms and personal baggage, but what was of peculiar value was the dispatch-book of General Pope which contained information of great importance to us."

That the dash by Col. W. H. F. Lee's command and the capture of General Pope's headquarters was a brilliant achievement for the Confederates, and a humiliating loss to the Union cause cannot be denied. But the attack made by Colonels Rosser and Brien upon the large and valuable trains of quartermaster and commissary stores and ammunition was a positive victory for the Union arms. This immense train was parked and corralled at several high points, say half mile southeast of Pope's headquarters near Cedar Creek. The attack was made about 10 o'clock at night and with great vigor, which continued for several hours. At one point of attack the train was guarded by four companies of the First Pennsylvania Rifles— better known as the Pennsylvania Bucktails, and one company (C) 2d Pennsylvania Cavalry, Capt. N. M. Rittenhouse. The Confederates charged many times upon these troops, to be as often repulsed; at the time the rain, the thunder and lightning were terrific; with each flash of lightning there was also a flash along the line of the Bucktails and Captain Rittenhouse's company. At another point were the trains of Generals Sigel and Milroy, in charge and command of Capt. Isaiah B. McDonald. The charge upon Captain McDonald's position, like the other just mentioned, was made with the fury and desperation of determined soldiers, but Captain McDonald was a brave and experienced soldier and did not lose his head; he had seen much service, having enlisted in the 17th Indiana Infantry in the three months' service and been continuously in the field in West Virginia since April, 1861. Captain McDonald had only about ninety men as a train guard, fifty of these were commanded by Lieutenant Sommerville of the 3d W. Va. Infantry, the balance of his guard, some 45, were from several other regiments in General Milroy's command. Captain McDonald was ably and loyally assisted by Lieut. John H. Shuttleworth, regimental quartermaster of the 3d W. Va. Infantry. Lieutenant Sommerville was complimented for his splendid defense of this train. Notwithstanding the Confederates outnumbered our train-guard four to one, no part of the train was captured or destroyed, save those at General Pope's headquarters.

On the morning of the 28th of August we find Milroy's brigade leading the advance towards Manassas, arriving within a mile of the junction at noon, where we halted to await further orders. The infantry was turned aside into the shade of the woods, General Milroy and a few of his field officers took a gallop up to the railroad station at the junction, where we found an immense amount of Government stores in the cars, which were yet burning, having been set on fire the previous night by the Confederates. At 3 P. M. orders were received to join the balance of the corps, then marching in the direction of New Market. Milroy here followed his usual tactics, and in place of marching along the main road, moved across the country and soon overtook them. After marching about an hour skirmishing began in front, and the battle of Manassas or second Bull Run was on. Milroy was ordered to take position on Schenck's left, when he pushed forward through the woods and underbrush in the direction of the Confederate firing, which seemed to recede as we advanced. It finally grew dark, but Milroy pushed on until it became terrific thunder of a desperate battle; still Milroy pushed on in the direction of the heavy firing, which suddenly ceased with great shouting, indicating a victory for the Confederates, as the shouting was the familiar "rebel yell." It was now 9 o'clock, and the darkness so dense that recognition of friend or foe was impossible. At this moment it was discovered that we were alongside of a Confederate regiment resting on their arms, which was revealed to us by the following dialogue: "Hello, what regiment?" "48th Alabama; who are you?" "3d Virginia, we want to take position far on your left;" and the 3d Va. (W. Va.) and the balance of Milroy's brigade hurriedly withdrew to his lines at the front of Sigel's corps. On the following morning (the 29th), at daybreak, we were ordered to proceed in search of the enemy; we had not proceeded far when we were greeted by a few straggling shots from the woods in front. Milroy was about to make a charge on the woods when he received orders to halt and let the men have breakfast. The hastily prepared meal was only finished when the enemy were discovered in force about three-quarters of a mile in front of us, upon our right of the pike leading from Gainsville to Alexandria. Milroy at once ordered up two batteries and opened upon them, causing them to fall back; he then moved forward his whole brigade, with skirmishers deployed, and continued to advance, the enemy falling back; whilst we were in this pursuit, a tremendous fire of small-arms on our right assured General Milroy that General Schurz was hotly engaged. Milroy immediately sent the 82d Ohio, Colonel Cantwell, and the 5th W. Va., Colonel Zeigler, to General Schurz's assistance; the 2d and 3d W. Va. were for the time held in reserve. But a few moments elapsed when the two regiments sent to assist Schurz were hotly engaged by the enemy who were strongly posted behind a railroad embankment, which afforded them an excellent breastwork; the result was that the two regiments were driven back by the terrible fire they met, but they soon rallied and charged again and again. In this last charge the brave Cantwell of the 82 Ohio was killed; at this moment the 2d W. Va. was sent to their support, but like the regiments that had preceded it, were met with such a destructive fire that they too were forced back. In the midst of this slaughter, Milroy came to the writer and with all the enthusiasm of his nature, said: "Major Lang, now is the opportunity for you to distinguish yourself. I want you to charge the railroad embankment just in front of our position, and see what is behind it." There was but one reply to such a command, and that was to charge. While arranging the companies that I was to guide, an incident in illustration of premonition of death on the battlefield was forcibly presented to me. Capt. David Gibson of Company H, 3d W. Va., approached me with a face as calm and spiritual as if he had been preparing for the march to the bridal altar, and said to me, "Major, I shall be killed in this charge." I endeavored to quiet his apprehension in some by-play of pleasant words, but he did not heed them, but forcefully said, "I tell you I am going to be killed in this charge, I knew it last night, I have known it all morning." The captain was as brave a man as ever drew sword, but on this occasion his voice and manner were so changed, that I begged him not to make the charge, but he would not listen to that. So, the charge began,—out of the wood, across the field, and before we had passed half the distance, a bullet struck him in the forehead, and brave Captain Gibson fell dead, face to the foe. The charging column continued, only a few scattering shots from the railroad met our advance until we were within 150 feet of the embankment, when immediately a deluge of bristling muskets poured over the embankment and sent such a crash of leaden hail into our ranks, that we beat a hasty retreat, leaving many of our men dead or wounded on the field; we had met "Stonewall" Jackson's own command. They did not follow us, but immediately fell back behind their embankment. By this time Milroy's brigade had been so cut to pieces and suffering for want of food and rest, that Milroy was compelled to rally his shattered remnant, and camp some three-quarters of a mile to the rear, where the almost famished men got time to eat a bite and drink muddy water from a pool, then to lie down and sleep soundly amid the roar of artillery and the rattle of musketry.

The next morning (the 30th) the brigade was brought into position assigned them, and remained in reserve until about 4 P. M., when the services of the brigade were called to check the retreating masses which had been driven back from the front, which was soon followed by an order to move off to the left on double quick; the enemy having massed their forces during the day in order to turn our left flank, Milroy formed his line of battle along an old country road, the left resting near the edge of the woods in which the battle was raging. Soon our troops came rushing, panic stricken, out of the woods, leaving Milroy's brigade to face the enemy, who had followed the retreating masses to the edge of the woods. The road just referred to in which our brigade was formed, was an old abandoned road through the fields, worn and washed from three to five feet deep, affording a splendid cover for the men; we opened fire on the enemy at short range, driving them back into the woods. But the enemy being reinforced from the masses in their rear, came on again and again, pouring in their advance a perfect hurricane of balls, which had but little effect on our men who were so well protected in their road entrenchment. But the steady fire of our brigade, together with that of a splendid brass battery on higher ground in our rear, which Milroy had ordered to fire rapidly with canister over the heads of his men, had a most withering effect upon the enemy, whose columns melted away and fast recoiled from repeated efforts to advance upon our road breastworks from the woods. But the fire of the enemy which had affected the men in the road so little, told with destructive results on the exposed battery in their rear. Nor did the mounted officers find their position protected in the slightest. General Milroy's horse was shot, Lieutentant-Colonel Thompson was wounded in the shoulder, my own horse shot down, Adj't Nathan Goff was more fortunate and escaped injury. But the fire from the enemy grew more terrific every moment, and soon the battery that had done such splendid service gave way, followed by a general stampede on our left, and shortly after our own line began to show distrust and started by two's and three's to leave the line. Adjutant Goff and myself, noticing this, made haste to check the break, and tried to rally them just over and behind a small rise in the ground. It was now after sunset, and the brigade having exhausted their ammunition, with no opportunity to bring forward a supply, and as the break was going on to the right of us and to the left of us, we withdrew in fairly good order, and soon joined a bewildering mass of artillery, infantry and cavalry, all seeming bent on the one single purpose, viz., to make the distance between the enemy and themselves as wide as possible. In great charity, darkness now interposed, petitioning peace between the contending armies.

After General Pope, perhaps no general officer gave up the fight so reluctantly as did General Milroy. He secured another horse on the field, whose rider probably had been killed, and rallying some volunteer aids around him, went from one command to another, and begging the use of a brigade would put it into the fight as willingly as if they were his own command. But it was too late, the second battle of Bull Run was lost to the Union.

General Pope with his Army of Virginia fought a gallant fight; no truer soldiers, no braver men ever drew sabre, carried a musket or fired a gun, than composed that splendid army. Milroy says of his own brigade, mainly West Virginians (with the 82d Ohio Infantry and the 12th Battery, Ohio L. A.): "The highest praise I can award to the officers and soldiers of my brigade, in all the hard service and fighting through which we have passed, is that they have bravely, cheerfully, patiently, and nobly performed their duty."

The following West Virginia troops (with their assigments) were engaged in this campaign, which terminated with the battle of Manassas, viz.:

1st West Va. Infantry, 4th Brigade, 3d Army Corps, Col. Joseph Thoburn commanding.

2d W. Va. Infantry,
3d W. Va. Infantry,
5th W. Va. Infantry,
1st W. Va. Cav., Co's C, E and L, } Independent Brigade, 1st Army Corps, Brig.-Gen'l R. H. Milroy commanding.

8th W. Va. Infantry, 3d Division, First Army Corps, Brig.-Gen'l Carl Schurz commanding.

1st W. Va. Cavalry, 9 companies, Cavalry Brigade, Gen'l John Buford commanding.

Battery C, 1st W. Va. Light Artillery, Reserve Artillery, Capt. Louis Schirmer commanding.

3d W. Va. Cavalry, Co. C, unattached, Jonathan Stahl commanding.

The loss in killed and wounded will attest the severity of the fighting during the Pope campaign, beginning August 16, 1862, to Sept. 2, inclusive:

Union—killed, 1747; wounded, 8452.

Confederates—killed, 1481; wounded, 7627.

The captured and missing are not given here, for the reason that the records are incomplete. But the Union loss was in excess of the Confederate.

After the battle of the 30th, Pope's entire army was ordered to retreat back across Bull Run to Centreville. On the 3d of September, Milroy's brigade was in camp near Fort Ethan Allen, Va., within the denfenses of Washington, and the Army of Virginia which had marched and fought and suffered so greatly was merged into the Army of the Potomac. Here General Pope, at his own request, was relieved of his command, and at the same time preferred charges of insubordination and negligence against Gen'l Fitz John Porter, on which the latter officer was court-martialed and cashiered.

The Army of Virginia was so much used up by its long campaigning that they were left in the defenses, while fresher troops met Lee in Maryland and defeated him at Antietam.

Milroy's brigade lay at Fort Ethan Allen, drilling, recuperating, and enjoying occasional visits to the capital until the 29th of September when we received orders to return to western Virginia.

CHAPTER XVI.

PERSONAL REMINISCENCES—(CONTINUED).

Arrival of Third Regiment at Clarksburg.—Ordered to Point Pleasant.—**Return to Buckhan-non.**—Gen'l Augustus Moor in Command of "Northern Brigade."—General Milroy Promoted and Sent to Winchester.—Soldiers Vote to Admit West Virginia to Statehood.—Gen'l B. S. Roberts in Command of "Fourth Separate Brigade."—War on Women and Children.—Imboden, Jones and Jackson's Raid.—Immense Destruction of Property.—General Averell in Command of Fourth Separate Brigade.—Transformation of Infantry Regiments to Cavalry.—Splendid Results Follow.

ILROY'S brigade boarded the cars at Washington, and arrived at Pittsburg at midnight Sept. 30, and my 3d Regiment at Clarksburg on the 1st of October, went into camp but did not remain long, for on the 3d of October the regiment was ordered to Point Pleasant, W. Va., opposite the mouth of Big Kanawha, where a threatened raid was anticipated by the enemy, but as the raid did not materialize the regiment was ordered to return to Clarksburg, arriving on the 13th. On the 15th, myself in command of the regiment, received orders to proceed to Buckhannon where we arrived on the 18th, when the regiment was divided into detachments to perform out-post duty at Buckhannon, Centreville, Bulltown, Sutton and Glenville, in W. Va. The other regiments of the brigade were cast for similar duty at other points along the border, and this service continued until about the 1st of April, 1863.

November 7th, 1862, General Milroy left our brigade and went to New Creek where he had eight regiments of infantry, two batteries and three companies of cavalry.

January 1st, 1863, he went to Winchester; here he received his commission as major-general,* to date from November 29, 1862.

In January, 1883, Gen'l Augustus Moor, with his old regiment, the 28th Ohio Infantry, came to Buckhannon, when he was assigned to our

---

* In the promotion of General Milroy to be a major-general, he was credited to West Virginia in place of Indiana. This very naturally created no little just indignation among loyal West Virginia soldiers, who believed their loyalty deserving that recognition. This feeling was not against Milroy personally; the West Virginia soldiers had great admiration for him, they recognized that he was a good man and a brave soldier. The displeasure was against the appointing authority.

T. F. L.

brigade, which was now designated the "Northern Brigade." General Moor proved to be an intelligent and efficient officer and gallant soldier, and was well liked by officers and men.

On March 12 an election was held in the camps, when the soldiers in the field were permitted to vote on the question of creating West Virginia into a separate state, and all the qualified voters availed themselves of this opportunity to attest their loyalty to the new state, and the result of that election demonstrated that the soldiers voted as they fought, and the new state received the unanimous vote of the soldiers.

General Orders No. 20, Headquarters Middle Department, 8th Army Corps, dated Baltimore, March 28, 1863, created the " 4th Separate Brigade," and assigned to its command Brig.-Gen'l Benjamin S. Roberts, who established his headquarters at Weston. The following regiments, batteries and detachments composed the brigade, viz.: 28th Ohio Inft., Col. A. Moor; the 2d W. Va. Infantry, Col. Geo. R. Latham; the 3d W. Va. Infantry, Lt.-Col. F. W. Thompson; the 8th W. Va., Lt.-Col. J. H. Oley; Ewing's Battery, Co. G, Light Artillery; Co. A, 1st W. Va. Cavalry, Captain Hagans; Co. E, 3d W. Va. Cavalry, Capt. Lot Bowen; Co. H, 3d W. Va. Cavalry, Lieutenant Flesher; Co. D, 1st Regt. Ill. Cavalry, Captain Schambeck.

General Roberts soon realized that his lot was cast in a community in which he had little or no military sympathy. And he began his military operations by making war upon the resident Secessionists, both men and women, forcing all who held Southern sentiments to leave their homes. Whilst there was a good deal of practical policy in this method to purge the state of those disloyal families who were making habitual mischief by carrying information and supplies from point to point in the mountains where they met their friends, and thus kept up a channel of communication that could only be broken by expelling them from the country, there was, nevertheless, in this method of ridding the community of disloyalty a question of just where to draw the line. Roberts made no distinction, and compelled many women who were quite regardful of their obligations to the Union to pack their trunks, and with their children forced them to abandon house and home and pass beyond our lines to the South. This indiscrimination touched the chivalric sense of justice and right of our soldiers, and Roberts was charged with making war on women and children instead of going after those who were in armed rebellion. But this method of putting down the war was short-lived. For, on the 24th of April, the combined forces of Imboden, Jones and W. L. Jackson, numbering about 4000 men, began their noted raid through the Middle Department. Their first attack was made on

Colonel Latham's command at Beverly, whose forces numbered 878 men, who made a gallant stand, and when finally forced, by reason of superior numbers, to withdraw, made a successful retreat. From the time of this attack on the 24th of April until the 14th of May, the Confederates seemed to have control of the situation, and went from place to place with an abandon of purpose and disregard of consequences or apprehension of danger from the Union arms. Colonel Latham with his command retired to Buckhannon, and Roberts called in his forces from Birch, Sutton and Bulltown to the same point.

On the 29th, Roberts' whole command had retired to Clarksburg, where he was reinforced by General Kenly's brigade; Clarksburg was the only town in many miles around that did not fall into the raiders' possession. There was not in all this raid any severe battle, in fact skirmishing between the forces at many points will fitly express the character of the fighting, consequently the number of killed and wounded was not great. But the raid was most disastrous in the destruction of many bridges on the Baltimore and Ohio and the Northwestern Virginia railroads. They captured 3100 head of cattle, 1500 head of horses, and the plundering of many stores throughout the country through which they passed was enormous. The money value of the property destroyed and carried off amounted to several millions of dollars.

Upon the retirement of the Confederates from the country, Roberts reoccupied Weston, Buckhannon, Beverly and other points formerly held by his forces. There was, on this occasion, no lack of gallantry or willingness to perform duty on the part of any of the officers or men of the regiments, batteries or detachments of the Union troops. To the contrary, there were many illustrations of bravery, energy and endurance. They were simply outnumbered and outgeneraled.

May 22, 1863, Brig.-Gen'l W. W. Averell reported at Weston, in compliance with the following order :

HEADQUARTERS, 8TH ARMY CORPS,
BALTIMORE, MD., May 18, 1863.

BRIG.-GEN'L W. W. AVERELL, *U. S. Volunteers.*

    General :

*   *   *   *   *   *   *   *   *   *   *   *

You will proceed to Weston, in western Virginia, or wherever else you may find Brig.-Gen'l B. S. Roberts, and relieve him of his command of the "Fourth Separate Brigade" of this Army Corps. On assuming command, you will establish your present headquarters at Weston or Buckhannon, or such other point as you may find it best to select south of the Baltimore and Ohio Railroad, drawing your supplies from the depot at Clarksburg. Your command, however, is intended to be, as far as it can be properly made so, a mobile force, and your service will be to keep that region of West Virginia between the railroad and the

Kanawha line clear of the enemy, preventing his invasions and supporting and co-operating with Brigadier-General Kelley, commanding on the line of the railroad, and with Brigadier-General Scammon, commanding on the Kanawha and Gauley Rivers. You may be called upon in emergency to follow the enemy, or to cross the mountains east of you, to aid in any movement in the direction of the valley of Virginia. On your left you will find it necessary to guard the passes and approaches by way of the Cheat River Mountain. Keeping these objects in view, it is left to your discretion to station your troops at such points as you may deem most advisable, keeping the body of them, however, together where it may become necessary and best to concentrate, covering your line of supplies.

You will inspect your command and report, at as early a day as possible, its exact condition and wants, with a view to having it supplied and put in the most effective condition. It is designed, as soon as practicable, by reinforcements, if they can be obtained by new organization and by all means of improvement, to convert or exchange the whole or greater part of your troops, so as to make yours a force of cavalry, with light artillery and with little or no infantry.   I am, very respectfully, your ob't servant,

WM. H. CHESEBROUGH,
Asst. Adjt.-General.

The following explains itself :

WAR DEPARTMENT,
WASHINGTON, *May* 19, 1863.

MAJOR-GENERAL SCHENCK, *Baltimore, Md.*

Brig.-Gen'l B. S. Roberts, U. S. Volunteers, will report in person to Maj.-Gen'l John Pope, commanding Department of the Northwest, Milwaukee, Wis., as soon as he is relieved from duty in the Middle Department. Please so order.

By order of Major-General Halleck,
J. C. KELTON, *Asst. Adjt. General.*

The two foregoing orders were hailed with demonstrations of genuine rejoicing by the officers and men of the Fourth Separate Brigade. General Averell's reputation as a gallant and successful cavalry fighter had preceded his coming by several months, and to be placed under such a leader was inspiring to these troops, who were at all times eager for the active operations of war. General Averell soon demonstrated the fact that he was master of the situation, and that he was not going to be a laggard in the management of the forces placed under his command. I feel that I would be indifferent to the best interests of the brigade, as well as to General Averell, did I not speak of both as we find them when he (Averell) assumed command. I shall write semi-officially as the following special order will indicate.

HEADQUARTERS, 4TH SEPARATE BRIGADE,
WESTON, W. VA., *May* 30, 1863.

SPECIAL ORDERS, }
   NO. 5. }

Major Theodore F. Lang, 3d Reg. W. Va. Vol. Inft., is hereby detailed as Acting Assistant Inspector General and Mustering Officer of the Brigade. Major Lang will report for orders and instructions by letter to Lieut.-Col. Donn Piatt, Inspector and Chief of Staff 8th Army Corps.   By command of Brig.-Gen'l Averell,

C. F. TROWBRIDGE,
Capt. and A. A. A. Gen'l.

Whilst my reference to the condition of the troops at the time contemplates all in the brigade, I shall especially speak only of the West Virginia regiments which had been early recruited, mustered into the service, and hurried away to the front. The ruling principle governing them at that time was to know how to make long marches, to endure hardships, and to load and fire *low* in time of battle. The master hand of discipline and drill had not been a part of their military experience. Therefore, when General Averell assumed command of these troops, he found himself with a brigade of loyal, courageous fighters, scattered through have a dozen counties, but who knew little of discipline, or of regimental or brigade maneuvers,—scantily supplied with approved arms, equipments, clothing, etc.

They were inefficient for any reliable defense of the country, and the utter hopelessness of any effort to take the offensive our experience had so recently demonstrated. My native pride and my devotion to my comrades would instinctively impel me to resent any imputation to them of wrongdoing or of indifference to duty. It was not that, but it was a fact, that all of the officers and enlisted men alike, were war students with no teachers among them of skilled warfare. General Averell was a West Point graduate, had been an instructor in the cavalry schools at Jefferson Barracks, Missouri, and Carlisle Barracks, Pennsylvania; he had also distinguished himself in New Mexico as an Indian fighter, and in the Civil War as Colonel of the 3d Pennsylvania Cavalry and Brigadier-General of Volunteers, serving in the Army of the Potomac. It will be seen, therefore, that he came to the command of the the 4th separate brigade with a ripe experience that fitted him well to build up a splendid brigade out of the best quality of "raw material."

How well he performed this service, the final results fully attested. He overcame the unfortunate conditions in which he found his troops, by concentrating them at three points, where they underwent a season of drill in the various arms of the service; they were also re-armed and equipped; 3000 infantry were changed into cavalry—marched 660 miles, had many skirmishes and fought the battle of Rocky Gap; all this within 80 days after he took command. Then followed the battles of Droop Mountain, Salem Raid, Wytheville, Lynchburg, Carter's Farm, Moorefield and others until Averell's cavalry became noted as a terror to the enemy, and at the same time, the admiration of the government. In another chapter will be found a biographical sketch of General Averell with a detailed account of some of his important operations, whilst in camp, on the march and upon the battlefield.

CHAPTER XVII.

PERSONAL REMINISCENCES—(CONTINUED).

Averell's Fighting Period.—His Assignment to the Kanawha Valley.—Sigel in Command of the Department of West Virginia.—Transfer of Author to Sigel's Staff.—Grant's Plan.—Sigel Leaves Martinsburg for Shenandoah Valley.—" Red Tape " in the Army.—Battle of New Market.—Defeat of Sigel by Breckinridge.—Roster of Union Troops Engaged.—Encamped at Strasburg.

THE period in which General Averell was in command,—first, of the " Fourth Separate Brigade," second, the " Fourth Division," and third, the " Cavalry Division," all of the 8th Army Corps, Department of West Virginia,—might be appropriately designated as the working, marching and fighting period of the West Virginia soldiery. For Averell had no inactive service ; he was on the go, both in summer's heat and winter's storm. My position of Inspector called for incessant labor, while on the march as A. D. C. and when in camp for a few days, to inspect and condemn unserviceable horses, mules, wagons, ambulances, ordnance, equipments, quartermaster and commissary stores, in fact, any and everything that was found in the command to be unserviceable. My term on the staff of General Averell continued till the 8th of June, 1864. On the 19th of April, 1864, however, at Martinsburg, I was temporarily detached to serve upon the staff of Maj.-Gen'l Franz Sigel, who had been placed in command of the Department of West Virginia, he having made a request upon General Kelley for a detail of officers for duty upon his staff, who were familiar with the Shenandoah valley.

On the 19th of April with a part of his cavalry, General Averell left Martinsburg for the Kanawha valley, where he was assigned to the command of all the cavalry there, under Gen'l Geo. Crook. On the 25th of April, General Sigel arrived at Martinsburg. I reported to him, in compliance with instructions, for duty upon his staff ; at the same time I protested to him that my place to render effective service was with General Averell, and begged to be permitted to follow him ; when Sigel replied very pleasantly but firmly that he could not let me go ; and, as if to reconcile me, proffered to make me " chief of headquarters," whatever that was ; at any rate, I was treated with a great deal of deference, and my service upon his staff was rendered very pleasant, especially as I had associated with me that genial gentleman and good soldier, Col. David H. Strother (Port Crayon). The 26th, 27th and 28th I spent with the General visiting the camps ; on the 27th, a review of all the troops stationed at Martinsburg took place.

At this time General Grant had planned a movement all along the line ; Generals Crook and Averell were to move from the Kanawha, on the 20th of May, via Lewisburg ; Colonel Harris was to make a demonstration from Beverly, and Sigel to move up the Shenandoah valley at the same date. He was expected to join Crook and Averell at Staunton or at some point to the southward. In conformity with this program, Sigel, on the 29th, left Martinsburg with his command and encamped at Bunker Hill, 12 miles south of Martinsburg. May 1st, marched to Winchester, headquarters camped on lawn at Hollingsworth's Mills. For the edification of the novice in military affairs, I will reproduce the following correspondence as illustrating the effect of "red tape" in the accomplishment of a small affair, to wit :

HEADQUARTERS, DEPARTMENT OF W. VA.,
NEAR WINCHESTER, VA., *May* 2, 1864.
LIEUT. THOS. H. WELSTED,
A. A. A. Gen'l.
Please detail for service at these headquarters a competent horse shoer; have him report at the earliest convenience. Respectfully,
T. F. LANG,
Major and Chief of Head.-Qrs.

HEADQUARTERS, DEPT. OF W. VA.,
NEAR WINCHESTER, VA., *May* 2, 1864.
LIEUT. WELSTEAD,
A. A. A. Gen'l.
Please send the horse shoer you have detailed for these Headquarters, and have him report here within an half hour. Also explain the reason why he has not reported before this. Respectfully,
T. F. LANG,
Maj. and Chief of Hd.-Qr.

HEADQUARTERS,
CAMP NEAR WINCHESTER, *May* 2d, '64.
Respectfully referred to Colonel Taylor, Comdg. 1st Cavalry Division, who is directed to comply with the within instructions.
This paper to be returned with report of action.
By command of Major-General Stahel.
THOS. H. HALSTEAD, *A. A. A. G.*

HD.-QRS., CAVALRY DIVISION,
WINCHESTER, *May* 2, 1864.
Respectfully referred to Colonel Wynkoop, who will have this man sent within the time specified ; will return this paper with report as to reason he has not been sent.
By order of Col. R. F. Taylor.
JESSE F. WYCKOFF, *A. A. A. Gen'l.*

HD.-QRS., 3RD CAVALRY BRIGADE,
CAMP NEAR WINCHESTER, *May* 2, 1864.

Respectfully returned. The order received this morning detailing a blacksmith, was not complied with at the time in consequence of conflicting orders from Maj.-Gen'l Stahel to the effect that every man in this command should appear upon review. Immediately after review the detail was promptly complied with from these Headquarters, and not until receipt was it known that he had not reported. He was sent at once to report to Major Lang.

JOHN E. WYNKOOP, *Col. Comdg. 3d Brigade.*

HEADQUARTERS, CAVALRY DIVISION,
May 2, 1864.

Respectfully returned with explanation of Colonel Wynkoop. The delay in the return of paper was caused by our Orderly with whom Colonel Wynkoop returned this paper among other envelopes.

R. F. TAYLOR, *Col. Comdg. Cav. Div.*

HEADQUARTERS,
CAMP NEAR WINCHESTER, *May* 2, 1864.

Respectfully returned to Major Lang, Chief of Staff, whose attention is invited to endorsement of Colonel Wynkoop, Comdg. Brigade, and Colonel Taylor, Comdg. Division Cavalry, which explain the cause of delay.

Respectfully,

THOMAS H. WELSTEAD, *A. A. A. Gen'l.*

We remained at this camp (Winchester) until May 8th. On the 9th, marched 15 miles to Stone House, 3½ miles north of Strasburg. Remained at this camp till the 10th. On the 11th, moved at 6 A. M., arriving at Woodstock at 4 P. M. Advance guard had some skirmishing with the enemy. Camped on lawn at Chaney's residence ; remained here the 12th, 13th and 14th. On the 14th, Col. Augustus Moor was ordered to take command of three regiments of infantry, 1000 cavalry and six pieces of artillery, and march to Mount Jackson to ascertain and feel the position and strength of the enemy under Imboden, reported to be posted on Rude's Hill. Colonel Moor left camp near Woodstock at 11 A. M., with the 1st W. Va. and 34th Mass. regiments of infantry and two sections of Battery B, Md. artillery ; Colonel Wynkoop with 300 cavalry and one section of artillery. Maj. Timothy Quinn, 1st N. Y., with 600 cavalry, was already in his (Colonel Moor's) front.

At Edenburg the 123d Ohio infantry was added to Colonel Moor's command. At 3 P. M., heavy firing was heard at the front, indicating that Major Quinn was engaging the enemy. Colonel Wynkoop was ordered by Colonel Moor to push forward to the support of Major Quinn, who was driving the enemy's skirmishers steadily before him until New Market was reached, when Colonel Wynkoop's and Major Quinn's skirmishers occupied the town. Colonel Moor, arriving with his infantry and artillery, selected a favorable position and opened fire with his artillery. Imboden soon answered furiously with his battery ; the firing soon ceased, however, and Imboden retired.

After dark, Colonel Moor changed his line of battle more to the front, near the Shenandoah River, when the command was ordered to rest in perfect order of battle without fires. At about 8 P. M., a line of Confederates approached across an open field, on Colonel Moor's front, with the evident purpose to turn Colonel Moor's position he had occupied before sunset. This attack was immediately in front of the 1st W. Va. infantry, Maj. Edward W. Stephens in command. Colonel Moor ordered him to remain quiet, until the enemy had come near enough to give them a volley, which was well executed. About 10 P. M. Colonel Moor's whole front was attacked with infantry and artillery ; the Confederates, however, had to retreat in confusion ; the firing was distinctly heard at General Sigel's headquarters at Woodstock.

At 4 o'clock A. M. on the 15th, General Sigel ordered me to take one dozen orderlies and proceed to the front, ascertain the extent of the skirmishing between Colonel Moor and the enemy (General Sigel did not believe there was much of a force in front of Colonel Moor), and to send messengers back to him with all information. Upon my arrival at Colonel Moor's position, I learned from him that Imboden had left his front about midnight, but that Quinn's cavalry, who had been scouting to the front, had captured a deserter, who reported that Imboden and Echols had been reinforced by General Breckinridge, and was then about four miles south of New Market, and advancing to attack Colonel Moor. I wrote this information and sent a messenger with it, double quick, to General Sigel. I then took a position upon an elevated point with the remainder of my orderlies ; I did not have long to wait until I discovered the enemy placing their skirmish line across the entire valley ; this information I at once wrote and sent my second orderly in full haste to General Sigel, informing him that a battle would be fought soon and suggested that he push forward his entire command at a double quick. Soon thereafter I saw the enemy placing his first line of battle, stretching across the valley.

This information I hurriedly penned and sent it with my third messager, as before, to General Sigel. The messenger had only gone, when I witnessed the second line of battle form as the first had done, indicating a large force; this important information I sent by the fourth messenger. In a few moments the skirmish lines were engaged, and at the same moment a piece of artillery opened upon me and my orderlies, who had occupied an exposed position. I had at this time become impatient because neither General Sigel nor his troops had come to the front. I then sent the fifth messenger and urged more positively than before our critical situation, and went so far as to overstep my position as A. D. C. to say to General Sigel that he must bring up his entire force, telling him to place his artillery and cavalry in the road, with his infantry on either side in the fields, and to come at once, otherwise he would be too late.

General Stahel with his cavalry was the first to arrive. Soon after General Sigel with his staff and bodyguard came on the field with a great flourish. I met him at once. He was at first disposed to make light of my frequent messages; he told me I was excited. I did not get excited on the battlefield. I pointed out to him the two long lines of battle the enemy had placed in his front, when he seemed to awaken to the importance of his situation, and realized that his command had its match or more, and he began to maneuver his troops. Colonel Moor's line was ordered to another position farther to the rear. Finally our regiments and batteries leisurely began to come into line, but too late. The enemy had made a vigorous assault, and notwithstanding Sigel displayed great personal bravery, and his troops engaged stood gallantly to their work, Sigel, with his detachments was simply fighting a concentrated force—formed at its leisure—and the day was lost. Sigel had sufficient troops to have beaten the Confederates under Breckinridge had he brought them into the fight. But, from either over-confidence in his own strength, or lack of confidence in the strength of the enemy, permitted his splendidly equipped army to be beaten and hurled down the valley, with a loss of about 600 killed and wounded.

The following troops constituted Sigel's command, and all of them—officers and men—who were engaged fought a good fight:

FIRST INFANTRY DIVISION.

Brig.-Gen'l Jeremiah C. Sullivan, *Commanding.*

First Brigade.	*Second Brigade.*
Col. Alexander Moor.	Col. Joseph Thoburn.
18th Conn., Major Henry Peale.	1st W. Va., Lt. Col. J. Weddle.
28th Ohio, Lieut-Col. G. Becker.	12th W. Va., Col. W. B. Curtis.
116th Ohio, Col. Jas. Washburn.	34th Mass., Col. Geo. D. Wells.
123d Ohio, Maj. Horace Kellogg.	54th Pa., Col. J. M. Campbell.

FIRST CAVALRY DIVISION.

MAJOR-GEN'L JULIUS STAHEL, *Commanding.*

First Brigade.

COL. WILLIAM B. TIBBITS.

1st N. Y. (Veteran), Col. Robt. F. Taylor.
1st N. Y. (Lincoln), Lt.-Col. Alonzo W. Adams.
1st Md. P. H. B., (detachment), Maj. J. T. Daniel.
21st N. Y., Major Charles G. Otis.
14th Pa. (detachment), Lt.-Col. Wm. Blakely.

Second Brigade.

COL. JOHN E. WYNKOOP.

Detachments 15th N. Y., 20th Pa., 22d Pa.

ARTILLERY.

1st W. Va. Light, Battery D, Capt. John Carlin.
1st W. Va. Light, Battery G, Capt. C. T. Ewing.
Md. Light, Battery B, Capt. A. Snow.
New York Light, 30th Battery, Capt. A. Von Kleiser.
5th U. S., Battery B, Capt. H. A. DuPont.

After the battle General Sigel, with his troops, fell back to Edenburg, and on the 16th retired leisurely to Stone House, north of Strasburg, where we remained in camp until the 26th of May.

CHAPTER XVIII.

PERSONAL REMINISCENCES—(CONTINUED).

General Hunter in Command.—Advance up the Shenandoah Valley.—Battle of Piedmont.—
Hunter Occupies Staunton.—Crook and Averell Join Hunter.—Return of the Author to
West Virginia.—Mustered out of Service.

WAR DEPT., ADJT.-GENERAL'S OFFICE,
WASHINGTON, *May* 19, 1864.

GENERAL ORDERS, }
   NO. 200.   }

By direction of the President, Maj.-Gen'l D. Hunter, U. S. Volunteers, is assigned to the Command of the Department of West Virginia.

By order of the Secretary of War,

E. D. TOWNSEND,
Assistant Adjutant-General.

In compliance with the above order, on the 21st of May, General Hunter arrived at Strasburg and relieved General Sigel of his command, General Hunter retaining, with two exceptions, Sigel's staff officers. General Hunter brought with him as A. A. General the well-known author Col. Charles G. Halpine (Miles O'Riley) and Major Samuel W. Stockton of the regular Army.

General Hunter began at once to reorganize his command, sent all tents and unservicable stores to the rear, and had his troops provided with new shoes, etc.

On the 26th of May, General Hunter moved southwest 13 miles to Pew's Run, where we remained until the 29th, when we broke camp at 5 A. M., arriving at Mount Jackson at 2 P. M.; found a small force of the enemy occupying Rude's Hill, soon dispersed them and went into camp.

On the 30th, visited the battlefield of New Market, found many of our wounded doing well; remained in camp at Rude's Hill until the 1st of June.

June 2d, left Rude's Hill at 5 A. M., marched to Harrisonburg, 15 miles; met the enemy in small force. They occupied, however, a strongly intrenched position at Mount Crawford, on the North River, where it is crossed by the Valley Turnpike; his right at Rockland Mills, his left at Bridgewater. While in Harrisonburg we stopped at the principal hotel, where we paid for board $20 per day, Confederate money.

On the 4th, General Hunter spent the day in ascertaining the enemy's force and position. Early in the morning a force of cavalry was sent to Mount Crawford to amuse him while General Hunter moved his column by a side road and crossed the Shenandoah at Port Republic by the use of pontoon bridges. This movement was so little expected that we found at the place a large supply train of the enemy. Our advance cavalry captured the larger part of it, which consisted of supplies and horses. We encamped about one mile south of Port Republic. A large woolen factory, run by the Confederate Government, was destroyed. June 5th, advanced on the Staunton road, met the enemy at Meridian at 6 A. M., sharp skirmish with advance, engagement became general at 9 A. M. near the village of Piedmont, seven miles southwest of Port Republic. The enemy were in force, advantageously posted. The battle opened with artillery; the enemy using several guns of long range and heavy caliber. At 10 o'clock the first brigade of infantry under Colonel Moor advanced on our right, and drove the enemy from his advanced position in a woods behind his line of defenses—constructed of fallen timber and fence rails. Colonel Thoburn with the second brigade of infantry took position in the woods on elevated ground on our left ready for action when and where most needed. At 11.30 the fine work of our artillery had silenced the enemy's batteries, and the cavalry under Major General Stahel was massed in rear of the infantry on our right. General Hunter with his staff conducted the battle from a central position in the low ground, where all parts of the field were easily watched. Maj. Samuel W. Stockton, A. D. C., and myself were General Hunter's chief couriers and advisers, and we made frequent trips from the immediate scene of battle to General Hunter's position.

At one o'clock, *Colonel Moor's first brigade made a vigorous charge across an open field upon the enemy's line, but were repulsed, when they fell back to their original position. I witnessed this disaster and detected danger to our arms. I then hurried to General Hunter and begged him to put Colonel Thoburn's brigade into the fight (up to this time Thoburn's command had not fired a shot); Hunter protested that to move Thoburn would be to uncover his left and leave that part of the field unprotected. It was then suggested to dismount Stahel's cavalry and put them into the fight along with the first brigade. This was done, and the dismounted cavalry, with the first brigade made the second charge upon the enemy's same position, but

* Attached to Colonel Moor's brigade in the battle of Piedmont were four batteries of the 5th N. Y. heavy artillery, serving as infantry ; viz., battery A, Capt. I. H. Graham; battery B, Capt. Geo. P. Mott; battery C, Capt. H. L. Emmons, and battery D, Capt. Oliver Cotter; these companies participated in the several charges made that day.

they were beaten back as before, General Stahel wounded and our forces much disheartened. I again went to General Hunter and informed him that unless Thoburn's brigade was put into the fight that the day was lost to us.

It was then 1.30 P. M., the enemy was observed to be massing his force at the position from which we had twice been driven. General Hunter then, with reluctance, directed me to go to Colonel Thoburn and put his brigade into the fight. I hastened to Thoburn and conducted his command from its concealed position in the woods, across the narrow valley, up the hill, directly on the right flank of the enemy's position. But, in the meantime, say about 2 P. M., the enemy had made a desperate assault upon Colonel Moor's first brigade and dismounted cavalry, which gallantly sustained themselves, assisted by Von Kleiser's N. Y. Battery, and a cross fire from Morton's and Carlin's Batteries on our left. So intense and eager were the enemy engaged with our front, that they permitted Thoburn to cross over the valley unseen by them; their first knowledge of his advance was when he opened fire upon them not over 50 yards distant from their right flank. At this moment the first brigade, Stahel's and Wynkoop's cavalry, charged, and in less than 10 minutes all was over. The enemy fled in confusion over a steep bank into the river, leaving over 1000 prisoners in our hands, including 60 officers. The killed and wounded were estimated at 600 men. Brig.-Gen'l W. E. Jones, commanding Confederate forces, was killed, his body fell into our hands, and was buried near the town.

The enemy had between 6000 and 7000 men, and 16 guns, among them two 20-pounder Parrotts.

I witnessed here what I had not seen on any battlefield before, nor since, it was this: Confederates who were in line just behind the rail breastworks, literally torn to pieces and their clothing on fire, caused by the bursting shells of our artillery.

An incident, illustrating the possibilities and the uncertainties of war, presented itself to me at the close of this battle, that is worthy of a place in these pages. During the winter and early spring, while General Averell and his command were stationed at Martinsburg, the General and his staff were on several occasions entertained at the pleasant and hospitable mansion (Boydville) of Mrs. Charles James Faulkner. This delightful home, like many others along the border states, was broken by the ruthless hand of sectional opinion. The distinguished statesman Hon. Charles James Faulkner and his two sons had left their home for the purpose of upholding the right of Secession, and they were sincere enough, and brave enough to buckle on their swords and fight as their convictions dictated. Mrs. Faulkner and her daughters, however, remained at home, and their native hospitality gave a welcome to either Union or Confederate gentlemen, whether in or out of the army.

When, therefore, General Sigel had made his arrangements to move up the valley I called to pay my respects and say "good bye" to Mrs. Faulkner and her daughters. When in the course of conversation I intimated that we were probably going into the Shenandoah Valley, Mrs. Faulkner informed me that her son, E. Boyd Faulkner, was in the valley, and she made the request that, in case he was killed or captured, I should care for him and notify her. Realizing that this was a one-sided contract, I suggested that the misfortunes of war might find me killed or captured. "Oh, in that event Boyd will take care of you," she said. So when the battle was over, aud the Confederate prisoners were massed and surrounded by our soldiers, my attention was attracted towards one of the Confederate officers—tall and straight as an arrow, a perfect type of the soldier, who was gesticulating and making a loud speech to his hapless comrades. I inquired of one of the prisoners as to who the noisy party was, when I was informed that it was Major E. Boyd Faulkner. I at once made my way to him, introduced myself, told him of my promise to his mother, and I kept my word so far as I could during a forced march, and when I arrived at Beverly ten days later, the first telegraph station, I telegraphed Mrs. Faulkner the particulars, and informed her that she could see her son at Grafton on the 16th. Mrs. Faulkner and daughter arrived there on that day, with a bountiful supply of comforts for him.

On June 6th, General Hunter occupied Staunton with but little resistance. Having belonged to a W. Va. regiment that had for more than two years maintained a cherished desire to take Staunton, I requested General Hunter to let me select a squadron of cavalry and lead the charge into the city; my request was readily granted, so I was the first Union soldier during the war to enter Staunton, except as a prisoner, or as a disguised scout. My entry into the city was by the main road under a bridge; a squadron of cavalry contested my entrance with a brisk fire, but they made a hasty exit as my squadron advanced; we captured 18 Confederate cavalry.

Upon taking possession of Staunton 400 sick and wounded Confederates fell into our hands—they were paroled; also fell into our hands large quantities of commissary and ordnance stores, which were destroyed or distributed among the troops. All the railroad bridges, and depots and public workshops, and public factories in the city and vicinity were also destroyed.

On the 7th, at 10 A. M., Hunter moved his entire command 5 miles on the Buffaloe Gap road; the enemy left in the direction of Lexington. We halted two hours, and returned to Staunton and occupied the camp ground which we had left in the morning.

On the 8th, Generals Crook and Averell, with their commands in fine condition, joined Hunter at Staunton, having marched from the Kanawha, destroying many miles of the Virginia and Tennessee railroad, and the Virginia Central at Goshen.

On the 8th and 9th, General Hunter gave his hard worked command a much needed rest, at the same time reorganizing the combined forces of Crook and Averell with his own command, and on the morning of the 10th started on "Hunter's celebrated Lynchburg campaign."

From Staunton (on the 15th) Hunter sent back, by way of Buffalo Gap and Beverly, a convoy of wagons, 1200 prisoners, and many refugees, guarded by 800 men, whose terms of enlistment had expired, the whole under the command of Col. A. Moor of the 28th Ohio Vol. Inft.; General Stahel accompanied this command.

Taking advantage of the opportunity, I accompanied Colonel Moor's command to West Virginia, my term of enlistment having expired some months. Having spent the entire day of the 9th in taking the friendly hand of comrades and saying that hard word "good bye" to those with whom I had spent nearly two years of service, I reluctantly left the scenes of long weary marches and desperate battles to once more seek the ways of peace.

In addition to the official reports of General Hunter's operations, I was the bearer of many letters and messages to friends at home; also the following complimentary orders issued by Generals Hunter and Averell:

HEADQUARTERS, DEPT. OF W. VA.,
SPECIAL ORDER, }   STAUNTON, VA., *June* 8, 1864.
  NO. III.   }

Leave of absence for twenty days is hereby granted to Major T. F. Lang, 6th W. Va. Cavalry, at the expiration of which leave he will report to the Commanding Officer of his regiment to be mustered out on the expiration of the term of his regiment.

The Major-General Commanding parts with regret from Major Lang, in whom he has found a brave, faithful and efficient officer, zealous in the cause of his country and prompt in the discharge of every duty.

By order of Major-General Hunter,
CHAS. G. HALPINE, *A. A. G.*

HEADQUARTERS, 2D CAV. DIV.: DEPT. W. VA.,
GEN'L ORDER, }   STAUNTON, VA., *June* 9, 1864.
  NO. 13.   }

Major T. F. Lang is hereby relieved from duty as A. A. I. Gen'l of this Division, by reason of the expiration of the term of service of his regiment. The necessity which compels the departure of this officer is deeply regretted by the Brig.-Gen'l Comdg. His gallantry has been conspicuous upon so many fields, and he has illustrated his devotion to the cause, and to the interest of this Division through so many difficulties for a long period; that he has won the esteem of all, and his separation is regarded as an irreparable loss to the command.

It is hoped that the Government may not long be deprived of the services of this zealous and efficient officer.

By Command of Brig-Gen'l W. W. Averell,
WILL RUMSEY, *A. A. G.*

We left Staunton at 5 A. M., via Buffalo Gap to Calf Pasture River, 21 miles; found the road blockaded in many places.

On the 11th, we went to Monterey, 28 miles; this was a hard day's march, many of our broken down horses gave out and were left on the road; the wagons were burned.

On the 12th, arrived at Greenbrier river, a distance of 24 miles.

On the 13th, marched to Huttonsville.

On the 14th, arrived at Beverly; sent Captain Gear with a detachment of the 21st N. Y. on a hazardous mission, with mail and despatches to General Hunter who was then far to the southward.

The 16th found us at Grafton where I took leave of Colonel Moor who proceeded to Camp Chase, Ohio, with his regiment and the prisoners.

I hastened to Clarksburg to meet my family, whom I had not seen in many months. After a few days of rest I took advantage of my leave and visited Cumberland, Martinsburg and Baltimore.

Returning on the 20th of July to Webster, where my regiment was encamped, where we remained until the 8th of August, when the regiment went to Wheeling to be mustered out of service.

On the 18th of August, 1864, received my final discharge, having served over three years continuously, in the field winter and summer, performing the most exacting duties required of the soldier the best I knew.

CHAPTER XIX.

ORGANIZATION OF THE PEIRPOINT GOVERNMENT.

Preservation of Loyalty Along the Slave States.—Meetings Held in all the Counties in the Western Part of the State.—Assembling of Delegates at Wheeling, May 13th.—Dr. John W. Moss made Presiding Officer.—Other Officers and Committees Selected.—Denounced Secession and Pledged Loyalty to the Government.—A General Convention to Assemble at Wheeling June 11th.—Governor Letcher Alarmed.—Anticipated Armed Revolt.—Orders Major Boyken to Seize Arms at Wheeling.—Exciting Controversy in the Convention in Relation to Plans.—Hon. John S. Carlisle and Hon. Waitman T. Willey Lead Opposing Elements.—Harmony Restored.—Convention Adjourns.—The Meeting was of National Importance.—Peirpoint's Plan.—Portentious Events Just Prior to the Election.—Demand on the President for Troops.—Canvassing for Governor.—Convention Meets on 11th of June.—Members Required to take an Oath to Support the Constitution of the United States.—The Offices of Governor, Lieutenant-Governor and other State Officers Declared Vacant.—Francis H. Peirpoint Selected Governor of Virginia.—Biographical Sketch of Governor Peirpoint.—Enters upon the Duties of his Office.—Notifying President Lincoln of his Election.—Receives Congratulations from the President.—Authorized to Raise Troops for the United States Government.—Financial Trouble Overcome.—United States Senators Elected.—The Restored Government Recognized.—They were Ready to Divide the State.

T is doubtful whether any single incident of importance in the early period of the Rebellion contributed so largely to the preservation of loyalty along the line of slave States, which bordered upon the free States, as did the prompt action of western Virginia in their defense and maintenance of the Constitutional rights of the National Government.

In Chapter III of this work reference has been made to a meeting held at Clarksburg on the 22d of April, when Hon. John S. Carlisle offered a series of resolutions, which were adopted, calling an assembly of delegates of the people at Wheeling, for May 13th, to take action in opposition to the Ordinance of Secession adopted at Richmond on the 17th of April. Meetings were held in all of the western counties of the State, and delegates were designated from each county to attend said assembly at Wheeling.

At a meeting at Kingwood, in Preston county (May 4), it was declared that the separation of western from eastern Virginia was essential to the maintenance of their liberties; they also resolved, " to so far defy the insurgent rulers of the State as to elect a representative in the National Congress." Similar sentiments were expressed at other meetings. This call for the 13th of May was made to take place a fortnight before the day appointed for the popular vote on the Secession Ordinance in Virginia.

To the meeting of that convention all looked forward with hope; that was thought to be the rallying point from which all succeeding movements would take their origin. The morning of the 13th of May brought to Wheeling its swarm of delegates and a deluge of its own excited inhabitants. Great enthusiasm prevailed, and all interested were eager for the work to begin. Promptly at 11 o'clock A. M. the delegates met at Washington Hall. The large building was filled with anxious people, who showed by their countenances the depth of their feelings and the weight of their responsibilities. The delegates were plain, unassuming men; they possessed those traits of character which makes honesty the accompaniment of simplicity. Above all, they were filled with a noble spirit caught from their constituents, an undying attachment to the Government of their fathers.

The meeting was called to order by Chester D. Hubbard, of Ohio county, on whose motion William B. Zinn, of Preston county, was called to preside. Rev. Peter T. Laishley, of Monongalia county, himself a delegate, invoked the aid of Deity on the deliberations, a pious act of faith not without its usefulness in estimating the character of the delegates and the rectitude of their motives.

A committee on permanent organization and representation was appointed. At the afternoon session Dr. John W. Moss, of Wood county, was reported for permanent president; Colonel Wagner, of Mason, Marshal M. Dent, of Monongalia, and G. L. Cranmer, of Ohio county, were appointed as secretaries. The president on being escorted to the chair addressed the convention in a speech that impressed all with the solemn importance of the action which they were called upon to consider. The clergymen of the city were requested, by motion, to open each day's session with religious exercises. The committee on credentials reported duly accredited delegates from twenty-six counties, as follows: Hancock, Brooke, Ohio, Marion, Monongalia, Preston, Wood, Lewis, Ritchie, Harrison, Upshur, Gilmer, Wirt, Jackson, Mason, Wetzel, Pleasants, Barbour, Hampshire, Berkeley, Doddridge, Tyler, Taylor, Roane, Fayette and Marshall.

A committee, consisting of one member from each county represented, was appointed on State and Federal relations. The following persons composed it: Campbell Tarr, Brooke county; W. T. Willey, Monongalia; John S. Carlisle, Harrison; J. J. Jackson, Wood; Charles Hooton, Preston; Daniel Lamb, Ohio; Geo. McPorter, Hancock; Joseph Macker, Mason; D. D. Johnson, Tyler; James Scott, Jackson; G. W. Bier, Wetzel; R. C. Holliday, Marshall; A. S. Withers, Lewis; E. T. Trahorn, Wirt; F. H. Peirpoint, Marion; S. Dayton, Barbour; G. S. Senseney, Fayette; J. S. Burdette, Taylor; S. Cochran, Pleasants; A. R. McQuilkin, Berkeley; J. E. Stump, Roane; S. Martin, Gilmer; A. B. Rohrbough, Upshur; O. D. Downey, Hampshire; Mr. Foley, Ritchie.

The delegates numbered nearly five hundred loyal men, and their action was marked with a decision of purpose that suggested that they had met for the transaction of business. They denounced the Ordinance of Secession, and pledged their loyalty to the National Government and their obedience to its laws.

It was also determined that if the Ordinance should be approved by the popular vote of Virginia, that this preliminary conference request the people of all the counties represented to appoint delegates on the 4th day of June, to a general convention to assemble in Wheeling on the 11th of the same month. There was remarkable unanimity of sentiment in the convention against longer submitting to the control of the Secessionists. And this stubborn resistance thoroughly alarmed the disunionists at Richmond. Governor Letcher anticipated an armed revolt in that section, and it was in deference to this opinion that he (Letcher) sent orders to Maj. F. M. Boykin at Grafton to seize arms in possession of the State militia at Wheeling, arm such men as might rally to his camp, and to cut off telegraphic communication between Wheeling and Washington.

Notwithstanding the unanimity of sentiment in relation to the resistance of the Secessionists, there sprang up on the second day of the convention an excited controversy as to the plan to be adopted for immediate action. "There were those who came to the convention with the recollections of wrongs and insults burning in their memories. This class of men came to vote for an immediate and unqualified division of the State, however violent or revolutionary it might appear. Some delegations, indeed, came to the city with a banner flying at their head, endorsed, "New Virginia, now or never." This party had a powerful leader in the Hon. John S. Carlisle, smarting from the injustice and contumely that he had experienced in the convention at Richmond. His plan was to immediately adopt a constitution and form of government for the counties represented, and proceed to fill the offices by temporary appointment. This was a popular idea with the mass of the convention, and it became almost perilous to oppose it; those who ventured to do so subjected themselves for the time to the liability of having imputations cast upon their loyalty. But there was a minority, respectable both as to members and intelligence, who felt and saw the irreparable mischief that would follow in the train of such a course. This party found a leadership in the Hon. W. T. Willey, of Monongalia, whose more equable temperament

FRANCIS H. PEIRPOINT
Loyal Governor of Virginia

enabled him to discern the true point of distinction between spasmodic disruption and authorized resistance.   It was argued that the proceeding urged by the majority was wholly unwarranted by the call that had led to this assemblage; that the delegates had not been appointed with this view nor empowered to act with such extreme vigor; that this was but an informal meeting of the people, not legally convened, and could not bind the people to acquiesence either in law or reason, or by any known rule or precedent; that no vote had yet been taken by the people on the Ordinance of Secession, and hence the State of Virginia had a Government under the Constitution of the United States at Richmond; that the Federal Government would not recognize a state created thus, because it was not after the mode prescribed in the Constitution of the United States.

*   *   *   *   *   *   *   *   *

"On the third day, the debate was continued, but in a better spirit; the voice of better counsels was beginning to prevail, and all felt the imperative necessity of some action and that it should be, so far as the same was possible, harmonious in its character."*

At this time the Committee on State and Federal Relations made their report to the convention, which proved a happy blending of all opinions, and the members thereafter were quite harmonious, transacting the business of the convention to the satisfaction of all.   After but little discussion, the report of the committee was adopted by the body.

A Central Committee of Safety was appointed as follows: John S. Carlisle, James S. Wheat, Chester D. Hubbard, Francis H. Peirpoint, Campbell Tarr, George R. Latham, Andrew Wilson, S. H. Woodward and James W. Paxton.

A vote of thanks was tendered to the citizens of Wheeling for their hospitality; also, to the president and other officers of the body.   Several eloquent speeches were made.   A prayer was then offered invoking the blessings of Heaven upon the labors of the meeting.   The "Star Spangled Banner" was sung by the united voices of over a thousand people; three cheers were given for the Union, and amid a blaze of enthusiasm the convention adjourned *sine die*.

This meeting was of National importance.   The great daily papers of Boston, New York, Philadelphia, Pittsburg, Cleveland, Columbus, Cincinnati and Chicago had their reporters there.   An intense Union feeling was developed and it greatly encouraged the sentiment in the North.

From the close of the convention till the election, which took place on the 23d of May, the country was in a feverish excitement.   In the North-

* From Judge J. Marshall Hagan's "Formation of West Virginia."

west the feeling against Secession became an absolute passion. Nothing could withstand the tremendous weight of public sentiment so unequivocally placed in the balances against it. A Committee of Safety had been appointed by the convention organized, and that committee in turn appointed a sub-committee to remain in Wheeling to take charge of affairs.

  *Then the next day when the sub-committee met, some one who had heard that Peirpoint had a plan of action, asked him to explain it. He admitted that he had, and that it was this: "On principle the loyal people of the State are entitled to the protection of the laws of the State and the United States. When our convention assembles on the 11th of June, I have no doubt we will know that the Governor of the State has joined the Southern Confederacy. The convention will pass resolutions declaring, in the language of the Declaration of Independence that 'he has abdicated his office by joining a foreign state,' and that it is the right of this convention to appoint a Governor and Lieutenant-Governor, and pass such other ordinances as are necessary to turn out of office all disloyal men and to fill them by loyal men, and do anything else that may be necessary. Our actions must go to the whole State. We will call the Legislature together immediately, if neces-·sary. You observe the convention is composed of double the number of delegates of the lower house. It may be we will need a legislature and convention both at once. We will elect Senators to fill the places made vacant by resignation of Hunter and Mason. We will commission our members elected and send them to Congress. The Governor will call upon the President for military aid to suppress the rebellion. In the meantime, we will get the United States Army to occupy the Monongahela and Kanawha valleys, drive the Rebels beyond the mountains, and we will organize below. Now, if we carry out the program, we will represent this State of Virginia, and divide the State by the consent of Congress and the consent of the Legislature of Virginia." The committee unanimously assented, and worked diligently, attending to all the details necessary to strengthen the Union cause.

  On Saturday before the fourth Thursday in May, election day, Peirpoint's friends at Fairmont thought it safe for him to come home and stay until the election. There was great commotion on the day before the election, and a regiment from Georgia and the valley of Virginia arrived at Philippi and Grafton. A large Rebel meeting was held in Fairmont the same evening. Threats were freely made. About 2 o'clock at night a lady

  * By permission from Frank S. Reader's History of the 5th W. Va. Cav.

living near called to Peirpoint and told him that she had been watching all night; that she heard of threats, and feared that he would be killed, or his home burned that night. He told her not to be alarmed, that they would not hurt him; but he watched from that to daylight, got an early breakfast, and went to his office. A friend came in excited and declared there was present danger, and insisted on his leaving at once on the train for Wheeling. He went and got to the office of the committee at Wheeling at half past 3 P. M. The committee was there. They gibed him about not being at home voting. He replied, "The time of voting is past. I move that Mr. Carlisle be sent at once to Washington to demand troops to drive the Rebels out of western Virginia." Carlisle readily consented to go on the next train at 8 o'clock that night. He had to go by Harrisburg and Baltimore. He got to Washington at 3 P. M. next day. He told the hackman to drive him to the White House as quick as his horses could go; got there and inquired for the President; was informed he could not see the President, as all the Cabinet were there in Cabinet meeting. Carlisle said he wanted to see all the Cabinet and the President together, and demanded that his card be taken in. The President called him in. "Well," said the President, "Mr. Carlisle, what is the best news in West Virginia?" Carlisle, without answering that question, said: "Sir, we want to fight. We have one regiment ready, and if the Federal Government is going to assist us we want it at once." "You shall have assistance," said the President. This was on Friday afternoon. On Sunday morning United States troops from Ohio and Indiana crossed the river at Wheeling and Parkersburg, and on the third of June the first fight in the state came off at Philippi.

Before the assembling of the convention, a number of Union gentlemen in Wheeling held a kind of informal caucus and discussed the men who would likely be prominent for Governor. They finally agreed on Peirpoint, and appointed a gentleman to see him and ascertain if he would accept; if so they would work to that end. Peirpoint was seen, the matter submitted; he declared "that he had never thought of occupying the place. He had been looking to older men." After hearing all his friends had to say, he replied: "I am in for the war to lead or drive, and if the convention so orders, I will do the best I can." Two days before the meeting of the convention, the members began to arrive in Wheeling. The first question to leading Union men was, "What are we going to do?" They were told to see Peirpoint; he had worked up a plan of action. So they went to him singly and by numbers. He explained the proposed action in detail. All inquired, "Have you consulted the President or any of his Cabinet?" He answered, "No. We don't want to consult them. This action by our enemies will be called revolutionary. The Government of the United States is watched in this country and Europe, and we don't want to compromise it in any way. But we will submit our work and I will guarantee its acceptance."

The convention assembled on the 11th of June, 1861. It was agreed that all the members before taking their seats, should take an oath to support the Constitution of the United States as the supreme law of the land, notwithstanding anything to the contrary in the Ordinance of Secession passed at Richmond on the 17th of April, 1861. About thirty-five counties were represented, and every delegate elected, but one, took his seat. Hon. A. I. Boreman was elected president of the convention. Appropriate committees were appointed on fundamental principles and plan for reorganizing the State. The committee went to work in earnest, and in a few days they reported in substance that the loyal people of the State were entitled to the benefit of State and National Government; that the offices of Governor and Lieutenant-Governor were vacant by reason of the officers who were elected to their places having joined a foreign government; and that it was the duty of the convention to elect a Governor and Lieutenant-Governor for six months, until the offices could be filled by an election of the people. They made it the duty of the Governor to require all the officers in the State to take the oath to support the Constitution of the United States as the supreme law of the land; and the restored government of Virginia as vindicated by the convention assembled at Wheeling on the 11th of June, 1861, notwithstanding anything to the contrary in the ordinance passed at Richmond on the 17th of April, 1861. It was made the duty of the Governor on the refusal of any office-holder of a state or county office to take this oath to declare the office vacant and order an election to fill the vacancy with a loyal man. By the 21st all the preliminaries were completed, speeches of explanation made and election of Governor ordered for that day. Peirpoint was asked privately to leave the hall.

Daniel Lamb, Esq., nominated him, in a short speech, for Governor of the Restored Government of Virginia. No other nomination was made and the vote was unanimous. Peirpoint was sent for and informed of the action of the convention by the president, who asked him if he was ready to take the oath of office. He said he was. The oath was then administered on the president's platform in the presence of the convention. Peirpoint turned to the convention and said he thanked them for this expression of their confidence, and would serve them to the best of his ability.

William Lazier was selected as one of the Governor's Council, and L. A. Hagans, Preston, Secretary of State.

Francis Harrison Peirpoint was born in Monongalia county, Va., about five miles east of Morgantown, January 25, 1814. The same year his father, Francis Peirpoint, and mother, Catherine, removed into Harrison county, three miles southwest of what is now Fairmont. They settled in a log cabin in an unbroken forest. In 1827 his father removed to what is now Fairmont, W. Va. What work Francis did until thirteen years old, was on the farm. After he was of school age, he went about two and one-half miles to a log school house, four terms of three months each, in the winter time. From thirteen years old to twenty-one and one-half he worked in his father's tanyard, then he started on foot to seek an education at Allegheny College, at Meadville, Pa., about one hundred and eighty miles distant. He remained at Allegheny College four and one-half college years, and was graduated in the class of 1839, visited home three times, in vacation, traveling as he first started most of the distance. After he left college he taught school for three years in Virginia and Mississippi. In political opinion he was a Whig. His father taught him that slavery was a moral, social and political evil. During his college life this sentiment was increased. While riding in Mississippi, his personal observations of the institution intensified this sentiment. After leaving college and while teaching, he studied law. In consequence of the failing health of his father, he returned home in 1842, and was admitted to the bar in that year. He was an amateur politician, though never a candidate for office, and frequently addressed the people on political subjects. He was placed by his party on the State electoral ticket for President, in 1848. His district contained ten counties, six mountain counties of which were overwhelmingly Democratic. It was proposed and agreed upon that the two electors should hold joint discussions of the points of difference between the parties, in all the counties in the district, at the county seats, and at such other points as they could attend. The meetings were largely attended and the canvass lasted over three months. Much of the capital of Democratic politicians then was to abuse abolitionists. Abolitionism was the sum of all villainies in politics. Socialism, free love, negro equality, slave insurrection and general spoliation of women and property, were attributed to designing abolitionists. But Peirpoint did not suffer himself to be put on the defensive, but assumed the aggressive at the start. Whatever accusations were brought against the abolitionists, he knew that the people of western Virginia knew the slavocracy of the State only by its oppression of the white laboring people; that the Democratic party had always held the political power in the State, and that the part east of the Blue Ridge, though largely in the minority in population, held controlling power in the Legislature. The west had had but one United States Senator and never a judge of the Court of Appeals or a Governor. By the laws of the State, they to a great extent exonerated their slaves from taxation, and taxed all the laboring man had, from a pig to an engine. By law, a poor man with three sons over sixteen years, with himself, might be called to work the roads ten or twenty days in the year, while the gentleman owning two male slaves over sixteen years, was exempt from road working, and his land was seldom taxed for road purposes. The children were without free schools, and almost without schools of any kind. He pointed them to Pennsylvania and Ohio, with their free institutions; on the one side of an imaginary line you could see thrift, intelligence of the children and prosperity of the people; not so where slavocracy reigned. He declared that western Virginia wanted free schools, a sound currency and a tariff for protection. He continued this line of attack on the oppression of slave holders, through the local press and before the people, in 1852, 1856, and in the Governor's election in 1859. When the Democratic party divided in 1860, and nominated Breckinridge and Douglas for President, Peirpoint at once announced that the Breckinridge party ment secession, rebellion, division of the Union and war. He maintained this country could not be divided without war. Breckinridge Democrats vehemently denied this charge. Peirpoint pressed it the harder, so that when the Rebellion came, a large number of Democrats were on the Union side. He was not an Abolitionist in their sense of the term, but he hated the institution of slavery, the intolerant spirit of pro-slavery men, and their oppression. At the age of seventeen Governor Peirpoint joined the M. P. Church, was an active superintendent of the Sunday school for eighteen years before the war, has had a class ever since, and says that the most valuable knowledge is that received in this grand work. The Governor is now an honored resident of Fairmont, W. Va., and though beyond three score years and ten, is active in good works.

After his election, Governor Peirpoint at once entered upon the duties of his office. The collector of the port offered him an office, with a bare table, half quire of paper and pen and ink, in the custom house. Some friends came in to congratulate him, and some of them remarked that he was the first man they had ever known to thank men for putting a rope around his neck. The Governor replied that success was never convicted of treason. He immediately addressed a letter to the President of the United States, in substance informing him that there was an insurrection and rebellion in the State; that certain evil minded men in the State had banded themselves together and had joined with like minded men from other States; that they had formed strong military organizations and were pressing Union men into their army, and taking their substance to support their organizations; that their object was to overthrow the goverment of the State and United States, and that he had not sufficient military force at his command to suppress the rebellion. He called upon the President for military aid, and signed his letter, "F. H. Peirpoint, Governor of Virginia."

About the fourth day after, the Governor received a letter from Secretary of War (Cameron) acknowledging receipt of his letter, saying that he was directed by the President to congratulate the people of Virginia on their so soon resuming their relations with the United States Government, and authorizing Governor Peirpoint to raise voluntary regiments for the United States Army and to appoint company and field officers. This letter was read to the convention and greatly strengthened their faith in the movement.

The second week of the convention was nearing its close. Serious trouble was ahead. Landlords were informing members that they would expect their pay at the end of the second week. Money was exceedingly scarce. The Governor was informed of the situation. "Yes," said he, "I have been actively thinking about that. Tell them to hold on until next week." This was on Saturday. On Monday morning Governor Peirpoint said to Mr. P. G. Vanwinkle, "We must have money. I want you, after breakfast, to go with me to N. W. and M. M. banks, and endorse my notes for $5000, one on each bank. I intend to have $10,000 from these banks." Vanwinkle said he would do it. They got the cashiers together. The Governor told them what he wanted. They raised the objection that they could not make the loan to the State without a vote of the stockholders. The Governor replied: "I want it on my own individual note and Mr. Vanwinkle will endorse it. I want it to pay the mileage and *per diem* of the members of the convention. If my government succeeds you are sure of your money. If it does not succeed, your money is not worth a bubble." One of the cashiers replied: "You shall have five thousand from this bank, what shall we do with it?" The Governor replied: "Place to my credit officially and I will so draw my checks." The other cashier said he would like to do the same thing, but nearly all his directors were of the Secession party, and they would not meet until Thursday. Governor Peirpoint said, "Please give them my compliments, and tell them to place the money to my credit, and I don't want any higgling about it." On Wednesday the cashier informed him that $5000 was placed to his credit in the other bank. The Governor went immediately to the convention, asked the President to inform all the members that if they would get a certificate from the Sergeant-at-arms of the mileage and *per diem* due them, and bring it to the Governor, he would give them a check for the money. This gave great strength to the convention. Thus the Governor became Auditor and Treasurer also.

The convention adjourned to August 6. The Legislature of the Reorganized Government met on the 1st day of July, and elected Waitman T. Willey and John S. Carlisle United States Senators from Virginia, the acceptance of whose credentials, together with those of the Congressmen elected on the 23d of May, was the official recognition by the Government of the United States of the Reorganized Government of Virginia.

The Governor procured proper seals, and issued commissions to Senators and Representatives in Congress, who were admitted to seats in the extra session called by the President to meet on the 4th of July, 1861.

The Restored Government being recognized by the Legislative and Executive branches of the Federal Government, they were ready to divide the State.

CHAPTER XX.

WEST VIRGINIA, THE "CHILD OF THE STORM."

When Named.—Its Formation Not the Act of Any One Man, but of Enthusiastic, Determined Men.—President Lincoln Recognized the Importance of Preserving Loyalty upon the Border.—Ordinance Providing for the Formation of a New State Approved by the People.—Constitution Framed for the New Government.—Approved by Vote on the First Thursday in April, 1862.—Provisions of the Same.—Radical Changes in Organic Law.—The Memorial Asking the Erection of the New State Presented in the Senate by Mr. Willey.—His Eloquent Appeal.—Favorable Report of the Committee on Territories. —The Measure Discussed in Congress in Relation to Slavery.—Wide Divergence of Opinion in Heated Debate.—Finally Referred Back to the Convention and to the People.— The President Issues Proclamation on the 20th of April, 1863, Creating West Virginia a State in the Union.—State Officers Elected Fourth Thursday of May Following.— Arthur I. Boreman Installed Governor on the 20th of June.—Governor Peirpoint removed Seat of Government of Virginia from Wheeling to Alexandria.—Marvelous Growth of West Virginia, by Governor MacCorkle.

WEST VIRGINIA, the "Child of the Storm," received its name in the Convention of the 26th of November, 1861, that framed and proposed the Constitution for the said State. The formation of West Virginia was not the act of any one man, nor was it the act of the politicians of the State, as they were in the Rebellion. It was simply the carrying out of an enthusiastic determination of a large body of serious, determined men, who felt that they had been oppressed by the slave power of the State. The movement, therefore, for a new State readily assumed a form that promised success, and the people gave a hearty support to the cause. Its organization and admission to the Union would complete the chain of loyal commonwealths on the south side of Mason and Dixon's line, and would drive back the jurisdiction of rebellious Virginia beyond the chain of mountains and interpose that barrier to the progress of the insurrectionary forces westward and northward.

The provision in the Federal Constitution that no new State shall be formed within the jurisdiction of any other State without the consent of the Legislature of the State as well as of Congress, had always been the stumbling block in the way of West Virginia's independence. Despite the hostilities and antagonisms of the two populations, Virginia would insist on retaining this valuable section of country within her own jurisdiction. But now, April

15, by the chances of war, the same men who desired to create the new State were wielding the entire political power of Virginia, and they could naturally grant permission to themselves to erect a State that would be entirely free from the objectionable jurisdiction which for the time they represented. They were not slow to avail themselves of their opportunity.

President Lincoln recognized the great importance of preserving loyalty upon the border of the free States. As Delaware, Maryland, Kentucky and Missouri had been promptly placed under the control of governments friendly to the Union, the territory of Virginia adjacent to the loyal States gave to the President a great deal of anxious thought. Notwithstanding the action of the loyal people in the western part of the State, and the recognition given by Congress, the continued exercise of even a nominal jurisdiction so far north, by the State which contained the capital of the Southern Confederacy, would be a serious impeachment of the power of the National Government, and would detract from its respect at home and its prestige abroad.

The President desired most of all the establishment of civil government, with the reign of law and order everywhere recognized. It was, therefore, to him a matter of regret that the National Government was of itself capable only of enforcing military occupation, so far as related to Statehood.

The Peirpoint government, as it was now popularly termed, adopted an ordinance on the 20th of August, 1861, providing "for the formation of a new State out of a portion of the territory of this State." The ordinance was approved by a vote of the people on the fourth Thursday of October, and on the 26th of November the convention assembled in Wheeling to frame a Constitution for the new government. The work was satisfactorily performed, and on the first Thursday of April, 1862, the people approved the Constitution by a vote of 18,862 in favor of it, with only 514 against it. At this time there were more than 10,000 soldiers in the ranks of the Union Army from West Virginia who did not vote—had they done so, they would have voted solidly for the new State.

The work of the representatives of the projected new State being thus ratified, the Governor called the Legislature of Virginia together on the 6th day of May, and on the 13th of the same month that body gave its consent, with due regularity, to "the formation of a new State within the jurisdiction of the said State of Virginia."

The Constitution as adopted comprised many radical changes in the organic law as previously adopted in Virginia. It named forty-four counties absolutely to compose the State, and further provided that the counties of Pendleton, Hardy, Hampshire and Morgan should also be included if a majority of the votes cast at the election on the adoption of the Constitution in those counties should be in favor of that adoption. The old system of *viva voce* voting was abrogated, and that of the ballot substituted. The office of lieutenant-governor was abolished. The old county court system, which had become in Virginia a supremely antiquated folly, was dissipated by a healthier system of judicial circuits. A still greater change in the structure of the municipal body was effected in the erection of townships for the regulating of local affairs. Taxation was made equal and uniform for the first time in the history of their people. A check was placed upon the system of granting the credit of the State to corporations, which had enthralled Virginia in a debt of millions. No debts were to be contracted by the State, except to meet the the casual deficit, to redeem a previous liability, or to defend the State in time of war. An equitable proportion of the debt of Virginia prior to January 1st, 1861, was to be assumed by the new State. The vast schemes of land piracy which had so confused the titles to real estate west of the Alleghanies, and had so retarded the settling of the country, were wholly uprooted by a provision that no further entries upon waste and unappropriated lands should be made. But the feature of the instrument that demonstrates most clearly the spirit of enlightened patriotism and enlarged sense of genuine interest in the cause of humanity, was the liberal provision for the establishment of a system of free schools. All the proceeds of the public domain were appropriated to this object ; giving to it everything upon which the primary basis of a State is formed. The Legislature was also required to provide for the establishment of schools as soon as practicable, etc.

Such parts of the common law and statutory laws of Virginia as were in force at the time the Constitution went into operation, and not repugnant thereto, were to remain and continue the law of West Virginia until altered or repealed by the Legislature of the latter. These acts of the loyal people of West Virginia will be viewed by the impartial historian with wonderment and admiration ; in all they acted wisely and well. Beginning at the corner-stone of all true government, they layed it well in the consent of the governed.

The memorial of the Legislature, together with the act granting assent to the erection of the State of West Virginia, and the Constitution of the latter, were presented in the Senate by Senator W. T. Willey, on the 29th of May, 1862.

It is to be regretted that lack of space will not permit the insertion here of the full text of Senator Willey's splendid speech in behalf of the movement. After reviewing the preliminary operations on behalf of the people of West Virginia, he spoke as follows :

"Finally, sir, in obedience to the proclamation of the Governor, the Legislature of Virginia assembled at Wheeling on the 6th day of this month, and on the 13th day thereafter gave its consent to the formation of this new State, and has forwarded such consent to the Congress of the United States, together with an official copy of the Constitution adopted as aforesaid, with the request that the said new State may be admitted into the Union of the United States.

"And now it only remains for Congress to give its assent. Ought that assent to be given?

"Mr. President, before I answer this question, I desire to correct a misapprehension which I find is prevalent, not only throughout the country, but also here. It seems to be supposed that this movement for a new State has been conceived since the breaking out of the Rebellion, and was a consequence of it; that it grew alone out of the abhorrence with which the loyal citizens of West Virginia regarded the traitorous proceedings of the conspirators east of the Alleghanies, and that the effort was prompted simply by a desire to dissolve the connection between the loyal and disloyal sections of the State. Not so, sir. The question of dividing the State of Virginia, either by the Blue Ridge mountains, or by the Alleghanies, has been mooted for fifty years. It has frequently been agitated with such vehemence as to threaten seriously the public peace. It has been a matter of constant strife and bitterness in the Legislature of the State. The animosity existing at this time between the North and the South is hardly greater than what has at times distinguished the relations between East and West Virginia, arising from a diversity of interests and geographical antagonisms. Indeed, so incompatible was the union of the territory lying west of the Alleghany Mountains with the territory lying east thereof, under one and the same State municipality, that so long ago as 1781, several of the States insisted that Virginia should include in her act of cession all her trans-Alleghany territory, making the Alleghany mountains her western, as they were her natural boundary. A committee in the Federal Congress about this time made a strong report, suggesting such a boundary; and Mr. Madison records that— 'From several circumstances, there was reason to believe that Rhode Island, New Jersey, Pennsylvania, and Delaware, if not Maryland likewise, retained latent views of confining Virginia to the Alleghany Mountains.' " *

Mr. Willey showed that there was the requisite population to entitle the people to the privilege. The geographical position of the proposed territory was in favor of the admission. He said: "Look at the map. Observe how this territory lies, like a wedge driven in between the State of Ohio on one

* *Madison's Debates*, vol. 1, pp. 463–465.

WAITMAN T. WILLEY
U.S. Senator West Virginia

ARTHUR I. BOREMAN

War Governor West Virginia

side, and the States of Pennsylvania and Maryland on the other, and is completely cut off from all convenient intercourse with east Virginia by the Alleghany mountains.

"The people living within the limits of the projected new State never had, and never can have, any trade or commerce with eastern Virginia. The traffic and commerce between the two sections," he said, "had not amounted to fifty thousand dollars in the last twenty years. The natural and best markets of West Virginia are Baltimore, Pittsburgh and Cincinnati," etc.

The social difference on account of negro slavery indicated more fully perhaps than any other one the necessity for a division.

Continuing he said: "Mr. President, in view of these considerations, I think I am authorized to say that the division of the State of Virginia asked for is a physical, a political, a social, an industrial and commercial necessity. It is necessary for the preservation of harmonious and fraternal relations between the eastern and western sections of the State. It is indispensable to the development of the great natural resources of West Virginia, and to the prosperity and happiness of its inhabitants.

"And now, sir, a few words in relation to the resources of the new State. Its area will be at least respectable—greater than very many of the other States of the Union. It will contain about twenty-four thousand square miles. It will embrace immense mineral wealth. It will include waterpower more than sufficient to drive all the machinery of New England. It contains the finest forest of timber on the continent. It includes the Great Kanawha salines and the Little Kanawha oil wells. It abounds in iron ore; and its coal fields are sufficient to supply the consumption of the entire Union for a thousand years. Much of it is well adapted to the production of all the valuable cereals; and all of it is unrivaled for the growth of grass and for grazing."

Mr. Willey concluded his speech in the following eloquent wording:

"Sir, these counties of Western Virginia, knocking for admission into the Union as a new State, contain, in rich abundance, all the elements of a great commonwealth. Why have they remained undeveloped in the oldest State in the American Union? Why are our mines unworked? Why are our waterfalls forever wasting away, unappreciated by the skill of man, chafing and foaming in their channels, as if in conscious rage at the long neglect? The answer to these questions is an irrefutable argument in favor of the division desired. Unless the State is divided, these natural resources of wealth and power will forever remain undeveloped. Is this just to the people there? Is it just to the country at large?

"Thus, sir, we present our claims for this new State. We pray you to grant your assent. It will send a thrill of joy through three hundred thousand hearts, and it will do no injustice to any. Then, sir, will our invaluable virgin mines invite the espousal of your surplus capital, and our perennial streams will lend their exhaustless power to your manufacturing skill. Then shall we soon be able to say, in the jubilant language of the Psalmist: 'The pastures are clothed with flocks; the valleys also are covered over with corn; they shout for joy; they also sing.' Virginia—East Virginia, restored from her temporary aberration; West Virginia, like a newly discovered star—East Virginia and West Virginia, twin stars, shall henceforth shine with ever-brightening lustre in the republican zodiac of States encircling our western hemisphere."

The Constitution was referred to the Committee on Territories and a bill favorable to admission was promptly reported by Senator Wade of Ohio. "The measure was discussed at different periods, largely with reference to the effect it would have upon the institution of slavery, and Congress insisted upon inserting a provision that the children of slaves, born in the State after the fourth day of July, 1863, shall be free ; and no slave shall be permitted to come into the State for permanent residence therein." But this was not satisfactory; and Mr. Willey's proposition was amended so as to make it read as follows :

"The children of slaves born within the limits of this State after the fourth of July, 1863, shall be free; and all slaves within the said State who shall, at the time aforesaid, be under the age of ten years, shall be free when they arrive at the age of twenty-one years, and all slaves over ten and under twenty-one years, shall be free when they arrive at the age of twenty-five years; and no slave shall be permitted to come into the State for permanent residence therein." This substitute afterwards came to be designated as the "Willey amendment," not that it was his original creation, but he accepted it in that form in deference to the wishes of the Senate.

The bill with the amendments was fully discussed in the Senate, and in the House, and a wide divergence of opinion in heated controversy ensued. Mr. Carlisle, from some unexplained reason, had become violently opposed to the creation of the new State, and he assailed the measure now upon the ground that to admit the new State with this amendment would be to impose a Constitution upon the people of West Virginia, which, in this particular, had never been submitted to them, or ratified by them. His course, however, did not reflect the wishes of the masses of the people of the State. But "Mr. Willey received a substantial support from the members of the House of Representatives, representing the counties included in the limits of the new

State. The Hon. Wm. G. Brown, of Kingwood, and the Hon. Jacob B. Blair, of Parkersburg, aware of Senator Carlisle's defection, had prepared themselves for such a contingency." Fortunately the convention which framed the proposed Constitution of West Virginia had not finally dissolved, but had simply adjourned to be re-convened upon the call of a committee which had been appointed by the body for the purpose, whenever in their opinion it might be deemed necessary and expedient. Mr. Willey caused consternation among the opponents of the bill, when he asked leave of the Senate to introduce, by way of substitute for the original proposition pending, a new bill, which he had lying on his desk, referring the Constitution, as amended, back to the convention which formed it with the provision that, if that body should adopt it, and submit it again to the people, and they should ratify it as thus amended, the President of the United States, upon being properly certified of the fact, should make proclamation accordingly, fixing a certain day when West Virginia should become one of the United States.

The committee referred to did recall the convention. It met again at Wheeling, early in February, 1863. The vote on the Constitution, as amended was taken on the 26th of March, 1863. It resulted in the adoption by a majority of about twenty-seven thousand. The result having been certified to the President of the United States, as provided for by the act of Congress, he on the 20th of April following, issued his proclamation.

The convention, prior to adjourning, in February, 1863, provided for an election, to be held on the fourth Thursday of May following, to choose members of both branches of the Legislature, a Governor and other State officers, judges of the Supreme Court of Appeals, judges of the various circuit courts, and county officers. An election was accordingly held at that period, when members of the Senate and House of Delegates were chosen in nearly all of the counties. Hon. Arthur I. Boreman, of Wood county, was chosen as the first Governor of the State of West Virginia; Samuel Crane, of Randolph, Auditor; Campbell Tarr, of Brooke, Treasurer; J. Edgar Boyers, of Tyler, Secretary of State, and A. Bolton Caldwell, of Ohio, Attorney-General. Hons. Ralph L. Berkshire, of Monongalia, William A. Harrison, of Harrison, and James H. Brown, of Kanawha, were elected Judges of the Supreme Court of Appeals. These officers were all chosen without opposition. Judges were also elected in all of the circuits but two, which latter were in the disputed ground between the contending forces of the war.

" When, therefore, the period of sixty days from the date of the President's proclamation had elapsed, the 20th of June, 1863, the new State had a Government consisting of all the departments, Legislative, Executive and Judicial, provided for by the Constitution. The financial condition of the State was in splendid condition, as the General Assembly of Virginia, by an act, passed February 3, 1863, granted all the property and the proceeds of fines, forfeitures, confiscations and all uncollected taxes within the boundaries of the new State, to it. It also appropriated the sum of one hundred and fifty thousand dollars out of the Treasury to the State of Virginia, by an act passed February 4th, 1863. Governor Peirpoint removed the seat of Government of Virginia from Wheeling to Alexandria, prior to the inauguration of Governor Boreman, which took place on the 26th of June, 1863, in Wheeling, which had been designated by the Convention as the Seat of Government of West Virginia, until it should be permanently located by the Legislature. Both branches of the Legislature assembled on the same day and began the labor of altering the laws, and enacting such others as were necessary to conform to the requirements of the organic law and the condition of affairs."

A State seal, with an appropriate device, was adopted, inscribed, "STATE OF WEST VIRGINIA; MONTANI SEMPER LIBERI" (mountaineers are always free), and the new commonwealth took its place as the thirty-fifth State of the Union, covering an area of 23,000 square miles; population in 1890, 762,794.

The following letter from Govornor MacCorkle is given to show the wonderful growth in the State of West Virginia.

STATE OF WEST VIRGINIA.

In a national convention ten years ago a newspaper reporter mentioned a recalcitrant member as hailing from the "Little Wild State of West Virginia." Would that be true to-day?

The State is three times larger than Massachusetts.

In West Virginia there is the largest nail-mill in the world. There are invested in the industries of Wheeling alone ten milion dollars, with annual sales aggregrating fifty millions.

In 1880 railroad mileage was 691 miles; in 1892 it was 1700—the second State in the Union in railroad building.

In 1880 the "Big Injun" sand was not touched; to-day oil output is 625,000 barrels per month—the second oil producing State. The rich Gordon and Berea sands only touched in two places. The Sisterville field is to-day the greatest oil-producing field.

In 1880 we produced 1,404,008 tons of coal; 1892 produced 8,710,888 tons, making the ɪurth coal-producing State.

In 1880 we produced 121,715 tons of coke; 1892, 1,313,668 tons, making second coke State, New River coke outselling Connellsville in Chicago. The great Pittsburg seam scarcely touched.

We have 16,000 square miles of coals, making our coal area the greatest.

In Flat Top region, in 1880, there was nothing but a wilderness. Last year the coal output was 2,300,000 tons; the coke more than 400,000 tons.

We have the largest area of hard-wood in the Union, good iron ore, fine glass sand and salt water, splendid building stone.

Our taxes are only 3½ mills on the dollar for State purposes. Our school system is excellent; with less than a million people, we spent last year $1,400,000 for education. The State has not a dollar of debt.

Our natural resources of forest, farm and mine are boundless, our people rapidly progressive; we have low taxes, a salubrious climate; no locusts, grasshoppers, cyclones, or droughts.

We offer the heartiest welcome to our Northern and Eastern friends desiring to change their homes. This welcome is especially extended to the small farmer; for him, in our fertile soil, is every possible hope of success, both in regular agricultural line and in fruits. The State is the gateway between the West and North, and it is right at the market.

WILLIAM A. MacCORKLE.

CHAPTER XX—(ADDENDA).

Veteran Newspapers in the Army in Western Virginia.—Influence of the Press in the Early Struggle.—The " Wheeling Intelligencer," " Cincinnati Gazette," " Cincinnati Commercial " and "Baltimore American," Pioneer Papers.—A. W. Campbell's Loyalty.—Whitelaw Reid, as Correspondent and Volunteer Aide-de-Camp, at Laurel Hill, Carrick's Ford, and Carnifex Ferry.—Murat Halstead's Intense Unionism.—C. C. Fulton's Influence.—Col. Bickham, Aid-de-Camp and Correspondent.

THAT the daily newspapers which had extensive circulation in the early struggle had great influence in moulding a popular Union sentiment in West Virginia cannot be truthfully denied. The pioneers, as we recall them, were *The Wheeling Intelligencer, Cincinnati Gazette, Cincinnati Commercial,* and *Baltimore American.* The *Wheeling Intelligencer* ranked first in the estimation of the soldiers, and it found its way into every camp in western Virginia. A. W. Campbell, Esq., the proprietor and editor, was one of the original stalwart Unionists who had great personal popularity and influence, which was not confined to the limits of western Virginia. His paper therefore was read as an authority on the great questions relating to the war, and throughout the Rebellion, and on until the present time, Mr. Cambell and his paper have adhered to the loyal principles he advocated during the war. Then follow the two Cincinnati papers referred to.

In those days the editor of the *Cincinnati Gazette* was Richard Smith, and the editor of the *Cincinnati Commercial,* was Murat Halstead. The two papers many years ago were consolidated under the present name, *The Cincinnati Commercial Gazette.* Until recently, the joint editors of *The Cincinnati Commercial Gazette* were Murat Halstead and Richard Smith. In the old days, however, the *Cincinnati Gazette* was the dignified, old conservative Whig organ; with the development of the free soil sentiment, it became Republican, and was a most zealous and loyal supporter of the war.

Attached to the reportorial staff of the Gazette, was a young man, Whitelaw Reid, who, by reason of the national prominence he has attained, is deserving of a passing notice in this article. He had been editing a country paper at Xenia, Ohio, the capital of his native county, until a short time before the outbreak of the war, and had then been at Columbus, as the Legislative correspondent of the *Cincinnati Gazette.* This led him to familiarity with the Southern uprising in Ohio, the development of the volunteer forces, the organization of volunteer camps, the plans of the Governor, etc. At the close of the Legislative session he became city editor of the *Gazette*, but within a few weeks was detached to accompany the first force sent into West Virginia. He joined General Thomas A. Morris, an old regular army officer who had been recalled to the service, and assigned to the command of the column operating from Grafton, by way of Philippi, on Laurel Hill. There were no quarters provided for a war correspondent in those early days, but General Morris, who knew all about young Reid, immediately appointed him a volunteer aide on his staff, gave him a sword and a fatigue cap, a tent at his headquarters, and a place in the mess, and told him that, under ordinary circumstances, he could mind his own business, but whenever needed, he would be called upon for work on the march and battlefield. Aide-de-camp Reid wrote regularly letters to the *Gazette*, over the signature of "Agate;" these graphic letters will be recalled with interest, not only by the West Virginia soldiers, but by the Ohio and Indiana troops as well. These letters were, as a rule, the first source of information about army movements to a great many of the people most keenly interested in them. He went with Morris during the advance on Laurel Hill, in pursuit of Garnett's flying army, and was in the fight when they were overtaken at Carrick's Ford, where Garnett fell while trying to rally his rear guard. Garnett had been a class-mate and room-mate, at West Point, of Major John Love, who was then Chief of Morris' staff. At Love's request, Morris detailed Aide Reid to accompany Garnett's body with a couple of cavalrymen through the intervening 30 miles to Rowlesburg, in the Cheat River country, whence it was sent by express to Governor Letcher, at Richmond.

Soon after this event Aide-de-camp Reid was sent to join General Rosecrans, who appointed him (Reid) to a similar position on his staff. It was at this time, at Clarksburg, that the author met Whitelaw Reid; both of whom were then enjoying the young romance of a struggle which soon ceased to be either young or romantic.

Reid continued to write letters for the same paper over the same signature about the next campaign, which resulted in the march of Rosecrans from Clarksburg to the Gauley, and in the sharp fight with Floyd and Wise, which ended in driving them from their intrenchments at Carnifex Ferry. In this action Aide-de-camp Reid carried the order from Rosecrans to Gen'l H. W. Benham, commanding the advance brigade, which led to the advance upon the intrenchments, in which Col. John W. Lowe, 12th Ohio Infantry, was killed. Colonel Lowe was the first Ohio field officer killed in the war; he fell at the head of his regiment, pierced through the forehead by the bullet from a sharpshooter's squirrel rifle. "Aide-de-camp" and "Correspondent" Reid remained with General Rosecrans in the Kanawha until the setting in of winter seemed to indicate the close of active military operations, when he tendered the resignation of his complimentary commission to General Rosecrans, that he might resume the more active duties of the pen.

The *Cincinnati Commercial* was more radical than the *Gazette*, and its utterances at the time tended to excite the passions of the already inflamed Union feeling among the soldiers.   The name of Murat Halstead, the editor, was as notorious for its intense loyalty to the Union, as was that of Horace Greeley, and the *Cincinnati Commercial* ranked in its loyalty with the *New York Tribune*, *Philadelphia Press* and *Chicago Tribune*.

Col. W. D. Bickham, of the *Cincinnati Commercial*, held a position to that paper corresponding to that held by Whitelaw Reid, of the *Gazette*. Bickham was the war correspondent of the *Commercial*, and was also made an aide-de-camp upon the staff of General Rosecrans.   He left Rosecrans along with Reid, and resumed his duties on the *Commercial*.   Colonel Bickham, after the war, purchased the *Dayton, O., Journal*, which he conducted with great energy and usefulness until his death.

The *Baltimore American*, another welcome visitor to the homes of the loyalists, and to the soldiers in the field, is well remembered by the author. Whilst conservative in tone, it gave a loyal support to the Government.   Mr C. C. Fulton, the manager and editor, was very close to President Lincoln and his cabinet, and enjoyed opportunities for obtaining valuable information accorded to few newspaper men.

CHAPTER XXI.

THE BALTIMORE AND OHIO RAILROAD AND ITS RELATIONS TO THE UNION.

The Bond Between the Government and the B. & O. Railroad Little Understood.—The Services of the Road of Inestimable Value to the Government.—The Mad Rush of Companies, Regiments and Brigades from the West to the Support of the National Capital Conveyed over this Single Track Road.—The Destruction of this Road Sought by the Confederates During the Entire War, and their Success would have Prolonged the War.—President John W. Garrett the Master-hand that Kept the Road in Operation and Held it for the Union.—Ably Assisted by Mr. King and Mr. W. Prescott Smith.—Stonewall Jackson Captures many Locomotives and other Rolling Stock and Conveys same to Southern Roads.—Mr. Garrett Consults with the Authorities at Washington when that City was Threatened with Capture.—Confederates from Winchester Demand from Mr. Garrett a Guarantee that National Troops should not Pass over the Road.—Harper's Ferry Abandoned by Confederates, and the Great Bridge Destroyed.—Great Destruction of the Road from Harper's Ferry to Grafton.—Riot in Baltimore on the 19th of April.—Enemies of the B. & O. Road other than Confederates.—The Pennsylvania Railroad and its Unwarranted Charges.—President Garrett Victorious.

PERHAPS there is no incident of the late war, properly within the scope of this work, so little understood as the relation to the Union of the Baltimore and Ohio Railroad. Indeed, there are few persons who are aware of any relation between the road and the Government. What service, will be asked, can a private corporation have performed to warrant so extended reference in a record of the late war? A corporation whose very purpose is one of peace—to carry passengers and transport freight from point to point. What can such a corporation have had to do with the conclusion of a civil war? It is believed that the following pages will justify the opinion that the services of this road were of inestimable value to the Government in its operations—not only along the line of the road, but its influence was far-reaching, and extended from the capital of the nation to all parts where troops and supplies were required. The reader must, therefore, remember these two leading facts: 1st, that railroad lines and water courses are essential in handling armies; 2d, that the Baltimore and Ohio Railroad was by far the most important road that figured in that great struggle. The road occupied a geographical position that can justly be termed the principal theatre of military operations of the war, and its stage settings contemplate the scenes of conflict of the contending armies in Maryland, Virginia, West Virginia, Tennessee, Kentucky and Missouri. For more than four years this single track road was the artery that conveyed the mad rush of the companies, regiments and brigades from the west to the support of the capital of the nation, and in turn would reconvey them, as necessity required, to fields of battle all along the border states.

During the entire war, from its inception to its close, this road was the objective point—the goal towards which the Confederacy bent its greatest energies, the destruction of which inspired its armies to deeds of gallantry and heroic endurance.

Admitting, then, the fact of the favorable geographical position of the road, and the importance which both the Unionists and the dis-Unionists assigned to it, let us pause to inquire, What would have been the result had the road fallen into the hands of the Secessionists? or, suppose the officers of the road had been disloyal to the Government, and had aided and abetted the cause of the Secessionists; we believe, had such conditions obtained, the war would undoubtedly have been greatly prolonged, if not materially changed in its results. Having noted the favorable geographical location of the road, let us next inquire as to who dictated the policy which made the road a weapon of aggression in the hands of the Government, who was it that determined the destiny of the road—controlled its splendid management, and determined that it should stand for, and not against the Union? For this was a service, in kind if not degree, as patriotic and as honorable as commanding the forces of the Government on the field. The personality that determined the policy of the B. & O. R. R. was President John W. Garrett, this was the master-hand that opened the throttle-lever of her engines and sped them on their patriotic work.

There were few men, if any, that stood so pre-eminently high in the councils of the nation—who rendered such inestimable service in advancing the best interests of the Government. He was one of Mr. Lincoln's trusted advisors; his relations to the President and Secretary of War Stanton were of the closest character. He was as much a part of Mr. Lincoln's Cabinet as any man in it, and was often called to Cabinet councils when questions of grave moment were to be discussed. He was at once advisor to the President, A.-de-C. to the Secretary of War, and to several commanding generals, besides manager in every detail of the Baltimore and Ohio Railroad. It is true that Mr. Garrett was ably assisted, especially by the services of Mr. King, 1st Vice-President, and by Mr. Wm. Prescott Smith, Master of Transportation, and by others; but it was, after all, a question of command and execution. When we take into consideration the fact that for four years contending armies, and occasional raids by the Confederates swept across the road, frequently many miles of track being torn up, bridges, culverts, and rolling stock destroyed, we marvel at the rapidity with which such damages to plant were repaired.

But such was the energy and foresight of President Garrett, that, when such disasters did occur (they having been anticipated by Mr. Garrett), his provision for repair was so complete that oftentimes the repair was made in less time than it required the enemy to inflict the damage. Duplicate bridges, etc., were always on hand, and a damage done one day would be repaired by the following day. The first loss of importance to the main stem of the road occurred about the middle of May, 1861, while "Stonewall" Jackson was in command at Harper's Ferry. General J. D. Imboden, C. S. A., in "Battles and Leaders of the Civil War," recites what he terms a bit of strategy which "Stonewall" Jackson practiced. He says : "From the very beginning of the war the Confederacy was greatly in need of rolling-stock for the railroads. We were particularly short of locomotives, and were without the shops to build them. Jackson, appreciating this, hit upon a plan to obtain a good supply from the Baltimore and Ohio Road. Its line was double-tracked, at least from Point of Rocks to Martinsburg, a distance of 25 or 30 miles. We had not interfered with the running of trains, except on the occasion of the arrest of General Harney. The coal traffic from Cumberland was immense, as the Washington Government was accumulating supplies of coal on the seaboard. These coal trains passed Harper's Ferry at all hours of the day and night, and thus furnished Jackson with a pretext for arranging a brilliant 'scoop.' When he sent me to Point of Rocks, he ordered Colonel Harper with the 5th Va. Infantry to Martinsburg. He then complained to President Garrett, of the Baltimore and Ohio, that the night trains, eastward bound, disturbed the repose of his camp, and requested a change of schedule that would pass all east-bound trains by Harper's Ferry between 11 and 1 o'clock in the daytime. Mr. Garrett complied, and thereafter for several days we heard the constant roar of passing trains for an hour before and an hour after noon. But since the 'empties' were sent up the road at night, Jackson again complained that the nuisance was as great as ever, and, as the road had two tracks, said he must insist that the west-bound trains should pass during the same two hours as those going east. Mr. Garrett promptly complied, and we then had, for two hours every day, the liveliest road in America.

"One night, as soon as the schedule was working at its best, Jackson sent me an order to take a force of men across to the Maryland side of the river the next day at 11 o'clock, and, letting all west-bound trains pass till 12 o'clock, to allow none to go east, and at 12 o'clock to obstruct the road so that it would require several days to repair it. He ordered the reverse to be done at Martinsburg. Thus he caught all the trains that were going east or west between those points, and these he ran up to Winchester, thirty-two miles on the branch road, where they were safe, and whence they were removed by horse-power to the railway at Strasburg. I do not remember the number of trains captured, but the loss crippled the Baltimore and Ohio Road seriously for some time, and the gain to our scantily-stocked Virginia roads of the same gauge was invaluable." Destructive as this incident proved to be, it did not suggest to Mr. Garrett to fold his hands and permit his road to lie idle. But we find him in communication with the authorities at Washington urging the restoration of his road, and the authorities were ready and willing conferees, for they knew that without the co-operation and aid of the Baltimore and Ohio the Government would seriously be hindered in collecting and transporting the troops and supplies required to maintain its enormous armies.

Washington City was threatened several times with capture, and twice actually surrounded by the Confederate cavalry, when this single-track road would be found equal to the emergency, and President Garrett and his able assistants, with a wisdom and courage overreaching all difficulties, invariably brought relief on time to save the capital. For this splendid service, rendered in defense of the Nation's capital, the entire management of the road is entitled to the fullest measure of praise.

LOYAL TO THE UNION.

Notwithstanding the Confederates, early in the conflict, held the road in their grasp from Harper's Ferry to Grafton, and alternately made overtures of friendly import or threatened destruction if the road did not grant certain demands, still President Garrett ignored their friendship as he disregarded their threats. Through all he was unalterably for the Union, and never lost faith in the ultimate triumph of the Nation's cause.

On the 18th of April, 1861, the day following the adoption of the Ordinance of Secession by the Virginia Convention, some leading Virginians from Winchester came down to Baltimore and demanded from Mr. Garrett guarantees that no National troops or munitions of war should be permitted to pass over the Baltimore and Ohio Railroad. This demand was accompanied by a threat that, if it was not complied with, the Virginians would destroy the magnificent bridge of the road at Harper's Ferry. Mr. Garrett was inflexible, and declined the guarantees demanded of his road.

On the 2d of May, 1861, Lt.-Col. Geo. Deas, Inspector-General, C. S. A., in his official report to General Lee, at Richmond, recommended

JOHN W. GARRETT
President Baltimore & Ohio Railroad

.

" that Harper's Ferry be abandoned, remove machinery, destroy the buildings, blow up the bridge, and move out into the valleys, and thus manœuvre against the advancing enemy ; in addition to which a force should be sent at once up the Baltimore and Ohio Railroad to blow up the tunnels and burn the bridges on Cheat River and otherwise cause such damage to the road as to render impossible the passage of a force from Wheeling or Parkersburg."

On the 13th of June, the threat of the Winchester delegation, and the recommendation of Inspector Deas, was carried out. General Joseph E. Johnston, then in command at Harper's Ferry, destroyed the splendid and costly bridge. Two days later, on the approach of the Union forces under General Robert Patterson near Williamsport, and under Colonel Lew Wallace at Romney, General Johnston, considering the position untenable, withdrew the Confederate army to Winchester.

At the outbreak of the war there was but one railroad connection from the north, east and west, with Washington City, and that the Baltimore and Ohio—a single track road. During the exciting period incident to the 19th of April, 1861, when the 6th Mass. Regiment encountered the mob in Baltimore and all was confusion and dire apprehension at Washington, somehow Mr. Garrett was never at a loss to know just what to do. He was personally acquainted with Mr. Lincoln long before he became President, and when he issued his proclamation, calling for 75,000 troops, Mr. Garrett assured him that every demand on the road should be promptly complied with, notwithstanding the menace of the Virginia authorities. It must be remembered that the destruction of the railroads north and east of Baltimore City during the exciting period of the 19th of April was the work of excited and disloyal officials of Baltimore City and of the State, influenced at the time by a mob, and not by Confederate soldiers.

Enemies of the Baltimore and Ohio Railroad.

The military forces of the South were not the only enemies, nor were they the most dangerous the Baltimore and Ohio Railroad had to contend with. Rival roads, both east and west, it seems, would have sacrificed the capital to have gained a vantage over their successful rival, and their methods were more to be dreaded than were the Confederate soldiery, for they made their attack in secret and by written charges which they could not sustain. It has already been stated that the destruction of bridges on the railroads entering the city of Baltimore was by excited city and State officials, etc.; there could not have been the slightest room for a charge that the officers of the Baltimore and Ohio Railroad had even indirectly been responsible for the destruction of any part of any railroad.

The following extract from a letter written to the Secretary of War is only a specimen of a number of similar letters:

PHILADELPHIA, *April* 23, 1861.

HON. SIMON CAMERON, *Secretary of War.*

Dear Sir:—Since I wrote my last of this date, I have been informed that the Baltimoreans and Marylanders have destroyed the whole of the bridges on the Northern Central. This seems to have been a mere spite action, and must convince the Government that those loyal to the Government in Maryland are in a vast minority. As soon as the capital is safe from attack, it seems to me that the Government should at once turn on Baltimore and place it under martial law, and require that it should pay all damages to the railroads it has destroyed, and to their business.

*   *   *   *   *   *   *   *   *   *   *

The War Department should at once destroy, if it has not already done so, the bridges on the main stem of the Baltimore and Ohio Railroad as high up as Harper's Ferry.

*   *   *   *   *   *   *   *   *   *   *

If you are in want of railway men to control the road (Annapolis branch, via Annapolis Junction), or locomotives or cars to work it, they can immediately be sent down from here, with competent and loyal enginemen.

*   *   *   *   *   *   *   *   *   *   *

Yours truly,   J. EDGAR THOMPSON,
President Penna. Central Railroad.

A rivalry that would assail a competing corporation at such a time, and under such circumstances, can be contemplated with feelings of genuine condemnation. The insinuation that the officers of the Baltimore and Ohio Railroad were disloyal to the Government was entirely unjustifiable, when it was known that the reverse was the case ; for, as early as April, at a regular monthly meeting of the directors of the road, it was officially announced that, thereafter, no person should be appointed to any position, or employed in any capacity by the officers of the company except loyal citizens of the United States. At the same meeting the following order was promulgated: "That the display of the American flag, as heretofore, at prominent stations of the company is hereby approved, and that, as the company regains possession of its road, the National flag shall be displayed at its principal stations and shall so continue until otherwise ordered by the board."

In another letter to Secretary Cameron, of the same date as the one heretofore quoted, Mr. Thompson writes: "Mr. Palmer informs me that you have not taken military possession of the Washington Branch of the Baltimore and Ohio Railroad Company, and the Annapolis Road; if you have no superintendent fit to control such an enterprise, I would mention Joseph D. Potts, now in Baltimore, at the Northern Central Railroad office, and T. H. Duprey, here in Philadelphia."

Perhaps the most complete refutation of the charge of disloyalty made by the rival roads against the B. & O. was the message of Governor Letcher to the Virginia Legislature, at about the same date these charges were made. He said: "The Baltimore and Ohio Railroad has been a positive nuisance to this State, from the opening of the war to the present time, and, unless its management shall hereafter be in friendly hands, and the government under which it exists be a part of our Confederacy, it must be abated. If it should be permanently destroyed, we must assure our people of some other communication with the seaboard." And about the same date a crushing rebuke was administered by President Lincoln to a delegation of Baltimore politicians (who visited him to acquaint him of Mr. Garrett's disloyalty) when he said: "When any of you have done half as much to aid this Government as John W. Garrett, I may consider your request."

Another very potent argument, in which the eastern railroads realized that the B. & O. was not so disloyal after all, was in 1862, when General Lee marched his army into Maryland, and an invasion of Pennsylvania was threatened; the Pennsylvanians learned a very important lesson, which was, that, if the Confederates once became in permanent possession of the B. & O. Road, the Southern army would overrun Pennsylvania and, as a result, her railroads, bridges over the Juniata, the tunnels, depots and shops would fall victims of the Confederacy.

But enough has been written on the subject of disloyalty of the Baltimore and Ohio officials—neither President Garrett or his company were guilty of the charge.

CHAPTER XXII.

LOYALTY OF PRESIDENT JOHN W. GARRETT TO THE UNION, AND HIS CLOSE RELATIONS TO PRESIDENT LINCOLN.

General Patterson's Advance on Williamsport.—Colonel Lew Wallace at Romney.—Magical Rebuilding of the B. & O. Railroad.—Battle of Bull Run Disastrous to the Union Cause. —Blockade of the Potomac and Quantico, Creek by Confederates.—The Emergency gives Scope to the Fertile Resources of President Garrett.—100,000 Men and 60,000 Animals to be Fed.—Damage Inflicted by Confederates.—Early Official Action of the Directors of the Road for the Union.—Records of the War Department Filled with Correspondence between the Executive Mansion, War Department and President Garrett.—Generals Halleck, McClellan, Fremont, Kelley, Crook and Others Communicate with Mr. Garrett.—Strategy of Mr. Garrett in Securing Communication Between the War Department and General Meade at Gettysburg.—Gigantic Achievements of the B. & O. Road in Transporting Troops and Army Supplies from the Army of the Potomac to the Relief of General Rosecrans at Chattanooga, Tenn.—President Garrett's Personal Account of this Great Feat.—Gratitude of Secretary Stanton.—The Final Review at Washington, D. C.—Garrett and Stanton at the Bier of the Martyr President.

MMEDIATELY upon the advance of General Patterson near Williamsport, and of Colonel Wallace at Romney, and upon the withdrawal of General Johnston from Harper's Ferry to Winchester in June, 1861, the Baltimore and Ohio Railroad Company began to rebuild the destroyed portion of its road. And soon thereafter the camp-fires of the Federal troops seemed to burn brighter by reason of the gladsome whistle of the locomotives of the Baltimore and Ohio Road.

Before the completion of these repairs, however, the disastrous battle— to the Union Army—at Bull Run was fought, and the Unionists retreated into Maryland in the immediate vicinity of Washington City, where they remained until March, 1862. The Confederates now saw their opportunity, as they believed, to place Washington City in a state of blockade by erecting batteries on the Potomac, at Quantico Creek and other points, thereby hoping to starve out the Union forces in and around Washington; and they were successful only to the extent of causing a great deal of inconvenience and some suffering to McClellan's Army, which, at this time, amounted to about 100,000 men and 60,000 animals. This emergency gave scope to the fertile resources of President Garrett. This immense army of men and animals must be fed. Our base of supplies was mainly the far west, and the Baltimore and Ohio Road, with its single track traversing a country largely in sympathy with the enemy, was the main avenue through which this immense amount of supplies was to come, but the road proved equal to the emergency. During this critical period Mr. Garrett sacrificed the comforts of his home for Camden Station, where, days and nights, he could be found, taxing his great physical capacity to its fullest endurance in order to provide for this great army of consumers. Supplies poured in from both extremities of the road. From the far west came the products of her farms—horses, mules, flour, corn, meal, lard, bread, beef, pork, clothing, medical stores, etc. From the north and east, by fleets of vessels daily to Locust Point, cargoes of arms of every grade, clothing, boots and shoes, harness, wagons, ambulances, etc., which was shipped over the Washington branch, requiring from 300 to 400 cars daily.

(And in addition to all this, there were periods during the blockade when wagon trains numbering 100 would be sent from Baltimore to Washington in order to supply some urgent necessity.) In order to protect stores, and to guard against the raids of the enemy, nearly every mile of railroad and turnpike was guarded by a soldier.

DAMAGE INFLICTED BY CONFEDERATE SOLDIERS.

The damage sustained during the war to the Baltimore and Ohio Road was enormous. The fine bridge at Harper's Ferry was twice destroyed, the extensive machine-shops and engine-houses at Martinsburg were razed to the ground. In 1862–3 the road sustained its severest losses; 42 locomotives and tenders, 386 cars, 23 bridges, embracing 127 spans and a total length of bridge of 4713 feet, 36 miles of track, the telegraph and water stations for over an hundred miles were totally destroyed. Notwithstanding all this destruction, the business management of President Garrett in transporting troops and supplies was so effective that the directors of the road were able to declare a small dividend. In his annual report for 1863, Mr. Garrett said: "It is gratifying and proper to inform the stockholders that the first six months of the fiscal year presented a large and profitable traffic, and that notwithstanding the interruption of its business and immense destruction of its property and the grave and varied embarrassments complicating the management, the board have been able to meet all the engagements of the company, and expect to continue to maintain its credit and financial position at that high and reliable standard so important to all the great interests involved."

The records of the War Department are filled with the correspondence between the Executive Mansion and the War Department and President Garrett. We also find him in communication with Generals Halleck, McClellan, Fremont, Kelley, Hooker, Crook and many other commanding generals. It was no uncommon occurrence to find Mr. Garrett the first to convey information of the approach of the enemy to the Federal authorities, and his suggestions as to the probable intentions of the enemy and his recommendations as to the placement of the Union forces were always considered of the greatest importance. Indeed, his ready knowledge of military matters was wonderful for one who had not received a military training. This aptness in President Garrett, in connection with his duties as manager of his railroad, was the secret of his frequent calls to Washington for consultation by the President and Secretary Stanton, notably such instances as the critical times when the troops in the Shenandoah Valley were hurried to Washington after the second battle of Bull Run ; again, when Banks was being driven from the valley by Stonewall Jackson ; again, when the 11th and 12th Corps were transferred from the Army of the Potomac to the west to the relief of Rosecrans, and when Early was threatening Washington via Monocacy, and when Sheridan at Winchester called for the 19th Army Corps. An incident that illustrated Mr. Garrett's versatility to provide means in cases of great emergency is given here, as possessing special interest. During the Gettysburg campaign in 1863, when that place was surrounded by General Lee's army, the railroads and the telegraph wires were destroyed in every direction around Gettysburg, and there was no easy means of communication between Washington and General Meade, Commander of the Union forces and his army. After an interview between Secretary Stanton and Mr. Garrett the following telegrams, via Baltimore, will explain how these two officials overcame the difficulty, and brought General Meade in ready communication with Washington.

BALTIMORE, MD., *July*, 1, 1863.
(Received 8.30 *P. M.)*

HON. E. M. STANTON, *Secretary of War.*

I have conferred with the acting Superintendent of the Northern Central Railroad, Mr. Young, and with Superintendent Shoemaker of the Express Company. I have arranged that a locomotive be started from Bolton Station at 9 this P. M., and that express company will send by that engine 12 active horses for service between Westminster and General Meade's headquarters ; the messengers also go on this train. Will you have your first message at telegraph office, Bolton, by that hour? The parties will arrange that an engine shall leave Baltimore and Westminster, respectively, every three hours, waiting, however, with fast engine at Westminster for the reply to the despatch which you may now send, unless you instruct otherwise. Mr. Young states that the Western Maryland Railroad is very deficient in sidings, but has promised, after full discussion of the difficulty, to do all that is practicable, and hopes fully to accomplish your wishes. Should you prefer a later hour for starting, please so direct.

J. W. GARRETT, *President.*

WAR DEPARTMENT, *July* 1, 1863.—11.24 P. M.
JOHN W. GARRETT, ESQ., BALTIMORE.

You will please accept thanks of this Department for your energetic and successful arrangements for communicating with General Meade. They are entirely satisfactory. General Halleck has availed himself of the facilities you provided.

EDWIN M. STANTON, *Secretary of War.*

To mention in detail the many incidents in which President Garrett and the Baltimore and Ohio Road performed conspicuous service would fill a book containing more pages than this volume contemplates. A single episode in the history of the road in the war will, however, illustrate, and we shall take for the purpose the removal of the 11th and 12th Corps from the Army of the Potomac to Chattanooga, Tennessee, in September, 1863.

The history of this marvelous *feat* in transporting an army which had not been excelled in this or any other country, is this: General Rosecrans had been defeated in the battle of September 19th and 20th at Chickamauga by General Bragg's army, but Rosecrans had gained Chattanooga, recently abandoned by Bragg. The Confederates having been reinforced, General Bragg held the key to the outlet of Chattanooga. The Government at Washington had grave apprehensions that Rosecrans would abandon Chattanooga and attempt a retreat, which, it was conceded, would be not only a mistake, but a positive calamity to Rosecrans' army. Prof. Draper, in his "History of the Civil War," says: "At a consultation President Lincoln seemed almost in despair. 'I advise' said Stanton 'that a powerful detachment should be sent from the Army of the Potomac to open the road.' Lincoln smiled incredulously; Halleck considered such an attempt impracticable. 'I do not,' said the Secretary of War, 'offer you this opinion without first having thoroughly informed myself of all the details. I will undertake to move 20,000 men from the Army of the Rapidan and place them on the Tennessee, near Chattanooga, within nine days.' Not without reluctance did Lincoln give his consent that the 11th and 12th Corps should be moved." And this is how it was done :

WAR DEPARTMENT,
WASHINGTON, D. C., *September* 23, 1863—11.15 P. M.
JOHN W. GARRETT, ESQ., BALTIMORE.
Please come to Washington as quick as you can, and bring Smith with you.
EDWIN M. STANTON.

CAMDEN STATION, BALTIMORE, *September* 24, 1863.
(*Received* 8.25 *A. M.*)
HON E. M. STANTON.
I am on 8 o'clock train from Baltimore, and expect to be at Department at 10 o'clock with our master of transportation ; have arranged for full information regarding engines and cars.* J. W. GARRETT.

*We do not find any record of it, but the most plausible inference is that Secretary Stanton and President Garrett had been in consultation prior to this summons, else why should the Secretary of War (as just mentioned by Prof. Draper) have spoken so confidently as "having thoroughly informed himself." And Mr. Garrett as fully admits it, when, in his reply, he says : "I have arranged for full information regarding engines and cars."
T. F. L.

Mr. Garrett's summons was evidently to attend a Cabinet meeting, which subsequent events show was a full one, and, in addition to the Cabinet, were several army officers. The official telegrams sent out that day (Sept. 24th) following the Cabinet meeting were numerous, and indicate that the movement had been definitely decided upon. The 11th and 12th Corps of Meade's Army of the Potomac were ordered to proceed at once. The two corps were placed under the command of Maj.-General Hooker. The transfer of this army by Mr. Garrett westward to the Tennessee was accomplished with marvelous expedition, and to do this it was necessary to connect diverging railroads by improvised tracks; he built temporary bridges across large rivers, passed through a half dozen states, and although accompanied by its artillery, trains, baggage, and animals, this army moved from the Rapidan in Virginia to Stevenson in Alabama, a distance of 1192 miles, in seven days, crossing the Ohio River twice.

The following interesting account from the ready pen of J. Thomas Scharf, Esq., will no doubt be read with interest:

The real facts attending this transfer of troops were given to the writer by the late John W. Garrett in an interview at the Southern Hotel in St. Louis, May 20, 1882.

" On that occasion," said Mr. Garrett, " I was summoned by telegraph to Washington city and responded in person, having made the run in 52 minutes by special train. Repairing to the Executive Mansion I was invited to attend a Cabinet meeting, at which there were present, as I now recall the scene, Generals Halleck and Hooker and several others, besides the President and and his full Cabinet. The subject under discussion, I was informed, was the possibility of transferring two army corps, numbering between 25,000 and 30,000 men, from the east to the west, in time to be made available for the assistance and relief of Rosecrans at Chattanooga, and as the Cabinet officers of the army present could not settle the question of transportation and time, they had summoned me.

" I arrived at the very moment when they were at issue as to the possibility of making so large a transfer in so short a time. In response to their questions, I replied that I could put 30,000 men in Louisville, Ky., in ten days, provided I was clothed with absolute power over the whole route, as well as all military authority, not even excepting that of General Halleck, then general-in-chief; that the lines of railroad and telegraph should be under my sole control and command, and should be protected at night at threatened points with lanterns to warn the approach of any danger; that no military officer should give any order not subject to my control, and that I be empowered **to seize and run cars, stop the mail and passenger trains, government freights** and all other trains upon the road; that further authority be given me to seize wagons, lumber, and impress men on the Ohio river for the purpose of building a bridge.

FIGHTING JOE HOOKER'S CAMPAIGN.

"The Secretary of War, who was much pleased at the prospect of accomplishing this great feat of transportation contrary to the expressed opinion of General Halleck, replied that he would grant me everything and hold me responsible for success. General Hooker, who was to command the expedition, replied that while he had great respect for me personally, he would not, as long as he held the rank of major-general, become the subordinate of any civilian, and that he would there and then tender the resignation of his commission if any such authority was to be given to me. I replied that it was only with such authority that I would be responsible for the success of the movement, and that without that authority I would not attempt the transfer of so many troops in such a short time.

"It was because I knew that absolute authority over every appliance for the movement, as well as every man to be moved, was necessary, that I insisted on dictatorial powers. That I was not mistaken was made apparent at the very outset of the movement, when it became necessary to threaten several colonels with arrest and report to the War Department for slowness in movement and disposition to retard and embarrass the transfer; and again, at Grafton, a train was stopped by telegraph from a general officer until he could catch up with his command. Such interference, you can see, would have been fatal to the operations of a movement of 30,000 men over more than 1000 miles along a single-track railroad, as well as dangerous to the lives of large numbers.

"Mr. Stanton settled the matter with General Hooker in a private interview, upon returning from which he asked me to recommend four men of prominence for appointment as captains on the staff of General Hooker.

"Clothed with full power over men, material and railroad, I repaired to Camden Station, Baltimore, and there took up my abode, and did not leave the station, except to go to Washington, for five days, sleeping in my chair when I could and eating at the depot as opportunity offered. I dispatched Mr. Wilson, master of transportation, to the Ohio river, with power to seize flatboats and lumber and to construct a bridge over the river to be in readiness for the first train of cars that arrived with troops; and when, on the third day of my labor, I repaired to Washington to attend a Cabinet meeting, I was met by Mr. Stanton and General Halleck with the remark: 'Well, you have failed! It is impossible to have the bridge completed over the Ohio before the troops arrive there on the cars!' I was surprised, and almost confused. Something, I thought, had gone wrong or been omitted, and yet I could not think where or by whom the error or omission had been made. However, while the discussion was going on, we were interrupted by the hurried entrance of a messenger with a dispatch for me, announcing the completion of the bridge and the passage of the troops without the least delay.

"The entire two corps were landed safely in Louisville within the time stipulated by me, without accident or injury."

SECRETARY STANTON'S GRATITUDE.

WAR DEPARTMENT,
WASHINGTON CITY, *September* 27, 1863.—6.40 P. M.
JOHN W. GARRETT, ESQ., BALTIMORE.

I have only to say that all your proceedings are cordially approved, and the energy and skill manifested by you and your assistants and subordinates receives the admiration and thanks so well merited.

EDWIN M. STANTON, *Secretary of War.*

Colonel D. C. McCullum, United States Military Superintendent of Railroads, did not hesitate to say "that, in his judgment, this was by all question the most important and most successful transportation movement ever conducted in this country, and, so far as he was aware, had not been excelled in the military annals of Europe. For his services upon this occasion Mr. Garrett received the grateful thanks of President Lincoln and his Cabinet." The author regrets that limited space will not permit a more extended mention of this interesting railway—war history. It is proper, however, to say that President Garrett and the Baltimore and Ohio road continued to be a military necessity to the Union cause until the close of the war. To President Garrett, more than any one military officer, is due the preservation of the Capital during Early's and Breckenridge's raid in 1864.

The removal of the 23d Army Corps in January, 1865, from the Western Army at Eastport, Miss., to Washington City, was an achievement equal to the transportation of the 11th and 12th corps, heretofore described.

On the last day of May, 1865, after the review at Washington, the Baltimore and Ohio was called upon to convey to their homes the immense number of 120,000 men, a million pounds of baggage, 1100 horses, all of which were safely transported within a fortnight to their destination. The friendly relations between President Lincoln and President Garrett remained unbroken to the last, and when the assassin's bullet took the life of the lamented Lincoln, his faithful friends and co-workers, Garrett and Stanton, were unfeigned mourners at the bier of the great and good martyr.

CHAPTER XXIII.

FIRST REGIMENT W. VA. CAVALRY VOLUNTEERS.

Roster of the Field, Staff and Company Officers of the First Regiment West Virginia Cavalry Volunteers, Showing the Alterations and Casualties Therein from the Date of Original Organization of Said Regiment to the Date of Muster Out, July 8, 1865.

Date of Commission.	Names and Rank.	Co.	Remarks.
	Colonels.		
Sept. 7, 1861.	Henry Anisansal,		Resigned August 6, 1862.
Oct. 16, 1863.	N. P. Richmond,		Resigned March 18, 1863, re-commissioned June 12, 1863, again resigned Nov. 7, 1863.
Dec. 23, 1863.	Henry Capehart,		Brevetted Major-General.
	Lieutenant-Colonels.		
Sept. 7, 1861.	N. P. Richmond,		Promoted to Colonel.
Oct. 16, 1862.	John S. Krepps,		Resigned May 22, 1863.
June 16, 1863.	Joseph Darr, Jr.,		Resigned July 3, 1864.
Aug. 1, 1864.	Charles E. Capehart,		
	Majors.		
Sept. 30, 1861.	John S. Krepps,		Promoted to Lieutenant-Colonel.
Sept. 25, 1861.	Joseph Darr, Jr.,		Promoted to Lieutenant-Colonel.
Nov. 11, 1861.	Benj. F. Chamberlain,		Resigned Oct. 1863.
Dec. 8, 1862.	Josiah Steele,		Died of wounds received in action.
June 6, 1863.	Charles E. Capehart,		Promoted to Lieutenant-Colonel.
Aug. 12, 1863.	Harvey Farrabee,		Mustered out at expiration of term of service.
Nov. 25, 1865.	William C. Carman,		Mustered out on account of wounds received in action.
	1st Lts. and Adj'ts.		
Oct. 1, 1861.	Christopher C. Krepps,		Promoted to Captain, Co. F.
Feb. 20, 1862.	David Mequillet,		Promoted to Captain, Co H.
Jan. 1863.	Sidney W. Knowles,		Killed in action at Gettysburg.
Aug. 12, 1863.	Richard B. Sowers,		Resigned October 30, 1864.
Feb. 9, 1865.	Frank C. Robinson.		
	1st Lts. and R. Q. M.		
Oct. 4, 1861.	William Fleming,		Resigned January 6, 1862.
Dec. 7, 1861.	Thomas Bensall,		Resigned July 1, 1862.
July 19, 1862.	S. C. W. Dunlevy.		
	1st Lts. and Reg. Com.		
Nov. 3, 1862.	Henry C. Durritt,		Promoted to Captain, Co. A
Feb. 23, 1865.	Adam C. Woodcock.		
	Surgeons.		
Sept. 18, 1861.	Henry Capehart,		Promoted to Colonel.
Feb. 2, 1864.	Perrin Gardner.		

Date of Commission.	Names and Rank.	Co.	Remarks.
	Assistant Surgeons.		
Sept. 30, 1861.	Hiram D. Enochs,		Resigned July 10, 1862.
Oct. 6. 1861.	John R. Nickel,		Never joined Regiment for duty.
July 19, 1862.	Perrin Gardner,		Promoted to Surgeon.
Feb. 11, 1864.	Arthur Titus,		Promoted to Surgeon, 3d W. Va. Cavalry.
Feb. 14, 1864.	Zachariah A. White.		
	Chaplains.		
Oct. 21, 1861.	David Truman,		Resigned July 17, 1862.
Oct. 10, 1862.	F. W. Vertican,		Resigned Oct. 1863.
Nov. 28, 1863.	David Truman.		
	Captains.		
Oct. 2, 1861.	J. Lowrie MeGee,	A	Promoted to Major, 3d W. Va. Cavalry.
April 2, 1863.	Harrison H. Hagans,	A	
Sept. 25, 1861.	Harvey Farrabee,	B	Promoted to Major.
Aug. 12, 1863.	Hugh P. Boone,	B	
Sept. 28, 1861.	Isaiah Hill,	C	Resigned April 21, 1862.
May 28, 1862.	Hoffman Atkinson,	C	Resigned July 19, 1862.
June 30, 1862.	William C. Mullen,	C	Dismissed Oct. 14, 1862.
Jan. 12, 1863.	William A. McCoy,	C	Resigned November 7, 1864.
Dec. 18, 1864.	Francis M. Work,	C	
Oct. 3, 1861.	William C. Carman,	D	Promoted to Major.
Feb. 3, 1864.	Earl W. Shaffer,	D	Dismissed May 18, 1865.
Nov. 1861.	William N. Harris,	E	Killed in action at Gettysburg.
Aug. 12, 1863.	Newberry W. Wheeler,	E	
Oct. 16, 1861.	Robert Ward,	F	Resigned Dec. 27, 1861.
Feb. 20, 1862.	Christopher C. Krepps,	F	Dismissed Jany. 21, 1863.
Nov. 25, 1863.	William P. Wilkin,	F	Resigned February 27, 1865.
Oct. 7, 1861.	Thomas Winters,	G	Resigned June 30, 1862.
June 30, 1862.	Josiah Steele,	G	Promoted to Major.
Jan. 6, 1863.	John A. Byers,	G	Mustered out at expiration of term of service.
Sept. 28, 1861.	Isaac P. Kerr,	H	Resigned September 30, 1862.
Jany. 12, 1863.	David Mequillet,	H	Honorably discharged, on account of wounds received in action.
May 15, 1865.	Wilmon W. Blackmar,	H	
Oct. 16, 1861.	William A. West,	I	Resigned April 22, 1862.
May 22, 1862.	William B. Harrison,	I	Resigned March 1, 1863.
April 1, 1863.	Dennis Delaney,	I	Killed in action at Wytheville, Va.
Sept. 23, 1863.	Walter A. Powell,	I	Honorably discharged.
Feb. 9, 1865.	Henry C. Durritt,	I	
Oct. 2, 1861.	Weston Rowand,	K	Mustered out at expiration of term of service.
Feb. 7, 1865.	Fabricius A. Cather,	K	
Nov. 16, 1861.	Jocob S. Shuman,	L	Resigned June 21, 1862.
Aug. 11, 1862.	John S. Cunningham,	L	Resigned February 7, 1863.
June 6, 1863.	John Seltzer,	L	Mustered out January 8, 1865.
Feb. 23, 1865,	John J. McDonald,	L	
Oct. 19. 1861.	John Hess,	M	Resigned March 4, 1862.
Aug. 12, 1863.	S. B. Howe,	M	Killed in action at Appomattox C. H.

Date of Commission.	Name and Rank.	Co.	Remarks.
	Captains.		
June 11, 1862.	Thos. H. Reeves,	N	Resigned July 4, 1862.
Nov. 25, 1863.	James Dean,	N	
	First Lieutenants.		
Oct. 2, 1861.	George H. King,	A	Resigned December 5th, 1861.
Dec. 27, 1861.	Harrison H. Hagans.	A	Promoted to Captain.
April 3, 1862.	Jacob Jennewine,	A	Resigned October 1, 1862.
Oct. 16, 1862.	Nimrod N. Hoffman,	A	Mustered out at expiration of term of service.
Nov. 12, 1864.	Thomas H. B. Lemley,	A	
Sep. 25, 1861.	Parker Ackley,	B	Resigned April 22, 1862.
May 13, 1862.	Arthur S. Palmer,	B	Transferred to Co. C.
Jany. 12, 1864.	Hugh P. Boone,	B	Promoted to Captain.
Aug. 12, 1863.	Samuel Grim,	B	Resigned Feb. 26, 1865.
Sep. 28, 1861.	Josiah Steel,	C	Promoted to Captain, Co. G.
June 30, 1862.	William A. McCoy,	C	Promoted to Captain.
Jany. 12, 1863.	Maxwell Carroll,	C	Transferred to Co. F.
May 13, 1862.	Arthur S. Palmer,	C	Resigned November 16, 1863.
Jan. 29, 1864.	Francis M. Work,	C	Promoted to Captain.
Dec. 18, 1864.	William H. Foulke,	C	
Oct. 3, 1861.	Earl W. Shaffer,	D	Resigned September 29, 1862.
Nov. 11, 1862.	A. W. Richardson,	D	Dismissed July 10, 1863.
Feb. 3, 1864.	Charles A. Armstrong,	D	
Nov. 18, 1861.	Newberry W. Wheeler,	E	Promoted to Captain.
Nov. 25, 1863.	Joseph Humphrey,	E	Mustered out at expiration of term of service.
Oct. 16, 1861.	Augustus Norton,	F	Resigned July 10, 1862.
Jan. 12, 1863.	Maxwell Carroll,	F	Resigned on account of wounds received in action.
Aug. 12, 1863.	William P. Wilkin,	F	Promoted to Captain.
Nov. 25, 1863.	Stephen Malone,	F	
Oct. 7, 1861.	William E. Feazel,	G	Resigned June 21, 1862.
June 20, 1862.	William St. Clair,	G	Mustered out at expiration of term of service.
Sept. 28, 1861.	Archibald Skiles,	H	Resigned June 30, 1862.
Dec. 11, 1862.	James F. Poole,	H	Dismissed January 10, 1863.
Feb. 8, 1864.	Harry W. Fuller,	H	Resigned February 24, 1865.
Oct. 16, 1861.	Horatio N. Mackey,	I	Resigned April 23, 1862.
June 26, 1862.	Walter A. Powell,	I	Promoted to Captain.
Jan. 6, 1863.	William E. Guseman,	I	Died of wounds received in action.
June 8, 1865.	Benjamin F. Sapp,	I	
Oct. 2, 1861.	Charles D. Lawsen,	K	Deserted May 14, 1863.
Aug. 12, 1863.	Anderson Dawson,	K	Dismissed February 18, 1864.
March 11, 1864.	Fabricius A. Cather,	K	Promoted to Captain.
Feb. 23, 1865.	William Golden,	K	
Nov. 16, 1861.	John S. Cunningham,	L	Promoted to Captain.
Aug. 11, 1862.	John Seltzer,	L	Promoted to Captain.
Aug. 12, 186s.	John T. McDonald,	L	Promoted to Captain.
Oct. 19, 1861.	John Geyer,	M	Resigned December 11, 1861.
Dec. 17, 1861.	Robert W. Playford,	M	Resigned February 28, 1862.

Date of Commission.	Names and Rank.	Co.	Remarks.
	First Lieutenants.		
June 30, 1862.	Henry Guesather,	M	Resigned Aug. 3, 1862.
Dec. 11, 1862,	S. B. Howe,	M	Promoted to Captain.
Aug. 12, 1863.	Gottlieb Wipf,	M	
June 11, 1862.	Joseph H. Wilson,	N	Dismissed August 10, 1863.
Nov. 25. 1863.	Samuel B. Paxton,	N	
	Second Lieutenants.		
Oct. 2, 1861.	Jacob Jennewine,	A	Promoted to 1st Lieutenant.
Oct. 3, 1862.	Nimrod N. Hoffman,	A	Promoted to 1st Lieutenant.
Oct. 16, 1862.	John H. Conn,	A	Mustered out at expiration of term of service.
Sep. 25, 1861.	Hugh P. Boone,	B	Promoted to 1st Lieutenant.
Jan. 12, 1863.	W. W. Wilson,	B	Resigned Jannary 1, 1865.
Feb. 23, 1865.	James P. Allum,	B	
Sep. 28, 1861.	William C. Mullen,	C	Promoted to Captain.
June 30, 1862.	George W. Chandler,	C	
Oct. 3, 1861.	Chas. A. Armstrong,	D	Promoted to 1st Lieutenant.
Feb. 3, 1864.	Eugene Gallaher,	D	
Nov. 18, 1861.	Sidney W. Knowles,	E	Promoted to 1st Lieutenant and Adj't.
Jan. 12, 1863.	Hiram Robinett,	E	Resigned October 28, 1863.
March 14, 1864.	Arthur S. Palmer,	E	Honorably discharged.
March 22, 1865.	Coza G. Walsh,	E	
Oct. 16, 1861.	Samuel Lyda,	F	Transferred to Co. H.
Dec. 11, 1862.	William H. Allen,	F	Resigned March 4, 1863.
Dec. 18, 1864.	William Saunders,	F	
Oct. 7, 1861.	Willliam H. Shanley,	G	Resigned April 26, 1863,
May 28, 1862.	John A. Byer's,	G	Promoted to Captain.
Jan. 12, 1863.	Irwin C. Swintzel,	G	Deceased.
Aug. 12, 1863.	John McNaughton,	G	Mustered out at expiration of term of service.
Sep. 28, 1861.	William H. Murphy,	H	Resigned July 4, 1862.
Oct. 16, 1861.	Samuel Lyda,	H	Mustered out August 31, 1862.
Oct. 17, 1862.	Henry J. Leasure,	H	Resigned April 6, 1864.
April 8, 1864.	Wilmon W. Blackmar,	H	Promoted to Captain.
Oct. 16, 1861.	Dennis Delaney,	I	Promoted to Captain.
April 1, 1863,	Charles H. Livingston,	I	
Jan. 23, 1864.	Benjamin F. Sapp,	K	Promoted to 1st Lieutenant
Oct. 2, 1861.	Anderson Dawson,	K	Promoted to 1st Lieutenant.
Aug. 12, 1863.	John Smith,	K	Killed in action, June 20, 1864.
Dec. 18, 1864.	William Golden,	K	Promoted to 1st Lieutenant.
Sep. 10, 1864.	Isaac N. Fordyce,	K	
Nov. 16, 1861.	John Seltzer,	L	Promoted to 1st Lieutenant.
Aug. 11, 1862.	John J. McDonald.	L	Promoted to 1st Lieutenant.
March 1, 1864.	Sylvester W. Donley,	L	Killed in action, near Winchester.
Feb. 20, 1865.	John W. Glendening,	L	
Oct. 19, 1861.	Henry Guenther,	M	Promoted to 1st Lieutenant.
June 30, 1862.	Gottlieb Wipf,	M	Promoted to 1st Lieutenant.
March 22, 1865.	Jacob E. Israel,	M	
June 11, 1862.	S. B. Howe,	N	Promoted to 1st Lieutenant.
March 4, 1864.	Charles B. Smith,	N	

Regimental History.

Dr. Henry Capehart, whose portrait appears in these pages, is by birth and education a Pennsylvanian, born in the county of Cambria, March 18, 1825. He located as a physician in Bridgeport, Ohio, in September, 1849, from whence he entered the military service, and was commissioned surgeon of the First West Virginia Cavalry, September 10, 1861. He was a fine horseman, and an ardent admirer of the noble animal.

The regiment was recruited from the western counties of Pennsylvania, eastern Ohio, and western Virginia, at a time when the Government was not organizing cavalry regiments. It was composed of superior material, mostly young men from the farms, experienced horsemen and marksmen, who could break and tame the wildest colt, or pierce the head of a squirrel in the top of the tallest hickory with a rifle-bullet. When the regiment entered the field mounted and equipped, with its complement of field, staff and line officers, and led by Prof. Carl Colby's famous silver cornet band, all mounted on milk-white horses, the regiment well caparisoned, with jingling and flapping trappings, the riders all young and handsome, it was as beautiful and inspiring an organization as ever graced the armies of the United States. This the citizens of Clarksburg, Cumberland, Martinsburg and Winchester will no doubt cordially admit, though the uniforms may not have been of their favorite color.

Its first active service was in the mountains of West Virginia, by detachments, scouting and doing picket and outpost duty to the various infantry commands holding the mountain passes and guarding the Baltimore and Ohio Railroad. These duties in the wild, mountainous region, infested with Confederate scouts, guerillas and bushwhackers, soon developed in the officers and men that individuality, courage and daring which distinguished them throughout the period of their service.

In the spring of 1862, it was brigaded with other cavalry regiments, under the command of General Hatch, and participated in the operations in the valley of the Shenandoah and its neighborhood under Generals Shields, Banks, McDowell, Schenck and Fremont, though some of the companies were separated. Capt. C. C. Krepps, with a company of the regiment, put the enemy's cavalry, panic stricken, to flight, and gained possession of the bridge at Port Republic, and but for orders to the contrary, would have destroyed it, thereby cutting off the retreat of Stonewall Jackson. In the darkness of the night preceding the battle of Cedar Mountain, Captains Steele and C. C. Krepps, with two companies, rode through General Jackson's camps, creating great apprehension and confusion, at the same time capturing a number of prisoners. As our army was retreating from second Bull Run, the regiment met the then famous Black Horse Cavalry in a hand-to-hand charge, and damaged it so badly that it was never again heard of under that name. This marked the regiment for outpost duty in the defenses of Washington, and Fairfax Court House, Centerville and Chantilly, with frequent reconnoissances to Warrenton, Salem, Aldie, and Upperville. The brilliant Colonel Mosby, while at Warrenton Junction, his favorite stamping ground, once fell upon the regiment (in a surprise) when the men were preparing their mid-day meal and grazing their horses, but, springing to arms, fighting at a disadvantage, on foot and utterly unprepared, repulsed and drove Mosby's command, capturing some thirty prisoners, including the celebrated Lieut. Dick Moran, mortally wounded, when we followed him (Moseby) in a horse race for several miles.

In the spring of 1863 the regiment received its Spencer rifles, which added materially to its efficiency in its subsequent fights under the reckless and dashing Kilpatrick. It bore the leading part in repelling a charge of Gen'l J. E. B. Stuart's cavalry in the streets of Hanover, Pa., taking Colonel Payne and over a hundred of his men prisoners. It covered and held our guns against Stuart's charge at Hunterstown, Pa. It was conspicuous for holding the low gap at the left of Round Top the last day's fight of Gettysburg, against vastly superior numbers; repeatedly repelling assaults, and finally forming an important part of the charging column under the glorious Farnsworth, who penetrated the enemy's lines near the Devil's Den, and hastened the retreat of the Confederate army from the battle-field of Gettysburg. It was also foremost in the charging and fighting of Kilpatrick's division in its pursuit of Lee's army. At the pass of Monterey, single-handed, during the night of the 4th of July, under Maj. Charles E. Capehart, it captured or destroyed upward of eight miles of Lee's ammunition and supply train, and took as prisoners an entire Confederate brigade, with its commanding general. It also fought with the best at Boonesboro, Hagerstown, Williamsport and Falling Waters.

In the Mine Run campaign the regiment did its full share of duty. The army going into winter quarters the regiment was sent home on veteran furlough. To speak of individual acts of gallantry would be to mention almost every officer and private in the regiment. It may be said, too, that it was always accorded the first rank in every command with which it was associated. It was always conspicuous in the advance against the enemy, covering the rear in a dangerous retreat, and led in more than one forlorn hope. It was never in retreat except before overwhelming numbers, while on no occasion did it lose its organization, and was as nearly invincible as any body of men ever was. Indeed, at a banquet to the regiment in Wheeling

HENRY CAPEHART
Brevet Major General U.S.Volunteers

L.M. Strayer

HENRY CAPEHART
Colonel 1st West Virginia Cavalry
Medal of Honor Greenbrier River May 22, 1864

at this time, one of the speakers, a minister of the gospel, remarked that 'the bare thought of the boys paring their nails made him sad for he regarded it as a waste of so much brave material.'

General Davies, of Kilpatrick's division, having reported that Surgeon Capehart, through a knowledge of the country roads, and some adroit strategy, as well as fighting, had saved his command from capture on Meade's retreat from Mine Run, and with recommendations from Kilpatrick, Custer, Pleasonton and others for exceptional military aptitude, the surgeon became the colonel of the veteran First West Virginia Cavalry. Recruited to the strength of 1200, the regiment took part under Generals Crook and Averell in the raid against the railroads of southwestern Virginia. At the same time General Sigel moved up the Shenandoah Valley, which was a part of the grand movement of all the armies under Grant. Sigel was defeated by Breckinridge; Colonel Strother, the celebrated author, facetiously remarked: "Crook was tearing up the railroads and Sigel was tearing down the turnpike." In General Hunter's movement on Lynchburg, the regiment charged round the city. In the retiring movement, it recaptured artillery that had been taken from our army, drove the enemy by hard blows from the gaps on the line of march, and in not a few desperate encounters covered the retreat of Hunter's famine-stricken and wasting army, and so punishing the enemy as to cause him to abandon pursuit. It resumed the struggle in the valley of the Shenandoah, on its return from Hunter's ill-starred campaign; met the enemy's cavalry at Bunker's Hill, drove it to Stephenson's Depot, and when the infantry arrived, fought and carried the left of the line against cavalry and infantry in the brilliant and hard-contested victory of General Duval over General Ramseur, capturing many prisoners. Two days later it roconnoitered as far as Cedar Creek, and made its way back to Winchester in complete order, though hotly pursued all the way by a much larger force of the enemy's cavalry. Had the information obtained been accepted by General Crook, his retreat across the Potomac a day or two later would have been avoided. In the engagement and retreat out of the valley the cavalry covered the flank and rear of Crook's army.

The enemy's cavalry, under Generals Bradley T. Johnston, Imboden and McCausland, having invaded Maryland and Pennsylvania, and burnt Chambersburg, General Averell was sent to intercept them. After recrossing the Potomac, the enemy passed south of Cumberland, captured and destroyed our station of supplies at New Creek, and reached Moorefield, where they rested in fancied security, enjoying the rich fruits of the raid. Averell was ordered from Washington to pursue and attack them to the death wherever found. Their outpost and picket was captured before day by the First West Virginia

Cavalry without firing a shot.   They were then charged and routed on one side of the river at early dawn.   Fording the river, the First West Virginia charged Imboden and McCausland on the other side, who had now become aroused, and formed to meet us.   We swept the enemy's battle-line from the wheat-field and their ambush in the cornfield and timber, chased them rapidly up the slope, through the woods, crowded them on to the narrow mountain road, pursuing the remnants over six miles.   The enemy believed that no quarter would be given on account of having burned Chambersburg, hence, comparatively few offered to surrender, and an unexampled number, therefore, were killed outright, though many were wounded and hundreds were taken prisoners, while all the booty with which they had been laden, from a spool of cotton to a bolt of silk, was spilled, leaving in our hands artillery, flags, guns and equipage.

In Sheridan's victory of the Opequon, or Winchester, over Early, the cavalry played an important and decisive part; Custer's bugles sounding the charge revived the drooping spirits of the somewhat discouraged infantry; the First West Virginia Cavalry carried everything in its front, scaling the heights and taking the forts.   It was here that the brilliant and daring fighter Lieutenant Donnelly fell.

After the battle of Fisher's Hill, General Sheridan relieved General Averell from the command of his division.   Whereupon Col. Wm. H. Powell was placed in command of the division, and Col. Henry Capehart transferred to the Third Brigade, composed of the First, Second and Third West Virginia and the First New York Lincoln Cavalry, all tried regiments; the First New York, as well as the West Virginia regiments, having gained unusual distinction.   The colonel's brother, Maj. Charles E. Capehart, who succeeded to the command of the First West Virginia, came from the West, soon after recovering from wounds received at Donelson.   An athlete and of great physical strength, with a keen eye and a cool head, and an accomplished swordsman, probably no one in either army rode harder or straighter or wielded a more deadly sabre, or who could dare and do more with a regiment than he could with the First West Virginia Cavalry.   Later, General Sheridan was pleased to designate it as "Capehart's Fighting Brigade."

The brilliant cavalryman and author, Captain King, writing recently of the brigade, says that "he envied its leader his command," and that "its doings were as familiar to him as household words."   Under its new leader it soon became conspicuous in the army, and the pride of West Virginia; but a mark for the slings and detestation of disloyal Virginia.   On the first day of its new leadership it knocked out Generals Imboden, Johnston and McCausland, and drove them on the run for fifteen miles, capturing many prisoners, and everything they had on wheels. At Nineva, it met the brigade of General Tibbits in flight down the valley before General McCausland. Taking the fight off Tibbits' hands, the West Virginia Brigade brought McCausland's onward career to a very sudden termination; whipped him to disorderly flight, captured over 400 prisoners, including 21 commissioned officers; took his artillery, battle flags and ambulances, and hunted him eight miles in less than forty minutes. This Sheridan pronounced the cleanest victory of the Shenandoah.

In the morning of the "phenomenal battle" of Cedar Creek, it held securely all the fords from Buckton to Front Royal, without allowing so much as a hoof of the enemy's cavalry to pass over, not, however, without killing and wounding a number of them as day was breaking—much to Early's disappointment, as he counted on their co-operation. Later in the day it rode with Custer on the left, and also with him on the right, in the charge that was decisive of the battle. After several important reconnoissances, it went into winter quarters near Winchester for a brief period.

The bold Colonel Moseby has certainly no good reason for recalling a certain Thanksgiving Day about this time with any pleasurable or glorious emotions. "The boys" had just finished dinner, supplied by the U. S. Sanitary Commission, and were reveling in the happy sensations produced by the consumption (with a perfect appetite) of turkey and cranberry sauce, prime roast beef, plum pudding and other things, at this time particularly appreciated by them. Moseby, having either captured or routed a foraging party of the Sixth Corps, came riding down in hot pursuit; drove in the cavalry division picket, and even fired into General Tibbits' headquarter tents. First in the saddle, the First West Virginia fell upon the bold marauder, forced him to disgorge his captures of men and wagons, took some of his men, and drove him for ten or twelve miles, when not a vestige of him or his command was visible, escaping by the by-ways, the ravines and the woods; his escape was due to the fleetness of his steeds. In winter quarters the regiment reached its highest state of discipline and drill, equaling any in the service. General Sheridan not only pronounced it his "fighting brigade," but, on seeing still more of it, claimed it to be the most efficient brigade of cavalry in the service of the United States.

As the movement of Grant, at Petersburg, was beginning, the brigade was assigned to the division commanded by General Custer. On the third day's march, taken out of its proper place in the column, the brigade started, at three o'clock in the morning, in the lead of Sheridan's 12,000 cavalry, moving up the valley, with orders to move with great caution, as the enemy were known to be near and in considerable force. Camp was hardly more than cleared before the blaze of rifles from either side illuminated the woods in the gloom of an extremely dark morning. A sweep forward and General Rosser was again running for dear life. The crossing at Mount Crawford was fortified, and the bridge, with the flooring taken up, was prepared for burning by the enemy. Swimming the swollen river, the First West Virginia and First New York attacked the enemy in flank and put him to rout, taking many prisoners, when the flames were subdued, the floor of the bridge relaid, and the column, with its artillery and wagons, passed on undisturbed. General Rosser was pursued on the run for twenty miles, and so closely that he failed to burn or injure the bridge over Middle River. General Early now collected all the force he had at his disposal, in a stronghold at Waynesborough, where he had erected substantial fortifications, well supplied with cannon, and resolved to defend the position to the last extremity. Custer, with his division alone, appeared in his front. Sending a brigade to demonstrate on the flank, at the sound of Custer's bugle-blast the rest moved for the works; Capehart's brigade charging through the enemy and fording the river, reached their rear. Dazed and confounded by Custer's brilliant audacity, they threw their hats in the air, cheering and applauding the deed, and surrendered to the extent of some 1400, with their fortifications, cannon and equipments; the unquestionably courageous Early (Rosser with him) escaping in flight.

Under orders from Custer, Capehart passed Rock Fish Gap, a position of such strength that it might have been held against great odds for an indefinite period, and continuing, at Greenwood, a depot of supplies, we captured a locomotive and cars, with several pieces of artillery. General Early having reached Greenwood Station, left there accompanied by a salute from the rifles of the advance of the First West Virginia. The affair was all over before Sheridan heard of it. When he came up, he threw his arms around Custer's neck, thanking him effusively, adding that it had taken a load from his mind, as he expected considerable difficulty in getting possession of the Gap, and anticipated a delay of at least some days before accomplishing it. The West Virginia Brigade camped for the night at Afton Station, where its colonel, with his staff, had the felicity of partaking of a wedding supper with the bride, bridesmaids and other charming ladies, in a cottage draped with clinging vines, amid rocks and trees, all of which was enlivened by the beautiful music of the brigade band.

The tempting viands, untouched by the groom and his male companions, who had levanted at the approach of the detested West Virginians, were tastefully laid on the table in the dining room. The airy spirit of the fair young ladies was at first decidedly chilly and forbidding, corresponding well with

L.M. Strayer

CHARLES E. CAPEHART

Lieutenant Colonel 1st West Virginia Cavalry

Medal of Honor Monterey, Pa. July 4, 1863

HARVEY FARRABEE
Major 1st West Virginia Cavalry

the cold, drizzling rain, of freezing mud and darkness without. Their hearts soon melted, however, before the warm-hearted and attractive young soldiers; brave all of them, in war, but mild in peace, who had in a measure forced their company upon the fair ladies, and with song, music and dance, all went merry as a marriage bell till break of day, when the boys were again in the saddle on the march. The continuation of the movement was comparatively an unobstructed, triumphal progress, though leaving more or less of terror, and the distruction of public buildings, railroads and the canal in its path, carrying thousands of slaves, men, women and babes to freedom. Passing hard by the gates of the Confederate capital, and in view of the stupendous fortifications of Richmond and Petersburg, Grant's great guns from his works boomed out on the air in recognition of Sheridan's arrival, which must have fallen on Lee's ears as portents of his fast-coming doom. Waiting for a supply train, now necessary in the altered circumstances, having hitherto lived on the enemy, Custer's troopers, at least, met with profuse hospitality from their comrades of the cavalry of the Army of the Potomac.

We were freely reminded that we would meet here a very superior class of troops, in the veteran regiments of the Confederate army, as compared with those we had vanquished in the Shenandoah. We replied that little things like that had no terror for us, we simply proposed to whip Lee's cavalry wherever we met them. Approaching Dinwiddie C. H., the West Virginia Brigade was in charge of the supply train, which had literally to be carried through the deep mud and quicksand of that region. A hurrying aide relieved our brigade of this duty by another force, and ordered us to report with all possible haste to General Sheridan—near the Court House. When near there, General Custer came galloping down the White Oak road from General Sheridan, and pulling up his horse, communicated orders to move the brigade up the road to oppose the advancing enemy, and said at the same time, laughing, "General Sheridan and those fellows up there don't know whether school is going to keep or not," to which the West Virginia colonel replied: "Well, General, it will keep a while, anyway, when the boys get there." Most of Sheridan's force (the infantry not yet up) was retreating before the enemy, both infantry and cavalry, and some of it badly scorched and cut up, and all in a bad enough way. Our West Virginia brigade took position at the intersection of the Chamberlain Creek and White Oak roads, repulsed the enemy's cavalry charge with heavy slaughter, and stood there like a fortress, repelling repeated attacks of both infantry and cavalry. During the night it held the extreme advance single-handed, while its band enlivened the darkness and gave the impression to the enemy of on infantry reinforcement, the enemy sullenly retiring before morning. At Five Forks, one of the most important battles of the war, as to its far-reaching effect, that was fought, the brigade, with Wells' brigade, charged (mounted) the enemy's right flank, where were Fitzhugh Lee, R. H. Lee and Rosser, and quickly routed them, to which, as Custer says, " the victory was mainly due." Lieutenant W. W. Blackmar, who was transferred from the cavalry in the south-west, and commissioned in the 1st W. Va. cavalry, and now of Capehart's staff, was promoted by Custer on the field of Five Forks for brilliant personal daring ; during the entire engagement he rode in the front rank in the thickest of the fight, and without a superior for ability.

General Sheridan, however, more than a mile away, has it that the cavalry here was held in check; and through some inexplicable blunder has Coppinger marked on the map in his memoirs as in command of the West Virginia Brigade, instead of its commander Capehart. Coppinger never had any connection with the West Virginia Brigade, and never was in command of a brigade, while it is not probable that he led a mounted charge during his career. In the preparation of Sheridan's memoirs (made hastily), he also commits several important errors. In regard to the extraordinary success at Little Sailor's Creek, relating to the cavalry, Sheridan was over two miles distant; here he has the opposing forces in entirely different positions from the true ones (of course inadvertently). The record, however, if meager, due to the rush of events, confirms the facts as here given. In the morning, not without some fighting and loss of life, the 1st West Va., cut out from Lee's army an immense train and 13 pieces of splendid artillery, some of it never having been fired, and imported from England. In the afternoon Ewell's Corps was facing the rear, toward Richmond, and the 6th Corps was battering away with artillery, at pretty long range, with little or no effect, Ewell being in a strong position on high ground on the opposite side of the creek. In the assault afterwards the 6th Corps met a bloody repulse, which General Sheridan, back with General Wright, was overlooking. On the same side of the creek with Ewell, and in his rear, at right angles to him, was Anderson's Corps, in triple line, with some temporary intrenchments of rails and earth, preparing to sweep the cavalry from the line of retreat. Anderson's Corps was composed in part of Pickett's Division, immortal for the charge at Gettysburg. None of the Union cavalry, excepting the West Virginia Brigade, was in close proximity to the enemy, or in at the death, though the 1st New Jersey, of Crook's Division, made a gallant, if ill-directed charge off on the left, but was swept off the field with heavy loss; and Anderson's road was clear, though of course threatened. The West Virginia Brigade, under cover of a declivity, got within short rifle-range of Anderson's Corps, and was breathing the horses. The

Colonel (a solitary horseman is seldom fired on by a large body of men) passed over the brow of the hill and was making a circuit to reconnoiter the enemy, when, to his surprise, Anderson's men rose and delivered a fire, and in looking back he saw that it was directed at Custer, who had unexpectedly arrived with his body-guard, carrying fluttering battle-flags captured from the enemy, his horse was just falling to the ground and giving the peculiar shriek of death, with a bullet through its heart. The Colonel hurrying up to Custer, suggested that the moment was opportune for a charge, the enemy's muskets being in considerable part empty, to which he answered, with the characteristic smile of battle on his face : "Charge 'em, charge 'em."

The command numbered about 1400. The formation, already made, one regiment in line, supported in center by two regiments in column of squadrons, and one regiment supporting the right of line, also in column of squadrons. The undertaking, an onset against seven or eight times its numbers of Lee's veterans. Colonel Capehart in the forefront, with his bugler, Tom Custer and Colonel Allen, of the Second West Virginia, on either side; at the blast of the bugle, 5000 iron hoofs were in motion. The speed increasing from a trot to a mad run, though the order perfect, the troopers, with sabres flashing, the firing of pistols and carbines, shouts and yells—with all the noise and uproar possible—surged over the works and rode smashing through the battle-lines, sabering and shooting all who offered resistance; the Confederates, thrown off their balance and panic-stricken, the little handful ten times magnified in its audacity, the enemy began throwing down their arms and surrendering wholesale, though not without several isolated encounters to the death, in one of which Tom Custer received a bullet in the cheek, which came out near the ear ; shooting his antagonist dead, he came smiling, and waving his captured battle-flag.

Captain Stevens, of the First New York, took in General Ewell and staff, who stood in rear of his own corps, confronting the Sixth, across the creek, and Anderson's left. On the colonel of the brigade coming up, he sent members of his staff, with some of the colonel's, through his command, now with the cavalry in rear and the Sixth Corps in front, and the truce men communicating to the Sixth Corps, Ewell's command laid down its arms to the West Virginia Brigade; the full numbers surrendering, with those from Anderson, to the brigade, amounting to about 8000, including Ewell and seven other general officers; an event that at any other time would have sent the North wild with enthusiasm, but with the events pending, exciting but little attention. The Sixth Corps took no prisoners and the rest of the cavalry comparatively few, and those mostly stragglers. Ewell's command, having fought off the Sixth Corps, with Sheridan and Wright, more or less successfully, and marched off the field by officers of the West Virginia Brigade, was for the most part unaware of its surrender until it was ordered to stack arms and had marched some distance from them to a meadow on the Harper farm. It will, however, be admitted that the Sixth Corps has the most brilliant history of any corps in the army, if it was not in it with Custer's men. Custer, prevented by the death of his horse from riding in the charge with his body-guard, soon came up and engaged in a somewhat prolonged conversation with General Ewell, who believed the end was near. Generals Kershaw and Pickett, the latter of Gettysburg fame, were among the captured. Pickett remarked to General Ewell in regard to the West Virginia Brigade: "General, this cavalry pays no more attention to battle-lines than if we were men of straw." In recognition of the kindness and courtesy of Captain Stevens to General Ewell, his distinguished captive presented him with his field glass, accompanied with a kindly note.

From Namozine Church to Deep Creek the brigade had the advance and drove the cavalry before it, while taking many prisoners.

Custer marched both by night and by day. In a sharp skirmish with the First and Second Brigades, at Appomattox Station, he captured the trains of supplies coming up from Lynchburg on the railroad to meet Lee, the West Virginia Brigade supplying the engineers to run off the trains.

On the approach of night, Custer learned that Lee's reserve artillery and trains lay directly in his front, on the road to Lynchburg, whither Lee was directing his wasting and famishing army. Guarding this reserve was a strong force of infantry and artillery. Forming line, the West Virginia Brigade moved in intense darkness through the forest until nearing a field, when it was met by a blaze of canister and musketry, which developed the position of the enemy's guns and battle-line, and proved the signal for a charge, with the result of driving the enemy from the field in disorder, taking many prisoners and the guns. Following up the success rapidly, the brigade rode over the reserve with little or no opposition; taking possession of the numerous wagons and cannon, with the teams of horses all attached ready to move, and now across Lee's line of retreat, it picketed well out towards Appomattox Court House and within a short distance of the Confederate army. Relieved by Smith's Brigade, of Crook's Division, it partook of coffee and an hour or two's rest.

In the gray of morning, the West Virginia Brigade is again in the saddle. Custer's Division is probably the most efficient body of horse for its numbers the world has ever seen; horses and men are worn and jaded by constant hard marching and hard fighting, both by night and by day, and the uniforms and accoutrements are worn, battered and tarnished by hard

WILMON W. BLACKMAR
Captain 1st West Virginia Cavalry
Medal of Honor Five Forks, Va. April 1, 1865

GEORGE A. CUSTER
Brevet Major General U.S.A.

knocks, exposure to all sorts of weather and mud; but hope beats high and nerves both horses and men to deeds of reckless daring, even those most faint of heart. You see Custer at the head of the column: he with the long, flow-ing, yellow hair—a model of a cavalryman—if wearing more gold lace than is customary, and finer dress; but he wears it well, and his body-guard is still in his train, with the fluttering battle-flags taken from the enemy. He is con-ducting the division out along the higher ground to Clover Hill, on Lee's flank, with the intention of leading a charge into the Confederate army. The sun at Appomattox is beginning to light up the scene, over the somewhat depressed plain, in which lies Appomattox Court House and the army of the doomed Confederacy. At some distance to the rear and right of Custer, you see another large body of cavalry. It is the division of the slower and more conservative, but sturdy, Devin, which is supporting Custer. Now look somewhat further to Custer's rear, slightly southwest of the court house. They are Birney's colored troops, on the double-quick,—somewhat obscured by the woods, their tongues out and white eyes bulging, and panting from their rapid marching, looking more determined than the blood-hounds of the enemy that have hunted their race in the preceding generations. Birney, under Sheridan's orders, is placing them facing the court house and across the highway to Lynchburg, by which Lee hopes to make his retreat; the remainder of the 24th Corps following near by.

General Smith, with his command, is considerably to the front of the colored troops, his artillery injudiciously advanced. The Fifth Corps, under the splendid and untiring Griffin, are marching as if their lives depend upon it; they had been marching and fighting since reaching the Peninsula—three years ago—when, at Gaines' Mill, single-handed, they fought Lee's army to a drawn battle; and at Malvern Hill, with no more than their original numbers, routed Lee in confusion, and if their leader had had his way, Lee would have been destroyed. Away across the woods, nearly east of the court house, and out of sight, is the Second Corps, under the brave and accomplished soldier Humphreys, in close proximity to Lee's rear, and ready to spring on him at a word, they who had waded through fire and blood under Hancock. Not far away, under the fine soldier Wright, is the Sixth Corps, whose record for hard marching and hard fighting is unexcelled, if equaled, part of whom stood alone with the cavalry in stemming Jubal Early's victorious tide at Cedar Creek.

The sun at Appomattox is now out in full force, its rays reflecting from the bayonets, guns and equipment of the vast array. And all the panoply of war is seen—horse, foot and artillery—with its various attendants. Yet, to an on-looker taking in the general scene, all is silent as death—quiet enjoined on either side and the ground more or less yielding; not so much as the curling smoke or the sound of a solitary rifle-shot. The troops are seemingly moving to their appointed places as stalking phantoms of dead and gone armies marshaling for the Last Judgment.

General Gordon, in the van of the Confederate army, has been quietly preparing to break through and sweep their enemy from Lee's way of retreat. Almost without a sign of warning, and hardly expected, rifles are cracking and cannon are roaring. Gordon is making his assault. Smith, before pointed out, comes tumbling back with the loss of artillery and some killed and wounded, and is passing away to the left, while Lee's cavalry is driving Crook back with the remainder of his command in more or less confusion. But staggering before the hot fire of Birney's colored troops, who swarm out to meet him, with other infantry confronting, Devin and Custer in flank and rear, the latter saluted by Confederate batteries, Gordon is tumbling back broken and disordered, all hope gone; and even pursued in some cases, with the capture of some of his officers, greatly to the wounding of their dignity—by colored troops.

But see! A white flag is up. The mounted officer who bears it is coming from the direction of the court house, towards Custer's column. He reaches it at the head of the West Virginia Brigade. Colonel Capehart and the officer proceed along the column to Custer. He said to Custer: "I have the honor to bear the compliments of General Longstreet to the officer in command, and to say that Generals Lee and Grant are in correspondence touching the surrender of the Confederate Army of Northern Virginia, and to request a cessation of hostilities until the result is made known." If that is so, it seems a breach of good faith that they have been trying to fight their way out in the meantime. Custer, his face beaming with animation, grippling the rim of his hat with his right hand and giving it a few spasmodic jerks, as was his habit, replies: "Tell General Longstreet that I am not in command of all the forces here, but that I am on his flank and rear with a large cavalry force, and that I will accept nothing but unconditional surrender." But, turning to Colonel E. W. Whitaker, his chief of staff, he says to him: "Go over with this officer and bear my message to General Longstreet." Becoming impatient, Custer turns over the command to Capehart (who commands the division to the end, Custer's authority having been enlarged, leads in the finale, grand review at Washington) and says to him: "I am going over to see what is going on," following his chief of staff, having communicated what had occurred to Sheridan. On taking command, Capehart throws out a skirmish line to the outer edge of the timber between him and the enemy, which becomes immediately engaged in a brisk fusilade. The advance brigade is promptly ordered to their support: and a charge is on the point of being made. The fire reaching Sheridan's ears, he is saying to some Rebel officers, considerably to the left rear of Capehart's column: "Oh, that's some of Merritt's" (Merritt commanding the cavalry nominally) "cavalry making a charge" as if he would rather have a fight than not; and a man or two killed of no moment anyway. But the rattle-headed Confederate colonel in front of Capehart, swearing and talking of death in the "last ditch" in preference to surrender, is finally squelched by peaceful means, with the assistance of the same officer who had appeared with the flag of truce, and all is again tranquil.

Custer is having words somewhat warm with Longstreet, and more or less suspecting that there may be a scheme on foot to gain time and make another attempt to break the meshes in which Lee is enveloped, and demands from Longstreet immediate surrender or direful consequences; Longstreet parleying and fencing, unwilling to surrender to Sheridan, much less to Custer, or giving the cavalry the credit of bringing it about, only desirous of having it effected by Lee and Grant themselves.

Make way! Grant, the great commander of all the armies of the Republic, is coming through the lines; unassuming, muddy, shabby in dress, and mounted on his well known pony, though as daring a rider as any in all his hosts, with his staff, all in finer array than himself. The impetuous Sheridan, his Irish blood at boiling point, is suspicious of some unfair play, and is desirous to cut the knot by the sword. Grant, more wise, and always perfectly balanced, quiets him down, and proceeds with him and other high officers in his train to meet Lee (resplendent in a new and gorgeous uniform), at the McLean house. The surrender is consummated and the war practically ended.

To give even the leading results in the career of the regiments composing the West Virginia Brigade, not forgetting the exceptionally gallant regiment, the 1st N. Y. Lincoln, would require a volume. Colonel Capehart, in his congratulatory order and farewell address to the division, which had captured in the final campaign more men, cannon, battle-flags and other material of war than all the rest of the army combined, said: "All I ask of the historian is that he write me the commander of the Third Cavalry Division." And it may be said that the West Virginia colonel who succeeded him, uses in his office the chair in which Grant sat while conferring with Lee, and drawing and signing the terms of the surrender at the McLean house.

Grant had brought the greatest war of modern times to a close within a year; and would doubtless have captured or destroyed Lee during that memorable summer, but for some of those purely accidental circumstances to which war is proverbially subject, with the failure of certain subordinates to meet reasonable expectations.

And while Sheridan and Sherman have sounded their own trumpets; and not always with a full measure of justice to Grant, as well as their subordinates, Grant was the genius, the reliance, the tenacity and courage, the electric power that strengthened all, from Sherman and Sheridan to the private in the ranks, to fight on and endure to the end.

The following are Custer's recommendations for Capehart's promotion and his order, printed from the autograph, assigning the command of the division to him:

[EXTRACT.]

HEADQUARTERS 3D CAVALRY DIVISION,
MIDDLE MILITARY DIVISION, *April* 18, 1865.

HON. E. M. STANTON,
　　Secretary of War.

I have the honor to submit the following recommendations for the promotion of officers of my command.

First. That Colonel H. Capehart, 1st Virginia Cavalry, Commanding 3d Brigade of this Division, be promoted with full rank of Brigadier-General U. S. Volunteers, to date from March 1, 1865. Colonel Capehart, by his skill in handling his brigade, and in the personal gallantry displayed in the engagement at Mt. Crawford, on the 1st of March, by which the enemy were driven with heavy loss from the burning bridge and the way opened before us in our march up the valley, was the first to inaugurate that series of successes which characterized our movement to the James River. At Waynesboro, he bore a leading part in effecting the rout and capture of Early's forces. In the late campaign from Petersburg to Appomatox Court House, Colonel Capehart has been second to none in the display of marked ability, untiring zeal and energy, as well as unsurpassed personal gallantry and daring. At Dinwiddie Court House he was particularly conspicuous. At Five Forks I attribute our success mainly due to the united efforts of Colonels Capehart and Wells. While at Sailor's Creek the brunt of the engagement was born by Colonel Capehart's Brigade, which in every charge was led by its gallant commander. At Appomattox Station, the 8th inst., Colonel Capehart again rendered himself conspicuous by his skill and bravery, and to him is much of the credit due, for the successful termination of that obstinate engagement, which resulted in our capturing twenty-four pieces of artillery, beside a large number of prisoners, wagons, etc., to say nothing of the influence this engagement had in deciding the fortunes of the following day.

I earnestly trust this recommendation will be favorably considered.

　　　　　　　　　　G. A. CUSTER, *Brevet Major-General.*

HEADQUARTERS 3D CAVALRY DIVISION,
APPOMATTOX COURT HOUSE, *April* 9, 1865.

COLONEL CAPEHART, *Commanding 3d Brigade.*

Colonel: In accordance with orders from Major-General Sheridan, I have been placed in command of the 1st and 3d Divisions of Cavalry. You will, on receipt of this order, assume command of the 3d Cavalry Division.　　　　Very Respectfully,

　　　　　　　　　　G. A. CUSTER, *Brevet Major-General.*

CHAPTER XXIV.

SECOND REGIMENT W. VA. CAVALRY VOLUNTEERS.

Roster of the Field, Staff and Company Officers of the Second Regiment West Virginia Cavalry Volunteers, Showing the Alterations and Casualties Therein from the Date of Original Organization of Said Regiment to the Date of Muster Out, June 30, 1865.

Date of Commission.	Names and Rank.	Co.	Remarks.
	Colonels.		
Sept. 16, 1861.	William M. Bolles,		Resigned June 25, 1862.
July 18, 1862.	John C. Paxton,		Dismissed May 7, 1863.
May 18, 1863.	Wm. H. Powell,		Promoted to Brig. Gen'l.
	Lieutenant-Colonels.		
Sept. 16, 1861.	John C. Paxton,		Promoted to Colonel.
Aug. 19, 1862.	Rollin L. Curtis,		Resigned Oct. 25, 1862.
Dec. 5, 1862.	Wm. H. Powell,		Promoted to Colonel.
May 18, 1863.	David Dove,		Resigned July 5, 1864.
July 14, 1864.	John J. Hoffman,		Mustered out at expiration of term of service.
Nov. 26, 1864.	James Allen,		Mustered out at expiration of term of service.
	Majors.		
Oct. 2, 1861.	Rollin L. Curtis,		Promoted to Lieutenant-Colonel.
Oct. 2, 1861.	John J. Hoffman,		Promoted to Lieutenant-Colonel.
Feb. 5, 1862.	Henry Steinbach,		Mustered out February 23, 1864.
Aug. 19, 1862.	Wm. H. Powell,		Promoted to Lieutenant-Colonel.
Jany. 2, 1863.	John McMahon,		Dismissed April 25, 1864.
April 29, 1864.	James Allen,		Promoted to Lieutenant-Colonel.
July 14, 1864.	Chas. E. Hambleton,		Mustered out at expiration of term of service.
Nov. 26, 1864.	Edwin S. Morgan,		Mustered out at expiration of term of service.
	1st Lts. and Adj'ts.		
Oct. 25, 1861.	John P. Merrill,		Resigned June 5, 1862.
Nov. 5, 1862.	Elijah F. Gillon,		Resigned Sept. 7, 1864.
Nov. 12, 1861.	Earl A. Cranston,		Resigned June 2, 1862.
Oct. 25, 1861.	George E. Downing,		Resigned May 1, 1862.
	1st Lts. and R. Q. M.		
Oct. 2, 1861.	Sayres G. Paxton,		Mustered out at expiration of term of service.
Oct. 23, 1861.	William Holden,		Resigned March 13, 1862.
	1st Lts. and Reg. Com.		
Jan. 2, 1863.	George S. South,		Mustered out at expiration of term of service.
	Surgeons.		
Oct. 25, 1861.	Thomas S. Neal,		Resigned February 9, 1863.
Jan. 17, 1863.	Matthew McEwen.		
	Assistant Surgeons.		
Nov. 6, 1861.	Lucius L. Comstock,		Promoted to Surgeon, 8th W. Va. Infantry.

Date of Commission.	Names and Rank.	Co.	Remarks.
	Assistant Surgeons.		
March 6, 1863.	Ozias Nellis,		Mustered out at expiration of term of service.
May 18, 1863.	Edward L. Gillian.		
	Chaplain.		
Oct. 2, 1861.	Charles M. Bethauser,		Resigned Oct. 12, 1862.
	Captain.		
Oct. 19, 1861.	James L. Wallar,	A	Dismissed April 25, 1864.
April 29, 1864.	William V. Johnston,	A	Mustered out at expiration of term of service.
Nov. 26, 1864.	Alberto Campbell,	A	
Nov. 22, 1861.	Wm. H. Powell,	B	Promoted to Major.
Oct. 9, 1862.	Chas. E. Hambleton,	B	Promoted to Major.
July 14, 1864.	Israel B. Murdoch,	B	Mustered out at expiration of term of service.
Jan. 7, 1865.	Will. S. Merrill,	B	Resigned June 14, 1865.
Nov. 22, 1861.	Thomas Neal,	C	Resigned July 22, 1862.
June 26, 1862.	James Allen,	C	Promoted to Major.
April 29, 1864.	James A. Morrison,	C	Mustered out at expiration of term of service.
Nov. 5, 1862.	Edwin S. Morgan,	C	Promoted to Major.
Jan. 7, 1865.	Ebenezer E. Wilson,	C	
Oct. 19, 1861.	Henry S. Hamilton,	D	Resigned.
May 18, 1863.	Alex. H. Ricker,	D	Transferred to Co. H.
Nov. 24, 1863.	James A. Umpleby,	D	Mustered out at expiration of term of service.
Nov. 26, 1864.	John McNally,	D	Mustered out at expiration of term of service.
Nov. 22, 1861.	Andrew Scott,	E	Resigned January 12, 1862.
Jan. 27, 1863.	Jeremiah Davidson,	E	Promoted to Major, 79th O. V. I.
May 18, 1863.	Joseph Ankrom,	E	
Nov. 22, 1861.	Arthur D. Eells,	F	Resigned May 6, 1862.
June 26, 1862.	Oliver H. P. Scott,	F	Resigned December 23, 1862.
April 1, 1863.	George Millard,	F	Mustered out at expiration of term of service.
Nov. 26, 1864.	Henry F. Swentzel,	F	
Oct. 19, 1861.	John McMahan,	G	Promoted to Major.
Jan. 2, 1863.	Jasper A. Smith,	G	Resigned May 14, 1863.
May 18, 1863.	Joseph Ankrom,	G	Transferred to Co. E.
Nov. 2, 1864.	Jasper A. Smith,	G	
Nov. 22, 1861.	David Dove,	H	Promoted to Lt. Col.
Nov. 24, 1863.	James A. Umpleby,	H	Transferred to Co. D.
May 18, 1863.	Alex. H. Ricker,	H	Mustered out at expiration of term of service.
Nov. 22, 1861.	Newton J. Behan,	I	Resigned October 23, 1864.
Nov. 5, 1862.	Wm. M. Fortescue,	I	Mustered out at expiration of term of service.
Nov. 22, 1861.	Silas H. Emmons,	K	Resigned Oct. 17, 1862.
Nov. 5, 1862.	Edwin S. Morgan,	K	Transferred to Co. C.
Oct. 16, 1861.	Geo. W. Gilmore,	L	Mustered out at expiration of term of service.
Nov. 2, 1864.	Jasper A. Smith.	M	Transferred to Co. G.
	First Lieutenants.		
Oct. 19, 1861.	Lewis E. Campbell,	A	Resigned Feb 28, 1863.
May 18, 1863,	Alexander Ward,	A	Mustered out at expiration of term of service.
Nov. 26, 1864.	Elihu D. Robinson,	A	
Nov. 22, 1861.	Chas. E. Hambleton,	B	Promoted to Captain.

Date of Commission.	Names and Rank.	Co.	Remarks.
	First Lieutenants.		
July 31, 1862.	P. F. Roherbacker,	B	Resigned Feb. 24, 1863.
May 18, 1863.	Israel B. Murdoch,	B	Promoted to Captain.
July 14, 1864.	Edwin A. Rosser,	B	
Nov. 22. 1861.	Jeremiah M. Boyd,	C	Mustered out at expiration of term of service.
Nov. 26, 1861.	Ebenezer E. Wilson,	C	Promoted to Captain.
Jan. 7, 1865.	Abijah B. Farmer,	C	
Oct. 19, 1861.	George W. Snyder,	D	Resigned Feb. 24, 1863.
May 18, 1863.	James M. Merrill,	D	Transferred to Co. K.
Nov. 5, 1862.	John McNally,	D	Promoted to Captain.
Nov. 26, 1864.	Samuel McVey,	D	
Nov. 22, 1861.	Andrew A. Fouts,	E	Dismissed Feb 26, 1862.
May 29, 1862.	Jasper A. Smith,	E	Promoted to Captain, Co. G.
Jan. 2, 1863.	Jeremiah Davidson,	E	Promoted to Captain.
Jan. 27, 1863.	Joseph Ankrom,	E	Promoted to Captain, Co. G.
May 18, 1863.	John D. Barber,	E	Killed in action near Winchester.
July 12, 1864.	Wm. S. Merrill,	E	Promoted to Captain, Co. B.
Jany. 7, 1865.	James W. Hicks,	E	
Nov. 22, 1861.	Oliver H. P. Scott,	F	Promoted to Captain.
June 26, 1862.	Wm. M. Fortescue,	F	Promoted to Captain, Co. I.
Nov. 5, 1862.	George Milliard,	F	Promoted to Captain.
April 1, 1862.	Lloyd B. Stephens,	F	Resigned July 13, 1864.
Nov. 26, 1864.	Charles C. Clise,	F	
Oct. 19, 1861.	Geo. B. Montgomery,	G	Resigned Feb 24, 1863.
May 18, 1863.	John J. Medlicott,	G	Honorably discharged, Sept. 27, 1864.
Nov. 2, 1864.	Milton McMillin,	G	
Nov. 22, 1861.	John Walden,	H	Resigned Oct. 22, 1862.
Nov. 5, 1862.	James A. Umpleby,	H	Promoted to Captain.
April 29, 1864.	James W. Ricker,	H	Mustered out at expiration of term of service.
Nov. 22, 1861.	John W. Neal,	I	Resigned May 5, 1862.
June 26, 1862.	George K. Weir,	I	Killed in action at Fayetteville, Va.
Oct. 9, 1862.	Wm. V. Johnston,	I	Promoted to Captain, Co. A.
April 29, 1864.	Saml S. Hawk,	I	Mustered out at expiration of term of service.
Nov. 22, 1861.	William Yard,	K	Resigned September 30, 1862.
Nov. 5, 1862.	John McNally,	K	Transferred to Co. D.
May 18, 1863.	James M. Merrill,	K	Mustered out at expiration of term of service.
Oct. 16, 1861.	James Abraham,	L	Mustered out at expiration of term of service.
Sep. 26, 1864.	Jasper A. Smith,	M	Promoted to Captain.
Nov. 2, 1864.	Milton McMillin,	M	Transferred to Co. G.
	Second Lieutenants.		
Oct. 19, 1861.	Charles A. Hudson,	A	Resigned September 30, 1862.
Oct. 9, 1862.	Alexander Ward,	A	Promoted to 1st Lieutenant.
May 18, 1863.	James W. Ricker,	A	Promoted to 1st Lieutenant, Co. H.
April 29, 1864.	Ebenezer E. Wilson,	A	Promoted to 1st Lieutenant, Co. C.
Nov. 26, 1864.	Abijah B. Farmer,	A	Promoted to 1st Lieutenant, Co. C.
Jan. 7, 1865.	Emerson McMillin,	A	
Nov. 22, 1861.	James Allen,	B	Promoted to Captain, Co. C.

Date of Commission.	Names and Rank.	Co.	Remarks.
	Second Lieutenants.		
June 26, 1862.	Israel B. Murdoch,	B	Promoted to 1st Lieutenant.
May 18, 1863.	James A. Morrison,	B	Promoted to Captain, Co. C.
April 29, 1864.	Wm. S. Merrill,	B	Promoted to 1st Lieutenant, Co. E.
Nov. 26, 1864.	Martin Kramer,	B	
Nov. 22, 1861.	William Church,	C	Resigned September 30, 1862.
Oct. 9, 1862.	Harvey J. Fulmer,	C	Mustered out at expiration of term of service.
Nov. 26, 1864.	George Freeman,	C	
Oct. 19, 1861.	Edwin S. Morgan,	D	Promoted to Captain, Co. K.
Jan. 2, 1863.	James A. Hoover,	D	Mustered out at expiration of term of service.
Nov. 26, 1864.	W. S. McClanahan,	D	
Nov. 22, 1861.	Joseph Ankrom,	E	Promoted to 1st Lieutenant
Jan. 27, 1863.	Henry F. Swentzel,	E	Promoted to Captain, Co. F.
Nov. 26, 1864.	James W. Hicks,	E	Promoted to 1st Lieutenant.
May 18, 1863.	Alberto Campbell,	E	Promoted to Captain, Co. A.
Jan. 7, 1865.	John M. Corns,	E	
Nov. 22, 1861.	Wm. M. Fortescue,	F	Promoted to 1st Lieutenant.
June 26, 1862.	George Millard,	F	Promoted to 1st Lieutenant.
Nov. 5, 1862.	Lloyd B. Stephens,	F	Promoted to 1st Lieutenant.
April 1, 1863.	Oliver C. Ong.	F	Mustered out prov. G. O. War Dept.
Nov. 26, 1864.	Elisha T. Fisher,	F	
Oct. 19, 1861.	Jeremiah Davidson,	G	Promoted to 1st Lieutenant, Co. E.
Jan. 2, 1863.	John J. Medlicott,	G	Promoted to 1st Lieutenant.
May 18, 1863.	Alberto Campbell,	G	Transferred to Co. E.
Sep. 30, 1864.	Wm. J. Kirkendall,	G	
Nov. 22, 1861.	James A. Umpleby,	H	Promoted to 1st Lieutenant.
Nov. 5, 1862.	Geo. W. Shoemaker,	H	Died of wounds received in action.
Oct. 24, 1863.	Charles C. Clice,	H	Promoted to 1st Lieutenant, Co. F.
Nov. 22, 1861.	John A. Lowe,	I	Resigned September 30, 1862.
Oct. 9, 1862.	Jonathan B. Carlisle,	I	Mustered out prov. G. O. War. Dept.
Nov. 22, 1861.	John McNally,	K	Promoted to 1st Lieutenant.
Nov. 5, 1862.	Walter Christopher,	K	Prisoner of war, captured July 4, 1863, at Fayetteville, W. Va.
Aug. 22, 1861.	Lewis M. Dawson,	L	Dismissed October 31, 1861.
Oct. 22, 1861.	Isaac N. Fordyce,	L	Dismissed November 19, 1862.
Sept. 30, 1864.	Wm. J. Kirkendall.	M	Transferred to Co. G.

Joseph J. Sutton, *History of the Second Regiment West Virginia Cavalry Volunteers*

JOHN C. PAXTON
Colonel 2nd West Virginia Cavalry

L.M. Strayer

WILLIAM H. POWELL
Colonel 2nd West Virginia Cavalry
Brevet Major General U.S. Volunteers

Gen. Wm. H. Powell.

Gen'l Wm. H. Powell was born May 10, 1825, in Monmouthshire, South Wales, Great Britain, of Welsh ancestry, "a gallant, Christian race, patterns of every virtue, every grace, ever loyal to God and country." He emigrated with his parents to America in 1830. His early life, covering the period of 1833 to 1843, was spent in Nashville, Tennessee, since which he has resided in Virginia, Ohio and Missouri; his present home, since 1876, is Belleville, Illinois. His entire manhood life, save the four years he devoted to saving " the old flag " in 1861 to 1865, has been devoted as an iron manufacturer and mechanical engineer. At the age of 25 he was employed to superintend the erection of the original Benwood Iron and Nail Works, near Wheeling, West Virginia, and following the completion of these works, the the erection of the Blandy & Sturgess Rail Mill, and the construction of the first nail works at Ironton, Ohio, known as the Belfont Iron and Nail Works. In 1857, he was chosen by the Lawrence Rolling Mill Company as its general manager and financial agent, which position he relinquished, August 1, 1861, to enter the service of the United States, to suppress the rebellion inaugurated in the Southern States.

His effort in obtaining recruits enabled him to report with a company at Parkersburg, Va., for organization and muster, September 16, 1861. Under President Lincoln's call of July 2, 1861, the formation of a regiment for the cavalry arm of the U. S. service was begun about August 1, in southern Ohio. Three companies were recruited in Lawrence County, two in Meigs, one in Jackson, one in Vinton, one in Washington, and one in Morgan. The remainder of the regiment was composed largely of volunteers from Putnam and Monroe counties, West Virginia. When this body was ready for organization and commission, application was made to Governor Dennison, of Ohio, to complete the organization. This he declined to do, saying that the governors of all the Northern States had received instructions from the War Department to recruit no more cavalry, and that they were also advised that all cavalry organizations in excess of forty regiments would be mustered out of the service.

Application was then made to F. H. Peirpoint, provisional governor of that portion of Virginia now known as West Virginia, the latter State not having been admitted to Statehood until June 20, 1863. Governor Peirpoint, with the consent of the Secretary of War, accepted the organization as cavalry, ordering the same into camp quarters at Parkersburg, where ten companies reported about the middle of September, 1861.

On the 15th of December the regiment was ordered into winter quarters at Guyandotte, Va. The organization was a fine body of Ohio soldiery, and many were the regrets expressed that it could not have been mustered into service as an Ohio regiment. Yet, neither during the progress of the war nor since its close, have we had the slightest cause to complain of our treatment at the hands of the loyal people of the little mountain State, born amid the throes of war, rocked and shaken with the roar of cannon, whose soil drank the blood of many of her own gallant and loyal sons.

With the exception of an occasional unimportant scouting expedition, and co-operation with Col. James A. Garfield, on the 7th and 8th of January, 1862, in his movements against General Humphrey Marshall, in north-eastern Kentucky, where the first blood of the regiment was spilled by the killing of two men, Amos McKee, of Co. B, and Albert Leonard, of Co. C, and the wounding of five others, the command was not disturbed in its drill exercise and preparation for subsequent service during the winter. During the month of April, 1862, the regiment was divided into battalion organizations. The Second Battalion, composed of Co's. A, D, E, G and K, under command of Lieutenant-Colonel Paxton, accompanied by Maj. R. L. Curtis, was ordered to report to Gen'l J. D. Cox, at Flat Top Mountain. In a few days thereafter, Colonel Bolles, accompanied by Major Hoffman, in command of the First Battalion, composed of Co's. B, C, F, H and I, broke camp under orders to report to Lieutenant-Colonel Elliott, at Gauley Bridge, who, in command of the 47th O. V. I. was *en route* to Meadow Bluffs, Greenbrier County. On the eve of May 11, Major Hoffman commanding the cavalry, moved forward form Meadow Bluffs via the Blue Sulphur Springs route, and Colonel Elliott proceeded via the Lewisburg pike, under instructions to meet at the junction of the two roads at Handley's house, near Lewisburg. The commands met as ordered before break of day on the 12th. Edgar's Rebel Infantry battalion, and Captain White's cavalry company were encamped within speaking distance of the junction, advised of the approach of the Union troops by some of their pickets that had escaped capture. Those captured had informed Colonel Elliott of the position of the enemy; at daylight the Rebel line was charged and scattered in all directions. Captain Powell was ordered out in pursuit of the Rebel cavalry, and drove them to and through the town of Lewisburg, to within one mile of the White Sulphur Springs, capturing quite a number of prisoners in this wild and exciting chase. The command returned to Meadow Bluffs, where, on the 16th of May, Col. Geo. Crook arrived with other troops, and organized the 3d Brigade of the Kanawha Division, comprising the 36th, 44th and 47th O. V. I. and First Battalion 2d W. Va. Cavalry and a battery of artillery, and began his reconnoissance in force against Jackson River Depot. The infantry moving via the pike, and the cavalry on the old Sweet Spring road, under orders to form a junction at Callahan's Station. *En route* to the station Captain Powell commanded the advance guard of twelve men. On nearing the station, late in the afternoon, six Rebel captains of "the Moccasin Ranger" organization were surprised and captured after a serious contest, after Captain Powell charged upon the station and captured two other officers and twenty-five men. A halt was made to await the arrival of the main force, which, on coming up after dark, went into camp. The command moved forward next morning upon Jackson River Depot, but on learning that there were no Rebel troops in that immediate section, and that General Heth, with a considerable force, was moving in the direction of Lewisburg, Colonel Crook hastened back to Meadow Bluffs, to make the necessary preparation to give his old class-mate at West Point a warm reception.

On the early morn of May 23d, Colonel Crook placed his command in line just as General Heth gained the summit of the hill east of the town, and quickly formed his line of battle about midway between the summit and the eastern edge of the village, placing his guns near the eastern edge of the town. Crook quietly moved his command under cover of the buildings on the west side of the village and awaited Heth's attack, which was promptly made, and as promptly met by Crook in a gallant charge of the 36th, 44th and 47th Ohio Volunteer Infantry, capturing the enemy's guns, and pushed his line forward driving Heth and his entire force in utter rout, the cavalry pushing the enemy back over Greenbrier River in the direction of Union. Thus the victory was quickly achieved. The time occupied in this engagement did not exceed 30 minutes from the time Heth gained the summit until he was driven back over it. The enemy's loss was 80 killed, 100 wounded, 157 prisoners, 4 guns, 25 horses and 300 stand of small-arms. Union loss—13 killed, 50 wounded, 6 prisoners. Colonel Crook slightly wounded. The brigade returned to its camping grounds at Meadow Bluffs, May 29th.

Aside from active cavalry scouting, and the visit in force made by Colonel Crook, accompanied by his brigade on the 24th of June to his distinguished friend, General Heth at Union, who, in preference to waiting Crook's arrival, had sought a hiding place in some distant mountain the day previous. On learning of the enemy's flight, Colonel Crook returned to Meadow Bluffs. The infantry force quietly rested until the 14th of August, on which date Gen'l J. D. Cox was ordered to report with the Kanawha Division, except the 44th and 47th Ohio Volunteer Infantry and 2d Virginia Cavalry, at Washington City. The latter regiments were ordered into camp at the Kanawha Falls, under command of Col. J. A. J. Lightburn.

Early in September, the camp was filled with rumors of the coming of General Loring, with a Rebel force, *via* Flat Top Mountain, to drive the Yanks into Ohio, which induced Lightburn to move his force down the river to "Soup Creek." On the 13th the rumor materialized into fact; the enemy attacked the Union position. Colonel Lightburn declined to contest the Rebel advance and retreated to Charleston, and on his arrival ordered the transports with supplies and sick in hospital *en route* to Gallipolis, Ohio. then crossed the Elk River and destroyed the bridge, moved down the river to Pocatalico, thence across the country to Racine, Ohio.

Two days previous to General Loring's attack, Lightburn was advised of Jenkins' Rebel cavalry raid to the Ohio River near Guyandotte, and sent Colonel Paxton with eight companies of the Second Virginia Cavalry to look after him. Colonel Paxton pushed forward rapidly on the pike leading from Charleston via Coalsmouth to Guyandotte on the Ohio River. On approaching within a few miles of Barboursville, General Jenkins' force, 1200 strong, was reported to be quartered near the latter place. Captain Powell (now major, having received his promotion June 25, in command of Company B) being in the advance, halted to await Colonel Paxton's arrival with the command which failed to close up until after dark. The conference was short. Major Powell advanced rapidly, drove in the Rebel pickets and charged the camp, driving the entire force up the Guyandotte River, and was in peaceable possession of the Rebel camp on Colonel Paxton's arrival, losing but one man killed in the charge. Returning from this movement against the enemy to report to Colonel Lightburn, on reaching Coalsmouth, the transports were met *en route* out of the Kanawha river, and the first news of the evacuation of the Kanawha Valley by the Union troops was received with orders to Colonel Paxton to escort the transports out of the Kanawha River. On reaching Thirteen Mile Creek, the regiment, save a suitable guard, left with the transports, moved across the country to Letart Falls on the Ohio River, thence down the Virginia shore to Point Pleasant at the mouth of the Kanawha River. The Second Virginia Cavalry Regiment did not disgrace its war record by forsaking the sacred soil of Virginia by crossing the Ohio river into Ohio, notwithstanding its orders to do so.

The brigade reassembled at Point Pleasant. The inexcusable driving out process experienced under Colonel Lightburn induced the assignment of Gen'l Q. A. Gilmore, U. S. A., to the command of the troops at Point Pleasant, who was soon relieved by General Milroy, and he in a few days relieved by Gen'l J. D. Cox, who, on the 20th of October, after a reorganization of the troops proceeded to Charleston, where it was ordered into winter quarters, the Second Virginia Cavalry being ordered into winter quarters at Camp Piatt, 12 miles above, on the Kanawha River.

On the 16th of November Gen'l George Crook, having been promoted to the rank of brigadier-general of volunteers, relieved General Cox in the command of the Kanawha Division.

Having completed the campaign work of 1862 in the Kanawha Valley, as was supposed, much to the surprise and gratification of the boys, they were in the saddle and on the road in obedience to the following order:

HEADQUARTERS KANAWHA DIVISION,
CHARLESTON, KANAWHA CO., VA., *November* 23, 1862.

SPECIAL ORDER }
   NO. — }

Col. Jno. C. Paxton, commanding the Second Regiment Loyal Virginia Cavalry, will proceed with all the serviceable men of his regiment to-morrow morning, Nov. 24, to Cold Knob Mountain, in Greenbrier County, Va., *via* the Summerville and Lewisburg road, leav- the Kanawha River route at Cannelton. On Cold Knob Mountain you will overtake Col. P. H. Lane, commanding the 11th O. V. I., ordered to that point to reinforce your command. From which position you will proceed against the camps of the 14th Rebel Virginia Cavalry Regiment, located in the Sinking Creek Valley, some two miles apart in winter quarters, recruiting. Break up the organization if possible.

GEORGE CROOK,
Commanding Kanawha Division.

Leaving the camp at early morn, Summerville was reached at 8 P. M. that day, having traveled sixty miles over rough roads, camped there that night; broke camp early on the following morn, encountered a small Rebel squad *en route*, took them in and passed on, halted during the afternoon to feed and rest; then pressed forward through a heavy snow storm through the afternoon and night of the 25th, arriving at the summit of Cold Knob Mountain early forenoon of the 26th, where the command overtook Col. P. H. Lane, 11th O. V. I. ordered to this point from Summerville, to reinforce the cavalry movement, which regiment, in consequence of the deep snow and great suf- fering experienced, returned from Cold Knob to Summerville that morning. The advance upon the Rebel camp in the valley was promptly organized. Major Powell, in command of twenty men of company G., commanded by Lieut. Jeremiah Davidson, constituted the advance guard *en route* down the mountain side; a Rebel scouting party of four men were met, two were cap- tured, from whom the exact status of the enemy was learned. On nearing the foot of the mountain the two escaped scouts were seen in the distance leasurely approaching their camp; the smoke of which was perceptible to the advance guard. Major Powell halted a moment to allow the two scouts to pass around a point out of view of his movement, then pushed rapidly forward to said point, from which he gained full view of the Rebel camp, with the aid of his field glass; judging of the action of the camp, he felt assured that his close proximity was not known in the camp. Appreciating the golden opportunity, seeing that the regiment was not in supporting distance, the Major announced his purpose to his little heroic band. They promptly answered: " We will follow where you lead." The line was formed and the camp, 500 strong, was assailed. The enemy, surprised, capitulated on condition of the protection of their lives, before Colonel Paxton and the regiment reached the camp. Thus, Major Powell, with Lieutenant Davidson and twenty men of Company G, 2d Regiment Virginia Calvary, did on the 26th of Nov., 1862, without the loss of a life or the firing of a gun or revolver, accomplish one of the most brilliant and successful feats in the war of 1861 and 1865, for which daring exploit Gen'l W. H. Powell wears a badge bearing the following inscription: " The Congress to General William H. Powell, and 2d Regiment West Virginia Cavalry Volunteer, Sinking Creek, Virginia, Nov. 26, 1862," granted by reason of the following endorsement:

CHICAGO, ILL., *Feb.* 2, 1889.

My Dear Powell: I have read your paper on the Sinking Creek raid with much interest and pleasure for I have always regarded the part you took in that expedition as one of the most daring, brilliant and successful of the whole war.

Yours sincerely,

GEORGE CROOK.

January 15, 1863, General Crook ordered Colonel Paxton in command of his regiment on an expedition to Peter's Mountain *via* Meadow Bluffs, Alderson Ferry and Centreville. Companies B and H, under command of Lieutenant-Colonel Powell, who received his commission as lieutenant-colonel, dated October 25, 1862, for his daring gallantry in the Sinking Creek raid November 26, 1862, to succeed Lieut-Col. R. L. Curtis (resigned), were ordered to make a feint upon Lewisburg, and to burn Hanley's house and Teamster's barns near Lewisburg, to draw the troops of the enemy from their camps at Centreville and Union, in Monroe County to Lewisburg, to allow Colonel Paxton and his troops to pass through Centreville. The feint was a success, but the expedition in the main proved a failure on account of the heavy snows and extreme cold weather.

In the latter part of January, Lieutenant-Colonel Powell, under orders, proceeded to Wheeling on official business pertaining to the more efficient arming of the regiment; in this absence from his command, he contracted a severe cold and an attack of bilious fever, that proved so serious as to induce

L.M. Strayer

EDWIN S. MORGAN
Major 2nd West Virginia Cavalry

WILLIAM V. JOHNSTON
Captain 2nd West Virginia Cavalry

the tender of his resignation as lieutenant-colonel, about the middle of April.

During his absence from camp at home, and previous to the acceptance of his resignation, Gen'l E. P. Scammon, then commanding the Kanawha troops, ordered Colonel Paxton and regiment on a reconnoissance to Lewisburg; encountered the enemy near Brush Mountain, was surprised and suffered a disastrous defeat of 14 killed and severely wounded, and a number taken prisoner. On his return to camp, upon making his report, he was by order of General Scammon peremptorily dismissed from the service. Whereupon the regiment petitioned General Scammon and Governor Peirpoint to urge upon Lieutenant-Colonel Powell to withdraw his resignation as lieutenant-colonel, and to accept a commission as colonel of the regiment and return to the command, which he was induced to accept, receiving his commission as colonel of the Second Regiment Virginia Volunteer Cavalry, under date of May 13, 1863.

First Wytheville Raid.

July 13, an expedition was organized, consisting of the 34th Ohio Volunteer Infantry, Lieutenant-Colonel Franklin commanding (mounted for this expedition), seven companies of the 2d Regiment West Va. Cavalry (West Virginia having become a State June 30, 1863), commanded by Colonel Powell, and two companies of the 1st Regiment West Va. Cavalry, under command of Captain Delaney. Commanded by Col. John T. Toland, it began its movement against Wytheville, Va., on the Virginia and Tennessee Railroad. A number of small bodies of the enemy were encountered *en route*, many of whom were captured and paroled. The command suffered some loss at Raleigh C. H. through lack of proper precaution, evidencing the worthlessness of temporarily mounted infantry as cavalrymen.

The expedition reached Wytheville in the forenoon of the 18th; on nearing the village the advance 34th Ohio Volunteer Infantry encountered a feeble skirmish line on the crest of a low ridge that obstructed a view of the town. A halt was made, Colonel Powell received orders to move his command to the front to charge into the town. Colonel Powell suggested to the commanding officer to dismount the 34th Ohio Volunteer Infantry to drive the enemy from the crest of the ridge, that a knowledge of the position and strength of the enemy might be ascertained. The suggestion was unheeded and the order to charge repeated. The charge was made, the enemy was driven from his position, his guns and many prisoners taken. But the loss sustained was heavy and totally unjustified. The gallant Colonel Powell was severely wounded in leading the charge, and Colonel Toland killed soon after he reached the head of the line to assume command. The Union loss was killed in action, including Colonel Toland, 6; wounded in action, including Colonel Powell, 18.

Colonel Powell and the wounded Assistant-Surgeon O'Nellis were taken to Richmond, Va. as soon as able to be moved. The command under Lieutenant-Colonel Franklin returned to the Kanawha Valley.

Colonel Powell was held as a prisoner of war until the 29th of January, 1864. When, after great and repeated efforts he was paroled for thirty days to visit Washington City to effect the exchange of Richard H. Lee, then a prisoner on Johnsons Island. During Colonel Powell's sojourn in Libby prison he was confined in a cell in the basement of the building for thirty-seven days, and made to subsist on coarse corn bread and water, with no bed or bunk to lie down on, his supply of water was furnished him but once a week, one ordinary bucketful every Sunday morning, out of which he drank, and in which he washed his face and hands. The exchange was effected, and Colonel Powell, after a short visit at his home in Ironton, Ohio, returned to the Kanawha Valley and assumed command of his regiment March 20, 1864, which gave him a magnificent reception.

In His Visit at Home

His friends in the Lawrence Iron Works, over which he presided prior to the war, presented him a gold watch, bearing the inscription on the inner case: "Col. W. H. Powell, 2d Virginia Cavalry, from his friends of the Lawrence Iron Works, Ironton, Ohio, February 22, 1864. Always on time." The citizens at large, gave him $300 to purchase a horse and equipments; John Peters, Chaplain McCabe's father-in-law, a beautiful sabre, belt and sash and a brace of Colt's ivory mounted 44 calibre navy revolvers.

Gen'l Geo. Crook, having returned to the command of the corps in the Kanawha Valley, organized a cavalry movement (under Gen'l W. W. Averell) against Saltville, on the Tennesee and Virginia Railroad, and moved out from Camp Piatt April 30, while General Crook made an advance upon Dublin Depot. The latter achieved a brilliant success over Gen'l A. G. Jenkins' Rebel force in which engagement General Jenkins received his death wound. The former movement against Saltville was not made. General Averell withdrew the cavalry from its advance upon Saltville, and proceeded to make an attack upon Wythevlle, *via* Cove Gap, in which he was frustrated by reason of the occupancy of the Gap by a strong force of the enemy, anticipating his movements. On approaching the latter place it was found to be strongly fortified by the enemy, under Gen'l Jno. H. Morgan (of the Indiana and Ohio raid notoriety), whose advantageous position in Cove Gap rendered Averell's attack upon the objective point impracticable. General Averell, however, made an attack upon the enemy's position, which was stubbornly contested for four hours, in which engagement Averell received a wound across his forehead compelling his retirement from command during the battle, and in view of General Duffie's conspicuous absence, the command devolved upon Colonel Powell, whose active and determined movements baffled and successfully held in check the persistent attempts of the enemy to drive him from his position until darkness closed the engagement. During the night General Averell crossed the mountain and fell back to Blacksburg, *en route* to Lewisburg. In General Averell's report of this engagement at Cove Gap, he complimented the conduct of Colonel Powell and his regiment as follows (see Adjutant-General's Report, West Virginia, page 540): " The General commanding desires to express his high appreciation of the skillful evolution of the 2d Regiment, West Virginia Cavalry, under Colonel Powell, upon the field of battle. It was a dress parade that continued without disorder under a heavy fire for four hours."

On the 31st of May, Crook's entire force (Army of West Virginia) was again on the move, under orders to report to General Hunter at Staunton in a movement against Lynchburg, Va. On reaching Staunton, the cavalry force was reorganized; two divisions were created, commanded respectively by Generals Averell and Duffie, the latter for special separate service in the movement against Lynchburg; the former operated with the main force. Colonel Powell was assigned to the command of the Third Brigade, composed of the First, Second and Third Regiments, West Virginia Cavalry, Averell's Division, Army of West Virginia.

On the approach of the advance of the main force at Lexington, the enemy made but feeble resistance; Powell's brigade drove the enemy's cavalry a few miles beyond the city and returned to headquarters. At early morn of the 13th, the cavalry advanced on Buchanan, *en route* overtook McCausland's Rebel cavalry; Colonel Powell's brigade being in the advance, drove the enemy across the James River, who fired the bridge as he passed over, making it necessary for the Union troops to ford the stream. On reaching Buchanan, several batteaux loaded with stores of various descriptions were captured. The cavalry remained here until the morning of the 15th, then crossed the Blue Ridge between the Peaks of Otter to " Fancy Farm" to await the arrival of the main column. On its arrival at dark, Colonel Powell's brigade was ordered forward to Liberty, where the Rebel cavalry was encountered and driven off to find some other quarters for the night.

On the 16th, the main cavalry column advanced to Liberty, rebuilt the bridge over Little Otter River, forded Big Otter and attacked McCausland, driving him from New London. General Imboden's report that "the enemy's (Union) troops, after a short engagement gave way, losing a dozen men," and that "a double line of the enemy's infantry overlapped his right, forcing his retreat," is not correct; there were no infantry in the engagement at New London.

On the morning of the 17th, Colonel Powell's brigade in the advance, pushed McCausland and Imboden's cavalry force back to and beyond the stone church, within four miles of Lynchburg, and halted at the church until General Averell came forward with the remainder of his division and the 91st O. V. I., formed his line of attack and charged the Rebel line, driving it in great confusion towards the city, in which charge Col. Jno. A. Turley, 91st O. V. I., was wounded. On the arrival of the main army, Generals Crook and Averell urged an advance upon Lynchburg that evening, which was unheeded by General Hunter, who ordered the army into camp for the night. In the early morn of the 18th, Colonel Powell, in command of his brigade and two guns, moved out under orders on the road leading to Lynchburg *via* Campbell Court House to attack the Rebel works on south side of the city. He overtook General Imboden's cavalry at Campbell Court House in position behind the buildings. Powell immediately brought his guns to bear upon the court house and other buildings, resulting in the hasty display of Imboden's truce flag, which was respected by Colonel Powell upon condition that the enemy would evacuate the village in 10 minutes. He then drove Imboden back upon Lynchburg rapidly; on reaching a point within view of the city, the advance halted until the column closed up. In the meantime, a messenger from General Averell overtook the command with orders to Colonel Powell to return to army headquarters. *En route* to New London, on the road to Liberty, procuring a colored man as guide, the brigade passed to the left within sight of the Rebel camp fires at the stone church about midnight, overtaking Hunter's army at New London in camp near daybreak.

General Hunter retreated to the Kanawha Valley *via* Liberty, Bonsack, Salem, Newcastle and Lewisburg, reaching Charleston June 29, with an army sadly demoralized and half starved, all feeling, as freely expressed, that with General Crook in command the army would not have deserted the Valley of Virginia at Salem. General Hunter's forces moved out of Charleston, July 12, *en route via* Ohio River to Parkersburg, thence *via* Baltimore and Ohio Railroad to Martinsburg, where it arrived on the 18th.

July 20. General Averell, commanding a brigade composed of the 9th West Va. Infantry Volunteers, 91st and 34th Ohio Infantry Volunteers, and the Second Cavalry regiment, in advancing up the valley encountered the Rebel General Ramseur's Division, 5600 infantry, 8 guns and 1600 cavalry strong, in position on Carter's farm, four miles north of Winchester. The enemy, after a severe contest and heavy loss, was routed and driven from the field. Rebel loss, 217 killed and wounded, 200 prisoners, four guns and 800 stand of small-arms. Union loss, 60 killed, 157 wounded. Union force engaged 2000 infantry, 800 cavalry, no artillery.

In the entire campaign in the Shenandoah Valley, beginning July 20, 1864, under Hunter, and from the 7th of August until the close of the war, under Gen'l Phil. H. Sheridan, at Appomattox, serving in the Second Cavalry Division, Army of West Va., under Gen'l W. W. Averell and Gen'l W. H. Powell as commanders, in Sheridan's Cavalry Corps, the Second Regiment West Va. Cavalry, under its commander, Col. W. H. Powell, and under his command as brigade and division commander, won enduring renown from its Commanders-in-Chief, Powell, Averell, Crook, Torbert and Sheridan, in the main battles of Lewisburg, Wytheville, Sinking Creek raid, Lynchburg, Carter's Farm, Winchester, Moorefield, Martinsburg, Bunker Hill, Kearnstown, Winchester (July 24, 1864), Moorefield, Stevenson's Depot, Opequon (September 19), Fisher's Hill, Mount Jackson, Forrest Hill, Weyer's Cave, Cedar Creek, Nineveh, Rude's Hill, Liberty Mills and Five Forks, and 46 other severe and important engagements, as evidenced by the following recommendations received by its commanding officer for promotion.

[COPY.]

HEADQUARTERS, 2D CAVALRY DIVISION IN THE FIELD,
DEPARTMENT W. VA., *Sept.* 3, 1864.
BRIG.-GEN'L L. THOMAS, *Adj't.-Gen'l.*

General:—I have the honor to request that Col. W. H. Powell, 2d West Va. Cavalry, be appointed a Brigadier of Volunteers. He has been in the service three years, and his term of service is about to expire. For that appointment he has every recommendation. He has always distinguished himself in battle ; has been wounded and suffered in prison. He is a gentleman of high character, and one of the best brigade commanders that I know. The cavalry arm of the service can ill afford to lose so excellent an officer.

(Signed)   W. W. AVERELL, *Brig.-Gen'l.*

[ENDORSEMENTS.]

HEADQUARTERS, DEPARTMENT W. VA.
NEAR BERRYVILLE, VA., *Sept.* 5, 1864.

Colonel Powell has served with me often since the commencement of this war. He has distinguished himself in every battle he was engaged in under me. He has been recommended by me on several occasions, for promotion. I regard him as one of the best cavalry officers I have ever seen in the service.

(Signed) GEO. CROOK, *Brevet Major-General,*
Army of West Virginia.

HEADQUARTERS, MIDDLE MILITARY DIVISION,
SHENANDOAH VALLEY, *Sept.* 5, 1864.

I have enquired particularly in reference to this officer's conduct heretofore, and of his abilities and good soldierly conduct, and recommend him for the additional grade.

(Signed) P. H. SHERIDAN, *Maj.-Gen'l Commanding.*

It is said Colonel Powell now commands a brigade, and these recommendations being so good and ample, give him a brevet appointment, if a full commission is impracticable.

(Signed) A. LINCOLN, *President United States.*

Col. Wm. H. Powell received his commission as brigadier-general October 19, 1864. At the close of the campaign in the Shenandoah Valley, General Powell, by reason of death and severe illness in his family, was reluctantly constrained to leave the service, and return to his bereaved and stricken family. Having tendered his resignation January 5, he received the following kindly expressed regrets from his corps and army commanders:

HEADQUARTERS, CAVALRY CORPS, MIDDLE MILITARY DIVISION,
WINCHESTER, VA., *January* 14, 1865.

BRIG.-GEN'L W. H. POWELL, *Commanding 2d Cav. Div.*

General:—Your resignation having been accepted, I feel I should be doing myself an injustice did I permit you to leave the service of the United States and my command, without tendering you an expression of my appreciation of your valor and ability as a soldier, your zeal, efficiency and untiring energy as a cavalry commander.

During the period of your service under my command, you have more than sustained the reputation so justly given you by your former commander, and have merited and won the commendation of your superiors. Thrown suddenly in command of your division, in the midst of active operations, and during a campaign most severe, but never exceeded in brilliancy, your labors have been incessant, but at all times performed with an alacrity, skillfulness and honesty of purpose which have invariably crowned your efforts with success, winning for you an enviable and lasting reputation. I now part with you with great regret, earnestly trusting that your career in civil life may be as brilliantly successful.

I am truly and sincerely your friend,

(Signed) A. T. S. TORBERT, *Brevet Maj.-Gen'l,*
Chief of Cavalry Command.

HEADQUARTERS, ARMY OF THE SHENANDOAH, *July* 15, 1865.

My Dear General:—I greatly regret the necessity which compelled you to leave the public service. The regret is not only for the loss I myself sustain, but the loss to the public service. I desire to express to you my heartfelt thanks for your faithful support, and for your gallantry which has contributed so much to make the victories of the Shenandoah Valley decisive. Should you again enter the service, I would consider myself fortunate in having you under my command.

Very truly,

PHIL. H. SHERIDAN, *Maj.-Gen'l, U. S. A.*

BRIGADIER-GENERAL POWELL, *Comdg. 2d Cav. Div.*

CHAPTER XXV.

THIRD REGIMENT W. VA. CAVALRY VOLUNTEERS.

Roster of the Field, Staff and Company Officers of the Third Regiment West Virginia Cavalry Volunteers, Showing the Alterations and Casualties Therein from the Date of Original Organization of Said Regiment to the Date of Muster Out, June 30, 1865.

Date of Commission.	Names and Rank.	Co.	Remarks.
	Colonel.		
March 10, 1865.	John L. McGee.		
	Lieutenant-Colonels.		
June 15, 1862.	David H. Strother,		Resigned September 10, 1864.
July 18, 1863.	John L. McGee,		Promoted to Colonel.
May 1, 1865.	John S. Witcher.		
	Majors.		
March 25, 1862.	John L. McGee,		Promoted to Lieutenant-Colonel.
July 29, 1863.	Lot Bowen,		Resigned December 12, 1864.
July 29, 1863.	Seymour B. Conger,		Killed in action at Moorefield, W. Va., August 7, 1864.
April 13, 1864.	John S. Witcher,		Promoted to Lieutenant-Colonel.
Dec. 15, 1864.	Charles E. Anderson,		
May 23, 1865.	Charles W. White,		
May 23, 1865.	John L. Hurst.		
	1st Lt. and Adj't.		
June 25, 1862.	Barna Powell.		Honorably discharged January 1, 1864.
	1st Lts. and R. Q. M.		
Sept. 11, 1863.	Lee Haymond,		Promoted to Captain and C. S. U. S. V.
Nov. 26, 1864.	Samuel C. Mellor.		
	1st Lt. and Reg. Com.		
Oct. 7, 1863.	David M. Drake.		Honorably discharged.
	Surgeons.		
April 22, 1864.	Thomas Morton,		Mustered out at expiration of term of service.
May 17, 1865.	Arthur Titus.		
	Assistant Surgeons.		
July 8, 1862.	Thomas Morton,		Promoted to Surgeon.
April 22, 1864.	David S. Pinnel,		Resigned December 23, 1864.
April 16, 1864.	Benoni Parkinson,		Promoted to Surgeon, 17th W. Va. Infantry.
Jan. 25, 1865.	Aaron W. Davis.		

Date of Commission.	Names and Rank.	Co.	Remarks.
	Chaplain.		
July 1, 1864.	William Slaughter.		
	Captains.		
Dec. 27, 1861.	Everton J. Conger,	A	Promoted to Major, 1st D. C. Cavalry.
April 20, 1865.	Joseph Robbins,	A	
Oct. 3, 1862.	Charles W. White,	B	Promoted to Major.
April 20, 1865.	Andrew J. Adams,	B	
March 14, 1862.	William B. Shaw,	C	Resigned May 24, 1862.
May 28, 1862.	Jonathan Stahl,	C	Resigned October 23, 1862.
Nov. 22, 1862.	Seymour B. Conger,	C	Promoted to Major.
March 1, 1864.	Peter Tabler,	C	
Oct. 22, 1862.	James R. Utt,	D	Killed in action May 16, 1863.
July 18, 1863.	George W. McVicker,	D	
Oct. 28, 1862.	Lot Bowen,	E	Promoted to Major.
Jan. 23, 1864.	Timothy F. Roane,	E	
Nov. 25, 1862.	Samuel C. Means,	F	Permanently detached, Order Sec. of War.
Sept. 2, 1863.	John S. Witcher,	G	Promoted to Major.
July 6, 1864.	John Harshbarger,	G	
Feb. 19, 1863.	W. H. Flesher,	H	Resigned June 16, 1865.
Oct. 27, 1865.	Charles E. Anderson,	I	Promoted to Major.
Feb. 15, 1865.	George A. Sexton,	I	
Sept. 12, 1863.	David B. Wolf,	K	Dismissed, October 29, 1864.
Nov. 26, 1864.	Benja. C. Smith,	K	
April 20, 1865.	Francis J. LeSage,	L	
Aug. 8, 1864.	John L. Hurst,	M	Promoted to Major.
May 23, 1865.	Jacob W. Heavner.	M	
	First Lieutenants.		
Dec. 27, 1861.	Seymour B. Conger,	A	Promoted to Captain, Co. C.
Nov. 22, 1862.	Wm. W. Barrett,	A	Mustered out at expiration of term of service.
March 9, 1865.	James Devoir,	A	
Oct. 3, 1862.	George W. Artis,	B	Resigned May 18, 1863.
July 15, 1863.	John P. Johnson,	B	Killed in action near Salem, Va.
Feb. 15, 1865.	George W. Wilson,	B	
March 14, 1862.	John E. Hoffman,	C	Killed in action November 24, 1863.
Jany. 26, 1864.	John E. Bowers,	C	Mustered out at expiration of term of service.
Sep. 8, 1864.	Albert Teets,	C	
Sep. 22, 1862.	Geo. W. McVicker,	D	Promoted to Captain.
July 18, 1863.	McGill Clark,	D	
Oct. 28, 1862.	Timothy F. Roane,	E	Promoted to Captain.
Jan. 23, 1864.	Leonard Clark,	E	Killed in action at Moorefield, W. Va.
Sep. 24, 1864.	George W. Starr,	E	
Nov. 25, 1862.	Luther W. Slater,	F	Resigned Janury 18, 1863.
Feb. 26, 1863.	James S. Perry,	F	Permanently detached, Order War Dept.
Feb. 16, 1865.	Stephen Ripley,	F	
Dec. 6, 1862.	John S. Witcher,	G	Promoted to Captain.

Date of Commission.	Names and Rank.	Co.	Remarks.
	First Lieutenants.		
Oct. 24, 1863.	John Harshbarger,	G	Promoted to Captain.
Dec. 20, 1862.	William H. Flesher,	H	Promoted to Captain.
Feb. 19, 1863.	Aaron W. Davis,	H	Promoted to Assistant Surgeon.
Feb. 15, 1865.	Andrew J. Adams,	H	Promoted to Captain, Co. B.
Oct. 12, 1863.	George A. Sexton,	I	Promoted to Captain.
Sep. 12, 1863.	James P. Matthew,	K	Mustered out at expiration of term of service.
June 9, 1865.	Richard B. Little,	K	
April 8, 1864.	Jacob W. Heavner,	M	Promoted to Captain.
May 23, 1865.	Claudius B. See.	M	
	Second Lieutenants.		
Jan. 10, 1862.	Wm. W. Barrett,	A	Promoted to 1st Lieutenant.
Nov. 22, 1862.	Benjamin C. Smith,	A	Promoted to Captain, Co. K.
March 15, 1865.	Lewis S. Jenkins,	A	
Oct. 23, 1862.	Daniel J. Martin,	B	Dismissed September 12, 1864.
March 30, 1865.	Thomas M. Goff,	B	
March 14, 1862.	Joseph A. Benson,	C	Resigned May 24, 1862.
Nov. 20. 1862.	John E. Bowers,	C	Promoted to 1st Lieutenant.
Feb. 12, 1864.	Albert Teets,	C	Promoted to 1st Lieutenant.
Oct. 22, 1862.	McGill Clark,	D	Promoted to 1st Lieutenant.
July 18, 1863.	Joseph Robbins,	D	Promoted to Captain, Co. A.
Dec. 1, 1862.	Wm. E. Lovett,	E	Discharged by order General Sheridan.
Nov. 25, 1862.	Daniel M. Keys,	F	Permanently detached by order Sec. War.
March 11, 1865.	William P. Hubbard,	F	
June 19, 1863.	Francis J. LeSage,	G	Promoted to Captain, Co. L.
May 23, 1865.	James C. Swintzel,	G	
Feb. 19, 1863.	Andrew J. Adams,	H	Promoted to 1st Lieutenant.
Feb. 15, 1865.	Alfred Boregard,	H	
Oct. 27, 1863.	Nathan Rexroad,	I	
Sep. 12, 1863.	Henry A. Wolfe,	K	Killed in action February 20, 1864.
March 26, 1864.	John M. Capito,	K	Dismissed September 12, 1864.
Nov. 14, 1864.	Ira E. Freeman,	K	Dismissed April, 1865.
May 23, 1865.	Edgar L. Clayton,	K	
March 27, 1865.	William Knox,	L	
April 13, 1864.	Samuel A. Childers.	M	Resigned June 17, 1865.

THE THIRD WEST VIRGINIA CAVALRY.

The 3d West Virginia Cavalry was organized in the spring of 1862, with David H. Strother, lieutenant-colonel; John L. McGee, major and Barna Powell, adjutant.

Lieutenant-Colonel Strother had a national reputation as an artist and litterateur, and was among the first in this country to illustrate his own literary productions of Southern life and events, prior to the war, in *Harper's Magazine* under the *nom de plume* of "Porte Crayon." During the two first years of the regiment's service it was doing guard and scouting duty by company detachments, which were stationed from the Shenandoah to the Kanawha Valleys; during this time Colonel Strother was performing special service on the staff of Generals Averell, Sigel and Hunter.

Colonel McGee had seen much active service in the war prior to his promotion into the 3d Cavalry Regiment. He also served as " chief of staff " with General Milroy.

On the 18th of July, 1861, Company A, 1st West Virginia Cavalry, recruited and mustered in at Morgantown, W. Va., was the first cavalry organization raised in the State; it was mustered into service as the "Kelley Lancers," J. L. McGee, captain; and at once reported to Gen'l B. F. Kelley, at Grafton, whence it was ordered to New Creek (Keyser), W. Va., and on General Kelley's advance on Romney, took part in that expedition, and together with the Ringgold cavalry charged the enemy's works. This charge was delivered with fine spirit and most satisfactory results, the whole of the enemy's artillery, stores and flags being taken without the loss of a man.

General Kelley, in his official report to the War Department remarks: "I must be pardoned, however in calling the attention of the country to the brilliant charges of the cavalry under Captains Keys and McGee. I venture to say they are unsurpassed by any in the annals of American warfare."*

This advance was soon followed by the surprise of the Rebels at Blues Gap; in which the Lancers were again conspicuous, resulting in the capture of a number of prisoners, three pieces of artillery and the entire camp equipage of the enemy, and driving the Rebel forces to the eastern slope of the Alleghanies, thus transferring the field of active operations to the Valley of Virginia.

Captain McGee was promoted to major of the 3d West Virginia Cavalry, October 2, 1861.

The several companies and battalions in the Third Regiment rendered conspicuous service. As early as June, 1862, Company C, Capt. Seymour

* Romney, October 28, 1861, Rebellion Record, vol. 5, sec. 1, page 380.

B. Conger, was attached to General Fremont's command. When in pursuit of "Stonewall" Jackson in his retreat up the Shenandoah Valley, Captain Conger and his company frequently engaged the enemy, and received special mention from General Fremont, upon the occasion of a splendid dash made by the company at the bridge near Mount Jackson; when the retreating enemy had fired the structure, Captain Conger's gallant charge saved the bridge, and General Ashby barely escaped capture.

Capt. Lott Bowen, Co. E, displayed the qualities of the brave soldier in the vicinity of Weston, Sutton and Bulltown in western Virginia under General Roberts. Lieut. Timothy F. Roane, in command of the same company, charged, routed, killed and captured many of Imboden's and Jackson's troops near Clarksburg, at Simpson's Creek and Jane Lew, in the early part of May, 1863. In the reorganization of the Army of the Potomac, January 31st, 1863, Companies A and C were detailed for special duty at General Sigel's "Grand Reserve Division" headquarters. Company H, in command of Capt. W. H. Flesher, was at Parkersburg from May 1 to August 31, 1863; Company G, Capt. John S. Witcher, was in Col. Rutherford B. Hayes' Brigade in the Kanawha Valley.

In June, 1863, Captain Conger, with Companies A and C, was attached to General Pleasanton's Corps, Buford's Division, Colonel Devin's Brigade, and participated in the battles of Brady Station, Beverly Ford, Stevensburg and Upperville, Virginia.

A characteristic episode of the war, and one which very forcibly illustrates the estimation in which the West Virginia troops were held, occurred while General Milroy was in command at Winchester. A reconnoissance of considerable force had been repulsed with very serious loss to our troops, and it was determined to send out a strong force to develop the full strength of the enemy. The general, looking over the detail which had been made for the expedition, remarked that he would like to have some West Virginia boys at the front of this movement. Colonel McGee, Inspector-General, and Chief of the Staff of the Division, at once volunteered to take command of the advance guard with three companies of West Virginia Cavalry, one company of the 1st West Virginia and two of the 3d West Virginia Cavalry; it was so ordered, and the three companies, about 60 men all told, took the road far in advance of the main column.

At Fisher's Hill two Rebel pickets were observed, and Colonel McGee deployed his command sending out parties to either side, while, with about thirty men, he took up the march to the summit, which was approached by a narrow road cut in a precipitous side of the hill. When near the summit the two men in advance dashed back in perfect panic, shouting the report that

JOHN L. McGEE
Colonel 3rd West Virginia Cavalry

DAVID H. STROTHER
Lieutenant Colonel 3rd West Virginia Cavalry

they were followed by a thousand Rebs in full charge. To countermarch on this narrow road in the presence of the enemy was impossible, so the only alternative was to fight. Colonel McGee at once gave the order and with drawn sabre led the charge.

Just at the summit the road turns sharply out of the wood leading thence straight away over an open plateau: at this turn the opposing parties were first disclosed to each other, separated about 50 yards, the Rebs were in full charge and the charge of the West Virginians was delivered with such impetuosity, that the Rebel column was split and doubled back upon itself, and no more spirited hand-to-hand fight was seen during the war than that here enacted, and it was kept up with most heroic vigor until the enemy was completely routed and sent flying up the valley. It was afterward learned that the Rebel force numbered about 100 men, commanded by Major Myers, and their loss was one killed, several wounded and five prisoners; while we had two men seriously wounded, one mortally, one horse killed; the horse ridden by Colonel McGee in the charge received five bullet wounds, but the rider escaped unhurt.

One More of the Same Kind.

Lee, in his advance into Maryland detached Ewell's Corps (variously estimated at from 35,000 to 50,000 men) to pick up Milroy on the way. This they found no light morning's work. But after three days' hard and continuous fighting against hopeless odds, Milroy, with ammunition exhausted, completely surrounded and cut off from supplies or communication, determined to hold a council of war.

But before going into the council, Colonel McGee told the author that the general took him aside, and in the most impressive manner, told him: "I have been persuaded to call a council of war. It may decide to sur-render, but I will never surrender to any d——d Rebels. If the council decide to surrender, I want you to get your three companies of West Virginians together, and at their head we will go to Harper's Ferry or to hell."

In narrating the incident the colonel remarked that although he had been for three days almost constantly under fire and two nights on the outpost line, he would have most cheerfully accepted the challenge, never doubting that they would reach their proper destination. But fate ordered otherwise, and the next morning the general broke the Rebel line and marched with 5000 men of his command into the Union lines.

April 16, 1864, Major Lott Bowen, at Buckhannon, was ordered by General Sigel to proceed with his battalion to Clarksburg, thence by river and railroad to Charleston, Kanawha. May 10, 1864, the regiment, in command of Major Conger, was with General Averell in the battle of Wytheville, Va. Averell made special mention of the regiment in this.

At Staunton, Va., June, 1864, the regiment was assigned to Col. W. H. Oley's 2d Brigade, thence to the Kanawha Valley, under Oley and Duffie. August 7, 1864, General Averell fought the battle of Moorefield, W. Va. The 3d Cavalry was in command of Major John S. Witcher. The fight was one of the most signal victories for the Union cause during the war. General Averell in his report of the battle says:

" The brigadier-general commanding congratulates the officers and men of the division upon the brilliant success achieved by their victory at Moorefield, on the morning of the 7th inst.   . . .   But with our exultations is mingled a profound grief at the loss of Major Conger, 3d West Virginia Cavalry, who found death as he had always wished, in the front of battle, with heart and hand intent upon the doing of his duty. Brave, steadfast and modest, when he fell this command lost one of its best soldiers, and his regiment and general a friend. The men who followed him in the charge will never forget his glorious example, or that of the gallant Lieutenant Leonard Clark, who fell by his side."

In the reorganization of the Army of West Virginia, August 31, 1864, Gen'l George Crook, commanding; General Averell, commanding division; Col. Wm. H. Powell, commanding the Second Brigade, in which the Third West Va. Cavalry was a part under command of Maj. Lott Bowen. And still later, on the 19th of September, the same organization was preserved except the Third Cavalry, which was commanded by Maj. John S. Witcher, and Col. Henry Capehart commanding Second Brigade.

At the battle of Fisher's Hill, September 22, Lieut.-Col. McGee was in command of the Third Cavalry. On September 23, 1864, General Averell was succeeded in command of his division by Col. Wm. H. Powell.

During the months of January and February, the Third Regiment under Lieutenant-Colonel McGee, were stationed near Winchester, Va., doing picket duty, making frequent reconnoissances up the valley.

On February 27th, the regiment broke camp and moved with the cavalry corps commanded by Major-General Sheridan up the valley to Staunton, and participated in the battle at Waynesboro, Va., on the 2d of March, defeating General Early, and pushing on the same evening to Greenwood Depot. The next day the command moved to Charlottesville, and thence with the command of General Sheridan on his great raid, which resulted in the destruction of more than fifty miles of the James River Canal, many miles of railroad, besides other public property.

The command arrived at "White House" on the 19th of March, where it remained in camp until the 24th, marched thence *via* Charles City Court House, and crossed the James River at Deep Bottom.

On the morning of the 1st of April, a desperate engagement took place, in which the Third Cavalry bore a conspicuous part. On April 2d, at Ford's Station, the Third Regiment, under Lieut.-Col. John S. Witcher, charged and drove a brigade of Confederate cavalry, killing the Confederate General Pegram. The regiment continued to do duty in all the exciting and closing scenes terminating with the surrender at Appomattox on the 9th of April.

The regiment participated in the Grand Review at Washington on the 23d of May, 1865. The regiment was mustered out on the 23d of June, 1865, at Wheeling, W. Va.

The regiment lost during the war in killed and died of wounds, six officers and forty enlisted men ; died of disease or in prison, one hundred and thirty-six.

CHAPTER XXVI.

FOURTH REGIMENT W. VA. CAVALRY VOLUNTEERS.

Roster of the Field, Staff and Company Officers of the Fourth Regiment West Virginia Cavalry Volunteers, Showing the Alterations and Casualties Therein from the Date of Original Organization of Said Regiment to the Date of Muster Out, June 23, 1864.

Date of Commission.	Names and Rank.	Co.	Remarks.
	Colonel.		
Nov. 20, 1863.	Joseph Snider.		
	Lieutenant-Colonel.		
Aug. 29, 1863.	Samuel W. Snider.		
	Majors.		
Sept. 1, 1863.	Nathan Goff, Jr.		
Sept. 1, 1863.	Charles F. Howes,		
Nov. 27, 1863.	James A. Smith.		
	1st Lieut. and Adj't.		
Aug. 20, 1863.	Wm. McGee.		
	1st Lieut. and R. Q. M.		
July 11, 1863.	Thomas Bonsal.		
	1st Lieut. & Reg. Com.		
Oct. 2, 1863.	W. H. B. South.		
	Surgeon.		
Aug. 17, 1863.	David S. Pinnell.		
	Assistant Surgeon.		
Nov. 14, 1863.	David Shanor.		
	Chaplain.		
Aug. 29, 1863.	Jeremiah L. Simpson.		
	Captains.		
July 18, 1863.	William H. Shanley,	A	
July 22, 1863.	Jeremiah L. Simpson,	B	Appointed Chaplain.
July 31, 1863.	Robert C. Arbucle,	C	
Aug 27, 1863.	Calvin A. Hutchinson,	D	
Aug. 14, 1863.	John F. Wanless,	E	
Aug. 29, 1863.	James A. Smith,	F	Promoted to Major.
Dec. 18, 1863.	James H. Hibbetts,	F	
Aug. 29, 1863.	James H. Algeo,	G	
Aug. 27, 1863.	Michael Donohoe,	H	
Aug. 29, 1863.	Morris M. Snider,	I	
Aug. 29, 1863.	Joseph S. P. Barker,	K	
Aug. 29, 1863.	John S. McDonald,	L	
Nov. 27, 1863.	William King.	M	

Date of Commission.	Names and Rank.	Co.	Remarks.
	First Lieutenants.		
July 18, 1863.	David H. Dawson,	A	
July 22, 1863.	William J. Morgan,	B	
July 31, 1863.	Scott A. Harter,	C	
Aug. 5, 1863.	William L. Theis,	D	
Aug. 14, 1863.	John L. Hurst,	E	
Aug. 29, 1863.	James H. Hibbetts,	F	Promoted to Captain.
Dec. 22, 1863.	Richard B. Hewitt,	F	
Aug. 29, 1863.	Francis A. Barnes,	G	
Aug. 29, 1863.	Joseph A. Summers,	H	
Aug. 29, 1863.	Joseph Lamont,	I	
Aug. 29, 1863.	Decatur S. Elliott,	K	
Aug. 29, 1863.	Francis Harris,	L	
Oct. 21, 1863.	Tappan W. Kelley.	M	
	Second Lieutenants.		
July 18, 1863.	William H. Travis,	A	
Aug. 5, 1863.	Granville Brown,	B	
July 31, 1863.	Thomas E. Davis,	C	
Aug. 29, 1863.	Elias L. Davis,	D	
Aug. 10, 1863.	Lorenzo D. Westfall,	E	
Aug. 29, 1863.	Daniel P. James,	F	
Aug. 29, 1863.	Thomas J. Sprague,	G	
Aug. 29, 1863.	Marshall Allen,	H	
Aug. 29, 1863.	Andrew J. Vickers,	I	
Aug. 29, 1863.	Thomas Buchanan,	K	
Aug. 29, 1863.	William Varley,	L	
Nov. 27, 1863.	Joseph H. Barker.	M	

THE FOURTH WEST VIRGINIA CAVALRY.

The Fourth W. Va. Cavalry was organized August, 1863, as a one year regiment. The field officers were Joseph Snider (formerly of the 7th W.Va. Infantry), colonel; Samuel W. Snider, lieut.-col.; Nathan Goff, Jr. (of the 6th West Va. Cavalry), Charles F. Howes and James A. Smith, majors.

The regiment served in General Kelley's command and did splendid service. The principal event in which the regiment took part occurred when in the performance of escort duty, January 30, 1864, while conducting a supply train from New Creek to Petersburg; when at Medley, 2½ miles below Moorefield Junction, Colonel Snider, who was in command of the train guard, met at this point Lieutenant-Colonel Quirk, commanding 23d Illinois Infantry, falling back before the advance of the enemy. Colonel Snider being the ranking officer took command of the forces, and at once formed line of battle in the following order: The 23d Illinois, Lieutenant-

Colonel Quirk, on the left. A detacment of the 2d Maryland in the center, four companies of the 4th W. Va. Cavalry, occupying the right ; two companies of the 4th W. Va. Cavalry were placed in position on the right flank, as was also a detachment of the Ringgold Battalion, Lieutenant Spear. Two companies of the Fourth were ordered to take position on the left flank. The two remaining companies of the Fourth were placed in rear of the center to be used as the exigencies of the engagement might demand. Colonel Snider had scarcely gotten his command in position when the enemy opened upon him with two pieces of artillery; their infantry advancing at the same time, was met by a galling fire from Snider's front, and caused them to fall back. Thrice the enemy tried the same thing with the same results. During the engagement in front the enemy was extending his flanks to the right and to the left, either of which outnumbered Snider's command. The result was that Colonel Snider was compelled to withdraw his command in order to prevent capture. He lost his train, but he made a gallant defense; he was, however, fighting more than double his own command. The loss in this engagement was five killed, thirty-four wounded, and a large number captured. Among the latter was the gallant young Major Nathan Goff, Jr.

No apology will be offered for the somewhat extended reference to Major Goff which follows, for it is doubtful if West Virginia has given the nation a more distinguished son than he, having rendered his State and Nation most brilliant service no less in peace than in war.

General Goff seems to have been born under a lucky star. His father, no less than his uncle for whom he is named, were well to do and influential citizens when he was born. Many more of his kindred were independent and powerful socially. Hence the lines of his youth were cast in pleasant places. Most boys who started with the advantages he had would have made but little of themselves ; probably he would not had he not begun and continued as though his future depended entirely upon his own exertions. Early in his boyhood he took to his books, and was sent to the best schools of his native town, and later attended the Northwestern Academy, at Clarksburg, and was under the care of Dr. Gordon Battelle, its principal. There he laid the foundation of a good education. As a boy he was studious, yet full of fun and fight. He never seemed to take the family bent for business, but started early for a profession. In 1859, he entered the popular and national College at Georgetown, D. C. Here the outbreak of the war found him. He at once took sides with the Union. Early in April, 1861, and while the guns of Sumter were echoing over the land, he threw aside his books, went home, and in May enlisted as a private soldier in company G, Third Virginia Union Infantry. This was a step hardly to be expected of one so

NATHAN GOFF Jr.
Major 4th West Virginia Cavalry
Brevet Brigadier General U.S. Volunteers

SAMUEL W. SNIDER
Lieutenant Colonel 4th West Virginia Cavalry

situated in life as was young Goff. He had youth, and health and wealth; in fact, everything that would seem to have the power to allure him from the struggles of war.

The author of " Loyal West Virginia from 1861 to 1865 " is well qualified to speak of young Goff, residing from boyhood in the same city— Clarksburg, Va. Enlisting together in the same regiment, serving together throughout the war, we can say that the army may have contained more conspicuous names, but it contained no braver soldier, no truer hearted, manlier man than Nathan Goff, Jr. He was only nineteen years of age, and still more youthful in appearance when he joined the army, but his superior soldierly qualities early brought him to the front, and he was elected second lieutenant of his company. A year later, he was commissioned first lieutenant and adjutant. With his regiment he participated in the battles of McDowell, Cross Keys, Front Royal, Warrenton Springs, Rappahannock Station, Second Bull Run, Rocky Gap, Droop Mountain and other engagements of greater or lesser note. In 1864, he was promoted to major of the Fourth West Virginia Cavalry. In the engagement near Moorfield—already referred to—Major Goff's horse was shot; falling upon the major's leg, he could not extricate himself, and he was taken prisoner and sent to Libby prison at Richmond, Va.

This capture marks an event in his life that will live during all time. He shared the fate of other Union prisoners for a time; but there was a change when the Federal forces captured Major Armsey, a Confederate, who was also a West Virginian, and lived in the adjoining county to Goff. He and some others were tried as spies, and condemned to death, by the Union authorities.

Then Goff and several more Federal officers were consigned to close confinement, and notified that when the Federal sentence against Armsey and the other Confederates, for whose safety they were held, was carried into effect, they would be put to death as an act of reprisal. For months Goff lived in the shadow of death, subjected to all the rigors and privations incident to the limited ability of the enemy to supply their prisoners with the necessaries of life.

His imprisonment tended to bring out his strongest traits of character; he never flinched or murmured, but waited upon his fate like a strong man. He was a great favorite among the prisoners before his solitary confinement began, and his selection as a hostage for Major Armsey caused great feeling among them, as well as at his home, where he was so well known and a general favorite. As soon as the Federal Government had been notified that he would be shot if Armsey was executed, naturally his powerful friends made great efforts to save his life. For weeks the decision hung in the balance a hair's weight would have turned, and he and his comrades were suffering not only the tortures of half-fed, closely confined prisoners of war, but a terrible uncertainty as to their fate, that was even worse than prison treatment. It was while this suspense was irksome and all absorbing that he gave evidence of a strength of character as unexpected as it is rare in man. In a letter to President Lincoln in relation to his confinement, now on file in the War Office, the following striking passage occurs:—

"If Major Armsey is guilty he should be executed, regardless of its consequences to me. The life of a single soldier, no matter who he may be, should not stand in the way of adherence to a great principle."

After months of confinement, an exchange of Armsey for Goff was arranged, and each officer returned to his regiment.

When Goff reached Washington, after his imprisonment, he was sent for by President Lincoln, and there occurred between the President and the young officer a most remarkable scene. Goff, who was intent upon effecting the release of his comrades whom he had left in prison, made the interview the occasion of depicting to the Executive the sufferings of our prisoners. His eloquent recital of their hardships brought tears to the eyes of the great-hearted President, and even moved the stoical Stanton, who was present. The result of this appeal was that arrangements were soon after made for an exchange of prisoners, which was promptly afterwards carried into effect.

Not very long after his return north, Goff joined his regiment, which he found at Grafton. But a little time had elapsed after his return, when Major Armsey, for whom he had been held as a hostage and exchanged, was again captured by the Union forces and was placed in jail at Clarksburg. The news had no sooner become known among the people, that the man for whom Goff had so greatly suffered was in their power, than his life was in danger. Just at this time Goff happened to come down from Grafton to his home, and he at once stayed the fury of the citizens by saying to the angry crowd: "Let no friend of mine lay a hand upon this man; he is entitled to our protection, as a prisoner of war." The act and these words, beyond all question, saved the life of Armsey, as the latter has many times since testified.

This incident in the life of the young soldier shows the inherent manhood of his character while yet a boy. Forgetting the hardships he had endured, he remembered only that by the laws of war this prisoner had done nothing to forfeit his life, and he used, as he had need, all of his great personal popularity among his townsmen to save his life. He left the army not long after this incident, after having been made a brevet brigadier-general of Volunteers, for gallant and meritorious services on the field.

JOHN W. MOSS
Colonel 2nd West Virginia Infantry
Colonel 5th West Virginia Cavalry

CHAPTER XXVII.

FIFTH REGIMENT W. VA. CAVALRY VOLUNTEERS.

Roster of the Field, Staff and Company Officers of the Fifth Regiment West Virginia Cavalry Volunteers (late 2d Regiment, West Virginia Infantry), showing the Alterations and Casualties therein from the Date of Original Organization of Said Regiment to the Date of Consolidation with the 6th Regiment, West Virginia Cavalry, December 14, 1864.

Date of Commission.	Names and Rank.	Co.	Remarks.
	Colonels.		
July 3, 1861.	John W. Moss,		Resigned May 20, 1862.
May 24, 1862.	George R. Latham,		
	Lieutenant-Colonels.		
July 3, 1861.	Robert Moran,		Resigned May 20, 1862.
June 30, 1863.	Alexander Scott,		Mustered out at expiration of term of service.
	Majors.		
July 3, 1861.	James D. Owen,		Resigned July 7, 1862.
July 31, 1862.	Thomas Gibson,		Resigned to accept promotion.
Nov. 11, 1862.	Henry C. Flesher,		Resigned Feb. 22, 1863.
March 16, 1863.	Patrick McNally,		Died of wounds received in action at Rocky Gap. Va.
April 25, 1864.	Douglas D. Barclay,		Mustered out at expiration of term of service.
	Fist Lieuts. and Adjts.		
July 3, 1861	Henry G. Jackson,		Resigned Oct. 8, 1862.
Nov. 26, 1861.	Charles McC. Hays,		Resigned Jan. 11, 1862.
Feb. 7, 1862.	David F. Williamson,		Resigned March 25, 1862.
June 9, 1862.	John Combs,		Promoted to Captain,
April 27, 1864.	John C. French,		Declined promotion, not mustered.
	1st Lieut. & R. Q. M.		
July 27, 1861.	Webster A. Stevens.		Resigned.
July 26, 1862.	Alexander J. Pentecost,		Mustered out at expiration of term of service.
	Surgeons.		
July 25, 1861.	Robt. W. Hazlett,		Resigned March 2, 1863.
March 13, 1863.	Eli N. Love,		Mustered out at expiration of term of service.
	Asst. Surgeons.		
Aug. 6, 1861.	Sample Ford,		Resigned Sept. 18, 1862.
Dec. 20, 1862.	Eli N. Love,		Promoted to Surgeon.
Sep. 20, 1862.	Theodore Millspaugh,		Mustered out at expiration of term of service.
	Chaplain.		
Aug. 23, 1861.	John W. W. Bolton,		Mustered out at expiration of term of service.
	Captains.		
	Albert C. Hays,	A	Resigned July 22, 1861.
Aug. 28, 1861.	William Otto,	A	Resigned March 13, 1862.
April 20, 1862.	John A. Hunter,	A	Relieved from Command, August 1, 1863.

Date of Commission.	Names and Rank.	Co.	Remarks.
	Captains.		
Aug. 18, 1863.	Oliver R. West,	A	Mustered out at expiration of term of service.
Aug. 28, 1861.	George R. Latham,	B	Promoted to Colonel, May 20, 1862.
May 20, 1862.	Daniel Wilson,	B	Resigned April 22, 1863.
Jan. 27, 1864.	Amos B. Hammer,	B	Mustered out at expiration of term of service.
Aug. 2, 1861.	Edward Planke,	C	Resigned March 5, 1863.
April 4, 1863	James K. Billingsley,	C	Mustered out at expiration of term of service.
Aug. 2, 1861.	Thomas Gibson, Jr.	D	Promoted to Major, July 7, 1862.
July 31, 1862.	Douglas D. Barclay,	D	Promoted to Major, May 1, 1864.
April 27, 1864.	John R. Frisbee,	D	Mustered out at expiration of term of service.
June 24, 1861.	Simpson Hollister,	E	Resigned December 1, 1862.
Oct. 14, 1861.	Thomas E. Day,	E	Recommissioned in 6th Cavalry.
July 4, 1861.	Alexander Scott,	F	Promoted to Lieutenant-Colonel, May 20, 1862.
Nov. 26, 1862.	Thomas B. Smith,	F	Recommissioned in 6th Cavalry.
June 30, 1862.	Henry C. Flesher,	F	Promoted to Major, November 9, 1862.
	James D. Owens,	G	Promoted to Major.
Aug. 2, 1861.	Chatham T. Ewing,	G	Transferred to 1st W. Va. Lt. Art.
Aug. 2, 1861.	Patrick McNally,	H	Promoted to Major, March 24, 1863.
March 16, 1863.	Joseph M. Bushfield,	H	Relieved February 18, 1864.
April 27, 1864.	John Combs,	H	Mustered out at expiration of term of service.
Aug. 28, 1861.	Louis E. Smith,	I	Resigned November 23, 1862.
Dec. 23, 1862.	Norval W. Truxal,	I	Mustered out at expiration of term of service.
July 28, 1861.	John P. Kiger,	K	Resigned Jan. 8, 1862.
Feb. 7, 1862.	Andrew Grubb,	K	Mustered out at expiration of term of service.
	First Lieutenants.		
March 1, 1862.	Oliver R. West,	A	Promoted to Captain.
Aug. 27, 1861.	David L. Smith,	A	Promoted to Captain and C. S, Aug. 18, 1863.
June 30, 1862.	Amos B. Hammer,	B	Promoted to Captain.
Aug. 28, 1861.	Fabricius A. Cather,	B	Resigned May 20, 1862.
Aug 2, 1861.	August Rolff,	C	Resigned September 10, 1862.
Sep. 23, 1862.	Henry Schultz,	C	Relieved December 9, 1863.
March 16, 1863.	Lewis P. Salterback,	C	Mustered out at expiration of term of service.
April 17, 1862.	Douglas D. Barclay,	D	Promoted to Captain, July 7, 1862.
July 7, 1862	John R. Frisbee,	D	Promoted to Captain May 1, 1864.
April 27, 1864.	Jacob Colmer,	D	Mustered out at expiration of term of service.
Aug. 2, 1861.	David Ecker,	D	Resigned April 17, 1862.
	Henry G. Jackson,	E	Appointed Adjutant, August 23, 1861.
June 24, 1861.	Hamilton B. James,	E	Killed in action at Bull Run, August 29, 1862.
Sept. 23, 1862.	Charles H. Day,	E	Transferred to Co. F.
Dec. 20, 1862,	John C. French,	E	Mustered out at expiration of term of service.
July 4, 1861.	John A. Hunter,	F	Promoted to Captain, Co. A.
Sept. 23, 1862.	Chas. H. Day,	F	Transfered to Co. I.
April 27, 1864.	Wm. Schmolze,	F	Mustered out at expiration of term of service.
Aug. 3, 1861.	Alfred Seckman,	G	Killed in action, Alleghany Mountains.
Jan. 11, 1862.	Howard Morton,	G	Transferred to 1st West Virginia Lt. Art.
Aug. 2, 1861.	Henry C. Flesher,	H	Promoted to Captain, Co. F.

Date of Commission.	Names and Rank.	Co.	Remarks.
	First Lieutenants.		
June 30, 1862.	Joseph M. Bushfield,	H	Promoted to Captain, March 24, 1863.
March 16, 1863.	Louis P. Salterbach,	H	Transferred to Company C.
Feb. 7, 1862.	Norval W. Truxal,	I	Promoted to Captain.
Aug. 28, 1861.	Abraham A. Devore,	I	Resigned October 10, 1861.
	David F. Williamson,	I	Promoted to Adjutant.
Dec. 23, 1862.	James K. Billingsley,	I	Transferred to Company C.
Sept. 23, 1862.	Charles H. Day,	I	Honorably discharged for wounds received in action.
July 27, 1861.	Andrew Grubb,	K	Promoted to Captain.
Feb. 7, 1862.	Arthur J. Weaver,	K	Killed in action, Noevmber 6, 1863.
	Second Lieutenants.		
Aug. 22, 1861.	Oliver R. West,	A	Promoted to 1st Lieutenant.
July 9, 1862.	James Black,	A	Relieved May 30, 1863.
Sept. 1, 1863.	James R. Hutchinson,	A	
Aug. 2, 1861.	Daniel Wilson,	B	Promoted to Captain.
June 30, 1862.	Asbury C. Baker,	B	Resigned Dec. 19, 1862.
Sept. 1, 1863.	Felix H. Hughes,	B	Mustered out at expiration of term of service.
Aug. 2, 1861.	Christian Petry,	C	Resigned July 25, 1862.
Sept. 23, 1862.	Christian Vierheller,	C	Resigned April 11, 1863.
March 26, 1864.	Geo. H. Kirkpatrick,	C	
Aug. 2, 1861.	Douglas D. Barclay,	D	Promoted to 1st Lieutenant.
Sept. 23, 1862.	John R. Frisbee,	D	Promoted to 1st Lieutenant.
April 2, 1862.	Joseph M. Bushfield,	D	Transferred to Company H.
Aug. 20, 1862.	A. J. Chambers,	D	Relieved September 29, 1862.
Oct. 9, 1862.	Jacob Colmer,	D	Promoted to 1st Lieut., and mustered out at expiration term of service.
June 24, 1861.	Basil T. Bowers,	E	Resigned December 10, 1861.
Jan. 13, 1863.	James B. Smith,	E	Promoted to Captain, 6th W. Va. Cavalry.
July 4, 1861.	Douglas G. Smythe,	F	Resigned June 17, 1862.
June 30, 1862.	Thomas B. Smith,	F	Promoted to Captain.
June 30, 1862.	William Schmolze,	F	Promoted to 1st Lieutenant, mustered out at expiration term of service.
Aug. 2, 1861.	Jacob G. Huggins,	G	Resigned March 22, 1862.
May 28, 1862.	Samuel J. Shearer,	G	Transferred to 1st W. Va. Light Artilery.
Aug. 2, 1861.	John Combs,	H	Promoted to Adjutant.
June 7, 1862.	Charles H. Day.	H	Transferred to Company E.
Sept. 23, 1862.	John C. French,	H	Promoted to 1st Lieutenant.
Nov. 26, 1862.	Andrew P. Russell,	H	Mustered out at expiration of term of service.
Aug. 28, 1861.	Norval W. Truxal,	I	Promoted to 1st Lieutenant.
Dec. 23, 1863.	James B. Montgomery,	I	Mustered out at expiration of term of service.
July 27, 1861.	Arthur J. Weaver,	K	Promoted to 1st Lieutenant.
Feb. 7, 1862.	David A. Jennings,	K	Resigned Janury 22, 1863.
Feb. 19, 1863.	Daniel K. Shields,	K	Relieved June 3, 1863.

The Second Virginia Infantry.

The Second Virginia Infantry, afterwards the Fifth West Virginia Cavalry, was the first regiment in the State enlisted for the three years service, and the first one mustered in under Governor Peirpoint. Companies A, D, F and G came from Pittsburg, Pa.; Company I from Greenfield and California, Washington County, Pa.; Company H from Ironton, Ohio; Company B from Grafton, Va.; Company C from Wheeling, Va.; Company E from Monroe and Belmont Counties, Ohio, and Wetzel, Taylor and Ritchie Counties, Va.; and Company K from Parkersburg, Va., and Bridgeport, Ohio. The companies met together at Beverly, Va., in the latter part of July, and were organized as the Second Regiment Virginia Infantry.

The muster out rolls show a total enrollment of 1069 men from first to last, of whom about 65 were discharged before the arduous campaigns of 1862 began, and Company G was detached for artillery service, making the real strength of the regiment, April 1st, 1862, about 900 men. As a rule, when a West Virginia regiment was once formed and mustered into the service, it had to depend on its original members for its future strength. But few recruits were received, and as comrades fell in battle, or by disease, their places were forever left unfilled, sad reminders of the horrible realities of war. In this regiment, but 19 recruits were received in the whole of the three year's service. Of this number, 189 were killed and died from disease and in Confederate prisons. It was a regiment of comparatively young men, the average age being about 24 years, a large number of them being but boys of eighteen, while a few had reached the age of forty. They were young, active, strong and intelligent, the making of a splendid regiment, and their work for three years fully confirmed all that was expected of them. Some of the companies of this regiment enjoyed special distinction in the early part of their service. Company A claims the credit of killing the first armed Confederate soldier.

At Glovers Gap, between Wheeling and Grafton, on the Baltimore and Ohio Rail Road, the company was detached to guard that important position, and more particularly to break up a Confederate military organization, known to be in that section, under command of Captain Christian Roberts. On the morning of May 27, a detachment of the company under command of Lieutenant West encountered Captain Roberts and a portion of his command, and in the fight that followed, Captain Roberts was killed, being the first armed Confederate soldier that fell in the war. Jackson, the slayer of the gallant Colonel Ellsworth, killed a few days previously, was a civilian, while Captain Roberts was a regularly mustered officer of the Confederacy.

ALEXANDER SCOTT
Lieutenant Colonel 5th West Virginia Cavalry

WILLIAM SCHMOLZE

First Lieutenant 5th West Virginia Cavalry

Company B claims to have had killed the first enlisted man in the U. S. volunteer service in the war. The company was at Fetterman, W. Va. On the night of May 22, Daniel Wilson and Bailey Brown, of the company, walked down towards Fetterman, and encountered the Confederate picket on the railroad in the east end of town, where Daniel W. S. Knight and George Glenn, of Captain Robinson's Confederate company, 25th Virginia, were on guard. Knight ordered them to halt. Instead of doing so, they continued to advance, Knight repeating his order, until they got close to the pickets, when Brown fired his revolver shooting Knight through the ear. Knight, who was armed with an old-fashioned smooth-bore flint-lock musket, loaded with slugs, returned the shot, killing Brown almost instantly. He was enrolled as a member of his company, May 20, 1861, though the company was not mustered in until the 25th. His death occurred on May 22, while that of the gallant Colonel Ellsworth did not occur until the 24th, two days later.

Company I was organized April 27, 1861, and immediately offered its services to the country, but was not accepted because of Pennsylvania's quota being filled, and was one of the first companies organized in the country that entered the three years' service. When mustered into the service the pay of the men began with April 27, they having, at their own expense, in the meantime been drilling and preparing for service. The company was called "the boatmen," when met by the three months' volunteers in western Virginia, because of their having come from the Monongahela River, many of whom followed that occupation and were a hardy set of men.

The regiment lay in camp at Beverly from the latter part of July until September 12, when it was sent to Elkwater, where General Reynolds was fortified against Gen'l Robt. E. Lee, to help drive the enemy's forces from Cheat Mountain. Early in the morning of the 13th, the 2d Va. in the lead, with the 3d Ohio, charged up and over a foot hill of the mountain, driving the Confederates from their hot breakfast in confusion. Soon afterward the enemy were driven from their stronghold, and to this regiment is due, in part, by its impetuous andvance, the honor of administering the first defeat to General Lee.

On December 13th, it took part in the battle on the summit of the Allegheny Mountains, remaining at Elkwater until January 7, 1862, during which time several important expeditions were made, and the whole section cleared of the marauding bands of Confederates. January 7th, the regiment went to the fort on Cheat Mountain Summit, the highest camp of the war, while the Confederates were encamped on the Allegheny Mountains, 20 miles distant, remaining there scouting, etc., until April 5th, when the onward movement toward Staunton began.

Gen'l John C. Fremont took command of the "Mountain Department," including the Cheat Mountain force, March 29th, and the regiment was with him until superseded by Gen'l John Pope, taking part in the battles of Monterey and McDowell, the advance up the Shenandoah and the battle of Cross Keys.

Under General Pope, it was in General Milroy's brigade, leading the column and took part in the battles of Kelly's Ford, White Sulphur Springs, Waterloo Bridge, Groveton and Bull Run. The regiment lost 24 killed and 90 wounded in these battles, more than one-third of the losses of the brigade. After the Bull Run battle the regiment was placed in the defenses at Washington, and returned to West Virginia, September 30th, arriving at Beverly October 29th.

April 24, 1863, the command was attacked by a superior force of Confederates and compelled to leave Beverly, returning to that place May 21st, and remaining there until ordered to Grafton to be mounted, in which time scouting expeditions were so numerous that it was difficult to keep run of them.

May 23, 1863, Brig.-Gen'l W. W. Averell was assigned to the command of the Fourth Separate Brigade, composed of mounted infantry and cavalry, of which the Second Virginia became a part, operating in western Virginia. In addition to scores of scouting expeditions, the most notable of the battles and expeditions of this brigade were the battle of Rocky Gap, August 26 and 27, in which the regiment lost five killed and 18 wounded; the battle of Droop Mountain, November 6, the regiment losing nine killed and 15 wounded, out of 200 men engaged; and the famous Salem raid, from December 8 to 25, 1863, in which the regiment lost but one man wounded and 17 captured. The command then went to Martinsburg, W. Va., where by special order of the War Department, each man that was on the Salem raid received, gratis, one pair of shoes and a suit of clothing, to replace those lost and worn out on the expedition. General Order No. 39, War Department, dated January 26, 1864, was issued, changing the Second Virginia Infantry to the Fifth West Virginia Cavalry. At noon, March 19, 1864, the brigade left Martinsburg and went to Charleston, W. Va., arriving there April 30, 1684. In the spring and summer of 1864, the regiment took a gallant part in the battle of Cloyd Mountain in May, and in the expedition of Gen'l David Hunter to Lynchburg.

After this the companies whose term of service had expired were mustered out of the service, and the re-enlisted men, about 200 in number, were consolidated with the Sixth West Virginia Cavalry in September. The regiment had a service of which any troops might be proud, and fully sustained its reputation for courage, efficiency and staying qualities. In the history of this noble regiment, Governor Pierpoint has the following to say of it: "Some that came to Wheeling were mere boys. Major Oakes, the mustering officer, a very judicious man, told me that some of the boys ought to be home with their mothers, but they persevered, and those boys came out veterans. It was the first regiment I had mustered in, the three month's regiments being formed before I became governor. Those that came from Pennsylvania were in citizens' light clothing, and there was a great deal of hardship and destitution until clothing was issued to them, which was some time after their mustered in.

There was one pleasing feature of the troops from the two States, Ohio and Pennsylvania, that was their perfect assimilation in spirit and purpose. The Pennsylvanians seemed to feel that they were with the Virginians to defend the Virginia homes from invasion, and partook of all the enthusiasm of the Virginians in the fight. Whenever I heard of a fight where the Second Virginia or Fifth Cavalry, after they became mounted, was, I heard a good report of them. They were reported brave to recklessness sometimes. It was said of them that whenever they got in a close place, every man was a general, and that they were almost invincible. They certainly achieved some victories that seemed in the beginning hopeless."

CHAPTER XXVIII.

SIXTH REGIMENT WEST VIRGINIA CAVALRY VOLUNTEERS.

Roster of the Field, Staff and Company Officers of the Sixth Regiment West Virginia Cavalry (late 3d Regiment West Virginia Infantry), Showing the Alterations and Casualties therein, from the Date of Original Organization of Said Regiment to the Date of Consolidation with the 5th Regiment, West Virginia Cavalry, December 14, 1864.

Date of Commission.	Names and Rank.	Co.	Remarks.
	Colonel.		
July 12, 1861.	David T. Hewes,		Dismissed February 15, 1864.
	Lieutenant-Colonels.		
July 23, 1861.	Frank W. Thompson,		Mustered out at expiration of term of service.
Oct. 27, 1864.	Rufus E. Fleming,		
	Majors.		
July 23, 1861.	Chas. E. Swearingen,		Resigned July 17, 1862.
Aug. 7, 1862.	Theodore F. Lang,		Mustered out at expiration of term of service.
March 11, 1864.	Hauson W. Hunter,		Mustered out at expiration of term of service.
Oct. 27, 1864.	Peter J. Potts,		
	1st Lieut. and Adj't.		
July 12, 1861.	Theodore F. Lang,		Promoted to Major, August 7, 1862.
Aug. 7, 1862.	Nathan Goff, Jr.		Promoted to Major, 4th W. Va. Cavalry.
Oct. 24, 1863.	Dennis B. Jeffers,		Promoted to Captain, Company C.
Jan. 14, 1864.	Hiram J. Willey.		
	1st Lieut. and R. Q. M.		
Aug. 5, 1861.	John H. Shuttleworth,		Mustered out at expiration of term of service.
	Surgeons.		
July 30, 1861.	Dennis B. Dorsey,		Resigned August 5, 1862.
Oct. 25, 1862.	Ebenezer C. Thomas,		Mustered out at expiration of term of service.
Oct. 4, 1864.	Abel H. Thayer.		
	Assistant Surgeons.		
Oct. 25, 1862.	Ebenezer C. Thomas,		Promoted to Surgeon.
Oct. 29, 1862.	Galelma Law,		Promoted to Captain, Company K.
Sep. 14, 1862.	Abel H. Thayer,		Promoted to Surgeon.
	Chaplains.		
July 24, 1861.	James W. Curry,		Resigned August 3, 1862.
Oct. 3, 1862.	Andrew J. Lyda,		Resigned April 29, 1864.
	Captains.		
	Frank W. Thompson,	A	Promoted to Lieutenant-Colonel.
Aug. 5, 1861.	James J. Thompson,	A	Mustered out August 15, 1864.

Date of Commission.	Names and Rank.	Co.	Remarks.
	Captains.		
Aug. 5, 1861.	N. A. Shuttleworth,	B	Resigned June 5, 1862.
June 30, 1862.	W. W. Werninger,	B	Resigned November 9, 1862.
Dec. 10, 1862.	Louis A. Myers,	B	Mustered out August 16, 1864.
Aug. 5, 1861.	Isaiah Kirk,	C	Resigned July 23, 1862.
Aug. 7, 1862.	Jacob G. Cobun,	C	Died from wounds received in action.
Jan. 19, 1864.	Dennis B. Jeffers,	C	Mustered out at expiration of term of service.
Aug. 5, 1861.	Dennis A. Litzinger,	D	Resigned June 15, 1862.
Sep. 12, 1862.	John W. Perry,	D	Resigned September 19, 1862.
Nov. 28, 1862.	Andrew J. Squires.	D	
Aug. 5, 1861.	Sylvester B. Phillips,	E	Resigned November 8, 1862.
Dec. 10, 1862.	Peter J. Potts,	E	Promoted to Major.
Aug. 5, 1861.	Cyrus Webb,	F	Resigned April 4, 1862.
May 28, 1862.	Daniel Sheets.	F	Mustered out at expiration of term of service.
Aug. 5. 1861.	Alex. C. Moore,	G	Appointed Captain, Battery E, 1st W. Va. Light Art., September 23, 1862.
Sep. 23, 1862.	Rufus E. Fleming,	G	Promoted to Lieutenant-Colonel.
Nov. 1, 1864.	James S. Law,	G	
Aug. 5, 1861.	Henry C. Hagans,	H	Resigned.
July 12, 1861.	Charles E. Swearingen,	H	Promoted to Major.
Aug. 7, 1862.	David Gibson,	H	Killed in action at Bull Run, Aug. 29, 1862.
Sep. 12, 1862.	Levi L. Bryte,	H	Dismissed.
Oct. 6, 1864.	Wm. H. Kantner,	H	
Oct. 5, 1861.	Wm. J. Purdy,	I	Resigned February 6, 1862.
Feb. 21, 1862.	Hanson W. Hunter,	I	Promoted to Major.
March 26, 1864.	Louis B. Purdy,	I	Mustered out at expiration of term of service.
Aug. 5, 1861.	Moses S. Hall,	K	Promoted to Lieut.-Col. 10th W. Va. Inft.
June 30, 1862.	Josiah M. Woods,	K	Resigned April 27, 1863.
May 30, 1863.	Galelma Law,	K	Mustered out at expiration of term of service.
May 9, 1864.	Jacob S. Hyde,	L	Died at Annapolis, Md.
	First Lieutenants.		
Aug. 5, 1861.	Aaron C. Pickenpaugh,	A	Mustered out at expiration of term of service.
Aug. 5, 1861.	W. W. Werninger,	B	Promoted to Captain.
June 30, 1862.	Louis A. Myers,	B	Promoted to Captain.
Dec. 10, 1862.	Henry F. Mayers,	B	Mustered out at expiration of term of service.
Aug. 5, 1861.	Jacob G. Cobun,	C	Promoted to Captain.
Aug. 7, 1862.	Dennis B. Jeffers,	C	Promoted to Captain.
April 6, 1864.	David E. McGinnis,	C	
Aug. 5, 1861.	John W. Perry,	D	Promoted to Captain.
Nov. 28, 1862.	James W. Hollis,	D	Mustered out at expiration of term of service.
Nov. 11, 1864.	Robert F. Lindsey,	D	
Aug. 5, 1861.	Claudius B. See,	E	Resigned March 22, 1862.
Dec. 10, 1862.	Bartholomew Clark,	E	Killed in action.
Aug. 5, 1861.	Daniel Sheets,	F	Promoted to Captain.
May 28, 1862.	Asa Coplin,	F	Died of wounds received in action.

Date of Commission.	Names and Rank.	Co.	Remarks.
	First Lieutenants.		
Nov. 15, 1862.	Curtis Davidson,	F	Mustered out at expiration of term of service.
Nov. 26, 1864.	George Bumgarner,	F	
Aug. 5, 1861.	Wm. L. Hursey,	G	Resigned July 30, 1862.
Aug. 20, 1862.	David Hewes,	G	Resigned October 3, 1862.
Dec. 10, 1862.	Henry C. Link,	G	Mustered out at expiration of term of service.
Nov. 1, 1864.	Arthur E. Wells,	G	
Aug. 5, 1861.	David Gibson,	H	Promoted to Captain.
Aug. 7, 1862.	C. B. Hadden,	H	Dismissed July 6, 1863.
April 6, 1864.	Wm. H. Kantner,	H	Promoted to Captain.
Aug. 5, 1861.	Hanson W. Hunter,	I	Promoted to Captain.
Feb. 21, 1862.	Louis B. Purdy,	I	Promoted to Captain.
	Robert F. Lindsey,	I	Promoted to Captain, 6th Cavalry.
Aug. 5, 1861.	James Z. Browning,	K	Resigned April 10, 1862.
June 30, 1862.	John Emory Day,	K	Died from wounds received at second battle of Bull Run.
Nov. 28, 1862.	John Sommerville,	K	Promoted to Captain.
March 9, 1864.	John S. Wotring,	L	Resigned.
	Second Lieutenants.		
Aug. 5, 1861.	John C. Davis,	A	Resigned May 20, 1862.
May 15, 1862.	Nicholas B. Medara.	A	
Aug. 5, 1861.	Louis A. Myers,	B	Promoted to 1st Lieutenant.
June 30, 1862.	Henry F. Mayers.	B	Promoted to 1st Lieutenant.
Dec. 20, 1862.	James S. Law,	B	Promoted to Captain, Co. G.
Aug. 5, 1861.	Elisha M. H. Brown,	C	Resigned March 18, 1862.
April 4, 1862.	Dennis B. Jeffers,	C	Promoted to 1st Lieutenant.
Aug. 7, 1862.	David E. McGinnis,	C	
Aug. 5. 1861.	George W. Artis,	D	Resigned March 7, 1862.
Sep. 12, 1862.	James W. Hollis,	D	Promoted to 1st Lieutenant.
Nov. 28, 1862	John Hinebaugh,	D	Mustered out at expiration of term of service.
Nov. 11, 1864.	Samuel R. Hanen,	D	
Aug. 5, 1861.	Randolph See,	E	Resigned Sept. 1862.
Nov. 28, 1862.	Bartholomew Clark,	E	Promoted to 1st Lieutenant.
Dec. 19, 1862.	Marshal Gould,	E	Mustered out at expiration of term of service.
Nov. 1, 1864.	Alonzo C. Bunton,	E	
Aug. 5, 1861.	Asa Coplin,	F	Promoted to 1st Lieutenant.
May 28, 1862.	Curtis Davidson,	F	Promoted to 1st Lieutenant.
Nov. 15, 1862.	James R. Jones,	F	Died August 6, 1863.
Nov. 26, 1864.	Porter Flesher,	F	
Aug. 5, 1861.	Nathan Goff, Jr.	G	Promoted to Adjutant.
Aug. 7, 1862.	Rufus E. Fleming,	G	Promoted to Captain.
Sep. 23, 1862.	Henry C. Link,	G	Promoted to 1st Lieutenant.
Dec. 10, 1862.	William E. Bryson,	G	Resigned April 25, 1863.
Sep. 25, 1863.	Benj. F. Wicks,	G	Mustered out at expiration of term of service.
Nov. 1, 1864.	John W. Kidwell.	G	

Date of Commission.	Names and Rank.	Co.	Remarks.
	Second-Lieutenants.		
Aug. 5, 1861.	Christopher B. Hadden,	H	Promoted to 1st Lieutenant.
Aug. 7, 1862.	Levi L. Bryte,	H	Promoted to Captain.
Sep. 12, 1862.	Wm. H. Kantner,	H	Promoted to 1st Lieutenant.
Nov. 1, 1864.	R. W. Blue	H	
Aug. 5, 1861.	Louis B. Purdy,	I	Promoted to 1st Lieutenant.
Feb. 21, 1862.	Benj. T. Lydick,	I	Resigned January 18, 1863.
Jan. 28, 1863.	Robert F. Lindsey,	I	Promoted to 1st Lieutenant.
Aug. 5, 1861.	Ephraim McClaskey,	K	Died September 1861, from wounds received in action.
March 8, 1862.	Josiah M. Woods,	K	Promoted to Captain.
Oct. 11, 1861.	Charles Hewitt,	K	Resigned February 10, 1862.
June 30, 1862.	John Sommerville,	K	Promoted to 1st Lieutenant.
Nov. 28, 1862.	Jacob W. Core,	K	Mustered out at expiration of term of service.
March 8, 1864.	Eli L. Parker,	L	Promoted to Captain.

THE THIRD REGIMENT WEST VIRGINIA INFANTRY

(AFTERWARDS 6TH WEST VIRGINIA CAVALRY).

Governor Peirpoint entrusted the formation of this regiment to Col. David T. Hewes, of Clarksburg, a gentleman well known in the State, with a reputation for skill in military tactics, having for many years held an important office in the militia of the State. The camp or rendezvous, named "Camp Hewes," was located near the city, and was well supplied with tents and other necessaries for the comfort of the men. As this was the second regiment raised (the first—Colonel Kelly's—being a three months' regiment), recruited under the three years' call, there was little difficulty in procuring the full complement of ten companies. The following will show from what counties they were recruited:

Co. A, Monongalia County; Co. B, Harrison County; Co. C, Preston County; Co. D, Preston County; Co. E, Upshur County; Co. F, Taylor and Harrison Counties; Co. G, Harrison County; Co. H, Monongalia County, and border of Pennsylvania; Co. I, Marshall County; Co. K, Ritchie County.

The full quota of companies for the Third Regiment was secured about the 1st of July, when the regiment was organized by general consent by the selection of the following field and staff officers; David T. Hewes, colonel; Frank W. Thompson, lieutenant-colonel; Charles E. Swearingen, major; Theodore F. Lang, adjutant; John H. Shuttleworth, regimental quartermaster; D. B. Dorsey, surgeon; Rev. James W. Curry, chaplain.

The formation of the regiment completed, its term of service in camp was short-lived. The field and staff officers made Clarksburg headquarters for a time, but the companies were required for immediate service for the protection of the border counties against the marauding bands of guerrillas that infested that part of the State. So, without the ceremony of a regular muster-in—no authorized mustering officer being at hand—the several companies when full would select their officers, A. Werninger, a city justice of the peace, would administer an oath to support the Constitution of the United States, and, with but a day or two of drilling in the facings, they would be supplied with Springfield muskets, altered from the old flint-lock, and hurried away to perform the most exacting and dangerous duty known to the service.

For several months the regiment did this work, occupying the border from Philippi to Suttonville, a distance of one hundred miles.

About the 10th of September came the gladsome order to report for duty at the front. For several weeks prior to this date the officers of the regiment had been urging the authorities to relieve our scattered regiment from the irksome duties of fighting guerrillas, and to permit us to take the field as a consolidated regiment. Beverly was designated as the point at which the regiment was to assemble.

The regiment remained in camp at this place a short time, which was spent in drilling and scouting, when it went into winter quarters in General Milroy's brigade at Camp Elkwater. The regiment remained at Elkwater until about the 1st of April, at which time orders were issued. Milroy's command was ordered to advance to the front, when the Third Regiment with the balance of Milroy's brigade turned their faces, on April 5, towards Staunton, marching on the Cheat Mountain and Staunton turnpike. Arriving the following day at Monterey, the command remained there a fortnight or more, soldiering under difficulties that were seldom excelled in the hardships of a soldier's life. The enemy were in strong force at McDowell, 10 miles away, and on the Shenandoah Mountain, 20 miles distant.

On the 12th of April at Monterey we had quite a lively fight; the enemy, 1000 strong, making an attack upon our position, but they were handsomely repulsed by Milroy's forces. On the 30th of April, Milroy moved his forces to McDowell and went into camp for the night.

On the 1st of May the command was early under arms, and the way to Staunton looked clear, but at the moment when the order of march was given, a dispatch from General Fremont commanding the Mountain Department caused a halt, and the day was spent impatiently waiting; the second day likewise, and thus for several days did we linger in temporary camp

FRANCIS W. THOMPSON
Lieutenant Colonel 6th West Virginia Cavalry

John Parsley, Poolesville, Md.

ABEL H. THAYER
Surgeon 6th West Virginia Cavalry

LOUIS A. MYERS
Captain 6th West Virginia Cavalry

John Parsley, Poolesville, Md.

HENRY C. LINK
First Lieutenant 6th West Virginia Cavalry

awaiting orders, and not till the 7th did we get orders to move, and then the orders were not general.

The 3d W. Va., 32d and 75th Ohio were advanced to Shaw's Ridge and Shenandoah Mountain in the direction of Staunton. Our scouts soon brought the information that Stonewall Jackson had joined General Johnson, and that their combined forces were advancing towards McDowell, when the three advance regiments were ordered to fall back on McDowell. On the next morning (May 8th) the enemy was seen in force upon the Bull Pasture Mountain, about one and three-fourths miles distant from McDowell, on right and front. About 10 A. M. General Schenck arrived, and the morning and forenoon were taken up in skirmishing. About 3.30 P. M. General Milroy discovered that the enemy were preparing to place a battery that would command our whole encampment, when he received permission from General Schenck to make a reconnoissance for the purpose of obtaining information as to the position and strength of the enemy. Just here I will state that General Schenck, being the ranking officer, became the commander-in-chief of the forces. The troops placed by General Schenck at Milroy's disposal were the 3d W. Va., 25th, 75th and 32d Ohio, of Milroy's brigade, and the 82d Ohio, of Schenck's brigade. These regiments were by no means full, various companies of each being detailed for special duty.

It only required a few minutes for Milroy to ascertain what he was so anxious to know, and the battle proved to be one of the most stubbornly contested, for the numbers engaged, that took place during the war. The 25th and 75th Ohio, the former under command of Lieut.-Col. W. P. Richardson, and the latter under command of Col. N. C. McLean and Maj. Robert Reily, led in the attack. They advanced in the most gallant manner up the face of the steep hill and attacked the enemy in their front. Numbering less than 1000 men, unprotected by any natural or artificial shelter, they advanced up a precipitous mountain side upon an adversary protected by intrenchments hastily thrown up and the natural formation of the mountain, and drove them (being at least twice their numerical strength) over the crest of the mountain, and for one and a half hours maintained—while exposed to a deadly fire—the position from which they had so bravely driven the foe.

At about 4 o'clock, perceiving that the enemy's force was being constantly increased, the 82d Ohio, Colonel Cantwell; 32d Ohio, Lieut.-Col. E. H. Swinney, and 3d West Virginia, Lieut.-Colonel F. W. Thompson, were ordered to turn the right flank of the enemy. They obeyed the order with the greatest alacrity, but the enemy observing the design, and having a much superior force, in a handsome manner changed his front to the rear. These three regiments, however, attacked them briskly, and kept up a destructive fire that caused the enemy to waver several times; but fresh reinforcements being brought up by them, and a portion of the same coming down the turnpike, the 3d West Virginia became exposed to their fire in its front and rear; unable, however, to withstand the fire of the 3d West Virginia, the latter reinforcements joined the main body of the Confederates and the contest become general and bloody. From 3.30 P. M. to 8.30 P. M. this small force engaged with undaunted bravery a force of the enemy which could not have been less than 6000 men, and maintained the position from which they had driven them, displaying a courage and zeal which has merited the thanks of the country, and proved themselves true representatives of the American citizen soldier.

After nightfall the engagement still continued, the firing of our men being guided only by the flashes of the enemy's musketry, until the ammunition of almost all the men engaged was wholly exhausted, when, having achieved the purpose of the attack, our forces were recalled, retiring in good order, bringing with them their dead and wounded. Whilst the report of this engagement has thus far been general, giving to each regiment engaged its just meed of praise, we cannot dismiss the account without referring to a few incidents that came immediately under the writer's observation relating to the 3d West Virginia regiment. The attack by the enemy upon our rear, above referred to, was a desperate position for a regiment to be placed in, and nothing but the most intense devotion to duty by both officers and men held them in place. Firing first to the front, and then turning to the rear, the unerring aim of our men did its work, and the "rear" party broke and left that part of the field. As has already been stated, the enemy were protected by a natural position on top of the mountain, while the 3d West Virginia regiment was partly in an open field and partly (say one company) in a wood, our whole front not being over 100 yards from the enemy. The fight in our front was peculiar in this, that the enemy fired by regiment, and in this order: when they were ready to fire, they would advance quickly to the top of the mountain, exposing just enough of their persons to enable them to discharge their guns; when the volley would be fired, they would as quickly retire from view. In that manner the 3d West Virginia regiment was engaged with at least two, perhaps three, regiments of the foe.

This must have been so, for the time that would elapse between volleys was not sufficient to enable one regiment to reload. But our own boys soon got the hang of it, and awaited each time the coming of the exposure; our men loaded and fired at will.

As we were in an open field, without breast-works or other protection, we must have suffered greatly but for the fact of the haste with which the enemy fired. The leaden hail went mostly above our heads, and that part (the left) of the regiment referred to as being in the wood, verified this assertion by their appearance when they left the field after the battle, for their caps and shoulders were covered with the bark and buds and twigs of the trees.

And here again we were arrayed against the 31st Virginia (Confederate) regiment referred to in a former chapter as having been mainly recruited by residents from Clarksburg. So close together were the two regiments that they recognized and called to each other.

It required no military genius to grasp the situation and determine upon a retreat from that point. The enemy occupying a natural position for either offensive or defensive operations, with an army of 7000 men against our two small brigades, aggregating only 3700 men, Generals Schenck and Milroy, wisely taking advantage of the darkness of the night, withdrew our little army along the road through the narrow gorge which afforded the only egress from the valley in which McDowell is situated, in the direction of Franklin. This withdrawal was effected without the loss of a man, and without the loss or destruction of any public property, except of some stores, for which General Milroy was entirely without the means of transportation. The withdrawal to Franklin was made by easy marches on the 9th, 10th and 11th, the enemy all the time cautiously pursuing. The night march after the battle was of course one of great fatigue, for the men were already worn out with the marching and fighting, with little sleep and little to eat, but at 8 o'clock on the morning of the 9th, 13 miles from McDowell, a halt was made for rest and rations till 2 P. M. Upon reaching Franklin, on the 11th, we found that the enemy had followed with a heavy force, and were preparing to attack us. For two days demonstrations were made at different points of our position, but nothing more than skirmishing occurred, when on the night of the 13th the enemy retired to the southward; and thus ended the operations of our army "on to Staunton."

At Franklin, immediately following the battle of McDowell, General Fremont was placed in command of the Mountain Department when he reorganized his command. General Milroy commanded a brigade in which the Third West Virginia formed a part. The regiment took part in Fremont's race up the Shenandoah Valley in pursuit of Stonewall Jackson. It bore a gallant part at the battle of Cross Keys, was continued in Milroy's brigade, in the Pope campaign, taking part in all the battles of that period, viz.: Crooked Creek, Sulphur Springs, Rappahannock Station, Freeman's Ford, Hedgeman's River, Waterloo Bridge, Warrenton Springs, Broad Run, Gainsville, Manassas or Second Bull Run, August 28 to 30. After the

Bull Run defeat the regiment was put in camp at Fort Ethan Allen near Washington.

September 30, the regiment left Fort Ethan Allen for West Virginia, arriving at Clarksburg on the 1st of October; after a few days' rest was ordered to Point Pleasant, soon to return to Clarksburg and Buckhannon, when the regiment was divided into detachments to perform out-post duty at Buckhannon, Centreville, Bull Town, Sutton and Glenville. In this detached condition the regiment was respectively in the brigades of General Milroy, Col. A. Moor and Gen'l B. S. Roberts.

On May 18th, Brigadier-General Averell was placed in command of the Fourth Separate Brigade, with headquarters at Weston. The regiment under Averell's management was called together again, and in November, 1863, was changed to mounted infantry, and in January, 1864, to the 6th Cavalry.

Under Averell the regiment took a conspicuous part—Lieutenant-Colonel Thompson in command—in all of Averell's raids, to Rocky Gap, Droop Mountain, Salem raid, Moorefield, and in all the operations in the Shenandoah Valley, and in Kelley's and Crook's department.

From the formation of the Mountain Department in May, 1862, under Fremont, until after the battle of Cloyd Mountain in May, 1864, this regiment and the 2d W. Va. Infantry were in the same brigade. When the regiments were mounted in June, 1863, and the 2d became the 5th W. Va. Cavalry, the 3d became the 6th W. Va. Cavalry, the two regiments bearing the same relative rank as when infantry. The two regiments were thus constantly together for over two years, and when their time of enlistment expired, the veterans and recruits of the two regiments were consolidated, taking the name of the 6th W. Va. Cavalry. (See 6th W. Va. VETERAN Cavalry, Col. R. E. Fleming, commanding.)

CHAPTER XXIX.

SEVENTH REGIMENT W. VA. CAVALRY VOLUNTEERS.

Roster of the Field, Staff and Company Officers of the Seventh Regiment West Virginia Cavalry (late Eighth Regiment West Virginia Infantry), Showing the Alterations and Casualties Therein from the Date of Original Organization of Said Regiment to the Date of Muster Out, August 1, 1865.

Date of Commission.	Names and Rank.	Co.	Remarks.
	Colonel.		
March 1, 1863.	John H. Oley,		Brevetted Brigadier-General.
	Lieutenant-Colonels.		
Nov. 27, 1861.	Lucian Losier,		Dismissed August 24, 1862.
Oct. 2, 1862.	John H. Oley,		Promoted to Colonel.
March 1, 1863.	John J. Polsley.		
	Majors.		
Oct. 29, 1861.	John H. Oley,		Promoted to Lieutenant-Colonel,
Oct. 2, 1862.	John J. Polsley,		Promoted to Lieutenant-Colonel.
March 1, 1863.	Hedgeman Slack.		
June 20, 1864.	William Gramm.		
Oct. 27, 1864.	Edgar P. Blundon.		
	1st Lt. and Adj'ts.		
Dec. 21, 1861,	John J. Polsley,		Promoted to Major.
Oct. 2, 1862.	Jacob M. Rife,		Promoted to Captain, Co. C.
Aug. 17, 1863.	Alonzo M. Wilson,		Promoted to Captain, Co. E.
	William A. Walton,		Transferred to the line.
Aug. 12, 1864.	George W. Brown,		Promoted to Captain, Co. A.
April 29, 1865.	Daniel W. Polsley.		
	1st Lts. and R. Q. M.		
Nov. 14, 1861.	William C. Kimball,		Promoted to C. S. U. S. A.
June 20, 1864.	John W. Wingfield.		
	1st. Lieut. and R. C. S.		
Dec. 14, 1864.	John McCombs.		
	Surgeons.		
Nov. 6, 1861.	Charles A. Barlow,		Resigned April 5, 1862.
May 6, 1862.	James Putney,		Resigned September 19, 1862.
Oct. 22, 1862	Lucius L. Comstock.		
	Assistant Surgeons.		
May 23, 1862.	James H. Rouse,		
Nov. 11, 1862.	Louis V. Stanford.		
	Chaplain.		
March 1, 1863.	Andrew W. Gregg.		

Date of Commission.	Names and Rank.	Co.	Remarks.
	Captains.		
Dec. 3, 1861.	Richard H. Lee,	A	Dismissed.
April 29, 1865.	George W. Brown,	A	
Dec. 3, 1861.	Moses H. Wood,	B	Resigned Jan. 17, 1862.
Feb. 15, 1862.	William Gramm,	B	Promoted to Major.
Oct. 27, 1864	Edward P. Wilbur,	B	
Jan. 14, 1862.	Hedgeman Slack,	C	Promoted to Major.
Aug. 17, 1862.	Jacob M. Rife,	C	Transferred to Company F.
June 20, 1864.	Charles A. Smith,	C	
Jan. 14, 1862.	Isaac M. Rucker,	D	Resigned November 6, 1862.
Jan. 31, 1863.	John M. Reynolds,	D	Mustered out at expiration of term of service.
Feb. 18, 1865.	George W. Karnes,	D	
Jan. 14, 1862.	Julien E. Curtiss,	E	Killed in action.
Oct. 3, 1862.	Wm. L. Gardner,	E	Killed in action at Droop Mountain.
Nov. 27, 1863.	Alonzo M. Wilson,	E	
April 4, 1862.	Edgar B. Blundon,	F	Promoted to Major.
Aug. 17, 1863.	Jacob M. Rife,	F	
July 9, 1862.	James S. Cassady.	G	
July 8, 1862.	Andrew W. Gregg,	H	Commissioned Chaplain.
Feb. 25, 1863.	William H. H. Parker,	H	Killed in action at Droop Mountain, Va.
Nov. 27, 1863.	Fletcher C. Lanham,	H	Mustered out at expiration of term of service.
April 29, 1865.	Charles Stover,	H	
Jan. 31, 1863.	Francis Mathers,	I	
March 19, 1863.	Elias Powell,	K	
May 21, 1864.	Isaac M. Rucker,	L	
Oct. 27, 1864.	William A. Walton,	M	
	First Lieutenants.		
Dec. 3, 1861.	James Abbott,	A	Resigned May 5, 1862.
March 19, 1863.	William A. Walton,	A	Promoted to Captain, Company M.
Oct. 27, 1864.	John L. McVey,	A	
Dec. 3, 1861.	James W. Nowlen,	B	Resigned September 19, 1862.
Oct. 3, 1862.	Joseph S. P. Barker,	B	Resigned Feb. 28, 1863.
March 19, 1863.	Edward P. Wilbur,	B	Promoted to Captain.
Dec. 14, 1864.	Wm. V. B. Bias,	B	
Jan. 14, 1862.	A. B. Williams,	C	Resigned June 18, 1862.
July 9. 1862.	Charles A. Smith,	C	Promoted to Captain.
Dec. 14, 1864.	Sprague Lawrence,	C	
Jan. 14, 1862.	John M. Reynolds,	D	Promoted to Captain.
Aug. 17, 1863.	Isaac A. Wade,	D	Mustered out at expiration of term of service.
Feb. 18, 1865.	William A. Bias.	D	
Jan. 14, 1862.	William L. Gardner,	E	Promoted to Captain.
Oct. 3, 1862.	Alonzo M. Wilson,	E	Promoted to Captain.
Aug. 17, 1863.	John F. Grayum,	E	
April, 4, 1862.	Jacob M. Rife,	F	Commissioned Adjutant.
Dec. 15, 1862.	Fletcher C. Lanham,	F	Promoted to Captain, Co. H.
Aug. 23, 1864.	William H. Newcomb,	F	

Date of Commission.	Names and Rank.	Co.	Remarks.
	First Lieutenants.		
July 9, 1862.	David R. Noble,	G	Resigned February, 9, 1863.
Feb. 25, 1863.	Solomon Priester,	G	Died of typhoid fever at Point of Rocks.
Sept. 22, 1864.	James D. Fellers,	G	
Nov. 28, 1862.	William S. Dunbar,	H	Resigned June 22, 1863.
July 9, 1862.	Wm. H. H. Parker,	H	Promoted to Captain.
Aug. 19, 1863.	Charles Stover,	H	Promoted to Captain.
Dec. 5, 1863.	Jacob Webb,	H	Mustered out at expiration of term of service.
April 29, 1865.	Achilles McGinness.	H	
Jan. 15, 1862.	Ferdinand Neumann,	I	Killed in action April 11, 1862.
July 9, 1862.	Francis Mathers,	I	Promoted to Captain.
Jan. 31, 1863.	John A. Morehart,	I	Killed in action August 28, 1863.
Jan. 25, 1865.	Nimrod Mason,	I	
	Elias Powell,	K	Promoted to Captain.
March 19, 1863.	Wm. A. Walton,	K	Transferred to Company A.
Sep. 22, 1864.	John A. Cobb,		Mustered out at expiration of term of service.
Jan. 25, 1865.	Henry L. Carter,	K	
April 8, 1864.	Isaac M. Rucker,	L	Promoted to Captain.
May 21, 1864.	Lewis A. Martin,	L	
Sep. 22, 1864.	George W. Karnes,	M	Promoted to Captain, Co. D.
April 7, 1865.	Charles W. Angel,	M	
	Second Lieutenants.		
Dec. 3, 1861.	Caleb H. Casdorph,	A	Mustered out, G. O. War Department.
March 31, 1865.	Reuben Harrison,	A	
Dec. 3, 1861.	William Gramm,	B	Promoted to Captain.
April 4, 1862.	Wm. H. H. Parker,	B	Promoted to 1st Lieutenant, Company H.
July 9, 1862.	Joseph S. P. Barker,	B	Promoted to 1st Lieutenant.
Oct. 3. 1862.	Edward P. Wilber,	B	Promoted to 1st Lieutenant.
March 19, 1863.	Joseph F. Hager,	B	Discharged for disability for wounds received in action.
April 29, 1865.	Jonathan J. Ball,	B	
Jan. 14, 1862.	Charles A. Smith,	C	Promoted to 1st Lieutenant.
July 9, 1862.	John W. Wingfield,	C	Promoted to 1st Lieutenant and R. Q. M.
June 20, 1864.	Sprague Lawrence,	C	Promoted to 1st Lieutenant.
Dec. 14, 1864.	Lafayette W. Pauley,	C	
Jan. 14, 1862.	Isaac A. Wade,	D	Promoted to 1st Lieutenant.
Aug. 17, 1863.	Harvey Reynolds,	D	Mustered out at expiration of term of service.
March 14, 1865.	Micahel Lee,	D	
Jan. 14, 1862.	Alonzo M. Wilson,	E	Promoted to 1st Lieutenant.
Oct. 3, 1862.	John F. Grayum.	E	Promoted to 1st Lieutenant.
Aug. 17, 1863.	Wm. H. Beckner,	E	
April 4, 1862.	Fletcher C. Lanham,	F	Promoted to 1st Lieutenant.
July 9, 1862.	Lewis V. R. Stanford,	F	Promoted to Assistant Surgeon.
Dec. 15, 1862.	Thomas Newcomb,	F	Died at Gallipolis, O., August 15, 1863.
Nov. 27. 1863.	Wm. H. Newcomb,	F	Promoted to 1st Lieutenant.
Aug. 23, 1864.	Robert C. Dawson,	F	Muster revoked by War Department.
May 19, 1865.	Thomas H. Burton,	F	

Date of Commission.	Names and Rank.	Co.	Remarks.
	Second Lieutenants.		
July 9, 1862.	Jeremiah Hare,	G	Resigned September 10, 1862.
Nov. 25, 1862.	Solomon Priester,	G	Promoted to 1st Lieutenant.
Feb. 25, 1863.	James D. Fellers,	G	Promoted to 1st Lieutenant.
Oct. 27, 1864.	John E. Swaar,	G	
Feb. 25, 1863.	Jacob Webb,	H	Promoted to 1st Lieutenant.
Dec. 5, 1863.	Charles Stover,	H	Promoted to 1st Lieutenant.
Sep. 22, 1864.	Nimrod Mason,	H	Promoted to 1st Lieutenant, Company, I.
Feb. 23, 1865.	Achilles McGinnis,	H	Promoted to 1st Lieutenant.
April 29, 1865.	Wm. P. Tyree,	H	
Jan. 31, 1863.	John Price,	I	Cashiered February 15, 1865.
March 14, 1865.	Matthew E. Cook,	I	
March 19, 1863.	John A. Cobb,	K	Promoted to 1st Lieutenant.
Sep. 22, 1864.	Henry L. Carter,	K	Promoted to 1st Lieutenant.
Jan. 25, 1865.	Hiram Lewis,	K	Transferred to Co. L.
May 21, 1864.	John D. Young,	K	Mustered out June 3, 1865.
May 21, 1864.	John D. Young,	L	Transferred to Company K.
Jan. 25, 1865.	Hiram Lewis,	L	
Nov. 26, 1864.	Charles W. Angel,	M	Promoted to 1st Lieutenant.
April 7, 1865.	Daniel W. Polsley,	M	Promoted to 1st Lieutenant and Adjutant.

THE EIGHTH WEST VIRGINIA INFANTRY,

(AFTERWARDS SEVENTH WEST VIRGINIA CAVALRY.)

The Eighth Regiment, Virginia Infantry, was organized in the Kanawha Valley, by Major John H. Oley, during the fall of 1861, headquarters being at Charleston. The regiment was ordered to New Creek in April, 1862, becoming apart of General Fremont's Mountain Department, and with the Sixtieth Ohio Infantry, was organized as an advance brigade, and placed under the command of Colonel Cluseret, A. D. C. to General Fremont. In the pursuit of Jackson up the valley, this brigade had the advance, and were engaged in several skirmishes with Ashby's cavalry, following him closely to Harrisonburg, where they engaged him, resulting in the death of Ashby. This brigade occupied the centre at the battle of Cross Keys and was complimented by General Fremont for its gallantry. The regiment became a part of General Bohlen's brigade, Sigel's corps, in Pope's campaign, and served with great gallantry in all the engagements of that campaign. On arriving at Washington City, the regiment was transferred to General Milroy's brigade, and returned with him to western Virginia, and was again assigned to duty in the Kanawha Valley. In November, 1862, it was transferred to Colonel Moor's brigade.

L.M. Strayer

JOHN H. OLEY
Colonel 7th West Virginia Cavalry
Brevet Brigadier General U.S. Volunteers

On the assignment of General Averell to the Fourth Separate Brigade, this regiment was mounted, and became a part of his brigade, as the Seventh West Virginia Cavalry, with which it served as long as the organization existed. The regiment spent the last years of its term in the Kanawha Valley, occupying the following different posts: Charleston, Coalsmouth, Windfield, Point Pleasant and Guyandotte. Early in January two or three brigades of Confederate troops were sent to winter in the counties immediately in the front of these posts, and the regiment was kept very actively engaged during the winter, to prevent incursions by them, and in the protection of loyal citizens and their property.

Several small engagements took place, in which a number of the enemy were killed, and about two hundred prisoners taken. About the 1st of February, six officers and nearly one hundred and fifty men were discharged by reason of expiration of term of service, but the regiment was immediately filled to the maximum by the muster-in of recruits.

From the time of the surrender of Lee's army the regiment was engaged in patrolling the twenty counties of southwestern Virginia, composing the District of Kanawha, for the purpose of paroling returned Confederates and maintaining order in the country—over five thousand Confederates were paroled by the officers of this regiment. In June, Colonel John H. Oley, who had been in command in the Kanawha Valley for a year previously, received an appointment as brevet brigadier-general, to rank from March 13, 1865, for gallant and meritorious services in West Virginia. The regiment was mustered out at Charleston, West Virginia, on the 1st day of August, 1865.

The regiment lost during the war: killed in battle and died of wounds, 5 officers and 28 enlisted men; died of disease or accident, 2 officers and 201 enlisted men; total, 236.

CHAPTER XXX.

SIXTH REGIMENT VETERAN CAVALRY.

Roster of the Field, Staff and Company Officers of the Sixth Regiment West Virginia Veteran Cavalry, Showing the Alterations and Casualties therein, from December 14, 1864 (Date of Consolidation with Fifth Regiment, West Virginia Cavalry), to December 31, 1865.

Date of Commission.	Names and Rank.	Co.	Remarks.
	Colonel.		
May 24, 1862.	George R. Latham.		Honorably discharged January 11, 1865.
	Lieutenant-Colonel.		
Oct. 27, 1864.	Rufus E. Fleming.		
	Majors.		
Oct. 27, 1864.	Peter J. Potts,		Resigned.
March 30, 1865.	Andrew J. Squires.		
March 29, 1865.	Thomas E. Day,		Resigned August 14, 1865.
	1st Lieut. and Adj't.		
Aug. 9, 1865.	R. L. Stealey.		
	1st Lieut. and R. Q. M.		
Oct. 5, 1864.	George Bumgardner.		Not Mustered.
	Surgeon.		
Nov. 26, 1865.	Abel H. Thayer.		
	Captains.		
Nov. 1, 1865.	John Somerville,	A	
Nov. 1. 1864.	James S. Law,	B	Mustered out.
March 30, 1865.	John W. Kidwell,	B	
Dec. 14, 1864.	Robert F. Lindsey,	C	
Nov. 28. 1862.	Andrew J. Squires.	D	Promoted to Major.
March 30, 1865.	Eli L. Parker.	D	
March 9, 1864.	Jacob S. Hyde,	E	Died at Annapolis, Md.
March 22, 1865.	Jehu F. Wotring,	E	Mustered out.
Oct. 6, 1865.	George M. Michael,	E	
Oct. 5, 1864.	W. H. Kantner,	F	Mustered out.
Aug. 9, 1865.	Richard W. Blue.	F	
Aug. 4, 1864.	Michael Donohue.	G	
Jan. 14, 1865.	James B. Smith.	H	
Oct. 10, 1864.	Thomas E. Day,	K	Promoted to Major.
April 18, 1865.	David J. M. Williamson.	K	
	First Lieutenants.		
Feb. 1, 1865.	Porter Flesher,	A	
Nov. 1, 1864.	Arthur E. Wells,	B	Resigned April 27, 1865.
Dec. 14, 1864.	Alonzo C. Bunten,	C	
Nov. 11, 1864.	Robert F. Lindsey,	D	Promoted to Captain, Co. C.

Date of Commission.	Names and Rank.	Co.	Remarks.
	First Lieutenants.		
Dec. 14. 1864.	Eli L. Parker,	D	Promoted to Captain.
March 30, 1865.	Samuel R. Hanen,	D	Resigned July 13, 1865.
March 9, 1864.	Jehu F. Wotring,	E	Promoted to Captain.
March 22, 1865.	George M. Michael,	E	Promoted to Captain.
Nov. 1, 1864.	W. W. Hickman,	F	Resigned July 14, 1865.
Oct. 6, 1865.	William S. Coburn,	F	
Aug. 4, 1864.	Henrie W. Brazie,	G	
Oct. 10, 1864.	George W. Miller,	H	
Oct. 10, 1864.	D. J. M. Williamson,	K	Promoted to Captain.
April 18, 1865.	Alstorpheus Werninger,	K	
	Second Lieutenants.		
Nov. 11, 1864.	Geo. Bumgardner,	A	Commissioned 1st Lieutenant and R. Q. M.
Nov. 1, 1864.	John W. Kidwell,	B	Promoted to Captain.
March 30, 1865.	Elisha C. Davidson,	B	
Nov. 1, 1864.	Alonzo C. Bunten,	C	Promoted to 1st Lieutenant.
Dec. 14, 1864.	W. W. Brown,	C	
Nov. 11, 1864.	Samuel R. Hanen,	D	Promoted to 1st Lieutenant.
March 30, 1865.	Frank Warthen,	D	
March 9, 1864.	Eli L. Parker,	E	Pomoted to 1st Lieutenand, Co. D.
Dec. 14, 1864.	George M. Michael,	E	Promoted to 1st Lieutenant.
March 22, 1865.	Magruder W. Selby,	E	
Nov. 1, 1864.	Richard W. Blue,	F	Promoted to Captain.
Aug. 20, 1864.	James W. Myers,	G	
Nov. 16, 1864.	Milton J. Thayer,	H	
Jan. 13, 1863.	James B. Smith,	K	Promoted to Captain, Co. H.
Feb. 1, 1865.	Alstorpheus Werninger,	K	Promoted to 1st Lieutenant.
April 18, 1865.	Peter Krouse,	K	

THE SIXTH WEST VIRGINIA VETERAN CAVALRY VOLUNTEERS,
JULY, 1864, TO JUNE, 1866.

The time of the non-veterans of the Sixth West Virginia Regiment expired in July, 1864. The regiment was reorganized at Cumberland, Md., in the same month. Those re-enlisting were formed into five campanies and two new companies added. The regiment was remounted at North Bridge, August 22, and ordered a few days later to report at New Creek where it was consolidated with the Fifth Regiment and was afterwards known as the Sixth West Virginia Veteran Volunteers, commanded by Colonel Latham.

In November, 1864, Colonel Latham, acting under orders from General Kelley, sent Lieut.-Col. R. E. Fleming, with about 300 men, to Burlington, W. Va., thence to march to Moorefield, in which vicinity a company of the enemy, under McNeill, was believed to be. Colonel Fleming detached 200 men under Major Potts to march by night to the rear of Moorefield, while he with the remaining 100 proceeded directly to Moorefield. Colonel Fleming reached the north bank of South Branch River in the evening of November 27, and there encamped. Hardly 20 minutes had elapsed after dismounting ere the scouts reported that a large force of Rebels lay just south of Moorefield. Hastily remounting, Colonel Fleming ordered a small detachment to cross the river and learn more certainly as to the whereabouts and number of the enemy. These soon returned with the information that General Rosser with 3000 or 4000 men was near at hand. The one piece of artillery was placed in position and the men drawn up on the river bank to await the attack of the enemy. Very soon General Rosser opened fire from the opposite side, which was returned. A vigorous fight was maintained until Colonel Fleming ascertained that detachments of the enemy were crossing both above and below him. Nothing remained for Fleming save to cut his way out in the face of this superior force. The only avenue of escape lay over a narrow wagon road through Milla Gap. Placing the artillery in front, a vigorous firing was kept up in the rear until the gap was reached. Here the artillery broke down and had to be abandoned. In this narrow pass, blockaded by the artillery, a hand-to-hand sabre fight occurred, in which some 50 men were killed, wounded or captured. Darkness ended the pursuit. The remnant retreated to New Creek, riding a distance of some 40 miles in four hours. Colonel Fleming reported to Colonel Latham that General Rosser was moving rapidly to New Creek with at least 3000 men.

The next morning, November 29, this same force captured New Creek, and some of the boys that escaped capture, after swimming or fording the Potomac River, rested their weary limbs in the mountains till the next day, when they returned to New Creek, where the camp was speedily reestablished. Colonel Latham was relieved from duty and the Sixth, under the command of Colonel Fleming, remained at New Creek doing garrison duty until January 12, 1865. Orders were then received to report at Sandy Hook, Md. On January 15, by order of General Crook, the horses were turned over and the regiment went into winter quarters at Remount Camp, Pleasant Valley, where it remained until April 4. Then marched to Harper's Ferry afoot; thence April 13 to Key's Ford, and after a night's rest, back to Remount Camp, and again supplied with horses.

Immediately after the assassination of President Lincoln, the Sixth was ordered to Washington, D. C. A detachment was sent in pursuit of Booth and his accomplices. Dr. Mudd was arrested at Surrattsville, and Booth chased from Maryland into Virginia. The Sixth now having its headquarters on 7th Street, sent out each morning a detachment for escort duty during the

GEORGE R. LATHAM
Colonel 5th West Virginia Cavalry
Colonel 6th West Virginia Veteran Cavalry

RUFUS E. FLEMING
Lieutenant Colonel 6th West Virginia Veteran Cavalry
Brevet Brigadier General U.S. Volunteers

trial of the conspirators in the assassination. And the entire regiment commanded by Colonel Fleming, did guard duty on Pennsylvania Avenue between the capitol and Georgetown during the "Grand Review."

On June 8th, orders were received to report at Cloud's Mills, Va. Four days later the Sixth returned to Washington, and camped near the south end of Long Bridge where it remained until June 12th. The boys who had reenlisted for "three years more or during the war," now thought the war over, and visions of home flitted through many a brain. But, alas, orders were received for this regiment, in company with the 2d Mass., the 14th Pa., and 21st N. Y., to go to Fort Leavenworth, Kansas, *via* Cincinnati and St. Louis. An incident of this trip was a collision on the night of June 20th, at Carlisle, Ill. Three men and seventy-three horses were killed. Daylight showed a mass of broken cars piled high upon each other. Upon the very top of one of these piles, thirty feet above the trestle, which was itself thirty feet above the ground, stood, unhurt, a gallant black steed, "Bismarck," the property of Lieutenant Brazie.

Fort Leavenworth was reached June 29th, and here they awaited further orders until July 16th. Then came the word that the Sixth should report at Fort Kearney on the Plains, where the work of subduing the hostile Indians awaited them.

The boys of the Sixth had fought many severe battles, endured long marches and untold hardships for Uncle Sam without a murmur. Now, the civil war having ended, many believed their duty was done. They declared they had not sworn to do duty against the savages and refused to move from Leavenworth.

Major Squires, in command of about one-third of the regiment, was sent to Fort Kearney, while Colonel Fleming remained with the rebellious two-thirds. By dint of much persuasion the objectors were soon brought to terms and moved forward to Julesburg. Major Squires' command crossed the Platte River and were assigned to escort duty for the overland mail, and as a reward for their obedience never encountered the Indians.

On the contrary, Colonel Fleming's command had several severe battles with the redskins on this side of the Platte, but in their new method of warfare they proved that the men whose state motto is " *montani semper liberi* " were equal to the conquering of a savage foe.

One incident occurring soon after the plains were reached, will long be remembered by those interested. While *en route* to Julesburg, Colonel Fleming with thirteen men and four Pawnee Indians turned aside for a hunt. After riding several miles they saw far ahead a wagon train on fire. Spurring onward it was soon found that the Indians had killed several of the teamsters and driven the rest to the river, and were making off with one hundred and twenty-five mules. Hoping to rescue the mules, Colonel Fleming ordered his men to follow, himself taking the lead. Soon they were in sight of the fleeing foe. Exultingly they followed, wondering to see hundreds of Indians running from a handful of men. Soon the Colonel's bump of caution suggested treachery, and riding to the top of a hill, he saw that they were being enticed into a narrow canon, while the surrounding bluffs showed hundreds of savages evidently arranging for their favorite method of encircling their pursuers. A halt was called and orders given to lead a hasty retreat; "speed away for your lives, the river banks is our only hope of escape," was the command. As they turned to obey the order, the Indians with horrid yells wheeled to follow. The air was full of flying arrows; with tingling scalplocks they urged their horses forward—thoughts of Bull Run, of Cross Keys, of New Creek, of all the dire disasters they had ever experienced flashed through their minds, but this was worse, for who can see a ray of glory in contemplating the loss of his scalp? "That was the only time in my war experience," said the Colonel, "that despair entered my mind", and his many narrow escapes were well known to all. He had ridden what proved to be a slow horse that morning—twice he dismounted, the little band forming a barricade to drive back the Indians—but not thus were the boys of the Sixth to perish. The river bank was gained and the Indians put to flight. In this hardly won escape much was learned of savage warfare that served to good purpose in future encounters. Several severe battles were afterwards fought in all of which the Sixth came off victors.

That part of the regiment under command of Major Squires, wintered at Fort Casper, Dakota, while Colonel Fleming's command remained at Julesburg and Cottonwood Springs. At the latter place the two commands were ordered to consolidate in March, 1866, thence to march to Fort Leavenworth, Kansas, a distance of 385 miles. This completed the service of the Sixth West Virginia Veteran Volunteer Cavalry. Mustered out at Fort Leavenworth, May 22, 1866, it was ordered to Wheeling, West Virginia, for pay and final discharge June 1, 1866. On the arrival at Wheeling, a banquet was tendered to the regiment at the McClure House. Before the boys separated, Col. R. E. Fleming was given a proof of the confidence and esteem of his fellow officers by receiving from them a handsome gold watch which he proudly wears to this day.

CHAPTER XXXI.

FIRST REGIMENT (THREE MONTHS' SERVICE) W. VA. INFANTRY.

Roster of the Field, Staff and Company Officers of the First Regiment West Virginia Infantry Volunteers (Three Months' Service), Showing the Alterations and Casualties therein, from the Date of Organization to the Date of Muster Out.

Date of Commission.	Names and Rank.	Co.	Remarks.
	Colonel.		
May 22, 1861.	Benjamin F. Kelley,		Promoted to Brigadier-General.
	Lieutenant-Colonel.		
July 18, 1861.	Henry B. Hubbard,		Commissioned Lt.-Col. of 3 yrs. organization.
	Major.		
June 1, 1891.	Isaac H. Duval,		Commissioned Major of 3 yrs. organization.
	1st Lieut. and Adj't.		
May 29, 1861.	John B. Lukens.		
	1st Lieut. and R. Q. M.		
May 27, 1861.	Isaac M. Pumphrey.		Appointed Major and Paymaster, U. S. A.
	Surgeon.		
	Joseph Thoburn.		Commissioned Colonel of 3 yrs. organization.
	Assistant Surgeon.		
Aug. 3, 1861.	John D. M. Carr.		
	Captains.		
May 10, 1861.	Andrew H. Britt,	A	
May 11, 1861.	Edward W. Stephens,	B	Commissioned Captain in 3 yrs. organization.
May 15, 1861.	Isaac N. Fordyce,	C	
May 15, 1861.	Mountford Stokeley,	D	
May 16, 1861.	Thomas C. Parke,	E	
May 17, 1861.	George C. Trimble,	F	Commissioned Major, 11th W. Va. Infantry.
May 18, 1861.	James Kuhn,	G	
May 21, 1861.	James F. Donnelly,	H	Commissioned Captain in 3 yrs. organization
May 21, 1861.	B. W. Chapman,	I	
May 23, 1861.	George W. Robinson,	K	
	First Lieutenants.		
May 10, 1861.	Joseph D. Britt,	A	
May 11, 1861.	Charles A. Griffin,	B	
May 15, 1861.	Thos. McK. McNeely,	C	
May 15, 1861.	Christopher H. Orth,	D	
May 16, 1861.	Oscar F. Melvin,	E	Commissioned Captain in 3 yrs. organization.
May 17, 1861.	Jacob Weddle,	F	Commissioned Captain in 3 yrs. organization.
May 18, 1861.	James C. White,	G	Commissioned Captain in 3 yrs. organization.
May 21, 1867.	Samuel B. Stidger,	H	

Date of Commission.	Names and Rank.	Co.	Remarks.
	First Lieutenants.		
May 21, 1861.	Thomas Lloyd,	I	Commissioned 2d Lieut. in 3 yrs. organization.
May 23, 1861.	Charles Bryson,	K	
	Second Lieutenants.		
May 10, 1861.	Thomas O'Brien,	A	
May 11, 1861.	Thomas H. Morton,	B	
May 15, 1861.	James W. Singleton,	C	Commissioned 2d Lieut. in 3 yrs. organization.
May 15, 1861.	John J. McCook,	D	
May 16, 1861.	Enos W. Melvin,	E	
May 17, 1861.	John B. Trimble,	F	Commissioned Captain in 3 yrs. organization.
May 18, 1861.	Albert W. Kuhn,	G	
May 21, 1861.	John S. McDonald,	H	Commissioned 1st Lieut. in 3 yrs. organization.
May 21, 1861.	Richard H. Brown,	I	
May 23, 1861.	Peter Crawford,	K	

THE FIRST REGIMENT OF VIRGINIA UNION VOLUNTEER INFANTRY.

The history of the First Regiment of Virginia Union Volunteer Infantry antedates the organization and formation of the new State. It was a part of the old Virginia military establishment, Governor Peirpoint having been appointed Provisional Governor of the State of Virginia by President Lincoln, the State government being established at Wheeling, by reason of that portion of the State east of the Alleghanies having joined its fortunes with the Confederacy through the operation of secession.

This regiment of Loyal Virginia Infantry was the first regiment organized on Southern soil for the defense of the nation under the call of President Lincoln. The regiment was organized at Wheeling, the first company being mustered into the service of the United States on May 10, 1861. On May 23, the organization of the regiment was complete, Colonel Benjamin F. Kelley being assigned to the command by the then Provisional Governor of Virginia, Francis H. Peirpoint.

The condition of the public mind in and about the city of Wheeling at the time this regiment was organized was such that grave fears were entertained by very many loyal people that it would be unsafe to send arms and equipments of war with which to equip this regiment, to the city of Wheeling. Several patriotic gentlemen whose loyalty never was questioned, residents of Wellsburg, the county seat of Brooke, the adjoining county on the north, made application to the Secretary of War, and through the kind offices of Governor Andrews, of Massachusetts, arms were secured for this regiment. They were sent to Wellsburg in the care of Messrs. W. H. Carothers and Cambell Tarr. Louis Applegate and Adam Kuhn were associated with them in the receiving and transferring of these arms by steamboat to Wheeling, where they were turned over to the regiment. On May 27, the regiment was placed under marching orders.

The good people of Wheeling had furnished them with a supply of blankets and clothing, but they were without knapsacks, haversacks, cartridge-boxes or any other of the habiliments of regularly organized troops, save that in their hands they clasped an old United States Springfield musket.

Colonel Kelley applied for transportation to the Baltimore and Ohio Railroad, which was refused upon the grounds that the railroad company proposed to remain neutral in the question of war as between the sections, the agent stating that an order had been issued that the road would not carry either troops or munition of war for either side. Colonel Kelley emphasized the following language in reply to the agent: "This is war. Railroad companies cannot be their own masters. They are to serve the government that guarantees to them possession and protection for their property. You have a train of cars in the depot to-morrow morning at four o'clock or I will place you in prison and take possession of your railroad by military authority." No further argument was needed. The agent communicated with the company and the cars were accordingly furnished and afterwards, throughout the entire war, the Baltimore and Ohio Railroad continued to perform any service necessary for the successful transaction of the war.

The regiment left Wheeling May 27th on the Baltimore and Ohio Railroad. They were joined at Benwood by some Ohio troops under Colonel Irvin, and two days afterwards, at Camp Buffalo, the 15th Ohio joined the command. On the 31st, Grafton was occupied by our troops, while the Confederates under Colonel Porterfield retired. On the morning of June 3, the first battle was fought at Philippi, West Virginia, in which the First Virginia participated, Colonel Kelley being wounded in the affray. Here is a notable incident in the history of the regiment. It was not only to bear in history the record of having been the first loyal regiment formed on Southern soil, but the additional historic incident is now given to it by reason of Colonel Kelley being the first officer wounded in the great War of the Rebellion.

It would be impossible to trace out the meanderings of this regiment through the three months' service that followed. Suffice it to say they participated in all the historic campaign of the early war in the mountains of West Virginia. The regiment completed its service and returned to Wheeling, where it was mustered out of service on the 28th day of August.

Of the three months' organization it is sufficient to say that Henry B. Hubbard, of Wheeling, was lieutenant-colonel; Isaac H. Duval, of Wellsburg, was major; John B. Lukens, of Wheeling, was adjutant; Isaac M Pumphrey was quartermaster; Dr. Joseph Thoburn was surgeon, and Dr. J. D. M. Carr, assistant-surgeon.

CHAPTER XXXII.

FIRST REGIMENT WEST VIRGINIA INFANTRY.

Roster of the Field, Staff and Company Officers of the First Regiment West Virginia Infantry Volunteers, Showing the Alterations and Casualties therein, from the Date of Original Organization of the Regiment to the Date of Consolidation with the Fourth Regiment, West Virginia Infantry, December 10, 1864.

Date of Commission.	Names and Rank.	Co.	Remarks.
	Colonel.		
Oct. 30, 1861.	Joseph Thoburn,		Killed in action at Cedar Creek, Va., Oct. 19, 1864.
	Lieutenant-Colonels.		
Nov. 2, 1861.	Henry B. Hubbard,		Discharged on Surgeon's certificate of disability, Oct. 3, 1862.
Dec. 4, 1862.	Jacob Weddle.		
	Majors.		
Nov. 2, 1861,	Isaac Hardin Duval,		Promoted to Col. 9th W. Va. Inft. Sept. 9, 1862.
Dec. 4, 1862.	Jacob Weddle,		Promoted from Captain Co. A. Promoted to Lieutenant-Colonel.
Dec. 4, 1862.	Edward W. Stephens,		Promoted from Captain, Co. F. Mustered out at expiration of term of service.
	1st Lieut. and Adj't.		
Nov. 13, 1861.	James McElroy,		Promoted to Captain, Co. D.
Sep. 23, 1862.	Henry J. Johnson,		Vice McElroy, promoted. Retained in service by order Sec'y of War, and transferred to 2d W. Va. Veteran Infantry.
	1st Lieut. and R. Q. M.		
Nov. 13, 1861.	Wm. T. Singleton,		Promoted to Captain, and C. S.
July 4, 1864.	Lucian Gray,		Vice Singleton, promoted,
	Surgeon.		
Oct. 29, 1861.	David Baguley,		Mustered out at expiration of term of service.
	Assistant Surgeons.		
Jan. 19, 1863.	A. W. D. Kraft,		Discharged March 19, 1863.
Oc.. 30, 1861.	S. B. Stidger,		Resigned July 10, 1862.
July 8, 1862.	James L. Gillespie,		Vice Stidger. Resigned Nov. 18, 1862.
Feb. 27, 1863.	John English,		Vice Gillespie, resigned.
	Chaplains.		
Feb. 19, 1862.	Gordon Battelle,		Died of disease.
Feb. 4, 1863.	William R. Howe,		Vice Battelle, deceased. Mustered out at expiration of term of service.
	Captains.		
Oct. 3, 1861.	Jacob Weddle,	A	Promoted to Major, Oct. 3, 1862.

Date of Commission.	Names and Rank.	Co.	Remarks.
	Captains.		
Nov. 25, 1862.	William J. Robb,	A	Promoted from 1st Lieutenant. Mustered out at expiration of term of service.
Nov. 26, 1861.	James C. White,	B	Resigned Jan. 16, 1863.
Feb. 19, 1863.	George W. White,	B	Vice J. C. White, resigned.
Oct. 21, 1861.	William Milhouse,	C	Discharged for disability Oct. 13, 1862.
Nov. 25, 1862.	William H. Orr,	C	Mustered out at expiration of term of service.
Nov. 5, 1861.	James F. Donnelly,	D	Died at Cumberland, Md., January, 1862.
Oct. 6, 1862.	John S. McDonald,	D	Resigned.
Nov. 25, 1862.	James McElroy,	D	Mustered out at expiration of term of service.
Nov. 20, 1861.	Wm. Morgan,	E	Resigned August 16, 1862.
Nov. 25, 1862.	John Craig,	E	Mustered out at expiration of term of service.
Nov. 1, 1861.	Edward W. Stephens,	F	Promoted to Major.
Feb. 4, 1863.	James E. Morrow,	F	Mustered out at expiration of term of service
Nov. 5, 1861.	Oscar F. Melvin,	G	Mustered out at expiration of term of service.
Nov. 6, 1861.	James M. Bowers,	H	Resigned July 28, 1862.
Sep. 10, 1862.	Thomas Reed,	H	Mustered out at expiration of term of service.
Nov. 6, 1861.	John B. Trimble,	I	Resigned.
Aug. 25, 1862.	John W. Dougherty,	I	Died at Annapolis, Md., 1864.
Dec. 11, 1861.	Richard Radcliff,	K	Mustered out at expiration of term of service.
	First Lieutenants.		
Oct. 3, 1861.	William B. Kelley,	A	Mustered out at expiration of term of service.
Nov. 26, 1861.	James McElroy,	B	Promoted to Captain, Co. D, Jany. 16, 1863.
Nov. 20, 1861.	John W. Dougherty,	B	Promoted to Captain, Company I.
Feb. 19, 1863.	Thomas H. McKee,	B	Mustered out at expiration of term of service.
Oct. 21, 1861.	William H. Orr,	C	Promoted to Captain.
Nov. 25, 1862.	James W. Singleton,	C	Mustered out at expiration of term of service.
Nov. 5, 1861.	John S. McDonald,	D	Promoted to Captain.
Feb. 6, 1862.	James Wilson,	D	Resigned.
Oct. 8, 1862.	Martin B. Helms,	D	Mustered out at expiration of term of service.
Nov. 20, 1861.	John F. Baer,	E	Resigned February 28, 1862.
Nov. 1, 1861.	Charles A. Freeman,	E	Mustered out at expiration of term of service.
Dec. 17, 1861.	Thayer Melvin,	F	Appointed A. A. General.
Nov. 24, 1861.	John W. White,	F	Resigned January 24, 1863.
Feb. 25, 1863.	Theodore L. Apple,	F	Mustered out at expiration of term of service.
Nov. 5, 1861.	Thomas Lloyd,	G	Mustered out at expiration of term of service.
Nov. 6, 1861.	Thomas Reed,	H	Promoted to Captain.
Sep. 24, 1862.	Henry H. Hornbrook,	H	Mustered out at expiration of term of service.
Nov. 22, 1861.	John W. Dougherty,	I	Promoted to Captain.
Nov. 6, 1861.	George James,	I	Mustered out at expiration of term of service.
Dec. 11, 1861.	James A. Lewis,	K	Mustered out at expiration of term of service.
	Second Lieutenants.		
Oct. 3, 1861.	John Barnes,	A	Killed in action at Port Republic, June 9, 1862.
July 8, 1862.	Thomas M. Simpson,	A	Mustered out at expiration of term of service.
Nov. 24, 1862.	Thos. H. McKee,	B	Promoted to 1st Lieutenant.
Feb. 19, 1863.	John F. Ryan,	B	Mustered out at expiration of term of service.
Nov. 6, 1861.	James W. Singleton,	C	Transferred to Company I.

Date of Commission.	Names and Rank.	Co.	Remarks.
	Second Lieutenants.		
July 8, 1862.	Robert W. Vance,	C	Resigned February 2, 1863.
Feb. 25, 1863.	Joseph B. Gordon,	C	
Oct. 21, 1861.	Burgess Stewart,	C	Resigned July 1, 1863.
Nov. 5, 1861.	Wm. D. Logsden,	D	Resigned January 1, 1862.
Jan. 23, 1862.	James Wilson,	D	Promoted to 1st Lieutenant.
Feb. 6, 1862.	James C. Connelly,	D	Dishonorably discharged January 29, 1863.
Nov. 5, 1861.	Chester B. Hall,	D	Mustered out at expiration of term of service·
Nov. 20, 1861.	John Craig,	E	Promoted to Captain.
March 10, 1862.	James E. Morrow,	E	Promoted to Captain.
Nov. 25, 1862.	John F. Baird,	E	Mustered out at expiration of term of service.
Nov. 1, 1861.	John W. White,	F	Promoted to 1st Lieutenant.
Feb. 25, 1863.	James L. Steel,	F	Mustered out at expiration of term of service.
Nov. 5, 1861.	Chester B. Hall,	G	Transferred to Company D.
Dec. 18, 1861.	William J. Robb,	G	Transferred to Company A.
Aug. 25, 1862.	Joseph O. Adams,	G	Mustered out at expiration of term of service.
Nov. 6, 1861.	Henry H. Hornbrook,	H	Promoted to 1st Lieutenant.
April 11, 1864.	William S. Murphy,	H	Mustered out at expiration of term of service.
Nov. 6, 1861.	James W. Singleton,	I	Promoted to 1st Lieutenant, Company C.
Nov. 25, 1862.	James M. Goudy,	I	Mustered out at expiration of term of service.
Dec. 11, 1861.	David Morgan,	K	Resigned February 1, 1862.
March 17, 1862.	Henry K. Weeden,	K	Dismissed March 7, 1864.
April 11, 1864.	John W. Plattenburg,	K	Mustered out at expiration of term of service.

THE FIRST WEST VIRGINIA IN THE THREE YEARS' SERVICE.

Immediately after the three months' men were discharged, on August 30, Dr. Joseph Thoburn, the former surgeon of the regiment, received the appointment of colonel for the purpose of reorganizing the regiment, which event was consummated about October 30, 1861. The regiment began its career in the three years' service by four companies being sent to the Little Kanawha, Wirt County, Virginia, to suppress insurrection and dispel a band of marauders known as moccasin rangers, who were devastating the country in the oil region about Burning Springs. The regiment was brought together by all the companies taking post at Romney in Hampshire County, Virginia, about November 12, where they became a part of the command of General Kelley, who was then occupying this advance position as a part of the defense line of the Baltimore and Ohio Railroad. Here, again, that wonderful history of which much has been written, but of which there remains much that never shall be told, was enacted. From the beginning of Kelley's first command at Romney to the close of the last scenes of the war at Appomattox, a part of this regiment participated in every engagement fought in the valley or the great campaigns which became a part of the history of the war, other than the army of the Potomac.

A short summary may give a faint idea of what the service of this regiment was. From Romney, in the winter of 1861 and 1862, to Patterson's Creek, where General Lander assumed the command of that grand division of men afterward known as Shields' Division, thrown together as a distinctive army; afterwards to Paw Paw Tunnel, where the lamented Lander died and then by the coming of General Shields, they began to weave history which stretched onward, covering the first battle of Winchester, March 23, 1862, where Stonewall Jackson was routed and driven from the field.

On June 9, at Port Republic, the troops of this division won for themselves an imperishable name. No battle of the war has crowded into it so much heroism and gallantry on the field, where our forces were greatly outnumbered. Our 3000 accomplished on that field that wonderful defense which the Confederates claim was the result of 10,000 men present. In July, 1863, the regiment went with a part of the divisions to join that of General Rickets, a part of McDowell's corps, Army of Virginia, in which command it participated in the battles of Cedar Mountain, Rappahannock Station, Thoroughfare Gap and the second battle of Bull Run, August 29 and 30.

At the close of the Bull Run campaign, the regiment was assigned to duty in the defense of Washington, being stationed at Arlington Heights. At this time it is worthy of note to say that the regiment came out of the second battle of Bull Run without a commissioned officer on duty. Sergeant Major Johnson commanded the regiment and marched it from Fairfax Station to Arlington Heights.

In October, 1862, the regiment was transferred from the defense of Washington to the Department of West Virginia, where they assisted in opening the Baltimore and Ohio Railroad to Harper's Ferry, and took post at North Mountain, being assigned to the Second Brigade of the First Division of the Eighth Army Corps. During the summer of 1863, they participated in the campaigns of that department, making many long and difficult marches, co-operating with the forces on the flank of Meade's army, during the Gettisburg campaign, taking post in August at Petersburg, West Virginia. On September the 11, at Moorefield, five companies of the regiment were captured by the Confederate forces under McNeill, with a part of Imboden's command. These five companies were taken to Richmond, a portion of the men being exchanged during the winter of 1863–64, but the eight officers there captured, excepting Captain Reed, Company H, were held prisoners of war until the close of the Rebellion.

The winter of 1863–64 was memorable in the regiment's history for the service rendered in the defense of the line of railroad, in resisting Confederate raids and preventing destruction of property. On the 25th of February, 1864, the regiment was sent to Wheeling on veteran furlough, and on the 1st of April it again entered active service, joining Sullivan's command at Webster, West Virginia, where it was attached to the Second Brigade, commanded by Colonel Thoburn. In May, 1864, it participated in Sigel's campaign in the Shenandoah Valley, taking part in the battles of New Market, May 14 and 15, and continuing in the same organization during the campaign of General Hunter, bearing an honorable part in the battles of Piedmont, June 5, and Lynchburg, June 17 and 18, retreating from Lynchburg to the Kanawha Valley.

In July and August it participated in the campaigns of General Crook against the Confederate General Early, in the Shenandoah Valley, and took part in the battle of Snicker's Ferry, July 18, and Winchester, July 24. In the months of August, September and October, it formed a part of the Army of West Virginia, in General Sheridan's department, and was actively engaged at Cedar Creek, August 12; at Berryville, September 3; at Charlestown, August 22 and at Halltown, August 26; at the battle of Opequon, September 19; Fisher's Hill, September 23, and Cedar Creek, October 19.

In this last engagement, Colonel Thoburn was killed, he being then in command of the First Division of the Army of West Virginia. On October 29, the regiment was sent to Cumberland, Maryland, where the three years' men not veteranizing were mustered out and the veterans were consolidated with part of the Fourth West Virginia Infantry, forming the Second Regiment of West Virginia Veteran Volunteers. In reviewing the history of this regiment, the field and staff, as composed at its organization, was Joseph Thoburn, colonel; Henry B. Hubbard, lieutenant-colonel, discharged on account of wounds, October 23, 1862; Isaac H. Duval, major, promoted to colonel of the Ninth Virginia Infantry, September 9, 1862; Jacob Weddel, major, November, 1862, also lieutenant-colonel, December 4, 1862; E. W. Stevens, major, December 4, 1862; James McElroy was the first adjutant of the regiment, November 13, 1861. He was succeeded by John W. Dougherty. Dougherty and McElroy both succeeding to captaincies in the regiment, Henry J. Johnson became adjutant, September 23, 1862. W. T. Singleton was the quartermaster, Dr. David Bagley, surgeon, and the following named persons were assistant surgeons at different dates: A. W. D. Kraft, S. B. Stidger, James L. Gillespie, John English. Revs. Gordon Battelle and Wm. R. Howe served the regiment as chaplains.

L.M. Strayer

JOSEPH THOBURN
Colonel 1st West Virginia Infantry
Mortally Wounded Cedar Creek, Va. October 19, 1864

WILLIAM B. KELLEY

First Lieutenant 1st West Virginia Infantry

The many changes which occurred in the line officers of the regiment would require too much space in this short article. Suffice it is to say that when the regiment closed its three years' term of service, not a single captain of the original ten was mustered out with his company. Most of the companies were commanded by men who either started as lieutenants, or had been promoted from the ranks.

SOME OF THE NAMES WORTHY TO BE MENTIONED AS CONNECTED WITH THE REGIMENT.

COL. BENJAMIN F. KELLEY.

Col. Benjamin F. Kelley was the first colonel. Mention being made of his service and wounds, we have here to add that he was nominated by President Lincoln to be a brigadier-general of volunteers at the same time at which General Grant and a number of others who became illustrious in the War of the Rebellion were named for like positions. General Kelley was confirmed by the Senate and as a brigadier-general he commanded many important armies during the progress of the war. He was the only brigadier-general that ever commanded a department as such, through the entire war, notably the Department of West Virginia in the summer of 1864. He was brevetted major-general and leaves a record for fidelity and devotion to the cause of the Union, sharing in the establishment of a new State—West Virginia. He now sleeps among more than 14,000 of his comrades at Arlington, where future citizens shall view his resting place and talk of his life service in the cause of liberty.

COL. JOSEPH THOBURN.

But few names in the annals of the war have clustered around them memories so strange and inexplainable as that of this gallant and loyal son of Virginia. He was on many battlefields, a leader worthy of his star, but facts over which political destinies seemed to hang, had kept from him the well-earned distinction of general, while he commanded a division of the army as a colonel longer than any man in the great Rebellion. It is said by a writer who is familiar with the records of the War Department, that this fact cannot be disputed. Colonel Thoburn was perhaps as well known as any colonel in the war ; although his services were confined exclusively to the soil of Virginia, yet he came in touch and in contact with the commanders of all the Eastern armies and held subordinate positions above his rank, temporarily commanding brigades and divisions at different times. He was a man of conscientious principles, lovable in his disposition and brave to a fault. He never lacked in popular esteem among the rank and file of the army. His death was announced by General Sheridan as a great calamity. West Virginia has no greater honor to perform than that of placing, somewhere within her borders, a suitable testimonial to the character of this man.

ISAAC H. DUVAL.

Isaac H. Duval, of Wellsburg, West Virginia, who entered the service as major in the three months' service with the First Virginia Infantry, re-entered the service in the same capacity with the regiment at the beginning of the three years' term. His genius as a soldier very soon brought him into prominence when the active hostilities of the war began to show of what metal men were made. Of all the names borne on the rolls of the First Virginia Infantry, perhaps the ideal soldier was found in the person of this man. Very early in 1862, Governor Peirpoint selected him as colonel of the Ninth West Virginia Volunteers. His soldierly bearing soon marked its characteristics upon the regiment, and it became known throughout the Army of West Virginia that there was none better than the Ninth. In the conflicts that followed in the campaigns of 1863-64, Colonel Duval was promoted to the rank of brigadier-general and upon him devolved important commands during that history made famous by Sheridan and Crook, which shall live in the annals of time. It is a strange coincidence that at the surrender of the last troops in the Department of West Virginia, it should fall to the lot of one of West Virginia's sons to receive the sword of the commander of the capitulating forces, when the climax of war was ended. General Duval, upon whom rested the command of Hancock's corps (General Hancock being absent), being stationed at Staunton, Virginia, at the time of the capitulation of Lee's army, threw his troops in the way of the Confederate General Rosser, who in the command of Lee's cavalry attempted to make his way west with a sufficient force to continue active operations, but was brought to bay and compelled to surrender. General Duval has lived to enjoy the honor and esteem of the people of West Virginia, he having represented them in the lower House of Congress, and in many ways filled places of trust and honor.

SUBALTERNS.

Among the subordinate officers there were many who entered the service as unknown striplings or boys from the schools and the shops, who placed themselves at the heads of companies and other subordinate commands that were as honorable to their service, by reason of their youth and opportunities, as though they had succeeded to greater commands.

RANK AND FILE.

In the rank and file there were men as true and loyal, as ever bore arms in the defense of liberty and free government. It may not be amiss to state that of the per cent. of battleflags captured in the war, it stands to the credit of West Virginia for having captured a greater number in proportion to the troops in the field than by the troops of any other State. The names of many of the First West Virginia Infantry are enshrined forever on fields that shall live as among the marked spots where the conflicts of men took place in the War of the Rebellion. It would be doing injustice to others that any should be named, for among the unknown who fell and sleep in unmarked graves, West Virginia's greatest glory is unhonored and unsung, but we can all say: "All hail to the sons of the storm-born State, who gave their lives that liberty might live and that West Virginia may ever continue among the family of States."

CHAPTER XXXIII.

FOURTH REGIMENT WEST VIRGINIA INFANTRY.

Roster of the Field, Staff and Company Officers of the Fourth Regiment West Virginia Infantry, showing the Alterations and Casualties therein, from the Date of Original Organization to the Date of Consolidation with the First West Virginia Infantry, December 10, 1864.

Date of Commission.	Names and Rank.	Co.	Remarks.
	Colonels.		
Aug. 14, 1861.	J. A. J. Lightburn,		Promoted to Brigadier-General, Volunteers.
May 9, 1863.	James H. Dayton,		Mustered out at expiration of term of service.
	Lieutenant-Colonels.		
Aug. 27, 1861.	Wm. H. H. Russell,		Resigned.
March 19, 1863.	James H. Dayton,		Promoted to Colonel.
May 19, 1863.	John L. Vance,		Mustered out at expiration of term of service.
	Majors.		
Aug. 27, 1861.	John T. Hall,		Killed in action.
Oct. 4, 1862.	James H. Dayton,		Promoted to Lieutenant-Colonel,
March 9, 1863.	John L. Vance,		Promoted to Lieutenant-Colonel.
May 9, 1863,	A. M. Goodspeed,		Killed in action at Vicksburg,
Aug. 17, 1863.	Henry Grayum,		Mustered out at expiration of term of service.
	1st Lieut. and Adj't.		
Aug. 22, 1861.	Philson B. Stanberry,		Honorably discharged.
Jan. 26, 1864.	Alpheus Beall,		Mustered out at expiration of term of service.
	First Lieut. and R.Q.M.		
Oct. 18, 1861.	Jesse F. Stevens,		Mustered out at expiration of term of service.
	Surgeons.		
Aug. 26, 1861.	D. R. Achley,		Resigned.
May 9, 1863.	John R. Philson,		
	Asst. Surgeons.		
Nov. 19, 1861.	John R. Philson,		Promoted to Surgeon,
May 9, 1863.	Homer C. Waterman,		Mustered out at expiration of term of service.
	Chaplain.		
Nov. 27, 1861.	George S. Woodhull,		Mustered out at expiration of term of service.
	Captains.		
	Henry S. Welton,	A	Resigned September 1st, 1861.
Sep. 1, 1861.	Tilton B. Rockhill,	A	Resigned November 30, 1862.
Dec. 31, 1862.	Martin V. Lightburn,	A	Mustered out at expiration of term of service.
July 5, 1861.	John L. Vance,	B	Promoted to Major.
March 19, 1863.	Barlow W. Curtis,	B	
July 5, 1861.	Thomas J. Smith,	C	Resigned November 20, 1862.
Dec. 31, 1862.	Barney J. Rollins,	C	Mustered out at expiration of term of service.

Date of Commission.	Names and Rank.	Co.	Remarks.
	Captains.		
July 8, 1861,	Arza M. Goodspeed,	D	Promoted to Major.
May 9, 1863.	John L. Mallernere,	D	Mustered out at expiration of term of service.
July 22, 1861.	Wm. R. Brown,	E	Promoted to Colonol, 13th W. Va. Infantry.
Oct. 4, 1862.	Ephraim C. Carson,	E	Resigned Jan. 3, 1863.
March 19, 1863.	Daniel A. Russell,	E	Mustered out at expiration of term of service.
Aug. 22, 1861.	Wm. H. H. Russell,	F	Promoted to Lieutenant-Colonel.
Sept. 1, 1861.	George W. Storey,	F	Resigned January 5, 1863.
March 19, 1863.	Wm. S. Hall,	F	Mustered out at expiration of term of service.
July 1, 1861.	Henry Grayum,	G	Promoted to Major.
Aug. 17, 1863.	William Grayum,	G	
Aug. 1, 1861.	Patrick H. Brunker,	H	Resigned January 5, 1863.
March 19, 1863.	Benjamin D. Boswell,	H	Promoted to Major, 2d Veteran Infantry.
July 10, 1861.	Alexander Vance,	I	Resigned February 16, 1863.
March 19, 1863.	Calvin A. Shepherd,	I	Mustered out at expiration of term of service.
July 22, 1861.	James H. Dayton,	K	Promoted to Major.
Oct. 4, 1862.	James J. Mansell.	K	Mustered out at expiration of term of service.
	First Lieutenants.		
Sep. 1, 1861,	Martin V. Lightburn,	A	Promoted to Captain.
Dec. 31, 1862.	John J. Sayre,	A	Mustered out at expiration of term of service.
July 5, 1861.	Wm. C. Bailey,	B	Resigned September 30, 1862.
Dec. 31, 1862.	Barlow W. Curtis,	B	Promoted to Captain.
March 19, 1863.	Wm. H. H. Sisson,	B	Mustered out at expiration of term of service.
July 5, 1861.	Barney J. Rollins,	C	Promoted to Captain.
Dec. 31, 1862.	Wm. L. McMasters,	C	Mustered out at expiration of term of service.
July 8, 1861.	John L. Mallernee,	D	Promoted to Captain.
May 9, 1863.	Geo. W. Hankinson,	D	Mustered out at expiration of term of service.
Aug. 22, 1861.	Ephraim C. Carson,	E	Promoted to Captain.
Oct. 4, 1862.	Daniel A. Russell,	E	Promoted to Captain.
Aug. 22, 1861	Philson B. Stanberry,	E	Promoted to Adjutant.
March 19, 1863.	James H. Ralston,	E	Resigned September 6, 1863.
Jan. 26, 1864.	Edward Mallory,	E	Mustered out at expiration of term of service.
July 30, 1861.	Wm. S. Hall,	F	Promoted to Captain.
March 19, 1863.	Finley D. Ong.	F	Died prisoner at Vicksburg, May 22, 1863.
Aug. 17, 1863.	George A. Scott,	F	Mustered out at expiration of term of service.
July 18, 1861.	John DeLille,	G	Resigned November 30, 1862.
Dec. 31, 1862.	Cincinnatus B. Blake,	G	Resigned April 3, 1863.
Aug. 17, 1863.	Calvin L. Lightburn,	G	
Nov. 5, 1861.	John B. Booram,	H	Resigned November 11, 1861.
Dec. 31, 1862.	Benjamin D. Boswell,	H	Promoted to Captain.
May 13, 1862.	H. F. Donnelley,	H	Resigned December 8, 1862.
March 19, 1863.	Michael Christopher,	H	Mustered out at expiration of term of service.
July 10, 1861.	Calvin A. Shepherd,	I	Promoted to Captain.
March 19, 1863.	James W. Dale,	I	Promoted to Captain, 2d Infantry.
July 22. 1861.	James J. Mansell,	K	Promoted to Captain.
Oct. 4, 1862.	Alpheus Beall,	K	Appointed Adjutant.
July 26, 1864.	Enoch Clice,	K	Mustered out at expiration of term of service.

Date of Commission.	Name and Rank.	Co.	Remarks.
	Second Lieutenants.		
June 17, 1861.	John W. Davis,	A	Resigned December 5, 1862.
Dec. 31, 1862.	Columbus Shrewsberry,	A	Resigned May 26, 1863.
Aug. 17, 1863.	John McDonald,	A	Mustered out at expiration of term of service.
July 5, 1861.	Barlow W. Curtis,	B	Promoted to 1st Lieutenant.
Dec. 31, 1862.	Wm. H. H. Sisson,	B	Promoted to 1st Lieutenant.
March 19, 1863.	Alex. Wartenburg,	B	Mustered out at expiration of term of service.
Oct. 1, 1861.	Wm. L. McMasters,	C	Promoted to 1st Lieutenant.
	Jesse V. Stevens	C	Promoted to 1st Lieutenant, and R. Q. M.
Dec. 31, 1862.	Robert Dyke,	C	Mustered out at expiration of term of service.
Oct. 25, 1861.	George W. Hankisson,	D	Promoted to 1st Lieutenant.
Aug. 17, 1863.	John N. Dean,	D	Promoted to 1st Lieutenant. 2d Vet. Infantry.
Aug. 22, 1861.	Ephraim C. Carson,	E	Promoted to 1st Lieutenant.
Aug. 22, 1861.	Daniel A. Russell,	E	Promoted to 1st Lieutenant.
Oct. 4, 1862.	James H. Ralston,	E	Promoted to 1st Lieutenant.
March 19, 1863.	Edward Mallory,	E	Mustered out at expiration of term of service.
July 30, 1861.	Finley D. Ong,	F	Promoted to 1st Lieutenant.
March 19, 1863.	George A. Scott,	F	Promoted to 1st Lieutenant.
Aug. 17, 1863.	Allen Bloomfield,	F	Mustered out at expiration of term of service.
July 28, 1861.	C. B. Blake,	G	Promoted to 1st Lieutenant.
March 19, 1863.	William Grayum,	G	Promoted to Captain.
Nov. 5, 1861.	H. F. Donnelly,	H	Promoted to 1st Lieutenant.
May 13, 1862.	Benjamin D. Boswell,	H	Promoted to 1st Lieutenant.
Dec. 31, 1862.	Michael Christopher,	H	Promoted to 1st Lieutenant.
Dec. 31, 1862.	Wm. R. Malone,	H	Mustered out at expiration of term of service.
July 10, 1861.	James W. Dale,	I	Promoted to 1st Lieutenant.
March 19, 1863.	Edward H. Trickle,	I	Mustered out at expiration of term of service.
July 22, 1861.	Alpheus Beall,	K	Promoted to 1st Lieutenant.
Oct. 4, 1862.	Enoch T. Clice,	K	Promoted to 1st Lieutenant.

THE FOURTH WEST VIRGINIA INFANTRY.

The Fourth West Virginia Infantry was organized August, 1861, with the following field officers: J. A. J. Lightburn, colonel; Wm. H. H. Russel, lieutenant-colonel, and John T. Hall, major.

The regiment did its first service in the Kanawha Valley, and hard service it was, too; guard duty, scouting, fighting, was the daily program.

On the 6th of August, 1862, Major Hall, with a force of forty-eight men, at Beach Creek, near Logan Court House, encountered 200 Confederated mounted infantry, under Colonel Stratton and Major Witcher. The fight was a stubborn one, Major Hall and two enlisted men were killed and twelve wounded. Of the Confederates, Major Witcher was killed; upon the death of their commander the Confederates retreated. In the death of

Major Hall, the 4th Regiment suffered a great loss. He was a graduate of West Point, was young, brave, and of course well qualified for all the duties of a soldier.

The next military experience of importance which the regiment was called upon to undergo, was " Colonel Lightburn's retreat from the Kanawha Valley." A few preliminary words will enable the reader to better comprehend the situation.

On July 1, 1862, General McClellan, after the battle of Malvern Hill, retreated to Harrison's Landing. McClellan remained in camp till the 4th of August, when he received orders from General Halleck, commander-in-chief, to evacuate Harrison's Landing, and report at Washington; the object of this move was to conform to President Lincoln's original plan to move overland to Richmond. Pope was then in command of the "Army of Virginia," and in the early part of August fought the battle of Cedar Mountain.

On the 28th, 29th and 30th of August the battle of Manassas—or Second Bull Run—was fought; Pope having been defeated, General Lee took advantage of the disaster to invade Maryland, and possibly take the capital at Washington. While these important movements were going on, General Cox was in command in the Kanawha Valley, with a force of 12,000 or 15,000 men.

In view of the danger threatening Washington, General Cox was withdrawn from the Kanawha with all the troops that could be spared to reenforce the defenses around Washington. Cox took with him about 10,000 men, and arrived in time to participate in the battles of South Mountain and Antietam. There remained in the Kanawha of Cox's forces the 4th, 8th and 9th West Va. Infantry, the 34th, 37th, 44th and 47th Ohio Infantry, and the 2d West Va. Cavalry, with eight mounted howitzers, three rifled and three smooth-bore field pieces of artillery.

Pursuant to General Cox's orders, August 17, 1862, Colonel Lightburn assumed command of the district. The forces were stationed as follows: 34th and 37th Ohio, with four mounted howitzers and two smooth-bore field pieces, under command of Col. E. Siber; 37th Ohio Infantry at Raleigh Court House, with two companies of infantry as a guard for trains at Fayette Court House; the 44th and 47th Ohio Infantry, with two companies of the 2d West Va. Cavalry at Camp Ewing, a distance of ten miles from Gauley Bridge, on the Lewisburg road, under command of Col. S. A. Gilbert; 44th Ohio Infantry, two companies of the 9th West Va. Infantry, and two companies of the 2d West Va. Cavalry, under command of Major Curtis, were stationed at Summerville. The remainder of the 9th and 4th West Va. and two companies of West Va. Cavalry were stationed at different points from Gauley Bridge to Charleston, including an out-post at Coal River in Boone County, with Colonel Lightburn's headquarters at Gauley.

Early in September, 1862, the Confederate General Loring, with an army estimated at from 8,000 to 10,000, men appeared in the Kanawha Valley. Colonel Lightburn began at once to prepare for a retreat, and for the protection of his immense stores, Loring was making a forced march. About the 10th of September he was at Raleigh, and later at Fayette, where Colonel Siber and his command (who had retired from Raleigh) were strongly intrenched. Colonel Lightburn, apprehensive that Siber would be surrounded and cut off, ordered him to evacuate Fayette and fall back to Charleston. Colonel Siber did fall back, closely followed by Loring all the way to Charleston.

The results of a raid in force, no matter by whom made is always the same. The story of rout and disaster, the excitement, hurry and confusion to both civilian and soldier always prevails; so, at this time we find all the people of Charleston in a condition of intense alarm. On the 13th, Colonel Lightburn had all the transportation at hand, transports and wagons loaded with the most valuable Government stores and ordered them in the direction of Point Pleasant. About 1 o'clock P. M., Colonel Lightburn crossed Elk River, and the torch was applied to the Government buildings containing the stores that could not be removed. The bridge across Elk River was then destroyed. Charleston is situated at the confluence of the Kanawha and the Elk, the two rivers forming at this junction very nearly a right angle. A turnpike follows the course of the Kanawha, and crosses the Elk at Charleston. Colonel Lightburn then formed his line of battle to the best advantage. The enemy, under Loring in front, outnumbered Lightburn and with Jenkins on the right flank, 1200 to 1500 strong, did not present encouraging conditions for Lightburn and his command.

The Confederates opened the engagement from a battery on a hill south of Charleston, our battery replying. The Confederates had a Parrot gun on the opposite side of the Kanawha. The firing from the artillery was rapid, considering the number of pieces engaged; the fire was continued until about 5 P. M. The infantry regiments were not hotly engaged, though skirmishing was kept up until darkness put an end to it, when the enemy fell back to Charleston.

Colonel Lightburn and his command made all out of the situation it was possible to make. The enemy in superior numbers did not act with much energy; they seemed content to remain in Charleston and be let alone, where they could procure plenty of salt for their armies. The Fourth West Virginia lost in this engagement six men killed and several wounded; the total

Mass. MOLLUS, USAMHI

JOSEPH A.J. LIGHTBURN
Colonel 4th West Virginia Infantry
Brigadier General U.S. Volunteers

JAMES H. DAYTON
Colonel 4th West Virginia Infantry

loss to the whole command in the several engagements was 25 killed, 95 wounded. Confederate loss, 18 killed, 89 wounded. From Charleston, Colonel Lightburn with his command and an immense train of 700 wagons, under cover of the night took up its line of retreat on the Ripley road, arriving at Point Pleasant on the 16th of the month.

Early in October, 1862, General Cox returned from the East and resumed command of the forces in the Kanawha, the Fourth West Virginia Infantry being a part of his command. He arrived at Charleston on the 20th of October, but found the place evacuated. In the latter part of November, Colonel Lightburn received orders to move his regiment to Fayette Court House. Upon its arrival the regiment began to prepare comfortable quarters for the winter, but, as the sequel will show, "there is nothing certain in war." On December 28, 1862, the 4th West Virginia, the 30th, 37th and 47th Ohio Infantry, under Brigadier-General Ewing, were ordered out of the Department of West Virginia and sent to General Grant's command on the Mississippi River, when they were attached to the 15th Army Corps. Soon following, Colonel Lightburn was promoted to brigadier-general of volunteers and was assigned to the command of Ewing's brigade. The Fourth Regiment, besides performing military duty proper, also took a part in fatigue duty in the construction of the canal opposite Vicksburg. The brigade was in Gen'l W. T. Sherman's corps. While the regiment was at Young's Point, La., sickness prevailed to an alarming extent, 31 men having died there during February and March. About the 10th of May, the Fourth, under command of Colonel Dayton, received orders to march to the front with General Lightburn's brigade, Blair's division, 15th Army Corps. On May 19th, the memorable assault on Vicksburg occurred. The Fourth Regiment was placed in the advance of Lightburn's brigade and charged the enemy's works. A few men scaled the parapet, among them Capt. Finley D. Ong, of Company F, and Britton Cook, a corporal of Company E, who entered the Confederate works; they were wounded and taken prisoners and died in the enemy's hands. The balance of the command was quickly repulsed. The regiment lost in this assault 25 killed and 10 mortally wounded. Maj. A. M. Goodspeed was among the killed. The 20th and 21st were spent in taking care of the wounded. On the 22d, the regiment participated in Grant's final assault on Vicksburg, losing three men killed and two mortally wounded. Adjutant P. B. Stanbury was among the wounded.

The regiment did heroic service during its term in the Western army, marching and fighting. It participated in the battles of Chattanooga, Rasacca, Dallas, Kenesaw Mountain. In the spring of 1864, the regiment returned to West Virginia, and after one month's veteran furlough, ordered to the Shenandoah Valley, and became a part of Hunter's command in Thoburn's division, and took part in the battles of Piedmont, Lynchburg, Kearnstown, Snicker's Gap, Berryville, Winchester and Cedar Creek.

The regiment's losses from its organization to its consolidation with the First West Virginia Infantry, which formed the Second Veteran Infantry, was: killed and died of wounds, three officers and 80 men; died of disease or accident, two officers and 156 men; total deaths, 241. The Second Veteran Regiment was mustered out of the service July 16, 1865.

CHAPTER XXXIV.

FIFTH REGIMENT W. VA. INFANTRY VOLUNTEERS.

Roster of the Field, Staff and Company Officers of the Fifth Regiment West Virginia Infantry Volunteers, Showing the Alterations and Casualties therein, from the Date of Original Organization of the Regiment to the Date of Consolidation with the Ninth Regiment, West Virginia Infantry, November 9, 1864.

Date of Commission.	Names and Rank.	Co.	Remarks.
	Colonel.		
Sep. 10, 1861.	John L. Zeigler,		Resigned April 14, 1863.
June 19, 1863.	Abia A. Tomlinson,		Mustered out at expiration of term of service.
	Lieutenant-Colonels.		
Sep. 10, 1861.	Stephen P. Colvin,		Resigned March 1, 1862.
March 10, 1862.	Abia A. Tomlinson,		Promoted to Colonel,
Aug. 17, 1863.	Wm. H. Enochs,		Com. Lieut.-Colonel, 1st W. Va., Vet. Inft.
	Majors.		
Sep. 10, 1861.	Ralph Ormstead,		Killed in action September 15, 1863.
Oct. 11, 1861.	Abia A. Tomlinson,		Promoted to Lieutenant-Colonel.
April 19, 1862.	Lorenzo A. Phelps,		Dismissed August 15, 1863.
	1st Lieut. and Adj't.		
Sep. 10, 1861.	Thomas N. Davey,		Resigned February 1, 1862.
April 19, 1862.	Samuel B. McColloch,		Transferred to the line.
April 17, 1863.	P. Davey,		Mustered out at expiration of term of service.
	1st Lieut. and R. Q. M.		
Sep. 10, 1861.	Zopher D. Ramsdell,		Mustered out and appointed C. S.
	Surgeon.		
Aug. 27, 1861.	Peras R. Randall,		Mustered out at expiration of term of service,
	Assistant Surgeons.		
Aug. 27, 1861.	Daniel Mayer,		Mustered out at expiration of term of service.
Sep. 4, 1862.	Charles D. Dalley,		Promoted Surgeon 13th W. Va. Infantry.
	Chaplains.		
Sep. 23, 1861.	James M. Kelley,		Resigned.
Nov. 22, 1862.	Joseph Little,		Com. Chaplain, 1st W. Va. Vet. Infantry.
	Captains.		
Sep. 23, 1861.	James C. McFadden,	A	Dismissed May 27, 1863.
Aug. 15, 1863.	Mark Poore,	A	Com. Captain, 1st W. Va. Veteran Infantry.
Sep. 23, 1861.	James E. Smith,	B	Resigned May 19, 1862.
June 26, 1862.	Robert B. McCall,	B	Mustered out at expiration of term of service
Sep. 23, 1861.	Woodson Powers,	C	Resigned February, 7, 1862.
Feb. 21, 1862.	Wm. T. McQuigg,	C	Mustered out at expiration of term of service.
Sep. 23, 1861.	Samul C. Miller,	D	Resigned April 12, 1863.
Aug. 17, 1863.	James B. Bazell,	D	Mustered out at expiration of term of service.

Date of Commission.	Names and Rank.	Co.	Remarks
	Captains.		
Sep. 23, 1861.	Lorenzo A. Phelps,	E	Promoted to Major.
Aug. 19, 1862.	Wm. H. Enochs,	E	Promoted to Lieutenant-Colonel.
Aug. 17, 1863.	Hamilton Willis,	E	Com. Captain, 1st W. Va. Veteran Infantry.
Sep. 23, 1861.	Joseph M. Kirk,	F	Resigned February 7, 1862.
Feb. 21, 1862.	E. R. Merriman,	F	Mustered out at expiration of term of service.
Dec. 7, 1861.	Thomas J. Ewing,	G	Resigned January 3, 1863.
March 4, 1863.	James Murphy,	G	Dismissed April 6, 1863.
Sep. 1, 1863.	James P. Waymer,	G	Com. Captain, 1st W. Va. Veteran Infantry.
May 17, 1862.	Henry Kenderlie,	H	Mustered out at expiration of term of service.
Jan. 15, 1862.	Francis M. Miles,	I	Resigned June 16, 1862.
July 10, 1862.	Wm. J. Dixon,	I	Mustered out at expiration of term of service.
Dec. 7, 1861.	Alfred F. Compston,	K	Mustered out at expiration of term of service.
	First Lieutenants.		
Sep. 23, 1861.	Benjamin A. Rodgers,	A	Resigned May 18, 1862.
July 10, 1862.	Wm. Schilling,	A	Mustered out at expiration of term of service.
Sept. 23, 1861.	Joseph P. Kendrick,	B	Resigned April 9, 1862.
May 17, 1862.	Robert B. McCall,	B	Promoted to Captain.
June 26, 1862.	Jos. F. Bancroft,	B	Transferred to Company D, Dec. 9, 1863,
March 26, 1864.	Francis L. Hersey,	B	Com. Adjutant, 1st W. Va. Veteran Infantry.
Sep. 23, 1861.	Jackson Mantrey,	C	Resigned February 7, 1862.
March 25, 1862.	Guy Rowe,	C	Mustered out at expiration of term of service.
Oct. 5, 1864.	Wm. F. Elswick,	C	Com. 1st Lieut., in 1st W. Va. Vet. Infantry.
Sep. 23, 1861.	Henry C. Neff,	D	Dismissed July 29, 1863.
June 26, 1862.	Joseph F. Bancroft,	D	Mustered out at expiration of term of service.
Oct. 5, 1864.	Alfred O. Enochs,	D	Com. 1st Lieut. in 1st W. Va. Vet. Infantry.
Sep 23, 1861.	Isaac N. McKendry,	E	Resigned May 19, 1862.
June 26, 1862.	Hamilton Willis,	E	Promoted to Captain.
March 18, 1862.	Henry H. Walcott	E	Died July, 1864, in Webster, Ohio.
Sep. 23, 1861.	Ira G. Copley,	F	Resigned March 20, 1862.
May 17, 1862.	W. H. H. Eba,	F	Resigned May 12, 1863.
July 5, 1862.	Samuel Johnson,	F	Transferred to Company G, Sept. 20, 1863.
Dec. 7, 1861.	John T. Swann,	G	Resigned February 7, 1862.
Feb. 21, 1862.	Henry C. Farmer,	G	Resigned May 14, 1863.
July 5, 1862.	Samuel Johnson,	G	Mustered out at expiration of term of service.
May 17, 1862.	Wm. J. Dixon,	H	Promoted to Captain, Company I.
July 5, 1862.	Samuel Johnson,	H	Transferred to Company F, June 20, 1863.
April 19, 1862.	Samuel B. McColloch,	H	Mustered out at expiration of term of service.
Oct. 5, 1864.	Wm. A. Zeigler,	H	Com. 1st Lieut. 1st W. Va. Veteran Infantry.
Jan. 15, 1862.	Jonathan Wood,	I	Resigned March 14, 1862.
March 18, 1862.	Henry H. Walcott,	I	Transferred to Company E.
Dec. 7, 1861.	Wm. H. Enochs,	K	Promoted to Captain, Company E.
June 16, 1862.	Samuel M. McCullough,	K	Mustered out at expiration of term of service.
	Second Lieutenants.		
Sep. 23, 1861.	Edward John,		Resigned April 8, 1862.
Aug. 13, 1862.	Wm. Kirkpatrick,	A	Disch. on account of disability, Sept. 29, 1862.
Oct. 12, 1862.	David J. Thomas,	A	Killed in action, Lynchburg, Va., June 18, 1862.

L.M. Strayer

ABIA A. TOMLINSON
Colonel 5th West Virginia Infantry

The Rutherford B. Hayes Presidential Center, Fremont, Ohio

JOSEPH LITTLE

Chaplain 5th West Virginia Infantry and 1st West Virginia Veteran Infantry

(Note Portable Field Organ)

Date of Commission.	Names and Rank.	Co.	Remarks.
	Second Lieutenants.		
Oct. 5, 1864.	George F. Jarrell,	A	Com 2d Lieut in 1st W. Va. Veteran Infantry.
Sep. 23, 1861.	Robert B. McCall,	B	Promoted to 1st Lieutenant.
May 17, 1862.	Joseph F. Bancroft,	B	Promoted to 1st Lieutenant.
June 26, 1862.	Mark Poore,	B	Promoted to Captain, Company A.
Oct. 24, 1863.	Francis L. Hersey,	B	Promoted to 1st Lieutenant.
Sep. 23, 1861.	Joseph Allen,	C	Died from wounds received in private quarrel, April 11, 1862.
May 22, 1862.	William E. Rowe,	C	Mustered out at expiration of term of service.
Sep. 23, 1861.	Andrew Griffith,	D	Resigned January 6, 1863.
Jan. 31, 1863.	Abraham W. Miller,	D	Killed in action near Browboro, Va.
Oct. 5, 1864.	John Zimmerman,	D	Com. 2d Lieut. in W. Va. Veteran Infantry.
Sep. 23, 1861.	William Willis,	E	Mustered out at expiration of term of service.
Oct. 5, 1864.	John Q. Hagerman,	E	Com. 2d Lieut. 1st W. Va. Veteran Infantry.
Sep. 23, 1861.	James Baisden,	F	Killed in action near Cassville, Va.
Oct. 30, 1861.	Benjamin R. Haley,	F	Resigned August 15, 1862.
Sep. 19, 1862.	Archibald Pack,	F	Mustered out at expiration of term of service.
Dec. 7, 1861.	James Murphy,	G	Promoted to Captain.
March 4, 1863.	James W. Waymer,	G	Promoted to Captain.
May 17, 1862.	Samuel Jones,	H	Mustered out at expiration of term of service.
Jan. 15, 1862.	Allen B. Hawes,	I	Resigned April 9, 1862.
April 19, 1862.	James D. McBride,	I	Resigned January 8, 1863.
March 4, 1863.	Wm. A. Zeigler,	I	Promoted to 1st Lieutenant, Company H.
Dec. 7, 1861.	James B. Bazell,	K	Promoted to Captain, Company D.
Aug. 17, 1863.	John M. Cloy,	K	Mustered out at expiration of term of service.
Oct. 5, 1864.	Andrew J. Johnson,	K	Com. 2d Lieut. 1st W. Va. Veteran Infantry.

THE FIFTH WEST VIRGINIA INFANTRY.

The Fifth West Virginia Infantry was organized at Ceredo, W. Va., during the summer of 1861, and was mustered into the United States service October 18, 1861, with the following field officers: John L. Zeigler, colonel; Stephen P. Colvin, lieutenant-colonel, and Ralph Ormstead, major. The regiment was engaged in protecting the loyal citizens of the Kanawha Valley, and ridding it of the Confederates, until ordered to Parkersburg on December 10. A principal part of the regiment was sent to New Creek and in February, 1862, accompanied Colonel Dunning of the Fifth Ohio, commanding brigade, on his expedition to Moorefield, against Colonel Harness of the Confederate army. On the 2d of May, the regiment left New Creek, and went to McDowell, joining the command of General Milroy, and taking part in the battle at that place, and after that battle became a part of General Milroy's brigade. They remained with the brigade all through Pope's campaign, participating in all the battles in which the brigade took a part, from

Cedar Mountain to the second battle of Bull Run, both officers and men being conspicuous for their soldierly conduct while in camp and on the march, and for gallantry upon the battlefield.

The regiment returned to the Kanawha Valley in October, 1862, and was detached from Milroy's brigade, and in May, 1864, it became a part of General Crook's command, participating in his expeditions. It took a part in General Hunter's advance on Lynchburg, and the battle at that place June 18. Returning, it proceeded with General Hunter's army to the Shenandoah Valley, forming a part of the Army of West Virginia under General Crook in the brigades commanded by Col. I. H. Duval, Ninth W. Va. Infantry, and Col. Rutherford B. Hayes, 23d Ohio Infantry. Colonel Hayes commanded the brigade for several months, during which time he fought a number of closely contested battles. The survivors of the regiment have cause for congratulation that they had served under a commander who not only illustrated the highest idea of the true soldier while on the field of battle, but when the war was over and the people of the nation had called the commander of the First Brigade, Army of West Virginia, to the Presidential chair, he illustrated the same high idea of American statesmanship in the exalted civil position that he had shown on the battlefield.

On the 9th of November, 1864, the Fifth and Ninth West Virginia Infantry were consolidated by order of the War Deparment, and designated the First Regiment West Virginia Veteran Infantry, and were mustered out of service July 21, 1865. The regiment lost during the war, killed and died of wounds four officers and 57 enlisted men; died of disease and accident, two officers and 88 enlisted men. Total, 151.

CHAPTER XXXV.

SIXTH REGIMENT W. VA. INFANTRY.

Roster of the Field, Staff and Company Officers of the Sixth Regiment West Virginia Infantry Volunteers, Showing the Alterations and Casualties therein, from the Date of Organization to the Date of Muster out, June 10, 1865.

Date of Commission.	Names and Rank.	Co.	Remarks.
	Colonel.		
Sep. 27, 1861.	Nathan Wilkinson.		
	Lieutenant-Colonels.		
Oct. 3, 1861.	John F. Hoy,		Mustered out at expiration of term of service.
Feb. 27, 1865.	Larkin Peirpoint.		
	Majors.		
Nov. 1, 1861.	John B. Frothingham,		Promoted to Lt.-Col., and A. A. D. C. U. S. A.
July 2, 1862.	John H. Showalter,		Mustered out at expiration of term of service.
Nov. 12, 1864.	Larkin Peirpoint,		Promoted to Lieutenant-Colonel.
April 20, 1865.	Edward A. Bennett.		
	1st Lt. and Adj'ts.		
Sep. 21, 1861.	Zenas Fish.		Resigned January 15, 1863.
Jan. 21, 1863.	James P. Wilkinson,		
	1st Lts. and R. Q. M.		
Sep. 21, 1861.	James P. Wilkinson,		Resigned January 17, 1863.
Jan. 3, 1862.	Wm. H. Adams.		
	Surgeons.		
Aug. 27, 1861.	Albert P. Wheeler,		Dismissed May 5, 1862.
Aug. 1, 1862.	Erasmus D. Safford,		Resigned July 20, 1864.
Dec. 14, 1864.	John T. Wharton.		
	Assistant Surgeons.		
Aug. 27, 1861.	John T. Wharton,		Promoted to Surgeon, December 14, 1864.
April 4, 1864.	David Shaner,		
	Chaplains.		
Dec. 13, 1861.	Ebenezer Mathers,		Mustered out at expiration of term of service.
Nov. 26, 1864.	Nixon Potts.		
	Captains.		
Oct. 3, 1861.	John H. Showalter,	A	Promoted to Major, July 22, 1862.
July 26, 1862.	John Fisher,	A	
Oct. 3, 1861.	Theophilus Jones,	B	Died at Philippi, Oct. 16, 1862, of self-inflicted wounds.
Jan. 28, 1863.	Edward A. Bennett,	B	Promoted to Major, April 25, 1865.
April 20, 1865.	Thomas T. Freeman,	B	
Oct. 3, 1861.	Thomas A. Maulsby,	C	Transferred to 1st W. Va. Artillery.
Sep. 2, 1864.	Josiah H. Bee,	C	Discharged by special order of War Dept.
Oct. 3, 1861.	William Skelton,	D	Mustered out at expiration of term of service.

Date of Commission.	Names and Rank.	Co.	Remarks.
	Captains.		
Sep. 10, 1864.	John Clark,	D	
Oct. 3, 1861.	Larkin Peirpoint,	E	Promoted to Major, November 18, 1864.
Dec. 15, 1864.	Geo. M. Ireland,	E	
Oct. 1, 1861.	William Hall,	F	
Oct. 1, 1861.	Wm. H. Mattingly,	G	Mustered out at expiration of term of service.
Oct. 14, 1864.	John T. Drake,	G	Discharged by special order of War Dept.
Dec. 27, 1861.	William Schockey,	H	
Dec. 27, 1861.	Charles J. Harrison,	I	Mustered out at expiration of term of service.
March 24, 1865.	John Donohoe,	I	
Dec. 27, 1861.	Joseph Reece,	K	Resigned October 25, 1862.
Nov. 10, 1862.	Joseph A. Faris,	K	Mustered out at expiration of term of service.
March 24, 1865.	Lovead D. Hathaway,	K	
Dec. 27, 1861.	John H. Dickey,	L	Discharged by order of Secretary of War.
May 28, 1863.	Wm. M. Treadway,	L	Mustered out at expiration of term of service.
Dec. 26, 1864.	C. F. A. Yahrling,	L	
Nov. 30, 1861.	John Carroll,	M	Mustered out at expiration of term of service.
Dec. 27, 1861.	George Kenney,	N	
Dec. 27, 1861.	Joseph M. Godwin,	O	Mustered out at expiration of term of service.
March 24, 1865.	Augustus F. Lang,	O	
Dec. 25, 1861.	Ewald Over,	P	Mustered out at expiration of term of service.
Feb. 21, 1865.	Edward Lindner,	P	
	First Lieutenants.		
Oct. 3. 1861.	John Fisher,	A	Promoted to Captain.
July 25, 1862.	Joseph N. Peirpoint,	A	Died at Fairmount, W. Va., Dec. 19, 1863.
Sep. 22, 1864.	Jacob F. Greiner,	A	
Oct. 3, 1861.	Harvey Cotton.	B	Dismissed April 9, 1863.
July 22, 1863.	Thomas T. Freeman,	B	Promoted to Captain, April 20, 1865.
April 20, 1865.	Adam Graw,	B	
Oct. 29, 1861.	A. J. Fleming,	C	Resigned July 7, 1862.
July 17, 1862.	Jesse F. Miller,	C	Resigned December 17, 1862.
Jan. 7, 1863.	George W. Graham,	C	Transferred to 1st W. Va., Artillery.
Sep. 26, 1864.	Silas B. Nicholson,	C	
Oct. 3, 1861.	Ezekiel Sheppard,	D	Mustered out at expiration of term of service.
Sep. 10, 1864.	Christian Hickman,	D	Discharged by special order of War Dept.
Oct. 3, 1861.	Lloyd Dotson,	E	Resigned January 15, 1862.
Jan. 17, 1863.	George M. Ireland,	E	Promoted to Captain, December 18, 1864.
April 20, 1865.	Nicholas Neidert,	E	
Oct. 1, 1861.	John H. Carrico,	F	
Oct. 1, 1861.	John T. Drake,	G	Promoted to Captain, October 14, 1864.
Oct. 14, 1864.	Peter E. Dils,	G	
Dec. 27, 1861.	James Humes,	H	Promoted to 15th W. Va. Infantry.
April 23, 1862.	Augustus F. Lang,	H	Promoted to Captain, Company O.
March 24, 1865.	Daniel S. Bush,	H	
Dec. 27, 1861.	James Neill,	I	Mustered out at expiration of term of service.
March 9, 1865.	Wm. A. Higgins,	I	
Dec. 27, 1861.	Joseph A. Faris,	K	Promoted to Captain, November 10, 1862.

Date of Commission.	Names and Rank.	Co.	Remarks.
	First Lieutenants.		
Jan. 26, 1863.	Lovead D. Hathaway,	K	Promoted to Captain, March 24, 1865.
March 23, 1865.	Valentine J. Gallion,	K	
Dec. 27, 1861.	Wm. M. Treadway,	L	Promoted to Captain, June 1, 1863.
May 28, 1863.	Wm. R. McDonald,	L	Mustered out April 17, 1865.
July 9, 1863.	John Donohoe,	L	Mustered out at expiration of term of service.
March 24, 1865	Virgil S. Brown,	L	
Oct. 28, 1861.	Isaac N. Estabrook,	M	Resigned February 19, 1862.
March 20, 1862.	John S. S. Herr,	M	Transferred to 1st W. Va. Artillery.
July 9, 1863.	John Donohoe,	M	Transferred to Campany L.
Dec. 27, 1861.	Jackson Moore,	N	
Dec. 27, 1861.	George W. E. Dorsey,	O	Promoted to Captain and C. S.
Aug. 1, 1864.	Joseph A. Annan,	O	
Oct. 24, 1861.	Edward Lindner,	P	Promoted to Captain.
Feb. 27, 1865.	Charles Klevis,	P	
	Second Lieutenants.		
Oct. 3, 1861.	Joseph N. Peirpoint,	A	Promoted to 1st Lieutenant.
July 22, 1862.	Jacob F. Greiner,	A	Promoted to 1st Lieutenant.
Sep. 22, 1864.	Benjamin F. Coogle,	A	
Oct. 3, 1861.	Jacob Johnson,	B	Dismissed April 1st, 1863.
April 11, 1863.	Thomas T. Freeman,	B	Promoted to 1st Lieutenant.
July 22, 1863.	Adam Graw,	B	Promoted to 1st Lieutenant.
April 20, 1865.	Elam P. Potts,	B	
Oct. 29, 1861.	Jesse F. Miller,	C	Promoted to 1st Lieutenant.
July 17, 1862.	George W. Graham,	C	Promoted to 1st Lieutenant.
Jan. 7, 1863.	James C. Means,	C	Transferred to 1st W. Va. Artillery.
Sep. , 1864.	Joseph A. Dougherty,	C	
Oct. 29, 1861.	Thomas B. Walters,	D	Discharged March 21, 1863.
April 11, 1863.	Benj. S. Cunningham,	D	Mustered out at expiration of term of service.
Oct. 3, 1861.	Joseph A. Summers,	E	Resigned January 15, 1862.
April 11, 1863.	Nicholas Neidert,	E	Promoted to 1st Lieutenant.
April 20, 1865.	James B. Weatfall,	E	
Oct. 1, 1861.	Thornton F. Hebb,	F	Discharged by order of War Department.
May 28, 1863.	Valentine J. Gallion,	F	Promoted to 1st Lieutenant.
March 24, 1865.	Jas. A. Bowermaster,	F	
Oct. 1, 1861.	Henry J. Hoy,	G	Dishonorably dismissed.
Oct. 27, 1862.	Peter E. Dils,	G	Promoted to 1s Lieutenant.
Oct. 27, 1864.	James Linhart,	G	
Dec. 27, 1862.	Henry Broemsen,	H	Mustered out at expiration of term of service.
Dec. 15, 1864.	Daniel S. Bush,	H	Promoted to 1st Lieutenant.
March 31, 1865.	Gilbert M. Sims,	H	
Dec. 27, 1861.	Wm. McMullen,	I	Resigned August 16, 1862.
Aug. 25, 1862.	Richard F. Green,	I	Mustered out at expiration of term of service.
Feb. 23, 1865.	Jesse F. Snodgrass,	I	
Dec. 27, 1861.	Wm. A. Higgins,	K	Mustered out at expiration of term of service.
March 24, 1865.	Allen T. Emery,	K	
Dec. 27, 1861.	Charles Chrisswell,	L	Resigned January 15, 1863.

Date of Commission.	Names and Rank.	Co.	Remarks.
	Second Lieutenants.		
Feb. 6, 1863.	Wm. R. McDonald,	L	Promoted to 1st Lieutenant.
May 28, 1863.	C. F. A. Yahrling,	L	Mustered out at expiration of term of service.
Feb. 21, 1865.	Virgil S. Brown,	L	Promoted to 1st Lieutenant.
March 24, 1865.	Robert C. Dunnington,	L	
Nov. 30, 1861.	John Donohoe,	M	Promoted to 1st Lieutenant.
July 9, 1863.	Virgil S. Brown,	M	Mustered out at expiration of term of service.
Dec. 27, 1861.	Jehu E. Parkinson,	N	Mustered out at expiration of term of service.
Dec. 15, 1864.	Vernon M. Clary,	N	
Dec. 27, 1861.	Jackson C. Saucer,	O	Mustered out at expiration of term of service.
Feb. 21, 1865.	John T. Athey,	O	
Dec. 25, 1861.	Henry Knapp,	P	Mustered out at expiration of term of service.
Feb. 21, 1865.	Joseph Crisswell,	P	

THE SIXTH WEST VIRGINIA INFANTRY REGIMENT.

The Sixth West Virginia Infantry Regiment was organized August, 1861, with the following field officers: Nathan Wilkinson, colonel; John F. Hoy, lieutenant-colonel, and John B. Frothingham, major, with 14 companies of 100 men each. The regiment was recruited and mustered into service with the express proviso that it was to serve as guard duty upon the lines of the Baltimore and Ohio and Northwestern Virginia Railroads. It did not, therefore, share in the hurry and enthusiasm of large bodies of troops together in battle, and when a detachment of them had the good fortune to strike the enemy, they were going it alone and unobserved, and did not receive the general commendation from superior officers, or receive the plaudits of the press of the country. Realizing this, the subordinate officers in command of scouting parties or the defenders of bridges and blockhouses failed to make formal reports of such incidents, and if they did make reports, those above them seemed to regard it as unimportant, and felt some delicacy about troubling headquarters or the official records with what then appeared comparative trifles, when the current news of the day was filled with accounts of greater events. But this failure of subordinate officers to make full and complete reports operated to do injustice in the light of history to this fine regiment. The author has been told by an officer of the regiment, that sometime after the close of the war, he with a small group of officers of the regiment went over the list as they could recall, and they counted 41 men that had been killed in action, whilst the number having died from wounds and disease was several hundred. The official record places the number at much less. Notwithstanding the charge of "Home Guards" that

Roger D. Hunt Collection, USAMHI

NATHAN WILKINSON
Colonel 6th West Virginia Infantry

was so often frivolously applied to this regiment, its mission was just as honorable, its duties as exacting, as was the service of regiments who were further to the front.

The Baltimore and Ohio Railroad was a necessity to the Union Army: the faithful guarding of it was a specific service that required tact, and it was better that that duty be entrusted to men made familiar by experience with every detail. There were many illustrations of gallantry displayed by both officers and men during the war. In addition to the officers named as "field officers," we recall Majors J. H. Showalter, Larkin Peirpoint and E. A. Bennett, and Captains Fisher, Skelton, Hall, Mattingly, Reece, Schockey, Harrison, Carroll, Kenney, Godwin, Lang, Over and others. During the latter years of the war, Colonel Wilkinson was in command of a brigade, so the command of the regiment was assigned to Major Showalter, who proved to be an intelligent, painstaking and gallant officer.

Col. John C. Rathbone, commanding at Spencer, in Roan County, in his report to General Kelley, May 31, 1862, says: "Captain Showalter, with 23 men acting as escort to a wagon train from Ravenswood to his headquarters at Spencer, was surrounded by over 100 Confederates under command of Captains Downs and Duskey. Captain Showalter showed fight and gallantly repulsed the Confederates, and held them in check, until Captain Showalter, under great difficulties, dispatched two messengers, Joseph H. Hershberger and Charles C. Eyster, for reenforcements. These messengers were fired upon, Eyster's horse was killed, when Hershberger stopped amid a shower of bullets and mounting Eyster upon his horse, the two dashed away to Spencer and returned with Lieutenant Lawson, Co. K, First West Virginia Cavalry, and 30 men to the relief of Showalter, who had with his 23 men defended his train. When the reenforcements arrived the enemy were driven off with considerable loss in killed and wounded, when the train with its valuable stores was brought safely to its destination.

It is a matter of truthful record that Capt. John Fisher with 35 men of his Company A, successfully held the town of Piedmont on the B. & O. Road, against the attack of the Confederates 300 strong under command of Major McDonald, but the account, if given in detail, would be a long one. The regiment is entitled to the highest honors for splendid service done.

Major Showalter, who was in command at Rowlesburg in April, 1863, became the object of much severe criticism at the time by reason of his retreat from that place to Morgantown, Pittsburg, Wheeling and return to Rowlesburg. The lapse of years and the official records of the War Department have furnished abundant evidence to show that Major Showalter and his command partook of the general stampede that prevailed at that time.

This was the period of the Jones-Imboden-Jackson raid into West Virginia; Latham had fallen back from Beverly, Roberts with his entire force retreated to Clarksburg, in fact a general stampede of the Union forces prevailed. We find by the records of the War Department that Major Showalter was in April, 1863, in command at Rowlesburg with 220 men. Gen'l W. E. Jones, with over 3000 Confederate cavalry, had left the Shenandoah Valley on this noted raid. Jones had disposed of his forces to strike the Baltimore and Ohio Railroad at several points simultaneously. He attacked Rowlesburg in person, with over 1000 cavalry, on Sunday, April 23, at noon. Major Showalter held the place, fighting continuously till darkness brought the battle to a close, when Jones retired to West Union, on the N. W. turnpike, six miles from Rowlesburg, leaving his dead and wounded in our hands.

To meet this attack, Showalter had divided his force into three parts. Sending Lieutenant McDonald, of Co. L, up the Cheat River road with a detachment who felled trees across the road, behind which he successfully repelled the cavalry charge; a small detachment was also at the iron trestle bridge who defended that important work against a much larger force. This piece of trestle-work was especially placed on the list by General Lee for destruction. Their implements for the prosecution of this work fell into Showalter's hands. Within the following two or three days, the operations of the raid extended from Harper's Ferry to Parkersburg, and north of the Baltimore and Ohio Railroad to Morgantown. Consternation reigned everywhere; it seemed to be catching, and that Major Showalter, after having been surrounded, with his small force, did what he believed was for the best, must be conceded. Certainly the charge of cowardice cannot be truthfully charged against Major Showalter.

The army may have contained more conspicuous regiments, but it contained no more faithful defenders of the nation's cause than the Sixth West Virginia Volunteer Infantry.

CHAPTER XXXVI.

SEVENTH REGIMENT W. VA. INFANTRY VOLUNTEERS.

Roster of the Field, Staff and Company Officers of the Seventh Regiment, West Virginia Infantry Volunteers, Showing the Alterations and Casualties therein, from the Date of Original Organization of Said Regiment to the Date of Muster Out, July 1, 1865.

Date of Commission.	Names and Rank.	Co.	Remarks.
	Colonels.		
Nov. 9, 1861.	James Evans,		Resigned August 2, 1862.
April 22, 1862.	Joseph Snider,		Mustered out by consolidation of regiment, September 7, 1863.
	Lieut.-Colonels.		
Sep. 16, 1861.	John G. Kelley,		Resigned September 10, 1862.
Oct. 21, 1862.	Jonathan H. Lockwood,		Mustered out at expiration of term of service.
Dec. 15, 1864.	Isaac B. Fisher,		Discharged by special order of War Dept.
Feb. 6, 1865.	Francis W. H. Baldwin,		
	Majors.		
Sep. 23, 1861.	Jonathan H. Lockwood,		Promoted to Lieutenant-Colonel.
Jan. 7, 1863.	James B. Morris,		Mustered out by consolidation of regiment.
May 2, 1865.	Marcus Fetty.		
	First Lts. and Adjt's.		
Nov. 27, 1861.	Alex. T. Marshall,		Resigned November 20, 1862.
July 10, 1863.	Robert J. Linton,		Mustered out at expiration of term of service.
Oct. 27, 1864.	George E. Bishoff.		
	1st. Lieut. and R. Q. M.		
Nov. 14, 1861.	Evans D. Fogle,		Resigned March 12, 1863.
April 3, 1863.	Henry Startzman,		Resigned August 14, 1863.
Sep. 4, 1863.	Robert Collins,		Mustered out at expiration of term of service.
Nov. 25, 1864.	Robert Henderson.		
	Surgeons.		
Nov. 14, 1861.	Isaac Scott,		Mustered out at expiration of term of service.
May 29, 1865.	David Shanor.		
	Assistant Surgeons.		
Oct. 4, 1861.	T. W. Ross,		Resigned August 8, 1862.
Dec. 4, 1862.	Wilson T. Hicks.		Mustered out by special order of War Dept.
	Chaplains.		
Jan. 4, 1862.	John W. Reger,		Resigned February 21, 1863.
March 11, 1863.	Samuel Steel.		
	Captains.		
Sep. 10, 1861.	Samuel W. Snider,	A	Resigned December 4, 1862.
Nov. 25, 1862.	Thomas Elliott,	A	Died.

Date of Commission.	Names and Rank.	Co.	Remarks.
	Captains.		
July 10, 1863.	Josiah F. Ravenscraft,	A	Died at Wheeling, April 18, 1864.
Jan. 8, 1863.	John Fordyce,	A	Mustered out at expiration of term of service.
Dec. 12, 1864.	Marcus Fetty,	A	Promoted to Major.
May 2, 1865.	Christopher C. Lee,	A	
Oct. 7, 1861.	Thomas Morris,	B	Promoted to Lieut.-Col., 15th W. Va. Inft.
Oct. 21, 1862.	Samuel Kraus,	B	Mustered out at expiration of term of service.
Oct. 27, 1864.	Francis W. H. Baldwin,	B	Promoted to Lieutenant-Colonel.
Feb. 18, 1865.	Jesse L. Barnett,	B	
Oct. 5, 1861.	Valentine Smith,	C	Resigned August 4, 1862.
Aug. 14, 1862.	Edwin A. Barr,	C	Resigned December 5, 1862.
April 3, 1863.	Felix E. Boyles,	C	Mustered out by consolidation of regiment.
March 10, 1863.	John W. Denny,	C	Died October 14, 1863.
Nov. 27, 1863.	Eli C. Henthorn,	C	Killed in action, October 5, 1864.
Oct. 27, 1864.	John C. Way,	C	Discharged on certificate of disability.
March 29, 1865.	Wm. A. Beagle,	C	
Nov. 2, 1861.	Isaac B. Fisher,	D	Promoted to Lieutenant-Colonel.
March 2, 1865.	Samuel Fisher,	D	
Sep. 18, 1861.	Henry B. Lazier,	E	Resigned January 26, 1863.
April 3, 1863.	Marcus Fetty,	E	Mustered out by consolidation of regiment.
May 2, 1865.	Richard C. Burton,	E	
Nov. 9, 1861.	James B. Morris,	F	Promoted to Major.
Jan. 8, 1863.	John Fordyce,	F	Transferred to Company A.
May 29, 1865.	John C. Felton,	F	
Nov. 19, 1861.	Solomon Spangler,	G	Resigned April 11, 1863.
May 29, 1865.	Richard Bingman,	G	
Jan. 3, 1862.	H. J. Bowers,	H	Resigned.
April 17, 1863.	Francis M. Roberts,	H	Killed in action at Chancellorsville.
July 10, 1863.	Francis L. Hicks,	H	Not mustered as Captain, mustered out as Second Lieutenant.
Dec. 7, 1861.	D. C. M. Shell,	I	Killed in action at Antietam.
Oct. 21, 1862.	James Watson,	I	
Jan. 3, 1862.	Jonathan Moore,	K	Resigned August 5, 1862.
Oct. 21, 1862.	John B. Williams,	K	Resigned October 23, 1862.
March 10, 1863.	John W. Denny,	K	Transferred to Company C.
	First Lieutenants.		
Sep. 10, 1861.	Thomas Elliott,	A	Promoted to Captain.
Nov. 25, 1862.	Samuel P. Elliott,	A	Resigned February 6, 1863.
June 2, 1863.	James. E. Murdock,	A	Mustered out at expiration of term of service.
Dec. 12, 1864.	Christopher C. Lee,	A	Promoted to Captain.
May 2, 1865.	Wm. H. Meighen,	A	
Oct. 7, 1861.	Wm. T. Head,	B	Resigned June 17, 1862.
Aug. 14, 1862.	Samuel Kraus,	B	Promoted to Captain.
Oct. 21, 1862.	James Prickett,	B	Mustered out on account of wounds received in battle.
April 17, 1863.	Parker J. Duff,	B	Resigned September 4, 1864.
Sep. 24, 1864.	F. W. H. Baldwin,	B	Promoted to Captain.

Date of Commission.	Names and Rank.	Co.	Remarks.
	First Lieutenants.		
Oct 27, 1864.	John R. Charlton,	B	Discharged on certificate of disability.
Feb. 18, 1865.	Jesse May,	B	
Oct. 5, 1861.	Edwin A. Barr,	C	Promoted to Captain.
Aug. 14, 1862.	James Swartz,	C	Killed in action at Antietam.
Oct. 21, 1862.	Felix E. Boyles,	C	Promoted to Captain.
April 3, 1863.	John F. Evans,	C	Mustered out on account of wounds received at Chancellorsville.
April 17, 1863.	Eli C. Henthorn,	C	Promoted to Captain.
Nov. 27, 1863.	W. H. Cunningham,	C	Mustered out at expiration of term of service.
Oct. 27, 1864.	William A. Beagle,	C	Promoted to Captain.
March 29, 1865.	Mark Hopkins,	C	
Nov. 2, 1861.	James Watson,	D	Promoted to Captain, Co. I.
Oct. 21, 1862.	J. F. Ravenscraft,	D	Promoted to Captain, Company A.
July 10, 1863.	Abraham Detrick,	D	Not mustered as 1st Lieutenant.
April, 3, 1863.	Alonzo M. Conway,	D	Resigned.
July 6, 1864.	Marcus Fetty,	D	Promoted to Captain, Company A.
Dec. 12. 1864.	Samuel Batten,	D	Promoted to Captain.
March 2, 1865.	Richard C. Burton,	D	Promoted to Captain, Company E.
May 2, 1865.	George Distler,	D	
Sep. 18, 1861.	Isaac Hastings,	E	Resigned May 26, 1862.
July 17, 1862.	Marcus Fetty,	E	Promoted to Captain.
July 10, 1863.	Charles A. Callahan,	E	Mustered out by consolidation of regiment.
May 2, 1865.	John D. Heslep,	E	
Nov. 9, 1861.	Ambrose A. Stout,	F	Resigned March 25, 1863.
April 17, 1863.	Vincent Stephens,	F	Mustered out by consolidation of regiment.
May 2, 1865.	John C. Felton,	F	Promoted to Captain.
May 29, 1865.	John J. Jenkins,	F	
Nov. 19, 1861.	John A. Fleakman.	G	Resigned February 1, 1863.
April 17, 1863.	Parker J. Duff,	G	Transferred to Company B.
May 29, 1865.	Calvin Coburn,	G	
Jan. 3, 1862.	George W. Taggart,	H	Resigned January 21, 1862.
Aug. 14, 1862.	John H. Montgomery,	H	Resigned March 23, 1863.
April 17, 1863.	Eli C. Henthorn,	H	Transferred to Company C.
Dec. 7, 1861.	A. A. Corrillo,	I	Resigned February 28, 1862.
May 22, 1862.	John Garvy,	I	Deceased.
April 3, 1863.	Alonzo M. Conway,	I	Transferred to Company D.
Jan. 3, 1862.	John B. Williams,	K	Promoted to Captain.
Oct. 21, 1862.	Cyrus B. Morgan	K	Resigned April 9, 1863.
July 10, 1863.	Abner M. Johnson,	K	Not mustered as 1st Lieutenant.
	Second Lieutenants.		
Sep. 10, 1861.	Charles Elliott,	A	Died, date unknown.
Aug. 14, 1863.	Samuel P. Elliott,	A	Promoted to 1st Lieutenant.
Nov. 25, 1862.	William Glover,	A	Resigned June 10, 1863.
April 17, 1863.	James E. Murdock,	A	Promoted to 1st Lieutenant.
June 2, 1863.	James W. Brown,	A	Not mustered.
July 10, 1863.	David F. Potter,	A	Killed in action at Cold Harbor, Va.

Date of Commission.	Name and Rank.	Co.	Remarks.
	Second Lieutenants.		
July 6, 1864.	George A. Connor,	A	Died at Washington, D. C., July 31, 1865.
Oct. 7, 1861.	Samuel Kraus,	B	Promoted to 1st Lieutenant.
Aug. 14, 1862.	James Prickett,	B	Promoted to 1st Lieutenant.
Oct. 21, 1862.	John Mathews,	B	Mustered out by consolidation.
March 10, 1863.	Abner M. Johnson,	B	Killed in action May 12, 1864.
July 6, 1864.	Francis W. Baldwin,	B	Promoted to 1st Lieutenant.
Sep. 24, 1864.	John R. Charlton,	B	Promoted to 1st Lieutenant.
Oct. 27, 1864.	Jesse L. Barnett,	B	Promoted to Captain.
May 29, 1865.	Martin L. Myers,	B	
Oct. 5, 1861.	Elmore Fetty,	C	Resigned.
July 17, 1862.	James Swartz,	C	Promoted to 1st Lieutenant.
Aug. 14, 1862.	Felix E. Boyles,	C	Promoted to 1st Lieutenant.
Oct. 21, 1862.	John F. Evans,	C	Promoted to 1st Lieutenant.
April 3, 1863.	Wm. H. Cunningham,	C	Promoted to 1st Lieutenant.
Sep. 24, 1864.	John C. Wray,	C	Promoted to Captain.
Oct. 27, 1864.	Robert Henderson,	C	Promoted to 1st Lieutenant and R. Q. M.
Dec. 12, 1864.	Mark Hopkins,	C	Promoted to 1st Lieutenant.
May 29, 1865.	Israll Wells,	C	
Nov. 2, 1861.	John W. Eddington,	D	Resigned February 28, 1862.
May 22, 1862.	James W. Coburn,	D	Resigned November 12, 1862.
April 3, 1863.	Samuel Fisher,	D	Mustered out by consolidation.
April 17, 1863.	Thomas Finn,	D	Discharged by reason of wounds received in action.
May 29, 1865.	George W. Powell,	D	
Sep. 18, 1861.	Anthony Jacquette,	E	Resigned May 26, 1862.
July 17, 1862.	Cyrus B. Morgan,	E	Promoted to 1st Lieutenant, Company K.
Oct. 21, 1862.	Francis L. Hicks,	E	Promoted to Captain, Company H.
July 10, 1862.	Clark Kelly,	E	Mustered out by consolidation.
May 2, 1865.	Preston Campbell,	E	
Nov. 9, 1861.	Bailes D. Thompson,	F	Resigned Oct. 13, 1862.
Jan. 8, 1863.	Vincent Stephens,	F	Promoted to 1st Lieutenant.
April 17, 1863.	George M. Shough,	F	Mustered out by consolidation.
May 2, 1865.	Brice H. Tarr,	F	
Nov. 19, 1861.	John W. Denny,	G	Promoted to Captain, Company K.
April 17, 1863.	Thomas Finn,	G	Transferred to Company D.
Jan. 3, 1862.	John H. Montgomery,	H	Promoted to 1st Lieutenant.
July 17, 1862.	Francis M. Roberts,	H	Promoted to Captain.
April 17, 1863.	Silas B. Nicholson,	H	Mustered out by consolidation.
Dec. 7, 1861.	Benjamin McDonald,	I	Resigned May 28, 1862.
July 17, 1862.	Abraham Detrick,	I	Mustered out by consolidation.
Oct. 21, 1862.	Robert Collins,	I	Promoted to 1st Lieutenant and R. Q. M.
Jan. 3, 1862.	Thomas Keyser,	K	Resigned June 2, 1862.
July 17, 1862.	Benjamin L. Shriver,	K	Killed in action at Antietam.
Oct. 21, 1862.	H. W. Heidelshimer,	K	Resigned February 6, 1863.
March 10, 1863.	Abner M. Johnson,	K	Transferred to Company B.
July 10, 1863.	James A. King,	K	Not mustered.

THE SEVENTH WEST VIRGINIA INFANTRY.

The Seventh West Virginia Infantry can easily be placed upon the list as the banner regiment that served from the State during the war. This estimate is based upon the fact that it participated in a greater number of the larger battles fought during the war, and as having lost the greatest per cent. of killed and wounded. The regiment was organized August, 1861, with Lieut.-Col. John G. Kelley and Maj. Jonathan H. Lockwood as field officers. On November 9, 1861, James Evans was commissioned colonel, resigning August 2, 1862. Joseph Snider became colonel of the regiment, August 22, 1862.

It served in West Virginia and the Shenandoah Valley until May, 1862, when it was assigned to Kimball's brigade, French's division, Second Army Corps, and joined McClellan's army at Harrison's Landing, just after the battle of Malvern Hill. At Antietam, September, 1862, the regiment lost three officers and 26 enlisted men killed, and four officers and 112 enlisted men wounded; *none missing.* In that battle Colonel Snider and Lieutenant-Colonel Lockwood had their horses killed under them. In Colonel Snider's report of the battle he says: "The Confederates endeavored to deceive us by hoisting a white flag, which for a moment caused our men to cease firing, during which time the enemy was discovered to be moving in large force with the view of flanking our left, which caused us to change the position of our left wing, this being done as speedily as possible, when we succeeded in driving the enemy back with great slaughter beyond their original position, where we held them until our ammunition was exhausted. During the engagement our colors were shot down three times, but were promptly hoisted each time, and were brought off the field with the regiment."

At Fredericksburg, Va., December, 1862, Lieutenant-Colonel Lockwood in his report of the battle says: "General Kimball, commanding brigade, ordered the Seventh Regiment to form on the right of the brigade; the line thus formed consisted of the 7th West Virginia, 24th and 28th New Jersey and 14th Indiana. About 12 M. the entire line was put in motion, moving by the right flank. By order of Colonel Snider, I took command of the right wing. As soon as we had crossed the canal, I filed the head of the line to the right. Our line of battle being formed, we moved up briskly over a distance of some 80 rods, under a most galling fire from the enemy's rifle pits and batteries in front, and a most terrible enfilading fire from his batteries on the right. Colonel Snider having been wounded, I assumed command and brought my regiment in good order on the line of the skirmishers, when, being in easy range of heavy forces of the enemy, concealed under good cover, my men suffered severely, but returned the enemy's fire promptly and with effect. A flank movement being attempted on our right, Lieutenant-Colonel Sawyer and myself moved our men in that direction. Our orders were to hold the ground at all hazards, which we did for a long time, when our cartridges being exhausted, we stood for some time with fixed bayonets to dispute any charge or assault upon our position. We were also to hold ourselves in readiness to charge the enemy with bayonets so soon as a charge along the line commenced. Between 4 and 5 o'clock P. M. we were withdrawn by order of Colonel Mason. Our loss in killed and wounded and missing was 51. Among the wounded I regret to mention Colonel Snider, Captain Watson, Lieutenant Detrick and Lieutenant Prickett. My officers and men behaved with admirable coolness and bravery, and deserve well of their country."

At Gettysburg, July, 1863, the Seventh West Virginia, under the command of Lieutenant-Colonel Lockwood, charged and drove back the Seventh Virginia (Confederate), wounding and capturing its colonel; also a Lieutenant Lockwood, a nephew of Lieutenant-Colonel Lockwood, who was wounded. In addition to Colonel Lockwood, the regiment lost five killed and 40 wounded. At the battle of Chancellorsville, Va., which continued five days, beginning May 7, the Seventh Regiment was constantly in the battle line, Colonel Carroll in command of the brigade. On the 3d of May, the brigade was ordered to form in line of battle, in an open field, fronting a wood, that lay between it and the enemy; the Seventh, under command of Colonel Snider, occupying a position on the left of the Fourth Ohio, and on the extreme left of the brigade. At 8 A. M., the entire line of the brigade was ordered to forward; it advanced into the wood, when it met the enemy advancing in large force towards our line, and when in close proximity to each other, the brigade opened on them with a volley of musketry that shook the ground they walked on. General Carroll immediately charged into them, putting them to flight, following them with a brisk fire, some of them falling dead, some wounded, while others threw down their arms, and throwing up their hands, ran into our lines, and many of them fell upon their faces and lay still until our column passed over them, when they would jump up and say: "They were where they wanted to be." In this advance, Carroll pursued them through the wood and beyond the Gordonsville plank road. The brigade captured in this charge 150 of the enemy, and recaptured a battalion of Zouaves, who had been surrounded by the enemy before our advance, also capturing a stand of colors belonging to the enemy. The Seventh Regiment occupying the enemy's first line of works, they opened upon the regiment with canister and grape and a heavy enfilading fire, and forced the

JOSEPH SNIDER
Colonel 7th West Virginia Infantry

JOHN G. KELLEY
Lieutenant Colonel 7th West Virginia Infantry

regiment to retire to the cover of the wood, where it held its position unt:l Colonel Carroll ordered it to withdraw from the field. On the 4th inst., in consequence of severe illness, Colonel Snider and Major Morris had to retire from the front, leaving the command of the regiment with Lieutenant-Colonel Lockwood.

On the 5th of May, the regiment recrossed the river at the United States Ford on pontoon bridges, and occupied its former camp. In this engagement the regiment lost one officer and two enlisted men killed, one officer and 16 men wounded.

Gen'l Alexander Hayes, commanding Third Division, Second Army Corps, in his report of the engagement at Morton's Ford on the Rapidan on February 6, 1864, referring to the Seventh Regiment, says: "I have neglectfully failed to call especial attention and notice to the conduct of the Seventh Regiment West Virginia Infantry, commanded by Lieut.-Col. J. H. Lockwood, of the First Brigade, distinguished always among the first and foremost in battle. They, with their gallant leader, had reenlisted for three years; the order for their return to their homes had been received and published; with a resolve to assist their old comrades in another day's trial they marched with us and returned, bearing with them to their homes one commissioned officer and 10 enlisted men wounded." Becoming much reduced in numbers, the Seventh Regiment was consolidated on September 5, 1863, into four companies, Lieutenant-Colonel Lockwood in command. By reason of which consolidation Colonel Snider, with other officers, was mustered out; Colonel Snider was then commissioned colonel of the Fourth West Virginia Cavalry. Three new companies were added to the Seventh Battalion in March, 1865.

It will be doing a simple act of justice to state that Lieutenant-Colonel Lockwood was in command of the regiment much of the time from its original formation in 1861 to its final muster out.

As an acknowledgment of the splendid service rendered by the battalion, it was furnished, in 1864, with Henry rifles—16-shooters; being thus armed it invariably occupied the advance, and was almost constantly on the skirmish line. The regiment served continuously in the Army of the Potomac, after July, 1862. From the 1st of January, 1865, to the date of muster out it was incorporated in the Second Army Corps, and participated in all the engagements with that corps in the final campaign against Richmond, maintaining during the whole time its well deserved reputation for gallantry. From the original formation to the final muster out, July 1, 1865, at Munson's Hill, Virginia, the Seventh participated in the following battles: Romney, W. Va.; Harrison's Landing, Va.; Antietam, Md.; Fredericksburg, Va.;

Chancellorsville, Va.; Gettysburg, Pa.; Mine Run, Va.; Morton's Ford, Va.; Wilderness, Va.; Front Royal, Va.; Po River, Va.; Spottsylvania, Va.; North Anna, Va.; Totopotomy, Va.; Cold Harbor, Va.; Petersburg, Va.; Deep Bottom, Va.; Ream's Station, Va.; Boydton Road, Va.; Strawberry Plains, Va.; Hatcher's Run, Va.; Sailor's Creek, Va.; Farmville, Va.; Appomattox, Va.

The regiment participated in the grand review at Washington City, on the 24th of June, 1865. The losses sustained during the war were, killed 142—14 per cent. of its enrollment. Total in killed and wounded, 522.

CHAPTER XXXVII.

NINTH REGIMENT WEST VIRGINIA INFANTRY VOLUNTEERS.

Roster of the Field, Staff and Company Officers of the Ninth Regiment West Virginia Infantry Volunteers, Showing the Alterations and Casualties therein, from the Date of Original Organization of the Regiment to the Date of Consolidation with the Fifth Regiment West Virginia Infantry, November 19, 1864.

Date of Commission.	Names and Rank.	Co.	Remarks.
	Colonels.		
Dec. 6, 1861.	Leonard Skinner,		Resigned Sept. 19, 1862.
Sep. 9, 1862.	Isaac Harden Duval,		Commissioned Colonel 1st W. Va. Vet. Inft.
	Lieutenant-Colonel.		
Nov. 12, 1861.	William C. Starr,		Mustered out at expiration of term of service.
	Major.		
Nov. 12, 1861.	Benjamin M. Skinner,		Mustered out at expiration of term of service.
	1st Lieut. and Adj't.		
Oct. 1, 1861.	Joseph C. Wheeler,		Resigned March 1, 1862.
Jan. 4, 1862.	Henrie W. Brazie,		Resigned March 14, 1863.
June 5, 1863.	Cary B. Hayslipp,		Promoted to Captain, Co. D, 1st W. Va. Veteran Infantry.
	1st Lieut. and R. Q. M.		
Dec. 6, 1861.	Joseph C. Merrill,		Mustered out.
	Surgeons.		
May 19, 1862.	William L. Grant,		Resigned Sept. 30, 1862.
Nov. 7, 1862.	Jonathan Morris,		Mustered out.
	Assistant Surgeons.		
Feb. 5, 1862.	Wm. L. Grant,		Promoted to Surgeon.
May 19, 1862.	James H. Hysell,		Promoted to Surgeon 1st W. Va. Vet. Inft.
	Chaplain.		
May 5, 1862.	John M. Phelps,		Resigned March 18, 1863.
	Captains.		
Jan. 4, 1862.	Samuel Davis,	A	Mustered out at expiration of term of service.
Jan. 14, 1862.	John W. Spencer,	B	Mustered out at expiration of term of service.
Feb. 8, 1862.	Nathan M. McLaughlin,	C	Resigned Dec. 9, 1862.
Jan. 10, 1863.	George W. Hicks,	C	Mustered out at expiration of term of service.
March 8, 1862.	John S. P. Carroll,	D	Promoted to Major, 1st W. Va. Vet. Infantry.
March 8, 1862.	John M. Phelps,	E	Commissioned Chaplain.
May 6, 1862.	William Engleman,	E	Resigned Aug. 31, 1863.
Feb. 1, 1864.	Oliver Phelps,	E	Commissioned Captain, 1st W. Va. Vet. Inft.
May 2, 1862.	Owen G. Chase,	F	Resigned October 5, 1862.
Nov. 10, 1862.	John W. Miller,	F	Mustered out at expiration of term of service.

Date of Commission.	Names and Rank.	Co.	Remarks.
	Captains.		
April 4, 1862.	Henry C. McWhorter,	G	Resigned on account of wounds, received in battle.
April 22, 1864.	William B. Wetzel,	G	Killed in action at Cloyd's Mountain.
May 2, 1862.	Joseph C. Wheeler,	H	Resigned August 2, 1862.
Sep. 12, 1863.	William G. Smith,	H	Died of wounds received in action.
Dec. 18, 1861.	William Turner,	I	Dismissed for absence without leave.
Nov. 25, 1862.	Allen F. Bratton,	I	Resigned Feb. 7, 1863.
Feb. 17, 1863.	William P. Pratt,	I	Mustered out at expiration of term of service.
May 6, 1862.	Thomas Boggess,	K	Resigned June 24, 1863.
Sep. 12, 1863.	Adonijah W. Rollins,	K	Dismissed October 8, 1864.
	First Lieutenants.		
Jan. 4, 1882.	Benjamin F. Stivers,	A	Mustered out at expiration of term of service.
Jan. 14, 1862.	Thomas J. Boatwright,	B	Resigned Dec. 9, 1862.
Jan. 10, 1863.	John C. Angel,	B	Mustered out at expiration of term of service.
Jan. 4, 1862.	Nathan M. McLaughlin,	C	Promoted to Captain.
Feb. 8, 1862.	George W. Hicks,	C	Promoted to Captain.
Jan. 10, 1863.	George W. Jenkins,	C	Commissioned 1st Lieutenant in 1st W. Va. Veteran Infantry.
Dec. 18, 1861.	Cary B. Hayslipp,	D	Appointed Adjutant.
March 8, 1862.	William Engleman,	E	Promoted to Captain.
May 6, 1862.	Oliver Phelps,	E	Promoted to Captain.
April 22, 1864.	John H. Lawhead,	E	Resigned October 5, 1864.
Dec. 28, 1861.	Owen G. Chase,	F	Promoted to Captain.
May 2, 1862.	John W. Miller,	F	Promoted to Captain.
Nov. 10, 1862.	George J. Walker,	F	Mustered out at expiration of term of service.
April 4, 1862.	Wm. B. Wetzel,	G	Promoted to Captain.
May 2, 1862.	James V. Hoover,	H	Resigned Oct. 17, 1862.
Dec. 19, 1862.	Wm. G. Smith,	H	Promoted to Captain.
April 22, 1864.	John W. Johnson,	H	Promoted to Captain 1st W. Va. Vet. Inft.
May 6, 1862.	Allen F. Bratton,	I	Promoted to Captain.
Feb. 5, 1863.	James Craig,	I	Resigned October 5, 1864.
May 6, 1862.	Adonijah W. Rollins,	K	Promoted to Captain.
	Second Lieutenants.		
Jan. 4, 1862.	James Ewing,	A	Mustered out at expiration of term of service.
Jan. 14, 1862.	Henry C. McWhorter,	B	Promoted to Captain Co. G.
Aug. 18, 1862.	John C. Angell,	B	Promoted to 1st Lieutenant.
Jan. 10, 1863.	Cornelius McConley,	B	Commissioned 1st Lieut. 1st W. Va. Vet. Inft.
Jan. 4, 1862.	George W. Hicks,	C	Promoted to 1st Lieutenant.
Feb. 8, 1862.	George W. Jenkins,	C	Promoted to 1st Lieutenant.
Jan. 10, 1863.	Benja. S. Cheuveront,	C	Dishonorably dismissed.
April 22, 1864.	Moses W. Davis,	C	Mustered out as supernumerary.
March 8, 1862.	William P. Pratt,	D	Promoted to Captain, Company I.
Feb. 17, 1863.	Henry C. Duncan,	D	Promoted to Captain Co. K, 1st W. Va. Veteran Infantry.
March 5, 1862.	Oliver Phelps,	E	Promoted to 1st Lieutenant.
May 6, 1862.	Joseph V. Rowley,	E	Resigned October 26, 1862.

Date of Commission.	Names and Rank.	Co.	Remarks.
	Second Lieutenants.		
Dec. 19, 1862.	Joseph H. Lawhead,	E	Promoted to 1st Lieutenant.
May 2, 1862.	Edmund F. Anderson,	F	Died at Charleston W. Va.
Sept. 27, 1862.	Snelling M. Smith,	F	Mustered out Oct. 30, 1864.
April 4, 1862.	Robert Laughlin,	G	Promoted to Captain Company I, 1st W. Va. Veteran Infantry.
May 2, 1862.	Wm. G. Smith,	H	Promoted to 1st Lieutenant.
Dec. 19, 1862.	Daniel Wilgus,	H	Resigned January 29, 1863.
Feb. 17, 1863.	John W. Johnson,	H	Promoted to 1st Lieutenant.
April 22, 1864.	Otho W. Karr,	H	Killed in action, August 26, 1894.
Sept. 24, 1864.	Stephen C. Hiltbruner,	H	Promoted to Capt. Co. C. 1st W. Va. Vet. Inft.
May 6, 1862.	George W. Hunter,	I	Resigned February 7, 1863.
May 6, 1862.	George Rhodes,	K	Resigned January 20, 1863.
Jan. 28, 1863.	Youthless Pullins,	K	Mustered out on Consolidation.

THE NINTH W. VA. VOLUNTEER INFANTRY.

The Ninth West Virginia Volunteer Infantry was organized December, 1861, with the following field officers: Leonard Skinner, colonel; William C. Starr, lieutenant-colonel; Benjamin, M. Skinner, major. The regiment was composed largely of refugees, who, having been driven from home, were fighting with a desperation that was not excelled by any troops in any army. The regiment served mainly in the Kanawha and Shenandoah Valleys under Crook, Hunter, Duval and others. It was especially distinguished for bravery at the battle of Cloyd's Mountain. Col. Carr B. White commanding the brigade, says in his report that the regiment carried the enemy's works on the right under fire that killed and wounded more than one third of the regiment, without an officer or man faltering, capturing two guns, one regimental flag, and many prisoners and is designated as one of the most gallant feats of the war. Its loss at this battle attests the desperate character of the assault: 45 killed, 144 wounded. In this action the color-guard entered the enemy's works in advance of the line, every one of them falling, killed or wounded, and after the fight, 21 men lay dead around the flag, 12 of whom were Confederates. Besides this battle the regiment bore a conspicuous part in the battles of Lynchburg, Kernstown, Winchester, Martinsburg, Hunter's raid, etc.

Gen'l I. H. Duval was commissioned colonel of the regiment, September 9, 1862, and although he served much of his term as brigade or division commander, the regiment was generally in his command. Of the regiments he commanded, General Duval says he served longer with the Ninth Regiment than the others, and led it in many hard fought battles; "we were in some defeats as well as many victories, and in our defeats and retreats the Ninth Regiment was never panic-stricken, but always came off as it went into battle, shoulder to shoulder. We never allowed the enemy to go through us in advancing or retreating."

The regiment's losses during the war were: killed and died of wounds, three officers and 96 enlisted men; died of disease or accident, one officer, 107 men. Total 207. The reenlisted veterans and recruits of the Ninth and Fifth Infantry Regiments were consolidated November 9, 1864, which formed the First West Virginia Veteran Infantry.

WILLIAM C. STARR
Lieutenant Colonel 9th West Virginia Infantry

MOSES S. HALL
Lieutenant Colonel 10th West Virginia Infantry

CHAPTER XXXVIII.

TENTH REGIMENT W. VA. INFANTRY VOLUNTEERS.

Roster of the Field, Staff and Company Officers of the Tenth Regiment West Virginia Infantry Volunteers, Showing the Alterations and Casualties therein, from the Date of Original Organization of the Regiment to the Date of Muster Out, August 9, 1865.

Date of Commission.	Names and Rank.	Co.	Remarks.
	Colonels.		
May 30, 1862.	Thomas M. Harris,		Brevetted Brigadier-General, Dec. 10, 1864. Com. Brigadier-General, March 29, 1865.
June 29, 1865.	Morgan A. Darnall.		
	Lieutenant-Colonels.		
Dec. 13, 1861.	Thomas M. Harris,		Promoted to Colonel.
May 30, 1862.	Moses S. Hall,		Mustered out at expiration of term of service.
March 24, 1865.	Morgan A. Darnall,		Promoted to Colonel.
July 3, 1863.	Lewis M. Marsh.		
	Majors.		
May 2, 1862.	Henry H. Withers,		Resigned November 25, 1864.
July 25, 1865.	Daniel Curran.		
	1st Lieut. and Adj't.		
Jan. 22, 1862.	Oliver P. Boughner,		Mustered out at expiration of term of service.
	1st Lieut. and R. Q. M.		
Dec. 14, 1861.	Samuel Adams,		Mustered out at expiration of term of service.
	Surgeons.		
May 8, 1862.	George C. Gans,		Died of disease, Oct. 4, 1864, at Harrisonburg, Va.
Oct. 24, 1864.	Jonathan R. Blair,		Mustered out at expiration of term of service.
July 6, 1865.	Ozias Nellis.		
	Assistant Surgeons.		
Jan. 3, 1862.	Wm. M. Worthington,		Resigned April 12, 1862.
April 28, 1862.	George C. Gans,		Promoted to Surgeon.
July 8, 1862.	Jonathan R. Blair,		Promoted to Surgeon.
Oct. 24, 1864.	Isaac W. Bouse,		Resigned November 28, 1864.
Jan. 13, 1865.	Ozias Nellis,		Promoted to Surgeon.
	Chaplain.		
Sep. 12, 1862.	John Branch,		Resigned Jan. 19, 1865.
	Captains.		
Feb. 12, 1862.	Morgan A. Darnall,	A	Promoted to Lieutenant-Colonel.
July 25, 1865.	Gwinn Minter,	A	
Dec. 26, 1861.	David Morgan,	B	Resigned August 12, 1862.
Sep. 12, 1862.	J. Loomis Gould,	B	Mustered out at expiration of term of service.
Dec. 12, 1861	Wm. D. Hall,	C	Dismissed August 1, 1864.
Oct. 27, 1864.	John H. Bailey,	C	Mustered out at expiration of term of service.

Date of Commission.	Names and Rank	Co.	Remarks.
	Captains.		
July 25, 1861.	Duncan Cunningham,	C	
Feb. 25, 1862.	Thomas D. Murrin,	D	Mustered out at expiration of term of service.
July 25, 1865.	Asa S. Hugill,	D	
April 2, 1862.	Lewis M. Marsh,	E	Promoted to Lieutenant-Colonel.
May 29, 1862.	Nimrod M. Hyer,	F	Mustered out at expiration of term of service.
July 21, 1862.	James M. Ewing,	G	Killed in action near Winchester, Va.
May 14, 1862.	Marshall W. Coburn,	H	Mustered out at expiration of term of service.
June 3, 1862.	James A. Jarboe,	I	Mustered out at expiration of term of service.
June 24, 1862.	Jacob P. Kuykendall,	K	Killed in action at Cedar Creek.
March 15, 1865.	Nimrod Kuykendall,	K	
	First Lieutenants.		
Feb. 10, 1862.	Joseph G. Bouse,	A	Resigned September 18, 1863.
Dec. 18, 1863.	Ausbin A. Wilson,	A	Mustered out at expiration of term of service.
July 25, 1865.	John E. Maxson,	A	
Dec. 26, 1861.	Chas. Morgan,	B	
Sep. 12, 1862.	Henry H. Lewis,	B	Mustered out at expiration of term of service. Muster revoked by War Department.
March 22, 1865.	David T. Peterson,	B	Resigned September 12, 1862.
Dec. 12, 1861.	Wm. C. Hebner,	C	Resigned August 12, 1862.
Sep. 12, 1862.	James P. Connolly,	C	Dismissed September 12, 1864.
Oct. 27, 1864.	Gwinn Minter,	C	Promoted to Captain, Company A.
May 9, 1865.	Duncan Cunningham,	C	Promoted to Captain.
Jan. 31, 1862.	Jedediah G. Waldo,	D	Dismissed December 9, 1863.
Jan. 14, 1864.	Daniel Curren,	D	Promoted to Major.
March 3, 1862.	Lewis M. Marsh,	E	Promoted to Captain.
April 2, 1862.	Eli Conoway,	E	Resigned January 18, 1863.
July 21, 1863.	Benjamin F. Shreves,	E	Resigned November 27, 1864.
Dec. 15, 1864.	David Patterson,	E	Resigned June 2, 1865.
Feb. 8, 1862.	Nimrod M. Hyer,	F	Promoted to Captain.
May 29, 1862.	Samuel A. Rollyson,	F	Mustered out at expiration of term of service.
April 25, 1862.	John McAdams,	G	Mustered out at expiration of term of service.
March 14, 1862.	Wm. M. Hays,	H	Mustered out at expiration of term of service.
April 22, 1862.	A. W. Barclay,	I	Died at Winchester, Va., April 19, 1863.
June 10, 1863.	John M. Jarboe,	I	Mustered out at expiration of term of service.
March 21, 1862.	Jacob P. Kuykendall,	K	Promoted to Captain.
June 24, 1862.	Thomas Hess,	K	Resigned October 23, 1864.
Nov. 25, 1864.	Nimrod Kuykendall,	K	Promoted to Captain.
March 22, 1865.	Thomas S. Nutter,	K	
	Second Lieutenants.		
Feb. 12, 1862.	Ausbin A. Wilson,	A	Promoted to 1st Lieutenant.
Dec. 18, 1863.	Ignatius C. Burbridge,	A	Dismissed November 25, 1864.
Dec. 26, 1861.	Henry H. Lewis,	B	Promoted to 1st Lieutenant.
Sep. 12, 1862.	David J. Ezekiel,	B	Mustered out at expiration of term of service.
Oct. 27, 1864.	Harrison F. Garrett,	B	Mustered out at expiration of term of service.
Dec. 12, 1861.	James Connolly,	C	Promoted to 1st Lieutenant.
Sep. 12, 1862.	John H. Bailey,	C	Promoted to Captain.

Date of Commission.	Names and Rank.	Co.	Remarks.
	Second Lieutenants.		
Nov. 25, 1864.	John E. Maxson,	C	Promoted to 1st Lieutenant, Company A.
Feb. 25, 1862.	Daniel Curran,	D	Promoted to 1st Lieutenant, Company A.
Jan. 23, 1864.	Joseph L. Ambrose,	D	Dismissed October 8, 1864.
Oct. 27, 1864.	Harrison F. Garrett,	D	Transferred to Company B.
April 19, 1862.	Benjamin F. Shreves,	E	Promoted to 1st Lieutenant.
July 21, 1862.	Charles B. McCollom,	E	Killed in action at Winchester, Va.
May 29, 1862.	Henry Bender,	F	Mustered out at expiration of term of service.
May 29, 1862.	Robert Varner,	G	Mustered out at expiration of term of service.
May 14, 1862.	Isaac Rollins,	H	Dismissed August 1, 1864.
Sep. 27, 1864.	Minter F. Marple,	H	Mustered out at expiration of term of service.
July 31, 1862.	John M. Jarboe,	I	Promoted to 1st Lieutenant.
June 10, 1863.	Michael Ahern,	I	Mustered out at expiration of term of service.
June 24, 1862.	Jeremiah H. Fluharty,	K	Resigned December 26, 1862.
Jan. 10, 1863.	Benjamin Moats,	K	Mustered out at expiration of term of service.

TENTH REGIMENT WEST VIRGINIA VOLUNTEER INFANTRY.

This regiment was recruited by T. M. Harris, who was a practicing physician at Glenville, Gilmer County, W. Va., at the breaking out of the war. At the solicitation of General Rosecrans, Dr. Harris visited Governor Peirpoint at Wheeling in the latter part of July, 1861, and obtained his consent to recruit a regiment for the Union service with the understanding that in the event of his success in recruiting a regiment he should receive a commission as its colonel.   He entered upon his work on the third day of August, 1861, and completed the organization of the 10th Regiment and received a colonel's commission to command the same, about the 3d of May, 1862.

The doctor had an extensive acquaintance with the country and the people and traveled over about 12 counties of the State, some of them several times, during the fall of 1861 and the winter of–1861 62, gathering recruits from the loyal portion of the population.   His first visit to a county was for the purpose of hunting out suitable men for his line officers.   In this work he used great discrimination and made very few mistakes.   The result was that his regiment, when organized, was under command of brave, intelligent and intensely loyal men.   In this way its future good record was assured.

The doctor found his task a tedious and difficult one.   He found plenty of loyal people, but at that early period of the war they were laboring under the delusion that the war would be a short one and there would be enough of troops raised in the States North and West to put down the rebellion without their aid.   He succeeded in getting four or five companies organized during the fall months of 1861, and these were put into service by the generals in command, at the request of the Governor, at points along the border line between the loyal and disloyal portions of the State, for the protection of the loyal people against guerilla raids. In this service they distinguished themselves as constituting a vigilant, intelligent and brave line of outposts. The service of this regiment after its organization in May, 1862, until June, 1864, was mostly in West Virginia. Having been recruited from the hardy mountaineers of the State, it was so particularly well adapted to the purpose of protecting the loyal interests against the enemy that the Governor was loth to give it up to any other service. It had the confidence of the loyal people who felt safe under its protection. In June, 1864, it was ordered to Martinsburg, and became incorporated into the organizations that were then being formed for operations against the enemy's threatened advance down the Shenandoah Valley and was finally incorporated in the command known in army orders as the "Army of West Virginia," under General Crook.

At the close of the Valley campaign in December, 1864, it was sent, under the command of its former colonel, now commanding a division, to City Point, where it became incorporated with the 24th Army Corps and it served in this corps during the remainder of its term of service. This regiment was noted for its prowess, courage, intrepidity and general reliability. It participated in many hard fought engagements and always came out with a splendid record. Most of its officers distinguished themselves for soldierly qualities and many of its private men won honorable mention. It was perhaps not excelled by any regiment in the service from this or any other State.

LIEUT.-COL. M. S. HALL, 10TH WEST VIRGINIA INFANTRY.

From the time that Colonel Harris was assigned to the command of a brigade, the command of the 10th Regiment devolved on its lieutenant-colonel, M. S. Hall. This officer was a native of Massachusetts who came to Virginia in 1845, being then 21 years old, and studied medicine with Dr. Harris, who had married his sister. He had been engaged in the practice of medicine for several years and was living at Harrisville, in the County of Ritchie, when the war broke out. He was among the pioneer Republicans of the State and being of an ardent temperament and very patriotic, he engaged in recruiting a company for the loyal service in May, 1861, and had it ready for muster in on the 4th of July, 1861. His first commission was that of captain and he was assigned to the command of Company K of the Third Regiment. This company had been recruited by him from the loyal young men of his acquaintance, mostly from the county of Ritchie and for three years of service. He continued in command of this company until the organization of the 10th

Regiment in May, 1862, when, at the solicitation of Colonel Harris, he was promoted to the lieutenant-colonelcy of the 10th. In this capacity he served until the expiration of the term of its enlistment. In every capacity in which he served, whether as line or field officer he distinguished himself for a loyal, intelligent, courageous and faithful discharge of duty. In every action in which his command was engaged, he won honorable mention. He was twice wounded near Duffield's Station; whilst engaged in resisting Early's advance to enable General Sigel's wagon train to cross the Potomac at Shepherdstown, he was struck by a minnie ball which broke the small bone of the forearm; and at Cedar Creek, on the 19th of October, he was again struck by a minnie ball which would have passed through the liver had its course not been deflected by the yielding of a rib causing it to follow the rib in its course and emerge from the opposite side, thus being guided in its course and prevented from entering the cavity of the body. Colonel Hall will be remembered by his comrades in the service as long as they shall live for his personal as well his soldierly qualities. He was a brave, open-hearted, considerate and good officer.

CHAPTER XXXIX.

ELEVENTH REGIMENT W. VA. INFANTRY VOLUNTEERS.

Roster of the Field, Staff and Company Officers of the Eleventh Regiment West Virginia Infantry Volunteers, Showing the Alterations and Casualties therein, from the Date of Organization of said Regiment to the Date of Muster Out, June 10, 1865.

Date of Commission.	Names and Rank.	Co.	Remarks.
	Colonels.		
Feb. 14, 1862.	John C. Rathbone,		Honorably discharged January 6, 1863.
Feb. 6, 1863.	Daniel Frost,		Killed in action at Snicker's Ferry.
Oct. 28, 1863.	Van H. Bukey,		Mustered out at expiration of term of service.
	Lieutenant-Colonels.		
Oct. 17, 1861.	John C. Rathbone,		Promoted ot Colonel.
May 24, 1862.	Daniel Frost,		Promoted to Colonel.
July 31, 1863.	Van H. Bukey,		Promoted to Colonel.
Feb. 7, 1865.	Wm. H. H. King.		
	Majors.		
Nov. 1, 1861.	George C. Trimble,		Dismissed January 4, 1863.
Feb. 26, 1863.	Van H. Bukey,		Promoted to Lieutenant-Colonel.
Nov. 20, 1863.	James L. Simpson,		Mustered out at expiration of term of service.
Feb. 7, 1865.	Michael A. Ayers.		
	1st Lt. and Adj'ts.		
Nov. 13, 1861.	T. A. Roberts,		Resigned October 9, 1862.
Nov. 5, 1862.	John H. McLaughlin,		Discharged May 18, 1865, by reason of wounds received in action at Cloyd's Mountain, Va.
	1st Lts. and R. Q. M.		
Jan. 3, 1862.	David Bell,		Mustered out at expiration of term of service.
Jan. 12, 1865.	Hugh P. Dils, Jr.		
	Surgeons.		
Oct. 27, 1862.	Andrew D. Voorheis,		Resigned October 17, 1863.
Jan, 12, 1865.	Erwin D. J. Bond.		
	Assistant Surgeons.		
Aug. 17, 1862.	Andrew D. Voorheis,		Promoted to Surgeon.
Mar. 7, 1863.	James A. Williamson,		Not mustered.
Feb. 3, 1864.	James Emory Kendall,		
Jan. 5, 1864.	Erwin D. J. Bond,		Promoted to Surgeon.
	Chaplain.		
Oct. 10, 1865.	Aaron J. Lyon,		Dismissed December 24, 1864.
	Captains.		
July 12, 1861.	John P. Baggs,	A	Dismissed April 4, 1863.
May 30, 1863.	William Cummings,	A	Mustered out at expiration of term of service.
Mar. 14, 1865.	George H. Purdy,	A	
Dec. 27, 1861.	James W. Myers,	B	Dismissed November 18, 1864.

Date of Commission.	Names and Rank.	Co.	Remarks.
	Captains.		
Dec. 27, 1861.	James L. Simpson,	C	Promoted to Major.
Jan. 20, 1864.	Jacob Clammer,	C	Mustered out at expiration of term of service
Aug. 20, 1862.	Van H. Bukey,	D	Promoted to Major.
April 1, 1863.	Alexander Moore,	D	Resigned October 2, 1864.
Oct. 27, 1864.	Levi Campbell, Jr.,	D	Mustered out at expiration of term of service.
Aug. 14, 1862.	David Deem,	E	Honorably discharged June 1, 1865.
Sep. 6, 1862.	Wm. F. Pell.	F	Discharged March 4, 1863, by Act of Congress.
July 16, 1863.	Fayette B. Stoddard,	F	
May 6, 1862.	John V. Young,	G	
Sep. 6, 1862.	Lewis Smith,	H	Dismissed September 14, 1863.
Oct. 12, 1863.	George W. Parriott,	H	Mustered out at expiration of term of service.
March 6, 1865.	Saml. K. Kirkpatrick,	H	
May 31, 1862.	Dixon R. King,	I	Mustered out at expiration of term of service.
Feb. 7, 1865.	Samuel L. Barber,	I	
Sep. 23, 1862.	Alfred Gilpin,	K	Resigned June 10, 1863.
July 16, 1863.	James W. Williamson,	K	Resigned March 20, 1865.
May 8, 1865.	Newton Poling,	K	
	First Lieutenants.		
Sept. 9, 1863.	Andrew Q. Mountz,	A	Resigned January 29, 1865.
Jan. 25, 1865.	Michael A. Ayers,	A	Promoted to Major.
April 25, 1865.	Albert W. Lemasters,	A	
Nov. 5, 1861.	Marlin Parke,	B	Dismissed Nov. 18, 1864.
May 8, 1865.	Daniel S. Haverty,	B	Resigned January 9, 1865.
Dec. 27, 1861.	James Robinson,	C	Resigned October 9, 1862.
Jan. 30, 1863.	Jacob Clammer,	C	Promoted to Captain.
Jan. 20, 1864.	Thornton Ferrell,	C	Mustered out at expiration of term of service.
Jan. 28, 1862.	Van H. Bukey,	D	Promoted to Captain.
Aug. 20, 1862.	Alexander Moore,	D	Promoted to Captain.
April 1, 1863.	James Barr,	D	Killed in action at Lynchburg, Va.
Aug. 15, 1864.	Levi Campbell, Jr.,	D	Promoted to Captain.
Oct. 27, 1864.	Christian J. Core,	D	Resigned March 29, 1865.
April 25, 1865.	William Geer,	D	
Aug. 14, 1862.	Philip F. Poe,	E	Dismissed November 28, 1864.
Jan. 20, 1865.	Madison H. Berry,	E	
Sep. 6, 1862.	Fayette B. Stoddard,	F	Promoted to Captain.
July 16, 1863.	Charles W. Kirby,	F	Killed in action at Winchester, Va.
Oct. 27, 1864.	William H. Collett,	F	
May 6, 1862.	Robert Brooks,	G	Resigned June 2, 1863.
Dec. 2, 1863.	Clark Elkins,	G	Mustered out at expiration of term of service.
March 9, 1865.	Van B. Morris,	G	
Nov. 16, 1861.	George W. Parriott,	H	Promoted to Captain.
Oct. 12, 1863.	John Holt,	H	Mustered out at expiration of term of service.
Nov. 9, 1861.	Dixon R. King,	I	Promoted to Captain.
May 31, 1862.	Wm. H. H. King,	I	Promoted to Lieutenant-Colonel.
March 22, 1865.	John W. King,	I	
Aug. 20, 1862.	James W. Williamson,	K	Promoted to Captain.

Date of Commission.	Names and Rank.	Co.	Remarks.
	First Lieutenants.		
July 16, 1863.	Newton Poling,	K	Promoted to Captain.
May 8, 1865.	James D. W. Riley,	K	
	Second Lieutenants.		
Nov. 9, 1861.	George W. Baggs,	A	Resigned Oct. 9, 1862.
March 1, 1863.	William Cummings,	A	Promoted to Captain.
May 30, 1863.	Andrew Q. Mountz,	A	Promoted to 1st Lieutenant.
Sep. 9, 1863.	James H. McGill,	A	Dismissed.
Sep. 7, 1864.	Michael A. Ayers,	A	Promoted to 1st Lieutenant.
Jan. 25, 1865.	George H. Purdy,	A	Promoted to Captain.
Dec. 27, 1861.	Samuel W. Ross,	B	Resigned September 5, 1864.
Sep. 10, 1864.	Daniel S. Haverty.	B	Promoted to 1st Lieutenant.
Dec. 27, 1861.	Nicholas Poling,	C	Resigned October 9, 1862.
Jan. 30, 1863.	Thornton Ferrell,	C	Promoted to 1st Lieutenant.
Jan. 20, 1864.	James F. McDonald,	C	Mustered out at expiration of term of service.
Oct. 9, 1862.	Charles B. Way.	D	Resigned September 30, 1863.
May 30, 1863.	Levi Campbell, Jr.,	D	Promoted to 1st Lieutenant.
Aug. 14, 1864.	Christian J. Core,	D	Promoted to 1st Lieutenant.
Sep. 27, 1864.	John S. Bukey,	D	Resigned May 18, 1865.
Jan. 27, 1865.	John D. Grim,	D	
July 29, 1862.	Thomas J. Robinson,	E	Resigned April 1, 1863.
May 30, 1863.	B. Taylor Frost,	E	Mustered out at expiration of term of service.
Dec. 19, 1864.	Madison H. Berry,	E	Promoted to 1st Lieutenant.
March 22, 1865.	James S. Newbanks,	E	
Aug. 20, 1862.	Charles W. Kirby,	F	Promoted to 1st Lieutenant.
July 16, 1863.	William W. Curtis,	F	Killed in action at New Creek, W. Va.
Aug. 13, 1864.	Wm. H. Collett,	F	Promoted to 1st Lieutenant.
Oct. 27, 1864.	William A. McCoy,	F	
July 23, 1862.	John S. Cunningham,	G	Promoted to Adjutant 13th W. Va. Infantry.
June 6, 1863.	Clark Elkins,	G	Promoted to 1st Lieutenant.
Dec. 2, 1863.	William G. McDaniel,	G	Mustered out at expiration of term of service.
April 2, 1862.	Bernard A. C. Pyles,	H	Resigned March 1, 1863.
April 13, 1863.	John Holt,	H	Promoted to 1st Lieutenant.
Oct. 12, 1863.	John H. Bloyd,	H	Mustered out at expiration of term of service.
May 31, 1862.	Uriah Lytle,	I	Mustered out at expiration of term of service.
Sep. 23, 1862.	Newton Poling,	K	Promoted to 1st Lieutenant.
July 16, 1863.	James D. W. Riley,	K	Promoted to 1st Lieutenant.

The Eleventh West Virginia Infantry.

The Eleventh Infantry was organized in May, 1862; its early service was in the western part of West Virginia, mainly on the line of the B. & O. R. R., in Wilkinson's brigade, Kelley's division, Eighth Army Corps. The following field officers were entrusted with its organization: John C. Rathbone, colonel; Daniel Frost, lieutenant-colonel; and George C. Trimble, major.

DANIEL FROST
Colonel 11th West Virginia Infantry
Mortally Wounded Snicker's Ferry, Va. July 18, 1864

Colonel Rathbone was honorably discharged January 6, 1863. On February 6, 1863, Lieutenant-Colonel Frost succeeded to the colonelcy. On the 9th of May, 1864, Col. H. G. Sickel, commanding brigade in the terrible battle of Cloyd's Mountain, in his report of same, makes special mention of the gallantry of Colonel Frost and his regiment. Six companies of the regiment, under Colonel Frost, participated in the advance from Lewisburg, June 1. 1864,—Col. Jacob M. Campbell's brigade, Crook's division—to Staunton, Va., having had considerable skirmishing *en route*, when the regiment, on June 8, joined General Hunter's command, remaining with Hunter in his expedition *via* Lexington to the Kanawha, where they arrived June 29, the regiment having marched 412 miles in the heart of the enemy's country, having lost in killed one officer (Lieut.James Barr, of Co. D), and five men, with 20 wounded.

At the battle of Snicker's Ferry, July 18, 1864, Col. Joseph Thoburn commanding division, Colonel Frost was in command of the Third Brigade, and while gallantly leading his command, fell mortally wounded. On the 28th of October, 1864, Lieut.-Col. Van H. Bukey was promoted to colonel of the regiment. Colonel Bukey had passed through all the grades of promotion from lieutenant to captain, to major, to lieutenant-colonel and colonel, in all of which he illustrated the best qualities of the brave soldier, remaining with his regiment until final muster out.

In March, 1865, the regiment was assigned to duty in the Army of the Potomac. The First Division of the Army of West Virginia embraced the 10th, 11th, 12th and 15th West Virginia Infantry Regiments, which was incorporated in the 24th Army Corps, and formed the Third Division of that corps, until it was broken up by the muster out of troops. The division was commanded in the final campaign of the war by Brevet Maj.-Gen'l John W. Turner. The 10th, 11th and 15th Regiments constituted the First Brigade of that division, under the command of Brevet Maj.-Gen'l Thomas M. Harris, formerly colonel of the 10th Regiment. In this campaign the regiment proved to be a gallant body of men. They took an active part in the fall of Petersburg, High Bridge, and at Appomattox. The regiment lost during its term of service, four officers and 63 enlisted men killed in battle, and died of disease or wounds, 148; total 215. It was mustered out June 17, 1865, at Richmond, Virginia.

CHAPTER XL.

TWELFTH REGIMENT W. VA. INFANTRY VOLUNTEERS.

Roster of the Field, Staff and Company Officers of the Twelfth Regiment West Virginia Infantry Volunteers, Showing the Alterations and Casualties therein, from the Date of Original Organization of Said Regiment to the Date of Muster Out, June 16, 1865.

Date of Commission.	Names and Rank.	Co.	Remarks.
	Colonels.		
Aug. 20, 1862.	John B. Klunk,		Resigned September 1, 1863.
Jan. 26, 1864.	William B. Curtis.		
	Lieutenant-Colonels.		
Aug. 23, 1862.	Robert S. Northcott,		Resigned January 5, 1865.
Jan. 25, 1865.	Richard H. Brown.		
	Majors.		
Aug. 25, 1862.	Francis P. Peirpoint,		Appointed Adjt.-Gen. of W. Va., June 16, 1863.
July 27, 1864.	William B. Curtis,		Promoted to Colonel.
Feb. 6, 1864.	Richard H. Brown,		Promoted to Lieutenant-Colonel.
Jan. 25, 1895.	William Burley.		
	First Lts. and Adjt's.		
Aug. 7, 1862.	Francis P. Peirpoint,		Promoted to Major.
Aug. 25, 1862.	George B. Caldwell,		Resigned Jany 8, 1865.
Feb. 1, 1865.	Henry R. McCord.		
	1st. Lieut. and R. Q. M.		
Aug. 5, 1865.	Nathan U. Thurber,		Resigned May 11, 1865.
May 17, 1865.	David B. Fleming.		
	Surgeons.		
Aug. 9, 1862.	John Frizzell,		Resigned September 15, 1862.
Sep. 16, 1862.	John C. Campbell,		Resigned March 12, 1863.
July 23, 1864.	Sampson P. Bryan.		
	Assistant Surgeons.		
Aug. 11, 1862.	Dwight Ruggles,		Resigned November 22, 1862.
Sep. 10, 1862.	Sampson P. Bryan,		Promoted to Surgeon.
Nov. 8, 1862.	Frederick H. Patton.		
July 23, 1863.	Alexander Neil.		
	Chaplains.		
Oct. 7, 1862.	Thomas H. Trainer,		Resigned December 25, 1862.
March 26, 1864.	Richard W. Wallace.		
	Captains.		
April 16, 1862.	Hagar Tomlinson,	A	Resigned November 1, 1864.
Nov. 16, 1864	William Burley,	A	Promoted to Major.
Jan. 25, 1865.	William L. Roberts,	A	
Aug. 22, 2862.	Martin P. Bonar,	B	Resigned January 25, 1863.
Feb. 11, 1863.	John C. Roberts,	B	Resigned on account of wounds.

Date of Commission	Names and Rank.	Co.	Remarks.
	Captains.		
Feb. 13, 1865.	Thomas A. Fleming,	B	
Aug. 23, 1862.	Erastus G. Bartlett,	C	
Aug. 20, 1862.	Wm. B. Curtis,	D	Promoted to Major.
Oct. 12, 1863.	Wm. A. Smiley,	D	Promoted to Paymaster U. S. A.
May 9, 1865.	David M. Blayney,	D	
Aug. 22, 1862.	Cornelius Mercer,	E	
Aug. 25, 1862.	Amos N. Pritchard,	F	Resigned March 24, 1865.
May 9, 1865.	Francis H. Peirpoint, Jr.,	F	
Aug. 25, 1862.	James W. Moffatt,	G	
Aug. 20, 1862.	Jacob H. Bristor,	H	
Aug. 28, 1862.	Richard H. Brown,	I	Promoted to Major.
Feb. 10, 1864.	John Henry Melvin,	I	
Aug. 29, 1862.	Thomas White,	K	Resigned August 1, 1863.
Oct. 28, 1863.	John B. Jester,	K	
	First Lieutenants.		
Aug. 16, 1862.	Thomas S. Magruder,	A	Resigded January 17, 1863.
Feb. 3, 1863.	William Burley,	A	Promoted to Captain.
Dec. 16, 1864.	Wm. H. Riggs,	A	
Aug. 22, 1862.	Nathan S. Fish,	B	Resigned February 3, 1863.
Feb. 11, 1863.	James W. Dunnington,	B	Dismissed May 28, 1864.
Aug. 6, 1864.	Henry C. Wallace,	B	
Aug. 23, 1862.	Wm. L. Roberts,	C	Promoted to Captain, Company A,
Feb. 1, 1865.	Michael Gardner,	C	
Aug. 20, 1862.	William A. Smiley,	D	Promoted to Captain.
Oct. 12, 1863.	David M. Blayney,	D	Promoted to Captain.
May 9, 1865.	James C. Peirson,	D	
Aug. 22, 1862.	Oscar H. Tate,	E	Dismissed March 6, 1863.
July 9, 1863.	James R. Durham,	E	
Aug. 22, 1862.	Thomas A. Fleming,	F	Promoted to Captain.
Feb. 13, 1865.	Francis H. Peirponit, Jr.,	F	Promoted to Captain.
May 9, 1865.	Duncan Cunningham,	F	Transferred to 10th W. Va. Infantry.
Aug. 25, 1862.	Van D. Hall,	G	Resigned February 13, 1865.
Feb. 13, 1865.	George W. Fortney,	G	
Aug. 20, 1862.	David Powell,	H	Mustered out by order War Department.
Feb. 13, 1865.	Thomas H. Means,	H	
Aug. 15, 1862.	John Henry Melvin,	I	Promoted to Captain.
Feb 10, 1864.	Milton B. Campbell,	I	Dismissed September 13, 1864.
Nov. 11, 1864.	William Hewitt,	I	
Aug. 29, 1862.	John B. Jester,	K	Promoted to Captain.
Oct. 28, 1863.	John R. Brenneman,	K	
	Second Lieutenants.		
Aug. 16, 1862.	William Burley.	A	Promoted to 1st Lieutenant.
Feb. 3, 1863.	Philip G. Bier.	A	Promoted to Captain and A. A. G. U. S. Vol.
April 6, 1864.	Thomas W. Manning,	A	Resigned November 16, 1864.
Dec. 16, 1864.	Joseph Caldwell,	A	Transferred to Company C.
Aug. 22, 1862.	John C. Roberts,	B	Promoted to Captain.

Date of Commission.	Names and Rank.	Co.	Remarks.
	Second Lieutenants.		
Feb. 11, 1863.	Henry T. Anshutz,	B	Honorably discharged.
Aug. 23, 1862.	John B. Lydick,	C	Resigned December 25, 1862.
Jan. 8, 1863.	James Whittingham,	C	Promoted to Captain and A. Q. M., U. S. Vols.
Oct. 24, 1864.	Henry R. McCord,	C	Promoted to 1st Lieutenant and Adjutant.
Dec. 16, 1864.	Joseph Caldwell,	C	Killed in the assault and capture of Ft. Gregg, whilst planting the regt'l. colors on the Ft.
Aug. 20, 1862.	David M. Blayney,	D	Promoted to 1st Lieutenant.
Nov. 23, 1863.	James C. Peirson,	D	Promoted to 1st Lieutenant.
Aug. 22, 1862.	James R. Durham,	E	Promoted to 1st Lieutenant.
July 9, 1863.	Asa S. Hugill,	E	Promoted to Captain and transferred to 10th W. Va. Infantry.
Aug. 25, 1862.	Thomas H. Haymond,	F	Resigned February 7, 1863.
March 4, 1863.	John T. Ben Gough,	F	Killed in action at Winchester.
Dec. 1, 1863.	Francis H. Peirpoint, Jr.,	F	
Feb. 13, 1865.	Duncan Cunningham,	F	Promoted to 1st Lieutenant.
May 9, 1865.	Craven Smith,	F	
Aug. 25, 1862.	Elam F. Pigott,	G	
Aug. 20, 1862.	Thomas H. Means,	H	Promoted to 1st Lieutenant.
May 9, 1865.	William D. Martin,	H	
Aug. 27, 1862.	Thomas W. Bradley,	I	Killed in action at Winchester.
Jan. 19, 1864.	Milton B. Campbell,	I	Promoted to 1st Lieutenant.
April 6, 1864.	William Hewett,	I	Promoted to 1st Lieutenant.
Nov. 11, 1864.	Josiah M. Curtis,	I	
April 29, 1863.	John R. Brenneman,	K	Promoted to 1st Lieutenant.
Oct. 28, 1863.	John A. Briggs,	K	

THE TWELFTH WEST VIRGINIA INFANTRY.

The Twelfth West Virginia Infantry was organized August, 1862, with John B. Klunk, colonel; Robert S. Northcott, lieutenant-colonel; and Francis P. Peirpoint, major. Its early service was performed in West Virginia in scouting, guard duty, etc. In January, 1863, we find the regiment at Winchester, in the Middle Department, Eighth Army Corps, General Milroy's division. In March, it is a part of Col. Geo. Hay's brigade, still at Winchester. May 11, it is at Clarksburg in General Roberts' command. June 1, at Grafton; again at Winchester, June 13 to 15, participating in Milroy's disastrous defense of that place, when the regiment lost two officers and six enlisted men killed, one officer and 35 wounded. In this engagement Lieut. James R. Durham, of Co. E, while gallantly leading his company in the fight was severely wounded in the right arm and hand.

On June 30, it was at Bloody Run, in Col. L. B. Pierce's brigade;

July 14, at Hagerstown, in Col. A. T. McReynold's brigade; August 31, at Martinsburg, in General Kelley's department; September 1, 1863, Colonel Klunk resigned. December 10, at Charlestown, in command of Major Curtis; December 31, in General Sullivan's division, Col. Geo. B. Well's brigade; January 26, 1864, Major Curtis promoted to colonel and in command of the regiment at Harper's Ferry. At New Creek, February 1, opposed to Early's and Rosser's advance upon that place. April 1, at Cumberland, in Colonel Thoburn's brigade, Sigel's department; April 15, at Webster and Beverly. May 15, at New Market, in the Shenandoah Valley, in the battle between Sigel and Breckinridge, two killed and fifteen wounded. July 18, at Snicker's Ferry, in Colonel Thoburn's brigade. July 24 and 25, at Kernstown in General Crook's command, Div.-Col. Wm. G. Ely's brigade, two killed, 19 wounded. September 19, at battle of Opequon, Lieutenant-Colonel Northcott commanding brigade. October 19, at battle of Cedar Creek, under General Sheridan, Colonel Curtis commanding brigade, Lieutenant-Colonel Northcott commanding regiment. In March, 1865, several West Virginia regiments were transferred to the Army of the Potomac, and were incorporated in the 24th Army Corps. The 12th Regiment was assigned to the 3d Brigade of that corps, under command of Col. William B. Curtis, of the 12th, as brigade commander.

While the brigade was in camp at New Market, Va., eight miles below Richmond, it received orders on the 27th of March to proceed at once to the left of our lines on Hatcher's Run, to co-operate in a general movement against the enemy. The advance troops struck the enemy's lines at the angle where their works began to retire, and crossed Hatcher's Run, silencing two forts, carrying one of them and the line of works between them by assault. The assault on the 2d of April, upon Forts Whitworth and Gregg, and two or three smaller works, were performed under the immediate observation of General Grant, who in his official report makes mention of the troops engaged. The Third Brigade (Colonel Curtis) captured Fort Whitworth and one or two smaller works, taking a large number of prisoners, whilst the 12th West Virginia Regiment, operating in this brigade, aided in taking Fort Gregg, and distinguished itself for gallantry in the desperate hand-to-hand conflict which the attack on that fort involved. The colors of the 12th West Virginia were the first planted on the works. The gallant color-bearer, Private J. R. Logsdon, of Co. C, was shot dead upon planting the colors there. Several other of the regiment were killed inside the fort, among whom were the gallant Lieut. Joseph Caldwell, of Co. C; Lieut. Josiah M. Curtis, Corporal Andrew Apple, and Private Joseph McCausland, of this regiment; each won from the Government a mark of distinction for their gallantry in this desperate conflict. Maj.-Gen'l John Gibbon, commanding the corps, presented to the regiment a golden eagle for their flagstaff, with the following inscription neatly engraved upon it, viz.: "Presented by Maj.-Gen'l John Gibbon to the 12th W. Va. Volunteer Infantry, for Gallant Conduct in the Assault upon Fort Gregg, April 2, 1865."

The regiment was mustered out of the service at Burksville, Va., June 16, 1865. The regiment lost during the war, killed and died of wounds, three officers and 56 men; died of disease, 131 men. Total 190.

CHAPTER XLI.

THIRTEENTH REGIMENT W. VA. INFANTRY VOLUNTEERS.

Roster of the Field, Staff and Company Officers of the Thirteenth Regiment West Virginia Infantry Volunteers, Showing the Alterations and Casualties therein, from the Date of Original Organization of the Regiment to the Date of Muster Out, June 22, 1865.

Date of Commission.	Names and Rank.	Co.	Remarks.
	Colonel.		
Sep. 16, 1862.	William R. Brown.		
	Lieutenant-Colonels.		
Aug. 20, 1862.	James R. Hall,		Killed in action at Cedar Creek, Va.
Oct. 27, 1864.	Milton Stewart.		
	Majors.		
March 11, 1864.	William P. Rucker,		Resigned November 23, 1864.
Dec. 13, 1864.	Albert F. McCown,		Resigned February 13, 1865.
March 10, 1865.	Lemuel Harpold.		
	1st Lieut. and Adj't.		
July 23, 1862.	William I. Mathews,		Promoted to Captain, Company H.
June 6, 1863.	John S. Cunningham,		Resigned January 10, 1865.
Jan. 20, 1865.	Francis W. Sisson,		
	1st Lieut. and R. Q. M.		
Aug. 20, 1862.	Stephen Comstock.		
	Surgeons.		
Aug. 22, 1862.	Samuel G. Shaw,		Resigned September 29, 1863.
Feb 5, 1864.	Charles D. Dalley.		
	Assistant Surgeons.		
May 6, 1863.	Abraham D. Williams.		Resigned January 31, 1865.
Feb. 8, 1864.	Jacob Lallance.		
	Chaplains.		
March 20, 1864.	William W. Harper,		Resigned March 2, 1865.
April 5, 1865.	Abraham R. Crislip.		
	Captains.		
Sep. 9, 1862.	James W. Johnson,	A	Appointed in U. S. colored troops.
Aug. 14, 1863.	Greenbury Slack,	A	Killed in action at Winchester.
Oct. 30, 1864.	George Danner,	A	
Aug. 25, 1862.	Milton Stewart,	B	Promoted to Lieutenant-Colonel.
Oct. 31, 1864.	William C. Greenlee,	B	
Sep. 12, 1862.	Van D McDaniel,	C	Died at Point Pleasant, W. Va., 1863.
Sep. 25, 1863.	Lemuel Harpold,	C	Promoted to Major.
Feb. 18, 1865.	William M. Hovey,	C	
Sep. 12, 1862.	Simon Williams,	D	Resigned on Surgeon's certificate of disability.
Jan. 20, 1865.	Henry C. Williamson,	D	
Oct. 8, 1862.	John D. Carter,	E	Resigned on Surgeon's certificate of disabiiity.

Date of Commission.	Names and Rank.	Co.	Remarks.
	Captains.		
Oct. 31, 1864.	John H. Rosler,	E	
Oct. 8, 1862.	Albert F. McCown,	F	Promoted to Major.
Dec. 14, 1864.	Timothy Russell,	F	
Jan. 27, 1864.	Allen C. Mason,	G	
Nov. 5, 1862.	Taylor W. Hampton,	H	Resigned March 10, 1863.
April 1, 1863.	William I. Mathews,	H	
Dec. 18, 1863.	William E. Feazel,	I	Resigned Dec. 19, 1864.
Jan. 7, 1865.	Peter Darnel,	I	
Feb. 9, 1864.	Henry Stump,	K	Resigned on certificate of disability.
Oct. 31, 1864.	Joseph E. McCoy,	K	
	First Lieutenants.		
Sep. 9, 1862.	Greenbury Slack,	A	Promoted to Captain.
Aug. 14, 1863.	George Danner,	A	Promoted to Captain.
Oct. 31, 1864.	Samuel S. Mathers,	A	
Sep. 12, 1863.	Lovell C. Rayburn,	B	Died from wounds received at Winchester.
Oct. 31, 1864.	Alfred F. Sullivan,	B	
Sep. 12, 1862.	Lemuel Harpold,	C	Promoted to Captain.
Sep. 25, 1863.	William M. Hovey,	C	Promoted to Captain.
Feb. 18, 1865.	John P. Wood,	C	
Sep. 12, 1862.	James W. Hanna,	D	Discharged on account of physical disability.
Feb. 7, 1865.	Michael Roseberry,	D	
Oct. 8, 1862.	William N. Hawkins,	E	
Oct. 8, 1862.	Timothy Russell,	F	Promoted to Captain.
Dec. 14, 1864.	Joseph Brumley,	F	
Feb. 1, 1864.	John Jones,	G	Discharged by order of War Department.
March 18, 1865.	Edward B. St. John,	G	
Sep. 12, 1862.	Oliver W. Griswold,	H	Taken prisoner and killed while in prison.
April 3, 1864.	William Perdue,	H	Discharged by order of War Department.
March 18, 1865.	Jacob Plybon,	H	
Jan 21, 1863.	William E. Feazel,	I	Promoted to Captain.
Dec. 18, 1863.	Peter Darnel,	I	Promoted to Captain.
Jan. 7, 1865.	William Shannon,	I	
Sep. 30, 1863.	Henry Stump,	K	Promoted to Captain.
Feb. 1, 1864.	Joseph E. McCoy,	K	Promoted to Captain.
Oct. 31, 1864.	Wm. P. Cunningham,	K	
	Second Lieutenants.		
Sep. 9, 1862.	Theophilus Maher,	A	Resigned February 1, 1863.
Feb. 4, 1863.	Samuel S. Mathers,	A	Promoted to 1st Lieutenant.
Oct. 31. 1864.	Robt. H. Davis,	A	
Sep. 12, 1862.	Charles T. Latham,	B	Resigned January 18, 1865.
Feb. 7, 1865.	Robt. O. Boggess,	B	Transferred to Company E.
Oct. 31, 1864.	Silas Morgan,	B	
Sep. 12, 1862.	William E. Feazel,	C	Transferred to Company I.
Sep. 25, 1863.	John P. Wood,	C	Promoted to 1st Lieutenant.
Feb. 18, 1865.	Wm. McDaniel.	C	
Jan. 9, 1863.	George Snowden,	D	Resigned September 18, 1864.

L.M. Strayer

WILLIAM R. BROWN
Colonel 13th West Virginia Infantry

JAMES R. HALL
Lieutenant Colonel 13th West Virginia Infantry
Killed Cedar Creek, Va. October 19, 1864

Date of Commission.	Names and Rank	Co.	Remarks.
	Second Lieutenants.		
Oct. 31, 1864.	Michael Roseberry,	D	Promoted to 1st Lieutenant.
Feb. 7, 1865.	Hezekiah Scott,	D	
Oct. 28, 1862.	John H. Rosler,	E	Promoted to Captain.
Feb. 7, 1865.	Robert O. Boggess,	E	
Oct. 8, 1862.	Joseph Brumley,	F	Promoted to 1st Lieutenant.
Dec. 14, 1864.	Francis W. Sisson,	F	Promoted to 1st Lieutenant and Adjutant.
May 8, 1865.	Joseph Pounds,	F	
Jan. 27, 1864.	Arthur W. Darnell,	G	Discharged on account of physical disability.
March 18, 1865.	Joseph B. Gilpin,	G	
Dec. 5, 1862.	John B. Bumgardner,	H	Resigned December 31, 1862.
Jan. 9, 1863.	William Perdue,	H	Promoted to 1st Lieutenant.
April 8, 1864.	Harvey Dunkle,	H	
Dec. 18, 1863.	Wm. Shannon,	I	Promoted to 1st Lieutenant.
Jan. 7, 1865.	John H. Davis,	I	
Feb. 1, 1864.	Wm. W. Harper,	K	Appointed Chaplain of regiment.
April 29, 1864.	James Wilson,	K	Resigned October 18, 1864.
Oct. 31, 1864.	John M. Young,	K	

THE THIRTEENTH INFANTRY W. VA. VOLUNTEERS.

The Thirteenth Infantry Regiment was organized October, 1862, with the following field officers: William R. Brown, colonel; James R. Hall, lieutenant-colonel. The regiment served in the Kanawha Valley during the first year of the war, mostly doing guard duty and scouting by detachments of companies. In May, 1863, the regiment was placed in the brigade of Col. Rutherford B. Hayes, and continued to serve under Colonel Hayes for about 18 months. During this period the regiment experienced considerable hard service.

In May, 1864, the regiment, 720 men, received orders to march at 8 A. M. the following day. The march was *via* Lewisburg. Crossed the main Alleghanies, June 2; Hot Springs, June 4; skirmished with the enemy at Warm Spring Mountain; at Goshen on the Virginia Central Railroad on the 5th and 6th, the time being devoted to destroying the railroad. June 7, crossed the mountain at Pond Gap; arrived at Staunton June 8, where it joined General Hunter's command. On the 10th, Hunter started on his advance from Staunton; in a skirmish on that day, near the village of Newport, the regiment had several men wounded. June 11, was present at the battle of Lexington; crossed the James River at Buchanan on the 14th; crossed the Blue Ridge on the 15th; arrived at Liberty, county seat of Bedford County, on the 16th; the day was devoted to destroying the Virginia and Tennessee Railroad. June 17, at 10 P. M., the regiment was assigned its place in line of battle for the following day before Lynchburg. June 18, at sunrise, the enemy opened heavily with artillery. During the morning the regiment was deployed to the right of the town; at noon the force was concentrated at the centre; was again deployed in line of battle in front of the brigade at 1 P. M., and slowly advanced under a heavy artillery and musketry fire towards the enemy's works, and remained before the works until 8 P. M., when the regiment was ordered to take position one mile beyond the village of New London. Loss in this engagement six men wounded.

June 20, was at Buford's Gap. Recrossed the Alleghany Mountains in the evening of June 24; at Meadow Bluff, 25; crossed Gauley River, June 28; encamped below Elk River July 1. Distance marched since May 30, 480 miles. Colonel Hayes' brigade, to which this regiment was attached, on this expedition consisted of the 23d Ohio, Lieut.-Col. James M. Comly; 36th Ohio, Col. Hiram F. Devol; 5th West Virginia, Col. Abia A. Tomlinson; 13th West Virginia, Col. Wm. R. Brown. At the battle of Winchester, Va., on July 24 and 25, Col. Hayes' brigade was attached to Duval's division, Eighth Army Corps. The 13th Regiment displayed conspicuous gallantry in this battle. Colonel Hayes in his report of the engagement makes this special mention: "The 13th West Virginia Volunteer Infantry, Colonel Brown, was never in a general engagement before. The officers and men of this regiment, under the circumstances, I deem worthy of special commendation." The regiment lost in this engagement 14 killed, 50 wounded, 15 missing.

January 31, 1864, the regiment was in Col. Abia A. Tomlinson's First Brigade, still in Kelley's division. April 2, 1864, we find the regiment at Cumberland, Md., as part of General Sigel's command. At Cedar Creek, October 19, 1864, the regiment again showed its sticking qualities; Lieut.-Col. James R. Hall was killed in this engagement while gallantly leading his men.

The regiment lost during the war, 4 officers and 57 enlisted men killed in action; died of disease, 1 officer and 107 men. Total 169.

CHAPTER XLII.

FOURTEENTH REGIMENT WEST VIRGINIA INFANTRY VOLUNTEERS.

Roster of the Field, Staff and Company Officers of the Fourteenth Regiment West Virginia Infantry Volunteers, Showing the Alterations and Casualties therein, from the Date of Original Organization of said Regiment to the Date of Muster Out, June 27, 1865.

Date of Commission.	Names and Rank.	Co.	Remarks.
	Colonels.		
Aug. 20, 1862.	Andrew S. Core,		Discharged April 14, 1863, by special order of War Dept.
July 29, 1863.	Daniel D. Johnson.		
	Lieutenant-Colonels.		
Aug. 21, 1862.	Chapman J. Stuart,		Discharged April 14, 1863, by special order of War Dept.
July 20, 1863.	George W. Taggart,		
	Majors.		
Aug. 21, 1862.	Daniel D. Johnson,		Promoted to Colonel.
July 29, 1863.	Shriver Moore.		
	1st Lieut. and Adj'ts.		
Aug. 22, 1862.	Wm. H. Gillespie,		Discharged for the good of the service.
Dec. 14, 1862.	Hunter H. Moss.		
	1st Lieut. and R. Q. M.		
Aug. 20, 1862.	James E. Hooten.		
	Surgeons.		
Aug. 22, 1862.	John W. Moss,		Died of disease at Petersburg, Va.
Feb. 6, 1864.	James H. Manown.		
	Assistant Surgeons.		
Aug. 23, 1862.	Walter S. Welsh,		Promoted to Surgeon 15th W. Va. Infantry.
Nov. 22, 1862.	James L. Gillespie,		Resigned March 12, 1864.
June 5, 1863.	Charles A. Thacker,		Discharged for disability, January 18, 1865.
March 25, 1864.	James H. Brownfield.		
	Chaplain.		
Nov. 1, 1862.	John L. Irwin,		
	Captains.		
Aug. 19, 1862.	Jacob Smith,	A	
Aug. 21, 1862.	Clinton Jeffers,	B	Dismissed March 1, 1864.
April 8, 1864.	John D. Elliott,	B	
Aug. 22, 1862.	Oliver P. Jolliffe,	C	
Aug. 21, 1862.	George W. Taggart,	D	Promoted to Lieutenant-Colonel.
July 29, 1863.	Andrew Mather,	D	Killed in action near Winchester, Va.

Date of Commission.	Names and Rank.	Co.	Remarks.
	Captains.		
Aug. 17, 1864.	James H. Rider,	D	Appointed Capt. and A. A. G., U. S. Vols.
Aug. 25, 1862.	Shriver Moore.	E	Promoted to Major.
Aug. 12, 1863.	Wm. M. Powell,	E	
Sep. 2, 1862.	Elias Y. Satterfield,	F	Resigned Apr. 27, 1863.
May 26, 1863.	Esrom Arnett,	F	Resigned March 6, 1865.
Mar. 3, 1865.	David B. McIlwain,	F	
Sep. 15, 1862.	Jacob M. Reitz,	G	
Aug. 22, 1862.	Henry M. Ice,	H	Resigned February 28, 1865, on account of wounds received in action.
March 8, 1865.	James W. Shroyer,	H	
Sep. 10, 1862.	Elias C. Finnell,	I	
Sep. 16, 1862.	Alfred L. Hoult,	K	
	First Lieutenants.		
Aug. 19, 1862.	Wm. W. Lewis,	A	Died of disease, September 22, 1864.
Aug. 6, 1862.	Wm. P. Greene,	A	Died of wounds received in action at Fisher's Hill, Va.
Dec. 15, 1864.	Elijah L. Wade,	A	
Aug. 21, 1862.	John D. Elliott,	B	Promoted to Captain.
April 8, 1864.	John M. Jeffers,	B	
Aug. 22, 1862.	Granville Brown,	C	Discharged by order of Secretary of War.
Aug. 12, 1863.	George H. Hardman,	C	Killed in action, near Burlington, W. Va.
Nov. 28, 1863.	John W. Bishop,	C	Discharged on account of disability.
Mar. 8, 1865.	Isaac N. Holland,	C	
Aug. 21, 1862.	Andrew Mather,	D	Promoted to Captain.
July 29, 1863.	James H. Rider,	D	Promoted to Captain.
Aug. 26, 1864.	Reuben B. Taylor,	D	
Aug. 25, 1862.	Wm. M. Powell,	E	Promoted to Captain.
Aug. 12, 1863.	Wirt Morris,	E	Resigned March 29, 1864.
Mar. 26, 1864.	John W. Buck,	E	Killed in action at Carter's Farm, Va.
Aug. 6, 1864.	Zenas Martin,	E	
Sep. 2, 1862.	John M. Satterfield,	F	Resigned April 14, 1863.
May 26, 1863.	David B. McIlwain,	F	Promoted to Captain.
Mar. 3, 1865.	Thomas M. Reed,	F	
Sep. 15, 1862.	James W. Shroyer,	G	Promoted to Captain, Company H.
Mar. 8, 1865.	Wm. G. Lowther,	G	
Aug. 22, 1862.	Newton S. Beaty,	H	Dismissed.
Jan. 10, 1865.	George W. Jolliffe,	H	
Aug. 22, 1862.	Uriah Griffith,	I	Died of wounds received in action at Cloyd's Mountain.
Nov. 10, 1864.	James B. Fogle,	I	Dismissed January 10, 1865.
Mar. 3, 1865.	Silas W. Hare,	I	
Sep. 16, 1862.	John A. Wiley,	K	Dismissed by General Order of War Dept.
Aug. 12, 1863.	Cornelius M. Hoult,	K	
	Second Lieutenants.		
Aug. 19, 1862.	Eli Davis,	A	Discharged.
April 1, 1863.	William P. Green,	A	Promoted to 1st Lieutenant.

Date of Commission.	Names and Rank.	Co.	Remarks.
	Second Lieutenants.		
Aug. 6, 1864.	Elijah L. Wade,	A	Promoted to 1st Lieutenant.
Mar. 15, 1865.	Andrew J. Charter,	A	
Aug. 21, 1862.	John M. Jeffers,	B	Promoted to 1st Lieutenant.
Aug. 22, 1862.	Henry Bell,	C	Discharged.
Aug. 12, 1863.	Isaac N. Holland,	C	Promoted to 1st Lieutenant.
Aug. 21, 1862.	James H. Rider,	D	Promoted to 1st Lieutenant.
July 29, 1863.	Edward M. Hoit,	D	Discharged on account of wounds received in action at Cloyd's Mountain, Va.
Feb. 7, 1865.	Lewis Beckwith,	D	
Aug. 25, 1862.	Wirt Morris,	E	Promoted to 1st Lieutenant.
Aug. 12, 1883.	J. B. Williamson,	E	
Sep. 2, 1862.	Esrom Arnett,	F	Promoted to Captain.
May 26, 1863.	Thomas M. Reed,	F	Promoted to 1st Lieutenant.
Sep. 12, 1862.	Philip Sigler,	G	Resigned April 13, 1864.
Aug. 22, 1862.	Cornelius M. Hoult,	H	Promoted to 1st Lieutenant, Co. K.
Aug. 12, 1863.	Robert N. Hess,	H	Killed in action at Fisher's Hill, Va.
Oct. 27, 1864.	George W. Jolliffe,	H	Promoted to 1st Lieutenant.
Mar. 15, 1865.	Isaac N. Martin,	H	
Sep. 10, 1862.	Joseph R. Peck,	I	Resigned December 28, 1862.
Jan. 7, 1863.	Wm. S. Morrison,	I	Died from wounds received in action at Cedar Creek, Va.
Sep. 16, 1862.	John J. Wise,	K	Dismissed by G. O. of War Department.
Aug. 12, 1863.	G. W. Cunningham,	K	Dismissed by G. O. of War Department.
Nov. 29, 1864.	T. W. Boydston,	K	

THE FOURTEENTH W. VA. INFANTRY.

The Fourteenth W. Va. Infantry was organized August, 1862, with the following field officers: Andrew S. Core, colonel; Chapman J. Stuart, lieutenant-colonel, and Daniel D. Johnson, major. The regiment served mainly in West Virginia, in Gen'ls I. H. Duval's and George Crook's divisions, Eighth Army Corps. The regiment was one of West Virginia's busy, fighting regiments, its loss in killed and wounded during the war testifying to the truth of this statement. A few of the principal battles in which it was engaged, were: Burlington, Winchester, Fisher's Hill, Cedar Creek, Carter's Farm, Cloyd's Mountain and others, the officers generally showing good judgment and gallant conduct on the battefield.

Colonel Core, having by request received his discharge, April 14, 1863, Maj. Daniel D. Johnson was promoted to colonel and served gallantly to the close of the war. Lieut.-Col. George W. Taggart, whose portrait accompanies this sketch, was an active officer of the regiment, and in the absence of the colonel, Colonel Taggart was to be found at the head of the regiment, displaying at all times military skill. He was on several occasions complimented in orders by his superior officers.

Many of the company officers performed deeds of heroism that are worthy of record. Capt. Jacob Smith, of Co. A, is deserving a medal for gallantry in the following episode. In the spring of 1863, the captain with his company was ordered to Greenland Gap, W. Va., to reenforce a company of the 23d Illinois Infantry. The two companies were stationed in two log houses at the cut. The Confederate General Jones, with his command, appeared on the scene. He charged the two companies, and was driven back. He charged again and again, but was as often driven away by the well-directed fire of the two companies, with considerable loss. Jones demanded the surrender. The Illenois captain who ran short of ammunition, did surrender, he, being the senior officer, ordered Captain Smith to do likewise. But Captain Smith replied, "I have some ammunition left," and continued to fight. Jones threatened to blow the house to fragments, but Smith was resolute and continued to fight. Under cover of the large chimney, the Confederates approached the house and set it on fire. Still Smith declined to surrender, nor did he until his last cartridge was gone, when the gallant captain and his men left the burning building, now half consumed, stacked arms and gave themselves up as prisoners.

An incident in which the 14th Regiment bore a novel and unenviable part will be read with interest by those who participated. The affair happened near Winchester on the 24th of July, 1864. Colonel Johnson was in command of a brigade, Lieutenant-Colonel Taggart was in command of the regiment. Colonel Johnson's brigade was on the right of the line of battle, the 14th Regiment on the left of the brigade, some distance from the regiment next on its right, in one of those low places so numerous in the valley. When Colonel Taggart was assigned his position in line his orders were to "remain there until ordered away." The battle opened all along the line. The concealed position of the regiment was such that neither Colonel Taggart nor any of his command had observed that the entire line had fallen back nearly two miles. Notwithstanding his positive orders, Colonel Taggart had two things confronting him and he must choose between the capture of his regiment or to fight his way to the rear. The enemy were to the right and the left of him. A thick growth of friendly sycamore bushes that skirted the road on which the Confederate cavalry were then marching, sheltered the regiment from the view of the marching cavalry. So Colonel Taggart waited the opportunity and when a breach in the enemy's column presented itself the order was given, and over two fences, across the road, with one volley that startled the enemy, and the regiment was soon in line with the brigade, well pleased with its escape.

L.M. Strayer

DANIEL D. JOHNSON
Colonel 14th West Virginia Infantry

GEORGE W. TAGGART
Lieutenant Colonel 14th West Virginia Infantry

At Cedar Creek, on the night of August 14, 1864, General Crook ordered Lieutenant-Colonel Taggart, who was in command of the regiment, to move at one o'clock that night, cross the Shenandoah River, and reach Massanutton Mountain before daylight the next morning, to ascend the mountain and establish a signal station on the north point of it. The regiment moved and was under cover of the timber at the foot of the mountain before daylight. Company A, Captain Smith, was sent forward as an advance guard with a citizen as guide. The Captain misunderstood the instructions given him, and moved up the mountain at its north end, where from the summit some distance down there was no timber. The enemy had considerable force at that point; when Captain Smith came within range they fired upon him; the enemy were concealed behind rocks, and the captain was compelled to retire. However, the presence of Captain Smith at this point of the mountain enabled the regiment to pass around and reach the summit of the mountain a mile in the rear of the force that had fired upon Captain Smith, and a mile or more inside Early's lines.

The ascent of the mountain was hazardous; the under brush was so dense that it was with great difficulty a man could get through. The regiment, however, was equal to almost any demands upon it, and it finally reached the mountain top. Lieutenant-Colonel Taggart placed his regiment in a defensive position, and gave it over to Major Moore, while the colonel and the officers of the signal corps were providing for their position, when the Confederates discovered the force in their rear, and quietly made their way to within a short distance of Major Moore's line, and opened fire upon them. Major Moore at once advanced his men, and drove the enemy back to his breastworks of stone across the top of the mountain. There was a still larger force of the enemy lying under cover on a spur of the mountain towards Strasburg, which Major Moore could not see. But, before he went far enough to enable this force to get in his rear, Colonel Taggart, after a short engagement, wisely fell back. The regiment lost two men killed and several wounded. The regiment arrived in camp at 1 o'clock, after a hard march that brought poor returns. The regiment bore a conspicuous part at the battle of Carter's Farm, July 20, 1864, having 20 killed and 52 wounded, and at Cloyd's Mountain, May 9, 1864, where 13 were killed and 62 wounded.

The regiment lost during the war, killed in battle and died of wounds, 7 officers and 81 enlisted men; died of disease and accident, 1 officer and 156 enlisted men. Total deaths 245. The regiment was mustered out of service at Cumberland, Md., June 27, 1865. At the close of the war, Lieutenant-Colonel Taggart was promoted by Pesident Johnson brevet colonel for meritorious conduct in battle during the war.

CHAPTER XLIII.

FIFTEENTH REGIMENT W. VA. INFANTRY VOLUNTEERS.

Roster of the Field, Staff and Company Officers of the Fifteenth Regiment West Virginia Infantry Volunteers, Showing the Alterations and Casualties therein, from the Date of Original Organization of said Regiment to the Date of Muster Out, June 14, 1865.

Date of Commission.	Names and Rank.	Co.	Remarks.
	Colonels.		
Dec. 4, 1862.	Maxwell McCaslin,		Resigned Sept. 7, 1864.
Sep. 22, 1864.	Milton Wells,		Discharged April 6, 1865, on account of disability from wounds received in action.
	Lieutenant-Colonels.		
Sep. 6, 1862.	Maxwell McCaslin,		Promoted to Colonel.
Dec. 4, 1862.	Thomas Morris,		Killed in action at Snicker's Ferry Va.
Aug. 8, 1864.	Milton Wells,		Promoted to Colonel.
Sep. 22, 1864.	John W. Holliday.		
	Majors.		
Sept. 24, 1862.	Thomas Morris,		Promoted to Lieutenant-Colonel.
Oct. 16, 1862.	Milton Wells,		Promoted to Lieutenant-Colonel.
Aug. 8, 1864.	John W. Holliday,		Promoted to Lieutenant-Colonel.
Sep. 22, 1864.	Fenelon Howes.		
	1st Lt. and Adj'ts.		
Sep. 12, 1862.	John W. Holliday,		Promoted to Major.
Sep. 10, 1864.	Albert L. Wells.		
	1st Lts. and R. Q. M.		
	David H. Yant,		Resigned Jan. 10, 1863.
Jan. 29, 1863.	David Jenkins,		Dismissed August 1, 1864.
Sep. 7, 1864.	Philip H. Heermans.		
	Surgeons.		
Sep. 5, 1862.	David L. Starr,		Resigned March 1, 1863.
March 19, 1863.	Walter S. Welsh,		
	Assistant Surgeons.		
Nov. 11, 1862.	Robert G. Dovener,		Resigned Sept. 18, 1863.
Feb. 11, 1864.	James F. Howe,		Resigned Nov. 29, 1864.
Jan. 14, 1863.	James J. Johnson.		
	Chaplain.		
Jan. 24, 1863.	Gideon Martin.		
	Captains.		
Sep. 2, 1862.	James Humes,	A	Dismissed November 21, 1864.
Dec. 14, 1864.	Blackburn B. Dovener,	A	
Sep. 4, 1862.	Michael Eagan,	B	
Aug. 22, 1862.	James Devoir,	C	Discharged on account of physical disability.
Jan. 23, 1864.	John McCaskey,	C	

Date of Commission.	Names and Rank.	Co.	Remarks.
	Captains.		
Sep. 6, 1862.	Jasper Peterson,	D	Resigned October 23, 1863.
Oct. 27, 1863.	William J. Nicoles,	D	
Aug. 22, 1862.	Washington M. Paul,	E	Dismissed July, 1864.
Oct. 3, 1864.	Cornelius Gandy,	E	
Sep. 11, 1862.	Fenelon Howes,	F	Promoted to Major.
Jan. 18, 1865.	Fred. G. W. Ford.	F	
Sep. 18, 1862.	Sidney F. Shaw,	G	
Sep. 29, 1862.	John B. Lukins,	H	Discharged on account of physical disability.
May 8, 1865.	Alexander Frew,	H	
Sep. 19, 1862.	Henry Newman,	I	Discharged on account of physical disability.
Nov. 10, 1864.	Robt. L. Byrnes,	I	
March 17, 1864.	Sylvester Porter,	K	
	First Lieutenants.		
Sep. 2, 1862.	Blackburn B. Dovener,	A	Promoted to Captain.
May 12, 1865.	Edward L. Pratt,	A	
Sep. 4, 1862.	Wm. J. Nicoles,	B	Promoted to Captain Co. D.
Oct. 27, 1863.	John W. Detamore,	B	Discharged on account of physical disability.
Jan. 18, 1865.	Patrick Powers,	B	
Aug. 22, 1862.	John McCaskey,	C	Promoted to Captain.
Jan. 23, 1864.	Eli M. Bell,	C	Discharged on account of physical disability.
Jan. 18, 1865.	John S. McGill,	C	
Sep. 6, 1862.	Edward H. Hall,	D	Died of disease at Cumberland, Md.
Dec. 8, 1862.	William C. Batton,	D	Discharged by order of War Department.
Sep. 4, 1863.	Wm. D. Hoff,	D	
Aug. 22, 1862.	Cornelius Gandy,	E	Promoted to Captain.
Oct. 3, 1864.	A. E. Fortney,	E	Resigned May 31, 1865.
Sep. 11, 1862.	Daniel Boyles,	F	Dismissed February 25, 1864.
June 20, 1864.	Frederick G. W. Ford.	F	Promoted to Captain.
Jan. 18, 1865.	Charles M. Groves,	F	
Sep. 18, 1862.	James J. Fulton,	G	Discharged on account of physical disability.
Nov. 25, 1864.	Thomas P. Butcher,	G	
Sep. 29, 1862.	William L. Schoff,	H	
Sep. 11, 1862.	David E. Flack,	I	Resigned April 3, 1861.
June 6, 1863.	Daniel McGruder,	I	Resigned April 6, 1864.
June 20, 1863.	Robert L. Byrnes,	I	Promoted to Captain.
Nov. 10, 1864.	Thomas G. Nash,	I	
Feb. 23, 1864.	Sylvester Porter,	K	Promoted to Captain.
Mar. 7, 1864.	Robert M. Haveley,	K	Died of wounds received in action at Cloyd's Mountain, Va.
June 20, 1864.	Andrew W. Cotts.	K	Killed in action at Winchester, Va.
Aug. 12, 1864.	James R. Lazear,	K	
	Second Lieutenants.		
Sep. 2, 1862.	David Dawkins,	A	Resigned November 27, 1862.
Dec. 10, 1862.	Sylvester Porter,	A	Promoted to 1st Lieutenant, Co. K.
Sep. 12, 1864.	Harry Hinkley,	A	Dismissed November 22, 1864.
Feb. 7, 1865.	Edward L. Pratt,	A	Promoted to 1st Lieutenant.

Date of Commission.	Names and Rank.	Co.	Remarks.
	Second Lieutenants.		
Sep. 4, 1862.	John W. Detamore,	B	Promoted to 1st Lieutenant.
Oct. 27, 1863.	Patrick Powers,	B	Promoted to 1st Lieutenant.
Aug. 22, 1862.	Eli M. Bell,	C	Promoted to 1st Lieutenant.
Jan. 23, 1864.	John S. McGill,	C	Promoted to 1st Lieutenant.
Jan. 18, 1865.	Salem Grim,	C	
Sep. 6, 1862.	Wm. C. Batton,	D	Promoted to 1st Lieutenant.
Dec. 8, 1862.	Mifflin Cutright,	D	Resigned November 18, 1864.
Dec. 10, 1864.	Amos M. Penninger,	D	
Aug. 22, 1862.	James H. Jackson,	E	Resigned January 25, 1863.
Feb. 4, 1863.	Ashford E. Fortney,	E	Promoted to 1st Lieutenant.
Oct. 3, 1864.	Wm. F. Warthen,	E	
Sep. 11, 1862.	Fred. G. W. Ford,	F	Promoted to 1st Lieutenant.
June 20, 1864.	William G. W. Price,	F	Dishonorably dismissed.
Feb. 7, 1865.	Thomas T. Baker,	F	
Nov. 22, 1862.	Thomas P. Butcher,	G	Promoted to 1st Lieutenant.
Nov. 25, 1864.	Henry C. Scott,	G	
Sep. 29, 1862.	William Leonard,	H	Discharged on account of physical disability.
Jan. 23, 1864.	Thomas L. Higgins,	H	Discharged on account of disability.
Sep. 20, 1862.	Daniel Magruder,	I	Promoted to 1st Lieutenant.
June 6, 1863.	William D. Hoff,	I	Promoted to 1st Lieutenant, Co. D.
Sep. 4, 1863.	Robert L. Byrnes,	I	Promoted to 1st Lieutenant.
June 20, 1865.	Albert L. Wells,	I	Promoted to 1st Lieutenant and Adjutant.
Sep. 10, 1864.	Thomas G. Nash,	I	Promoted to 1st Lieutenant.
Nov. 10, 1864.	Isaac Winters,	I	
Feb. 23, 1864.	Robert M. Haveley,	K	Promoted to 1st Lieutenant.
March 7, 1864.	Jesse Jaco,	K	

THE FIFTEENTH WEST VIRGINIA INFANTRY.

The Fifteenth Infantry was organized September, 1862, with Maxwell McCaslin, colonel; Thomas Morris, lieutenant-colonel; the latter having won his advancement by meritorious conduct as captain in the Seventh West Virginia Infantry. Milton Wells, whose portrait accompanies this sketch, was commissioned major by Governor Peirpoint, October 16, 1862. Major Wells assisted in recruiting this regiment, and like Lieutenant-Colonel Morris, had seen hard service: first as a private of Company D, 27th Ohio Infantry; later was commissioned captain of the same company, serving as such with his regiment in Missouri until August, 1862, when he resigned to accept promotion in the 15th W. Va. Infantry, rendering special service as drill master. This regiment took an active and gallant part in all the battles of the Shenandoah Valley, from the time of its organization until the last battle of Cedar Creek.

MAXWELL McCASLIN
Colonel 15th West Virginia Infantry

MILTON WELLS
Colonel 15th West Virginia Infantry

At the battle of Snicker's Ferry, Va., July 18, 1864, Lieutenant-Colonel Morris was killed, and on August 8, 1864, Major Wells was promoted to lieutenant-colonel. On September 7, 1864, Colonel McCaslin resigned his commission, when Lieutenant-Colonel Wells succeeded to the colonelcy, and was in command of his regiment at the battle of Cedar Creek, October 19, 1864, and he was the first to discover the Confederate forces advancing on that notable morning, and ordered the firing of the first musketry in that engagement. As a result, his command was the only one in that engagement that left dead and wounded soldiers on the parapets. In this engagement, Colonel Wells lost all of his personal baggage, equipments, etc., but in the rally of the afternoon recaptured them, among which was his commission as colonel. It was found in the pocket of a prisoner, covered with mud and dirt, and in that condition it remains at this date, hung in a frame at the colonel's residence in Iowa. During the engagement of the afternoon of this day, Colonel Wells was wounded in the left hip, from which he endures much suffering at the present time. This regiment served mostly in the Eighth Army Corps in West Virginia, in Colonel Thoburn's brigade and division. In the spring of 1864, the brigade in which the 15th W. Va. was attached was transferred to the Army of the Potomac. On this march, Colonel Wells caught cold in his wound, when sciatica was produced and great suffering followed. On April 16, 1864, Colonel Wells was honorably discharged, because of disability produced by this wound.

This regiment served with distinction in the Army of the Potomac, in the 24th Corps, First Brigade, under the command of Brev. Maj.-Gen'l Thomas M. Harris, formerly colonel of the 10th W. Va. Infantry. The regiment was mustered out of the service at Richmond, Va., June 14, 1865, having lost in battle during its term of service three officers and 50 enlisted men; died of disease or accident contracted in the service one officer and 98 enlisted men. Total four officers, 148 enlisted men.

CHAPTER XLIV.

SIXTEENTH REGIMENT WEST VIRGINIA VOLUNTEERS.

Roster of the Field, Staff and Company Officers of the Sixteenth Regiment West Virginia Infantry Volunteers, showing the Alterations and Casualties therein, from the Date of Original Organization of said Regiment to the Date of Muster Out.

Date of Commission.	Names and Rank.	Co.	Remarks.
	Colonel.		
Sep. 25, 1862.	James T. Close.		
	Lieutenant-Colonel.		
Nov. 25, 1862.	Samuel W. Snider.		
	Major.		
Nov. 26, 1862.	Bernard C. Armstrong.		
	1st Lieut. and Adj't.		
Sep. 19, 1862.	A. G. Gaston,		Resigned.
June 6, 1863.	Joseph B. Hamilton.		
	First Lieut. and R.Q.M.		
Sep. 19, 1862.	Ceorge Cassady.		
	Surgeon.		
Nov. 25, 1862.	D. W. Kilmer.		
	Asst. Surgeon.		
Sep. 20, 1862.	William Osman.		
	Captains.		
Sep. 20, 1862.	Frank M. Malone,	A	
Sep. 20, 1862.	Albert C. Widdicombe,	B	
Oct. 17, 1862.	John H. Birrell,	C	
Oct. 17, 1862.	James H. Posey,	D	
Oct. 17, 1862.	Sigmund Elble,	E	
Nov. 3, 1862.	J. H. Behan,	F	
Nov 3, 1862.	Theodore Shaidley,	G	
Nov. 3, 1862.	James S. Beavers,	H	
Nov. 3, 1862.	Robert McIntyre,	I	
Nov. 3, 1862.	John W. Baden,	K	
	First Lieutenants.		
Sep. 20, 1862.	Samuel J. Malone,	A	
Sep. 10, 1862.	Charles F. Howes,	B	
Oct. 17, 1862.	James Morrow,	C	
Oct. 17, 1862.	Joseph Lamont,	D	
Oct. 17, 1862.	John McCormick,	E	
Nov. 3, 1862.	G. R. Robinson,	F	
Nov. 3, 1862.	Joseph Wagner,	G	Resigned March 12, 1863.

Date of Commission.	Names and Rank.	Co.	Remarks.
	First Lieutenants.		
Nov. 3, 1862.	E. R. Longley,	H	
Nov. 3, 1862.	Thomas O'Neill,	I	
Nov. 3, 1862.	Fred. B. Daily,	K	Resigned November 17, 1862.
	Second Lieutenants.		
Sep. 20, 1862.	Wm. H. Poynton,	A	Dismissed Nov. 17, 1862.
Nov. 26, 1862.	George A. Armes,	A	
Sep. 20, 1862.	Ward Bunting,	B	
Oct. 17, 1862.	S. H. Johnson,	C	Not mustered.
Dec. 15, 1862.	Alfred M. Sampson,	C	Resigned February 5, 1863.
March 9, 1863.	Morris M. Snider,	C	
Oct. 17, 1862.	Saml. J. Stinchcombe,	D	Dismissed February 22, 1863.
April 1, 1863.	Oscar F. Green,	D	
Oct. 17, 1862.	James Thompson,	E	Dismissed February 22, 1863.
Nov. 3, 1862.	G. B. Hamilton,	F	
Nov. 3, 1862.	Orin S. Baker,	G	
Nov. 3, 1862.	John L. Kalfuss,	H	
Nov. 3, 1862.	Nathaniel Wilson,	I	
Nov. 3, 1862.	W. C. Burroughs,	K	

THE SIXTEENTH WEST VIRGINIA INFANTRY.

The Sixteenth W. V. Infantry was organized and mustered into service October 25, 1862, with the following field officers: James T. Close, colonel; Samuel W. Snider, lieutenant-colonel; and Bernard C. Armstrong, major. The regiment served in the defenses of Washington during its term of service, in January, 1863, under Brig.-Gen'l R. Cowdin, afterwards in Col. Burr Porter's brigade. In April, 1863, was attached to the brigade of Colonel Tannatt. May 31, 1863, in General De Russy's brigade. The regiment lost during its term, by sickness, seven enlisted men.

CHAPTER XLV.

SEVENTEENTH REGIMENT W. VA. INFANTRY VOLUNTEERS.

Roster of the Field, Staff and Company Officers of the Seventeenth Regiment West Virginia Infantry Volunteers, Showing the Alterations and Casualties therein, from the Date of Original Organization of said Regiment to the Date of Muster Out, June 30, 1865.

Date of Commission.	Names and Rank.	Co.	Remarks.
	Colonel.		
Mar. 13, 1865.	Charles H. Day.		
	Lieutenant-Colonels.		
Sep. 10, 1864.	John S. McDonald,		Honorably discharged.
Mar. 13, 1865.	William T. Head.		
	Majors.		
Sep. 10, 1864.	Charles H. Day,		Promoted to Colonel.
Mar. 13, 1865.	Frank L. Hicks.		
	First Lts. and Adjt's.		
Aug. 13, 1864.	Charles H. Day,		Promoted to Major.
Sep. 13, 1864.	William T. Head,		Promoted to Lieutenant-Colonel.
Mar. 23, 1865.	Benjamin F. Latham.		
	1st. Lieut. and R. Q. M.		
Aug. 17, 1864.	Jacob W. Crane.		
	Surgeon.		
Dec. 15, 1864.	Benoni Parkinson.		
	Assistant Surgeons.		
Sep. 16, 1894.	James H. Ramsey.		
Mar. 29, 1865.	William Stewart.		
	Chaplain.		
Mar. 8, 1865.	Jeremiah L. Simpson.		
	Captains.		
Sep. 6, 1864.	Arthur O. Baker,	A	
Sep. 7, 1864.	Samuel B. Todd,	B	
Sep. 8, 1864.	Nathaniel D. Helmick,	C	
Sep. 9, 1864.	David W. Peden,	D	Resigned March 6, 1865.
Mar. 23, 1865.	Edward S. Rider,	D	
Sep. 9, 1864.	Frank L. Hicks,	E	Promoted to Major.
Mar. 23, 1865.	Alpheus Garrison,	E	
Sep. 10, 1864.	Morris M. Snyder,	F	
Feb. 18, 1865.	Hanson Crisswell,	G	
Feb. 21, 1865.	William D. Logsdon,	H	
Feb. 23, 1865.	Samuel Holt,	I	
Feb 21, 1865.	Scott A. Harter,	K	

Date of Commission	Names and Rank.	Co.	Remarks.
	First Lieutenants.		
Sep. 13, 1864.	Samuel A. Parriott,	A	
Sep. 7, 1864.	Andrew J. Nuzum,	B	
Sep. 8, 1864.	Henry Parkinson,	C	
Sep. 9, 1864.	Edward S. Rider,	D	Promoted to Captain.
Mar. 23, 1865.	Eldridge Carter,	D	
Sep. 9, 1864.	Harvey Staggers,	E	Discharged by order of the Secretary of War.
Sep. 10, 1864.	Thomas E. Davis,	F	
Feb. 21, 1865.	George McC. Jones,	G	
Feb. 21, 1865.	Francis Harris,	H	
Feb. 24, 1865.	Thomas Rogers,	I	
Feb. 21, 1865.	Welcome Lee Farnum,	K	
	Second Lieutenants.		
Sep. 13, 1864.	George W. Griffith,	A	
Sep. 7, 1864.	Benjamin F. Latham,	B	Promoted to Lieutenant and Adjutant.
Mar. 23, 1865.	John C. Kuh,	B	
Sep. 8, 1864.	Antony Raffo,	C	
Sep. 9, 1864.	A. H. McTaggart,	D	Resigned March 6, 1865.
Mar. 23, 1865.	John O. M'Gowan,	D	
Sep. 9, 1864.	Alpheus Garrison,	E	Promoted to Captain.
Sep. 10, 1864.	Hosea Matheny,	F	
Feb. 21, 1865.	Andrew J. Vickers,	G	
Feb. 21, 1865.	John W. Perry,	H	
Feb. 23, 1865.	Moses Tichnell,	I	
Feb. 26, 1865.	John Forman,	K	

THE SEVENTEENTH WEST VIRGINIA INFANTRY.

The 17th Infantry Regiment was organized in September, 1864. It remained in General Kelley's department during its term of enlistment. The regiment lost by disease and wounds 25 enlisted men.

CHAPTER XLVI.

FIRST REGIMENT W. VA. VETERAN INFANTRY VOLUNTEERS.

Roster of the Field, Staff and Company Officers of the First Regiment West Virginia *Veteran* Infantry Volunteers, formed by Consolidation of the 5th and 9th Regiments W. Va, Infantry, Showing the Alterations and Casualties in said Regiment, from November 8, 1864, Date of said Consolidation, to the Date of Muster Out, July 21, 1865.

Date of Commission.	Names and Rank.	Co.	Remarks.
	Colonels.		
Sep. 9, 1862.	Isaac Harden Duval,		Promoted to Brigadier-General.
Dec. 19, 1864.	William H. Enochs.		
	Lieutenant-Colonels.		
Aug. 17, 1863.	William H. Enochs,		Promoted to Colonel.
Jan. 4, 1865.	John S. P. Carroll.		
	Majors.		
Nov. 8, 1864.	John S. P. Carroll,		Promoted to Lieutenant-Colonel.
Jan. 4, 1865.	James P. Waymer,		
	1st Lieut. and Adj't.		
Nov. 1, 1864.	Francis L. Hersey.		
	1st Lieut. and R. Q. M.		
Nov. 1, 1864.	Hardin Kuhn,		Transferred to Company I, June 25, 1865.
Nov. 1, 1864.	John C. Bishop,		Transferred from Company I.
	Surgeon.		
Nov. 1, 1864.	James H. Hysell,		
	Assistant Surgeon.		
March 3, 1865.	Richard L. Meers.		
	Chaplain.		
Nov. 14, 1864.	Joseph Little.		
	Captains.		
Aug. 15, 1863.	Mark Poore,	A	
Feb. 1, 1864.	Oliver Phelps,	B	
Nov. 1, 1864.	Stephen C. Hiltbruner,	C	Resigned March 10, 1865.
March 29, 1865.	William A. Zeigler,	C	
Nov. 1, 1864.	Carey B. Hayslip,	D	Resigned March 10, 1865.
March 29, 1865.	Cornelius M. Conley,	D	
Aug. 17, 1863.	Hamilton Willis,	E	
Nov. 1, 1864.	Jacob May,	F	
Sep. 1, 1863.	James P. Waymer,	G	
Jan. 4, 1865.	William F. Elswick,	G	
Nov. 1, 1863.	John W. Johnson,	H	
Nov. 1, 1863.	Robert Laughlin,	I	
Dec. 12, 1864.	Henry C. Duncan,	K	
	First Lieutenants.		
March 26, 1864.	Francis L. Hersey,	A	Appointed Adjutant.

L.M. Strayer

BENJAMIN D. BOSWELL
Major 2nd West Virginia Veteran Infantry
Formerly Captain 4th West Virginia Infantry

L.M. Strayer

JOHN N. DEAN
First Lieutenant 2nd West Virginia Veteran Infantry
Formerly Second Lieutenant 4th West Virginia Infantry

Date of Commission.	Names and Rank.	Co.	Remarks.
	First Lieutenants.		
Nov. 1, 1864.	John Q. Hagerman,	A	
Dec. 12, 1864.	Cyrus Patridge,	B	
Jan. 10, 1863.	George W. Jenkins,	C	Died at Portland, Ohio.
Nov. 1, 1864.	Silman Andre,	D	Transferred to Company **F.**
Dec. 19, 1864.	Samuel T. Riggs,	D	Resigned July 7, 1865.
Sep. 5, 1864.	Alfred O. Enochs,	E	
Nov. 1, 1864.	Silman Andre,	F	
Sep. 5, 1864.	William F. Elwick,	G	Promoted to Captain.
Sep. 5, 1864.	William A. Zeigler,	G	Promoted to Captain, Company **C.**
Mar. 29, 1865.	Charles O. Phelps,	G	
Dec. 14, 1864.	Cornelius M. Conley,	H	Promoted to Captain, Company **D.**
Mar. 29, 1865.	David A. Johnston,	H	
Nov. 1, 1864.	John C. Bishop,	I	Appointed R. Q. M.
Nov. 1, 1864.	Hardin Kuhn,	I	
Sep. 5, 1864.	William A. Zeigler,	K	Transferred to Company **G.**
Jan. 4, 1865.	Andrew J. Johnson,	K	
	Second Lieutenants.		
Sep. 5, 1664.	George F. Jarrell,	A	Transferred to Company **G.**
Nov. 1, 1864.	James T. Hailey,	A	Transferred to Company **K.**
Jan. 4, 1865.	Columbus Enochs,	A	
Dec. 12, 1864	Vinin D. Gardner,	B	
Dec. 19, 1864.	Anthony O. Stiverson,	C	
Nov. 1, 1864.	David A. Johnson,	D	Promoted to 1st Lieutenant, Company **H.**
March 29, 1865.	Lorenzo D. Markin,	D	
Dec. 12, 2864.	Vinin D. Gardner,	E	Transferred to Company B.
Feb. 16, 1865.	George Wills,	E	
Nov. 1, 1864.	Charles O. Phelps,	F	Promoted to 1st Lieutenant, Company **G.**
Sep. 5, 1864.	George F. Jarrell,	F	
Sep. 5, 1864.	George F. Jarrell,	G	Transferred to Company **F.**
March 29, 1865.	John M. Truman,	G	
Sep. 5, 1864.	John Zimmerman,	H	
Nov. 1, 1864.	Lawrence Leppert,	I	
Sep. 1, 1864.	Andrew J. Johnson,	K	Promoted to 1st Lieutenant.
Nov. 1, 1864.	James T. Hailey,	K	

THE FIRST REGIMENT WEST VIRGINIA VETERAN INFANTRY.

The First Regiment West Virginia *Veteran* Infantry was formed by the consolidation of the Fifth and Ninth W. Va. Infantry Regiments, November 9, 1864, Col. Isaac H. Duval, of the Ninth, becoming colonel of the consolidated regiments. Colonel Duval was soon after promoted to brigadier-general, when, on the 19th of December, 1864, Lieut.-Col. William H. Enochs succeeded to the colonelcy. The regiment was assigned to the

First Brigade, commanded by Col. Rutherford B. Hayes; Second Division, General I. H. Duval commanding; and in the Department of West Virginia, Gen'l Geo. H. Crook, commander. The regiment was on duty the principal portion of its term of service in the Shenandoah Valley, and at Staunton, Virginia. Its losses were: died of wounds and disease, 40 men. It was mustered out of service July 21, 1865.

CHAPTER XLVII.

SECOND REGIMENT WEST VIRGINIA VETERAN INFANTRY.

Roster of the Field, Staff and Company Officers of the Second Regiment West Virginia *Veteran* Infantry Volunteers, formed by Consolidation of 1st and 4th Regiments W. Va. Infantry, Showing the Alterations and Casualties therein, from the 10th day of December, 1864, Date of Consolidation to the Date of Muster Out, July 16, 1865.

Date of Commission.	Names and Rank.	Co.	Remarks.
	Lieutenant-Colonel.		
Dec. 4, 1862.	Jacob Weddle.		
	Major.		
Dec. 23, 1864.	Benjamin D. Boswell.		
	1st Lieut. and Adj't.		
Sep. 23, 1862.	Henry J. Johnson.		
	1st Lieut. and R. Q. M.		
Nov. 15, 1863.	Lucian Gray.		Promoted to Captain, Company I.
	Surgeon.		
Dec. 23, 1864.	John English.		
	Assistant Surgeon.		
Jan. 4, 1895.	Homer C. Waterman.		
	Captains.		
March 19, 1863	Benjamin D. Boswell,	A	Promoted to Major.
Jan. 31, 1865.	James W. Dale,	A	
May 19, 1863.	Barlow W. Curtis,	B	
Aug. 17, 1863.	William Grayum,	C	
Nov. 15, 1864.	John W. Plattenburg,	D	
Nov. 17, 1864.	Richard S. Moore,	E	
Nov. 25, 1864.	William S. Murphy,	F	
Nov. 25, 1864.	Clarence E. Irwin,	G	
March 13, 1865.	Jacob Baltzell,	H	
April 6, 1865.	Lucian Gray.	I	
	First Lieutenants.		
March 19, 1863.	James W. Dale,	A	Promoted to Captain.
Jan. 20, 1865.	Wm. R. Malone,	A	Resigned April 12, 1865.
April 26, 1865:	Albert J. Hazleton,	A	
Dec. 31, 1862.	Wm. L. McMasters,	B	Mustered out January 10, 1865.
Jan. 31, 1865.	John N. Dean,	B	
Aug. 17, 1862.	Calvin L. Lightburn,	C	
Nov. 25, 1864.	Wm. H. Melvin,	D	
Nov. 15, 1864.	Wm. H. Chapman,	E	Acting R. Q. M.
Nov. 15, 1864.	Lucian Gray,	F	Appointed R. Q. M.

Date of Commission.	Names and Rank.	Co.	Remarks.
	First Lieutenants.		
April 20, 1865.	John N. McCarty,	F	
Nov. 26, 1864.	Peter Ripley,	G	
Nov. 25, 1864.	Jacob Baltzell,	H	Promoted to Captain.
April 17, 1865.	Wm. B. Ebbert,	H	
Mar. 13, 1865.	Gilbert L. Holmes,	I	
	Second Lieutenants.		
Dec. 31, 1862.	Wm. R. Malone,	A	Promoted to 1st Lieutenant.
Jan. 31, 1865.	Albert J. Hazelton,	A	Promoted to 1st Lieutenant.
April 26, 1865.	James V. Davis,	A	
Aug. 17, 1863.	John McDonald,	B	Transfered to Co. H., Jan. 5, 1865.
Aug. 17, 1863.	John N. Dean,	B	Promoted to 1st Lieutenant.
Jan. 10, 1865.	Allen Bloomfield,	B	Discharged on account of disability.
Mar. 29, 1865.	Easom Greenlee,	B	
Oct. 3, 1864.	James M. Hodge,	C	Resigned April 12, 1865.
April 26, 1865.	Samuel Rarden,	C	
Dec. 18, 1864.	Wm. J. Mulbey,	D	Dismissed May 21, 1865.
April 6, 1865.	T. H. S. Carmack,	D	
Dec. 18, 1864.	Upton Sutherland,	E	
Dec. 18, 1864.	John N. McCarty,	F	Promoted to 1st Lieutenant.
April 25, 1865.	Egbert P. Shetter,	F	
Dec. 16, 1864.	Samuel Mellon,	G	Cashiered, March 31, 1865.
April 6, 1864.	Philip A. Bier,	G	
Aug. 18, 1863.	John N. Dean,	H	Transferred to Co. B.
Aug. 18, 1863.	John McDonald,	H	Discharged on account of disability.
April 19, 1865.	Ralph Raffle,	H	
March 15, 1865.	John C. Hatley,	I	

THE SECOND REGIMENT WEST VIRGINIA VETERAN INFANTRY.

The Second Regiment, West Virginia *Veteran* Infantry was formed by the consolidation, on the 10th day of December, 1864, of the First and Fourth W. Va. Infantry Regiments, Lieut.-Col. Jacob Weddle, of the First Regiment becoming the commanding officer. The regiment served in General Kelley's command until the close of the war. The regiment's losses from wounds and disease, were 17. It was mustered out July 16, 1865.

CHAPTER XLVIII.

FIRST REGIMENT W. VA. LIGHT ARTILLERY VOLUNTEERS.

Roster of Commissioned Officers of the First Regiment West Virginia Light Artillery Volunteers, Showing the Alterations and Casualties therein, from the Date of Original Organization of the Companies Composing Said Regiment to the Date of their Muster Out, Respectively.

Date of Commission.	Names and Rank.	Co.	Remarks.
	Captains.		
Sep. 26, 1861.	Philip Daum,	A	Promoted to Lieutenant-Colonel.
July 10, 1862.	John Jenk,	A	Dismissed March 9, 1863.
Sep. 3, 1863.	George Furst,	A	
Oct. 16, 1861.	Samuel Davey,	B	Resigned April 1st 1862.
April 2, 1862.	Ernest M. Rossefy,	B	Never reported to company for duty.
Oct. 28, 1862.	John V. Keeper,	B	
Jan. 25, 1862.	Frank Buell,	C	Died from wounds received in action at Freeman's Ford, Va.
Oct. 16, 1862.	Wallace Hill,	C	
Aug. 19, 1862.	John Carlin,	D	
Oct. 2, 1862.	Alexander C. Moore,	E	
Oct. 3, 1861.	Thomas A. Maulsby,	F	Honorably discharged on account of wounds received in action at Martinsburg, W. Va.
Oct. 24, 1863.	George W. Graham,	F	
Aug. 2, 1861.	Chatham T. Ewing,	G	
Sep. 24, 1863.	James H. Holmes,	H	Discharged March 17, 1865.
	First Lieutenants.		
Sep. 26, 1861.	John Jenk,	A	Promoted to Captain.
Dec. 31, 1861.	William Derose,	A	Resigned January 6, 1862.
July 10, 1862.	William Weitzel,	A	Resigned January 14, 1863.
Jan. 24, 1862.	Christian Schwarz,	A	Dismissed March 9, 1863.
April 1, 1863.	George Furst,	A	Promoted to Captain.
Oct. 24, 1863.	Frederick Hoffman,	A	
Sep. 4, 1863.	Madison Carter,	A	Mustered out by G. O. War Department.
Sep. 28, 1861.	Samuel Davey,	B	Promoted to Captain.
Oct. 16, 1861.	John V. Keeper,	B	Promoted to Captain.
Nov. 8, 1861.	James M. Shipton,	B	Resigned January 14, 1862.
May 14, 1862.	P. C Pendleton,	B	Muster revoked October 28, 1862.
Sep. 20, 1862.	B. H. H. Atkinson,	B	Transferred to Battery E.
Jan. 25, 1862.	Dennis O'Leary,	C	
Jan. 25, 1862.	Wallace Hill,	C	Promoted to Captain.
Oct. 16, 1862.	John G. Theis,	C	Mustered out at expiration of term of service.
May 2, 1865.	John W. Jacobs,	C	
Aug. 19, 1862.	Ephraim Chalfant,	D	
Sep. 5, 1862.	Charles C. Theaker,	D	Dismissed February 25, 1864.

Date of Commission.	Names and Rank.	Co.	Remarks.
	First Lieutenants.		
March 26, 1864	J. Melvin Richards,	D	
Sep. 18, 1862.	George W. Burner,	E	Discharged on account of physical disability.
Oct. 17, 1862.	Francis M. Lowry,	E	Died at Clarksburg, W. Va., Feb. 28, 1865.
Sep. 20, 1862.	B. H. H. Atkinson,	E	
March 10, 1865.	John T. Latham,	E	
Jan. 7, 1863.	George W. Graham,	F	Promoted to Captain.
March 20, 1862.	John S. S. Herr,	F	Resigned September 13, 1863.
Sep. 4, 1863.	Madison Carter,	F	Transfered to Battery A.
Jan. 11, 1862.	Howard Morton,	G	
Aug. 11, 1863.	James H. Holmes,	H	Promoted to Captain.
Sep. 24, 1863.	George W. K. Smith,	H	Mustered out at expiration of term of service.
July 7, 1864.	John E. Morgan,	H	
Aug. 25, 1864.	George W. Burnett,	H	
	Second Lieutenants.		
Sep. 26, 1861.	William Derose,	A	Promoted to 1st Lieutenant.
Dec. 31, 1861.	Lewis Foerch,	A	Resigned April 26, 1862.
Dec. 31, 1861.	Christian Schwarz,	A	Promoted to 1st Lieutenant.
Jan. 24, 1862.	William Weitzel,	A	Promoted to 1st Lieutenant.
July 10, 1862.	Max Seivers,	A	Dismissed October 9, 1863.
July 10, 1862.	William Weissman,	A	Dismissed.
Sep. 30, 1863.	Frederick Hoffman,	A	Promoted to 1st Lieutenant.
Oct. 24, 1863.	Christian Koenig,	A	Resigned January 3, 1865.
Nov. 19, 1864.	James N. Gray,	A	
Nov. 8, 1861.	Alexander Brawley,	B	Resigned May 9, 1862.
Nov. 8, 1861.	Benjamin F. Thomas,	B	Resigned February 5, 1863.
March 18, 1863.	M. A. McLaughlin,	B	Mustered out at expiration of term of service.
July 10, 1862.	Joseph W. Daniel,	B	Killed in action at Droop Mountain.
July 10, 1862.	B. H. H. Atkinson,	B	Promoted to 1st Lieutenant.
Jan. 25, 1862.	John G. Theis,	C	Promoted to 1st Lieutenant.
Jan. 25, 1862.	William W. Withrow,	C	Resigned December 28, 1862.
Oct. 16, 1862.	Henry M. Langley,	C	Resigned April 22, 1863.
Jan. 12, 1863.	Wesley R. J. Miner,	C	Resigned April 4, 1863.
Dec. 1, 1863.	John W. Jacobs,	C	Promoted to 1st Lieutenant.
Dec. 1, 1863.	Theodore G. Field,	C	Mustered out at expiration of term of service.
Sep. 5, 1862.	Thomas Harris, Jr.,	D	
Aug. 19, 1862.	J. Melvin Richards,	D	Promoted to 1st Lieutenant.
March 26, 1864.	John L. Morrison,	D	
Sep. 18, 1862.	John T. Latham,	E	Promoted to 1st Lieutenant.
Oct. 17, 1862.	Mandaville J. Fogg,	E	Dismissed September 10, 1864.
Oct. 7, 1864.	Wm. A. McNulty,	E	
March 10, 1865.	Samuel A. Rapp,	E	
Jan. 7, 1863.	James C. Means,	F	Dismissed July 29, 1864.
May 28, 1862.	Samuel J. Shearer,	G	
Sep. 24, 1863.	Sigmond Gnam,	H	Mustered out at expiration of term of service.
July 7, 1864.	James B. Gorrell,	H	
Aug. 29, 1864.	John B. McNally,	H	Discharged March 16, 1865.

THE FIRST WEST VIRGINIA LIGHT ARTILLERY.

The First West Virginia Light Artillery was composed of eight companies. And, like the cavalry and infantry arms of the service from the State, proved themselves not only efficient in battle, but they were active, busy, conscientious soldiers in any capacity or place.

BATTERY A.

Battery A was organized and mustered into the service September 26, 1861, with Philip Daum, captain; John Jenk, first lieutenant and William Derose, second lieutenant.

But as early as July 3d, we find Daum with a section of his battery at Wheeling, W. Va. On the 20th of July this section was at Oakland and New Creek. October 4th, the battery was engaged at the battle of Greenbrier River and Elkwater, near Alleghany Mountains. October 28th, the battery was at Romney, Va. About February 1st, 1862, Captain Daum was promoted to lieutenant-colonel of the First W. Va. Light Artillery Regiment, and was made chief of artillery. Lieutenant Jenk was made Captain of Company A, March, 1862. The battery bore a gallant part at the battle of Kernstown, Va., March 23, 1862. January 13, 1863, the battery, Captain Jenk in command, was in Camp of Instruction under Gen'l Wm. F. Barry, near Washington, D. C.

March 9, 1863, Captain Jenk was dismissed the service. The battery remained in Camp of Instruction until September, 1863, when Lieut. George Furst was promoted to captain. December, 1863, the battery was again in the field, in Col. Geo. D. Wells' Brigade, Sullivan's Division, Kelley's Department. May 31, 1864, the battery was at Maryland Heights, where it remained on duty until October 17, 1864, when it was transferred from Harper's Ferry to Parkersburg, W.Va., thence to Charleston, when Captain Furst was ordered to report to Col. J. H. Oley, commanding 1st Separate Brigade. The battery remained in the Kanawha Valley until it was mustered out July 21, 1865.

BATTERY B.

Battery B was organized October, 1861, with Samuel Davey, captain; John V. Keeper, first lieutenant. Captain Davey resigned April 1, 1862, when Lieutenant Keeper was promoted to captain; at this time the battery was in Banks' 5th Army Corps, Shield's division. The battery was conspicuous for its good work at the battle of Kernstown, March 23, 1862.

January 31, 1863, it is found in the 8th Army Corps under General Schenck, and in Milroy's brigade, stationed at Winchester, Va. May 31,

1863, the battery was assigned to General Averell's command, remaining with that general for several months, participating in all of Averell's raids in the mountains of West Virginia. April 9, 1864, attached to Colonel Moor's brigade at Beverly. April 28th, at Webster.

June 10, 1864. One section, under Lieutenant Atkinson, on Hunter's Lynchburg campaign, under General Duffie. The battery was at Kernstown, July 23, 1864, in General Duffie's command. October 19, 1864, General Duffie in his farewell order to his command complimented the battery for splendid service rendered. October 20, 1864, assigned to Colonel Wynkoop's brigade.

December 31, 1864, this battery was consolidated with Battery E, Capt. Alexander C. Moore, the battery retaining the latter organization.

BATTERY C—(PEIRPOINT BATTERY).

Battery C (Peirpoint battery) was organized January 25, 1862, with Frank Buell, captain, and Dennis O'Leary and Wallace Hill, as first lieutenants. These officers were well fitted for the service. The two first named, Buell and O'Leary, having had service from the beginning of the war, in the 18th Ohio (three months' troops), they were both commissioned by Governor Peirpoint on the 19th of September, 1861, as captain and lieutenant respectively, as recruiting officers, when they went to Charleston to recruit the battery, where they remained until its enlistment was completed.

In April, 1862, the battery was ordered to Wheeling Island, where they were furnished with a full battery of six Parrot guns. Left Wheeling, May 2, 1862, for Franklin, Va., to join General Fremont's army; went with that general to Petersburg, Strasburg, Woodstock, Mount Jackson and New Market, having participated in harrassing Stonewall's Jackson's retreat up the valley at that time. On the 8th of June, 1862, was hotly engaged at the battle of Cross Keys, was under fire from half past eleven A. M. until half past four P. M. In this engagement the battery received a terrific charge by the enemy, and had it not been for the timely advance of the "Pennsylvania Bucktails" who gallantly drove back the advancing Confederates saved the battery from capture.

Following that battle the battery was engaged with Sigel and Pope, was in the battles of Port Republic, Luray, Cedar Mountain and Freeman's Ford. At this last engagement, August 22, 1862, the battery met with an irreparable loss—the brave Captain Buell was killed.

Two batteries had been driven by the Confederate guns from their position when Buell's battery was ordered to replace those which had been

L.M. Strayer

FRANK BUELL
Captain Battery C 1st West Virginia Light Artillery
Fatally Injured Freeman's Ford, Va. August 22, 1862

L.M. Strayer

WALLACE HILL
Captain Battery C 1st West Virginia Light Artillery

driven from their position. So rapidly and accurately did Buell handle his pieces that one of the enemy's batteries was silenced and the other disabled. The second last shot fired by the Confederates was a solid shot which struck Captain Buell's horse in the right shoulder killing the horse instantly, the animal falling upon the captain and crushing him so seriously that he died that evening. The last words spoken by Captain Buell were, "I want those batteries silenced, I want my boys to do it."

Captain Buell's remains were embalmed in Alexandria, Va., and sent to his old home where they were buried in the family lot on his farm. The members of his battery erected over the remains a handsome marble shaft.

The battery under Captain Hill, a brave and intelligent officer, who was soon promoted, fought in the battles of Sulphur Springs, Waterloo Bridge, and at the second battle of Bull Run. Lieutenant O'Leary at this time was on detached service as A. A. D. M. of reserve artillery, Army of the Potomac.

May 2, 1863, the battery was in that terrible two days' hard fighting at Chancellorsville, Va. The battery was served by Captain Hill and Lieutenants O'Leary and Theis; the battery was opposed by Stonewall Jackson's command, and after a severe struggle the battery was forced to retire, having lost one gun and two caissons. After a short rest the battery was again on the move, and we find it at Gettysburg, July 2 and 3, 1863. The battery had position on Cemetery Hill, the right resting on the cemetery and the left near the stone wall by the Jamestown road. The battery being the very center of that great battlefield, it was exposed to a front fire and a right and left enfilading fire as well. The battery did its part well, officers and men standing to their guns during the two days' fighting. After the battle of Gettysburg, the battery recrossed the Potomac into Virginia. The next and last battle in which the battery was engaged, was at Mitchell's Ford, when the Union arms were successful. During the winter of 1863–64, the battery reenlisted, and was ordered into the defenses of Washington, where it remained until June 28, 1865, when it was mustered out of service. The battery did its duty well.

BATTERY D.

Battery D was organized August 19, 1862, with John Carlin, captain; Ephraim Chalfant, first lieutenant, and J. Melvin Richards, second lieutenant. Having served in West Virginia, in May 9, 1863, it is stationed at Winchester, Va.; in January 1863, in Schenck's Eighth Army Corps, Milroy's brigade, at Winchester, and during the historical defense of that place by Milroy, June 13 to 15, when it rendered conspicuous service. Following is the official report of Captain Carlin of the operations of the battery in that engagement:

WASHINGTON, D. C., *July* 24, 1863.

I certify that I am in command of Battery D, First West Virginia Light Artillery, composed of six 3-inch rifled guns, and have been under the command of Major-General Milroy since October, 1862; was with his command at the battle of Winchester, on June 13 and 14; had at the commencement of the engagement about 300 rounds of ammunition per gun; fired during the two days' fighting about 265 rounds of ammunition per gun of different kinds. I had left in the chests when the action ceased on Sunday night, about 35 rounds per gun. I was ordered by Major-General Milroy, through Brigadier-General Elliott, on Monday morning, about 2 o'clock, to spike my guns, destroy what ammunition was on hand, cut up the harness, and take nothing away but the saddles and bridles, and the horses, with the men mounted on them; which order I complied with. Had I been allowed to do so, I could have taken my guns and equipment out when the order was given to evacuate, and, in my opinion, could have rendered good service in covering the retreat and engaging the battery of the enemy that made the attack upon General Milroy's forces on the Martinsburg Road, four miles from Winchester, Va., on the morning of July 15.

JOHN CARLIN,
Captain Co. D, 1st W. Va. L. A.

August 18, Captain Carlin and battery are at Wheeling, W. Va.; August 31, 1863, in Mulligan's brigade at New Creek; December 31, 1863, in Thoburn's brigade at New Creek; January and February at New Creek; April 4, 1864, still in Thoburn's brigade, Sigel's department; April 9, 1864, by order of General Sigel the battery was assigned to the command of General Sullivan; also on the same date Captain Carlin was assigned to the staff of Major-General Sigel as chief of artillery, and acting chief of ordnance. May 15, 1864, in Colonel Wynkoop's brigade at New Market August 5, at Piedmont, under General Hunter; June 10 to 23, in Capt. H. A. Dupont's artillery brigade, on Hunter's Lynchburg campaign. July 31, still with General Hunter. August 8, battery ordered from Parkersburg and Wheeling to recruit its numbers and to refit with new guns. September 13, 1864, Captain Carlin received orders at Wheeling to proceed with his command to Parkersburg, and take charge of fortifications at that post; to report to Colonel Wilkinson, where it remained until mustered out, June 27, 1865.

BATTERY E.

Battery E was organized by Capt. Alexander C. Moore, at Buckhannan, West Virginia, in August, 1862; who was commissioned captain of the battery September 23, 1862. Captain Moore was one of West Virginia's loyal sons who was among the first in the State to illustrate his loyalty to the government by the most practical methods then known; his early enlistment in the army, from the earlest moment of the Secession agitation in the South, Captain Moore was in line, defending the Constitution of the nation in eloquent pleadings upon the rostrum in the cities and towns throughout the counties of Harrison, Taylor, Lewis, Upshur, etc., and when recruits were called for, he enlisted company G, for the 3d West Virginia Infantry. Having commanded this company for one year in its active operations in the State, Captain Moore was well prepared to take charge of this new field of usefulness as an officer of Artillery. He had little trouble, and spent little time in recruiting his company E, among his neighbors and friends who knew him best at Buckhannan and adjoining counties. And even before he had instilled the first lessons of the Artillery school into his company, and before they had been mustered into service he was called upon to defend the town against the advance of the Confederate General Jenkins. Immediately upon the completion of the enlistment of his company, he was ordered to Wheeling, and there was fully equipped. Then the battery was ordered to Clarksburg, and in turn to New Creek and Romney. At the latter place, the battery became, in 1863, a part of Campbell's Fourth Brigade, First Division, Eighth Army Corps, serving with this brigade in the South Branch Valley, at Romney, Moorefield and vicinity, and with General Kelley in his campaign in the summer of 1863, to Cherry Run, Williamsport and Hedgesville on Lee's retreat from Gettysburg, returning with the brigade to the South Branch Valley, serving in that locality until the summer of 1864.

Upon General Hunter's return from Lynchburg, the battery was ordered to join the Army of West Virginia, and accompanied it to the Shenandoah Valley, taking part in the engagements with the enemy at Snicker's Ferry, Cedar Creek, Kernstown, Bunker Hill and Berryville. At this time the battery was attached to the Artillery Brigade of the Army of West Virginia; was then in the fall of 1864, ordered to Maryland Heights, where it remained until January 1865, when the battery was ordered to the Artillery Camp at Camp Barry near Washington, D. C., and remained there until the close of the war.

While at Maryland Heights, Battery B was consolidated with Battery E, by order of the War Department, the consolidated battery remaining Battery E, under the command of Captain Moore. Lieut. B. H. H. Atkinson and 55 men was the transfer from B. to E. While at Camp Barry, D. C., President Lincoln was assassinated, and a detail from the battery of Lieut. Samuel A. Rapp and 30 men constituted a portion of the escort as the " Guard of Honor " accompanying the remains of Mr. Lincoln from the White House to the Capitol. At the close of the war, President Johnson conferred upon Captain Moore the rank of brevet major " for faithful and meritorious services during the war."

Battery E was a good battery, composed of the intelligent, patriotic young men from the counties of Upshur, Harrison and Randolph. Officers and enlisted men were proud of each other, and there was no jealousy or bickering from the beginning to the end. Major Moore was a distinguished attorney at law when the war came, and his legal ability was occasionally during the war brought into service as the judge advocate of important courts-martial. The battery was mustered out of the service, June 28, 1865.

BATTERY F.

Battery F was originally Company C, Sixth West Virginia Infantry and was constituted, by order of the War Department, Company F, First West Virginia Light Artillery, about January 1, 1863, Capt. Thomas A. Maulsby retaining his rank in the transfer, as did also First Lieut. George W. Graham, and Second Lient. James C. Means. The battery proved to be as efficient as artillery as it had been as infantry.

The battery's first service, January 31, 1863, was in Col. B. F. Smith's brigade, stationed at Martinsburg, with one section at North Mountain. May 31, 1863, it is stationed at Berryville: June 14, 1863, the battery was in the disastrous engagement and retreat from Martinsburg, Gen'l Dan Tyler in command of brigade; in this affair Captain Maulsby had the misfortune to lose four of his guns. The battery, after 6 P. M. of the 14 of June, was divided, one section under the command of a lieutenant, facing to the west, covering some of the enemy's infantry and cavalry that were moving in that direction on Martinsburg. The other two sections, commanded by Captain Maulsby, were facing south, covering the Confederate forces that were passing either to amuse or attack the forces posted on the hill near the cemetery. The detached section was 150 yards to the rear of the sections under the immediate command of Captain Maulsby. Just before sunset, the Confederates for the first time showed that they had artillery in position, as they opened fire from six or eight guns with good range. The first shot passed over Captain Maulsby's four guns, and plunged into the detached section, killing and wounding some horses, and producing a bad effect in the infantry supports. For the next 20 minutes the two sections under Maulsby were engaged in rapid fire in order to hold the advancing Confederates in check, while Tyler's forces were in retreat. Captain Maulsby, who was severely wounded, by his conduct in this battle showed that he was a gallant soldier, but we have no report from him as to the particulars of the loss of his guns. But it is believed that Gen'l Dan. Tyler was at fault in keeping the two sections of the battery so long on the field.

L.M. Strayer

CHATHAM T. EWING
Captain Battery G 1st West Virginia Light Artillery

July 31, 1863, the battery is in Camp of Instructions at Washington, D. C., Lieut. J. S. S. Herr in command. August 31, 1863, same, Camp. Lieut. J. C. Means in command. October 13, 1863, Captain Maulsby was honorably discharged on account of wounds received in action at Martinsburg, June 14, 1863. October 24, 1863, Lieut. George W. Graham was promoted to captain. December 31, 1863, the battery is in Colonel Wilkinson's brigade, Captain Graham in command; February 1, 1864, in Thoburn's brigade at New Creek, one section at Beverly; May 31 to July 1, at Clarksburg; July 24 and 25, at Kernstown, Va.; July 31, 1864, at Maryland Heights. Mustered out of service, September 14, 1864.

BATTERY G, FIRST REGIMENT WEST VIRGINIA ARTILLERY

Had its origin in Pittsburg, Pa. When the first call for volunteers was made in Pennsylvania, the number of men responding was much greater than the quota of the State. Among the companies organized under this call was the Plummer Guards, so named in honor of a patriotic merchant, Joseph Plummer, who at his own expense furnished them with complete uniforms. Fearing that the war would be of short duration and that no more men would be needed by their own State, they offered their services to Governor Peirpoint of West Virginia and were promptly accepted, and were mustered into the service as Co. G. in the Second W. Va. Infantry. It was early in the month of May that the company embarked on the steamer John T. McCombs for Wheeling. When the company arrived in Wheeling, it was quartered for a short time on board the steamer Courier, and afterwards was transferred to Camp Carlisle on Wheeling Island. The company left Wheeling for the front on July 5, 1861. They went first to Webster and thence to Laurel Hill, thence to Rich Mountain and Beverly. Took part in the pursuit of Garnet's retreating forces. Wintered at Elkwater.

On December 13, 1861, a detail of the company took part in the battle of Alleghany Mountains. In the spring of 1862 they were put in charge of some old brass 6-pounder guns, and as artillerymen became so expert as to command the admiration of the various commanders under which they served. In fact, so efficient did they become, that the authorities transferred them to the First Virginia Artillery Volunteers, after which they were recruited to the full battery strength and a splendid equipment of guns given them.

They participated in all of General Milroy's battles and marches.

They were with Fremont in his campaigns, and with General Pope up to and including the second battle of Bull Run. They then returned to West Virginia and became part of General W. W. Averell's Cavalry Division, and under that gallant leader did grand service at Rocky Gap, Droop Mountain and Salem raid, not to mention numerous other engagements and expeditions. The Rocky Gap fighting by this battery has few parallels in the history of the Rebellion. The history of the Second Virginia and of Averell's cavalry is the history of Battery G.

The original officers of the company were Captain Chatham T. Ewing; 1st Lieutenant, Alfred Sickman; 2d Lieutenant, Jacob Huggins. Lieutenant Sickman was killed December 13, 1861, in the battle of Allegheny Mountains, and Howard Morton who did gallant service on the occasion was promoted to his place. Lieutenant Huggins resigned early in 1862, and Samuel J. Shearer, a brave and capable officer, succeeded him.

The battery was mustered out on August 8, 1864.

Maj. Howard Morton enlisted in Company G, Second Virginia Infantry, afterwards Battery G, First Artillery. After the battle of Allegheny Mountains he was promoted to first lieutenant, *vice* Sickman killed. He served the full three years, taking a commendable part in all of the campaigns and battles participated in by the company. He was in command of the battery in several engagements, notably those of Rocky Gap and New Market, where his skill and courage received the plaudits of his comrades and commanders. At the close of his services in West Virginia, he returned to Pennsylvania where he was commissioned major of the Fifth Pennsylvania Artillery, and in that capacity served with bravery and skill.

Major Morton was a soldier by inheritance. On his father's side he came from two Revolutionary soldiers and three ancestors who were distinguished in the French and Indian wars. On his mother's side he is descended from Abraham Clark, a signer of the Declaration of Independence, and from two more Revolutionary soldiers. He is at present first vice-president of the Pennsylvania Society of the Sons of the American Revolution, and is foremost in every good work which looks to the inculcation of true American principles in the rising generations. He resides in Pittsburg, is happily married and comfortably situated, and has two children, a boy and a girl.

BATTERY H.

Battery H was organized September, 1863, with James H. Holmes, captain; George W. K. Smith as first lieutenant. December 31, 1863, the battery is assigned to Maj. G. F. Merriam's artillery brigade, Genl B. F. Kelley's department.   May 6, 1864, the battery is ordered from Wheeling to New Creek, where it was assigned to man the guns of the fort at that place, which position it occupied until December 31, 1864.   On August 4, 1864, took part in the engagement of the attack upon New Creek, and November 28, 1864, were victims of the capture of that place by the Confederate Generals Rosser and Payne.   The battery remained in General Kelley's department during its term of service, and was mustered out July 11, 1865.

CHAPTER XLIX.

BREVET MAJ.-GEN'L BENJAMIN FRANKLIN KELLEY.

His Birth.—Early Education and Business Relations.—Successful Military Career Prior to the Civil War.—Colonel of the First Loyal Regiment South of Mason and Dixon's Line. —Early Operation in the Civil War.—Wounded at Philippi.—In Command of the Rail Road Division and of the Department of West Virginia.—Captured by the Confederates.—His Army Record a Series of Victories.—His Death and Burial at Arlington Va.—His Marriages and his Family.

GENERAL KELLEY, son of Col. Wm. Bowdoin Kelley and Mary Smith Kelley, was born in New Hampton, New Hampshire, in April, 1807; was a graduate of the celebrated Partridge Military Academy, and was brought while a youth to West Liberty, Ohio County, Virginia, where he was engaged in the store of Absalom Ridgley, the principal merchant of the county; later he was in the employ of John Goshorn, merchant, of Wheeling, and a partner in the firm of Goshorn, Kelley & Co.

Gen'l Kelley first joined the Guards' Military Company, of Wheeling, and ascended through the intermediate ranks to the command of the Fourth Virginia Regiment (uniformed militia). At the breaking out of the war, General Kelley was the B. & O. R. R. agent in Philadelphia, and returning home was commissioned colonel of the first loyal regiment south of Mason and Dixon's line. On May 25, 1861, by order of General McClellan he was directed to assume command of all the troops then in West Virginia and to advance on May 27. Colonel Kelley left Wheeling with his regiment, which was poorly equipped, no accoutrements, ammunition carried in pockets and the arms supplied to the regiment by Massachusetts as the general government was disinclined at that time to take what they thought was a risk in sending arms to Virginians. The First Virginia was followed the next day by the Sixteenth Ohio and Ninth Indiana. Grafton was held at that time by a Confederate force under command of Colonel Porterfield. With remarkable celerity—having to repair railroads and build bridges—Kelley reached Grafton on June 1, Colonel Porterfield having retreated to Philippi. Kelley marched all night through a drenching rain and attacked the enemy at 4 A. M. on the 3d; the surprise was complete and the enemy routed, many prisoners, a large amount of stores, arms, ammunition, wagons, etc., fell into

BENJAMIN F. KELLEY
Brevet Major General U.S.Volunteers

the hands of the Union forces. Colonel Kelley was severely wounded, at first thought to be fatally, having been shot through the right breast and upper part of lung. General McClellan telegraphed:

CINCINNATI, *June* 3, 1861.

To GEN'L T. A. MORRIS :

Say to Colonel Kelley that I cannot believe it possible that one who has opened his course so brilliantly can be mortally wounded. In the name of the country I thank him for his conduct which has been the most brilliant episode of the war thus far. If it can cheer him in his last moments tell him I cannot repair his loss and I only regret that I cannot be by his side to thank him in person. God bless him.

(Signed)   GEORGE B. MCCLELLAN,
                        Maj.-Gen. Comdg.

And in his report General McClellan commending him recommended his promotion to brigadier-general.

With the most excellent surgical skill and nursing Colonel Kelley gradually recovered from his wound. He was the first Union officer wounded in the war, and at the end of 60 days, having been appointed brigadier-general, he was able to assume the command of the R. R. Division with headquarters at Grafton, to which General McClellan assigned him when he left West Virginia to assume the command of the Army of the Potomac. It is proper to remark here that the B. & O. R. R. was the only avenue in all that section by which soldiers and supplies could be quickly transferred, hence to protect it became a matter of military necessity to the Union forces. This position involved the protection of the B. & O. R. R. from Cumberland to Wheeling and Parkersburg, and incidentally covering all the Pittsburg country and Northern Ohio, a most difficult and harassing duty but little appreciated at the time by the general public. On October 22, 1861, General Kelley received an order from General Scott to concentrate his forces at New Creek and attack and capture Romney, Va. This order was promptly obeyed and moving from New Creek on the 27th of October at 4 P. M., he attacked Romney. After a sharp engagement he defeated the enemy, capturing many prisoners and a large amount of stores, a section of a battery, etc., etc. The following telegram was received :

HEADQUARTERS, ARMY,
WASHINGTON, *Oct.* 30, 1861.

BRIGADIER-GENERAL KELLEY :

Your late movement upon and signal victory at Romney do you great honor in the opinion of the President and Lieutenant-General Scott. You shall be reenforced as soon as practicable; in the meantime, if necessary, call for any troops at Cumberland or New Creek.

By command,
                E. D. TOWNSEND, *A. A. G.*

General Kelley was now assigned to the command of the Department of Harper's Ferry and Cumberland. He remained at Romney until January 1, organizing and drilling troops, keeping a wary eye on Jackson at Winchester. From trouble with his wound he asked to be relieved and was succeeded by General Lander. In a couple of months after Lander's death, he was ordered back in command of First Division of Middle Department with headquarters at Harper's Ferry. This involved the command of all the troops in the Shenandoah Valley and in Maryland west of the Monocacy. On July 1, 1863, he was ordered to Clarksburg, being in command of the Department of West Virginia. During the whole time he commanded the Department of West Virginia his troops were almost constantly engaged in offensive or defensive operations. When General Lee's army crossed the Potomac in 1863, for the campaign which was stopped by the battle of Gettysburg, General Kelley was ordered by General Halleck to concentrate his forces and move to a point as near Hagerstown as would be judicious. He accordingly took position in the mountain pass of Fairview immediately west of Clear Springs; this was a forlorn hope and his orders were to attack (even if he lost his division) General Lee's rear as soon as Meade's guns gave the signal. General Meade called a council of war on Sunday night and Wadsworth, the only volunteer general in command of a corps, voted to attack; the regulars thought it too strong a position and doubted the persistency of the men. The attack was never made and General Lee crossed the Potomac. Halleck's report says: "The operations of our troops in West Virginia are referred to here as being intimately connected with the Army of the Potomac; the force there, being too small to attempt any important campaign by itself, has acted masterfully on the defensive in repelling raids and breaking up guerrilla bands. When Lee's army retreated after the battle of Gettysburg, General Kelley concentrated all his available forces on the enemy's flank, near Clear Springs, ready to cooperate in the proposed attack by General Meade. They also rendered valuable service in the pursuit after Lee had effected his passage over the Potomac. On the 18th of November, General Kelley attacked Imboden, in Hardy County, W. Va., completely routing him.

In December, 1863, General Kelley ordered General Averell to make what is now known as the Salem raid, which was successful. After the Confederate forces had burned Chambersburg, Pa., they moved on Cumberland, and on August 1, 1864, their forces attacked General Kelley at 4 P. M.; the action was continued until dark and the enemy were repulsed. Crossing the Potomac at Old Town, the enemy made for Romney and attacked New Creek unsuccessfully. In the meantime, General Averell, by General Hunter's orders, reported to Kelley and was ordered to pursue the retreating force; he overtook them at Moorefield and completely routed them. In recognition of the Cumberland and New Creek actions General Kelley was brevetted major-general. From this time out, General Kelley was employed in the defense of the railroad and the adjacent territory. Near the close of the war Generals Crook and Kelley were captured and taken to Richmond; they were at first held as hostages for some Confederate prisoners North, but finally, through the efforts of some of General Kelley's friends in Richmond, were paroled and sent North. After the war General Kelley was for some years superintendent of Hot Springs in Arkansas and the last years of his life were passed in Washington City and his summers at his farm at Swan Meadows, near Oakland, Md. He died in July, 1892, and was interred according to his oft expressed desire at Arlington, Va., "that he might rest at last among the soldiers."

General Kelley was 5 feet, 10½ inches in height, of a soldierly erect carriage, had dark eyes and hair and was in youth and old age a remarkable and distinguished looking man. He was a constant attendant at church, and a Christian gentlemen. It will be observed that General Kelley not only organized the first loyal regiment in the entire South but he also fought and won the first victory achieved by the loyal army on Southern soil; his record shows an unbroken series of victories, for, from the beginning to the end of the war, he was never once defeated. He was the first Union officer wounded in the war.

General Kelley's military family consisted, first, for a short time, of Captain Crossman and Capt. B. F. Hawkes, Eighth Ohio, as A. A. G., but for the greater part of his war service he had the valued services of Col. Thayer Melvin, since judge at Wheeling, as assistant adjutant-general; Capt. G. W. Harrison, since superintendent West Virginia Central R. R., was his assistant quartermaster-general; Capt. W. H. Hosack, assistant commissary-general; and Lieut. W. B. Kelley, Lieut. Chas. Freeman, Lieut. William Mathews, all of First Virginia Infantry, as aides-de-camp. And it is well to note the services of the Rev Mr. Wiley, now of Palatine, W. Va., well known among soldiers as General Kelley's chaplain.

General Kelley married Isabel Goshorn (died, 1858), of Wheeling, and had six children by her: Lieut-Col. John G. Kelley, Seventh West Virginia Volunteer Infantry; First Lieut. W. B. Kelley, First West Virginia Volunteer Infantry; Mary I., married to J. C. Sullivan, brigadier-general, U. S. V.; Benj. Franklin Kelley, Jr., lieutenant-colonel and quartermaster U. S. Vols.; Tappen Wright Kelley, captain Fourth Maryland Cavalry; M. Belle Kelley, married Capt. D. B. McIlwain, Fourteenth West Virginia Infantry; and after the war, General Kelley was married to Mary Clare Bruce, daughter of Col. Robt. Bruce, Second Potomac Home Brigade Maryland Volunteers.

CHAPTER L.

BREVET MAJ.-GEN'L THOMAS M. HARRIS.

General Harris a Disciplinarian.—General Fremont's Commendation in a Special Order.—
Commands a Brigade at the Battles of Opequon and Fisher's Hill.—Also Cedar Creek.—
Colonel Thoburn Wounded, Harris becomes a Division Commander.—In the 24th Army
Corps at City Point, Virginia.—Commissioned a Brigadier-General.—At Appomattox.—
A Member of the Commission that Tried the Assassins of President Lincoln.—Mustered
Out April 30th, 1866, Brevet Major-General.

ENERAL HARRIS, whilst colonel of the Tenth Regiment, established a character for energy and faithfulness in obeying orders.
He was always on hand for any duty to which he was assigned
and always received honorable mention for his intelligent and efficient obedience. He had so schooled his regiment in discipline and tactics that it had
early in the service established a character for reliability, and so this regiment got frequent opportunities to distinguish itself in the high places of the
field. Whilst in command of the " Mountain Department " under General
Fremont, he received the commendation of that officer in a special order for
his intelligent and efficient discharge of the duties to which he had been
assigned.

In June, 1862, Colonel Harris was in command of the forces stationed
at Buckhannon. His services at this time were especially valuable to the
government, by reason of the fact that that part of the State was infested
with leading Confederates, who sought to influence the country people for
miles around that it was to their personal interest and to the advancement of
the Confederate cause for them to join either the Confederate army, or to
engage as guerrillas. Recruiting stations were established in the fastnesses
of the mountains for this purpose, and some of the most influential men in
that vicinity were known to be engaged as recruiting officers. They found
little encouragement from the better element among the mountaineers willing
to enlist in the regular army, but they were quite successful in engaging the
lower element for the despicable purposes of guerrilla warfare.

Colonel Harris was directed by General Fremont, then in command of
the Mountain Department, to capture and break up these recruiting stations.
Colonel Harris' familiarity with that entire region fitted him well to perform
this service. He not only destroyed the recruiting stations, but he killed

THOMAS M. HARRIS

Colonel 10th West Virginia Infantry

Brevet Major General U.S.Volunteers

and captured many of the enemy and secured all the arms and ammunition at these stations, capturing three of the officers, viz.: Haymond, Coal and Goff. These men were well known in the community as F. F. V.'s, but it is not likely that their names will appear in the history of the Civil War as having contributed to the elevation of the Confederate cause.

When Colonel Harris' regiment was incorporated in the Army of West Virginia, he was assigned to the command of a brigade. He, with his command, won honorable mention at the battles of Opequon and Fisher's Hill. At the battle of Cedar Creek it was his command that was first struck by the enemy at daybreak, as its position was on the extreme left of our line. Being surprised and receiving a flank attack it could only get out of the way of the enemy as best it could. The flank attack being pushed by the enemy, the 19th Corps was in like manner broken up and routed. The enemy continuing to push his advantage broke up our line so far that only one division of the 6th Corps remained in its position on the extreme right. During this demoralization and retrograde movement of our disorganized forces, Colonel Harris distinguished himself by his efforts to arrest the movement in retreat and to establish nuclei for a reforming of our lines. Whilst thus engaged the flag of the division came to him from Colonel Thoburn, its commander, who had just been mortally wounded. Colonel Harris being the next in rank came thus into the command of the division.

At the close of the campaign of 1864, in the Shenandoah Valley, he received an order to report with his division to General Grant at City Point, and was assigned to the 24th Army Corps under command of General Gibbon. When preparation began to be made for the opening of the spring campaign, he voluntarily offered the command of his division to General Turner who was then serving as a staff officer, and he took command of a brigade under Turner. He was moved to do this by his knowledge of the fact that Generals Ord and Gibbon desired to give General Turner a command and from the fact that Turner not only held a commission as a general officer but was also a graduate of West Point, whilst he himself, though in command of a division, held only a colonel's commission.

As the term of four or five companies of his regiment was now about to expire, they having been mustered into the service on the 29th of March, 1862, and so he would be left without a command, Generals Ord and Gibbon undertook to secure his promotion. Having received the favorable endorsement of General Grant, the recommendation was forwarded to the Secretary of War, but came back with the endorsement: "There is no vacancy." A few days later, the Secretary visited the army and reviewed Colonel Harris' division. When the colonel turned off at the head of the review and took his position at the side of the reviewing officer, the Secretary said to him in a quiet way: "General Ord and General Grant have been urging your promotion but there was no vacancy. You will just stay here with your command and I will go home and make a vacancy. I will muster out some one whom we can spare." He received his commission of brigadier-general on the afternoon of the 29th of March, 1865, whilst on the march against Petersburg. At Appomattox it was his brigade that confronted Gordon on the road leading to Lynchburg, and he had the honor of silencing the last guns ever put in position by General Lee. Returning to Richmond after the surrender he was detailed to serve on the commission that tried the assassins of President Lincoln;* and then receiving an order to report to General Terry, was assigned to duty in the Freedmen's Bureau department, and was placed in command of the District of the Northern Neck, with headquarters at Fredericksburg. He remained in this service until Christmas, when he received a furlough to visit his family and to await orders. He was mustered out of the service by a general order dated April 30, 1866, and a few days later was tendered the appointment as lieutenant-colonel of the 31st Infantry in the reorganization of the army. This flattering appointment he felt constrained not to accept on account of his age and the condition of his health.

* General Harris has written and had published in book form "A History of the Great Conspiracy, and Trial of the Conspirators by a Military Commission" which is the fullest and most complete account of that great trial that has as yet been given.—AUTHOR.

CHAPTER LI.

MAJ.-GEN. GEORGE CROOK.

By 1ST LIEUT. L. W. V. KENNON, U. S. Army.

Birth and Education.—Service in California.—Volunteer Appointment.—Battle of Lewisburg.
—Battle of Antietam.—Cavalry Service with Army of the Cumberland.—Pursuit of
Wheeler.—New River Expedition.—Lynchburg Expedition.—Early's Advance on Wash-
ington.—Pursuit of Early.—Formation of Middle Military System.—Battle of the Opequon.
—Battle of Fisher's Hill.—Battle of Cedar Creek.—Command of Department of West
Virginia.—Capture and Exchange.—Command of Cavalry, Army of the Potomac.—
Surrender of Lee.—Subsequent Career.—Death.

EORGE CROOK was born near Dayton, in Wayne Township, Montgomery County, Ohio, on September 8th, 1828. He entered the
Military Academy at West Point in 1848, graduated in 1852, and
in the same year joined his regiment, the Fourth Infantry, at Benicia Barracks,
in California.

As it is proposed in these pages to give only a brief sketch of the career of
General Crook, his romantic and brilliant services against hostile Indians of
Oregon and California, during the nine years succeeding his graduation, are
passed over with the mention of the fact that they brought him wounds and
distinction, and an experience which was a valuable preparation for his subsequent duties in a larger field.

In 1861 the Rebellion broke out, and Crook, then a captain, hastened
east by way of Panama, half fearful lest the fighting should be over before
he could have opportunity to do his part in it.

In September he was appointed Colonel of the 36th Ohio Volunteer
Infantry, which he at once joined in Somerville, West Virginia. He at once
began the work of transforming the raw recruits who made up his command,
into trained and disciplined soldiers. During the winter he drilled his men
in a large building erected for the purpose, and by spring his command was
in condition to begin active operations at once.

On May 1st, 1862, he was appointed to the command of a provisional
brigade, and May 23d, he engaged the Rebel forces under General Heth at
Lewisburg. General Heth, in his report of this action, stated: "I attained,
without firing a shot that position in front of Lewisburg which I would have
selected. . . . Victory was in my grasp, instead of which, I have to

acknowledge a most disgraceful retreat." The Rebels were driven demoralized from the field. Their commander attributed his defeat to the untrained condition of his troops. The victory was the immediate result of the winter drills, which Crook's foresight had planned. Lewisburg was his first battle in the war, and for his gallant and meritorious services on this occasion, he was brevetted a major in the regular army. He was wounded in this affair, but remained on the field until the end of the fight.

He was next engaged in the Virginia campaign of September and October, 1862, his brigade participating in the battles of South Mountain and Antietam. For his gallant conduct in the latter he was brevetted a lieutenant-colonel in the regular army, and on September 7th was promoted to be Brigadier-General of Volunteers, his commission being specifically a reward for his gallant and meritorious services in the field.

From October, 1862, to February, 1863, he was engaged in clearing the State of West Virginia from guerillas and "bushwhackers." From March to July, 1863, he was in command of the Independent Division at Carthage, Tennessee, taking part in the Tennessee campaign with the Army of the Cumberland, and the advance on Tullahoma, June 24th to July 4th. On July 1st, he was placed in command of the 2d Cavalry Division of the Army of the Cumberland. In the active campaign which ensued, besides almost daily skirmishing, he was engaged in the action at Hoover's Gap, June 26th, the battle of Chickamauga, September 19th, and conducted the cavalry pursuit of General Wheeler.

In this pursuit the enemy was struck in quick succession at the foot of the Cumberland Mountains, September 31st, at McMinnville, October 4th, and at Farmington, October 7th. The campaign lasted but ten days, and for the skill and vigor with which it was conducted, and for his brilliant services at Farmington, Crook was brevetted a colonel in the regular army, and was complimented in orders by General Rosecrans "for inaugurating the new practice of coming to close quarters without delay."

During the ensuing two months he was engaged in clearing of guerillas the country between Shelbyville, Tennessee, and Rome, Georgia.

In February, 1864, General Crook was relieved from duty in the Department of the Cumberland, and was ordered to the Department of West Virginia, where he was assigned to command the Kanawha Division.

Early in May, 1864, with a force of about 6000 men of all arms, he started on the expedition to destroy the New River bridge. On the 9th, he encountered the enemy under Generals Jones and Jenkins, at Cloyd's Mountain, occupying a strongly intrenched position. About one half the command under Colonel White was directed against the enemy's right flank, while the remainder, under Duval, attacked in front. After a hard fight, the intrenchments were everywhere carried, and the enemy fled to Dublin, from which point he was quickly driven by Crook's pursuing troopers.

On the 10th of May the New River bridge was captured and burned after an artillery fight of a couple of hours. The Virginia and Tennessee Railway was destroyed for many miles, and this means of communication between the Eastern and Western Armies of the Confederacy lost to them. The object of the expedition being accomplished, the command withdrew to Meadow Bluff, where it arrived on the 19th of May.

General Sigel, in command of the Department, did not approve of this expedition, but Crook had undertaken it at the suggestion of Grant, who deemed it "the most important work Crook could do," and indeed had expressed this view to him before sending him to West Virginia.

In May, Sigel was defeated at New Market. He was relieved from command and succeeded by Hunter. The latter, after the battle of Piedmont, united with Crook at Staunton, and advanced upon Lynchburg, before which place he arrived June 17th.

Lee, finding his lines of supply threatened by Hunter's advance, detached Early, in command of the 2d Corps, to oppose it. He arrived at Lynchburg in time to meet the attack of Crook and Averell on the 17th. On the following day, Hunter attacked in force, but without being able to capture the town. Convinced that reinforcements had reached the place, Hunter withdrew through the Kanawha Valley to the Ohio, the retreat being covered by Crook and Averell, who repulsed the enemy's advance at Buford's Gap on the 21st.

Hunter's advance had been ordered by Grant to be made by way of Charlottesville, to which point Sheridan with the cavalry of the Army of the Potomac had been ordered to join him. For reasons which seemed good to him, he went by way of the Shenandoah Valley and Lexington. The junction with Sheridan was not made, therefore, and the circuitous route followed allowed reinforcements to reach Lynchburg before he could take it. Crook had advised him to proceed directly to Lynchburg, and Hunter was afterwards frank enough to own that had he followed General Crook's advice, he would have captured the city.

Early did not attempt to follow Hunter beyond Buford's Gap, but moved his command down the Shenandoah Valley, crossed the Potomac, overcame Wallace in a desperate fight at Monocacy, and on the 11th of July his troops formed in front of Washington. Deeming himself unable to capture the city, reinforced by the 6th Corps, he withdrew across the Potomac on the 12th.

In the meantime, Hunter had reached the Ohio, and taking the railway at Parkersburg, arrived at Martinsburg on the 11th.

Wright was placed in command of the troops to pursue Early. As Hunter was senior to Wright, it was thought advisable to leave him in command of the Department of West Virginia at Harper's Ferry, while Crook was assigned to command the troops of that Department in the field, and directed to report to Wright.

Early retreated slowly, and succeeded in slipping between the converging columns of his pursuers, and crossed the Shenandoah River, losing only a small portion of his immense booty to Crook's cavalry under Tibbets.

Wright and Crook united on the 16th, and on the 18th, the latter's command was sent ahead to verify Early's retreat. The enemy was encountered near Snicker's Ferry. Thoburn's division succeeded in crossing, but with so small a force, and unsupported by the 6th corps, he was forced to fall back. Averell, advancing up the Valley from Martinsburg, attacked Ramseurs' Division on the 20th, and drove him from the field in the brilliant action at Carter's Farm.

There was no further pursuit, and Early's retreat ended at Strasburg, where he arrived on the 22d of July.

Wright, deeming his mission accomplished, had already started for Washington. Crook took up a position at Kernstown.

Early, noting the cessation of the pursuit, and the division of the Union forces, quickly advanced on Crook, and with his superior numbers turned both his flanks and drove him back to Bunker Hill. Crook was fortunate in saving his artillery and his trains.

The cause of this defeat is obvious. Not only was Crook greatly outnumbered, but many of his troops were worse than useless, having been hastily assembled, and sent on from Washington in the hope that perhaps they might prove useful. On the field they broke and ran at the first fire, their officers even tearing their shoulder straps from their shoulders to escape notice and capture. Hunter severely criticised both officers and men of the "refuse force" sent from Washington, and stated that "it was only owing to the steadiness and good conduct of Crook's Kanawha infantry that the army was saved from utter annihilation."

By Hunter's direction, Crook took post at Sharpsburg, to hold the South Mountain Gaps.

Hunter had resented the selection of Wright, his junior, to command the troops in the field, and requested to be relieved from his command, suggesting that Crook be appointed his successor. In a telegram to the Secretary of War he said: "Brigadier-General George Crook was recommended for promotion for meritorious conduct at the battles of South Mountain and Antietam, by Generals Cox, Wright and Rosecrans for services in West Virginia, and by Generals Thomas and Grant for services in the Army of the Cumberland. I consider him one of the best soldiers I have ever seen, and one of the most reliable and well balanced of men. I think his capacity for usefulness is limited by his rank, and I think that his promotion to a superior command would be of great advantage to the public service, and of very especial benefit in this Department. I would earnestly request, therefore, that he be appointed a major-general." To this Stanton replied that it would have given him grest pleasure to promote General Crook long ago, but that the law limited the number of major-generals, and there was then no vacancy. General Crook would, however, be appointed a major-general by brevet, and assigned to command on his brevet rank, awaiting a vacancy for " a full appointment which no man in the service has more fairly won."

This was accordingly done, and on July 25th, Crook was specially assigned by the President to command in the Department of West Virginia, with the brevet rank of major-general, the brevet being conferred for gallant and distinguished services in West Virginia, for which also he was brevetted a brigadier-general in the regular army.

Meanwhile Early was again master of the valley; he invaded Maryland, burned Chambersburg, and interrupted traffic on the Baltimore and Ohio Railroad and the Chesapeake and Ohio Canal.

Wright and Crook were fruitlessly marched and countermarched under Halleck's orders, until they made a junction on the 29th of July.

Grant now determined to crush the daring and pertinacious Early, and consolidated all the troops operating against him into a single command, the Middle Military Division. He visited the headquarters of the new Division, ordered a concentration of troops at Halltown, and issued general instructions for the ensuing campaign. Gen'l P. H. Sheridan was assigned to the temporary command of the Division on August 7th, 1864.

On the 10th, Sheridan moved forward from Halltown. Early fell back to Fisher's Hill. Fearful of the expected reinforcement of Early, Sheridan withdrew to the Opequon on the 17th where he was attacked on the 21st, but without decisive result. During the night he withdrew to the intrenched position at Halltown.

Early's reinforcement had brought his force up to about 21,000 men of all arms. Sheridan was joined by Wilson's and Averell's Cavalry Divisions, and by Grover's Division of the 19th Corps, making his force about 55,000 men for field duty under his immediate command.

Early occupied the lower valley, Sheridan the line at Halltown. Here the opposing armies remained without decisive action for nearly a month. In extending the Union line to Berryville on the 3d of September, Crook ran against Anderson as the latter was starting on his return to Richmond. A spirited action ensued, which had the effect of delaying Anderson's return until a couple of weeks later.

On the 18th of September, Early was at Martinsburg where he again destroyed the railway and canal.

Grant had expected decisive action from Sheridan and his splendid command, and not understanding the necessity for further delay, went to Charlestown with a plan of battle drawn up to give to Sheridan. The latter explained that he had understood Grant's orders were not to attack until Early should detach part of his command. Grant gave the order to move at once, and returned to City Point. The next day orders were issued for an advance of the entire army. The advance was made and on September 19th, the two forces met in the

BATTLE OF THE OPEQUON.

Early in the morning Wilson's cavalry galloped through the Berryville gorge, and at dawn carried the earthworks at the head of this defile, and held the position, enabling the 6th and 19th Corps to pass through it, and to form line of battle in front of Winchester.

Early had learned of Grant's presence when at Martinsburg, and with soldierly intuition at once hurried his troops back towards Winchester and was enabled to present his whole strength to Sheridan.

At about noon both armies simultaneously attacked. The Federal lines were broken between the two corps engaged, but Russell's Division of the 6th Corps, in reserve, repulsed the Rebel advance, and saved the Army from defeat. In the attack Russell lost his life, and was succeeded by Upton.

Crook had been held at the Opequon crossing, with his two divisions of infantry under Thoburn and Hayes and DuPont's artillery, with orders to protect the ford.

On the failure of his attack, Sheridan feared that Early's troops returning from Martinsburg would strike him in flank, and he hastily sent for Crook, directing him to support the 19th Corps and be ready to meet a flank attack from the right.

At two o'clock, the first of the West Virginia men reached the field. Crook placed Thoburn's Division in support of the 19th Corps, and with the other crossed the Red Bud Run. He was surprised to find there no evidences

L.M. Strayer

GEORGE CROOK
Brevet Major General U.S.A.

of the enemy's presence, and he moved at once up the left bank of the river, until he reached a point on the left and rear of Early's line. He sent word to Sheridan that he had attained such a position, and would attack immediately, asking that he be supported by an advance of the whole line.

Crook's advance was led by Col. Rutherford B. Hayes, who crossed the Red Bud and assailed the enemy in most gallant manner. The fight was stubborn, the enemy taking refuge behind a series of parallel stone walls which served as intrenchments. Thoburn advanced at the same time and the enemy broke. The cavalry under Merritt, who was informed by Crook of the situation, joined in the attack. Early withdrew through Winchester, his retreat being covered by Ramseur's Division, which alone retained its organization. He saved his trains and most of his artillery. The West Virginia men were the first to enter Winchester in pursuit.

The battle had been saved by Russell and Upton, and won by Crook. It was, however, a dearly bought victory. The Union loss was more than 5000; the Confederates loss nearly 4000, half of whom were prisoners captured mostly by Crook's troops.

Although brilliantly decisive of the battle, the use made of Crook's troops was not as he had wished. He had strongly urged upon Sheridan the plan of moving his command along the Senseney road, and putting it across Early's line of retreat. Sheridan was so far influenced by this idea, as to state that he at first intended to make this move, but was compelled to bring Crook up to save his army from defeat. It would have been better, without doubt, even under the existing conditions, to have allowed Crook to attack as he desired, and Sheridan acknowledged later that by doing so he might have captured the bulk of Early's army.

BATTLE OF FISHER'S HILL.

Early withdrew to Fisher's Hill, followed by Sheridan, and on the 22d of September the two armies fronted each other, on opposite sides of the Tumbling Run ravine.

Early's position was one of very great natural strength, and this was increased by trenches which reached from the Shenandoah to the foot of the Little North Mountains. Sheridan, however, determined to attack, and selected Crook's command to lead. At what point the assault was to be directed is doubtful, though it was somewhere on Early's front. Wherever it was, Crook objected most strenuously, on account of the great and certain loss it would cause in his command. Moreover, he had reconnoitered toward the Back Road, and had conceived the idea of placing his troops on the left and rear of the enemy's line as he had done at the Opequon. Sheridan did not think the plan was feasible, but finally yielded to the arguments of Crook and Hayes, and somewhat reluctantly gave authority to the former to carry out his plan.*

This was about two o'clock in the afternoon, and Crook hastened to fulfill his promise of a decisive victory with slight loss. Success depended mainly on the secrecy with which the move could be executed, and here Crook's experience in wild warfare in California served him in good stead. The enemy had signal stations on the mountains, on both sides of the valley, and it was necessary to move two divisions so as to avoid discovery by their sharp eyed occupants. Crook, on foot, personally led his men through ravines, woods and brush to the mountain, then along its side under cover of the woods until the enemy's dismounted cavalry pickets were encountered. The column was then faced to the left, and with a yell, the little army of West Virginia rushed down the mountain, carrying dismay and disaster to the confident Rebels who deemed themselves secure in their chosen " Gibraltar of the Valley."

On rushed the exultant West Virginians across the low rolling foothills and valleys at the head of Tumbling Run, up the slopes of the plateau where lay the enemy's main forces, rolling them back in confusion, taking no time to form lines, nor giving time to the enemy to organize resistance, until their entire line broke and fled wildly, some up the valley, more across the river to the shelter of the Massanutten Mountains. Crook pressed on to the pike, in rear of the right of Early's position at the beginning of the attack. His men followed the enemy a short distance, but being exhausted from their four mile charge, and night coming on, they bivouacked by the side of the pike, where they were passed by the other corps, who cheered them as they went by.

In this battle the Union loss was about 500. The Rebel loss was about 1400 men, 1100 of whom were prisoners, and 20 guns.

* Crook was always preeminently a man of action and found great difficulty in expressing his views in spoken words. Hayes was a lawyer and talker by profession, and Crook would at times call Hayes to speak for him. The present is a case in point, and Hayes, with less of the respect for rank inbred in the West Pointer, expressed his views in the freest manner. During the conversation with Sheridan, Crook turned to Hayes and said: "Col. Hayes, I want you to tell Gen'l Sheridan what you think of putting our men in on the enemy's front." Hayes said at once: "General, it would be simply murder." He warmly seconded Crook's idea of a flank attack, and stated that the West Virginia troops were mostly mountaineers, all of them had grown accustomed to service in the mountains, and that the move through the woods and brush along the mountain side was entirely practicable with such troops. The move could result in slight loss if unsuccessful, and might produce great results if successful. On this presentation of the case Sheridan finally yielded and gave the authority asked for.

A salvo of fifteen hundred guns was fired by direction of the Secretary of War, to celebrate the victory at Fisher's Hill. It was indeed most complete. It was also a victory won by the Army of West Virginia, on a plan conceived and executed by its commander, General Crook. The West Virginia troops alone could not, of course, have won this battle. The other corps held and occupied the enemy in front, and subsequently joined in the attack, especially Rickett's Division of the 6th Corps, which being on the right, was enabled to get into the action. That the West Virginia troops passed from the extreme left to the extreme right of the enemy's line, and that his fugitives fled to the Massanutten Mountains for safety, sufficiently indicates where the credit of the victory belongs.

Sheridan acknowledged this at once. On the day following the battle he telegraphed to Grant a request that Crook be appointed "to the full rank of major-general. His good conduct and the good conduct of his command turned the tide of battle in our favor both at Winchester and Fisher's Hill."

General Early also stated that it was Crook's force which ruined him at Winchester, and that at Fisher's Hill "the movement on my left flank was again made by Crook." For his gallant and meritorious services in this battle, Crook was brevetted a major-general in the regular army. The brevet rank of Brigadier-General, U. S. A., was conferred for gallant and meritorious services in the campaign in West Virginia.

The battle of Fisher's Hill gave the Union forces control of the valley; its stores of grain, provisions and supplies of all kinds were destroyed. The army then withdrew down the valley, and took up a position at Cedar Creek.

Battle of Cedar Creek.

Early quickly gathered his scattered forces and slightly reinforced by troops from Richmond returned to his former position at Fisher's Hill and planned an attack on the Union lines which, for brilliancy of conception and daring of execution, finds few parallels in history.

The Union lines extended along the bluffs overlooking Cedar Creek and the flatter country on its farther side, the 19th Corps on the right of the turnpike, the Army of West Virginia on its left, with one division of the latter thrown forward to a point overlooking the bend of the creek and its junction with the Shenandoah. The 6th Corps was in camp well to the right and rear of the 19th Corps.

During the night of the 18th of October Early secretly moved his army forward from Fisher's Hill; Wharton followed the pike, Kershaw the dirt road from Strasburg to the ford opposite Thoburn's position, and Gordon a trail along the foot of Massanutten Mountain, twice crossing the Shenandoah, to a point on the road from Bowman's Ford to the Cooley house.

At day-break Kershaw surprised and overran Thoburn's Division. Those who were not captured, escaped by flight and joined the other division in the rear. Here Crook and Hayes formed a line which fought desperately, but Gordon striking it in flank and rear, compelled it to give way. At the same time Wharton fell on the 19th Corps; it too broke, and the whole line was pushed rapidly back.

The 6th Corps on the extreme right, and more than two miles from the point of first attack, had time to form line. It gallantly resisted the enemy's advance, but it also was compelled to fall back.

Fighting against heavy odds,* Early was compelled to put all of his force in the first attack, and for this reason was unable to keep up the continuous pressure on the Union lines which alone would enable him to reap the fruits of his victory. The success of Gordon and Kershaw had carried them across the pike from the right to the left of the army, and disorganized by their very success, it became necessary to reform the lines, which were now placed nearly perpendicular to the pike on its west.

The time so allowed the Union force, was employed by Wright, in command during Sheridan's temporary absence in Washington, in disposing his troops to meet a further advance of the enemy. The whole of the cavalry was transferred from the right to the left to cover the pike, this being the key to the position.

The failure of Wharton's assault on Lewis Grant's Vermonters marked the end of Early's success, and Wright gave orders to prepare for a counter-attack. At this juncture Sheridan arrived on the field, and assumed command. He approved Wright's orders, but delayed the attack until one division of the cavalry should be returned to the right, and the stragglers more completely organized.

In the new line, the 19th Corps was on the right, the 6th in the center and the Army of West Virginia on the left.

At four o'clock the advance was begun. Gordon's division on the left first gave way, and Early's army, enveloped on both flanks by the Union cavalry, broke and ran.

At Strasburg the infantry pursuit stopped. DuPont's Artillery, which had been saved by the skill of its commander from the wreck of the morning, shelled the retreating enemy from the banks of Cedar Creek, while the cavalry continued its captures until late at night.

---

* The Union force present for duty was about 35,000 men; the Confederate strength was less than 20,000.

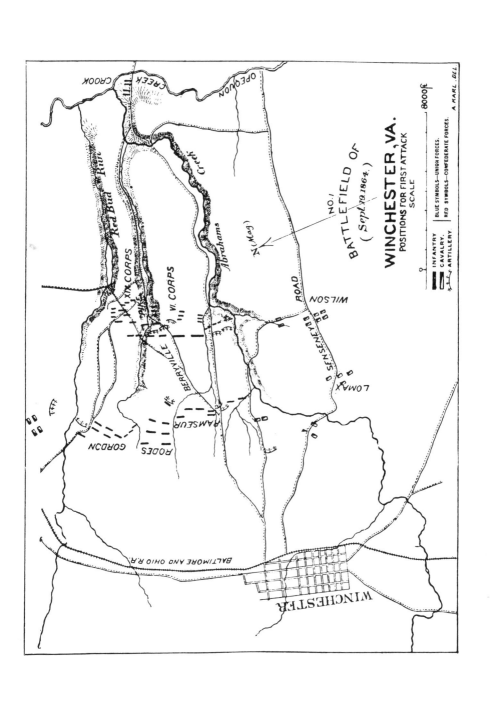

WINCHESTER, VA.
POSITIONS FOR FIRST ATTACK
BATTLEFIELD OF
(Sept 19 1864.)
SCALE
0   8000ft

INFANTRY   BLUE SYMBOLS—UNION FORCES.
CAVALRY.   RED SYMBOLS—CONFEDERATE FORCES.
ARTILLERY.   A. MARL. DEL.

CROOK
CREEK
CREEK
OPEQUON
Red Bud Run
Abrahams
Creek
N (Mag)
NO.1
XIX CORPS
VI. CORPS
WILSON
SENSENEY ROAD
LOMAX
BERRYVILLE
RAMSEUR
RODES
GORDON
BALTIMORE AND OHIO R.R.
WINCHESTER

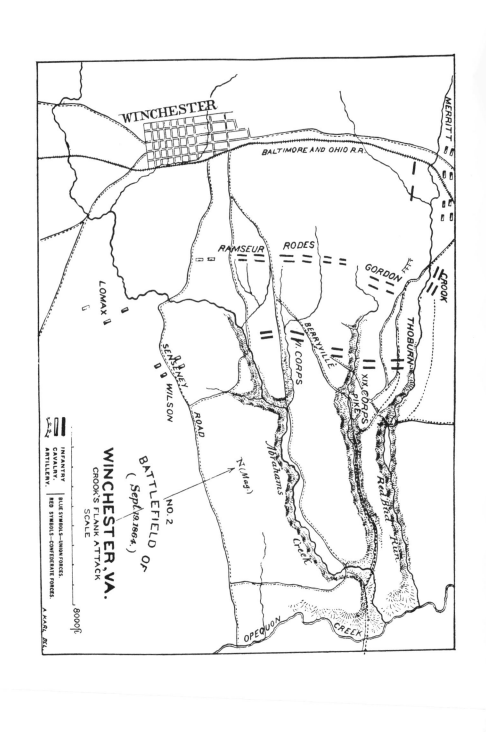

WINCHESTER

BALTIMORE AND OHIO R.R.

MERRITT

RAMSEUR   RODES

GORDON

CROOK

LOMAX

THOBURN

SENSENEY
WILSON
ROAD

VI. CORPS

BERRYVILLE
PIKE

XIX CORPS

N (Mag.)

Abrahams
Creek

Red Bud Run

OPEQUON   CREEK

BATTLEFIELD OF
(Sept. 19, 1864.)

NO. 2

WINCHESTER, VA.

CROOK'S FLANK ATTACK

SCALE

8000 ft

INFANTRY
CAVALRY.
ARTILLERY.

BLUE SYMBOLS—UNION FORCES.
RED SYMBOLS—CONFEDERATE FORCES.

A. KARL, DEL.

Early bivouacked at Fisher's Hill and the next day withdrew to New Market, having lost 1860 in killed and wounded, 1200 in prisoners, many wagons, and 24 guns, besides 23 of those he had captured in the morning.

The Union loss was 5665 in killed, wounded and missing, of whom 858 were from the Army of West Virginia.

To understand the first success of Early's attack it must be stated that Sheridan believed the fighting in the valley was over ; that a "Rebel advance down this valley would not take place," and, as late as the 17th, stated that the enemy was again retreating up the valley. The Army of West Virginia, the 19th Corps and two cavalry divisions were deemed sufficient to hold the valley, and the 6th Corps was started back for City Point, Crook being selected to command the forces remaining at Cedar Creek.

At this juncture Grant renewed his orders for Sheridan to operate against Gordonsville and Lee's lines of supply. This induced Sheridan to return the 6th Corps to Cedar Creek, and it was placed in camp to the right and rear of the intrenched lines occupied by the remainder of the army.

On the 15th Sheridan left for Washington where he was summoned to confer with the authorities regarding plans for future action, Wright, the senior officer present, taking command in his absence.

A reconnoissance on the 13th found the enemy in force, with infantry, artillery and cavalry at Hupp's Hill. After that, daily reconnoissances from both flanks failed to discover the enemy, although he was, during the whole period encamped, at Fisher's Hill.

On the 16th a message was intercepted from the Confederate signal station on Three Top Mountain, showing that they were still there at least. The message purported to be from Longstreet, and indicated that he was on his way to join Early. This was enough to insure the taking of extraordinary precautions, and Sheridan, then absent, sent back all the cavalry to Wright, and ordered him to make his position strong. " Close in Powell, . . . Look well to your ground and be well prepared."

On the 18th a reconnoissance made by one of Crook's brigades found no trace of the enemy in his old camp at Hupp's Hill. The cavalry also reported no enemy in its front. The impression was that Early could not maintain his command so far to the front, and that he would be compelled to withdraw for that reason. Both the army and its commander were beguiled into the belief that he had done so.

For still further assurance, Wright ordered reconnoissances to be made on the 19th to be pushed as far as Fisher's Hill. On that morning however, the Confederate attack was made. As the army was surprised, the precautious taken, though perhaps unusual, were evidently inadequate.

Against an advance along either the pike or the dirt roads from Strasburg the left was very strong; so strong that Wright telegraphed on the
16th: "I shall only fear an attack on my right, which I shall make every
preparation against and resisting." As for the left, Crook indeed intrenched
his position, and carried his lines well to the rear, but Wright felt so secure
there that he even neglected to close in Powell as expressly ordered by
Sheridan. This left this part of the position uncovered save by the ordinary
infantry pickets, whose line extended only to Cedar Creek. The cavalry
pickets beyond had been removed. Crook reported the denuded condition of his front, and was promised that the cavalry should be replaced.
This was not done, however, and while there were two strong divisions of
cavalry on the right, the left was uncovered.

The absence of these cavalry pickets enabled Early to cross both the
creek and the larger river without detection, while the darkness and fog
aided his enterprise, prevented his discovery by the infantry pickets until
his attack was made.

Thoburn's officer-of-the-day heard sounds from near the river, and went
with a patrol to investigate its cause, but in the dense obscurity of the morning, he was captured without being able to give the alarm. When the
pickets learned of the enemy's presence, they could do no more than fire
and retreat, and the Confederate troops would reach the trenches as soon as
they.

Again, it must be said that the position of the left of the line was faulty,
and for this Sheridan himself was responsible, since he personally selected
the positions and designated the troops to occupy them. Crook had objected
to the exposed position of Thoburn's Division, but was promised a protecting
line of cavalry pickets. To oppose an advance down the pike, the line was
admirably selected, and Thoburn's position commanded the ground to the
river in his front, but it was detached from any support; a deep ravine separated it from the rest of the army, and if flanked, the only hope of safety lay
in instant withdrawal. Any attempt to hold it under such conditions must
result in the capture of the entire force. The proper position for Thoburn
was on the left of the main line, extending toward the Cooley house. Had
he been so placed, Gordon could not have struck the flank and rear of the
Union lines, and the battle might there have been fought and won.

As it was, the West Virginia men did all that could have been done by
any troops, and the testimony of a Rebel officer who opposed them in their
desperate resistance at the pike, was that he saw there the hottest fire and the
fiercest fight of the war. Aroused from sleep at dawn, assailed by over-
powering numbers in front, in flank and in rear, they fought well, and gave

time to the 6th Corps to prepare for the assaults made on its lines. It may be remarked also that, in spite of its exposed position, the Army of West Virginia lost but seven guns, while the 6th Corps lost six, and the 19th Corps eleven.

It should be remembered, too, that they had but two small divisions of infantry in the battle, and these were still further reduced by large detachments; an entire brigade of Thoburn's Division was at Winchester, his total strength was about 1500 men, and the first attack fell on this weakened division.

Though driven back they were not demoralized; they did not feel as if they had had a fair chance; they did not feel whipped and longed only to be led against the enemy. When Sheridan came on the field, Crook, who shared the feeling of his men, strongly favored the idea of attacking at once. They were the first troops that Sheridan found in line on his arrival.

Though in diminished numbers, the West Virginia troops were gallantly in at the finish, with undiminished pluck.

It would be erroneous to hold them responsible for the morning's disaster, and Sheridan stated that the battle might have happened exactly as it did, had he himself been present at the time.

The causes of the disaster may be briefly stated to be the faulty position of the Union lines, the false sense of security as to the left, resulting in a failure to close in Powell and an unprotected condition of this point, and to faulty methods in the use of guards and cavalry to secure the safety of the army. In the last respect the Confederate service was greatly superior to that of their opponents.

After the battle of Cedar Creek there was little serious fighting in the valley, and the armies remained quiet, with the exception of Early's advance to Middletown in November, where he remained for a couple of days and then withdrew to New Market. In December, a futile cavalry raid was made towards Gordonsville. In the same month the greater part of the infantry of both armies was sent to City Point and Richmond respectively.

Crook, who had been promoted to the rank of major-general on October 21st, 1894, resumed the direct command of the Department of West Virginia, with headquarters at Cumberland. The winter months were spent in compiling the formal reports and returns pertaining to his Department.

Towards the end of February, Sheridan was preparing for his final cavalry raid up the valley to Richmond, and Crook was ordered to take his place. He accordingly turned over the command of his Department to General Kelley, and started for Winchester.

Partisan troops under McNeill had cut the railway, and Crook returned to Cumberland for the night, to wait until the track should be repaired. To this accidental circumstance he owed the mischance of being captured, for at about three o'clock on the following morning, February 21st, 1865, Crook and Kelley, Colonel Melvin and others, were surprised in their beds at their hotel, and carried off as prisoners of war to Richmond.

The capture was made by a party of eight of McNeill's men, and was planned and executed by Chas. J. Dailey, a resident of Cumberland and a soldier under McNeill. West Virginia is a rough, mountainous country with few good roads. It was the chosen home of the bushwhacker, and throughout the war Northern vigilance could never quite free the State from them. With Southern sympathizers both north and south of the Potomac, spies passed freely far into the Union lines, and Southern guerillas visited their families in towns under Federal rule.

Cumberland lay in the heart of the mountains, easy of access by trails scarce known to any but natives. The quarters of the Union generals were known to the Rebels, who, advised by friends or by their own observation, knew their daily customs, and it was easy for a small band to surprise and overpower the picket at the entrance of the town and enter the quarters of the Union generals. The latter, awakened with pistols presented at their heads, could do naught but submit to their captors.

In a moment they were away, and mounted on swift horses, were soon beyond reach of pursuit, although the alarm was given within ten minutes after their departure. So quietly and quickly was the exploit performed that persons sleeping in the adjoining rooms were not disturbed.

The Secretary of War was at first strongly minded to dismiss both generals, but Grant was unwilling that this should be done, and soon had Crook exchanged in order to have his services in the final campaign about to begin. Scarce three weeks passed, therefore, before he was found again on duty with the Union army. Hancock had been placed in command at Winchester, but a place was found for Crook in the forces about Richmond, and on March 27th, 1865, he assumed command of the Second Cavalry Division, which was increased later by the addition of Mackenzie's Division. This command constituted the cavalry of the Army of the Potomac.

Crook had already won laurels in command of cavalry, and in the brief campaign which ensued he gave fresh proof of his energy and skill. In the days preceding the surrender at Appomattox he was constantly in evidence, the battles of Dinwiddie Court House, March 31st, Jetersville, April 5th, Sailor's Creek, April 6th and Farmville, April 7th, attesting his activity and valor. It was almost a continuous fight for two weeks, and finally, on the 9th of April, it was Crook's force which Lee found across his line of retreat, and which held him until the advance of the infantry convinced him that the case was hopeless, and that at last the end had come.

The war was over. Crook had fought it through; in the East and in the West; with the Army of the Cumberland, the Army of West Virginia, and the Army of the Potomac. He had fought with cavalry and with infantry, and with all arms combined. With all he had proved himself a thorough soldier and skillful general, and was always greater than the position he filled. Against anything like equal numbers, he had been invariably victorious, and often so against superior numbers. His successive promotions were earned many times over by hard service and brilliant successes. His conduct at Lewisburg, Antietam, Farmington, Cloyd's Mountain, the Opequon, Cedar Creek and other fields all mark him an able leader, while it has been said that "the annals of war present perhaps no more glorious victory" than Fisher's Hill, which was fought on his plan and won by his troops.

In 1865 and 1866 Crook was in command of the District of Wilmington, N. C. In the latter year he was mustered out of the Volunteer service; the great armies of the Rebellion were disbanded and in peaceful pursuits expended the developed energies of the war in extending he National greatness. Crook was at this time a lieutenant-colonel of the 23d regular infantry, and was at once sent west to engage in a more arduous warfare, against savage Indians. In this field he acquired a fame unequaled by any American soldier.

In the northwest he quickly subdued the Snake River Indians in a sharp winter campaign.

His successes caused him to be ordered to Arizona, where the Apaches had defied the Mexicans since the days of Cortes, and where he was to teach them the power of the pale-faced American. Arizona was made habitable for white men by his rapid and effective subjugation of the Indians, and for his great work he was promoted by Grant, then President, from the grade of lieutenant-colonel to that of brigadier-general.

He was called wherever there was hard work to be done, and soon was north operating against the Sioux, who were taught to fear the might and respect the worth of the "Gray Fox."

Again called to Arizona, he reduced the Chiricahuas, the last remaining band of hostile Apaches, who had been excepted by War Department orders from his previous operations, and peace reigned in Arizona for the first time in her history.

No part of the great West was unknown to him. In every part he has conquered the savage enemies of the Government, and opened the way to civilization. His great reputation acquired in dealing with Indians shows the humane breadth of his character, for it was due not simply to his unequaled military skill in subduing them, but also to his patient tact in their management, and in his well-directed efforts to uplift them from barbarism and start them on the road to a higher life.

His work was rewarded by promotion to the highest grade of the Army. On the 6th of April, 1888, he was made a major-general, and assumed command of the Division of the Missouri, with headquarters at Chicago, Illinois.

There he died on the 21st of March, 1890.

Simple in manner, quiet in his tastes, abstemious in his habits, loved by all who came to know him well, skillful in civilized war, preeminent in wars against savages, profound in his knowledge of Indian character, just and truthful in his dealings with them and with all the world, he left, when he died, a place that could not be filled in the hearts of his friends, nor in the military service of his country.

CHAPTER LII.

COL. JACOB HORNBROOK.

Colonel Hornbrook's Early Trials.—Successful Business Man.—His Intense Loyalty in 1860.
—In the Convention that Nominated Lincoln for President.—Active in Promoting the
Reorganization of the State.—Aide-de-Camp to Governor Peirpoint.—A Member of the
West Virginia Legislature.—His Death and Burial at Greenwood near Wheeling, W. Va.

OL. JACOB HORNBROOK, the "Soldier's Friend," was born
October 7, 1812, and in youth and early manhood had many trials
and vicissitudes; but with indomitable perseverance, inherited from
his Huguenot ancestors, he finally succeeded and was for a large part of his
career a successful merchant. His earliest trip was to New Orleans on a
flat boat, a six months' trip from which he returned with 600 silver dollars, a
pet bear, a barrel of bear's oil, and some dozens of bottles of lemon juice,
all of which brought high prices on his return to Wheeling, and were quickly
turned into cash. With his brother Thomas he started the wholesale house
of J. & T. Hornbrook, at Wheeling, and in connection built and navigated
the steamboat "Merchant" as a trading boat; her cabins were store rooms for
the sale of goods. Colonel Hornbrook retired in 1859 with a competence.
Always an active man he threw himself into the contest that came upon us
in 1860, contributing his time and money to the cause of liberty; and, at a
time when the advocacy of liberty was dangerous in Virginia, Colonel Hornbrook was an outspoken and active member of the "wide awakes." Colonel
Hornbrook represented a district of Virginia in the convention that nominated Abraham Lincoln and with great ardor assisted in all that could promote his election. With Cassius M. Clay, his brother Thomas, Edward
Norton and others, the money was raised to keep the *Intelligencer* on its feet
at a time when it was in great straits. When the war broke out Colonel
Hornbrook assisted in the reorganization of the State and the recruiting of
troops; his time and money were always to be had when needed. Being
appointed an aide with rank of colonel of cavalry by Governor Peirpoint, he
was assigned as State agent to look after our soldiers, more particularly the
wounded ones; he brought home the money for the soldiers from the pay
tables that was needed for their families and with his daughter, Mrs. Kelley,
paid it to them, serving during the war without compensation.

This sketch is too brief to recount Colonel Hornbrook's service to his State and to her soldiers.   In many a West Virginia home Colonel Hornbrook's memory is prized and tender recollections remain of "The Soldier's Friend." After the war, Colonel Hornbrook served in the Legislature from Ohio County.   Colonel Hornbrook was six feet tall, very spare in his habits, light brown hair, of a most genial nature, and with a heart overflowing with goodness to his fellow man.   A successful merchant, a faithful friend, and in all the relations of life an honest man.   He died at the home of his daughter, in Philadelphia, on November 3, 1888, and was buried at Greenwood near Wheeling, W. Va.

> " His daily prayer, far better understood
> In acts than words, was simply *doing good* ;
> So calm, so constant, was his rectitude,
> That by his loss alone we know its worth
> And feel how true a man has walked with us on earth."

JACOB HORNBROOK
Colonel U.S. Volunteers

CHAPTER LIII.

MAJ.-GEN'L R. H. MILROY.*

Birth and Early Life of General Milroy.—Graduated with the Degrees of Master of Military Science, Civil Engineering and Bachelor of Arts.—Studied Law.—Went to Texas.—In the War with Mexico.—Married May, 1849.—Circuit Judge.—In the Civil War.—Captain and Colonel.—At Grafton and Philippi.—A Brigadier-General.—At Elk Water.—New Creek and Winchester.—A Major-General.—Episode at Winchester.—Censured by his Superiors.—Honorably Acquitted.—In Nashville, Tenn.—Encounter with General Forrest.—Returned to his Home in Indiana.—In Washington Territory.—His Bravery Conceded.—Died, March, 1890.—Relations to the Second West Virginia Infantry.

OBERT HUSTON MILROY, son of Gen'l Samuel and Martha Milroy, was born in Washington County, Ind., June 11, 1816, about seven months before the territory was admitted as a State. His father was a hard-working, successful farmer, was a member of the first constitutional convention of Indiana, and afterward for a number of years was a member of the legislature of that State, and at one time speaker of the House. The son aided the father in all the hard work of the farm until his 25th year. Prior to this he had received only a country schooling, but for years had been strongly desirous to secure an education at West Point, or at some college. But his father being a self-educated man, refused this desire of the son, for the reason that he believed that a collegiate education was more injurious than beneficial, and pointing to his fine library told Robert to educate himself. During the winter of 1840–41, his father sent him to Pennsylvania to visit two half uncles, and to collect from them a balance of $200 due from his grandfather's estate, which his father told him to appropriate to his own use in visiting the large Eastern cities. But on receiving the money Robert determined to use it in obtaining his highest desire, a collegiate military education. He had heard favorably of Norwich Military University at Norwich, Vt., Capt. A. Partridge, formerly superintendent at West Point, president, and went there and entered for study. By intense application to study, almost day and night, for two years and seven months, he was graduated with the degrees of Master of Military Science, Master of Civil Engineering and Bachelor of Arts. After vainly trying to get a com-

* For the following interesting sketch of General Milroy, we are indebted to Frank S. Reader, Esq., author and historian of the Fifth West Virginia Cavalry.—T. F. L.

mission as lieutenant in the regular army, he returned home in the spring of 1844 and began the study of law. In the spring of 1845 he went to Texas, took the oath of allegiance to "The Lone Star," and voted for its annexation to the United States. In the fall of that year he returned home on account of the death of his father, and resumed the study of law. On the breaking out of the war with Mexico, he promptly raised a company of volunteers and was mustered into the service of the United States for one year as captain of Company C, First Indiana Infantry, a part of the Indiana brigade of Brig.-Gen'l Joe Lane. When the year was up, Captain Milroy recruited another company for the war, but it was not accepted. After the muster out of his company, Captain Milroy returned to his home in Delphi, Ind., and again resumed the study of law. He attended a course of instruction in the Law Department of the Indiana State University during the winter of 1848–49, and was graduated with the degree of Bachelor of Law.

In May, 1849, he was married to Miss Mary Jane Armitage, of Delphi, and was admitted to the practice of law soon thereafter. In the fall of that year he was elected a member of the conventiou to remodel the constitution of his State. In 1852, he was appointed circuit judge, and upon the expiration of his term, in 1854, he moved to Rensselaer, Ind., where he continued the practice of law, until the breaking out of the rebellion, in April, 1861. Seeing clearly several months prior to that event, that war was inevitable, Judge Milroy, on February 4, 1861, issued a stirring call for the prompt organization of volunteer companies all over the State, to be ready with the volunteers of other States, to crush the coming rebellion in its infancy, and requested that all men qualified for military service, who desired to join such a company at Rensselaer, to give or send their names to him, and as soon as a sufficient number of names was received, a meeting would be called for the election of officers, which was done.

This was the first call made for volunteers for the great war. When war came, Indiana was called on for 60 companies of three months' troops, and Captain Milroy at once tendered his already organized company, which was mustered into the service April 24, 1861, as a part of the Ninth Indiana Infantry, of which Captain Milroy was elected colonel. He soon received an order to report with his regiment to Col. B. F. Kelley, at Grafton, Va., and crossed the Ohio River into Virginia, May 30, reporting to Col. Kelley June 1. He took a part in the battle of Philippi, the first of the war, and his regiment was in the advance in the pursuit of General Garnett, who was killed at Carrick's Ford. The three months' regiments then returned home.

Colonel Milroy went home with his regiment, but before disbanding, requested them to reenlist for three years, and by September 12, he had his regiment filled to the limit.   He was appointed brigadier-general to date from September 3, but was not assigned to the command of a brigade until October 10, remaining with his regiment.   He reported to General Reynolds at Elkwater on September 19, and took part in all the campaigns of that section. On December 10, General Reynolds was transferred to another field, and General Milroy was left in sole command of the Cheat Mountain region. He fought the battle of Allegheny Mountain, December 13, and directed the expedition to Huntersville, December 31, after which the troops went into quarters for the winter.   The history of General Milroy from this time until the return to western Virginia, after the Second Bull Run, is that of our West Virginia Brigade, which he led in every battle and on every march. The full account may be seen in PERSONAL REMINISCENCES OF THE AUTHOR and other chapters of this work, all of his official papers that can be reached, being quoted almost in full.

November 7, 1862, General Milroy left the West Virginia Brigade, and went to New Creek, where he had eight regiments of infantry, two batteries and three cavalry companies under his command.   On December 11, he moved his command from New Creek to Petersburg, and while there sent out scouting parties to Franklin, Brock's Gap settlement and Wardensville, and captured a number of prisoners.   On the 21, he sent General Cluseret with his brigade to Strasburg, which he captured, and then to Winchester, which he occupied December 25, where General Milroy went January 1, 1863. Here the general received his commission as major-general, to date from November 29, 1862, and was presented with a very fine sword by the officers of his command, as a mark of their confidence and esteem.   He was very active while here and did good service.

As there has been a great deal of criticism of the action of General Milroy at Winchester from June 12 to 16, 1863, it is but just to state briefly some facts relating to it.   In volume 7 of the ''Rebellion Records,'' will be found General Milroy's report and letter relating to the affair, which the survivors of his old command would do well to read, as a vindication of their beloved general, whose memory has been aspersed without cause.   General Milroy had a positive order to remain at Winchester, and never received orders to evacuate it.   In obedience to the order he remained there, until he demonstrated the impossibility of remaining longer without being annihilated, or compelled to surrender.   The former was not demanded for the good of the service, and the latter with him was impossible.   He had less than 7000 effective men, and with that small force would not have deemed it his duty to await the approach of Lee's army had he known they were coming that way.   He had a right to expect that if Lee's army advanced against him from Hooker's front, that he would be informed of it by the general-in-chief, through General Schenck, but no such information was ever received. General Milroy knew nothing of the presence of Lee's army until the end of the second day's fighting, when he captured some prisoners from whom he learned he was fighting Lee's army which then had him surrounded. He fought them till 8 o'clock on the evening of the third day when his ammunition and provisions, and all hope of succor, being exhausted, he cut his way out at daybreak on the fourth day, June 15, 1863, and got through with over 6000 effective men, who were on duty in July, as was amply proven before the Court of Inquiry called at his request in August, 1863. As soon as the general-in-chief, Halleck, learned that Milroy had arrived at Harper's Ferry, he telegraphed General Schenck in terms very insulting to Milroy, to give him no command at that place. By orders from General Schenck, he then proceeded to Baltimore, thence to Bloody Run in Bedford County, Pennsylvania, where some 3000 of his command were, that had come through by way of Hancock. He was actively employed, and was preparing to move to the attack on a considerable Rebel force in McConnelsburg, where he received an order on the 26th, from General Couch, in whose department he was then acting, to turn over his command to Colonel Pierce, Twelfth Pennsylvania Cavalry, and report at once to General Schenck in Baltimore, which he did, when by order of the general-in chief, he was placed in arrest. Thus it was for doing his duty, and staying the advance of Lee's army of 60,000 men for four days, which delay enabled General Meade to gain time and interrupt Lee's march, and choose the ground to fight the great pivotal battle of the war at Gettysburg, he was placed in arrest like a felon, and his command by his absence greatly crippled in its efficiency, and he made the victim of malice. There being no charges or causes assigned in the order of arrest, and none being furnished after repeated demand, General Milroy demanded a court of inquiry, to investigate and report upon the evacuation of Winchester. This court was ordered August 4, 1863, and completed its labors September 7, and by its findings and report, and the opinion of President Lincoln thereon October 27, General Milroy was wholly exonerated from all blame. It was an astounding affair, and an act of injustice to a brave and patriotic general, that the exigencies of the service could not excuse.

On May 13, 1864, after being out of command 10 months and 17 days, he received orders to report to Major-General Thomas, at Nashville, Tenn., for duty, where he arrived on the 22d. While General Milroy was in command in Tennessee, his time was occupied in guarding the various lines of transportation, and occasionally in heavy skirmishing with guerrillas. In September he had several engagements with Generals Williams and Wheeler,

ROBERT H. MILROY
Major General U.S. Volunteers

and later fought Generals Forrest and Bates. On December 7 he had a desperate encounter with Bates, near Murfreesboro, in which Bates and Forrest were defeated with heavy loss. This was the last regular battle General Milroy was in, though he remained in command at Tullahoma and Nashville till July, 1865, and resigned on the 18th of that month, and was mustered out July 26, 1865. General Forrest said of him that Milroy was the only Union general that ever defeated him in a fair fight.

After leaving the service, he remained in Tennessee for some time, and then returned to his old home in Delphi, Ind., where he resumed the practice of law. In July, 1872, he was appointed superintendent of Indian affairs for Washington Territory, and moved his family to Olympia, where he resided up to the time of his death. He held this office for two years, when it was abolished. Afterwards he was appointed United States Indian agent for the Yakima agency, and held this office till President Cleveland removed him in September, 1885, for "offensive partisanship." After this he practiced law up to the time of his death, which occurred at Olympia, March 29, 1890, aged 73 years, 9 months and 18 days.

General Milroy was one of the bravest and noblest men of our country. The writer, and the other members of the Second Virginia, had ample opportunity to see the general's bravery tested, and every one will unhesitatingly agree that he was the bravest and coolest man they ever saw in the storm of battle. No braver warrior than General Milroy ever buckled on a sword. His fame is fixed in the annals of his country and in the hearts of soldiers, all of whom loved him as a father, and followed him wherever he called, with implicit faith in his judgment and courage. An experienced officer and thoughtful writer of the Union army, who knew from personal service under Milroy at Winchester, what kind of a commander and fighter he was, has written the following: "Had Gen'l R. H. Milroy been put in command in a place which his genius and ability fitted him to fill, he would have been the Murat of America. There was not an officer in the army of the Union that excelled him in dash and true native courage."

General Milroy was a profoundly religious man. He was cast on the sea of doubt and skepticism for a number of years, but returned to his early faith and became a member of the Presbyterian church, under the ministry of Rev. J. R. Thompson, of the State of Washington.

The Second Virginia Infantry never served under a general for whom the men had so great an affection. It was the regard of men for a friend, and that he was their friend is the testimony of every member of the old regiment. The affection was returned by the noble general, who spoke of them as "my boys," and to whom he had but to speak and they would follow him into the very jaws of death. In a letter to the Historian from one of the general's family, the writer says: "It seems to me that father spoke more frequently of the Second Virginia Infantry than he did of all the other regiments he commanded. There seemed to be more persons in it that he individually remembered and thought a great deal of." When the general was requested to write some of the early events of his life for this history, though very feeble he expressed a desire to do so, "because," as he said, "the old Second Virginia Infantry asked for it," and his son said he was willing to do anything he could for the old regiment, "for there was time when he knew the regiment would do anything he asked them to do."

———

That General Milroy maintained his position at Winchester against such an overwhelming army was largely due to the magnificent fortifications of the place. The credit of this piece of engineering is due to Captain W. Angelo Powell, who displayed a skill in the construction of said works that was pronounced by prominent generals and engineers of the army to be the very best constructed during the war. Captain Powell was not only a skilled engineer, but he displayed conspicuous gallantry upon many battlefields.

CHAPTER LIV.

GENERAL I. H. DUVAL.

His Birth and Early Life.—In the Rocky Mountains.—In Texas among the Indians.—With Lopez in Cuba.—Volunteer in the Army.—Captain and Major in the First West Virginia Infantry.—Colonel of the Ninth Infantry and First Veterans.—In the Eighth Army Corps.—At Port Republic and Opequon.—In Command of Hancock Veteran Corps.—At Staunton, Va.—Capture of General Rosser's Cavalry.—Attempt to Assassinate General Duval.—Elected to Congress.—A Useful Life.

GENERAL I. H. DUVAL was born in Virginia, but left home at an early age for the Far West. He spent 14 years in the Rocky Mountains and on the prairies. Immediately after the annexation of Texas he collected hostile Indians for the Government for the purpose of making treaties, and brought in delegations from 20 different tribes living on the frontier of Texas. He commanded the first company that crossed the plains from Texas to California after the discovery of gold. He had no guide, and traveled the whole distance with the aid of a small pocket compass. He joined the Lopez insurrection in Cuba, and escaped execution by a mere scratch. He returned to this country and entered the U. S. army on the first call for troops. Captain Duval was elected major of the First W. Va. three months' regiment; reappointed major of the three years' regiment, and later appointed colonel of the Ninth W. Va. Infantry, also colonel of the First W. Va. Veterans. He was promoted from time to time up to major-general by brevet.

While he held the rank of colonel, he commanded at different times the First and Second Divisions of the Eighth Army Corps; was on two occasions assigned by special order to the command of the corps in the absence of General Crook; was wounded twice, once at Port Republic, in the foot, and through the left thigh at the battle of the Opequon; had eleven horses killed and wounded under him during the war; was assigned to the new Hancock Veteran Corps, and led it down the valley with orders to get in the rear of Richmond to prevent General Lee's escape should he attempt to get away from General Grant, who was then pressing Lee in front of Richmond. It was expected that General Hancock would have overtaken and assumed command of his forces before Duval reached his destination. At Staunton, Va.,

Duval learned of General Lee's surrender, and realized that Hancock's Veteran Corps would not be required for the service which they expected to perform. Duval was in command and captured General Rosser's cavalry, paroled several thousand Confederate soldiers and captured several trains loaded with iron, leather, guns and army supplies belonging to the Confederate States of America.

While at Staunton an attempt was made to assassinate General Duval· While sitting in the house of a loyal citizen a shot was fired at him, the bullet passing between his arm and body, into the back of the sofa upon which he was sitting.

For several months after peace was declared, General Duval had charge of a subdivision, with headquarters at Wheeling, W. Va., having served four years and nine months in the army, having fought in 34 battles. After the war, General Duval was elected to Congress from the first district of West Virginia; also served four terms in the Legislature of the State and two terms in the State Senate; was adjutant-general of the State for two years, U. S. assessor two years, and 14 years collector of internal revenue for the first district of West Virginia. General Duval told the author that he was most fortunately situated during his service in the war. He had been supported by gallant and efficient officers and men, and his success was mainly due to them. From the start to the finish they never hesitated to do all that was required of them. Their loyalty to country and flag could not be questioned, they were at all times ready to endure hardships, to march and starve, to suffer and to die, if necessary, in upholding the Nation's honor.

L.M. Strayer

ISAAC H. DUVAL
Brevet Major General U.S. Volunteers

CHAPTER LV.

BREVET MAJ.-GEN'L W. W. AVERELL.

His Genealogy.—Early Education.—A School Teacher.—At West Point.—Graduation and Assignment.—At Jefferson Barracks, Mo., and Carlisle, Pa.—In New Mexico Fighting Indians.—Wounded by Navajoes.—An Invalid Two Years.—In the Union Army.—Messenger to Texas.—Exciting Experience in the Far West.—At Washington, D. C., as Mustering Officer.—At First Battle of Bull Run.—Colonel Third Pennsylvania Cavalry.—In Command of First Cavalry Brigade.—Brigadier-General U. S. Vols.—In Command in West Virginia.—Transforming Infantry into Cavalry.—Averell on Lee's Flank after Gettysburg.—Capture of Confederates near Winchester.—Frank S. Reader, Provost-Marshal. —Expedition to and Battle of Rocky Gap.—Compliments to Regimental and Staff Officers.—Official Report of Confederate General Jones.

ILLIAM W. AVERELL descended from New England families. His father was a pioneer of western New York and his grandfather a soldier of the Revolutionary War from Connecticut. His great grandfather wedded a daughter of Josiah Bartlett, the first governor of New Hampshire under the constitution, whose name appears second on the Declaration of Independence. His grandmother was a Turner of Mayflower memory, and his mother a Hemmenway, a name borne by one of the oldest New England families. His father hewed a farm out of the wilderness in Steuben County, New York., early in the century, and became the first postmaster and the first magistrate in the town of Cameron, which offices he held for many years, rearing a family of five children, and died in 1887, aged 92 years. William had the benefit of an academic education, and taught school during two winter terms when he was 15 and 16 years of age, and surveyed lands and roads during the summer. In 1851, at the age of 18, he entered West Point, and was graduated in 1855. While he maintained a fair standing in his class, he devoted all his spare time to a comprehensive course of reading, which the great library at West Point permitted him to enjoy. Fond of athletic sports, he excelled in horsemanship, and stood at the head of a class of five riders. On graduation he was assigned to the regiment of mounted riflemen, now the Third United States Cavalry, whose colonel was then W. W. Loring. He was ordered to the Cavalry School, at Jefferson Barracks, Mo., whose superintendent was Col. Charles A. May, of the Second Dragoons. The school was removed to Carlisle Barracks, Pa., in December, 1855, and Lieutenant Averell remained with it as adjutant until August, 1857. Fitzhugh Lee, W. H. Jackson, D. H. Maury, C. H. Tyler and many other dashing cavalry officers, served at the school while Averell was adjutant. In the autumn of 1857, he joined his regiment in New Mexico, and assumed command of a company, of which both his senior officers were absent; the captain, Andrew Porter, on leave in Europe, and the first lieutenant, Gordon Granger, on recruiting service. An incursion of Kiowa Indians into the valley of the Rio Grande in December, 1857, gave Averell his first chance in an Indian fight, which he embraced by destroying the band and capturing the chief in a hand-to-hand encounter. For this exploit he was honorably mentioned in general orders from General Scott, commander-in-chief of the army. The outbreak of the Navajo tribe in 1858, opened an active field for "The Rifles," as his regiment was familiarly called, and Averell was engaged in about 25 combats with that powerful tribe, and was mentioned in general orders several times for his gallant conduct. His frontier experience was terminated by a wound received in a night attack of Navajoes on his camp, October 8, 1858, which resulted in the fracture of his left thigh, and put him upon crutches for nearly two years. In 1861, Lieutenant Averell went to Washington to see Mr. Lincoln inaugurated, and witnessed the struggles of many of his old Southern comrades and friends, to escape the social and political toils which drew them into secession and rebellion. Although still on sick leave, and an invalid and lame, when Fort Sumter was fired upon, he at once reported for duty, and was selected by General Scott as bearer of dispatches to Col. W. H. Emory, then in northern Texas and the Indian nation, commanding the First Regiment of cavalry and the First Regiment of infantry, the only portions of our little army in that region which had escaped the disgraceful surrender of Twiggs. Emory's command was isolated by the intervening turbulence of secession in southern Missouri and Arkansas, and a special messenger was decided upon as the only means of communication. Making his way through these States with a variety of adventures, young Averell reached Fort Smith to find it in the hands of a Confederate force under Colonel Boreland from Little Rock, and our troops some hundreds of miles out on the wild and perilous frontier. Purchasing a horse, he escaped from the town, swam the Poteaux River, which was booming, and the bridge burned. He was pursued and captured 50 miles out on the Wachita trail, escaped to the San Bois Mountains, which he crossed to the north, was again pursued on the Arbuckle trail, but escaped at the expense of becoming lost for 48 hours, but constantly making his way westward. In a blind ride through a savage country, infested with wild beasts and murderous men, for over 260 miles, he found the command he was seeking to the southeast of Fort Arbuckle, surrounded by Texans and frontier Secessionists. The anxieties of the command were dispelled and its march taken up to the northward. Averell parted with the command on reaching Kansas and hastened to Washington, He was employed in mustering in volunteer regiments until recalled to become adjutant-general of the regular brigade at the first battle of Bull Run, and after that adjutant-general to the Governor of Washington, and provost-marshal of the Army of the Potomac. In August, 1861, he was appointed colonel of the Third Pennsylvania Cavalry, and shortly after had the Eighth Cavalry added to his command, forming the first brigade of cavalry organized in the war. He led the advance into Manassas, March, 1862, and served with the cavalry during the Peninsula campaign. He was promoted to brigadier-general United States Volunteers, September 26, 1862, and served in the Army of the Potomac until he was appointed to the command of the Fourth Separate Brigade in West Virginia, May 16, 1863.

This new brigade formed for General Averell was composed of the Second, Third and Eighth Loyal Virginia Infantry, the Fourteenth Pennsylvania Cavalry, Gibson's Battalion of Cavalry and Battery G,W.Va. L. A. The intention was to organize a force that would be able to meet the Confederate partisan rangers on their own ground, and as these regiments were so intimately acquainted with all the ins and outs of the warfare of the mountains, they were selected for this exceedingly difficult, arduous and dangerous service.

In order to carry into effect this new organization, General Averell proceeded at once to transform the three infantry regiments into mounted infantry, which was accomplished with as little delay as possible. Horses and equipments were soon procured. The soldiers being mostly native West Virginians, were as a rule good horsemen, and readily became efficient riders. The matter of drilling the men in the new tactics was the most serious part of the transformation, but the men were willing students and soon learned to be efficient cavalrymen.

On July 7th, General Averell with all of his brigade except the Second Virginia, was ordered east to harass the lines of General Lee, in his retreat from Gettysburg. While not permitted to take a part in that memorable battle, the brigade rendered efficient service on Lee's flank, causing him considerable trouble and loss. Gen'l H. W. Halleck, in his report to the Secretary of War, November 15, 1863, thus concisely states the services of this brigade in that campaign:

"The operations of our troops in West Virginia are here referred to as being intimately connected with those of the Army of the Potomac. The force being too small to attempt any important campaign by itself, has acted mostly upon the defensive, in repelling raids and breaking up guerrilla bands. When Lee's army retreated across the Potomac in July last, Brigadier-General Kelley concentrated all his available forces on the enemy's flank, near Clear Spring, ready to co-operate in the proposed attack by General Meade. They also rendered valuable services in the pursuit, after Lee had effected his passage of the river."

The troops were forwarded as rapidly as possible, but arrived too late at Williamsport, Md., to do any service there, Lee's army having crossed the river and was on its way south. General Averell with his brigade hastily retraced his steps, aiming to reach the valley and attack Lee's forces in that locality. On the 18th he captured a number of prisoners, and on the 19th found the enemy on the Martinsburg road, having some severe skirmishing and driving them, capturing many more prisoners. The next day a large force of the Confederates attacked Averell and he was compelled to fall back, with considerable fighting during the night. On the 24th he again advanced and continued a forward movement until he reached Winchester on the 30th, camping and reconnoitering at various intermediate points. During the stay here a great many Confederate deserters came to our lines, who were sent to the rear, and a large number of prisoners were paroled.

Mr. Frank S. Reader, who was assistant provost-marshal at the time, said: "It was a part of my duty in camp to look after paroling of prisoners, care of deserters and to hear the complaints and woes, and request for passes, of the citizens of the surrounding country. At this point the number of exceedingly and obtrusively 'loyal' people that annoyed General Averell's headquarters, might have led to the belief that that part of the beautiful valley was the home of all the loyalty of Virginia; but the loyalty was not of the kind to inspire confidence, and the utmost care was required that no advantage was secured by the enemy by means of passes." The command lay here until the 5th of August.

EXPEDITION TO AND BATTLE OF ROCKY GAP.

The following is General Averell's report of this expedition, the best account of the raid and battle that the author has ever seen:

HEADQUARTERS, 4TH SEPARATE BRIGADE, 8TH ARMY CORPS.
BEVERLY, W. VA., *September* 1, 1863.

On August 5 I left Winchester and marched over North Mountain to Wardensville, 28 miles. A lieutenant and 10 men of Imboden's command were captured on the way by Captain Von Koenig who led the advance during the day. I arrived at Moorefield with my command at 8.30 P. M., on the 6th, after a tedious march of 30 miles over a difficult road. At Lost River a company of the Fourteenth Pennsylvania was sent to Moorefield, *via* Harper's Mills, where it captured a lieutenant and a party of the enemy, but subsequently falling into

WILLIAM W. AVERELL
Brevet Major General U.S.A.

an ambush after dark, lost its prisoners and 13 men captured. Four of the Fourteenth Pennsylvania were wounded, and three of the enemy were killed and five wounded. On the 9th, I left Moorefield and marched to Petersburg, 11 miles, leaving Gibson's battalion on the South Fork. My command was at this time badly in want of horse shoes and nails, clothing and ammunition, requisitions for which had been made by my quartermaster, at Cumberland, on the 7th. The order of Brigadier-General Kelley to move was received on the 15th, at Petersburg, but it was not until noon of the 17th that horse-shoe nails arrived. Some ammunition for Ewing's battery was also received, but I was unable to increase my supply for small-arms which amounted to about 35 cartridges to each man. This was sufficient for any ordinary engagement, but we had a long march before us entirely in the country occupied by the enemy, and I felt apprehensive that the supply would be exhausted before the expedition should be ended. It was my opinion that the delay, which would ensue by awaiting the arrival of the ammunition, would be more dangerous to us than undertaking the expedition with the supply we had. Therefore on the 18th, Colonel Oley, of the Eighth West Virginia, was sent with his regiment up the North Fork of the South Branch of the Potomac, and Gibson's battalion up the South Fork, and on the morning of the 19th I moved with the Third West Virginia, Fourteenth Pennsylvania Cavalry and Ewing's battery nearly to Franklin, sending forward two squadrons to destroy the saltpeter works, five miles above.

On the 20th I proceeded up the South Branch to Monterey, over a rough road, the Eighth West Virginia and Gibson's battalion joining the column on the march. A few guerrillas were captured on the road. At Monterey the quarterly court was found in session. Upon my arrival it was adjourned and the principal officials arrested. It was learned that Imboden had been there the day previous to hold a conference with Maj.-Gen'l Samuel Jones, upon the subject of attacking me at Petersburg. The road to Huntersville was taken on the 21st, as far as Gibson's store, my advance, conducted by Lieutenant Rumsey, aide-de-camp, driving about 300 of the enemy before it, during the march, to within five miles of Huntersville. Our casualties during the day were only four wounded and six horses killed and disabled, although constantly annoyed by shots from guerrillas who infested the bushes along the way. Learning, during the night of the 21st, that the enemy had assumed a position in a ravine, about three miles from Huntersville, which was difficult to carry on account of the precipitous character of the sides, I made a false advance on the 22d, with Gibson's battalion, while the main body, taking a by-road to the right, reached Huntersville without meeting resistance, rendering the position of the enemy useless to him, and causing him to retire in haste towards Warm Springs. Colonel Oley, with the Eighth West Virginia and one squadron of the Third West Virginia, was sent after the retreating enemy and overtook his rear guard at Camp Northwest, from whence it was driven several miles. Camp Northwest was burned and destroyed, with commissary buildings and stores, blacksmith shops, several wagons, a number of Enfield rifles, gun equipments and a quantity of wheat and flour at a mill close by. A large number of canteens, stretchers and hospital supplies fell into our hands.

The 23d was spent at Huntersville awaiting the arrival of the Second and Tenth West Virginia. The Tenth and a detachment of about 350 of the Second West Virginia and a section of Keeper's battery arrived during the day from the direction of Beverly. The Second had 40 rounds of ammunition per man, with 1000 rounds additional, which were transferred to the Third West Virginia. During the day a reconnoissance, under Lieutenant-Colonel Polsley, Eighth West Virginia, was made toward Warm Springs. One lieutenant and five men of the enemy were captured, and 12 killed and wounded. Our loss was only five horses shot. On the 24th the march was resumed toward Warm Springs, through which Jackson and his forces were driven over the mountains east of that place toward Millborough.

Our losses during the day were two men severely wounded, some slightly hurt and a few horses shot. Captured many arms, saddles and other stores from the enemy. The forces under Jackson having been driven out of Pocahontas County too soon to permit them to form a junction with any other bodies of the enemy, and the prospect of overtaking him being very small, I determined to turn my column towards Lewisburg, hoping that my movement up to the Warm Springs had led the enemy to believe that I was on my way to his depots in the vicinity of Staunton. I relied also on some co-operation from the direction of Summerville. I therefore sent the Tenth West Virginia back to Huntersville, and on the 25th made a rapid march of 25 miles to Callaghan's in Allegheny County, destroying the saltpeter works on Jackson's River, on my way. Arrived at Callaghan's, reconnoitering parties were sent to Covington and Sweet Springs. Some wagons of the enemy were captured near Covington, and the saltpeter works in that vicinity destroyed.

At 4 A. M. on the 26th my column was formed, en route to White Sulphur Springs. The road crossed two mountain ranges before 10 miles had been traveled over. About 9.30 A. M., when about 12 miles from Callaghan's, a message from Captain Von Koenig was received by me at the head of the column, that the enemy were resisting his advance and desiring re-enforcements. A squadron of the Second was sent on at a trot, and a squadron of the Eighth ordered forward. A few minutes elapsed when the enemy's cannon announced his purpose of disputing our farther progress and indicated his strength. I at once started the column forward at a rapid gait down through a narrow pass, which soon opened out into a little valley a mile long, inclosed on each side by rugged rocky heights, covered with a stunted growth of pine, oak und chestnut trees. At the opening, the projectiles from the enemy's cannon first struck the head of our column. A jutting cliff on the right afforded protection for the horses of the Second and Eighth, and the dismounted men of the Second were at once ordered to the summit of the ridge, and the squadron of the Eighth dismounted to the hill on our left.

A section of Ewing's battery was brought up rapidly and planted on the first available position, where it opened briskly and with great accuracy. The squadron of the Eighth, ordered to the left, mistook the direction in some way, and found itself on the right with the Second West Virginia. The main body of the Eighth West Virginia, led by Colonel Oley, however, soon made their way to the crest on our left. The Third West Virginia and Fourteenth Pennsylvania were ordered forward, came to the front and dismounted very soon. I beg to call your attention to the fact that my column of horses, nearly four miles long, was now in a narrow gorge, and that during the time necessary for the Third West Virginia and Fourteenth Pennsylvania to arrive at the front, it was necessary that Ewing, supported only by the advance guard, should maintain his position against an attack of the enemy's artillery and infantry combined. The Second on the right and the Eighth on the left, afforded some support, but Ewing's battery, with canister, not only resisted the approach of the enemy, but actually advanced upon him, in order to obtain a better position, and held him at bay until the arrival of the Fourteenth Pennsylvania and Third West Virginia, which were at once deployed to the right and left of the road, thus filling up the gap in my line. The enemy gave away his position to us and endeavored to assume another about half a mile in rear of the first, with his right resting upon a rugged prominence, his center and left protected by a temporary stockade, which he had formed of fence rails. I resolved to dislodge him before he should become well established, and then, if possible, to rout him from the field. One of the guns of Ewing had burst, and the other five were advanced to within 600 yards of the enemy. Capt. Von Koenig was sent to advance the Third and Eighth, and orders were sent to the right also to advance. Gibson's battalion was thrown into a house and the surrounding enclosures which stood in front of the enemy's centre. The enemy clung tenaciously to the wooded hill on their right, and Gibson's battalion was driven from the house by a regiment of the enemy, which at that moment arrived upon the field. I immediately caused the house to be set on fire by shells, which prevented the enemy from occupying it. The right was able to gain only a short distance by hard fighting. It then became an affair of sharpshooters along the whole line at a distance of less than 100 yards. The effort which my men had made in scaling a succession of heights on either hand, had wearied them almost to exhaustion. A careful fire was kept up by small-arms for three hours, it being almost impossible for either side to advance or retire. During this time I reconnoitered the position, going from the hills on the right to the left. At about 4 P. M. I determined to make another effort to carry the position. A squadron of the Fourteenth Pennsylvania, which had not been dismounted, was brought up and instructions sent to the commanders along the line that a cavalry charge was about to be made on the enemy's center, and directing them to act in concert. The charge was splendidly made by Captain Bird, of the Fourteenth Pennsylvania cavalry, who led his men until he came to a stockade which the enemy had thrown across the road. Orders had been given to the officers commanding the regiments on the right, to press forward at the same time and endeavor to gain the Antony's Creek road, which came in on the enemy's left. The order to the Second to advance was conveyed by Lieutenant Combs, the adjutant of that regiment, who delivered the order to that portion of the regiment nearest him. Major McNally on the right, and Lieutenant Combs on the left, of the regiment, with less than 100 men, advanced on the enemy's line and drove them out of the stockade, leaving Major McNally mortally wounded in the hands of the enemy. The effect of the cavalry charge was to cause about 300 of the enemy to run away from the stockade, exposing themselves to a deadly fire from the Fourteenth Pennsylvania, Colonel Schoonmaker, but their position was soon regained by their reserves. No united effort was made to attain the road on the extreme right, as directed. Reports soon reached me from all parts of the line that ammunition was falling short. The slackened firing of the enemy evidently indicated that his supply was not plentiful. The night came with no change in position, and no tidings from the west, whence General Scammon was expected. During the night all the ammunition in the wagons was brought up and equally distributed, and every available man brought to the front. It was quite evident to my mind that if the resistance of the enemy was kept up, I could go no farther in that direction. It was impossible to retire during the night without disorder, and perhaps disaster. By remaining until morning two chances remained with me : first, the enemy might retreat, and, second, Scammon might arrive. The morning showed us that both chances had failed, that the enemy had received ammunition, and that re-enforcements were coming to him from the direction of Lewisburg. The battle was renewed, but every arrangement made in rear for a prompt withdrawal. The ambulances loaded with wounded, the caissons, wagons, and long columns of horses were placed in proper order upon the road, details made for the attendance of the wounded, trees prepared to fell across the gorge when our artillery should have passed, and commanding officers received their instructions. The enemy's re-enforcements arrived and attempted to turn my left about 10 A. M. At 10.30 o'clock the order to retire was given, and in forty-five minutes from that time my column was moving off in good order, my rear guard at the barricades repulsing the enemy's advance twice before it left the ground. Successive barricades were formed and my column reached Callaghan's about 5 P. M., where it was halted, fires built, and the men and horses given the first opportunity to eat for thirty-six hours. After dark the fires were left burning and the column took the road to Warm Springs. A scouting party of the enemy in front of us had left word with the citizens that Jackson was at Gatewood's, with a strong force. This shallow attempt at deception did not deter us from marching to that point, where we arrived at daylight on the 28th. At

9 A. M. the march was resumed to Huntersville without interruption, but with considerable annoyance from guerrillas. At evening we marched to Greenbrier Bridge, or Marlin's Bottom, where Colonel Harris, with the Tenth West Virginia, was posted. The ensuing day the command moved to Big Springs, where it was ascertained that a party of the enemy had entered the road before us for the purpose of blockading it. At 2 A. M., on the 30th, we were again *en route*, and at daylight came upon a blockade, half a mile long, made by felling large trees across the road. While delayed in cutting it out the animals were fed and a strong blockade made in rear. The command arrived at Beverly on August 31, having marched, since June 10, 636 miles, exclusive of the distance passed over by railroad, and of the marches made by detachments, which would increase the distance for the entire command to at least 1000 miles. This command has been mounted, equipped and drilled; marched over 600 miles through a rugged mountainous region, fighting the enemy almost daily; had one severe battle; destroyed the camps of the enemy; captured large amounts of supplies and 266 prisoners, in less than eighty days. The strength of the enemy opposed to me in the engagement at Rocky Gap was 2500, as near as could be ascertained by observations and from the reports of prisoners, and also from statements of Rebel officers. I did not have 1300 men in the front the first day. . . .

Among those who particularly distinguished themselves in action for gallantry and ability, I would mention the following officers, viz.: Capt. Paul Von Koenig, aide-de-camp, killed, First W. Va. Artillery; Capt. C. T. Ewing, wounded, Second W. Va. Mounted Infantry; Maj. F. P. McNally, died of wounds, Eighth W. Va. Mounted Infantry; Capts. W. L. Gardner, W. H. H. Parker, and Lieut. J. A. Morehart, killed, Fourteenth Pa. Cavalry; Capt. John Bird, wounded and prisoner; Lieuts. John N. McNutt, M. W. Wilson, James Jackson, and Jacob Schoop, wounded.

I was greatly indebted to the following named officers for their untiring energy and hearty co-operation during the battle: Lieut.'s J. R. Meigs, of the Engineers, U. S. Army, and Will Rumsey; Capt. C. F. Trowbridge and Lieut. L. Markbreit, aides-de-camp; Maj. Theodore F. Lang, acting assistant inspector-general; Lieut. Geo. H. North, assistant quartermaster; Cols. J. N. Schoonmaker, 14th Pa. Cav., and J. H. Oley, 8th W. Va. Mounted Inft.; Lieuts. J. Combs, adjutant, 2d W. Va. Mounted Inft., and B. H. H. Atkinson, Battery B, 1st W. Va. Artilery.

*   *   *   *   *   *   *   *   *   *   *

WM. W. AVERELL,
Brigadier-General of Volunteers.

The following is the report of Maj.-Gen'l Sam. Jones, commanding the Confederate forces of the battle:

On the evening of August 23 I received information from Col. Wm. L. Jackson that Brig.-Gen'l Averell, U. S. Army, with a force estimated at over 4000 men, consisting of cavalry, mounted infantry and artillery, was in motion from the direction of Moorefield. So far as I could ascertain, General Averell was on a raid towards Staunton. He had driven Colonel Jackson from Hightown and his camp near Huntersville, and the latter had fallen back to Gatewood's on Back Creek, on the road from Huntersville to Warm Springs. I had a few days previously ridden over that road, Colonel Jackson accompanying me part of the way, and from my own observations and his representations, believed that he could detain the enemy on that road long enough to enable me to send a force to his assistance or place it in the rear of the enemy. I accordingly ordered the First Brigade of my command, Col. George S. Patton, commanding, to move by the Antony's Creek road. I joined the brigade myself on that road on the 25th. On the morning of that day I received a dispatch from Col.

Jackson, dated at 9 o'clock on the previous day, at Gatewood's. He informed me that he had driven back the enemy's skirmishers to his old camp near Huntersville. The tenor of the dispatch induced me to believe that he could not only check the opposing force at Gatewood's but could move up and join the First Brigade at the intersection of the Antony's Creek road from Huntersville to Warm Springs. I dispatched him, informing him of the movement of that brigade, directed him, if possible, to join it at the junction of the roads above mentioned. I have reason to believe that he never received my dispatch, and that it was intercepted by the enemy. While on the march on the 25th, information was received, which I deemed reliable, that the enemy had not only driven Colonel Jackson from Gatewood's but had forced him beyond Warm Springs. Still remaining under the impression that the destination of the enemy was Staunton, the First Brigade was ordered to turn off from the Antony's Creek road and take a shorter route to Warm Springs. After 10 o'clock that night information was received which satisfied me that the enemy had abandoned the pursuit of Colonel Jackson and that while the First Brigade was marching toward Warm Springs, General Averell was advancing from Warm Springs to Callaghan's. I immediately ordered Colonel Patton to return on the Antony's Creek road in the hope of intercepting the enemy on the road from the Warm to the White Sulphur Springs. By a night march our advance guard reached the intersection of the latter named road at the same instant that the head of Averell's column debouched from the defile through the Allegheny Mountains on the road from Callaghan's. General Averell endeavored to force his way through, but the First Brigade was quickly placed in position, when an engagement commenced, which, for five hours, was very warm and continued at intervals until dark. That night the troops occupied the same position that they had taken in the morning. The enemy made two vigorous attacks the next morning which were handsomely repulsed, when he abandoned his position and retreated towards Warm Springs. My cavalry and artillery were ordered in pursuit. For about ten or eleven miles the road passes through a narrow and thickly wooded defile. The enemy availed himself of the advantage offered to retard pursuit by felling trees across the road.

The report of General Jones shows his losses to be 20 killed, 129 wounded and 13 captured—a total of 162.

CHAPTER LVI.

BREVET MAJ.-GEN'L WM. W. AVERELL—(CONTINUED).

Droop Mountain Campaign.—General Averell's Official Report.—Salem Raid.—Winter Soldiering.—Destruction of Railroad between Richmond and Knoxville.—Thrilling Report of General Averell.—Gen'l Sam. Jones' Dispatch.—The Richmond *Examiner's* Sarcastic Comment.—Weather Intensely Cold.—Averell at Martinsburg.

HE months of September and October were ones of intense activity, consisting of heavy picket duty, arduous scouting and severe drilling. Scouting was the regular order, and it was the exception when one or more scouting parties were not out in the mountains or valleys, watching the movements of the Confederates who were constantly hovering about. On the 1st of November, 1863, orders were issued to take the road again to the southward.

The following is General Averell's report of this expedition:

On the 1st day of November, I left Beverly with my command consisting of the Twenty-Eighth Ohio Volunteer Infantry, Col. A. Moor; Tenth West Virginia Volunteer Infantry, Col. T. M. Harris; Second West Virginia Mounted Infantry, Lieut.-Col. A. Scott; Third West Virginia Mounted Infantry, Lieut.-Col. F. W. Thompson; Eighth West Virginia Mounted Infantry, Col. J. H. Oley; Fourteenth Pennsylvania Cavalry, Col. J. N. Schoonmaker; Gibson's Battalion and Batteries B and G, First West Virginia Light Artillery, Capts. J. V. Keeper and C. T. Ewing. The command moved on the Staunton pike to Greenbrier Bridge, and thence by Camp Bartow and Green Bank to Huntersville, driving before them the enemy's pickets, and capturing or dispersing the guerrilla bands which infest that part of the country. The command reached Huntersville at noon of the 4th, and it was there ascertained that Lieutenant-Colonel Thompson, of Jackson's command, was at Marlin's Bottom, with a force of about 600 men. I at once sent the Fourteenth Pennsylvania Cavalry and Third West Virginia Mounted Infantry on the direct road to Mill Point, to cut off Thompson's retreat toward Lewisburg, and the Second and Eighth West Virginia Mounted Infantry and one section of Ewing's battery to Marlin's Bottom, to attack him at that place. At 9 o'clock I received information from Colonel Oley, Eighth West Virginia Mounted Infantry, commanding detachment to Marlin's Bottom that the enemy had retired toward Mill Point, blockading the road in their rear. A dispatch from Colonel Schoonmaker, Fourteenth Pennsylvania Cavalry, received about midnight, informed me that Thompson had effected a junction with the remainder of Jackson's command, and that it was all in position in his front and threatening an attack. The infantry and Keeper's battery were moved about 3 A. M. to join Schoonmaker, and Oley was ordered to cut out the blockade and march to the same point as fast as possible. I reached Mill Point with the infantry and Keeper at 8 A. M. on the 5th, and found that they had just arrived, and that the enemy were retiring. This was Thursday, the 5th of November. We were thirty-four miles from Lewisburg, at which point it had been directed that my force should arrive on Saturday, at 2 P. M. It was not thought proper to press the enemy vigorously on this day, in order to keep him as far as possible from Lewisburg, and not to permit him to be re-enforced from that direction, and to gain the advantage which would follow from the arrival at Lewisburg of the force under General Duffie from the Kanawha Valley. An attempt was, however, made to capture the force under Jackson by sending three mounted regiments to cut off his retreat. The rapidity of the enemy's movements made this attempt unsuccessful, and he succeeded in reaching Droop Mountain, upon the summit of which he made a stand. My advance was withdrawn from the fire of his artillery and the attack postponed until the ensuing day. On the morning of the 6th, we approached the enemy's position. The main road to Lewisburg runs over Droop Mountain, the northern slope of which is partially cultivated nearly to the summit, a distance of two-and-one-half miles from the foot. The highway is partially hidden in the views from the summit and base in strips of woodland. It is necessary to pass over low rolling hills and across bewildering ravines to reach the mountain in any direction. The position of the enemy was defined by a skirmishing attack of three companies of infantry. It was thought that a direct attack would be difficult.

The infantry and one company of cavalry were therefore sent to the right to ascend a range of hills which ran westward from Droop Mountain, with orders to attack the enemy's left and rear. To divert the enemy's attention from this, the Fourteenth Pennsylvania and Keeper's battery made a successful demonstration upon his right. The remainder of the command prepaired for action. While these movements were progressing, the arrival of re-enforcements to the enemy was announced by the music of a band, the display of battle-flags and loud cheers of the Rebels on the top of the mountain. The attack of our infantry, 1175 strong, was conducted skillfully and resolutely by Col. A. Moor. The guide who had been sent with him proving worthless, he directed his column, nine miles over the mountains and through the wilderness to the enemy's left, led by the flying pickets and the sound of his cannon. The intermittent reports of musketry heralded the approach of Colonel Moor to his destination, and at 1.45 P. M. it was evident from the sound of the battle on the enemy's left and his disturbed appearance in front, that the time for the direct attack had arrived. The Second, Third and Eighth West Virginia dismounted, were moved in line obliquely to the right up the face of the mountain, until their right was joined to Moor's left. The fire of Ewing's battery was added to that of Keeper's. At 3 P. M. the enemy were driven from the summit of the mountain upon which they had been somewhat protected by rude breastworks of logs, stones and earth. Gibson's battalion and one section of Ewing's battery were at once ordered to pursue the routed Rebels. Fragments of each regiment were already eagerly in pursuit. The horses of Second, Third, Eighth and Fourteenth were brought up the mountain as soon as possible. The infantry pushed forward, and as soon as details had been made for succoring the wounded and burying the dead, the entire command followed the enemy until dark. It appeared from the reports of prisoners that the enemy's force had consisted of the Fourteenth Virginia Cavalry, Twenty-second Virginia Infantry, Derrick's Battalion, Edgar's Battalion, Jackson's Brigade and seven pieces of artillery; in all about 4000 men. His loss in killed and wounded was about 250, one piece of artillery and one stand of colors. Several men of my command reported having seen and measured two other pieces of artillery abandonded by the enemy and secreted by the wayside. Time was not had, however, to look after them. I did not desire to reap more than the immediate fruits of victory that evening. It was yet twenty miles to Lewisburg, and I hoped that by letting the enemy alone during the night, he might loiter on the route and be caught the next day between my command and the force expected from the Kanawha Valley. As we went down the mountain the following morning, we could see the smoke of several camp fires along the mountains to the eastward, showing that the enemy had been somewhat dispersed. On the 7th I moved rapidly forward over an excellent road toward Lewisburg. The Fourteenth, which was in advance, reached that place at 2 P. M., and found Gen'l Duffie with four regiments and one section of artillery already in possession of the town. He had reached it at 10 P. M., capturing a few stragglers and such material as the enemy had been unable to remove in his flight. I learned that a small portion of the enemy's main body had passed through Lewisburg in great disorder early on the morning of the 7th on their way to Dublin. I also learned that Gen'l Lee had promised Brig.-Gen'l Echols ample re-enforcements at or near that point. I determined to move with my whole command to that place, and accordingly set out on the morning of the 8th. After proceeding a few miles, a formidable blockade was encountered through which it was necessary to cut a passage. General Duffie reported his command as unfit for further operations, as his infantry had but one day's rations and was so exhausted as to be able to march only ten miles per day. My own infantry was encumbered with the prisoners, captured property and material. I therefore ordered General Duffie to retire to Meadow Bluff, and Colonel Moor, with the Twenty-eighth Ohio Volunteer Infantry, Tenth West Virginia Volunteer Infantry and Keeper's Battery to return to Beverly, taking with him all the prisoners and such of the wounded from the battle of Droop Mountain as could be transported. Colonel Moor brought from Hillsborough fifty-five of our own and one Rebel wounded. He left with those who were too badly wounded to bear transportation, Assistant Surgeon Blair, Tenth West Virginia Volunteer Infantry, and supplied them with all the rations, hospital stores and medicines which could be spared. His command reached Beverly on the 12th, bringing with it all the prisoners, property, etc., which had been captured up to the arrival of my command at Lewisburg. With the cavalry, mounted infantry and Ewing's battery of my command, I moved *via* White Sulphur Springs to near Callaghan's, passing through the battle ground of Rocky Gap on my way. At White Sulphur I retook the wounded of my command who had been left after the battle of Rocky Gap in August last. At Callaghan's on the morning of the 9th I learned that General Imboden, with from 900 to 1500 men, was at Covington on his way to re-enforce Echols at Union.

Not deeming his command of sufficient importance to delay my march, and knowing the impossibility of bringing him to a fight, I sent two squadrons of the Eighth West Virginia Mounted Infantry, under Major Slack, to drive him away from my line of march. This was accomplished after a sharp skirmish, in which Imboden was reported wounded, and one lieutenant and twenty men of his command were captured. From Callaghan's I moved by Gatewood's up the Back Creek road to Franklin; the main body of the command moved through Monterey and joined me about eight miles beyond that place. At Hightown I met Colonel Thoburn, with a brigade of infantry and two pieces of artillery, whom I directed to return to Petersburg. My command reached Petersburg on the 13th where it was supplied with rations and forage. On the 17th I arrived at New Creek, bringing with me about 150 captured horses and 27 prisoners, exclusive of those which were sent from Lewisburg with Colonel Moor. Several hundred cattle were captured on the march.

Since leaving Beverly, seventeen days, we marched 296 miles, a part of the time suffering intensely from the cold, constantly subjected to the hidden attacks of bushwhackers, and having fought one of the most gallant and triumphant little battles of the war.

THE SALEM RAID.

General Burnside was besieged at Knoxville, Tenn., by Confederate General Longstreet, and in order to raise the siege by cutting off the latter's supplies, and compel him to move his base of supplies, General Averell was directed to cut the railroad, and interrupt communication between Richmond and Knoxville, at all hazards, even if his whole force was captured or destroyed. By a dispensation of Providence, General Averell was enabled not only to accomplish the plans laid down, and the results desired, but as well to return to our lines with the loss of a very small number of his men, and none of his artillery. There was no single incident during the war, that was attended with greater perils, in which greater suffering to both man and beast were experienced than this raid furnished. No better history of the event can possibly be written than the thrilling report of General Averell, which we give in full:

HEADQUARTERS, FIRST SEPARATE BRIGADE, DEPARTMENT OF W. VA.,
MARTINSBURG, W. VA., *December* 31, 1863.

Captain: I have the honor to submit the following report of the operations of my brigade since the date of its arrival at New Creek, W. Va., November 18. Having been notified by the brigadier-general commanding the department, that active service would be expected of me very soon, measures were at once taken to place the command in as good condition as possible, but owing to the meagre supply of horses, shoes, nails, coal and forges furnished, and the shortness of the time allowed, the mounted forces of the brigade were but poorly prepared to make a long march on the 6th of December, when I received orders to move on the 8th. My orders did not contemplate the movement of any co-operative forces excepting a small force under Colonel Thoburn, but after representing to the department commander the importance of such movements, and my desire that they should be made, he kindly invited me to accompany him to his headquarters at Cumberland and arrange a plan for them. I went with him to Cumberland on the evening of the 6th, and drew up a plan which was briefly as follows, viz.: Brigadier Scammon, commanding forces in the Kanawha Valley, to be at Lewisburg on Saturday, December 12; to look out northward and endeavor to intercept the enemy from that direction; to remain until the 18th, taking advantage of any opportunity to strike the enemy in the direction of Union or elsewhere. Colonel Moor to be at Marlin's Bottom, Friday, December 11; to feel the enemy in the direction of Lewisburg on the 12th and 13th; to remain near Frankfort until the 18th, and on his return to bring off the wounded left after the battle of Droop Mountain. Brigadier-General Sullivan, commanding forces in the Shenandoah Valley, to be at Woodstock on Friday, December 11, to make careful demonstrations until the 18th, when he was to move toward Staunton, and threaten the same boldly on the 20th and 21st. The command of Colonel Thoburn was to turn off at Monterey, and moving toward Staunton, keep the attention of the enemy fixed upon the Parkersburg pike. A copy of the above plan was given to the department commander and I received his promise that his orders should be given in accordance with it, with the exception of Moor's and Thoburn's commands, which were to receive orders from me. It was thought that between the two demonstrations of the Kanawha and Shenandoah forces, I might pass the enemy's lines without delay, and that the threatening of Staunton on the 20th and 21st with the operations in the direction of Union, would divert the enemy from offering any great resistance to the return of my fatigued command.

The Second West Virginia Mounted Infantry, Lieutenant-Colonel Scott; Third West Virginia Mounted Infantry, Lieutenant-Colonel Thompson; Eighth West Virginia Mounted Infantry, Colonel Oley; Fourteenth Pennsylvania Cavalry, Lieutenant-Colonel Blakely; Major Gibson's battalion of cavalry, and Ewing's battery set out from New Creek on the morning of the 18th of December, with fair weather, but with many misgivings on account of our poor condition to overcome the weary distances and confront the perils incident to such an expedition. During the march of two days to Petersburg, constant exertions were made to complete the shoeing of the horses, but lack of means and material rendered it impracticable to attain the desired object. At Petersburg, on the 10th, the command of Colonel Thoburn, about 700 strong, joined mine, and together we proceeded southward, arriving nearly at Monterey on the 11th. The most of my train was placed in charge of Colonel Thoburn and, on the morning of the 12th, my command and his started in a severe and discouraging rain storm, Thoburn toward McDowell, and my command down Back Creek. The secluded road which runs along and across this now swollen stream, was pursued the ensuing day without any incident worthy of note, until our arrival at Gatewood's where the rear guard of Jackson's forces, flying from the advance of Moor, was encountered and dispersed, and four wagons destroyed loaded with ammunition and stores. The storm continued on the 14th, and Jackson's River was found hardly fordable. Upon arriving at Callaghan's, reports reached us that Scammon had advanced and occupied Lewisburg, and that the Rebel forces, commanded by General Echols, had retired toward Union, under order from Maj.-Gen'l Sam. Jones. We halted a few hours to rest and feed the animals, and to make a false advance in the direction of Covington. At 2 A. M., December 15, the column was in motion upon a dark and difficult road, which runs up Dunlap Creek to the pike, connecting the White with the Sweet Sulphur Springs. We reached the beautiful valley of the Sweet Sulphur, about 10 A. M., and halted two hours, availing ourselves of the plentiful forage found there. * * * * * * * *

At the Sweet Springs it was learned that Echols' forces were encamped four miles from Union, to the northward, and that General Scammon had retired from Lewisburg. The road to Newcastle was taken at 1 P. M., and near the summit of the Sweet Springs Mountain a Rebel quartermaster met us and was captured, which assured me that our advance was unknown as yet to the enemy. From the top of this mountain a sublime spectacle was presented to us. Seventy miles to the eastward the Peaks of Otter reared their summits above the Blue Ridge, and all the space between was filled with a billowing ocean of hills and mountains, while behind us the great Alleghanies, coming from the north with the grandeur of innumerable tints, swept past and faded in the southern horizon. When within twelve miles of Newcastle another halt was made to feed and rest, while a squadron advanced toward Fincastle, conveying to the enemy a false impression, and bringing to us some sixty horses and some prisoners. Newcastle was passed during the night, and efforts were made to reach Salem by daylight in the morning. A party of Rebels, under Captain Chapman, reconnoitered our advance during the night, and all were captured except their leader, who, declining to surrender, was killed. The head of my column was preceded by vigilant scouts, armed with repeating rifles, mounted upon fleet horses, who permitted no one to go ahead of them.

We approached Salem unheralded, and the whistling of locomotives could be heard from that point long before it was reached by us. Four miles from Salem, a party of Rebels from the town in quest of information concerning the Yankees, met us. From some of these it was learned that the division of Gen'l Fitzhugh Lee had left Charlottesville on the 14th to intercept my command, and that a train loaded with troops was momentarily expected at Salem to guard the stores at that point. I hastened with my advance, consisting of about 350 men and two 3-inch guns, through the town to the depot. The telegraph wires were first cut—the operator was not to be found—the railroad track torn up in the vicinity of the depot, one gun placed in battery and the advance dismounted and placed in readiness for the expected train of troops. An inspection and estimate of the stores contained in the depot and two large buildings adjacent were made, and upon a subsequent comparison of notes taken, found to be as follows:—2000 barrels of flour, 10,000 bushels of wheat, 100,000 bushels of shelled corn, 50,000 bushels of oats, 2000 barrels of meat, several cords of leather, 1000 sacks of salt, 31 boxes of clothing, 20 bales of cotton, a large amount of harness, shoes, saddles, equipments, tools, oil, tar, and various other stores and 100 wagons. A train from Lynchburg, loaded with troops, soon approached. My main body was not yet in sight, and it was necessary to stop the train ; a shot was fired at it from one of the guns, which missed; a second went through the train diagonally, which caused it to retire, and a third and last shot hastened its movements. My main body arrived, and parties were sent four miles to the eastward and twelve miles to the westward to destroy the road. The depots with their contents were burned ; three cars standing upon the track, the water-station, turn-table and a large pile of bridge timber and repairing material destroyed. Five bridges were burned and the track torn up and destroyed as much as possible in six hours. The "yanks" with which we had provided ourselves, proved too weak to twist the U rails, and efforts were made to bend them, by heating the centres, with but partial success. A few small store houses, containing leather and other valuable articles, were destroyed in the vicinity. The telegraph wires were cut, coiled and burned for over half a mile. Private property was untouched by my command, and the citizens received us with politeness.

It was intimated to some inquisitive ones that we were going back by Buchanan, but about 4 P. M. my command quitted the work of destruction and returned upon the road it came some seven miles, when it halted for the night. The last eighty miles had been marched in about thirty hours. Little sleep had been enjoyed by my men during five days and nights ; it was necessary to pause and collect our energies for the return. During the night of the 16th it rained heavily, and also the ensuing day and night. My column was caught in the many windings of Craig's Creek, which was now swollen to a dangerous torrent which uprooted trees and carried them away. Heavy caissons were swept down the stream, and great exertion and skill were required to save them. In the river and in the rain forty-eight hours, it was impracticable to keep our ammunition dry, and my command, drenched, muddy and hungry arrived at Newcastle about sun-down on the 18th, in a miserable condition to make the march before us. Information that Fitzhugh Lee was at Fincastle reached me at Newcastle, and that Jones was between me and Sweet Springs. At 9 P. M. while a false advance was made toward Fincastle, my column took the road to Sweet Springs. We soon encountered and drove the enemy's pickets about twelve miles, to the junction of the road with the Fincastle pike, to the Sweet Springs. The command halted and built camp fires.

The condition of my ammunition made it prudent for me to avoid a fight. It was evident from a survey of the enemy's positions, that I could not get to the Sweet Springs without a contest, and that with Lee only a few miles to my right and rear. Two ways were left, both difficult and obscure : one to the southwest leading around Jones' right, through Monroe and Greenbrier Counties ; the other, northeast to the Covington and Fincastle pike, which I took, as it was the most direct and dangerous, consequently the safest if I could only make the march. We left our camp fires burning and went forward in the darkest and coldest night we had yet experienced. Thirty miles through the forest and frost, brought us to Fincastle pike about noon of the 19th. It was yet 15 miles to the bridge. The river was reported unfordable on account of the depth of the water and the obstructions formed by the ice. I had carefully calculated the possible marches of the enemy, and felt certain that we could make the march through the points they deemed most secure, but no halt could be made. When eight miles from the river a force of 300 mounted Rebels opposed our advance. As soon as they were broken, they were closely pursued at a gallop to the first bridge, five miles below Covington, and thence to the bridge at Covington, both of which were saved from destruction, although faggots had been piled upon them ready to burn. The head of my column reached the first bridge about 9 P. M. and three officers and six orderlies were sent back to keep it closed up.

The approach to the river is through a gorge which opens to the stream a mile below the first bridge. There the pike from Covington passes along the right bank to Clifton Forge and Jackson's River Depot, where Jackson was supposed to be with about 1000 men. I sent a company upon the road to Clifton Forge, with orders to dismount and move out three-fourths of a mile and hold the road until the colomn passed. A captured dispatch from Maj.-Gen'l Sam. Jones to Major-General Early, at Millborough, confirmed my opinion with regard to the position of the enemy, and gave me the information that General Early's division had been added to the forces opposed to my return. The dispatch is as follows:

ON TOP OF THE SWEET SPRINGS MOUNTAIN,
Dec. 19, 1863—7 A. M.

General: The enemy drove the pickets about 12 miles from here, near Mrs. Scott's, in the direction of Newcastle, about 2 o'clock this morning. General Echols has a strong position here and I think can effectually block this way to them. To avoid him, I think it probable that the enemy may attempt to escape by Covington or by Clifton Forge. Colonel Jackson's troops are at Clifton Forge. I would suggest, instead of keeping any force at the Warm Springs you would place it at Morris Hill and picket at Callaghan's. I presume that you are in communication with Colonel Jackson, and he may be able to give you information of the enemy's movements. I expect to ascertain the enemy's movements in the course of the morning. If he attempts to avoid Echols here and escape by Callaghan's we can reach Callaghan's before he can. Echols will hold the place here until he ascertains the enemy's movements. It is possible that they will attempt to pass Echols' right by Gap Mills, by passing one of the many gorges in these mountains to the south of this position between Echols and McCausland, who is at Newport, in Giles County. If he does that, he will pass out by the western portion of Monroe and Greenbrier; if he does so, you cannot touch him. Under all the circumstances of the case, as I see them now, I think that you should have a force at Morris Hill and a strong picket at Callaghan's. The enemy were certainly at Newcastle at sundown yesterday.

They cannot pass Echols here. They may escape by Clifton Forge or by Covington, if you do not prevent them. Echols will give you all the aid that he can. We are closer to the enemy than you are, and will be more likely to know their movements. I will endeavor to keep you informed. A portion of our small mounted force has been directed, if the enemy attempts to pass from Newcastle direct to Covington, or by Clifton Forge, to fall back in front of them so as to give Colonel Jackson and you the earliest information.

The operator at Jackson's River will use every effort to get the above to General Early and a copy to General Jackson. Colonel Jackson must have a copy of it.

SAM. JONES, *Major General.*

I relied somewhat upon the demonstration which was to be made against Staunton on the next day. I also thought that General Scammon might divert the force under Echols from interfering with mine. In both these trusts I was at fault. From all the information I have been able to collect, I believe the Kanawha force retired from Lewisburg on the 13th without waiting until the 18th as prearranged, and without making an effort in the direction of Union. The detachment sent from the command of General Sullivan was too feeble to make the threat upon Staunton of sufficient avail to keep Early from besetting my command upon its return. Instead of approaching Staunton on the 20th and 21st, it was retiring through New Market on the 20th. The dispositions of the Rebels had been prompt and skillful; Rossers brigade had crossed the Rappahannock at Fredericksburg on the 14th, made some demonstrations upon the Orange and Alexandria railroad near Bull Run; thence passed the Blue Ridge through Ashby's Gap; were stopped by the high water in the Shenandoah, and moved up by Front Royal to cut off the detachment from Harper's Ferry. The division of Early left Hanover Junction on the 15th; arrived at Staunton the same night; marched to Buffalo Gap the ensuing day, and thence to the Warm Springs and Millborough. Fitzhugh Lee's division leaving Charlottesville on the 14th, came into the valley, where it was decei ed by Thoburn's presence and diverted by the detachment from Sullivan's command for a day or two when it set out for Buchanan.

At Jackson's River, though trusting in the co-operation of the Kanawha and Shenandoah forces, I acted as though they would be of no assistance to me, which was indeed the case. My column, nearly four miles long, was hastened across the first bridge. When all had passed but my ambulances, a few wagons and a regiment in the rear, an attack was made by Jackson's force. The company on the Clifton Forge road was driven away : three ambulances were captured, and an effort was made to take the bridge which was unsuccessful. A night attack is always appalling, even to experienced troops. Unavailing efforts were made to open communication with the regiment cut off until morning, when it appeared that the enemy was determined to maintain his position upon the high cliffs which overlooked the bridge. During the night the balance of my command had been concentrated upon Callaghan's, and an efficient defense established upon all the roads approaching that point. Finding it impossible to dislodge the enemy as long the bridges remained, I directed them to be destroyed. The enemy at once left the cliffs and endeavored to reach the flank and rear of the regiment which remained on that side. Orders were sent to the regiment to swim the river or come to me over the mountain around the bend ; and after destroying the train, it swam the river with the loss of four men drowned. When nearly across a formal demand from General Early was received by the officers commanding the rear guard to surrender, addressed to the commanding officer of the United States forces. As my column was then in motion over the Alleghanies, no formal reply was returned to the demand.

During the night attack five officers and 119 men were lost by being captured. It was thought that had the regiment in rear been advanced steadily forward, these captures might have been mostly prevented, and we should not have been obliged to destroy our wagons and ambulances the following day. The road over the Alleghanies led us to Antony's Creek, between the White Sulphur Springs and Huntersville. A force of the enemy was reported at Gatewood's, which is twelve miles east of Huntersville. My command was yet thirty miles from that point. If I could cross the Greenbrier and reach Marlin's Bottom before the enemy my command would be safe. By a very obscure road the Greenbrier was reached and crossed on the 21st, opposite Hillsboro, and we encamped for the night at the northern base of Droop Mountain. My scouts thrown out kept me informed of the enemy's movements and positions.

For thirty hours after my command left Callaghan's, the enemy made great efforts to intercept my force, but they generally took wrong roads. The citizens who knew the country best regarded our capture as unavoidable. It was expected, as may be seen from the orders given Colonel Moor by me, that he would remain near Droop Mountain until the 18th, but owing to orders he received from the general commanding the department, subsequent to the reception of mine, he also retired on the 14th, thus leaving no co-operative forces except Colonel Thoburn's, in the positions I had reason to expect them to be on the 20th and 21st. Unaided, with a weary command of 2500 men, I had marched through a difficult country in which not less than 12,000 Rebels were maneuvered to effect my capture.

On the way to Edray, my rear guard experienced some trifling attacks on the 22d. The road thence to Beverly was a glacier, which was traversed with great difficulty and peril. The artillery was drawn almost entirely by dismounted men during the 23d and 24th. Couriers had been sent forward to Beverly to bring out subsistence and forage, which we succeeded, after extreme hardships, in meeting on the 24th. The officers and men undertook all that was required of them and endured all the sufferings from fatigue, hunger and cold with extraordinary fortitude, even with cheerfulness. The march of 400 miles, which was concluded at Beverly, was the most difficult I have ever seen performed. The endurance of the men and horses was taxed to the utmost, yet there was no rest for them. Believing that some retaliatory operations would be at once inaugurated by the enemy, I telegraphed to the general commanding the department that I thought it advisable to get my command into the valley as soon as possible, and set out for Webster, whence, by means of the railroad, I arrived at Martinsburg just in time to confront the enemy, who was advancing toward this place.

*I desire to mention the names of my staff officers, to whom I am greatly indebted for their thoughtful and untiring aid to me throughout this expedition :—Capt. Will. Rumsey, assistant adjutant-general and aide-de-camp ; Lieut. L. Markbreit, acting assistant adjutant-general ; Capt. W. H. Brown, assistant quartermaster ; Lieut. H. N. Harrison, acting assistant engineer ; Capt. L. A. Myers, provost-marshal ; Lieut. H. Koenigsberger, acting commissary of subsistence ; Lieut. G. H. North, ordnance officer, and Surgeon W. D. Stewart, medical director. The services of Lieut. J. R. Meigs, Engineers, and of his assistant, Henry Topping, Esq., were invaluable to me.

In concluding my report, I beg leave to thank the Honorable Secretary of War for his kindness in directing the quartermaster's department to furnish the men of my command, engaged in the recent expedition, with a suit of clothing *gratis.* No necessity was ever more pressing, or more promptly supplied ; no charity more timely, or more gratefully received. I am, Captain,

Very respectfully, your obedient servant,

Captain T. Melvin,   Wm. W. Averell,
  Assistant Adjutant-General.   *Brigadier-General.*

Averell had outwitted the men who attempted his capture, and it was a bitter dose for the Confederates. The Richmond *Examiner* of December 28th had the following sarcastic article on the failure to capture Averell:

"The great General Averell has gone, not 'up the spout,' but back into his den. Cast your eye upon a map, and I'll tell you how he went and how he came. He came from New Creek, a depot on the Baltimore and Ohio railroad, in the county of Hardy, along the western base of the Shenandoah Mountains through Covington to Salem, burnt things generally and returned over nearly the same route. Imboden seized the gap where the Parkersburg turnpike crosses the Shenandoah, and prevented a raid on Staunton. Averell left five hundred men to hold Imboden there, and pushed on toward Salem. That general could not pursue without uncovering Staunton—the forces

*Major Theodore F. Lang, acting assistant inspector-general, was left in command at New Creek during this raid.

threatening nearly equaling his own. General Lee was informed of the situation of affairs. Here commences the reign of major-generals and military science. Maj.-Gen. Jubal A. Early came. Maj.-Gen. Fitzhugh Lee came. Brigadier-General Walker came. Brigadier-General Thomas came. Their staffs came. They all took a drink. General Early took two. Brigadier-General Wickham came. Colonel Chambliss, commanding brigade, came. They smiled also.

"When Averell was opposite Staunton, Fitz. Lee was at Ivy depot, on the Virginia Central railroad, a day's march from that town. A fortunate occurrence, indeed. Everybody thought Averell was 'treed' now. He passed through Brown's Gap and struck the valley turnpike at Mount Crawford, eight miles above Harrisonburg—a miserable mistake. One day's march lost. He then marched toward Harrisonburg—then towards Staunton. Another day gone for nothing. He finally reached Staunton, where he ought to have been on the first night. Still there was plenty of time to cut Averell off. Lee and Imboden marched day and night to Lexington, and then towards Covington. They have yet time enough to intercept.

"Here was committed the fatal and foolish blunder. While Lee and Imboden were on the road to Covington, in striking distance of that place, word was sent the Yankees are marching towards Buchanan, instead of Covington. No man ought to have put credence in a statement so utterly absurd as that the enemy were going from Salem to that place. Such a statement pre-supposes Averell deliberately placing himself past escape, and therefore run raving mad. Such improbable rumors should never be entertained a moment, much less made the basis of important military movements. The order was obeyed. The troops turned and marched back, and at night were neither at Buchanan nor Covington.

"The story is told in a few words. The Yankees passed through Covington, and, and to their great amusement, escaped. The rumor about Buchanan was the tale of some frightened fool. The enemy, in terror and demoralization, fled from Salem at full speed, destroying their train and artillery. Jackson knocked some in the head; the citizens beat the brains out of others; one farmer in Alleghany killed six; some were scattered in the mountains, and are being picked up here and there; the rapid stream drowned many, but the main part have gone whence they came, wondering how they did get away. It is hardly necessary to add, the humblest private in the ranks, if he possessed sense enough to eat and drink, not only could, but would have managed better. Old Stonewall would have marched on, caught and killed the Yankees. What Lee thought the writer don't know. They who know, say Imboden begged to go to Covington. He made it plain to the dullest mind that the Buchanan story was past belief. What's done is done.

"No language can tell the suffering of our men. They were in the saddle night and day, save a few hours between midnight and day. They were beat up by their officers with their swords—the only means of arousing them numb and sleepy. Some froze to death, others were taken from horses senseless. They forded swollen streams, and their clothes, stiff frozen, rattled as they rode. It rained in torrents, and froze as it fell. In the mountain paths the ice was cut from the roads before they ventured to ride over. One horse slipped over the precipice—the rider was leading him—he never looked over after him.

"The whole matter is summed up in a couple of sentences. Averell was penned up. McCausland, Echols and Jackson at one gate, Lee and Imboden at the other. Some ass suggested he might escape by jumping down the well and coming out at Japan, *i. e.*, go to Buchanan. Early orders them to leave a gate open and guard the well. He did not jump in. Meanwhile, the Yankees coolly came up the valley, through Edenburg, New Market, up to Harrisonburg, within 25 miles of Staunton—'these headquarters.' This was bearding the lion in his den. Jubal took the field, at the head of Company Q and a party of substitute men, farmers and ploughboys, called 'home guards.' The Yankees got after him and the ' major-general commanding' lost his hat in the race. The last heard of him he was pursuing the enemy with part of his division—footmen and cavalrymen—with fine prospects of overtaking them somewhere in China, perhaps about the 'great wall.' The Yankees were retreating toward the 'Devil Hole.' Early bound for the same place. They did very little damage in the valley. Here is the moral. The marshals under Napoleon's eye were invincible—with separate commands, blunderers. A general of division, with Gen'l Robert E. Lee to plan and put him in the right place, does well. Moseby would plan or execute a fight or strategic movement better than Longstreet at Suffolk and Knoxville, Jubal Early at Staunton."

The command left Beverly on December 27, in a heavy rain, and on the 28th reached Webster. From there they went to Martinsburg, Va. The trip to Martinsburg was a very severe one, the cold being intense, so much so that bread froze in the box cars in which the men were transported. It will never be forgotten by those who participated in it. Upon reaching Martinsburg, the brigade went into camp without tents or covering of any kind, and suffered severely. Fuel was scarce, and there was really no condition of comfort.

CHAPTER LVII.

BREVET MAJ.-GEN'L WM. W. AVERELL—(CONTINUED).

Commanding all the Cavalry of the Fourth Division, 8th Army Corps.—Active Service of his Command.—Generals Rosser, Fitz. Lee, Imboden, Jones and others.—Cole's Maryland Cavalry.—Martinsburg to the Kanawha Valley.—General Crook in Command.—Battle of Wytheville, Va.—Destruction of Bridge at New River.—General Averell's Congratulations to his Troops.—General Crook Congratulates.—Lynchburg, Virginia, Campaign.—From the Kanawha to Staunton.—Suffering of Barefooted Soldiers.—Crook and Averell Join Hunter at Staunton, Va.—Reorganization of Hunter's Command.—March on Lynchburg.—Retreat of Confederates.—Attack McCausland at New London.—Withdrawal of Hunter's Forces to the Westward and to the Kanawha.

FROM January 1 to April 19, 1864, General Averell commanded all the cavalry of the Fourth Division, 8th Army Corps, with headquarters at Martinsburg, West Va. During this period his cavalry were seldom idle, Generals Rosser, Fitz. Lee, Imboden, Jones, and other Confederate officers made frequent incursions towards Winchester, Harper's Ferry, New Creek, and at several other points along the Baltimore and Ohio Railroad. Averell was on the alert, however, and his cavalry was generally near the Confederates during their raids.

Besides Averell's regular command there were several regiments that displayed great activity in the Shenandoah and neighboring communities. Conspicuous among these was Cole's Maryland Cavalry Regiment, and the Confederates under Rosser, Imboden, McNeill, Gilmor, McCausland, Jones, Mosby and the guerrilla bands had just cause to know and dread this gallant regiment; indeed it became something of a habit when the Union commanders would learn of a raid by the Confederates within our lines, to at once send Cole's Cavalry to meet and disperse them. Col. Henry A. Cole, Lieut.-Col. George W. F. Vernon and Maj. Oliver A. Horner were the brave field officers that led this gallant regiment in their many victories.

On April 19th, General Averell left Martinsburg under orders to join General Crook in the Kanawha Valley, when he was placed in command of "The Cavalry Division of the Kanawha." Receiving orders from General Crook at Charleston, West Va., Averell, on the 1st of May, proceeded to Camp Piatt, ten miles above, with the brigades of Brigadier-General Duffie and Colonel Schoonmaker, numbering in all 2079 officers and men, and 400 of the Fifth and Seventh West Va. Cavalry, under Col. J. H. Oley.

During the day and night of the first and most of the second day, the miscellaneous transportation furnished was put together, and loaded with rations and forage, which were intended to supply the command with six days' rations of subsistence and four of forage after leaving Logan Court House, but owing to the miserable condition of the teams and wagons furnished and the heavy roads, it was found that the command had only about four days' subsistence and one and a half days' forage with which to start from that point on the 5th. Sending back the wagons from Logan, and taking along a detachment of the Third West Virginia Cavalry, under Major Conger, which had been stationed there, Averell proceeded towards Wyoming Court House, meeting a scouting party of the enemy on the way.

From near Wyoming Court House on the 6th, Colonel Oley was sent towards Princeton to form a junction with General Crook's column, while the division found its way over pathless mountains and up tortuous streams to Abb's Valley, in Tazewell County, where it arrived on the evening of the 7th, capturing scouts of the enemy and one company of the 8th Virginia (Confederate) Cavalry on picket. The march was resumed on the 8th, and some Kentucky troops of the enemy driven, with a loss to them of four killed and five wounded, to Tazewell Court House, a distance of fifteen miles. It was then ascertained that forces had been assembled at Saltville, under command of Gen'ls John H. Morgan and W. E. Jones, to the number of 4500, and that the approaches from the north were well defended with earthworks and artillery. Information was also obtained from deserters and captured mails that the enemy was fully informed of our strength and intentions. Believing that it would be impracticable to carry the works about Saltville without infantry and artillery, and that a surprise was out of the question, General Averell abandoned that project and marched to Wytheville, in order to prevent the enemy from concentrating against the column of General Crook, capturing a train of wagons on the way.

Arriving near Wytheville on the afternoon of the 10th, Averell attacked a force stated by Confederate newspapers to have numbered 5000, under Generals Morgan and W. E. Jones, on their way eastward. This force was mostly infantry, with three pieces of artillery, and posted in an admirable position for defense or attack, impossible to turn with cavalry. The 14th Pa. and 1st West Va. Cavalry, under Colonel Schoonmaker, opened the battle, while the brigade of General Duffie was formed in line of battle. The 2d West Va. Cavalry, under Colonel Powell on the left, mounted; the 34th Ohio Infantry, dismounted, on the right, and the 3d West Va. Cavalry occupying the extreme left. The enemy pressed upon both flanks and advanced in three lines sheltered by fences in front. The field was maintained four hours, the vigor of the enemy gradually decreasing. At dark there was some prospect of our being able to drive him, but after dark he retired, and Averell marched his command to Dublin, where he arrived on the evening of the 11th. Our loss in the battle was about 114 officers and men killed and wounded.

We crossed New River, swollen by recent rains, on the morning of the 12th. The baffled columns of Morgan and Jones arrived on the left bank soon after, but the river had become impassable, and they had leisure to view the ruins of the railroad and bridges, which all the energies and skill of their superior forces had failed to avert. As our ammunition was nearly exhausted, Averell deemed it proper to join Crook's command, which, after a very difficult march, was accomplished on the 15th at Union, having marched 350 miles over a region almost impassable and destitute of supplies. Nearly thirty miles of the journey was made by file on foot over unfrequented paths. The mountain streams were frequently unfordable, and a few men and horses were lost by drowning. The command performed this arduous work with uncomplaining fortitude.

General Averell expressed in general orders his appreciation and thankfulness to officers and men for their devotion and heroism. He said: "Your country will remember your heroism with gratitude, and the noble sacrifices and sufferings of our fallen comrades will be cherished forever in our memories. The 14th Pa. and 1st West Va. Cavalry first received the shock of the battle, while the 2d and 3d West Va. Cavalry and 34th Ohio Mounted Infantry, established a line which the enemy had reason to respect and remember. Great credit is due to the brigade commanders, Brigadier-General Duffie and Colonel Schoonmaker."

He further says: "He desires, without making an invidious distinction, to express his high appreciation for the steady and skillful evolutions of the 2d West Va. Cavalry, under Col. W. H. Powell, upon the field. It was a dress parade which continued without disorder under a heavy fire during four hours."

In his report of the expedition against the Virginia and Tennessee Railroad, Gen'l G. Crook says: "Brig.-Gen'l W. W. Averell deserves particular mention for his severe and perilous marches, and his encounter with the enemy at the different points."

LYNCHBURG, VIRGINIA, CAMPAIGN.

On the 1st of June, 1864, Averell's division consisted of the brigades of General Duffie, Colonels Schoonmaker and Oley, and were encamped at Bunger's Mills, Greenbrier Co. Va., waiting for supplies from Charleston of horses, shoes, clothing, etc. General Crook's division crossed the river on that day, leaving Averell to bring up his rear detachments and supplies, which did not arrive. The detachments and supplies for which the command had so long waited failing to arrive, Averell followed Crook's division on the 3d to White Sulphur Springs with 3200 mounted and 1200 dismounted men; 600 men were without shoes, and many other articles of clothing were much needed. From the 18th of May until this day the division had waited near Lewisburg, upon half rations most of the time, for necessary supplies of horse shoes, nails and clothing; but owing to the miserable, inadequate and insufficient transportation furnished from the Kanawha, Averell was obliged to set out again almost as destitute as when he arrived. The march from Sulphur Springs to Staunton was made in five days via Morris' Hill, Warm Springs, Goshen and Middlebrook. The barefooted men suffered terribly, but without complaint, on this march. At Staunton the much needed supplies were received. Here also, when the forces of Crook and Averell joined General Hunter, the cavalry divisions were reorganized. Averell's division was as follows: First Brigade, Colonel Schoonmaker, 14th Pennsylvania Cavalry, 8th Ohio mounted infantry; Second Brigade, Colonel Oley, 7th West Virginia Cavalry, 34th Ohio Mounted Infantry, 3rd West Virginia Cavalry, 5th West Virginia Cavalry; Third Brigade, Col. W. H. Powell, 1st West Virginia Cavalry, 2d West Virginia Cavalry.

At the request of Major-General Hunter, commanding the department, General Averell on the 9th submitted a plan of operations, the purpose of which was the capture of Lynchburg, and the destruction, of railroads runring from that place in five days. The plan was accepted by General Hunter and on the 10th the command of General Hunter began its forward march to Lynchburg. Averell's division marched via Summerdean to Belleview. On the 13th the division moved toward Buchanan, driving General McCausland in disorder across the James River. He was pursued the last eight miles to Buchanan at a gallop, Averell's advance endeavoring to save the bridge at that place, but the flying forces of McCausland set it on fire before he himself had crossed, obliging him to ford the river to escape capture. The 14th was occupied in destroying some important iron furnaces in the neighborhood of Fincastle. On the 15th Averell followed Crook's division over the Blue Ridge between the Peaks of Otter to Fancy Farm.

The following morning Averell pushed on through Liberty, rebuilt the bridge over Little Otter River, forded Big Otter, and attacked McCausland at New London, about dark. He had been re-enforced by Imboden, with 400 men and two guns, but relinquished his position after a short action, in which he lost about a dozen men. At sunrise on the 17th Averell moved by the old road toward Lynchburg, some two miles to the right of Crook, who moved on the direct road from New London. The enemy resisted our advance at every step after arriving within eight miles of the city, but it was not until the command came in sight of the stone church, four miles from Lynchburg, that he seemed determined to give battle. Averell constantly advised General Crook of his progress, and after a brief reconnoissance of position, opened the attack.

The ground was difficult for cavalry, and its peculiar formation made the following disposition necessary: Schoonmaker's brigade furnished a strong skirmish line, mounted, across the open ground, supported by squadrons with intervals in columns of fours, open order, ready to charge or dismount to fight; Oley's brigade on the right, in column; Powell's on the left, in the same order. The enemy retired as the attack was developed, with very little skirmishing, but as it approached the crest of the hill upon which the church stands a rapid artillery fire was opened upon Averell, and their small-arms became unmasked. Schoonmaker's and Oley's brigades dismounted and ran to the front; the section of artillery with the division galloped up to the church, supported by Powell, and opened its fire. The enemy signally failed in his ruse to draw Averell into a position from which he expected to drive him. After a short but sharp contest the enemy was driven nearly a mile toward Lynchburg. Crook brought up two brigades, which were soon deployed and advanced to the support of Averell's line, and two of his batteries also arrived at the front. The enemy, driven to his field works, received re-enforcements and confidently advanced to charge Averell's line. Had the infantry support been in position, to have carried on our success then, we might have achieved some important advantage. As it was, Averell had a hard struggle to maintain his position until the infantry arrived, but with it came the dusk of evening, and although the boldness of the enemy was severely punished, our attack was delayed until the morning.

During the night of the 17th and the day of the 18th until 4 P. M., the enemy busied himself with throwing up earthworks, when he advanced from his works, making an attack, which was quickly repulsed. It was evident, however, that too many lives must be expended to carry the enemy's position.

General Hunter, therefore, gave orders to withdraw westward along the Virginia and Tennessee Railroad, and left Averell as a rear guard to the column, which position was maintained until Liberty was reached. Upon the arrival of the army at this place, it halted to rest west of the town. At the time Averell made the request that a brigade of infantry be left to support him, anticipating an attack from the indications in his rear; but for some reason the request was not granted, and unaided Averell's division stood the brunt of a severe attack for two hours. Schoonmaker's brigade especially distinguished itself by its obstinate resistance. Averell's ammunition failing, the division was withdrawn behind Crook's, which had been formed in line of battle a mile in the rear. Averell's loss in this severe engagement was 122.

On the morning of the 20th, the march was resumed in the direction of Buford's Gap, and the march continued, being interrupted constantly, however, as the column proceeded to Salem, to Fincastle, Newcastle, Sweet Springs, White Sulphur Springs, Lewisburg. This expedition of General Hunter was conspicuous for the great suffering and hardships to men and beasts, the great loss of life and property with no adequate return.

CHAPTER LVIII.

BREVET MAJ.-GEN'L W. W. AVERELL—(CONTINUED).

Itinerary of the Second Cavalry Division.—Defeat of Ramseur's Division at Stephenson's Depot.—Defeat of Generals McCausland and Johnson at Moorefield.—General Sheridan in Command in Middle Military Division.—Averell at Martinsburg.—Sheridan Humiliates Averell.—Averell Relieved.—His Closing Statement.—Jealousy in the Army.—Gallant Service Ignored.—Averell's Farewell Order.

ITINERARY of the Second Cavalry Division, General Averell commanding, July 2 to September 23, 1864: At Charleston, Kanawha County, W. Va., from July 2 to the 8th; left Charleston for Parkersburg on Tuesday, July 8, with his division; left Parkersburg July 15 for Martinsburg; arrived at that place on the 17th following, and immediately established pickets across the Shedandoah Valley south of Martinsburg; July 20, defeated Ramseur's division at Stephenson's Depot, capturing four guns and 250 prisoners; July 22 and 23, slightly engaged; July 24, battle of Winchester; division retired to Martinsburg, covering the rear of the Army of West Virginia. July 25, retired through Martinsburg; slightly engaged July 26, crossed the Potomac and encamped at Hagerstown. July 29, driven from Hagerstown by Confederate cavalry under McCausland. July 30, chased McCausland through Chambersburg, and *via* New London, London and (31st) McConnellsburg to Hancock, from which place he was driven by the attack of the division on the 31st. On the 3d of August, still pursuing the enemy. On the 4th of August, crossed the Potomac at Hancock, taking route *via* Bloomery Gap to Bath. At Springfield on the 5th, losing during the day 100 horses from exhaustion. On the 6th arrived at Romney; during the afternoon a messenger from the enemy was captured, with an order from General McCausland, which gave the information that McCausland's and Gen'l Bradley T. Johnson's brigades were posted three and four miles north of Moorefield. Moved on the 7th and attacked the forces of McCausland and Johnson. The victory was complete, driving and pursuing the enemy 10 miles east of Moorefield. Three battle-flags were captured with four pieces of artillery (all the enemy had), 420 prisoners, including six field and staff and 32 company officers and over 400 horses.

August 7, Maj.-Gen'l P. H. Sheridan, in compliance with orders from the War Department, assumed command of the Middle Military Division, with headquarters at Harper's Ferry. August 8, General Averell was ordered to concentrate his division at Hancock, Md. On the 14th, the division reached Martinsburg on its march to join General Sheridan, who was then near Cedar Creek, but received orders here, to remain in Martinsburg and refit his division for the field. From the date of assuming command of the Middle Military Division, General Sheridan exhibited a disposition to censure General Averell and to humiliate him, by a failure to give recognition for victories won, as well as to censure him for unavoidable failures. The breach begun thus early between those two generals, was brought to a humiliating termination to Averell and the soldiers of his command on the 23d of September, by an order of General Sheridan, relieving General Averell of the command of his division. In his official report (after being relieved) of the operations of his division just prior to his retirement, General Averell makes the following closing summary statement:

"I have in the above report introduced some details which would have been excluded were it not for the peculiar circumstances under which it is written. An officer who has served the Government nine years, who has suffered from wounds in battle, cannot without any assigned cause or pretext be suddenly relieved from the command of a division whose record tells of nothing but success and victories without having his sensibilities outraged and his reputation jeopardized. It is natural that the War Department should ask the wherefore for such action, and it is proper that I should state as explicitly as possible the reasons so far as known to me. I have evidence that it was determined to relieve me in order to make Brigadier-General Torbert chief of cavalry before Major-General Sheridan assumed command of the Middle Military Division. My success at Moorefield; achieved with an exhausted division against twice its numbers, probably caused a hesitation in my removal. The note of Major-General Sheridan, dated August 28, exhibits his readiness to avail himself of any pretext to censure me, and his reply to my explanation shows how completely his purpose was baffled. Major-General Sheridan illegally assumed the prerogative of the President of the United States and ordered me to report to a junior officer on the 23d of August without any just cause. While I had the entire country on the right flank of the army to guard up to the 19th of September, and had the orders of the major-general commanding to attack the enemy whenever I had an opportunity, my successes were barely mentioned, my activity was covertly censured, and an unjust impression to rest in the mind of the general-in-chief (Grant) to the extent of causing him to send an optional order for my relief. It was, I believe, admitted on the 19th of September on both sides, that our cavalry attack was the key to the victory which we won, and I think it was obvious that the success of that attack, as to time and place, was mainly attributable to the exertions of my division; yet, although I was the ranking officer of cavalry making the attack, the mention of my name in the dispatches was studiously avoided.

"Finally, the angry and discourteous note of the 23d was addressed to me to give the pretext implied therein a *quasi* establishment in history, and before time was given me to reply the order was issued, which, trampling upon my record and upon all military courtesy and justice, consigned me to the ignominy of idleness."

It was one of the unfortunate conditions that prevailed to a large extent in the army during the war that jealousy and personal preferment should have controlled the actions of officers in authority in place of recognizing loyalty, courage, capacity and endurance. This reference applies mainly to the regular army officers—the volunteer generals, to their credit, did not share to any considerable extent in this West Point ambition. That a gallant officer, as General Averell had proved himself to be, who had marched and fought, had swam and slid and rolled, had advanced in columns and in single file, over bloody battlefields and mountain paths, under a burning sun, and through winter's storm and snow, to meet and defeat the foe, should have been the victim of this prejudice and jealousy, was an outrage—not only towards General Averell, but upon the gallant legions of West Virginians, Pennsylvanians and Ohioans that had followed the gallant leader for so long a period. And since the war, it seems to have been the unmindful fashion of the writers of war reminiscences to completely ignore all military operations in West Virginia, except those which took place in the Shenandoah Valley near the close of the struggle, and the public mind has thus been led to group all events in that region that were worthy of memory into that brief period, and even soldiers who shared in the hardships and glories of Rocky Gap, Droop Mountain, Salem raid, Carter's Farm, Moorefield and Winchester, where bloody fields were won and batteries and flags were captured, have been somewhat prone to acquiesce in a forgetfulness of heroic deeds which could not be placed to the credit of a factious favorite.

When Averell was relieved from the command of his division the same order relieved him of all credit of directing its previous endeavors. As to the general personally, he has endured and survived with the comfort of the dead, and many a pang has touched the hearts of his heroic division so isolated from all notice or commendation of its splendid gallantry, dreadful fatigues and occasional starvation, and of the recognition which has been denied them in the popular annals of the war.

The following farewell order, issued by General Averell, addressed to his division, is given as a fitting *finis* to this sketch. The delicate and tender wording of which could only emanate from a brave and generous heart:

HEADQUARTERS, 2d CAVALRY DIVISION, DEPARTMENT OF W. VA.

IN THE FIELD, *September* 23, 1864.

GENERAL ORDERS, }
    No. 33.   }

In accordance with Special Orders No. 41, Headquarters Middle Military Division, of this date, I hereby relinquish the command of this division. In doing so, I request the offi. cers and men to accept my sincere thanks for the uniform obedience and respect they have shown to my orders, and the personal kindness they have always extended to myself. I shall never forget, my comrades, what I owe to you, whatever of reputation or rank I have gained during the last year was given to me by this command. Since the 1st of May, we have marched over 1800 miles, 500 comrades who have fallen in 20 battles attest the devotion with which you have done your duty; and seven battle-flags, 13 cannon and over 1500 prisoners captured from the enemy exhibit some of the results of your work. My associations with you will hereafter be among my most cherished memories, and I shall read the record of your deeds from day to day with eager interest. My regret in severing the ties that bind us is somewhat lessened by the knowledge that I am leaving you in the hands of that tried and trusty soldier, Col. W. H. Powell, in whom the utmost confidence may be placed. I would rather serve in your ranks than leave you, but I am only permitted to say farewell.

WM. W. AVERELL,

Brevet Major-General.

INDEX OF REGIMENTS.